KEEPING ★ SCORE

FILM MUSIC 1972-1979

JAMES L. LIMBACHER

The Scarecrow Press, Inc.
Metuchen, N.J., & London 1981

Library of Congress Cataloging in Publication Data

Limbacher, James L
Keeping score.

Discography: p.
1. Moving-picture music--Bibliography.
I. Title.
ML128.M7L5 016.7828'5 80-26474
ISBN 0-8108-1390-4

Manufactured in the United States of America

TABLE OF CONTENTS

INTRODUCTION

Keeping Score takes up where Film Music: From Violins to Video left off and covers the period from 1972 to 1979.

The last seven years have seen a large growth in interest in the science and art of composing for films, and this is reflected in the number of new composers who were not listed in the first book.

The most interesting phenomenon of the seventies was the formation of a group of film-music organizations to perpetuate the works (and in some cases memories) of some of the major film composers. Other groups were formed to produce and distribute hitherto-unavailable recordings of film music and reissues of older soundtracks.

Among the organizations that produced newsletters telling of the latest information on their favorite film-music composers were the John Barry Appreciation Society, the Elmer Bernstein Film Music Collection, The Miklos Rozsa Society, The Max Steiner Music Society, and the Korngold Society. The Miklos Rozsa Society also provided tapes of concert performances of Rozsa's works, while the Entr'acte Recording Society and the Elmer Bernstein Film Music Collection provided commercial discs of various works not previously recorded and reissues of older scores.

The last seven years have brought forth another phenomenon--that of the "private label" and "bootleg" recordings of film-music soundtracks. While many are legitimate reissues and the subject of great rejoicing for film-music lovers, others are underground pressings for which no royalties are offered to the composers or performers.

In any case, these soundtrack albums sold well, and interest in film music and its composers is now at an all-time high. The lucky record collector who bought a copy of The Bad Seed when it was issued by RCA Victor in 1956 can now rejoice that it is worth over $100 on today's market. As soon as it is reissued by RCA (or other authorized distributor), its value will decrease. Issuing it on a pirated label does not seem to cause the same decrease.

Despite the proliferation of musical scores in contemporary films, some scores are still in the junk category. To seem "with it," some producers have hired rock groups to drop casually into a recording studio and "compose and perform" a film score in one operation. The results usually sound unsatisfactory (and sometimes downright incompetent) since film composing is an exact art and science, not an electronic jam session. Even though these albums are poor, many are included in this book, along with the unusual names that some of these groups go by.

Record companies still "rearrange" scores to fit albums and many times will "augment" the music to fill out a record album. Not much can be done about this except to refrain from buying these "rip-off" albums. This type of album is also listed in this book for the sake of completeness.

Another important event since the last edition of this book is the formation by the American record industry of the "White House Record Commission." At regular intervals the industry provides a new series of the best-recorded works in various categories (classical, popular, film music, folk, etc.). The compiler of this book was honored to be appointed to this commission and to be at the White House when the initial collection was presented to the President of the United States for use by the presidential family in its own living room.

The collection remains at the White House and will not be taken away when a President leaves office.

What film-music albums were chosen to grace the President's record collection? These are the basic ones included: Born Free, Breakfast at Tiffany's, Doctor Zhivago, Exodus, For Whom the Bell Tolls, Gone with the Wind, The Graduate, A Man and a Woman, Midnight Cowboy, Mondo Cane, Never on Sunday, The Pink Panther, Romeo and Juliet, and 2001: A Space Odyssey. New albums will be added approximately every four years.

KEEPING SCORE

There are always problems in a book such as this one. Because so many films under the studio system had several house composers working on the same film, exact credits as to who did what are difficult to find. Universal and Columbia films of the forties were especially problematical; Gershenson and Bakaleinkoff are still listed for many of these titles, although they were not the composers in most cases. Just who were the composers of many of these scores may never be known for certain.

In other cases, some of the composers of the early thirties were more "providers" than actual composers. Abe Meyer, for instance, was a man who provided various standard agitatos and stings for Poverty Row films, but he is listed again for the sake of completeness rather than overpowering musical talent.

In the seventies many of the sleaziest pornographic feature films played background music by Steiner, Mockridge, Tiomkin, Rozsa, Herrmann, and others, lifted from their major scores. These, of course, are not listed under the names of these estimable composers.

Classical composers whose compositions were used in films but not written for them, have been eliminated after readers convinced the author that Chopin, Vivaldi, and Tchaikovsky never heard of a click track.

In regard to corrections to the first edition, it was decided to relist the entry with the corrected information. This means that the entry in <u>Keeping Score</u> supersedes the material in Film Music: From Violins to Video. When the cumulative edition comes out, the earlier entry will be discarded. The next edition will be both cumulative and computerized.

There have been several format changes in this edition. For instance, all titles are printed with the articles (the, a, an, der, die, el, gli, la, le, etc.) at the end in anticipation of computerization. Also, the designations of foreign recordings have been changed from an adjective at the beginning to a noun at the end--e.g., Italian Cetra 2576 is now Cetra 2576 (Italy).

ACKNOWLEDGMENTS

In preparing this new book, the compiler found soulmates all over the world who are just as fanatic about film music as he himself is. These people not only made suggestions, criticisms, and comments, but made additions and corrections, gave moral support, and once in a while even paid a compliment.

Their contributions are acknowledged here and now. My thanks to M. V. Baker, Dr. Charles Berg, Brian Burney, Ronald L. Bohn, Howard Crossland, Thomas de Mary, Jonathan Groucutt, Wolfram and Volker Hannemann, G. Roger

Hammonds, Steve Harris, David Hummel, Mark Koldys, Clifford McCarty, Martin Marks, James Marshall, William H. Rosar, Robert Seeley, Winston Sharples, Jr., and Luc van de Ven.

Special thanks must be given to my friends Thomas J. Moore, who helped with the discography; Charles G. Banciu, who helped with the composer index (as he did in the first edition); and Patrick Caraher and Wilfred Souchereau, who helped with the final checking and indexing.

And now let's start keeping score ...

WINNERS OF THE ACADEMY AWARD

FOR BEST ORIGINAL FILM SCORE

(The musical scoring award was established in 1934 and went to an operetta, One Night of Love. In 1935 it was given in earnest.)

1935 The Informer (Max Steiner)
1936 No composing award
1937 No composing award
1938 The Adventures of Robin Hood (Erich Wolfgang Korngold)
1939 Stagecoach (Richard Hageman, W. Franke Harling, John Leipold and Leo Shuken)
1940 No composing award
1941 All That Money Can Buy (The Devil and Daniel Webster) (Bernard Herrmann)
1942 Now, Voyager (Max Steiner)
1943 The Song of Bernadette (Alfred Newman)
1944 Since You Went Away (Max Steiner)
1945 Spellbound (Miklos Rozsa)
1946 The Best Years of Our Lives (Hugo Friedhofer)
1947 A Double Life (Miklos Rozsa)
1948 The Red Shoes (Brian Easdale)
1949 The Heiress (Aaron Copland)
1950 Sunset Boulevard (Franz Waxman)
1951 A Place in the Sun (Franz Waxman)
1952 High Noon (Dimitri Tiomkin)
1953 Lili (Bronislau Kaper)
1954 The High and the Mighty (Dimitri Tiomkin)
1955 Love Is a Many-Splendored Thing (Alfred Newman)

1956 Around the World in 80 Days (Victor Young)
1957 The Bridge on the River Kwai (Malcolm Arnold)
1958 The Old Man and the Sea (Dimitri Tiomkin)
1959 Ben-Hur (Miklos Rozsa)
1960 Exodus (Ernest Gold)
1961 Breakfast at Tiffany's (Henry Mancini)
1962 Lawrence of Arabia (Maurice Jarre)
1963 Tom Jones (John Addison)
1964 No composing award
1965 Doctor Zhivago (Maurice Jarre)
1966 Born Free (John Barry)
1967 No composing award
1968 The Lion in Winter (John Barry)
1969 Butch Cassidy and the Sundance Kid (Burt Bacharach)
1970 Love Story (Francis Lai)
1971 Summer of '42 (Michel Legrand)
1972 Limelight (Charles Chaplin, Raymond Rasch, and Larry Russell)
1973 The Way We Were (Marvin Hamlisch)
1974 The Godfather, Part II (Nino Rota and Carmine Coppola)
1975 Jaws (John Williams)
1976 The Omen (Jerry Goldsmith)
1977 Star Wars (John Williams)
1978 Midnight Express (Giorgio Moroder)
1979 A Little Romance (Georges Delerue)

NECROLOGY OF

FILM-MUSIC COMPOSERS

Richard Addinsell (1904-1977)
George Anthiel (1900-1959)
Constantin Bakaleinikoff (1898-1966)
Hubert Bath (1883-1945)
Arnold Bax (1883-1953)
Giuseppe Becce (1887-unknown)
Sir Arthur Benjamin (1893-1960)
Lord Berners (1883-1950)
Sir Arthur Bliss (1891-1975)
Marc Blitzstein (1905-1964)
Sir Benjamin Britten (1913-1976)
Valentino Bucchi (1916-1976)
Mario Castelnuovo-Tedesco (1895-1968)
Francis Chagrin (1905-1972)
Charles Chaplin (1889-1977)
Eric Coates (1886-1957)
Anthony Collins (1893-1964)
Sir Noel Coward (1899-1973)
Marcel Delannoy (1898-1962)
Francois de Roubaix (1939-1975)
Vasant Desai (1914-1975)
Paul Dessau (1894-1979)
Adolph Deutsch (1898-1980)
Robert Emmett Dolan (1908-1972)
Hanns Eisler (1898-1962)
Duke Ellington (1899-1974)
Don Ellis (1934-1978)
Percy Faith (1908-1976)
Jerry Fielding (1822-1980)

Nat Finston (1891-1980)
Leo F. Forbstein (unknown-1949)
Benjamin Frankel (1906-1973)
Giovanni Fusco (1906-1968)
Walter Goehr (1903-1960)
Allan Gray (1902-1973)
Bernard Green (unknown-1975)
John Greenwood (1889-1975)
Ferde Grofe (1892-1972)
Louis Gruenberg (1884-1964)
Vince Guaraldi (1928-1976)
Richard Hageman (1882-1966)
Leigh Harline (1907-1969)
W. Franke Harling (1887-1958)
Fumio Hayasaka (1914-1955)
Lennie Hayton (1908-1971)
Ray Heindorf (1909-1980)
Bernard Herrmann (1911-1975)
Paul Hindemith (1895-1963)
Frederick Hollander (1896-1976)
Arthur Honegger (1892-1955)
Jacques Ibert (1890-1962)
John Ireland (1879-1962)
Sir Ernest Irving (1878-1953)
Maurice Jaubert (1900-1940)
Bernhard Kaun (1899-1980)
Aram Khachaturian (1903-1978)
Kryzsztof Komeda (1932-1969)
Erich Wolfgang Korngold (1897-1957)
Joseph Kosma (1905-1969)
Constant Lambert (1905-1951)
Walter Leigh (1905-1942)
Oscar Levant (1906-1972)
Louis Levy (1893-1957)
Malcolm Lockyer (1923-1976)
Gary McFarland (1933-1971)
Bruno Maderna (1920-1973)
Albert Hay Malotte (1895-1964)
Muir Mathieson (1911-1975)
Hans May (1891-1959)
George Melachrino (1909-1965)
Darius Milhaud (1892-1974)
Cyril Mockridge (1896-1979)
Enzo Musetti (1893-1961)
Oliver Nelson (1932-1975)
Alfred Newman (1901-1970)
Ildebrando Pizzetti (1880-1968)

Francis Poulenc (1899-1963)
Serge Prokofiev (1891-1953)
Erno Rapee (1891-1945)
Alan Rawsthorne (1906-1971)
Hugo Reisenfeld (1879-1939)
Franz Reizenstein (1911-1968)
Johnny Richards (1911-1968)
Nino Rota (1911-1979)
Erik Satie (1966-1925)
Paul Sawtell (1906-1971)
Victor Schertzinger (1880-1941)
Walter Schumann (unknown-1958)
Vincente Scotto (1876-1952)
Matyas Seiber (1905-1960)
Yuri Alexandrovich Shaporin (1889-1966)
Dmitri Shostakovich (1906-1975)
Leo Shuken (1906-1976)
Louis Silvers (1889-1954)
Frank Skinner (1898-1968)
Eric Spear (unknown-1969)
Johnnie Spence (1935-1977)
Max Steiner (1888-1971)
Leith Stevens (1909-1970)
Robert Stolz (1880-1975)
Herbert Stothart (1884-1949)
Oscar Straus (1870-1954)
Igor Stravinsky (1882-1971)
Irvin Talbot (1896-1975)
David Tamkin (unknown-1975)
Dimitri Tiomkin (1899-1979)
Ernst Toch (1887-1964)
Georges van Parys (1902-1970)
Ralph Vaughan Williams (1872-1958)
Oliver Wallace (unknown-1963)
Edward Ward (unknown-1971)
Franz Waxman (1906-1967)
Kurt Weill (1900-1950)
Stanley Windt (unknown-1970)
Herbert Windt (1894-1965)
Hugo Winterhalter (1909-1973)
Jean Yatove (unknown-1978)
Victor Young (1900-1956)
Wolfgang Zeller (1893-1967)

BIBLIOGRAPHY

(Below are some of the more recent books on the subject of film music, both newly written and newly reissued.)

Bazelon, Irwin. Knowing the Score (Van Nostrand Reinhold, 1975).

Berg, Charles M. An Investigation of the Motive for and the Realization of Music to Accompany the American Silent Film 1896-1927 (Arno, 1976).

Beynon, George W. The Musical Presentation of Motion Pictures (Schirmer, 1921).

Elsas, Diana (ed.). Factfile: Film Music (American Film Institute, 1977).

Evans, Mark. Soundtrack: The Music of the Movies (Hopkinson and Blake, 1975).

Foort, Reginald. The Cinema Organ, 2d ed. (Vestal, 1970).

Hagan, Earle. Scoring for Films (Criterion, 1972; with recordings).

Harris, Steve. Recorded Music for Motion Pictures, TV and the Theater (A-1 Record Finders, 1976).

McCarty, Clifford. Film Composers in America, rev. ed. (DaCapo, 1972).

Skiles, Marlin. Music Scoring for TV and Motion Pictures (Tab, 1976).

Thomas, Tony. Music for the Movies (Barnes, 1973).

FILM TITLES AND DATES

A. T. S. (1943)
A. W. O. L. (1972)
A . . . Is for Apple (1963)
A Belles Dents (1966)
A Propos d'Une Riviere (1955)
A Toute Heure en Toute Saison (1961)
Aaron Loves Angela (1975)
Abbott & Costello Meet Dr. Jekyll and Mr. Hyde (1953)
Abbott & Costello Meet the Invisible Man (1951)
Abbott & Costello Meet the Mummy (1955)
Abby (1974)
Abdication, The (1974)
Abduction (1975)
Abductors, The (1972)
Abie's Irish Rose (1928)
Abilene Town (1946)
About Seven Girls (1974)
Abraham and Isaac (1948)
Absent-Minded (1970)
Absolutely Natural (1969)
Absolutely, Tomorrow (Ashita Koso) (1968)
Accuser, The (1977)
Ace Eli and Rodger of the Skies (1973)
Ace High (Quattro dell'Ave Maria, I) (1969)
Ace of Aces (1933)
Aces High (1976)
Ach wie ist's Moglich Dann (1914)
Acrobat, The (1979)
Across 110th St. (1973)
Across the Great Divide (1976)
Act of Vengeance (1974)
Actors and the Savages, The (1975)
Actualities Gauloises (1952)
Actualities Prehistoriques (1947)
Actualities Romaines (1947)
Adele Hasn't Had Her Supper Yet (1978)
Adios Amigo (1976)
Adios Gringo (1967)
Adolescent, The (1979)
Adolescents, The (1960)
Adolescents, The (1976)
Adoption, The (1975)
Adoption, The (1978)
Adorable (1933)
Adult Fun (1972)
Advantage, The (1978)
Adventure in Capri (1959)
Adventure in Diamonds (1940)
Adventure in Washington (1941)
Adventure Is Adventure (1972)
Adventures of a Dentist (1978)
Adventures of a Photographer, The (1960)
Adventures of a Wilderness Family, The (1976)
Adventures of Barry McKenzie (1972)
Adventures of Captain Marvel (1941)
Adventures of Chico (1938)
Adventures of Marco Polo, The (1938)

Adventures of Picasso, The (1978)
Adventures of Sherlock Holmes, The (1939)
Adventures of Sherlock Holmes' Smarter Brother, The (1975)
Affair in Monte Carlo (1952)
Affair of Susan, The (1935)
Affairs (1979)
Affairs of Cappy Ricks, The (1937)
Affairs of Jimmy Valentine, The (1942)
Affairs of Martha, The (1942)
Affection (1973)
Africa (1967)
African Queen, The (1951)
After the Rain (1978)
After the Thin Man (1936)
After Tonight (1933)
Afyon Oppio (1978)
Against a Crooked Sky (1975)
Agatha (1979)
Agaton Sax and the Bykoebing Village Festival (1976)
Age for Love, The (1931)
Age of Indiscretion (1935)
Age of Innocence, The (1934)
Agent 69 Jensen in the Sign of Sagittarius (1978)
Agent 69 Jensen in the Sign of Scorpio (1977)
Aggie Appleby, Maker of Men (1933)
Aggression (1975)
Agony of Mr. Boroka, The (1973)
Aguirre, the Wrath of God (1973)
Ah, Si! ... E Io Lo Dico a Zorro! (1979)
Air Pattern--Pacific (1943)
Airport 1975 (1974)
Airport '77 (1977)
Ajuricaba (1977)
Akenfield (1975)
Al Kautsar (1977)
Albert Peckingpaw's Revenge (1967)
Aldevaran (1975)
Alechinsky After Nature (1970)
Alex and the Gypsy (1976)
Alexander (see Very Happy Alexander)
Alexandria ... Why? (1979)
Alfie Darling (1975)
Alfredo, Alfredo (1973)
Algerian War, The (1972)
Ali the Man: Ali the Fighter (1975)
Alias Mr. Twilight (1946)
Alias the Deacon (1940)
Alibi per Morire, Un (1962)
Alice Adams (1935)
Alice Doesn't Live Here Anymore (1974)
Alice in Spanish Wonderland (1978)
Alice, or the Last Escapade (1977)
Alice's Adventures in Wonderland (1972)
Alien (1979)
Alison's Birthday (1979)
All-American Chump (1936)
All-American Coed (1941)
All Ashore (1953)
All at Sea (1957)
All Men Are Enemies (1934)
All Nudity Will Be Punished (1973)
All Over Town (1937)
All People Will Be Brothers (1973)
All That Jazz (1979)
All the King's Horses (1935)
All the Loving Couples (1968)
All the President's Men (1976)
Alle Origini Della Mafia (1979)
Allergic to Love (1944)
Allonsanfan (1973)
Almost a Gentleman (1939)
Almost Perfect Pair, An (1979)
Almost Summer (1978)
Aloha Oe (1915)
Aloma of the South Seas (1941)
Alone (1976)
Alone at Daybreak (1978)
Along the Navajo Trail (1945)
Along the Rio Grande (1941)
Alvin Purple (1973)
Alvin Rides Again (1974)
Always a New Beginning (1974)
Amarcord (1974)

Amazing Dobermans, The (1976)
Amazing Exploits of the Clutching Hand, The (1936)
Amazing Grace (1974)
Amazing Mrs. Holliday, The (1943)
Amazons, The (1973)
Ambulance (1962)
Amelie's Trip (1975)
Amendment to the Law for the Defense of the State (1976)
America (1914)
America (1924)
American Dream, The (1976)
American Friend, The (1977)
American Guerrilla in the Philippines, An (1950)
American Nitro (1979)
American Success Company, The (1979)
American Surplus, The (1975)
American Tragedy, An (1964)
America's Fat (1976)
Americathon (1979)
Amici Miei (1975)
Amico, Stammi Lontano Almeno un Palmo (1972)
Amityville Horror, The (1979)
Amlash Enchanted Forest, The (1974)
Among People (1979)
Among the Living (1941)
Amore de Pluie, Un (1974)
Amorous Adventures of Don Quixote and Sancho Panza, The (1976)
Amulet of Ogum, The (1975)
Anatomy of a Motor Oil (1970)
Anche se Volessi Lavovare, Che Cosa Faccio? (1972)
And Baby Makes Three (1972)
And for a Roof, a Sky Full of Stars (1968)
And Hope to Die (1972)
... And Justice for All (1979)
And Now My Love (1975)
And One Was Beautiful (1940)
And the Rain Blots Out All the Traces (1973)
And They Lived Happily Ever After (1976)
Andes Odyssey, The (1976)
Angel and Woman (1978)
Angel Comes to Brooklyn, An (1945)
Angel from Texas, An (1940)
Angel Mine (1978)
Angela (1973)
Angels (1976)
Angels over Broadway (1940)
Angels with Broken Wings (1941)
Anges Gardiens (1964)
Angry Man, The (1979)
Angry Youth (1972)
Anguish (1976)
Anima Nera (1962)
Anima Persa (1977)
Animal, The (1977)
Animal Kingdom, The (1932)
Anna and the Wolves (1973)
Anna Karenina (1975)
Anne of Green Gables (1934)
Anne of Windy Poplars (1940)
Anni Ruggenti (1962)
Annie Oakley (1935)
Anno Domini 1573 (1976)
Another Face (1935)
Another Man, Another Chance (1977)
Another Smith for Paradise (1972)
Anschi and Michael (1977)
Ant and the Aardvark, The (1968)
Ant from U. N. C. L. E., The (1968)
Ante Up (1975)
Anthology of Italian Cinema, The (1958)
Antipolis (1952)
Antiseptics in Hospital (1970)
Antoine and Sebastien (1973)
Anton the Magician (1978)
Antonio and Sebastian (1974)
Antonio Gaudi: An Unfinished Vision (1974)
Antonio Gramsci--The Days of Prison (1977)
Antony and Cleopatra (1914)
Antony and Cleopatra (1972)
Antti the Treebranch (1977)
Anuity, The (1972)
Any Gun Can Play (1967)
Apache Gold (1963)
Apache Kid, The (1941)

Ape and Superape (1973)
Aphonyo (1976)
Apocalypse des Animaux, L' (1973)
Apocalypse Now (1979)
Appassionata (1974)
Apple Dumpling Gang, The (1975)
Apple Pie (1975)
Apple, the Stem and the Seeds, The (1974)
Apple War, The (1972)
Appointment in Berlin (1943)
Appointment with a Shadow (1958)
Apprentice Sorcerers, The (1977)
Apprenticeship of Duddy Kravitz, The (1974)
Arabian Adventure (1979)
Arabian Nights, The (1974)
Arabian Tragedy, An (1912)
Are These Our Children? (1931)
Arid Land (1972)
Arizona Cyclone (1941)
Arizona Legion (1939)
Arizona Terrors (1942)
Arizona Trail (1943)
Arizonian, The (1935)
Arkansas Judge, The (1941)
Arkansas Traveler, The (1938)
Armaguedon (1977)
Arnold (1973)
Around the World in 80 Minutes (1931)
Arrah-na-Pough (1911)
Arrive Before Daybreak (1978)
Arsenal (1928)
Arson Gang Busters (1938)
Art of Killing, The (1978)
Artists and Models Abroad (1938)
Artless One, The (1972)
As Husbands Go (1933)
As the Moon (1977)
As We Forgive (1926)
Ascent, The (1977)
Ash Wednesday (1973)
Ashanti (1979)
Assassin, The (1961)
Assassin of Rome, The (1973)
Assassination, The (1972)
Assassination in Sarajevo (1976)
Assassination of Metteotti, The (1973)
Assassination of Trotsky (1972)
Assault on Agathon (1976)
Associate, The (1979)
Asya's Happiness (1978)
At Home Among Strangers (1974)
At Night All Cats Are Gray (1977)
At Sword's Point (1952)
At the Beginning of Summer (1979)
At the Brink of the Brink of the Bench (1979)
At the Earth's Core (1976)
At the Front in North Africa (1943)
At the Service of Spanish Womanhood (1978)
Ataud del Vampiro, El (Vampire's Coffin, The) (1959)
Atlantic Salmon, The (1956)
Atom Age Vampire (1960)
Attack in the Pacific (1945)
Attack of the Giant Leeches (1959)
Attack of the Killer Tomatoes (1979)
Attenti al Buffone (1975)
Attico, L' (1963)
Attila '74 (1975)
Au Guadalquivir (1965)
Audience, The (1972)
Audrey Rose (1977)
August and July (1973)
Autobiography of a Princess (1975)
Autostop Sosso Sangue (1977)
Autour d'un Recif (1949)
Avalanche (1978)
Avalanche Express (1979)
Avatar Botanique de Melle Flora, L' (1965)
Avenger, The (1933)
Average Man, An (1977)

Baara (1979)
Baba Yaga (1973)
Babatu (1976)
Babe (1975)
Baby, The (1972)

Baby Blue Marine (1976)
Baby Sitter, The (1975)
Baby Snakes (1979)
Bachelor Bait (1934)
Bachelor Daddy (1941)
Bachelor Mother (1939)
Bachelor Party, The (1957)
Bachelor's Daughters, The (1946)
Backfire (1964)
Bad (1977)
Bad Charleston Charlie (1973)
Bad Company (1972)
Bad Guy (1937)
Bad Guys, The (1979)
Bad Man, The (1941)
Bad Men of Deadwood (1941)
Bad Men of Missouri (1941)
Bad News Bears, The (1976)
Bad News Bears Go to Japan, The (1978)
Bad News Bears in Breaking Training, The (1977)
Bad One, The (1930)
Bad Spirits of the Euphrates, The (1978)
Bad Starters, The (1976)
Badge 373 (1973)
Badlands (1973)
Badlands of Dakota (1941)
Bahama Passage (1941)
Bailiff of Griefensee, The (1979)
Baker's Hawk (1977)
Ball of Fire (1942)
Ballad of Emile, The (1966)
Ballad of the Daltons, The (1978)
Ballerina ed il Buon Dio, La (1958)
Bamboo Gods and Iron Men (1974)
Band Plays On, The (1934)
Bandit Trail, The (1941)
Bang the Drum Slowly (1973)
Banished (1978)
Banjo on My Knee (1936)
Bank Shot (1974)
Banked Fires (1972)
Bar at the Crossing, The (1972)
Barbarian, The (1933)
Bare Knuckles (1978)
Baree, Son of Kazan (1925)
Barefoot Adventure (1961)
Barefooten Gen (1976)
Barnacle Bill (1941)
Barney (1977)
Barnyard Follies (1940)
Barocco (1976)
Baron Blood (1972)
Barricade at Pont du Jour, The (1978)
Barrier (1966)
Barrier (1979)
Barrier, The (1926)
Barry Lyndon (1975)
Barry McKenzie Rides Again (1974)
Base of the Air Is Red, The (1977)
Basketball Stars (1974)
Bat People, The (1974)
Batingaw (1974)
Batman (1943)
Battle Beyond the Sun (1963)
Battle Cry of Peace, The (1915)
Battle for the Railway (1978)
Battle of Algiers, The (1967)
Battle of Britain, The (1969)
Battle of Midway, The (1942)
Battle of Neretva (1969)
Battle of the Amazons (1973)
Battle of the Planet of the Apes (1973)
Battle of the Volga, The (1959)
Battleflag (1977)
Battlestar Galactica (1979)
Baxter! (1973)
Baxter, Vera Baxter (1977)
Bay of Marbles, A (1975)
Bayou (1957)
Be Blessed (1978)
Be Yourself (1930)
Beach Guard in Winter, The (1976)
Beachcomber, The (1939)
Bears and I, The (1974)
Beast, The (1974)
Beast Must Die, The (1974)
Beast of Morocco (1966)
Beasts (1977)
Beasts Are on the Streets, The (1978)
Beat Girl (see Wild for Kicks)
Beau Ideal (1931)
Beau Masque (1972)
Beau Militaire, Le (1968)

Beauty and the Beast (1962)
Beauty for the Asking (1939)
Because of the Cats (1973)
Becky Sharp (1935)
Bedside Head (1972)
Bedside Highway (1972)
Bedside Romance (1973)
Bedside Sailors (1976)
Bedtime Story (1941)
Bee at the Beach (1950)
Before Dawn (1933)
Before the Day Breaks (1977)
Before the Revolution (1964)
Begone Dull Care (1948)
Behind the News (1940)
Being There (1979)
Bel Paseo, Il... (1977)
Belfer (1978)
Bell, The (1973)
Bell Jar, The (1979)
Belladonna (1973)
Belle of the Nineties (1934)
Bells on Their Toes (1952)
Beloved Elektra (1975)
Beloved Love (1977)
Beloved Lover (1979)
Belstone Fox, The (1973)
Ben (1972)
Ben and Benedict (1977)
Beneath Western Skies (1944)
Bengal Brigade (1954)
Bengal Tiger, The (1972)
Benjamin (1973)
Benji (1974)
Bequest for a Village (1969)
Berlinger (1976)
Bernice Bobs Her Hair (1976)
Best Friends (1974)
Best Friends (1975)
Best Years, The (1949)
Betia, La (1972)
Betrayal (1929)
Betrayers, The (1962)
Betsy, The (1978)
Between Heaven and Hell (1976)
Between Men (1915)
Between Midnight and Dawn (1950)
Between Miracles (see Per Grazia Ricevuta)
Between Night and Day (1975)
Between the Lines (1977)
Beware the Blob (1972)
Beware: When a Widow Falls in Love (1975)
Beyond and Back (1978)
Beyond Fear (1975)
Beyond Good and Evil (1977)
Beyond the Bridge (1976)
Beyond the Door (1974)
Beyond the Door (1975)
Beyond the Great Wall (1964)
Beyond the Poseidon Adventure (1979)
Beyond the Sun (1975)
Beyond Time (1974)
Biches, Les (1968)
Bicyclettes de Belsize, Les (1969)
Bidone, Il (The Swindle) (1962)
Bielles des Sables (1952)
Big Bad Mama (1974)
Big Bird Cage, The (1972)
Big Blockade, The (1941)
Big Brother Ching (1975)
Big Bus, The (1976)
Big Carnival, The (Ace in the Hole) (1951)
Big City (1937)
Big Doll House, The (1971)
Big Fix, The (1978)
Big Game, The (1936)
Big Guy (1939)
Big Jim McLain (1952)
Big Lie, The (1951)
Big Mama (1979)
Big Sentiments Make for Good Sports (1973)
Big Sleep, The (1978)
Big Thumbs (1977)
Big Trees, The (1952)
Big Wednesday (1978)
Big Wheel, The (1949)
Bigamist, The (1953)
Bikini Beach (1964)
Bilbao (1978)
Bilitis (1977)
Bill of Divorcement, A (1940)
Billion Dollar Hobo (1978)
Billy in the Lowlands (1979)
Billy Jack Goes to Washington (1977)
Billy the Kid Returns (1938)
Billy the Kid vs. Dracula (1965)
Billy Two Hats (1973)

Bim (1976)
Bingo Long Traveling All-Stars and Motor Kings, The (1976)
Bio-Graphia (1975)
Biography of a Bachelor Girl (1935)
Birch Interval (1976)
Bird, The (1965)
Bird Life in Mauritania (1963)
Bird of Paradise (1932)
Birdman of Alcatraz (1962)
Birds, The (1972)
Birds Do It, Bees Do It... (1974)
Birds of a Feather (see Cage aux Folles, La)
Birds of Baden-Baden, The (1976)
Birds, the Bees, and the Italians, The (1967)
Birth of a Nation, The (1915)
Biscuit Eater, The (1972)
Bishop's Bedroom, The (1977)
Bismarck (1914)
Bit Between the Teeth, The (1979)
Bite the Bullet (1975)
Bitter Love (1974)
Bitter Tea of General Yen, The (1933)
Bittersweet Love (1976)
Black and White in Color (1976)
Black and White Lite Days and Nights (1978)
Black Arrow (1944)
Black Banana, The (1977)
Black Belly of the Tarantula, The (1972)
Black Belt Jones (1974)
Black Bird, The (1975)
Black Bunch, The (Jungle Sex) (1972)
Black Caesar (1973)
Black Castle, The (1952)
Black Cat, The (1941)
Black Christmas (1974)
Black Crook, The (1916)
Black Diamond, The (1977)
Black Diamonds (1940)
Black Eye (1974)
Black Fantasy (1972)
Black Friday (1940)
Black Girl (1972)
Black Godfather (1974)
Black Hole, The (1979)
Black Horse Canyon (1954)
Black Jack (1973)
Black Jack (1979)
Black Lash, The (1952)
Black Litter (1977)
Black Magic 2 (1977)
Black Mama, White Mama (1973)
Black Oak Conspiracy (1977)
Black Orpheus (Orfeu Negro) (1959)
Black Panther, The (1977)
Black Pirate, The (1977)
Black Sabbath (1964)
Black Samson (1974)
Black Shampoo (1976)
Black Sheep, The (1968)
Black Sheep, The (1979)
Black Shield of Falworth, The (1954)
Black Six, The (1974)
Black Stallion, The (1979)
Black Sun (1978)
Black Sunday (1977)
Black Thursday (1974)
Black Vampire, The (1953)
Black Victory (1976)
Black Windmill, The (1974)
Blackmail (1939)
Blackout (1978)
Blacula (1972)
Blade (1973)
Blaise Pascal (1972)
Blazing Magnum (1976)
Blazing Saddles (1974)
Blind Date (1959)
Blindman (1972)
Blockhouse, The (1973)
Blond Cheat (1938)
Blonde Inspiration (1941)
Blonde Savage (1947)
Blondie for Victory (1942)
Blondie Has Servant Trouble (1940)
Blondie Knows Best (1946)
Blondie on a Budget (1940)
Blondie Plays Cupid (1940)
Blondy (1975)
Blood and Guts (1978)
Blood Drinkers, The (Vampire People, The) (1966)

Blood Fiends (1966)
Blood for Dracula (1974)
Blood in the Streets (1976)
Blood Money (1933)
Blood Money (1954)
Blood of Dracula's Castle, The (1967)
Blood of the Railroad Workers (1979)
Blood on Satan's Claw, The (1971)
Blood Pie (1971)
Blood Relatives (1978)
Blood Sabbath (1971)
Blood Stains in a New Car (1975)
Bloodbrothers (1978)
Bloodhounds of Broadway (1952)
Bloodline (1979)
Bloodsuckers (1971)
Bloody Vampire, The (1961)
Blow for Blow (1972)
Blowdry (1976)
Blue Bird, The (1976)
Blue Collar (1978)
Blue Country (1977)
Blue Ferns, The (1977)
Blue Fin (1978)
Blue Summer (1973)
Bluebeard (1972)
Bluebeard's Eighth Wife (1938)
Blueprint for Murder (1953)
Blues Pattern (1956)
Bob & Daryl & Ted & Alex (1972)
Bobbie Joe and the Outlaw (1976)
Bobby Deerfield (1977)
Bobby's War (1974)
Bobo, Jacco (1979)
Body, The (1973)
Body Disappears, The (1941)
Body of My Enemy, The (1976)
Bokyo (1975)
Bolero (1934)
Bomb, The (1969)
Bomber and Paganini (1977)
Bombs Over Burma (1942)
Bonanza (1960)
Bone (1972)
Bons Ami, Les (1958)
Book of Good Love, The (1975)
Book of Numbers (1973)
Boom (1972)
Boom, Il (1963)
Boomerang (1979)
Boon, The (1979)
Bootleggers (5 Sons of Dogs) (1974)
Bootleggers, The (1974)
Boquitas Pintadas (1974)
Bora Bora (1968)
Border Cafe (1937)
Border Crossing, The (1979)
Border G-Man (1938)
Border Legion, The (1940)
Border Vigilantes (1941)
Bordertown Trail (1944)
Born Again (1978)
Born Losers (1967)
Born to Be Bad (1934)
Born to Be Wild (1938)
Born to Buck (1968)
Born to Kill (1975)
Born to Raise Hell (1975)
Borrowers, The (1973)
Borsalino and Co. (1974)
Boscop Diagram, The (1976)
Bosko Buha (1979)
Boss, The (1958)
Boss and the Worker, The (1975)
Boss of Boomtown (1944)
Boss' Son, The (1978)
Boston Strangler, The (1968)
Bottleneck (1979)
Bougnats, Les (1966)
Boulevard Nights (1979)
Bound for Glory (1976)
Bowery, The (1933)
Bowery Boy (1940)
Boxcar Bertha (1972)
Boxer, The (1977)
Boy and His Dog, A (1975)
Boy in the Tree (1961)
Boy Slaves (1939)
Boy Ten Feet Tall, A (1965)
Boy Who Cried Werewolf, The (1973)
Boy Who Saved a Nation, The (1937)
Boys (1977)
Boys from Brazil, The (1978)
Boys in Company C, The (1978)
Brannigan (1975)
Bras de la Seine, Les (1955)

Brass Target (1978)
Bravados, The (1958)
Brave One, The (1956)
Bravo Maestro (1978)
Bread and Chocolate (1974)
Bread and Stones (1979)
Bread of the Sky, The (1962)
Break of Hearts (1935)
Breaker, Breaker (1977)
Breakfast in Bed (1978)
Breakheart Pass (1976)
Breaking Away (1979)
Breaking Point (1976)
Breaking with Old Ideas (1976)
Breakout (1975)
Breakthrough (1979)
Breathless (1959)
Breezy (1973)
Breve Amori a Palma di Majorca (1959)
Bricklayers, The (1977)
Bride, The (1973)
Bride of Frankenstein (1935)
Bride Wore Black, The (1968)
Bride Wore Red, The (1937)
Bridge Too Far, A (1977)
Brief Season (1969)
Briere, La (1924)
Brigand, The (1952)
Bring Me the Head of Alfredo Garcia (1974)
Brink's Job, The (1978)
Britain at Bay (1940)
British Intelligence (1940)
Broadway to Hollywood (1933)
Broken Flag (1979)
Broken Lullaby (1932)
Bronte Sisters, The (1979)
Bronzes, Les (1978)
Brooklyn Orchid (1942)
Brother on the Run (1974)
Brother Rat and a Baby (1940)
Brother Sun, Sister Moon (1972)
Brothers (1977)
Brothers, The (1976)
Bruce Lee--True Story (1976)
Bruce Lee's Game of Death (1978)
Brutalization of Franz Blum, The (1975)
Brute Man, The (1946)
Brutes and Savages (1978)
Brutus (1976)
Bubble, The (1976)
Buck and the Preacher (1972)
Buck Benny Rides Again (1940)
Buck Rogers (1979)
Bucktown (1975)
Budapest Tales (1977)
Buddies (1976)
Budding Love (1977)
Buffalo Bill and the Indians, or Sitting Bull's History Lesson (1976)
Bug (1975)
Bugler of Battery B., The (1912)
Bugles in the Afternoon (1952)
Bugsy Malone (1976)
Bulldog Drummond in Africa (1938)
Bulldog Drummond Strikes Back (1934)
Bullet Code (1940)
Bullet for the General, A (1968)
Buque Maldito, El (see Ghost Galleon, The)
Burglars, The (1971)
Burgos Trial, The (1979)
Burma Convoy (1941)
Burn! (Queimada) (1970)
Burn, Samar, Burn! (1974)
Burned Bridge (1975)
Burned City, The (1976)
Burning (1979)
Burnt Offerings (1976)
Bus, The (1976)
Buster and Billie (1974)
Busting (1974)
But Aren't You Ever Going to Change, Margarita? (1978)
But Where Is Daniel Vax? (1974)
Butch and Sundance: The Early Days (1979)
Butcher, the Star and the Orphan, The (1975)
Butterflies Are Free (1972)
By Hook or By Crook (1976)
By Your Leave (1934)
Bye Bye Monkey (1978)

C. C. and Company (1970)
Cabiria (1913)
Cactus in the Snow (1972)
Caddie (1976)

Cage aux Folles, La (1978)
Cagliostro (1975)
Cahill, United States Marshall (1973)
Cain (1930)
Caio (1967)
Calaboose (1943)
Calamity (1978)
Califfa, La (1971)
California Dreaming (1979)
California Reich, The (1976)
California Split (1974)
California Suite (1978)
Caligula (1979)
Call Him Mr. Shatter (1976)
Call Me from Afar (1978)
Call Northside 777 (1948)
Call of Spring, The (1978)
Call of the Flesh (1930)
Call of the Rockies (1944)
Call of the Wild (1973)
Call of the Yukon (1938)
Call the Mesquiteers (1938)
Calling Dr. Death (1943)
Call-Up, The (1979)
Calm, Cool and Collected (see Femmes Fatales)
Calm Yourself (1935)
Calmos (see Femmes Fatales)
Calzonin Inspector (1974)
Camera Buff (1979)
Camouflage (1940)
Camouflage (1977)
Can I Do It ... Til I Need Glasses? (1977)
Can I Help You? (1966)
Canal, The (1979)
Cancel My Reservation (1972)
Candidate, The (1972)
Candide (1960)
Candleshoe (1977)
Cannibal Girls (1973)
Cannonball (1976)
Can't Help Singing (1944)
Cantagallo (1969)
Caone (1975)
Capricorn One (1978)
Captain, The (1972)
Captain Hurricane (1935)
Captain Is a Lady, The (1940)
Captain Kronos--Vampire Hunter (1972)
Captain Lightfoot (1955)
Captain Lust (1977)
Captain Midnight (1942)
Captain Mikula, the Kid (1974)
Captive City (1952)
Captured by Bedouins (1912)
Car, The (1977)
Car Wash (1976)
Caravan (1934)
Caravan to Vaccares (1974)
Caravans (1978)
Career Girl (1944)
Careful, Soft Shoulder (1942)
Carey Treatment, The (1972)
Carlos und Elisabeth (1924)
Carolina (1934)
Carolina Cherie (1973)
Carousella (1965)
Carpet on the Cloud, The (1976)
Carpetbaggers, The (1963)
Carrie (1976)
Carrot Queen, The (1978)
Carry On, Emmanuelle (1978)
Carry On, Screaming (1966)
Cars That Ate Paris, The (1974)
Carson City Kid, The (1940)
Casanova (1976)
Casanova and Company (1977)
Case Against Mrs. Ames, The (1936)
Case of the Full-Moon Murders, The (1973)
Case of the Mukkinese Battle-horn, The (1956)
Casey's Shadow (1978)
Casino Murder Case, The (1935)
Cass Timberlane (1948)
Cassandra Crossing, The (1977)
Castaway Cowboy, The (1974)
Castaways of Turtle Island, The (1976)
Castaways on Gilligan's Island, The (1979)
Castle of Purity (1974)
Castle of the Living Dead, The (1964)
Castle on the Hudson (1940)
Castles Through the Ages (1958)
Cat, The (1978)
Cat and the Mouse, The (Cat and Mouse) (1975)
Cat Ate the Parakeet, The (1972)
Cat from Outer Space, The (1978)
Cat Murkill and the Silks (1976)

Cat That Hated People, The (1948)
Cat Women of the Moon (1953)
Catastrophe 1999 (1977)
Catch My Soul (1974)
Catherine Inc. (1975)
Catherine the Great (1934)
Cats (Kattorna) (1964)
Cat's Play (1974)
Cattle Queen (1951)
Ce Cher Victor (1975)
Cecilia, La (1975)
Celestina (1976)
Cell Zero, The (1975)
Cesar and Rosalie (1972)
Cette Nuit-la (1958)
Chain of Life (1975)
Chained (1934)
Challenge of Greatness, The (1976)
Challenge to Be Free (1975)
Challengers, The (1968)
Champ, The (1979)
Champagne Waltz (1937)
Chance and Violence (1974)
Chance at Heaven (1933)
Chandu the Magician (1932)
Chang (1927)
Change of Heart (1934)
Chaplin Revue, The (1959)
Chaplinesque, My Life and Hard Times (1972)
Chaplin's Art of Comedy (1966)
Chapter Two (1979)
Chariots of the Gods (1973)
Charles and Lucie (1979)
Charleston (1978)
Charley and the Angel (1973)
Charley Moon (1956)
Charley One-Eye (1973)
Charley Varrick (1973)
Charley's Aunt (1941)
Charlie and His Two Birds (1973)
Charlie Brown Christmas, A (1970)
Charlie Chan at the Opera (1937)
Charlotte Lionshield (1979)
Charly and Steffen (1979)
Chasing Yesterday (1935)
Chasseur de Chez Maxim's, Le (1953)
Chato's Land (1972)
Chatter-Box (1977)
Che Guevara, El (1969)
Cheap (1974)
Cheaper by the Dozen (1950)
Cheating Cheaters (1934)
Cheerleaders, The (1973)
Chemins de Lumiere (1958)
Cherry, Harry and Raquel (1969)
Chess Players, The (1977)
Chetan, Indian Boy (1973)
Cheyenne Kid (1933)
Chi l'Ha Vista Morire? (1979)
Chicken, The (1963)
Chicken in the Rough (1950)
Child in the Crowd, A (1976)
Child Is a Wild Thing, A (1976)
Child Is Born, A (1940)
Child Is Ours, The (1973)
Child of the Night (1978)
Children of Agony (1977)
Children of Oblivion, The (1979)
Children of Rage (1975)
Children of Sanchez, The (1978)
Child's Play (1972)
Chimes at Midnight (Falstaff) (1967)
Chin, Chin, the Drunken Bum (1976)
China Behind (1974)
China Gate (1957)
Chinatown (1974)
Chinatown After Dark (1931)
Chinese Roulette (1976)
Chloe (1934)
Choca, La (1974)
Chocolate Eclair (1979)
Choice, The (1976)
Choirboys, The (1977)
Chomps (1979)
Chorus (1975)
Chosen Survivors (1974)
Christ Stopped at Eboli (1979)
Christiania (1977)
Christina (1974)
Christmas Eve (1947)
Christmas Holiday (1944)
Christopher Strong (1933)
Chronicle of a Latin-American Subversive (1976)
Chronicle of the Years of Fire (1975)

Chronik von Grieshuus (1925)
Chump at Oxford, A (1940)
Church Mouse, The (1934)
Chut (1972)
Ciao, You Guys (1979)
Ciel est par Dessus le Toit, Le (1956)
Cinderella Liberty (1973)
Cinema Cinema (1979)
Cinerama: South Seas Adventure (1958)
CirCarC Gear, The (1964)
Circumstantial Evidence (1935)
Circus, The (1928)
Circus Tent, The (1979)
Citadel of Crime (1941)
Cities (1970)
Cities and Years (1974)
Citizen Rebels, A (1974)
Citizen's Band (1977)
City of Bad Men (1953)
City on Fire (1979)
City Without Men (1943)
Clair de Femme (1979)
Clark (1977)
Clash by Night (1952)
Class of '44 (1973)
Class of Miss MacMichael, The (1978)
Claudine (1974)
Clear Horizons (1979)
Cleopatra Jones (1973)
Cleopatra Jones and the Casino of Gold (1975)
Clive of India (1935)
Clockmaker, The (1974)
Close Call for Ellery Queen, A (1942)
Close Encounters of the Third Kind (1977)
Closed Ward (1972)
Clown, The (1976)
Club Havana (1945)
Coach (1978)
Cock of the Air (1932)
Cockeyed Cavaliers (1934)
Coco la Fleur, Candidate (1979)
Code of the Prairie (1944)
Coffy (1973)
Cold Heart, The (1977)
Cold Homeland (1978)
Cold Journey (1975)
Cold Soup, The (1975)
Cold Storage (1950)
College Scandal (1935)
Colleges at War (1942)
Collina dei Comali, La (1979)
Colonel and the Werewolf, The (1979)
Colorado (1940)
Colors of the Rainbow, The (1974)
Colour (1975)
Coma (1978)
Comandementi per un Gangster (1968)
Come Back, Charleston Blue (1972)
Come Home and Meet My Wife (1974)
Come Impari ad Amare le Donne (1967)
Come On, Danger (1942)
Comes a Horseman (1978)
Cometogether (1971)
Coming Out Party (1934)
Commando (1963)
Commandos Strike at Dawn (1942)
Commare Secca, La (1962)
Comme un Boomerang (1977)
Commitment, The (1976)
Common Man, The (1975)
Communion (1977)
Companero (1975)
Comtesse Ursel (1913)
Concorde--Airport '79, The (1979)
Condemned to Live (1935)
Condemned Women (1938)
Confederate Ironclad, The (1912)
Confederation--The People Make History, The (1979)
Confessions of a Police Inspector to the District Attorney (1973)
Confessions of a Window Cleaner (1974)
Confessor, The (1973)
Confidences for Confidences (1978)
Congo Maisie (1940)
Conquered City (1962)
Conqueror, The (1916)
Conquerors, The (1932)

Conquest (1937)
Conquest of the Citadel, The (1977)
Conquest of the Planet of the Apes (1972)
Conquistadores, Les (1975)
Conrack (1974)
Conscript, The (1974)
Consequence, The (1977)
Consolation Marriage (1931)
Conspiracy (1939)
Constabulary, The (1975)
Contact (1973)
Context, The (1976)
Contraband (1940)
Contract, The (1978)
Contrechant (1963)
Conversation, The (1974)
Conversation Piece (1975)
Convoy (1978)
Cookbook of Birth Control, The (1975)
Cool Breeze (1972)
Cool Sound from Hell, A (1959)
Cool World, The (1963)
Cooley High (1975)
Coonskin (1975)
Cop (1976)
Cop, A (1972)
Cop or Hood (1979)
Cop Story (1975)
Cops and Robbers (1973)
Coquito, La (1978)
Corbeau, Le (1943)
Corky (1972)
Corleone (Father of the Godfather) (1978)
Corn Is Green, The (1945)
Corn Is Green, The (1978)
Cornbread, Earl and Me (1975)
Corner, The (1915)
Corpus (1979)
Corrida of Love (1976)
Corruption in the Halls of Justice (1975)
Corruption of Chris Miller, The (1973)
Corsair (1931)
Corvette Summer (1978)
Cosa Buffa, La (1972)
Could We Maybe (1976)
Counsellor, The (1973)
Count Dracula and His Vampire Bride (1978)
Count of Monte Cristo, The (1934)
Count of Monte Cristo, The (1976)
Count the Ways (1976)
Count Your Bullets (1972)
Countdown at Kusini (1976)
Counter Kill (1975)
Counterfeit (1936)
Countess Dracula (1970)
Country Inc. (1975)
Country Is Calm, The (1976)
Coup de Grace, The (1976)
Coupe a Dix Francs, La (see $2 Haircut, The)
Courage of Lassie (1946)
Courageous Dr. Christian, The (1940)
Course du Lievre a Tracers les Champs, La (1972)
Courtneys of Curzon Street, The (1947)
Courtship of Andy Hardy, The (1942)
Cousin, Cousine (1975)
Covered Wagon Days (1940)
Covert Action (1978)
Cowboy and the Lady, The (1938)
Cowboys, The (1972)
Cowboys from Texas (1939)
Crab Drum, The (1977)
Cracking Up (1977)
Cramp (1979)
Craze (1974)
Crazies, The (1973)
Crazy Days (1977)
Crazy Horse Paris--France (1977)
Crazy Joe (1974)
Crazy Sex (1976)
Crazy World of Julius Vrooder, The (1974)
Creature, The (1978)
Creature from the Black Lagoon, The (1954)
Creeping Flesh (1973)
Creeping Unknown, The (1955)
Crescendo (1972)
Cricket in the Ear (1976)
Crime Doctor's Courage (1945)
Crime of Dr. Crespi, The (1935)

Crime Ring (1938)
Crime School (1938)
Crime Without Passion (1934)
Crimebusters, The (1961)
Crimes of Petiot (1972)
Criminal, The (1960)
Criminal Records (1974)
Crippled Hand, The (1916)
Crocodile Tears (1965)
Croisiere pour l'Inconnu (1947)
Crooked Road, The (1940)
Cross Currents (1915)
Cross of Iron (1977)
Crossed Swords (1977)
Cross-Eyed Saint, The (1971)
Cruel Love (1978)
Cruel Sea (1972)
Cruise into Terror (1978)
Cry of the Black Wolves, The (1972)
Cry of the Heart (1974)
Cuba (1979)
Cuban Fight Against Demons (1972)
Cuban Love Song (1931)
Cuban Pete (1946)
Cubs, The (1975)
Cuccagna, La (1962)
Cuckoo Patrol (1965)
Culpepper Cattle Co., The (1972)
Cup Glory (1971)
Curio Lake, The (1974)
Curse of the Faceless Man, The (1958)
Curse of the Green Eyes, The (1965)
Curse of the Karnsteins, The (1963)
Curse of the Vampire (1960)
Curse of the Vampires (1970)
Curtain Call (1940)
Cyclops (1976)

D-Day Seen Through American Eyes (1962)
Dagmar Is Where It's At (1972)
Dagmar's Hot Pants Inc. (1971)
Dagny (1977)
Dakota (1974)
Damien--Omen II (1978)
Damnation Alley (1977)
Dan (1914)
Dance Class on Vacation, The (1978)
Dance of the Weed (1941)
Dancing Co-Ed (1939)
Dandy, the All-American Girl (see Sweet Revenge)
Dangerous Age, A (1957)
Dangerous Business (1946)
Dangerous Corner (1934)
Dangerous Game, A (1941)
Dangerous Holiday (1937)
Dangerous Kisses (1973)
Dangerous Years, The (1948)
Daniel Boone (1936)
Daniel in the Lion's Den (1948)
Dante, Mind the Shark (1978)
Daosawan, I Love You (1975)
Daredevils of the Red Circle (1939)
Daredevil's Time (1977)
Dark, The (1979)
Dark Journey (1937)
Dark Lady (1975)
Dark Past, The (1949)
Dark Places (1974)
Dark Streets of Cairo (1941)
Darkest Africa (1936)
Darshan (1974)
D'Artagnan (1915)
Darwin Adventure, The (1972)
Date with the Falcon, A (1942)
Daughter-in-Law (1976)
Daughter-in-Law, The (1972)
Daughter of the Gods, A (1915)
Daughter of the Sun God (1962)
Daughters, Daughters (1973)
Daughters of Darkness (1970)
Daughters of Satan (1972)
Daughters-in-Law (1972)
David (1979)
David Copperfield (1935)
David Copperfield (1970)
Dawn Has Not Broken Yet (1973)
Dawn of the Dead (1979)
Day and the Hour, The (1963)
Day at the Races, A (1937)
Day Does Not Die (1974)
Day for My Love (1977)
Day for Night (1973)
Day of Glory, The (1976)
Day of Infamy (1964)
Day of the Animals (1977)

Embryo (1976)
Emergency! (1977)
Emily (1976)
Emma Mae (1976)
Emmanuelle (1974)
Emmanuelle II--Joys of a Woman (1976)
Emperor, The (1979)
Emperor Jones, The (1933)
Emperor of the North (Pole), The (1973)
Emperor's Candlesticks, The (1937)
Empire of the Ants (1977)
Empreinte, L' (1908)
Empty Canvas, The (1964)
Empty Chair, The (1974)
Enchanted April (1935)
Enchanted Forest, The (1945)
Enclosure, The (1978)
Encounter (1971)
End, The (1978)
End of an Era, The (1957)
End of Autumn (1978)
End of Night (1976)
End of the Road (1954)
End of the World in Our Usual Bed in a Night Full of Rain, The (1978)
Endless Night (1971)
Endless Trail, The (1979)
Enemy Agent (1940)
Enemy Agents Meet Ellery Queen (1942)
Enemy of the Law (1945)
Enemy of the People, An (1978)
Enfants Gates, Des (see Spoiled Children)
Enforcer, The (1976)
Engagement, The (1970)
England Made Me (1973)
Enrico Cuisinier (1955)
Enrico Mattei Affair, The (1972)
Entanglement (1977)
Enter the Dragon (1973)
Entertainer, The (1975)
Entire Days in the Trees (1976)
Epidemic, The (1972)
Epilogue (1963)
Equus (1977)
Eric Soya's 17 (1967)
Erik the Conqueror (1962)
Ernesto (1979)
Erotic Adventures of Zorro, The (1972)
Erotikon--Karussel der Leidenschaften (1963)
Eruption (1961)
Escapade (1974)
Escape, The (1973)
Escape by Night (1937)
Escape from Athena (1979)
Escape to the Sun (1972)
Escape to Witch Mountain (1975)
Esercito di 5 Uomini (1971)
Espionage (1937)
Espy (1975)
Eternal Times (1975)
Etoiles en Croisette (1955)
Etudes (1963)
Europeans, The (1979)
Eva (1965)
Evaso, Le (see Widow Couderc, The)
Evelyn Prentice (1934)
Evening Land (1977)
Everlasting Glory, The (1975)
Every Inch a Lady (1975)
Every Little Crook and Nanny (1972)
Every Sunday Morning (1972)
Everybody Does It (1949)
Everybody He Is Nice ... Everybody He Is Beautiful (1972)
Everybody Rides the Carousel (1975)
Everybody's Doing It (1938)
Everything You Always Wanted to Know About Sex But Were Afraid to Ask (1972)
Everything's Ready, Nothing Works (1974)
Evictors, The (1979)
Evil, The (1978)
Evil Eye, The (1962)
Evolution of Snuff, The (1977)
Exclusive (1937)
Exclusive Story (1936)
Excuse Me, Are You For or Against? (1966)
Executive Action (1973)
Executive Suite (1976)
Exile Express (1939)
Exiled in a Central Avenue (1979)
Exiled to Shanghai (1937)

Exorcist, The (1973)
Exorcist II: The Heretic (1977)
Expert, The (1932)
Experts, The (1973)
Explosion (1978)
Explosive Generation, The (1961)
Extras, The (1978)
Extreme Close-Up (1973)
Eye of the Cat (1975)
Eyes of Laura Mars, The (1978)
Eyes of the Underworld (1943)
Eyewitness (1970)

F Is for Fairbanks (1976)
F. I. S. T. (1978)
F. J. Holden, The (1977)
F. T. A. (1972)
Fabiola (1922)
Fabulous Adventures of the Legendary Baron Munchausen, The (1979)
Factory Outing, The (1978)
Fair Today (1941)
Fairy Dance (1976)
Faithful Woman, A (1976)
Falcon's Brother, The (1942)
Fall, The (1972)
Fall, The (1978)
Fall, The (1979)
Fall In (1943)
Fall of the Roman Empire, The (1964)
Falling in Love (1961)
False Face (1976)
Family, The (1974)
Family Affair, A (1937)
Family Circus (1951)
Family Honeymoon (1949)
Family Honor, The (1977)
Family Nest (1979)
Family of North Country, The (1973)
Family Plot (1976)
Family Portrait (1976)
Family Secret, The (1951)
Family with 100 Children, The (1972)
Fanny Hill (1965)
Fanny Hill (1969)
Fan's Notes, A (1972)
Fantasie au Vieux-Colombier (1953)
Fantasies Behind the Pearly Curtain (1975)
Fantastic Balloon Trip, The (1976)
Fantastic Comedy (1975)
Fantasticna Balada (1958)
Far Country, The (1954)
Far from the Trees (1972)
Far Road, The (1978)
Far Shore, The (1976)
Far-West, The (1973)
Farewell Again (1937)
Farewell My Lovely (1975)
Farewell to Arms, A (1932)
Farewell to Yesterday (1950)
Farewell to Youth (1949)
Fargo (1952)
Fargo Kid, The (1940)
Farmer, The (1977)
Fast Break (1979)
Fast Charlie ... The Moonbeam Rider (1979)
Fat and the Lean, The (1961)
Fat City (1972)
Fatal Coma, The (1979)
Fatal Lady (1936)
Father Heart Wants to Get Married (1974)
Father Master (see Padre Padrone)
Father Sergius (1978)
Father Was a Fullback (1949)
Faustine and the Beautiful Summer (1972)
Faux Pas de Deux (1976)
Fear and Desire (1953)
Fear Is the Key (1972)
Fear of Fear (1976)
Fear on the City (1975)
Fed Up (1973)
Fedora (1978)
Feedback (1978)
Feedback (1979)
Feelings (1977)
Felicite (1979)
Felines, Les (1976)
Felix and Otilia (1972)
Fellini Roma (1972)
Fellini Satyricon (Satyricon) (1971)
Feminin-Feminin (1973)
Femme et le Patin, La (1929)
Femme Image, La (1960)

Femmes Fatales (Calmos) (1976)
Ferocious One, The (1974)
Fete Sauvage, La (1975)
Fever (1976)
Field Lilies (1972)
Fifth Commandment, The (1979)
5th Musketeer, The (1979)
Fifth Seal, The (1977)
Fifty-Fifty (1978)
Fifty-Year Barter, The (1937)
Fight for Freedom (1979)
Fight for Your Lady (1937)
Fight to the Death (1975)
Fighters, The (1974)
Fighting Dan McCool (1912)
Fighting Dervishes of the Desert, The (1912)
Fighting Devil Dogs (1938)
Fighting Mad (1976)
Fighting Marines, The (1935)
Fighting 69th, The (1940)
Fighting Vigilantes, The (1947)
Figlia del Capitano, La (1965)
Figures in a Landscape (1969)
Film, The (1975)
Filming "Othello" (1978)
Fils, Les (see Son, The)
Final Chapter--Walking Tall (1977)
Final Comedown, The (1972)
Finders Keepers (1952)
Finestra sul Luna Park, La (1956)
Finishing School (1934)
Fir Is Left, A (1970)
Fire (Feu) (1970)
Fire in the Middle (1978)
Fire Sale (1977)
Fire Trap (1935)
Fireball 500 (1966)
Firebrands of Arizona (1944)
Fireman, Save My Child (1932)
Firepower (1979)
Fire's Share, The (1978)
Fireworks Woman (1975)
First Circle, The (1973)
First False Step, The (1979)
First Lady (1937)
First Love (1940)
First Love (1977)
First Love (1978)
First Polka, The (1979)
First Star, The (1977)
First Step, The (1975)
First Time, The (1952)
First Time, The (1976)
First Time, on the Grass, The (1975)
Fish That Saved Pittsburgh, The (1979)
Fisherman's Wharf (1939)
Fist in the Pocket (1979)
Fit for a King (1937)
Five Days and Five Nights (1948)
Five Days from Home (1978)
5 Dolls for an August Moon (1972)
Five-Leaf Clover, The (1972)
Five-Man Army, The (1970)
5, 000, 000 Years to Earth (1968)
Five on the Black Hand Side (1973)
5 Sons of Dogs (see Bootleggers, The)
Five Steps (1968)
5, 000 Fingers of Dr. T, The (1952)
Flame (1975)
Flame, The (1947)
Flame Barrier, The (1958)
Flame of Barbary Coast (1945)
Flame of New Orleans, The (1941)
Flaming Signal, The (1933)
Flannagan (1976)
Flesh Gordon (1974)
Flesh of the Orchid, The (1975)
Flic Story, The (1975)
Flight (1960)
Flight, The (1978)
Flight to the Death (1975)
Flirt, The (1916)
Flirting with Fate (1938)
Flock (1972)
Floradora Girl, The (1930)
Flower of Holiness (1973)
Flunking Out (1977)
Flyers of the Open Skies (1977)
Flying Blind (1941)
Flying Cadets (1941)
Flying Carpet, The (1956)
Flying Devils (1933)
Flying Feet (1929)

Flying Tigers (1942)
Flying Torpedo, The (1916)
Flying with Music (1942)
Focal Point (1977)
Follow Me (1969)
Follow the Boys (1944)
Follow Your Heart (1936)
Food of the Gods, The (1976)
Foolish Years (1978)
For an Unimportant Reason (1974)
For Better or Worse (1975)
For Clemence (1977)
For Love One Dies (1973)
For the Love of Benji (1977)
For You I Die (1948)
Forbidden Planet (1956)
Forbidden Room, The (see Anima Persa)
Force of One, A (1979)
Force 10 from Navarone (1978)
Forced Landing (1941)
Foreigner, The (1978)
Foreplay (1975)
Forest Rangers, The (1942)
Foretold by Fate (1979)
Forever Young, Forever Free (1975)
Forever Yours (1945)
Forgotten Faces (1936)
Forgotten Girls (1940)
Forgotten Island of Santosha (1974)
Forsaking All Others (1934)
Fortune, The (1975)
40 Carats (1973)
40 Years Without Sex (1979)
Foul Play (1977)
Foul Play (1978)
Four Days to Death (1976)
Four Flies on Gray Velvet (1972)
Four Guns to the Border (1954)
Four in the Morning (1965)
Four Mothers (1941)
Four Musketeers, The (1975)
Four Seasons, The (1979)
Four's a Crowd (1938)
14, The (1973)
Fox in the Chicken Coop, The (1978)
Foxbat (1977)
Foxtrot (1976)
Foxy Brown (1973)
Framed (1940)
Framed (1975)
Francis (1950)
Francis Gary Powers: The True Story of the U-2 Spy Incident (1976)
Frank and Eva--Living Apart Together (1973)
Frank Buck's Jungle Cavalcade (1941)
Frankenstein (1931)
Frankenstein (1974)
Frankenstein and the Monster from Hell (1974)
Frankenstein--Italian Style (1977)
Frankenstein Meets the Wolf Man (1943)
Frankenstein: The True Story (1973)
Franz (1972)
Frasier, the Sensuous Lion (1973)
Fraulein Doktor (1969)
Freaky Friday (1976)
Freckles (1935)
Free for All (1976)
Free Man, A (1973)
Freebie and the Bean (1974)
Freewheelin' (1976)
French Connection II (1975)
French Postcards (1979)
Frenchie (1951)
Frenzy (1972)
Fresh Air (1956)
Friday Foster (1975)
Friday the 13th ... The Orphan (1979)
Fridericus Rex (1922)
Friendly Neighbors (1940)
Friends: Let's Go to the Party (1972)
Friends of Eddie Coyle, The (1973)
Fringe Benefits (1974)
Frisco Kid, The (1979)
Frisco Lil (1942)
Frisson des Vampires, Le (see Sex and the Vampire)
Fritz the Cat (1972)
Frogs (1972)
From a Roman Balcony (1960)

From Hell to Victory (1979)
From Noon Till Three (1976)
From the Mixed-Up Files of Mrs. Basil E. Frankweiler (1973)
From the Orient with Fury (1965)
From the Police, with Thanks (1972)
Front, The (1976)
Front Page, The (1974)
Frontier Badmen (1943)
Frontier Marshal (1939)
Frontier Revenge (1948)
Frontier Vengeance (1940)
Frontiers of Power (1967)
Fruit Is Ripe, The (1977)
Fuga, La (1964)
Fugitive, The (On the Night of the Fire) (1940)
Fugitive of the Plains (1943)
Full Circle (1977)
Full Confession (1939)
Fumo di Londra (1965)
Fun with Dick and Jane (1977)
Funeral Rites (1972)
Funny Note (1977)
Further Adventures of the Wilderness Family--Part 2 (1978)
Fury, The (1978)
Fury at Furnace Creek (1948)
Fuses (1977)
Futureworld (1976)
Fuzz (1972)

G-Men vs. the Black Dragon (1943)
Gable and Lombard (1976)
Gabriel over the White House (1933)
Gal Young Un (1979)
Galia (1967)
Galileo (1975)
Gallant Lady (1942)
Gallant Sons (1940)
Gambler, The (1974)
Gambling (1934)
Game Called Scruggs, A (1965)
Game of Love, A (1974)
Game of the Apple (1977)
Game Pass (1976)
Games of the XXI Olympiad Montreal 1976 (1977)
Gamin (Waif) (1978)
Ganga Zumba (1972)
Gangs of Chicago (1940)
Gangs of New York (1938)
Gangster Movie, The (1974)
Gangster's Apprentice, The (1976)
Ganja and Hess (1973)
Garden, The (1977)
Garden Murder Case, The (1936)
Garden of Torture, The (1976)
Garden That Tilts, The (1975)
Gas House Kids in Hollywood, The (1947)
Gas Lamps (1972)
Gas-Oil (1955)
Gaspards, Les (1974)
Gatefold Girl, The (1974)
Gates of Fire, The (1972)
Gateway (1938)
Gathering, The (1977)
Gator (1976)
Gaucho Jews, The (1975)
Gauchos of Eldorado (1941)
Gauntlet, The (1977)
Gay Blades (1946)
Gay Caballero, The (1940)
Gay Diplomat, The (1931)
Gay Lord Waring, The (1916)
Gay Vagabond, The (1941)
Gazoros, Serres (1974)
Gendarme and the Creatures from Outer Space, The (1979)
Genesis Children, The (1972)
Genius, The (1976)
Gentle Gangster, A (1943)
Gentleman from Indiana, The (1915)
Georg Hauser's Happy Minutes (1974)
George Who? (1973)
Georgia, Georgia (1972)
Georgie and the Dragon (1951)
Gerald McBoing Boing (1953)
Gerald McBoing Boing's Symphony (1953)
Germania (1914)
Get Carter (1973)
Get Charlie Tully (1976)
Get Out Your Handkerchiefs (1978)

Get Outta Town (1959)
Get to Know Your Rabbit (1972)
Get-Away, The (1941)
Getaway, The (1972)
Getaway, The (Derobade, La) (1979)
Getting There First (1971)
Getting Together (1976)
Ghost Comes Home, The (1940)
Ghost Galleon, The (El Buque Maldito) (1974)
Ghost Train (1976)
Ghost Valley Raiders (1940)
Ghost Walks, The (1934)
Ghoul, The (1975)
Giddyap (1950)
Gift of Gab, The (1934)
Gifts of an Eagle (1975)
Gildersleeve's Ghost (1944)
Giliap (1975)
Giordano Bruno (1973)
Giorno del Furore, Il (1973)
Giorno piu Corto, Il (1962)
Gioventu di Notte (1961)
Girl and the Dream Castle, The (1974)
Girl and the Gambler, The (1939)
Girl Can't Help It, The (1956)
Girl Fit to Be Killed, The (1976)
Girl Friends (1978)
Girl from God's Country (1940)
Girl from Havana, The (1940)
Girl from Manhattan, The (1948)
Girl from Monterey, The (1943)
Girl from Petrovka, The (1974)
Girl from San Lorenzo, The (1950)
Girl from the Mountains, The (1972)
Girl in Australia, A (1972)
Girl in Yellow Pajamas, The (1978)
Girl Named Poo Lom, A (1977)
Girl o' My Dreams (1934)
Girl of the Ozarks (1936)
Girl Passing Through, The (1972)
Girl Who Liked Purple Flowers (1974)
Girl with the Cello, The (1973)
Girl with the Long Hair (1975)
Girl with the Red Scarf, The (1978)
Girls Are for Loving (1973)
Girls at Arms (1975)
Girls at Arms, Part 2 (1976)
Girls at Sea (1977)
Girls' Dormitory (1936)
Girls for the Summer (1958)
Girls in the Sun (1968)
Giron (1974)
Giustiziere, Il (1962)
Give Us This Night (1936)
Give Us Wings (1940)
Glacier Fox, The (1979)
Glamour (1934)
Glass (1958)
Glass Cell, The (1978)
Glass Menagerie, The (1973)
Glass Mountain, The (1960)
Glass Sphinx, The (1967)
Gloria (1977)
Gloria Mundi (1975)
Gloria's Romance (1916)
Glorious Dust (1975)
Glory Brigade, The (1953)
Go Chase Yourself (1938)
Go for It (1976)
Go On Mama (1978)
Go See Mother ... Father Is Working (1978)
Go Tell the Spartans (1978)
Goalie's Anxiety at the Penalty Kick, The (1972)
Goat Horn, The (1972)
God Bless Each Corner of This House (1977)
God of Flower, The (Hanagami) (1977)
God Told Me To (1976)
God, Why Is There a Border in Love? (1979)
Goddesses, The (1973)
Godfather, The (1972)
Godfather II (1974)
Goin' Home (1976)
Goin' South (1978)
Goin' Surfin' (1975)
Goin' to Town (1935)
Going (1979)
Going for Broke (1977)
Going in Style (1979)
Going Places (1973)
Goke, Body Snatcher from

Hell (1968)
Gold (1974)
Gold Mine in the Sky (1938)
Gold Rush, The (1925)
Gold Rush Maisie (1940)
Golden Claw, The (1915)
Golden Fish, The (1959)
Golden Fleecing, The (1940)
Golden Fortress, The (1975)
Golden Girl (1979)
Golden Harvest (1933)
Golden Lady, The (1979)
Golden Mass, The (1975)
Golden Needles (1974)
Golden Nights (1976)
Golden Ophelia (1975)
Golden Swan (1977)
Golden Thing, The (1972)
Golden Voyage of Sinbad (1974)
Goldencauliflower Family Gets the Vote, The (1977)
Goliath and the Barbarians (1959)
Goliath and the Sins of Babylon (1963)
Goliath and the Vampires (1962)
Gone in 60 Seconds (1974)
Good and the Bad, The (1975)
Good Evening to Everybody (1976)
Good-for-Nothings (1978)
Good Guys and the Bad Guys, The (1976)
Good Guys Wear Black (1978)
Good Life, The (1964)
Good Luck, Miss Wyckoff (1979)
Good Morning (Ohayosan) (1975)
Good News (1979)
Goodbye Alicia (1977)
Goodbye, Emmanuelle (1978)
Goodbye, Flickmania (see So Long, Movie Friend)
Goodbye Girl, The (1977)
Goodbye, My Fancy (1951)
Goodbye Norma Jean (1976)
Goodbye ... See You Monday (1979)
Goodbye Singing, The (1975)
Goodnight, Ladies and Gentlemen (1977)
Gordon's War (1973)
Gosh (1974)
Got It Made (1974)
Grand Bouffe, Le (1973)
Grand Canary (1934)
Grand Jury (1936)
Grand Old Girl (1935)
Grand Ole Opry (1940)
Grand Piano, The (1979)
Grand Theft Auto (1977)
Grande Bourgeoisie, La (1975)
Grande Silenzio, Il (1968)
Grandma Schulz (1977)
Grandmother, The (1979)
Grandpa Goes to Town (1940)
Grass (1925)
Gravy Train, The (1974)
Gray Lady Down (1978)
Grayeagle (1977)
Greased Lightning (1977)
Greaser's Palace (1972)
Great Adventure, The (1974)
Great American Bugs Bunny-Road Runner Chase, The (1979)
Great American Cowboy, The (1974)
Great Day, The (1977)
Great Day in the Morning (1956)
Great Escape from Dien Pien Phu, The (1977)
Great Gatsby, The (1974)
Great Gildersleeve, The (1943)
Great Gundown, The (1977)
Great House, The (1975)
Great Jaspar, The (1933)
Great Love, The (1918)
Great MacArthy, The (1975)
Great McGonagall, The (1975)
Great Mr. Nobody, The (1941)
Great Northfield, Minnesota, Raid, The (1972)
Great Plane Robbery, The (1940)
Great Problem, The (1916)
Great Rights, The (1963)
Great Santini, The (1979)
Great Saturday, The (1976)
Great Scout and Cathouse Thursday, The (1976)
Great Scuttling, The (1972)
Great Swindle, The (1941)
Great Train Robbery, The (1941)
Great Train Robbery, The (1978)
Great Waldo Pepper, The (1975)
Great Waves Purify the Sand (1978)

Great White Hope, The (1970)
Great Ziegfeld, The (1936)
Greatest, The (1977)
Greatest Question, The (1919)
Greedy People, The (1977)
Greek Pearls, The (1968)
Greek Tycoon, The (1978)
Greeks Had a Word for Them, The (1932)
Green Belt, The (1941)
Green Cockatoo, The (1937)
Green Eyes (1934)
Green Jacket, The (1979)
Green Room, The (1978)
Green Swamp, The (1916)
Greetings and a Living (1974)
Grete Minde (1977)
Gridiron Flash (1934)
Griffin and Phoenix (1976)
Grip of Jealousy, The (1916)
Grizzly (1976)
Gromaire (1967)
Grotze Farmer, The (1975)
Groundstar Conspiracy, The (1972)
Groupie Girl (1970)
Growing Up Suddenly (1977)
Guappi, I (1979)
Guardian Angel, The (1979)
Guardian of the Wilderness (1977)
Guernica (1972)
Guess What Happened to Count Dracula? (1969)
Guest Workers (1974)
Guilty of Treason (1950)
Guinea Pig Couple, The (1977)
Gumball Rally (1976)
Gun, The (1978)
Gun Law (1938)
Gung Ho! (1946)
Guns of the Black Witch (1961)
Gus (1976)
Guttersnipes (1975)
Guy and a Gal, A (1975)
Guy Like Me Should Never Die, A (1976)
Gypsies Go to Heaven (1976)
Gypsy, The (1975)

H. C. Andersen in Italy (1979)
H. M. Pullham, Esq. (1941)
H. O. T. S. (1979)
Hail (1972)
Hail, Thieves (1973)
Hajduk (1975)
Half Naked Truth, The (1932)
Half Shot at Sunrise (1930)
Half Way to Shanghai (1942)
Halloween (1978)
Ham from the Ardennes (1977)
Hamburg Syndrome, The (1979)
Hamilton in the Musical Festival (1961)
Hamilton, the Musical Elephant (1961)
Hamlet (19[illegible]1)
Hamlet (1970)
Hamlet (1976)
Hammer (1972)
Hammersmith Is Out (1972)
Hand to Cut Off, A (1974)
Hands of Orlac, The (1960)
Hannibal (1973)
Hanover Street (1979)
Happiness Cage, The (1972)
Happiness Is So Near (1978)
Happy as the Grass Was Green (1973)
Happy Confusion (1978)
Happy Days (1974)
Happy Days (1976)
Happy Divorce, The (1975)
Happy Hooker, The (1975)
Happy Mother's Day ... Love, George (1973)
Happy New Year (1973)
Hard Part Begins, The (1973)
Hard Times (1975)
Hardys Ride High, The (1939)
Hare Census, The (1974)
Hark to the Cock (1978)
Harlem Wednesday (1958)
Harmony Abroad (1965)
Harper Valley P. T. A. (1978)
Harrad Experiment, The (1973)
Harrad Summer, The (1974)
Harry and Tonto (1974)
Harry and Walter Go to New York (1976)
Harry in Your Pocket (1973)
Hat Check Honey (1944)
Hatoko's Sea, The (1974)
Haunted Harbor (1944)
Have a Nice Weekend (1975)

Having Wonderful Time (1938)
Havoc (1972)
Hawaii Calls (1938)
Hawaii Five-O (1970)
Hawaiians, The (1970)
Hawk of the Wilderness (1938)
Hawmps (1976)
Hay Foot (1942)
Hazing, The (1977)
He Never Gives Up (1979)
He Walked by Night (1948)
Head over Heels (1979)
Headin' East (1937)
Headless Horseman, The (1975)
Headline Shooter (1933)
Heart Beat (1979)
Heartbreak Kid, The (1972)
Heartbreak People (1979)
Hearth Fires (1972)
Hearts Aflame (1922)
Hearts and Minds (1972)
Hearts High (1976)
Hearts in Bondage (1936)
Hearts of the West (1975)
Hearts of the World (1918)
Heat (1972)
Heat of Normandie St.-Onge, The (1976)
Heat's On, The (1943)
Heave Up (1978)
Heaven and Hell (1978)
Heaven Can Wait (1978)
Heavenly Bodies, The (1973)
Heavens and the Earth, The (1969)
Heavy Traffic (1973)
Heavy Trouble (1977)
Hedda (1975)
Helen Keller in Her Story (1956)
Hell Up in Harlem (1973)
Helldorado (1934)
Hellgate (1952)
Hello, Baby (1976)
Hello, Goodnight, Goodbye (1975)
Hello Jerusalem (1972)
Hello Sucker (1941)
Hellzapoppin' (1941)
Help! My Snowman's Burning Down (1964)
Hempas Bar (1977)
Hennessy (1975)
Henry Aldrich, Editor (1942)
Henry Aldrich Haunts a House (1943)
Henry Goes Arizona (1939)
Henry 9 Till 5 (1970)
Henry VIII and His Six Wives (1972)
Her First Romance (1940)
Herald of the Skies (1937)
Herbie Goes to Monte Carlo (1977)
Herbie Rides Again (1974)
Hercules at the Center of the Earth (1961)
Here Come the Tigers (1978)
Here Comes Every Body (1972)
Here Comes Mr. Jordan (1941)
Here Comes the Band (1935)
Here Is My Heart (1934)
Here's to Romance (1935)
Here We Go 'Round the Mulberry Bush (1968)
Heritage, The (1978)
Heritage of the Desert (1939)
Hero Ain't Nothin' but a Sandwich, A (1977)
Heroes (1977)
Heroes Are Not Wet Behind the Ears, The (1979)
Heroes of the Saddle (1940)
Heroine (1972)
Heroines of Evil, The (1979)
Herz aus Glas (1976)
He's My Guy (1943)
He's Quite a Man (1975)
Hester Street (1975)
Hex (1973)
Hey, Mister, I Am Your Wife (1976)
Hi, Gaucho (1935)
Hi, Neighbor (1942)
Hickey and Boggs (1972)
Hidden Power (1939)
Hide and Seek (1976)
Hide-Out (1934)
Hiding Place, The (1975)
Higgins Family, The (1938)
High and Dry (1951)
High and Low (1963)
High Anxiety (1977)
High Chaparral, The (1969)
High Conquest (1947)
High Flyers (1937)

High Plains Drifter (1973)
High Rise (1973)
High Street (1976)
High Velocity (1977)
Highways by Night (1942)
Hills Have Eyes, The (1978)
Hills of Oklahoma (1950)
Himiko (1974)
Hindenberg, The (1975)
Hippocrates (1972)
Hireling, The (1973)
His Family Tree (1935)
His Girl Friday (1940)
His Greatest Gamble (1934)
His Land (1970)
Histadruth (1945)
History of Postwar Japan as Told by a Bar Hostess, The (1974)
Hit (1973)
Hit Parade of 1941 (1940)
Hit Song (Schlager) (1979)
Hit the Road (1941)
Hitchhiker, The (1979)
Hitchhikers, The (1972)
Hitler, a Career (1977)
Hitler Around the Corner (1975)
Hitler: The Last Ten Days (1973)
Hitler's Children (1943)
Hitter, The (1979)
Hoa-Binh (1969)
Hoax, The (1972)
Hold That Ghost (1941)
Hole in the Wall, A (1978)
Holiday, The (1973)
Holiday for Lovers (1959)
Hollow Triumph (1948)
Hollywood Boulevard (1976)
Hollywood Cavalcade (1939)
Hollywood Stadium Mystery (1938)
Holocaust 2000 (1977)
Holy Alliance, The (1978)
Holy Mountain, The (1973)
Holy Office, The (1974)
Homage to Chagall--The Colors of Love (1977)
Home and Refuge (1977)
Home for Christmas (1975)
Home Movies (1979)
Home on the Range (1946)
Home, Sweet Home (1973)
Home Town Story (1951)
Homebodies (1974)
Homeland (1973)
Homeward in the Night (1977)
Homo Eroticus (1975)
Honey (1930)
Honeybaby, Honeybaby (1974)
Honeymoon (Taxidi Toy Melitos) (1979)
Honeymoon for Three (1941)
Honeymoon Trip, The (1976)
Honkers, The (1972)
Honky (1971)
Honolulu (1939)
Honor's Altar (1916)
Hooper (1978)
Hoopla (1933)
Hooray for Love (1935)
Hop Harrigan (1946)
Hop, the Devil's Brew (1916)
Hope (1978)
Hornet's Nest, The (1976)
Horrible Sexy Vampire, The (1970)
Horror, The (1933)
Horror Express (1973)
Horror Island (1941)
Horror of Dracula (1958)
Horror of the Blood Monsters (1970)
Horsemen, The (1971)
Hospitals: The White Mafia (1973)
Hot-Blooded Paolo (1973)
Hot Car Girl (1958)
Hot Channels (1973)
Hot Circuit (1972)
Hot-Head (1979)
Hot Lead and Cold Feet (1978)
Hot Parts (1972)
Hot Potato (1976)
Hot Rabbit, The (1974)
Hot Rock, The (1972)
Hot Stuff (1979)
Hot Tip (1935)
Hotel Pacific (1975)
Hotsy Footsy (1952)
Hottest Show in Town, The (1974)
Hound of the Baskervilles, The (1978)
Hour-Glass Sanatorium, The (1973)

Hour of Mary and the Bird of Gold, The (1976)
Hour of Parting, The (1973)
Hour of the Wolf, The (1979)
House (1977)
House, The (1975)
House Calls (1978)
House I Live In, The (1944)
House in the South, The (1975)
House of a Thousand Candles, The (1936)
House of Bamboo (1955)
House of Dracula (1945)
House of Fear (1944)
House of Frankenstein (1944)
House of Mystery, The (1934)
House of Sand, A (1962)
House of the Doves (1972)
House of the Lute (1979)
House of the Seven Gables, The (1940)
House on Bare Mountain (1962)
House on Skull Mountain, The (1974)
House That Dripped Blood, The (1971)
House Without Boundaries, The (1972)
Houses in This Alley (1978)
How Low Can You Fall? (1974)
How to Behave in a Fourposter Bed (1972)
How to Lose a Wife and Find a Lover (1978)
How to Make It (1968)
How to Marry a Millionaire (1953)
How to Seduce a Woman (1974)
How, When and With Whom? (1969)
How Wonderful to Die Assassinated (1975)
Howzer (1972)
Huckleberry Finn (1974)
Hudson's Bay (1940)
Hue and Cry (1978)
Hugo the Hippo (1976)
Hullabaloo over Georgie and Bonnie's Pictures (1979)
Hu-Man (1975)
Human Factor, The (1975)
Human Factor, The (1979)
Human Revolution, The (1974)
Hunchback of Rome (1960)
Hunchback of the Morgue, The (1973)
Hundred Days After Childhood, A (1975)
Hungarians, The (1978)
Hunger (1966)
Hungry Hank's Hallucination (1912)
Hungry Wives (1973)
Hunters, The (1977)
Hunters of the Deep (1955)
Hunting Accident, A (1978)
Hurricane (1978)
Hurricane (1979)
Hurricane, The (1937)
Hurricane Express, The (1932)
Hurricane Smith (1941)
Hurry, Charlie, Hurry (1941)
Hurry Up, or I'll Be 30 (1973)
Husbands Vacationing (1975)
Hustle (1975)
Hyena's Sun (1977)
Hypnotized (1932)
Hypochondriac, The (1979)
Hypothesis of the Stolen Painting, The (1979)

I Am a Delinquent (1977)
I Am a Fugitive from a Chain Gang (1932)
I Am Looking for My Own (1973)
I Am Suzanne (1934)
I Belong to Me (1978)
I Can't Give You Anything but Love, Baby (1940)
I Could Never Have Sex with Any Man Who Has So Little Regard for My Husband (1973)
I Cover Chinatown (1936)
I Cover the Waterfront (1933)
I Did It (1973)
I Did Kill Facundo (1975)
I Escaped from Devil's Island (1973)
I Fix America and Return (1974)
I Had a Feeling I Was Dead (1975)
I Killed Geronimo (1950)
I Killed Rasputin (1966)

I Like It That Way (1934)
I Live on Danger (1942)
I Love a Mystery (1945)
I Love You (1974)
I Love You, I Hate You (1968)
I Love You, I Love You Not (see Together)
I Love You No Longer (1976)
I Love You, Rosa (1972)
I Loved You Wednesday (1933)
I Married a Witch (1942)
I Married Adventure (1940)
I, Maureen (1978)
I Met Him in Paris (1937)
I Met My Love Again (1938)
I Miss You, Hugs and Kisses (1978)
I, Mobster (1958)
I Need You So Much, Love (1976)
I Never Cried Like This Before (1975)
I Never Promised You a Rose Garden (1977)
I Salute the Mafia (1965)
I Saw Her First (1975)
I Sing I Cry (1979)
I, Tintin (1976)
I Want a Solution (1974)
I Want to Be a Woman (1977)
I Want What I Want (1972)
I Was a Convict (1939)
I Will ... I Will ... for Now (1976)
Ice Castles (1978)
Ice Continent, The (1975)
Ice-Age (1975)
Icebreaker (1951)
Ice-Capades (1941)
Iceland (1942)
Icy Breasts (1974)
I'd Like to Have My Troubles (1975)
Idaho Transfer (1973)
Ideal Palace, The (1959)
Idealist, The (1976)
Idiot's Delight (1939)
If Don Juan Were a Woman (see Don Juan)
If Ever I See You Again (1978)
If I Had a Girl (1976)
If I Had a Million Rubles (1974)
If I Were to Do It Over Again (1976)
If Pigs Had Wings (1977)
If You Don't Watch Out (1950)
Ikarus (1979)
Il Faut Vivre Dangereusement (1975)
I'll Cry Tomorrow (1953)
I'll Force You to Leave (1978)
I'll Take Her Like a Father (1974)
I'll Wait for You (1941)
Illuminations (1976)
Illusions of a Lady (1974)
I'm a Woman Already (1975)
I'm Expecting (1979)
I'm Nobody's Sweetheart Now (1940)
I'm Still Alive! (1940)
Image, L' (1976)
Images (1972)
Immigrants, The (1978)
Immoral Tales (1974)
Immortal Garrison, The (1956)
Impiegato, L' (1959)
Impossible Is Not French (1974)
Impossible Object (1973)
Imprevisto, L' (1961)
Imputazione di Omicidio per uno Studente (1971)
In a Wild Moment (1977)
In Capo al Mondo (1962)
In Gay Madrid (1930)
In MacArthur Park (1977)
In Memoriam (1977)
In Mizzoura (1914)
In Old Caliente (1939)
In Old Cheyenne (1941)
In Old Colorado (1941)
In Old Kentucky (1920)
In Old Missouri (1940)
In Old Sacramento (1946)
In Praise of Older Women (1978)
In Search of Dracula (1975)
In Search of Justice (1979)
In the Driver's Seat (1973)
In the Fire Land (1976)
In the Grip of the Spider (1971)
In the Mouth of the World (1979)
In the Name of the Father (1971)
In the Name of the Fuhrer (1979)

In the Name of the Pope King (1978)
In the Realm of the Senses (1976)
In the Sign of Gemini (1975)
In the Sign of Taurus (1974)
In the Sign of the Lion (1976)
In the Year of the Lord (1969)
In Your Dad's Pocket (1973)
Inbreaker, The (1974)
Incident, The (1979)
Incorrigible (1975)
Incredible Journey of Dr. Meg Laurel, The (1979)
Incredible Melting Man, The (1978)
Incredible Shrinking Man, The (1957)
Independence (1976)
Independence Day (1976)
India Song (1975)
Indiscreet (1931)
Indiscreet (1958)
Inheritance, The (1976)
Inheritor, The (1973)
Inki (1975)
In-Laws, The (1979)
Inn of the Damned (1974)
Innocent, The (1976)
Innocent Bystanders (1973)
Innocent Sorcerers (1960)
Innocents with Dirty Hands, The (1975)
Insiang (1978)
Inside Amy (1975)
Inside Job (1973)
Inside Looking Out (1977)
Inside Out (1975)
Inside the Great Pyramid (1974)
Institution, The (1978)
Interior of a Convent (1978)
International Velvet (1978)
Internecine Project, The (1974)
Interval (1973)
Interview, The (1972)
Intolerance (1916)
Intruder, The (1976)
Intruders, The (1972)
Invasion of the Body Snatchers (1978)
Invasion of the Vampires, The (1962)
Investigator and the Woods, The (1976)
Invisible Agent (1942)
Invisible Enemy (1938)
Invisible Man Returns, The (1940)
Invisible Man's Revenge, The (1944)
Invisible Ray, The (1936)
Invisible Stripes (1939)
Invitation, The (1973)
Invito allo Sport (1979)
Io la Conoscevo Bene (1964)
Iphighenia (1977)
Irishman, The (1978)
Iron Buffalo, The (1977)
Iron Horse, The (1924)
Iron Mask, The (1929)
Iron Mistress, The (1952)
Iron Prefect, The (1977)
Is My Face Red? (1932)
Isabelle Devant le Desir (1975)
Island, The (1979)
Island at the Top of the World, The (1974)
Island in the Sky (1953)
Island of Aphrodite, The (1966)
Island of Dr. Moreau, The (1977)
Island of Doomed Men (1940)
Island of the Lost (1967)
Island of the Silver Herons, The (1977)
Islands in the Stream (1977)
Israel (1960)
Istanbul Express (1968)
It Ain't Easy (1972)
It All Adds Up (1976)
It Could Happen to You (1937)
It Had to Be You (1947)
It Happened All Night (1960)
It Happened in Hollywood (1973)
It Only Happens to Others (1971)
It Seemed Like a Good Idea at the Time (1975)
It Shouldn't Happen to a Vet (1976)
It Started with Eve (1941)
Italian Connection, The (1973)
Italian Graffiti (1974)
Italian of the Roses, The (1972)
Italiani Brava Gente (1965)
Itchy Fingers (1979)

It's a Long Time I've Loved You (1979)
It's a Wonderful World (1939)
It's Alive II (It Lives Again) (1978)
It's Me (1979)
It's Never Too Late (1977)
It's Not the Size That Counts (1974)
It's Showtime (1976)
I've Got You, You've Got Me by the Hairs of My Chinny Chin Chin (1979)

J. A. Martin, Photographer (1977)
J. D.'s Revenge (1976)
Jabberwocky (1977)
Jacare (1942)
Jack (1977)
Jack Armstrong (1947)
Jackson County Jail (1976)
Jacob the Liar (1975)
Jacob Two-Two Meets the Hooded Fang (1979)
Jacub (1977)
Jaguar (1942)
Jaguar Lives! (1979)
J'ai Mon Voyage (1973)
Jail House Blues (1942)
Jail Keys Made Here (1965)
Jalna (1935)
Jamilya (1972)
Jane (1915)
Jane Eyre (1934)
Jane Eyre (1970)
Janine (1962)
Japanese War Bride (1952)
Jaws (1975)
Jaws II (1978)
Jay Walker, The (1955)
Jazzoo (1968)
Jealousy (1979)
Jeanne Dore (1916)
Jeep Herders (1945)
Jeepers Creepers (1939)
Jennifer (1978)
Jenseits des Stroms (1922)
Jeremiah Johnson (1972)
Jeremy (1973)
Jerk, The (1979)
Jerusalem File, The (1972)
Jesse James at Bay (1941)
Jesse James Jr. (1942)
Jeu 1 (1962)
Jezebel (1938)
Jezebels, The (1974)
Jim, the World's Greatest (1976)
Jitterbugs (1943)
Joan of Ozark (1942)
Joan the Woman (1917)
Joao (1972)
Joe Dakota (1957)
Joe Kidd (1972)
Joe Panther (1976)
Joerg Ratgeb, Painter (1978)
John and Marsha (1974)
John Glueckstadt (1975)
John Needham's Double (1916)
Johnny Dark (1954)
Johnny Eager (1942)
Johnny Larsen (1979)
Johnny Vik (1973)
Jolly Bad Fellow, A (1964)
Jonah--Who Will Be 25 in the Year 2000 (1976)
Jonathan (1970)
Jonathan Livingston Seagull (1973)
Jongara (1974)
Jordan Is a Hard Road (1915)
Joseph Andrews (1977)
Josephine and Men (1956)
Joueur d'Echecs, Le (1927)
Jour en Suede, Un (1952)
Journal of Combat, The (1965)
Journalist (1979)
Journey (1972)
Journey, A (Tabiji) (1967)
Journey Among Women (1977)
Journey into Fear (1943)
Journey Through Rosebud (1972)
Journey Through the Past (1973)
Joy (1977)
Joy House (1964)
Joy of Letting Go, The (1976)
Joyride (1977)
Juan Moreira (1973)
Juan Perez Jolote (1977)
Juan Vicente Gomez and His Era (1975)
Judge and the Assassin, The (1976)
Judge Fayard Called the Sher-

iff (1977)
Judge Hardy and Son (1939)
Judge Hardy's Children (1938)
Judge's Friend, The (1979)
Judgment of an Assassin (1977)
Juggernaut (1974)
Jules Starts with Jules (1979)
Julia (1977)
Julie (1976)
Julie Glue Pot (1977)
Juliette and the Feel of the Times (1976)
Jumpin' at the Bedside (1976)
Jumping Ash (1976)
Jun (1979)
Jungle, The (1914)
Jungle Adventure Campa Campa (1976)
Jungle Captive (1944)
Jungle in the City, The (1975)
Jungle Raiders (1945)
Jungle Woman (1944)
Junior Bonner (1972)
Just a Gigolo (1979)
Just Another War (1970)
Just Crazy About Horses (1978)
Just for You (1952)
Just My Luck (1935)
Just Off Broadway (1942)
Just Out of Reach (1979)
Just Peter (1972)
Just Routine (1967)
Just the Beginning (1977)
Just You and Me, Kid (1979)
Justine (1974)
Justine (1976)
Justine de Sade (1972)

Kaigenieri (1973)
Kaleidoscope: Valeska Gert, For Fun--For Pleasure (1979)
Kangaroo (1952)
Kansas City Bomber (1972)
Kansas City Trucking Co. (1976)
Kansas Cyclone (1941)
Kansas Terrors, The (1939)
Karate Killers, The (1967)
Kashima Paradise (1973)
Kasper in the Underworld (1979)
Kassbach (1979)
Katsu Taiheiki (1974)
Katz and Karasso (1972)
Keep All Doors Open (1973)
Keep 'Em Flying (1941)
Keeper, The (1976)
Keeping Company (1940)
Keetje Tippel (1975)
Keiko (1979)
Kelly the Second (1936)
Ken Murray Shooting Stars (1979)
Kenny and Co. (1976)
Kentuckian, The (1955)
Kentucky Kernels (1934)
Kept Husbands (1931)
Key Is in the Door, The (1978)
Key Man, The (1955)
Key That Should Not Be Handed On, The (1977)
Key to Love, The (1978)
Keyhole (1974)
Khartoum (1966)
Kid, The (1957)
Kid Blue (1973)
Kid Comes Back, The (1938)
Kid from Kokomo, The (1939)
Kid Head (1975)
Kid Millions (1934)
Kidnapped (1938)
Kidnapped (1971)
Kids Are Alright, The (1979)
Kill! (1973)
Kill Barbara with Panic (1974)
Kill the Black Sheep (1972)
Kill Them All and Come Back Alone (1970)
Killer, The (1972)
Killer Elite, The (1975)
Killer Fish (1979)
Killer Force (1975)
Killer Inside Me, The (1976)
Killer That Stalked New York, The (1950)
Killing Game, The (Comic Strip Hero) (1968)
Killing Kind (1973)
Killing of a Chinese Bookie, The (1976)
Kind Lady (1935)
Kindaich Kosue no Boken (Adventure of Kindaich, The) (1979)

King and the Chorus Girl, The (1937)
King Kong (1976)
King of Chinatown (1939)
King of Hearts (1967)
King of the Congo (1929)
King of the Gypsies (1978)
King of the Mounties (1942)
King of the Newsboys (1938)
King of the Roaring Twenties (1961)
King of the Turf (1939)
King of the Wild (1931)
King, Queen, Knave (1972)
Kingdom of Naples, The (1978)
Kings Row (1941)
Kirlian Witness, The (1978)
Kiss, The (1929)
Kiss Before the Mirror, A (1933)
Kiss of Fire (1954)
Kisses for Breakfast (1941)
Kisses Till Monday (1974)
Klansman, The (1974)
Klara Lust (1972)
Kliou, the Tiger (1935)
Klute (1970)
Kneeler Peak (1977)
Kneuss (1978)
Knife in the Head (1978)
Knight Without Armor (1937)
Knights of the Range (1940)
Knute Rockne, All-American (1940)
Kongi's Harvest (1970)
Kristoffer's House (1979)
Kung Fu (1972)
Kuroneko (Black Cat) (1968)

Labyrinthe (1967)
Lacemaker, The (1977)
Laddie (1935)
Ladies in Distress (1938)
Lady and the Bandit, The (1951)
Lady Behave! (1938)
Lady Caliph (see Califfa, La)
Lady Caroline Lamb (1972)
Lady Consents, The (1936)
Lady from Kentucky, The (1939)
Lady from the Town, The (1979)
Lady Godiva (1956)
Lady Has Plans, The (1941)
Lady Ice (1973)
Lady in Question, The (1940)
Lady in Red, The (1979)
Lady in the Car with Glasses and a Gun (1970)
Lady of Secrets (1936)
Lady on the Bus (1978)
Lady Oscar (1979)
Lady Sings the Blues (1972)
Lady Vanishes, The (1979)
Lady with the Dog, The (1960)
Lady with the Lamp, The (1951)
Lady's Morals, A (1930)
Laia (1972)
Lake of Dracula (1971)
Lamore (1979)
Lancelot of the Lake (1974)
Lancer Spy (1937)
Land of Promise (1975)
Land of the Open Range (1942)
Land That Time Forgot, The (1975)
Land Unknown, The (1957)
Lantern Festival Adventure (1979)
Laramie Trail, The (1944)
Largo Retorno, Un (1975)
Lars Ole, 5c (1974)
Las Vegas Lady (1976)
Las Vegas Story, The (1952)
Last Affair, The (1976)
Last American Hero, The (1973)
Last Challenge of the Dragon, The (1978)
Last Days of Man on Earth, The (1975)
Last Days of Mussolini (1974)
Last Days of Pompeii, The (1913)
Last Days of Pompeii, The (1935)
Last Detail, The (1973)
Last Embrace (1979)
Laxt Exit Before Roissy (1977)
Last Exploits of the Olsen Gang, The (1974)
Last Gentleman, The (1934)
Last Hard Men, The (1976)
Last Love, The (1975)
Last Man on Earth, The (1964)
Last Mission of Demolitions

Man Cloud, The (1978)
Last of Sheila, The (1973)
Last of the Comanches (1953)
Last of the Cowboys, The (1977)
Last of the Mohicans, The (1936)
Last of the Pagans (1935)
Last Plantation, The (1976)
Last Remake of Beau Geste, The (1977)
Last Romantic Lover, The (1978)
Last Run, The (1971)
Last Snows of Spring, The (1973)
Last Supper, The (1978)
Last Tango in Paris (1972)
Last Tasmanian, The (1979)
Last Three Days, The (1977)
Last Tycoon, The (1976)
Last Wave, The (1977)
Last Winter, The (1978)
Last Woman, The (1976)
Last Word, The (1974)
Last Word, The (1979)
Last Years of Childhood, The (1979)
Late Blossom, The (1977)
Late Show, The (1977)
Laughing at Life (1933)
Laughing Boy (1934)
Laughing Policeman, The (1973)
Laughing Woman, The (1970)
Laurence (1962)
Lautare (1972)
Law and Order (1940)
Law Comes to Texas, The (1939)
Law of the Tropics (1941)
Lawbreakers, The (1960)
Lawless Valley (1938)
Lawyer, The (1978)
Lazy River (1934)
Leadbelly (1976)
Leather Pushers, The (1940)
Leave Us Alone (1975)
Lebanon--Why? (1978)
Lebende Leichnam, Der (1928)
Left-Handed (1972)
Left ... Right ... Sickness of the Body (1976)
Legacy (1975)
Legacy, The (1979)
Legacy of L. S. B. Leakey, The (1977)
Legato (1978)
Legend About the Death and Resurrection of Two Young Men, The (1972)
Legend of Boggy Creek, The (1972)
Legend of Frenchie King, The (1974)
Legend of Hell House, The (1973)
Legend of Nigger Charley, The (1972)
Legend of the Mountain (1979)
Legend of the Ubirajara (1976)
Legion of the Lawless (1940)
Lenin, You Rascal You (1972)
Lenny (1974)
Leon and the Rat, The (1976)
Leon la Lune (1956)
Leonor (1975)
Leopard, The (1972)
Leper (1977)
Let Go of My Beard (1975)
Let Joy Reign Supreme (1975)
Let Katie Do It (1915)
Let the Balloon Go (1976)
Let Us Live (1939)
Let's Do It Again (1975)
Let's Get Those English Girls (1976)
Let's Go, Barbara (1978)
Let's Leave the War in Peace (1977)
Let's Scare Jessica to Death (1971)
Letters from Mausia (1976)
Liaisons Dangereuses, Les (1959)
Lialeh (1973)
Libera, My Love (1975)
Liberty (1972)
Lickety Split (1974)
Lies My Father Told Me (1975)
Life and Times of Judge Roy Bean, The (1972)
Life Before Him (1977)
Life Changes (1976)
Life Goes On (1952)
Life Is Tough, Eh Providence?

(1972)
Life of a Shock-Force Worker, The (1972)
Life of Brian (1979)
Life of Chikuzan, The (1977)
Life of Emile Zola, The (1937)
Life of the Locusts (1965)
Life of the Party, The (1937)
Life Size (1974)
Life Study (1973)
Life Together (1958)
Life with Henry (1941)
Lifeguard (1976)
Lifespan (1975)
Lifetime, A (1974)
Ligabue (1978)
Light (1976)
Light at the Edge of the World, The (1973)
Light of Western Stars, The (1940)
Light on the Gallows, The (1977)
Light That Failed, Thc (1939)
Lightning Strikes Twice (1934)
Lilac Time (1928)
Lily and the Rose, The (1915)
Lily, Love Me (1975)
Limbo (1972)
Lina Braake--The Bank's Interests Can't Be the Interests Lina Braake Has (1975)
Lincoln Conspiracy, The (1977)
Linesman, The (1975)
Linus and the Mysterious Red Brick Housc (1979)
Lion and the Horse (1952)
Lion and the Virgin, The (1975)
Lipstick (1976)
Lisette (1961)
Lisztomania (1975)
Lit--Ze Bawdy Bed, Le (1975)
Little Archimedes, The (1979)
Little Ark, The (1972)
Little Cigars (1973)
Little Escapes (1979)
Little Friend (1934)
Little Girl in Blue Velvet, The (1978)
Little Malcolm (1974)
Little Man (1978)
Little Marcel (1976)
Little Men (1934)
Little Men (1941)
Little Mermaid, The (1976)
Little Mermaid, The (1977)
Little Minister, The (1934)
Little Mother (1972)
Little Old New York (1940)
Little Orphan Annie (1932)
Little Orvie (1940)
Little Red Riding Hood and Tom Thumb vs. the Monsters (1960)
Little Romance, A (1979)
Little Town of Anara, The (1978)
Live a Little, Steal a Lot (Murph the Surf) (1974)
Live and Let Die (1973)
Live Coal in the East (1975)
Live, Love and Learn (1937)
Lives of a Bengal Lancer (1935)
Living Dead at the Manchester Morgue, The (1974)
Living Free (1972)
Liza (1972)
Llano Kid, The (1939)
Location Hunting (1977)
Logan's Run (1976)
Lola's Lolos (1976)
Lollipop Cover (1966)
Lolly Madonna XXX (1973)
Lone Ranger, The (1938)
Lone Ranger Rides Again, The (1939)
Lone Star Raiders (1940)
Lone Wolf (1978)
Lone Wolf Returns, The (1935)
Lonely Heart, The (1973)
Lonely Hearts (1970)
Loner, The (1973)
Long Drive, The (1978)
Long Goodbye, The (1973)
Long Live Ghosts! (1979)
Long Live Hazana (1978)
Long Live Progress (1976)
Long Live the Island Frogs (1973)
Long Lost Father, The (1934)
Long Returning, A (1975)
Long Shot (1978)
Long Vacations of '36, The (1976)
Long Weekend (1978)
Long Weekend, The (La

Puente) (1977)
Longest Journey, The (1976)
Longest Night, The (1964)
Longest Yard, The (1974)
Look Who's Laughing (1941)
Looking for Mr. Goodbar (1977)
Looking Up (1977)
Looping (1975)
Looping the Loop (1929)
Loose Ends (1975)
Lord of the Rings (1978)
Lord Shango (1975)
Lords of Flatbush, The (1974)
Lost and Found (1979)
Lost Battalion (1962)
Lost Boy, The (Huckleberry Finn) (1974)
Lost City, The (1935)
Lost Honor of Katharine Blum, The (1975)
Lost Horizon (1973)
Lost Jungle, The (1934)
Lost Life, A (1976)
Lost Missile, The (1958)
Lost Paradise (1978)
Lost Squadron (1932)
Lotte in Weimar (1975)
Lottery Bride, The (1930)
Louis (1977)
Louvre Museum, The (1979)
Love (1974)
Love a la Carte (1960)
Love Affair (1939)
Love Among the Ruins (1973)
Love and Anarchy (1975)
Love and Bullets (1979)
Love and Cool Water (1976)
Love and Energy (1975)
Love and Faith: Lady Ogin (1979)
Love and Pain and the Whole Damn Thing (1973)
Love and Rage (1978)
Love and the Midnight Auto Supply (see Midnight Auto Supply)
Love at First Bite (1979)
Love at First Sight (1977)
Love by Rape (1970)
Love Finds Andy Hardy (1938)
Love Flower, The (1920)
Love Follows Pain (1977)
Love from a Stranger (1947)
Love, Honor and Oh, Baby! (1940)
Love in Four Dimensions (1965)
Love in Question (1978)
Love Is Blue (1977)
Love Lesson (1978)
Love of a Little Girl, The (1979)
Love of Captain Brando, The (1974)
Love of the Vampire, The (1961)
Love on the Run (1979)
Love, Swedish Style (1972)
Love Thy Neighbor (1940)
Love Under Fire (1937)
Loveland (1973)
Lovemakers, The (1961)
Lover, The (1972)
Lover, Wife (1977)
Lovers, The (1978)
Lovers in the Year I (1974)
Lover's Wind, The (1979)
Loves and Times of Scaramouche, The (1976)
Lovin' Molly (1974)
Loving Cousins (1976)
Lucie (1979)
Luck of the Irish, The (1948)
Lucky Boy (1929)
Lucky Devils (1933)
Lucky Devils (1941)
Lucky Lady (1975)
Lucky Luciano (1973)
Lucky Luke (1971)
Lucky Night (1939)
Lumiere (1977)
Lumiere des Justes, La (Light of Justice) (1979)
Luminous Procuress (1972)
Lust for a Campfire (1971)
Lust for Gold (1949)
Lycistrata (1972)
Lydia Bailey (1952)

M (1951)
M Squad (1957)
M. M. M. 83--Missions Mortale Molo 83 (1965)
Macao (1952)
MacArthur (1977)
McCullochs, The (1975)
McGuerins from Brooklyn,

The (1942)
Machine, The (1977)
Machine Gun Kelly (1958)
Machine Gun McCain (1970)
Machine Gun Stein (1979)
Mack, The (1973)
Mackan (1978)
Mackintosh and T. J. (1975)
Mackintosh Man, The (1973)
McLintock! (1963)
Macon County Line (1974)
McQ (1974)
Mad Adventures of Rabbi Jacob, The (1974)
Mad at the World (1955)
Mad Bomber, The (1973)
Mad Cage, The (see Cage aux Folles, La)
Mad Doctor, The (1941)
Mad Doctor of Market Street, The (1942)
Mad Dog (1976)
Mad Holiday (1936)
Mad Love (1935)
Mad Max (1979)
Madam Satan (1930)
Madame Butterfly (1932)
Madame Claude (1977)
Madame Kitty (1975)
Madame Rosa (1978)
Madame Sin (1972)
Madame Spy (1942)
Made (1972)
Made for Each Other (1939)
Madeline (1952)
Mademoiselle Mosquito (1956)
Madhouse (1974)
Madly (1970)
Mado (1976)
Madonna's Secret, The (1946)
Maestro di Vigevano, Il (1963)
Mafia (1969)
Mafia, The (1972)
Mafu Cage, The (1978)
Maggie, The (see High and Dry)
Magic (1978)
Magic Adventure, The (1973)
Magic Christian, The (1969)
Magician of Lublin, The (1979)
Magnificent Brute, The (1936)
Magnificent Doll, The (1946)
Magnificent Dope, The (1942)
Magnificent One, The (1973)
Magnificent Seven, The (1960)
Magnificent Seven Ride, The (1972)
Magnifique, Le (1976)
Magnum Force (1973)
Mahogany (1975)
Mai 68 (1974)
Maiden's War, The (1977)
Maids, The (1975)
Main Actor, The (1977)
Main Event, The (1979)
Main Street Lawyer (1939)
Main Thing Holiday (1972)
Main Thing Is to Love, The (1975)
Mais ou et Donc Ornicar (1979)
Maisie Was a Lady (1941)
Making of a President--1960, The (1964)
Male of the Century (1975)
Malenka, Niece of the Vampire (1969)
Malizia (1973)
Malpertius (1972)
Mama, I'm Alive (1977)
Mama Runs Wild (1938)
Mama Steps Out (1937)
Mama's Dirty Girls (1974)
Mamba (1930)
Mamma Roma (1962)
Mammals (1962)
Man, The (1972)
Man Against Man (1976)
Man and Boy (1971)
Man and War (Part 3) (1974)
Man Behind the Gun, The (1953)
Man Betrayed, A (1941)
Man Called Autumn Flower, A (1978)
Man Called Gringo, The (1964)
Man Called Noon, The (1973)
Man Friday (1975)
Man from Cheyenne, The (1942)
Man from Dakota, The (1940)
Man from Nowhere, The (1969)
Man from Oklahoma (1945)
Man from Swan Farm, The (1973)
Man from the East, A (1972)
Man from the Rio Grande, The (1943)
Man in the Middle (1964)
Man in the Saddle (1951)

Man in the Shadow (1957)
Man Is Dead, A (1973)
Man-Made Monster (1941)
Man Nobody Knows, The (1925)
Man of Conquest (1939)
Man of Courage (1943)
Man of Marble (1977)
Man on a Swing (1974)
Man on the Bridge (1976)
Man on the Roof, The (1976)
Man to Kill, The (1979)
Man Who Came from Ummo, The (1970)
Man Who Came to Dinner, The (1942)
Man Who Cheated Himself, The (1950)
Man Who Fell to Earth, The (1976)
Man Who Knew Love, The (1976)
Man Who Knew Too Much, The (1934)
Man Who Lost Himself, The (1941)
Man Who Loved Cat Dancing, The (1973)
Man Who Loved Women, The (1977)
Man Who Reclaimed His Head, The (1934)
Man Who Would Be King, The (1975)
Man Who Wouldn't Die, The (1942)
Man with the Axe (1979)
Man with the Golden Gun, The (1974)
Man Without a Name, The (1976)
Man Without a Star (1955)
Man You Love to Hate, The (1979)
Management Forgives a Moment of Madness, The (1979)
Manchu Eagle Murder Caper Mystery, The (1975)
Mandarine, La (1971)
Mandingo (1975)
Maneaters Are Loose, The (1978)
Mango Tree, The (1977)
Manhattan Melodrama (1934)
Manhattan Merry-Go-Round (1937)
Mani in Alto (1960)
Mani sulla Citta, Le (1963)
Manila Calling (1942)
Manitou, The (1978)
Manly Times (1978)
Manon (1926)
Manpower (1942)
Manrape (1978)
Man's Best Friend (1941)
Man's Castle, A (1933)
Manson (1972)
Manthan (1977)
Marathon Man (1976)
March on Paris 1914, The (1978)
March or Die (1977)
Marcia su Roma, La (1962)
Marco Polo (1976)
Marco's Theme (1972)
Margie (1940)
Marginal Ones, The (1978)
Maria (1975)
Marie-Ann (1978)
Marie the Doll (1976)
Marilyn and the Senator (1975)
Mark of the Wolfman, The (1968)
Marked for Murder (1944)
Marriage (1975)
Marriage a la Mode (1973)
Marriage Revolution, The (1975)
Marriage, Tel Aviv Style (1979)
Married and in Love (1940)
Married Bachelor (1941)
Married Before Breakfast (1937)
Marry the Girl (1937)
Marrying Kind, The (1952)
Martian Chronicles, The (1979)
Martin (1978)
Martin Luther (1925)
Martyrs of the Alamo, The (1915)
Mary, La (1974)
Mary, Mary, Bloody Mary (1975)
Mary of Scotland (1936)
Mary Regan (1921)
Maryland (1941)
Masquerader, The (1933)
Massacre at Central High (1976)
Massacre in Rome (1973)

Massacre River (1949)
Master and Margherita, The (1972)
Master Gunfighter, The (1975)
Master Touch, The (1974)
Matchless (1966)
Maternale (1978)
Matriarchy (1978)
Matrimony (1915)
Matter of Honor, A (1966)
Matter of Time, A (1976)
Matter of WHO, A (1962)
Mauahovsky Laughs (1976)
May (1976)
May I Have the Floor? (1976)
Mayuko, the Only One (1971)
Me (1975)
Me and Charley (1978)
Me and the Colonel (1958)
Me and the Mafia (1973)
Me, Too, I'm the Mafia (1974)
Meadow, The (Prato, Il) (1979)
Meal, The (1975)
Mean Dog Blues (1978)
Meanest Gal in Town, The (1934)
Meat (Fleisch) (1979)
Meatballs (1979)
Mechanic, The (1972)
Medic, The (Toubib, Le) (1979)
Medical Story (1976)
Meet the Boy Friend (1937)
Meet the Chump (1941)
Meet the Mayor (1938)
Meet the Missus (1940)
Meet the Wildcat (1940)
Meetings with Remarkable Men (1979)
Megalomaniac, The (1979)
Melancholy Baby (1979)
Melinda (1972)
Melodies of Veruski District (1974)
Melody and Moonlight (1940)
Melody Lingers On, The (1935)
Memories (1975)
Memories of Leticia Valle (1979)
Memories Within Miss Aggie (1974)
Men Against the Sky (1940)
Men and Women (1960)
Men Are Such Fools (1932)
Men in Her Life, The (1941)
Men of Texas (1942)
Men of the Timberland (1941)
Mepris, Le (1963)
Mercenaries, The (1967)
Mercy Island (1941)
Merry Monahans, The (1944)
Merry Wives of Windsor, The (1972)
Message, The (1976)
Message from Space, A (1978)
Messiah, The (1978)
Messiah of Evil (1975)
Messidor (1979)
Metamorphosis (1973)
Metamorphosis (1975)
Metamorphosis (1978)
Metamorphosis of Cloportes, The (1965)
Meteor (1979)
Mexican Spitfire (1939)
Mexican Spitfire Out West (1940)
Mexican Spitfire Sees a Ghost (1942)
Mexican Spitfire's Elephant (1942)
Michael Kohlhaas (1979)
Michael O'Halloran (1937)
Michael, the Brave (1973)
Michurin (Life in Bloom) (1947)
Mickey the Kid (1939)
Middle Age Spread (1979)
Midnight (1939)
Midnight Auto Supply (1978)
Midnight Court (1937)
Midnight Express (1978)
Midnight Man, The (1974)
Midnight Mary (1933)
Midnight Pleasures (1975)
Midnight Story, The (1957)
Midnight Warning (1932)
Midshipman Jack (1933)
Midstream (1929)
Midway (1976)
Might Makes Right (1975)
Mighty Barnum, The (1934)
Mighty Jungle, The (1959)
Mighty Treve, The (1937)
Mikey and Nicky (1976)
Milano Calibro 9 (1974)
Milarepa (1974)

Milk War in Bavaria (1979)
Millie's Daughter (1947)
Millionaire in Trouble (1978)
Millionaire Playboy (1940)
Millionaires in Prison (1940)
Mimi (see Dramma Borghese, Un)
Mimi, the Metalworker (1972)
Mina, Wind of Freedom (1977)
Minatomo Yoshitsune (1966)
Mind Your Back, Professor (1977)
Mine, The (1978)
Mine with the Iron Door, The (1936)
Miner's Daughter, The (1950)
Minister and Me, The (1976)
Minx, The (1972)
Mio (1972)
Miracle Man, The (1932)
Miracle on Main Street (1940)
Miracle Tree, The (1978)
Miracles of the Gods (1976)
Mirage (1972)
Mirror Mirror (1978)
Misfire (1977)
Misfire (1978)
Miss Maliway (1975)
Miss O'Gynie and the Flower Man (1974)
Miss Polly (1941)
Miss Salak Jitr (1979)
Miss V from Moscow (1942)
Missing Prisoners (1979)
Missing Ten Days (Ten Days in Paris) (1939)
Mission: Stardust (1968)
Missouri Breaks, The (1976)
Misteltoes (1979)
Mr. and Mrs. North (1942)
Mr. Billion (1977)
Mr. Bug Goes to Town (1941)
Mister Cinderella (1936)
Mr. District Attorney (1941)
Mr. District Attorney in the Carter Case (1941)
Mr. Dodd Takes the Air (1937)
Mr. Doodle Kicks Off (1938)
Mr. Dynamite (1941)
Mister 880 (1950)
Mr. Forbush and the Penguins (1972)
Mr. Klein (1976)
Mr. Majestyk (1974)
Mr. Moto's Last Warning (1939)
Mr. Ricco (1975)
Mr. Skitch (1933)
Mr. Sycamore (1975)
Mrs. Abad, I Am Bing (1976)
Mistress (1976)
Mistress, The (1976)
Mitchell (1975)
Mixed Company (1974)
Mob Town (1941)
Model Wife (1941)
Mohammad, the Messenger of God (1977)
Moi y'En a Vouloir des Sous (1973)
Mole People, The (1956)
Moliere (1978)
Molly (1951)
Molly and Me (1929)
Moment (1970)
Moment by Moment (1978)
Moments (1974)
Moments (1979)
Moments in a Matchbox (1979)
Mondo Balordo (1968)
Mondo Candido (1975)
Mondo Cane (1963)
Money from Home (1954)
Money! Money! Money! (1973)
Money Talks (1972)
Money to Burn (1940)
Monk, The (1973)
Monkey Bridge, The (1976)
Monkey Hustle, The (1976)
Monkey's Paw, The (1933)
Monolog (1973)
Monsieur Papa (1977)
Monster and the Ape, The (1945)
Monster Walks, The (1932)
Montana Moon (1930)
Monte Carlo (1930)
Montreal Main (1974)
Monty Python and the Holy Grail (1975)
Moods of Love (1977)
Mool-Dori Village (1979)
Moonlight Masquerade (1942)
Moonlight Murder (1936)
Moonlight Serenade (1979)
Moonraker (1979)
Moon's Our Home, The (1936)

Moonshine County Express (1977)
Moonstone, The (1934)
Moontide (1942)
Moonwalk One (1972)
Morals of Ruth Halbfass, The (1972)
Morbidness (1972)
More Blue Than Blue Color (1972)
More It Goes, the Less It Goes, The (1977)
More Than a Miracle (1967)
Moritz, Dear Moritz (1978)
Morning Schedule, The (1973)
Moscow Strikes Back (1942)
Moses (1976)
Most Beautiful Animal in the World, The (1975)
Most Dangerous Game, The (1932)
Most Important Event Since Man First Set Foot on the Moon, The (1973)
Motel's Invention (1974)
Mother and Daughter (1975)
Mother Carey's Chickens (1938)
Mother Didn't Tell Me (1950)
Motive for Revenge (1935)
Mount Hakkoda (1977)
Mountain Family Robinson (1979)
Mountain Man, The (1979)
Mountain Moonlight (1941)
Mountain Pass (1978)
Mouth to Mouth (1978)
Movie Movie (1978)
Moving Violation (1976)
Mummy's Boys (1936)
Mummy's Curse, The (1945)
Mummy's Ghost, The (1944)
Mummy's Hand, The (1940)
Muppet Movie, The (1979)
Murder at Midnight (1931)
Murder at the Vanities (1934)
Murder by Death (1976)
Murder by Television (1935)
Murder Clinic, The (1969)
Murder Is a Murder, A (1972)
Murder on a Honeymoon (1935)
Murder on Diamond Row (1937)
Murder on the Bridal Path (1936)
Murder on the Bridge (1975)
Murder on the Campus (1935)
Murder on the Orient Express (1974)
Murdered House, The (1974)
Murderess, The (1974)
Murph the Surf (see Live a Little, Steal a Lot)
Muscle Beach (1948)
Muscle Beach Party (1964)
Mushroom Eater, The (1976)
Muss 'Em Up (1936)
Mustang Country (1976)
Mustang: The House That Joe Built (1976)
Mutation, The (1974)
Mute, The (1976)
Mutiny in the Arctic (1941)
Mutiny on the Bounty (1935)
My Asylum (1979)
My Brilliant Career (1979)
My Brother Anastasia (1973)
My Brother Has a Cute Brother (1975)
My Daughter Hildegart (1977)
My Dear Friend (1977)
My Dear Miss Aldrich (1937)
My Dearest Lady (1972)
My Dog (1955)
My Father's Happy Years (1978)
My Fiance, the Transvestite (1975)
My First Sin (1977)
My Friend Pierrot (1960)
My Friends (1975)
My Gal Sal (1942)
My Heart Is Red (1977)
My Kingdom for a Cook (1943)
My Lady (1975)
My Lady's Past (1929)
My Little Loves (1974)
My Michael (1975)
My Mother, the General (1979)
My Name Is Nobody (1973)
My Own True Love (1949)
My Pal Trigger (1946)
My Sexy Girl Friend (1975)
My War--My Love (1976)
My Way (1974)
My Wife's Relatives (1939)
Myra Breckinridge (1970)
Mysteries (1979)
Mysterious Dr. Satan, The (1940)

Mysterious Island of Captain Nemo, The (1974)
Mysterious Miss X, The (1939)
Mysterious Mr. Moto (1938)
Mysterious Mr. Wong (1935)
Mysterious Monsters, The (1976)
Mysterious Rider (1938)
Mystery Liner (1934)
Mystery Mountain (1934)
Myth, The (1965)

N. P. (1971)
Nahia (1979)
Nail of Brightness, The (1975)
Naked Alibi (1954)
Naked Angels (1969)
Naked Ape, The (1973)
Naked Came the Stranger (1975)
Naked Hearts (1966)
Naked Vampires (1969)
Naked World of Harrison Marks, The (1965)
Nancy Drew, Reporter (1939)
Napoleon and Samantha (1972)
Nashville Coyote (1974)
Nasty Habits (1976)
Nata di Marzo (1957)
Nathalie Granger (1972)
National Class (1979)
National Health, or Nurse Norton's Affair, The (1973)
National Lampoon's Animal House (1978)
National Mechanics (1975)
Natives of Planet Earth (1973)
Natural Enemies (1979)
Naturally, It's Rubber (1964)
Navajo (1952)
Navajo Joe (1967)
Navajo Kid (1945)
Nazarene Cross and the Wolf (1975)
Necromancy (1972)
Necropolis (1969)
Ned Kelly (1970)
Neiges (1955)
Neither by Day nor by Night (1972)
Neither the Sea nor the Sand (1974)
Nelson Affair, The (1973)
Nene (1977)
Neptune Factor, The (1973)
Nest of Vipers (1979)
Network (1976)
Neutron and Fission, The (1965)
Nevada City (1941)
Never Give a Sucker an Even Break (1941)
Never Let Go (1960)
Never Say Die (1939)
Never Trust a Gambler (1951)
New Adventures of Tarzan, The (1936)
New Beaujolais Wine Has Arrived, The (1978)
New Centurions, The (1972)
New Clothes (1963)
New Frontier, The (1939)
New Lot, The (1943)
New Mexico (1951)
New Moon (1931)
New Ones, The (1973)
New Orleans (1929)
New Parthenon, The (1975)
New Spaniards, The (1975)
New Teacher, The (1975)
New York, New York (1977)
New York Town (1941)
Newcomers, The (1973)
Newman's Law (1974)
Newsfront (1978)
Next Man, The (1976)
Next Stop, Greenwich Village (1976)
Next Time I Marry (1938)
Niagara Falls (1941)
Nick Carter, Master Detective (1939)
Nickel Ride, The (1974)
Nickelodeon (1976)
Night at the Opera, A (1935)
Night Before, The (1973)
Night Before Christmas, The (1978)
Night Before the Divorce, The (1942)
Night Caller, The (1975)
Night Creature (1979)
Night Digger, The (1971)
Night Editor (1946)
Night Evelyn Came Out of the Grave, The (1972)
Night Flowers (1979)

Night Is a Sorcerer (1960)
Night Life of the Gods (1935)
Night Moves (1975)
Night of Counting the Years (1970)
Night of January 16th, The (1941)
Night of Nights, The (1939)
Night of Orange Fires (1975)
Night of St.-Germain des Pres, The (1977)
Night of the Devils, The (1971)
Night of the Lepus (1972)
Night of the Scarecrow, The (1974)
Night Plane from Chunking (1943)
Night Porter, The (1974)
Night Riders, The (1939)
Night Stalker, The (1972)
Night, the Prowler, The (1978)
Night Tide (1961)
Night Train (Pociag) (1959)
Night Watch (1973)
Nighthawks (1978)
Nightmare Castle (1965)
Nightmares (1979)
Nights and Days (1975)
Nightshade (1972)
Nightwing (1979)
Nine Months (1977)
9/30/55 (1977)
19 Red Roses (1974)
1900 (1976)
1941 (1979)
92 in the Shade (1975)
92 Minutes of Yesterday (1978)
99 and 44/100% Dead (1974)
Nini Tirabuscio, la Donna che Invento la Mossa (1970)
Nitra Sayan (1975)
Nitwits, The (1935)
No Deposit, No Return (1976)
No Hands on the Clock (1941)
No Longer Alone (1978)
No Man's Daughter (1976)
No Marriage Ties (1933)
No More Yesterdays (1935)
No Other Woman (1933)
No Pockets in a Shroud (1975)
No, the Case Is Happily Resolved (1973)
No Time for Love (1944)
No Time for Sergeants (1958)
No Trespassing (1978)
No Way Out (1973)
Nob Hill (1945)
Nocturnal Uproar (1979)
Nocturne (1972)
Noelleby Affair, The (1977)
Noi Donne Siamo Fatte Cosi (1971)
Noldebo Vicarage (1974)
Norma Rae (1979)
Norman ... Is That You? (1976)
Normans, The (1976)
Norseman, The (1978)
North Avenue Irregulars, The (1979)
North Dallas Forty (1979)
North of Nome (1936)
North Sea Is Dead Sea (1976)
Northern Lights (1978)
Northwest Rangers (1943)
Nosferatu, Phantom of the Night (1979)
Nostradamus and the Destroyer of Monsters (1961)
Nostri Mariti, I (1966)
Not as Wicked as All That... (1975)
Not Everything That Flies Is a Bird (1979)
Not Just Another Woman (1974)
Notes for an African Orestes (1970)
Nothing but the Truth (1975)
Nothing by Chance (1975)
Nothing Sacred (1937)
November 1828 (1979)
Now You See Him, Now You Don't (1972)
Nuclear Reactor, The (1966)
Nuda ogni Sera (1961)
Number One (1973)
Nuns of Saint'Archangelo (1973)
Nunzio (1978)

O. Henry's Full House (1952)
O Lucky Man (1973)
O, Madda (1977)
O. S. S. (1946)
Oasis (1972)
Obliging Young Lady, An (1942)
Obsession (1976)

Obsession (1979)
Occupation in 26 Pictures (1978)
Oceano (1971)
Odd Job, The (1978)
Oddballs, The (1974)
Ode to Billy Joe (1976)
Odessa File, The (1974)
Odyssey, The (1912)
Oedipus Orca (1977)
Of Death and Corpses (1979)
Of Men and Demons (1970)
Of Such Is the Kingdom (1948)
Off Bedside Limits (1975)
Off the Edge (1977)
Off the Record (1939)
Office Party, The (1976)
Office Picnic, The (1974)
Ogro (1979)
Oh, America (1975)
Oh, God! (1977)
Oh, Jonathan, Oh, Jonathan (1973)
Oh the Days (1978)
Oh! The Nomugi Pass (1979)
Oh, to Be on the Bandwagon (1972)
Ohanahan (1966)
Oklahoma Crude (1973)
Oklahoma Justice (1951)
Oklahoma Kid, The (1939)
Oklahoma Raiders (1944)
Old Barn Dance, The (1938)
Old Chisholm Trail, The (1942)
Old Comedy, The (1979)
Old Country Where Rimbaud Died, The (1977)
Old Dracula (1975)
Old-Fashioned Way, The (1934)
Old-Fashioned Woman, An (1974)
Old Homestead, The (1935)
Old House, The (1977)
Old Ironsides (1926)
Old Maid, The (1972)
Old Man Rhythm (1935)
Old Nest, The (1921)
Old Texas Trail, The (1944)
Old Woman, An (1978)
Oliver's Story (1978)
Olly, Olly, Oxen Free (1978)
Olsen Gang Goes to War, The (1978)
Olsen Gang Never Surrenders, The (1979)
Olsen Gang on the Track, The (1975)
Olsen Gang Outta Sight, The (1977)
Olsen Gang Runs Amok, The (1973)
Olsen Gang Sees Red, The (1976)
Olsen Gang's Big Score, The (1972)
Olympia-Olympia (1972)
Omar Gallato (1977)
Omen, The (1976)
On Friday at Eleven (1960)
On n'Enterre pas le Dimanche (1959)
On Stage, Everybody (1945)
On the Sideline (1977)
On the Sunny Side (1941)
On the Tip of the Tongue (1976)
On the Tracks of the Missing (1979)
On the Yard (1978)
On Top of All (1975)
Once (1973)
Once Before I Die (1966)
Once Before I Die (1970)
Once in a Blue Moon (1935)
Once in Paris (1978)
Once Is Not Enough (1975)
Once upon a Scoundrel (1973)
Once upon a Time (1976)
Once upon a Time (1979)
One and Only, The (1978)
One-Armed Boxer vs. the Flying Guillotine (1975)
One Big Affair (1952)
One by One (East Wind) (1974)
One Can Say It Without Getting Angry (1977)
One Day More, One Day Less (1973)
One Exciting Night (1922)
One Flew Over the Cuckoo's Nest (1975)
One Frightened Night (1935)
One Good Turn (1954)
One Hamlet Less (1973)
One Hour with You (1932)
100 Horsemen (1964)
122 Rue de Provence (1978)
One Is a Lonely Number (1972)

One Little Indian (1973)
One Man (1977)
One Man and His Bank (1965)
One Man's Law (1940)
One Man's Lifetime (1951)
One Must Live Dangerously (1975)
One Night in Life with One Woman (1976)
One Night, Three Women (1975)
One of Our Dinosaurs Is Missing (1975)
One of Our Spies Is Missing (1966)
One on One (1977)
One on Top of the Other (1972)
1 + 1 = 3 (1979)
One Silver Dollar (1975)
One Silver Piece (1976)
One Sings, the Other Doesn't (1977)
... One Third of a Nation... (1939)
1 2 3 Monster Express (1977)
One-Way Passage (1932)
One Who Came from Heaven, The (1974)
Onion Chase, The (1975)
Onion Field, The (1979)
Only 15 (1978)
Only God Knows (1974)
Only Once in a Lifetime (1979)
Only One, The (1976)
Only 16 (Part 2) (1977)
Only Way Home, The (1972)
Open Season (1974)
Opening Night (1977)
Opening of Misty Beethoven, The (1976)
Opening Tomorrow (1962)
Operation Black Panther (1977)
Operation Bororo (1973)
Operation Daybreak (1976)
Operation Heartbeat (1962)
Operation MJC (1965)
Operation Rose Rose (1974)
Operation Stadium (1977)
Operation Thunderbolt (1977)
Operation Time Bomb (1958)
Optimists, The (1973)
Opus 1 (1948)
Opus 65 (1952)
Orbita Mortal (1968)
Orca, the Killer Whale (1977)
Orchestra Rehearsal (1979)
Order and Security of the World (1978)
Orders, The (1975)
Ordinary Tenderness (1973)
Ordinateur des Pompes Funebres, L' (1976)
Ore dell'amore, Le (1963)
Orlak, the Hell of Frankenstein (1961)
Orphans of the Street (1938)
Orpheon (1966)
Oscar, Kina and the Laser (1979)
Otalia de Bahia (1976)
Other, The (1972)
Other Francisco, The (1975)
Other People's Money (1978)
Other Side of Midnight, The (1977)
Other Side of the Mountain, The (1975)
Other Side of the Mountain, Part 2, The (1978)
Other Side of the Underneath, The (1972)
Ottokar, the World Reformer (1978)
Our Modern Maidens (1929)
Our Neighbors, the Carters (1939)
Our Time (1974)
Our Time No. 1 (1967)
Our Wife (1941)
Our Willi Is the Best (1972)
Our Winning Season (1978)
Out California Way (1946)
Out of Season (1975)
Out of Whack (1979)
Out on Parole (1976)
Out West with the Hardys (1938)
Outcasts of Poker Flat, The (1952)
Outfit, The (1973)
Outlaw Blues (1977)
Outlaw Josey Wales, The (1976)
Outlaw Morality (1976)
Outlaws of Santa Fe (1944)
Outlaws of Sonora (1938)
Outlaws of the Cherokee Trail (1941)
Outrageous! (1977)

Outside Chance (1978)
Outside In (1972)
Outside of Paradise (1938)
Outside the 3-Mile Limit (1940)
Outsider, The (1979)
Outsiders (1977)
Over My Dead Body (1943)
Over the Edge (1979)
Over-Under, Sideways-Down (1977)
Overlord (1975)
Oz (1976)

Pablo (1978)
Pacific Challenge (1975)
Pacific Rendezvous (1942)
Pacifist, The (1972)
Paco (1975)
Padre Padrone (Father Master) (1977)
Page of Love, A (1977)
Paid in Full (1914)
Pain in the Neck, The (1973)
Pajama Party (1964)
Palm Beach (1979)
Palm Springs (1936)
Pals, The (1979)
Pals of the Saddle (1938)
Panama Lady (1939)
Pantelei (1978)
Paolo Barca, Schoolteacher and Weekend Nudist (1975)
Paolo il Caldo (see Hot-Blooded Paolo)
Paper Chase, The (1973)
Paper Flowers (1978)
Paper Tiger (1975)
Paperback Hero (1973)
Papillon (1973)
Par un Beau Matin d'Ete (1964)
Parachute Battalion (1941)
Parade (1974)
Parades (1972)
Paradine Case, The (1948)
Paradise (1976)
Paradise Alley (1978)
Paradise Square (1977)
Parallax View, The (1974)
Parallels (1962)
Paranoia (1966)
Paratrooper (Red Beret, The) (1954)
Paris des Mannequins, Le (1963)
Paris des Scandinaves, Le (1964)
Paris Honeymoon (1939)
Parisienne, La (1958)
Park, The (1977)
Parmigiana, La (1963)
Parole Fixer (1940)
Part 2, Sounder (1976)
Partisans (1974)
Partners (1976)
Parts the Clonus Horror (1979)
Pascual Duarte (1976)
Pasquelino: Seven Beauties (see Seven Beauties)
Passage, The (1979)
Passengers, The (1977)
Passion (1978)
Passion According to Matthew (1975)
Passion de Jeanne d'Arc, La (1928)
Passion Flower Hotel (1978)
Passover Plot, The (1976)
Passport to Alcatraz (1940)
Pastorale Hide and Seek (1975)
Pat Garrett and Billy the Kid (1973)
Patchwork Girl of Oz, The (1914)
Paths of War (1979)
Patrick (1978)
Paul and Michelle (1974)
Paula (1952)
Paulina 1800 (1972)
Pavlinka (1974)
Payoff, The (1978)
Peacemeal (1967)
Peaks of Zelengore, The (1976)
Pearl (1979)
Pearl in the Crown (1972)
Pearl of Death, The (1944)
Peasant on a Bicycle (1975)
Peau d'Ane (Donkey Skin) (1970)
Pebbles of Entretat (1972)
Peck's Bad Boy (1934)
Pedestrian, The (1974)
Pedro Paramo (1977)
Peeper (1975)
Peer Gynt (1915)
Peg O' My Heart (1922)
Pele (1977)
Penalty, The (1941)
Penguin, The (1965)

Penitente Murder Case, The (1936)
Penitentes, Los (1915)
Penitentiary (1979)
Pennies from Heaven (1936)
Penny Serenade (1941)
Pentecost Outing, The (1979)
Penthouse (1933)
People Are Funny (1946)
People from the Subway (1974)
People in Buenos Aires (1974)
People Meet and Sweet Music Fills the Air (1967)
People of the Wind (1976)
People, People, People (1975)
People That Time Forgot, The (1977)
People vs. Dr. Kildare, The (1941)
Pepita Jimenez (1975)
Peppermint Soda (see Diablo Menthe)
Per (1975)
Per Amore (1976)
Per Grazia Ricevuta (1971)
Percival le Gallois (1978)
Percy (1971)
Perfect Couple, A (1979)
Perfect Gentleman, The (1935)
Perilous Holiday (1946)
Perils of Nyoka (1942)
Perils of the Royal Mounted (1942)
Permette, Rocco Papaleo (1971)
Permission to Kill (1975)
Persecution and Assassination of Jean-Paul Marat as Performed by the Inmates of the Asylum of Charenton Under the Direction of the Marquis de Sade (1967)
Personal Affairs (1979)
Personal Opinion, A (1977)
Personality Kid (1946)
Personnel (1976)
Pete 'n' Tillie (1972)
Pete Roleum and His Cousins (1939)
Petersen (1974)
Petofi '73 (1973)
Petticoat Larceny (1943)
Petticoat Politics (1941)
Petty Girl, The (1950)
Petty Thieves (1977)
Phantasm (1979)
Phantastic World of Matthew Madson, The (1974)
Phantom, The (1943)
Phantom Cowboy, The (1941)
Phantom Empire (1935)
Phantom Love (1978)
Phantom of the Paradise (1974)
Phantom of the West (1931)
Phantom on Horseback, The (1977)
Phantom Raiders (1940)
Phantom Speaks, The (1945)
Phase VI (1974)
Photo Souvenir (1960)
Photo Souvenir (1978)
Photography (1974)
Piano in Midair, A (1977)
Pianorama (1973)
Picasso Summer (1969)
Piccadilly Incident (1946)
Pick a Star (1937)
Pick-Up (1968)
Pickup on South Street (1953)
Picnic (1955)
Picnic at Hanging Rock (1975)
Picture Brides (1934)
Picture Show Man, The (1977)
Pictures from a Strange Land (1972)
Piece of the Action, A (1977)
Pied Piper, The (1972)
Piedone lo Sbirro (1973)
Pierre of the Plains (1914)
Pierrot le Fou (1965)
Pig's War, The (1975)
Pim, Pam, Pum ... Fire! (1975)
Pink Panther Strikes Again, The (1976)
Pinocchio (1972)
Pioneer Trail (1938)
Pioneers, The (1977)
Pioneers of the West (1940)
Pipe Dreams (1976)
Pippi in the South Seas (1974)
Piranha (1978)
Pirates on Horseback (1941)
Pirosmani (1974)
Pistol, The (1973)
Pistol for Ringo, A (1966)

Pittsburgh (1942)
Pittsburgh Kid, The (1941)
Piu Bella Serata Della Mia Vita, A (1972)
... Piu Forte Ragazzi (1972)
Place Called Today, A (1972)
Place Without Limits, The (1978)
Plainsman, The (1966)
Plan 9 from Outer Space (1956)
Platanov (1977)
Play Girl (1932)
Play It Again, Sam (1972)
Players (1979)
Playgirl and the War Minister, The (1962)
Pleasantville (1976)
Please Believe Me (1950)
Pleasure Cruise (1933)
Plod (1972)
Plot, The (1973)
Plutonium (1979)
Plutopia (1950)
Poachers (1975)
Pocket Lover, The (1978)
Pocket Money (1972)
Polemonta (1975)
Police Inspector Accuses, A (1974)
Police Python 357 (1976)
Police Story (1973)
Police War, The (1979)
Policewoman (1974)
Policewoman (1975)
Polizia Incrimina, la Legga Assolve, La (1973)
Polly of the Circus (1932)
Polyolefins (1964)
Pom Pom Girls, The (1976)
Poor but Handsome (1956)
Poor Little Maria (1972)
Poor Lucas (1979)
Pop Always Pays (1940)
Pope Joan (1972)
Population Explosion (1967)
Porno at the School of Scandal (1974)
Port of Seven Seas (1938)
Portable Country (1979)
Porter, The (1978)
Portes Claquent, Les (1960)
Portia on Trial (1937)
Portnoy's Complaint (1972)
Portrait in the Rain (1978)
Portrait of Shunkin, A (1977)
Portrait of Teresa (1979)
Portrait of the Artist as a Young Man, A (1979)
Portrait Robot (1961)
Poseidon Adventure, The (1972)
Posse (1975)
Possession of Joel Delaney, The (1972)
Postman Didn't Ring, The (1942)
Potato Fritz (1976)
Powder River Rustlers (1949)
Powder Town (1942)
Powdersmoke Range (1935)
Power and the Glory, The (1933)
Power and the Truth, The (1972)
Power of the Whistler, The (1945)
Prairie Law (1940)
Prairie Pioneers (1941)
Praised Be What Hardens You (1972)
Predator, The (1976)
Pregnant by a Ghost (1975)
Prelude to War (1942)
Preludio a Espaja (1972)
Premiere Fois, La (see First Time, The)
Premonition, The (1975)
Preparation for the Festival (1978)
Present, The (1971)
Present Times (1972)
President Vanishes, The (1935)
President's Mystery, The (1936)
Pretty Good for a Human (1978)
Price of Power, The (1916)
Pride of St. Louis, The (1952)
Pride of the Blue Grass (1939)
Pride of the Navy (1939)
Prima Notte di Quiete, La (1972)
Prime Cut (1972)
Primitifs, du XIIIe, Les (1960)
Prince and the Pauper, The (1973)
Prince and the Pauper, The (see Crossed Swords)
Prince Ehtejab (1974)
Princess of the Dark, The (1917)
Princess O'Hara (1935)

Prison Nurse (1938)
Prison Ship (1945)
Prisoner of Second Avenue, The (1974)
Prisoner of the Harem (1912)
Prisoner of Zenda, The (1913)
Prisoner of Zenda, The (1922)
Prisoner of Zenda, The (1937)
Prisoner of Zenda, The (1979)
Private Affairs (1940)
Private Collection (1972)
Private Collections (1979)
Private Enterprise, A (1975)
Private Eyes, The (1977)
Private Files of J. Edgar Hoover, The (1977)
Private Life of Don Juan, The (1934)
Private Parts (1971)
Private Projection (1973)
Private Scandal, A (1931)
Private Vices, Public Virtues (1976)
Private War of Major Benson, The (1955)
Prize Fighter, The (1979)
Proceedings (1976)
Prodigal, The (1931)
Producers, The (1967)
Profiteer, The (1974)
Prometheus' Second Person (1975)
Promise, The (1978)
Promised Land, The (1974)
Promises in the Dark (1979)
Promissi Sposi, I (1938)
Proof of the Wild (1978)
Property Is No Longer a Theft (1973)
Prophecy (1979)
Proprieta non Piu un Furto, La (1973)
Prostitution (1976)
Proud Twins (1979)
Providence (1977)
Prowler, The (1951)
Psychic Killer (1975)
Public Enemies (1941)
Public Eye, The (1972)
Public Opinion (1935)
Puddin' Head (1941)
Pulp (1972)
Pumping Iron (1977)
Puppets Under Starry Skies (1978)
Pure and Simple (1930)
Pure S (1976)
Purgatory (1974)
Purple Taxi, The (1977)
Purple Vigilantes, The (1938)
Pursuit (1935)
Pursuit to Algiers (1945)
Pussy Talk (1975)
Puzzle of the Silver Half-Moon, The (1972)
Pyx, The (1973)

QB VII (1974)
Quadroon (1972)
Quadrophenia (1979)
Qualcono ha Tradito (1966)
Quarterback, The (1940)
Quarterly Balance-Taking (1975)
Quebec (1951)
Quebracho (1974)
Queen Bee (1978)
Queen of Blood (1966)
Queen Elizabeth (1912)
Queen of the Jungle (1935)
Questa Specie d'Amore (1972)
Question, The (1977)
Question Mark (1973)
Question of Rape, A (Le Viol) (1967)
Qui (1970)
Quiet Is the Night (1979)
Quiet Please, Murder (1943)
Quincy Adams Sawyer (1922)
Quintet (1979)
Quite Good Chaps (1972)

Ra Expeditions, The (1972)
Rabbi and the Shikse, The (1976)
Rabbit Test (1978)
Race for Space, The (1959)
Race for the Golden Flag (1969)
Race for Your Life, Charlie Brown (1977)
Race in the Head, The (1974)
Race with the Devil (1975)
Racers, The (1955)
Racing World (1968)
Racket Busters (1938)

Racketeers of the Range (1939)
Rafferty and the Gold Dust Twins (1975)
Rafter Romance (1933)
Raga (1971)
Ragazze Bruciate Verdi, Le (1961)
Ragazzi del Parioli, I (1958)
Rage (1972)
Rage (1979)
Rage in Heaven (1941)
Raggedy Ann and Andy (1977)
Raging Fists (1975)
Ragman's Daughter, The (1972)
Rags to Riches (1941)
Raiders of the Desert (1941)
Rain (1932)
Rain (1940)
Rainbow, The (1970)
Rainbow Boys, The (1973)
Rainbow on the River (1936)
Rainbow over Texas (1946)
Raining in the Mountain (1979)
Rainmakers, The (1935)
Rainy Love, A (1974)
Raising of Lazarus, The (1948)
Rak (1972)
Ramona (1928)
Rampart of Desire (1972)
Rancho DeLuxe (1975)
Rancho Notorious (1952)
Ranger and the Lady, The (1940)
Rango (1931)
Raomi (1978)
Ransom (see Terrorists, The)
Rare Bird, The (1973)
Rat, The (1938)
Ratataplan (1979)
Rationing (1944)
Ravaged Earth (1942)
Raven, The (see Corbeau, Le)
Raw Deal (1977)
Raw Edge, The (1956)
Rawhide Years, The (1956)
Ray of Sunlight, A (1979)
Real Life (1979)
Reason to Live, a Reason to Die, A (1974)
Rebel Jesus, The (1972)
Rebel Patagonia, The (1974)
Rebels, The (1979)
Reckless (1935)
Recollections (1978)
Recommendation for Mercy (1975)
Recourse to the Method, The (1978)
Red Beard (1966)
Red Beret, The (see Paratrooper)
Red Desert (1949)
Red Earth (1975)
Red Gold (1978)
Red-Haired Revolver (1974)
Red Mantle, The (1973)
Red Midnight (1978)
Red Morning (1934)
Red Planet Mars (1952)
Red Poppies on the Wall (1979)
Red River Range (1938)
Red River Robin Hood (1942)
Red River Valley (1941)
Red Rose, The (1973)
Red Seedlings (1979)
Red Skies of Montana (1952)
Red Snowball Tree, The (1974)
Red Sun (1971)
Red Sun (1975)
Red Sweater, The (Pull-Over Rouge, Le) (1979)
Red Zone (1976)
Redeemer, The (1966)
Redeemer, The (1977)
Redhead (1941)
Redskin (1929)
Reflection of Fear (1973)
Reform Candidate, The (1915)
Refugees (1963)
Regent's Wife, The (1975)
Reincarnation of Peter Proud, The (1975)
Release the Prisoners, It's Spring (1975)
Reluctant Gunfighter, The (1977)
Remains of the Shipwreck (1978)
Rembrandt--Fecit 1669 (1978)
Remember? (1939)
Remember Last Night? (1935)
Remember My Name (1978)
Remember the Day (1941)
Rendezvous (1935)
Rendezvous, The (1972)
Rendez-vous a Melbourne (1956)
Rendezvous with Annie (1946)

Rene the Cane (1977)
Renegade Ranger, The (1938)
Renegades of the Rio Grande (1945)
Repeated Absences (1972)
Report to the Commissioner (1975)
Reptilicus (1961)
Republic of Uzice, The (1974)
Request, The (1976)
Requiem for a Village (1976)
Rescue from Gilligan's Island (1978)
Rescuers, The (1977)
Restless Corpse, The (1979)
Resurrection (1931)
Resurrection of Eve (1973)
Resurrection of the Golden Wolf (1979)
Retour d'Ulysse, Le (1909)
Return (1973)
Return, The (1979)
Return from Witch Mountain (1978)
Return of a Man Called Horse, The (1976)
Return of Casanova (1978)
Return of Chandu, The (1934)
Return of Gilbert and Sullivan, The (1951)
Return of Jesse James, The (1950)
Return of Peter Grimm, The (1935)
Return of the Dragon (1974)
Return of the Big Blond, The (see Return of the Tall Blond, The)
Return of the Gunfighter, The (1967)
Return of the Pink Panther (1975)
Return of the Tall Blond, The (1974)
Return of the Texan (1952)
Return of the Vampire (1943)
Return to Campus (1975)
Return to Macon County (1975)
Return to the Beloved (1979)
Reunion in Vienna (1933)
Revenge (1979)
Revenge of the Cheerleaders (1976)
Revenge of the Pink Panther, The (1978)
Revengers, The (1972)
Revolt of the Thralls (1979)
Revolt of the Zombies (1936)
Revolution of the Seven Madmen, The (1973)
Revolver (1973)
Rhapsodie Hongroise (1929)
Rheingold (1978)
Rhinoceros (1974)
Rhythm in the Clouds (1937)
Rich Are Always with Us, The (1932)
Rich Kids (1979)
Richard Wagner (1913)
Riddle of the Sands, The (1979)
Ride a Crooked Mile (1938)
Ride a Wild Pony (1975)
Ride On, Vaquero (1941)
Riders of the Santa Fe (1944)
Riders of the Timberline (1941)
Riding on Air (1937)
Rig Move (1964)
Right of the Maddest, The (1973)
Right to Happiness, The (1919)
Right to Love, The (1972)
Right to Romance, The (1933)
Right to the Heart (1942)
Ring Around the Moon (1950)
Rings on Her Fingers (1942)
Ringside Maisie (1941)
Rio Grande (1950)
Rise, Fair Sun (1974)
Rites of May, The (1979)
Ritz, The (1976)
River, The (1929)
River, The (1979)
River of No Return (1954)
River's End (1940)
Road, The (1975)
Road Agent (1941)
Road Back, The (1937)
Road to Singapore (1940)
Road to Zanzibar (1941)
Roads of the South (1978)
Roar of the Dragon (1932)
Robbers of the Range (1941)
Robert and Robert (1978)
Roberte (1978)
Robin and Marian (1976)
Robin Hood (1922)
Robin Hood (1973)

Robin Hood of the Pecos (1941)
Robot Monster (1953)
Rock 'n' Roll Wolf (1978)
Rockabye (1932)
Rocketship X-M (1950)
Rocky (1976)
Rocky II (1979)
Rocky Mountain Rangers (1940)
Rogue Song, The (1930)
Rogue's Gallery (1944)
Rogues of Sherwood Forest (1950)
Rogue's Tavern (1936)
Roughly Speaking (1945)
Roland Rivas, Cab Driver (1974)
Roll, Thunder, Roll (1950)
Roller Boogie (1979)
Rollercoaster (1977)
Rolling Thunder (1977)
Roma (see Fellini's Roma)
Roma Bene (1971)
Romance in Manhattan (1935)
Romance in the Rain (1934)
Romance of Happy Valley, A (1919)
Romance of Lovers (1974)
Romance of the Rio Grande (1941)
Romance on the Run (1938)
Romantic Englishwoman, The (1975)
Rome: Armed to the Teeth (1976)
Rome Wants Another Caesar (1974)
Romeo and Juliet (1968)
Ronde de Nuit, La (1926)
Roof, The (1978)
Rooftops of New York (1960)
Rookie Cop, The (1939)
Rookies on Parade (1941)
Room Service (1938)
Room with a View on the Sea, A (1978)
Rooster Cogburn (1975)
Root, The (1975)
Roots (1976)
Roots of Blood (1979)
Roots: One Year Later (1977)
Roots 2 (1978)
Rose-Colored Telephone, The (1975)
Rose for Everyone, A (1967)
Rose of the Rio Grande (1938)
Rose-Tinted Dreams (1977)
Rosebud (1975)
Roseland (1977)
Rosemary (1958)
Roses of Danzig, The (1979)
Rough Day for the Queen (1973)
Rough Riders Round-Up (1939)
Roughly Speaking (1945)
Round Trip (1978)
Round-Up, The (1941)
Route de Suede, La (1952)
Routine Has to Be Broken (1974)
Rover, The (1967)
Rowdyman, The (1972)
Royal Divorce, A (1938)
Royal Flash (1975)
Royal Hunt, The (1977)
Rubber Gun, The (1977)
Ruby (1977)
Rufus (1975)
Ruling Class, The (1972)
Ruma Is Going (1968)
Run Away, I Love You (1979)
Run for the Roses (1978)
Run with the Devil (1959)
Runner Stumbles, The (1979)
Running (1979)
Running Fence (1978)
Rupert of Hentzau (1916)
Rural Teacher, The (1978)
Ruslan and Ludmila (1974)
Russian Roulette (1975)
Ruthless (1948)

S. O. S. (1975)
S. O. S. --Tidal Wave (1939)
S. T. A. B. (1976)
Sabata (1969)
Sabina, The (1979)
Sable Lorcha, The (1915)
Sacred Idol, The (1959)
Sacred Knives of Vengeance, The (1973)
Sad Young Men, The (1961)
Saddlemates (1941)
Sadie McKee (1934)
Sadist with Red Teeth, The (1971)
Saen Saeb Canal (1978)
Saga of Death Valley (1939)

Sagarana, the Duel (1974)
Sagebrush Law (1943)
Saharan Venture (1965)
Sai Thip (1979)
Sailor Who Fell from Grace with the Sea, The (1976)
Sailors on Leave (1941)
Sailor's Return, The (1978)
Saint Anne (Annee Sainte, L') (1976)
Saint-Germaine-des-Pres (1953)
Saint in Palm Springs, The (1941)
St. Ives (1976)
Saint-Paul-de-Vence (1949)
St. Pauli Report (1972)
Saint Strikes Back, The (1939)
Saint Takes Over, The (1940)
Saint-Tropez Blues (1960)
Saint-Tropez, Devoir de Vacances (1952)
Saint vs. the Vampire Women, The (1962)
Saint's Double Trouble, The (1940)
Sal-a-Malle-Ek (1965)
Salammbo (1925)
Sallah (1964)
Salo or 120 Days of Sodom (1975)
Salome (1953)
Salon Kitty (see Madame Kitty)
Salt Lake Raiders (1950)
Salut l'Artiste (see Hail the Artist)
Salvation (1973)
Salvatore Giuliano (1962)
Salzburg Connection, The (1972)
Samarang (1933)
Same Time Next Year (1978)
Sampan Boy (1950)
Samson (1914)
Samson and the Seven Miracles of the World (1962)
Samson and the Slave Queen (1962)
San Antonio (1945)
San Antonio Kid, The (1944)
San Francisco Docks (1941)
San Francisco Story, The (1952)
San Quentin (1937)
Sandstone (1977)
Sandy Gets Her Man (1940)
Sannikov's Land (1973)
Santa Fe Marshal (1940)
Santa Fe Stampede (1938)
Santee (1973)
Santi and Veena (1976)
Santo and Blue Demon vs. the Monsters (1968)
Santo and the Blue Demon vs. Dracula and the Wolf Man (1972)
Santo and the Revenge of the Vampire Women (1968)
Sapporo Winter Olympics (1972)
Saps at Sea (1940)
Saskatchewan (1954)
Satan's Brew (1976)
Saturday Night Fever (1977)
Saul and David (1968)
Savage, The (1975)
Savage Gold (1933)
Savage Is Loose, The (1974)
Savage Party, The (1976)
Savage Planet, The (1973)
Savage Sisters (1974)
Savage State, The (1978)
Savage Wild, The (1970)
Savages (1972)
Save the City (1977)
Save the Tiger (1973)
Saxophone (1978)
Say It with Flowers (1974)
Scalawag (1973)
Scale in Hi-Fi (1963)
Scandal Sheet (1952)
Scar, The (1977)
Scar, The (1978)
Scarecrow (1973)
Scarecrow in a Garden of Cucumbers (1972)
Scarlet Claw, The (1944)
Scarlet Empress, The (1934)
Scarlet Letter, The (1973)
Scatterbrain (1940)
Scattergood Meets Broadway (1941)
Scavenger Hunt (1979)
Scene Nun, Take One (1964)
Scenes of Fires (1978)
Scent of Earth, The (1978)
Scent of Woman (1974)
Schiava Io ce l'Ho e Tu No, La (1973)

Schlock (1973)
Schoolgirls Report III (1972)
Schoolmaster Hober (1977)
Schuldig (1913)
Scientific Cardplayer, The (1972)
Scobie Malone (1975)
Scorched Triangle, The (1975)
Scorchy (1976)
Score, The (1978)
Scorpio (1973)
Scorpion Sea (1975)
Scorpion Woods (1976)
Scott Joplin (1977)
Scoumoune, La (1972)
Scoundrel, The (1972)
Scrambled Eggs, The (1976)
Scratch a Tiger (1969)
Scream, Blacula, Scream (1973)
Scream of Silence, A (1979)
Screams of a Winter Night (1979)
Screw Driver, The (1941)
Scrounged Meals (1977)
Sea Gull, The (1973)
Sea Gull, The (1977)
Sea Gypsies, The (1978)
Sea Hawk, The (1940)
Sea Racketeers (1937)
Sea Spiders (1932)
Sea Urchin in the Pocket, A (1977)
Seabo (1977)
Sealed Lips (1941)
Search and Research (1967)
Search for Solutions, The (1979)
Season of the Senses (1969)
Sebastian (1968)
Sebastian (1976)
Seclusion Near a Forest (1976)
Second Awakening of Christa Klages, The (1978)
Second Best (1972)
Second Chance (1969)
Second Chance--Sea (1976)
Second Coming of Suzanne, The (1974)
Second Power, The (1977)
Second Truth, The (1966)
Second Wife (1936)
Second Wind (1976)
Second Wind, A (1978)
Secret, The (1974)
Secret, The (1979)
Secret Agent of Japan (1942)
Secret Agent Superdragon (1966)
Secret Life of Plants, The (1978)
Secret Love (1916)
Secret of Dr. Kildare, The (1939)
Secret of Madame Blanche, The (1933)
Secret of the Green Pins, The (1972)
Secret of the Sierra Dorada, The (1957)
Secret Rivals, The (1976)
Secrets (1933)
Secrets (1978)
Secrets of Scotland Yard (1944)
Secrets of the Wasteland (1941)
Section Speciale (1975)
Seducers, The (1968)
Seduction (1973)
Seduction of Joe Tynan, The (1979)
Seduction of Mimi, The (1974)
See Here, Private Hargrove (1944)
See You Tomorrow (1960)
Seed, The (1974)
Seedling, The (1974)
Seekers, The (1979)
Seizure (1974)
Sell-Out, The (1976)
Semi-Tough (1977)
Senilita (1962)
Sensations (1975)
Sentimental Story, A (1977)
Sentinel, The (1977)
Separate Peace, A (1972)
7 Morts sur Ordonnance (1975)
September Love (1978)
Sequoia (1935)
Serail (1975)
Sgt. Buntung (1979)
Sergeant Madden (1939)
Serious as Pleasure (1975)
Serpent, The (1973)
Serpent's Egg, The (1977)
Serpents of the Pirate Moon, The (1973)
Serpico (1973)
Servant and Mistress (1977)

Servants, The (1979)
Sette Baschi Rossi (1969)
Seven Alone (1975)
Seven Beauties (1976)
7 Days in January (1979)
7 Deaths by Subscription (1975)
Seven Freckles (1978)
Seven-Man Army (1976)
Seven Miles from Alcatraz (1943)
Seven Nights in Japan (1976)
Seven Per Cent Solution (1976)
Seven Samurai (1972)
Seven Sinners (1940)
Seven Ups, The (1973)
17 (see Eric Soya's 17)
Seventh Cross, The (1944)
Seventh Heaven (1927)
Sewers of Paradise, The (1979)
Sex and the Married Woman (1977)
Sex and the Vampire (1970)
Sex Crazy (1973)
Sex of Their Bodies (1972)
Sex Thief, The (1974)
Sextette (1978)
Sextool (1975)
Sexy Probitissimo (1964)
Shades of Silk (1979)
Shadow of Doubt (1935)
Shadow of the Castles (1976)
Shadow of the Eagle (1932)
Shadow of the Hawk (1976)
Shadows of a Hot Summer (1978)
Shadows of the Orient (1936)
Shaft in Africa (1973)
Shaft's Big Score (1972)
Shaggy D. A., The (1976)
Shampoo (1975)
Shamrock Hill (1949)
Shamus (1973)
Shanghai Joe (1974)
Shanks (1974)
Shaolin Abbot (1979)
Shaolin Rescuers (1979)
Shape of Things to Come, The (1979)
Shark's Treasure (1975)
She (1935)
She Married a Cop (1939)
She No Longer Talks ... She Shoots (1972)
Sheba Baby (1975)
Sheherazade (1928)
Sheik Steps Out, The (1937)
Sheila Levine Is Dead and Living in New York (1975)
Shenanigans (1977)
Shepherd of the Hills (1941)
Sheriff of Sundown (1944)
Sheriff of Tombstone (1941)
Sherlock Holmes and the Secret Weapon (1942)
Sherlock Jones (1975)
She's a Soldier, Too (1944)
She's Dangerous (1937)
She's Got Everything (1937)
Shiralee, The (1956)
Shirley Thompson vs. the Aliens (1972)
Shoot (1976)
Shoot It: Black, Shoot It: Blue (1974)
Shootist, The (1976)
Short and Sweet (1976)
Short Eyes (Slammer) (1977)
Short Memory (1979)
Shot in the Dark, A (1935)
Should Husbands Work? (1939)
Shout, The (1978)
Shout at the Devil (1976)
Show Business (1975)
Showdown, The (1940)
Showdown (1973)
Shriek in the Night, A (1933)
Shut Up, Gulls (1974)
Si le Vent te Faire Peur (1960)
Siberiade (1979)
Sidecar Racers (1975)
Sidewinder 1 (1977)
Siege of Petersburg, The (1912)
Siege of Tobruk, The (1942)
Sign of the Pagan (1954)
Signalet (1966)
Silence, A (1972)
Silence! The Court Is in Session (1972)
Silent Cry, The (1977)
Silent Movie (1976)
Silent One, The (1973)
Silent Partner, The (1979)
Silent Raiders (1954)
Silent Running (1972)
Silk Worms (1976)
Silly Billies (1936)

Silver Bears (1977)
Silver Dollar (1932)
Silver Lining (1932)
Silver Skates (1943)
Silver Streak, The (1934)
Silver Streak (1976)
Silver Threads (1937)
Simple Heart, A (1978)
Simple Histoire, Une (1957)
Simple Melody, A (1974)
Sinbad and the Eye of the Tiger (1977)
Sinful Dwarf, The (1973)
Sing and Like It (1934)
Sing Dance, Plenty Hot (1940)
Singapore Woman (1941)
Singer, The (1978)
Singer and the Dancer, The (1977)
Single Standard, The (1929)
Sins in the Family (1975)
Sins of Youth (1958)
Sirocco Blow, The (1979)
Sis Hopkins (1941)
Sister of Satan, The (1965)
Sisters (1973)
Sisters, or the Balance of Happiness (1979)
Sita's Wedding (1978)
Sitting Ducks (1979)
Sitting on the Edge of Tomorrow with the Feet Hanging (1979)
Sitting Target (1972)
Six Bears and a Clown (1976)
Six Faces of Terylene (1964)
Six-Gun Gold (1941)
Six O'Clock USA (1976)
Six Pack Annie (1975)
6,000 Enemies (1939)
16 Fathoms Deep (1948)
Sixth and Main (1977)
67 Days (1975)
Skatetown, U.S.A. (1979)
Ski on the Wild Side (1967)
Ski Patrol (1940)
Ski Total (1962)
Ski Troop Attack (1960)
Skipalong Rosenbloom (1951)
Skipper and Co. (1974)
Skirt Chaser, The (1979)
Sky Devils (1932)
Sky Giant (1938)
Sky High (1974)
Sky Murder (1940)
Sky over Holland (1967)
Sky Parade, The (1936)
Sky Riders (1976)
Skyjacked (1972)
Skyscraper (1959)
Slams, The (1973)
Slander House (1936)
Slap Shot (1977)
Slap the Monster on Page One (1972)
Slaughter (1972)
Slaughter of the Vampires, The (1962)
Slaughterhouse-5 (1972)
Slaughter's Big Rip-Off (1973)
Slave, The (1962)
Slave, The (1973)
Slave of Love, A (1978)
Slave Ship (1937)
Slavers (1977)
Sleep, Sleep My Love (1975)
Sleeper (1973)
Sleeping Car, The (1976)
Sleeping Dogs (1977)
Sleeping Dragon (1975)
Sleuth (1972)
Slightly French (1949)
Slightly Scandalous (1946)
Slightly Tempted (1940)
Slim (1937)
Slip-Up (1975)
Slippery When Wet (1959)
Slipstream (1974)
Slither (1973)
Slope in Spring, The (1971)
Sloppy Jalopy (1952)
Slow Dancing in the Big City (1978)
Slow Motion (1979)
Slum Boy (1976)
Slum People in the Sun (1979)
Slumber Party '57 (1977)
Small Change (1977)
Small Insect (1976)
Small Propeller, The (1967)
Small Timers, The (1978)
Small Town Girl (1936)
Small Town in Texas, A (1976)
Small World of Sammy Lee, The (1962)
Smartest Girl in Town, The (1936)

Smashing the Rackets (1938)
Smell of Wildflowers, The (1978)
Smemorato di Collegno, Lo (1962)
Smile (1975)
Smile Hello (1978)
Smile Orange (1976)
Smilin' Through (1932)
Smoke on the Potato Fields (1977)
Smokey and the Bandit (1977)
Smuggled Cargo (1939)
Smugglers (1972)
Snake Pit and the Pendulum, The (1967)
Snake Prince, The (1976)
Snap-Shot (1979)
Snapshots as Souvenirs (1979)
Sniper, The (1952)
Snow (1964)
Snow Job (Ski Raiders) (1971)
Snowball Express (1972)
Snowfall (1974)
Snowstorm (1977)
Snuffy Smith, Yard Bird (1942)
So Evil My Love (1948)
So Long, Blue Boy (1973)
So Long, Movie Friend (1979)
So Well Remembered (1948)
So You Won't Talk? (1940)
Society Doctor (1935)
Society Lawyer (1939)
Sodom and Gomorrah (1976)
Softening of the Egg, The (1975)
Soho Gorilla (1972)
Soil (1939)
Solaris (1977)
Soldier Brothers of Susanna, The (1912)
Soldier of Orange (1979)
Soldiers Never Cry (1979)
Soldiers of Fortune (1914)
Soleil de Pierre (1967)
Solemn Communion (1977)
Solomon King (1974)
Some Arpents of Snow (1973)
Some Call It Loving (1973)
Some Kind of Saint (1979)
Somebody Killed Her Husband (1978)
Somebody Up There Likes Me (1956)
Something Beautiful (1977)
Something for the Boys (1944)
Something Nice to Eat (1967)
Something Short of Paradise (1979)
Something to Hide (1972)
Something's Rotten (1979)
Sometime Sweet Susan (1974)
Somewhere Beyond Love (1974)
Somewhere, Someone (1972)
Somnabulists (1978)
Son, The (1973)
Son-Daughter, The (1932)
Son from Bergaarden, The (1975)
Son of Dracula (1943)
Son of Dracula (1974)
Son of Frankenstein (1939)
Son of Monte Cristo (1941)
Son of the Guardsman (1946)
Sonata over the Lake (1977)
Song Is Born, A (1948)
Song of Roland, The (1978)
Song of the Canary (1979)
Song of the City (1937)
Sonho de Vampiros, Um (1970)
Sonny and Jed (1974)
Son-Rise (1979)
Sons and Daughters (1967)
Sons for the Return Home (1979)
Sons of Fire (1975)
Sophia Loren in Rome (1965)
Sophie (1977)
Sorcerer (1977)
Sorority House (1939)
Sorpasso, Il (1962)
Sorriso del Grande Tentatore, Il (1979)
Sorrows of Young Werther, The (1976)
Soul Hustler (1973)
Soul of Nigger Charley, The (1973)
Souls at Sea (1937)
Sound Off (1952)
Sounder (1972)
Soup du Jour (1975)
Sourdough (1977)
South of Suez (1940)
South to Karanga (1940)
Southward Ho! (1939)
Souvenir of Gibraltar (1975)
Soylent Green (1973)
Space Cruiser Yamato (1977)

Space Monster (1964)
Spanish Revolt of 1836, The (1912)
Sparkle (1976)
Spartan Mother, A (1912)
Speak to Me of Love (1975)
Special Delivery (1955)
Special Delivery (1976)
Special Dispatch (1940)
Special Edition (1978)
Special Education (1977)
Spectre of Edgar Allan Poe, The (1974)
Speed (1936)
Speed Fever (1978)
Speedway (1929)
Spell, The (1977)
Spending Money (1976)
Sphinx, The (1933)
Spider Football (1977)
Spider Woman Strikes Back, The (1946)
Spikes Gang, The (1974)
Spiral (1978)
Spiral, The (1976)
Spiral of Mist, A (1977)
Spirit of the Beehive, The (1973)
Spirit of the Wind (1979)
Spoiled Children (1977)
Spook Who Sat by the Door, The (1973)
Spooks Run Wild (1941)
Sport Parade, The (1932)
Sport, Sport, Sport (1978)
Sporting Blood (1940)
Spring Day in Hell (1977)
Spring Parade (1940)
Springtime for Henry (1934)
Springtime in the Rockies (1937)
Spy Smasher (1942)
Spy Who Loved Me, The (1977)
S*P*Y*S (1974)
Squadron Antigangster (1978)
Squares (1972)
Squeeze, The (1977)
Squirm (1976)
S-s-s-s-s-s (1973)
Stadium Nuts (1972)
Stage Door (1937)
Stage to Chino (1940)
Stagecoach (1939)
Stagecoach Days (1938)
Stagecoach to Monterey (1944)
Stagecoach War (1940)
Stalker (1979)
Stand Up and Be Counted (1972)
Stand Up Straight, Delfina (1977)
Stand Up, Virgin Soldiers (1977)
Stanley and Livingstone (1939)
Star for a Night (1936)
Star of Midnight (1935)
Star Packer (1934)
Star Trek--The Motion Picture (1979)
Star Wars (1977)
Starcrash (1979)
Stardust (1974)
Stars and the Water Carrier, The (1974)
Stars in the Hair, Tears in the Eyes (1978)
Starship Invasions (1977)
Starting Over (1979)
State Fair (1933)
State of Siege (1973)
State Reasons (1978)
Stavisky (1974)
Stay As You Are (1978)
Stay Hungry (1976)
Steam Mare, The (1978)
Steel Arena (1973)
Stella Da Falla (1972)
Stella Dallas (1937)
Stepford Wives, The (1975)
Stepmother, The (1975)
Steppe, The (1978)
Steppenwolf (1974)
Sternstein Manor, The (1976)
Stevie (1978)
Stick-Up, The (1978)
Sting, The (1973)
Stolen Paradise (1941)
Stone (1974)
Stone Killer, The (1972)
Stony Island (1978)
Stop Calling Me Baby! (1977)
Storm at Daybreak (1933)
Storm Boy (1976)
Storm over Bengal (1938)
Storm over Tibet (1951)
Storm Warning (1940)
Stormtroopers (1977)
Stormy Wine (1976)
Story of Adele H., The (1975)

Story of Bicycles, The (1953)
Story of Chinese Gods, The (1976)
Story of Joanha, The (1975)
Story of Louis Pasteur, The (1935)
Story of "O," The (1975)
Story of Peaceful Genroku Era, The (1975)
Story of Taikoh, The (1965)
Story of the Age of Wars, The (1973)
Story of the Dragon, The (1976)
Story of the Taira Family, The (1972)
Straight Is the Way (1934)
Straight Time (1978)
Strait-Laced Girl, A (1977)
Strange Adventures of David Grey, The (see Vampyr)
Strange Affair of Uncle Harry, The (1945)
Strange City (1972)
Strange Door, The (1951)
Strange Events (1977)
Strange Letters (1977)
Strange People (1933)
Strange People (1976)
Strange Role, A (1977)
Strange Shadows in an Empty Room (1977)
Stranger in Town, A (1943)
Strangers (1972)
Strangers All (1935)
Stranger's Gundown, The (1974)
Strangers of the Evening (1932)
Strangler's Melody (1979)
Strauberg Is Here (1978)
Street Gangs of Hong Kong (1974)
Street of Missing Men (1939)
Street of the Crane's Foot (1979)
Street of Women (1932)
Street People (1976)
Streghe, Le (1966)
Strength of the Weak, The (1916)
Stronger Than Desire (1939)
Strongest Karate, The (1976)
Strongest Man in the World, The (1975)
Struggle (1975)
Student Body, The (1975)
Student von Prag, Der (1913)
Study in Terror, A (1966)
Stuff That Dreams Are Made Of, The (1972)
Stunts (1977)
Stupid Boy Friend, The (1976)
Stupid Life (1977)
Submarine D-1 (1937)
Submarine Patrol (1938)
Submersion of Japan (Tidal Wave) (1974)
Submission (1977)
Suburban Wives (1972)
Successive Slidings of Pleasure (1974)
Successo, Il (1963)
Such a Lovely Town... (1979)
Such Women Are Dangerous (1934)
Sudden Fury (1975)
Sudden Loneliness of Konrad Steiner, The (1976)
Sud-Express (1963)
Sued for Libel (1939)
Suez (1939)
Sugar, The (1978)
Sugar Hill (1974)
Sugar Is a Business (1971)
Sugarland Express, The (1974)
Suleiman the Conqueror (1963)
Sullivan's Empire (1967)
Summer Camp (1979)
Summer Guests (1976)
Summer Lightning (1972)
Summer Love (1958)
Summer of Love, A (1979)
Summer of Secrets (1976)
Summer Soldiers (1972)
Summer Wishes, Winter Dreams (1973)
Summerfield (1977)
Summertime Killer (1972)
Sun Comes Up, The (1949)
Sun of the Hyenes (see Hyena's Sun)
Sun on the Skin (1972)
Sun over the Swamp (1978)
Sunburn (1979)
Sunday Chronicle (1975)
Sunday in the Country (1975)
Sunday Woman (1976)
Sundowners, The (1960)

Sunrise at Campobello (1960)
Suns of Easter Island (1972)
Sunset in El Dorado (1945)
Sunset Murder Case, The (1938)
Sunset Trail (1938)
Sunstroke (1978)
Sup Sap Bup Dap (1975)
Super Cops, The (1974)
Super-Giant 2 (1956)
Super Super Adventure, The (1975)
Super Van (1977)
Superb Trip, The (1974)
Superbeast (1972)
Superdad (1974)
Superfly (1972)
Superfly T. N. T. (1973)
Superman (1978)
Supermarket (1974)
Supersonic Man (1979)
Supply Column Soldier, The (1976)
Supreme Kid, The (1976)
Surgeons (1978)
Surprise Sock (1978)
Survive! (1975)
Susanna tutta Panna (1957)
Suspiria (1977)
Sutjeska (1973)
Svedesi, Le (1961)
Swallows and Amazons (1974)
Swami (1977)
Swamp Water (1941)
Swap Meet (1979)
Swarm, The (1978)
Swashbuckler (1976)
Swedish Girls in Paris (1960)
Sweeney (1977)
Sweeney 2 (1978)
Sweet Creek County War, The (1979)
Sweet Jesus, Preacher Man (1973)
Sweet Movie (1974)
Sweet Punkin' (1976)
Sweet Revenge (1976)
Sweet Revenge (1979)
Sweet Smell of Success, The (1957)
Sweet Suzy (1973)
Sweet Woman (1977)
Sweetheart (1979)
Swell Guy (1947)
Swept Away (by a Strange Destiny in a Blue August Sea) (1974)
Swimming Pool, The (1977)
Swing High, Swing Low (1937)
Swing Out, Sister (1945)
Swinger, The (1972)
Swiss Affair, The (1978)
Swissmakers, The (1978)
Sword, The (1977)
Swords of Death (1972)
Symphony of Living (1935)
Symphony of Six Million (1932)
Syncopation (1942)
Szindbad (1972)

TNT Jackson (1975)
T. R. Baskin (1972)
T-Bird Gang, The (1958)
Tabu (1931)
Tachi and Her Fathers (1979)
Tailor from Ulm, The (1979)
Take a Hard Ride (1975)
Take All of Me (1978)
Take Care, France (1972)
Take Down (1979)
Take It Easy (1974)
Take Me to the Ritz (1977)
Take One (1977)
Take One Baby (1968)
Take 2 (1972)
Takeoff, The (1979)
Takiji Kobayashi (1974)
Taking of Christina, The (1976)
Taking of Pelham 1, 2, 3, The (1974)
Tales of Terror (1962)
Tales That Witness Madness (1973)
Talisman (1978)
Tall Blond Man with One Black Shoe, The (1973)
Tall Shadows of the Wind (1979)
Tamarind Seed, The (1974)
Tanasse Scatiu (1977)
Tanga Tika (1953)
Tanganyika (1954)
Tangled Destinies (1932)
Tangled Hearts (1916)
Tangsir (1974)
Tanks a Million (1941)
Tanner Steel Mill, The (1976)
Tant Qu'il y Aura de l'Angoisse

(1966)
Tant Qu'il y Aura des Capricornes (1961)
Tarzan and the She-Devil (1952)
Tarzan the Fearless (1933)
Tarzan's Secret Treasure (1941)
Tarzoon, the Snake of the Jungle (1975)
Taste of Blood, A (1967)
Taxi (1953)
Taxi Driver (1976)
Teacher, The (1978)
Teacher Nansen (1968)
Tears of Happiness (1974)
Telefon (1977)
Tell Him I Love Him (1977)
Tell It to a Star (1945)
Tell Me You Love Me (1974)
Tempest, The (1958)
Tempest, The (1979)
Tempi Duri per I Vampiri (1959)
Temptation (1967)
Temptations in the Summer Wind (1973)
Tempter, The (1974)
Temptress, The (1926)
10 (1979)
Ten Little Indians (1975)
10 Per Cent of Hope (1977)
Ten Seconds That Shook the World (1963)
Tenant, The (1976)
Tenants, The (1976)
Tender Cop (1977)
Tender Moment, The (1968)
Tenderness of Wolves, The (1973)
Tent of Miracles, The (1977)
Tentacles (1977)
Tentativo Sentimentale, Un (1963)
Teresa (1970)
Teresa the Thief (1973)
Terre Fleurie (1956)
Terres et Flammes (1951)
Terror (1977)
Terror (1978)
Terror by Night (1946)
Terror in the Haunted House (1958)
Terror in the Wax Museum (1973)
Terrorist, The (1963)
Terrorists, The (Ransom) (1975)
Tess (1979)
Test Pilot Pirx (1979)
Testament (1975)
Testimony of Two Men (1977)
Thai Tiger's Roar (1975)
Thanassi Get Your Gun (1972)
That Brennan Girl (1946)
That Brief Summer (1976)
That Certain Woman (1937)
That Dawn Should Be Peaceful (1972)
That Lady in Ermine (1948)
That Little Difference (1970)
That Long Night (1979)
That Lucky Touch (1975)
That Man Bolt (1973)
That Nazty Nuisance (1943)
That Sinking Feeling (1979)
That Summer (1979)
That's Enough, Man (1974)
That's the Way of the World (1075)
Thaw (1977)
Theater of Blood (1973)
Their Big Moment (1934)
Theodora Goes Wild (1936)
There Is No Forgetting (1976)
There Is No 13 (1974)
There Was a Lad (1978)
There's a Girl in My Heart (1950)
There's Always a Way to Find a Way (1973)
There's Always Tomorrow (1956)
There's Always Vanilla (1972)
These Glamour Girls (1939)
They All Come Out (1939)
They Are Their Own Gifts (1979)
They Died with Their Boots On (1942)
They Fought for Their Country (1975)
They Live by Night (1948)
They Made Her a Spy (1939)
They Made Me a Criminal (1939)
They Met in Bombay (1941)
They Only Kill Their Masters (1972)
They Shall Overcome (1974)
They Went That-a-Way and That-a-Way (1978)

Thief Who Came to Dinner, The (1973)
Thieves (1977)
Thing with Two Heads, The (1972)
Third After the Sun, The (1973)
Third Base (1978)
Third Door, The (1976)
Third Generation, The (1979)
Third Walker, The (1978)
Thirst (1979)
13 Days in France (1968)
Thirteen Women (1932)
13th Letter, The (1951)
39 Steps, The (1978)
This England (1940)
This Is a Hijack (1973)
This Is Cinerama (1952)
This Is Colour (1941)
This Is Korea (1951)
This Is Love, Isn't It? (1979)
This Is My Affair (1937)
This Is the Night (1932)
This Island Earth (1955)
This Kind of Love (1973)
This Property Is Condemned (1966)
This Side of Heaven (1934)
This Strange Passion (El) (1955)
This Thing Called Love (1941)
This Woman Is Mine (1941)
Thomas (1975)
Thomasine and Bushrod (1974)
Thoroughbreds Don't Cry (1937)
Those Dirty Dogs (1974)
Those Quiet Japanese (1972)
Those Were the Years (1975)
Those Wonderful Men with a Crank (1979)
Thou Shalt Not Kill (1939)
Thousands Cheer (1943)
Threat, The (1977)
Three Blind Mice (1938)
Three Card Monte (1978)
Three Cheers for the Irish (1940)
Three Days of the Condor (1975)
Three Godfathers, The (1936)
3 in the Cellar (1970)
Three into a Thousand (1970)
Three Little Bops (1956)
Three Live Ghosts (1929)
Three Live Ghosts (1936)
Three Men from Texas (1940)
Three Musketeers, The (1921)
Three Musketeers, The (1933)
Three Musketeers, The (1973)
Three Nights of Love (1964)
Three Rooms in Manhattan (1958)
Three Sisters (1967)
Three Smart Girls (1936)
Three Sons (1939)
Three Sons O' Guns (1941)
3:10 to Yuma (1957)
Three Texas Steers (1939)
Three the Hard Way (1974)
Three Tigers Against Three Tigers (1977)
Three Tough Guys (1974)
Three, Two, One (1975)
Three Wise Men, The (1976)
Three Worlds of Gulliver, The (1959)
Thrill of Brazil, The (1946)
Through Different Eyes (1942)
Through the Ashes of the Empire (1976)
Through the Looking Glass (1976)
Thruster, The (1977)
Thumb Tripping (1972)
Thunder (1929)
Thunder and Lightning (1977)
Thunder in the East (1953)
Thunder Town (1946)
Thunderbirds Are Go (1966)
Thunderbolt and Lightfoot (1974)
Thundering Fatty (see Dunderklumpen)
Thundering Hoofs (1942)
Thundering Trails (1943)
Ti-Cul Tougas (1977)
Ti Ho Sposato per Allegria (1967)
Tic Tac Toe (1979)
Tidal Wave (see Submersion of Japan)
Tidal Wave and West Wind (1976)
Ties for the Olympics (1977)
Tiger, The (1978)
Tiger and Crane Fists (1976)
Tiger Woman, The (1944)
Tiger's Way, The (1977)
Tight Shoes (1941)

Tiina (1977)
Tiko and the Shark (1966)
Til Divorce Us Do Part (1977)
Tilt (1979)
Timber (1967)
Timber Move (1965)
Timber Stampede (1939)
Time After Time (1979)
Time for Loving, A (1971)
Time Objectives (1965)
Time of Blue, The (1975)
Time of the Hunt, The (1972)
Time of the Vampires, The (1970)
Time of Violence (1964)
Time Out of Mind (1947)
Time Within Memory (1973)
Times Four (1970)
Times of the Constitution (1978)
Times Square Lady (1935)
Tin Drum, The (1979)
Tipchang (1974)
'Tis a Pity She's a Whore (Addio, Fratello Crudele) (1972)
Tit for Tat (1978)
Title Shot (1979)
To an Unknown God (1977)
To Be Free (1972)
To Beat the Band (1935)
To Find a Man (1972)
To Forget Venice (1979)
To Have and Have Not (1945)
To Kill in Silence (1972)
To Love (1964)
To Love Ophelia (1974)
To Search for a Golden Earth (1975)
Toast of New York, The (1937)
Together (1972)
Together? (1979)
Together Brothers, The (1974)
Together for Days (1972)
Toll of the Sea, The (1922)
Tom, Dick and Harry (1941)
Tom Sawyer, Detective (1938)
Tom Thumb (Petit Poucet, Le) (1972)
Tombstone Canyon (1932)
Tomorrow, Pheasant (1975)
Tomorrow's Children (1976)
Tonende Wells, Die (1928)
Tongues of Men, The (1916)
Tonight or Never (1931)
Tonight We Raid Calais (1943)
Too Many Husbands (1940)
Too Pretty to Be Honest (1972)
Too Skinny for Love? (1974)
Toolbox Murders, The (1978)
Top Dog (1978)
Top Flight (1964)
Top of the Heap (1972)
Top Secret--The History of German Resistance Against Hitler (1979)
Topo, El (1971)
Topper Returns (1941)
Topper Takes a Trip (1939)
Tora! Tora! Tora! (1970)
Torch High (1979)
Torment (1974)
Torndal Cousins, The (1973)
Tosca, La (1973)
Toto Diabolicus (1962)
Touch and Go (1955)
Touch of Class, A (1973)
Touchy (1976)
Tough Guy (1936)
Tourist Trap, The (1979)
Tovarich (1937)
Tower of London (1939)
Tower of the Devil (1969)
Towering Inferno, The (1974)
Towing (1978)
Town That Dreaded Sundown, The (1977)
Town Went Wild, The (1944)
Toy, The (1976)
Toys Are Not for Children (1972)
Traces (1972)
Track, The (1975)
Trackdown (1976)
Trader Horn (1973)
Traditions, My Behind (1979)
Tragedy of Big Eagle Mine, The (1913)
Tragedy of Love (1979)
Tragedy of the Desert (1912)
Trail Blazers, The (1940)
Trail of the Vigilantes (1940)
Trail to Gunsight (1944)
Train, The (1973)
Train in the Snow (1976)
Train Ride to Hollywood (1975)
Train Robbers, The (1973)

Traitement de Choc (1972)
Transatlantic Merry-Go-Round (1934)
Transgression (1931)
Transit Supervan (1969)
Trap, The (1966)
Trastevere (1972)
Trauma (1962)
Traveling Companions (1976)
Traveling Husbands (1931)
Travels with Anita (1979)
Travels with My Aunt (1972)
Tre per una Rapina (1964)
Tre Volti, I (1964)
Treasure, The (1972)
Treasure Island (1972)
Treasure of Matecumbe (1976)
Tree Without Roots, A (1974)
Trespassers, The (1976)
Trial by Combat (1976)
Trial of Billy Jack, The (1974)
Trial of the Catonsville Nine (1972)
Trial of the Judges, The (1974)
Triangle of Four (1975)
Trick Baby (1973)
Trifling Women (1922)
Trinity Is Still My Name (1972)
Trio Infernal, Le (1974)
Trip, The (1974)
Trip Through Purgatory (1974)
Tripes au Soleil, Les (1958)
Triple Cross (1967)
Triple Death of the Third Personage, The (1979)
Triple Echo, The (1973)
Triple Irons (1973)
Tripoli (1950)
Tristan et Iseult (1979)
Trocadero Lemon Blue (Trocadero Blue and Yellow) (1978)
Trompe d'Oeil (1975)
Trop c'est Trop (1975)
Trophy (1979)
Trotta (1972)
Trouble in Paradise (1932)
Trouble in Sundown (1939)
Trouble Man (1972)
Trouble Preferred (1948)
Trouble with Women, The (1947)
Trout (1978)
Truce, The (1974)
Truck Turner (1974)
True Confession (1937)
True Life of Dracula, The (1979)
True Story of Bernadette, The (1972)
True Story of Eskimo Nell, The (1975)
Trumpeter, The (1979)
Truster, The (1977)
Tu Seras Terriblement Gentille (1967)
Tugboat Annie Sails Again (1940)
Tulsa Kid, The (1940)
Tumbleweed Trail (1948)
Tunnelvision (1976)
Turkish Delight (1973)
Turn Back the Clock (1933)
Turn the Other Cheek (1975)
Turnabout (1940)
Turning Point, The (1977)
Tutti a Squola (1979)
Tutti i Colori del Buio (1972)
Tuxedo Junction (1941)
Twelve Crowded Hours (1939)
20 Mule Team (1940)
20, 000 Years in Sing Sing (1933)
23 Fireman's Street (1974)
27A (1974)
Twice a Woman (1979)
Twilight on the Prairie (1944)
Twilight on the Trail (1941)
Twilight's Last Gleaming (1977)
Twins of Evil (1972)
Two (1974)
Two Alone (1934)
$2 Haircut, The (1975)
Two-Gun Justice (1938)
Two-Gun Sheriff (1941)
Two Heartbeats (1972)
Two in the Dark (1926)
Two-Man Submarine (1944)
Two Men and a Maid (1929)
Two Men of Karamoja (1974)
Two-Minute Warning (1976)
Two of Them, The (1977)
Two People (1973)
Two Pieces of Bread (1979)
Two Seasons of Life (1972)
Two Seconds (1932)
Two Solitudes (1978)
Two Super Cops (1978)

Two Thoroughbreds (1939)
2076 Olympiad (1977)
Two Women (1975)
Typhoon (1940)

U. C. L. A. Story, The (1950)
U-Boat 29 (The Spy in Black) (1939)
U-Turn (1973)
Ugly, Dirty and Bad (1976)
Ulster (1940)
Ultimate Warrior, The (1975)
Ulzana's Raid (1972)
Uncle Joe Shannon (1978)
Uncle Tom's Cabin (1927)
Uncompromising Man, An (1979)
Under a Flag of Truce (1912)
Under Texas Skies (1940)
Under the Flag of the Rising Sun (1972)
Under Western Stars (1938)
Under Your Spell (1930)
Undercovers Hero (1975)
Undersea Kingdom, The (1936)
Underworld Story, The (1950)
Undine (1916)
Undying Monster, The (1942)
Unexpected Uncle (1941)
Unfinished Sentence in 141 Minutes, The (1975)
Unholy Garden, The (1931)
Unholy Partners (1941)
Unholy Rollers, The (1972)
Unidentified Flying Oddball, The (1979)
Union Station (1950)
United Family Awaits the Visit of Hallewyn, The (1972)
Unknown Ranger, The (1935)
Unknown Soldier's Patent Leather Shoes, The (1979)
Unmarried Woman, An (1978)
Unto a Good Land (1972)
Untypical Story, An (1978)
Up (1976)
Up from the Depths (1979)
Up 'n' at 'em, Amalie (1973)
Up the Sandbox (1972)
Up to His Ears (1965)
Up Wind (1979)
Upkeep (1973)
Uptown Saturday Night (1974)
Urbanissimo (1967)
Us Two (1979)
Utah (1945)
Utamaro's World (1946)
Utopia (1978)

VD (1973)
Valachi Papers, The (1972)
Valdez the Halfbreed (1973)
Valentino (1977)
Valerie and Her Week of Wonders (1970)
Valiant Is the Word for Carrie (1936)
Valise, The (1973)
Valley, The (1972)
Valley of Gwangi, The (1969)
Vampire (Upior) (1968)
Vampire and Sex, The (1968)
Vampire-Beast Craves Blood, The (1967)
Vampire Circus (1971)
Vampire for Two (1966)
Vampire Girls, The (1968)
Vampire Happening, The (1971)
Vampire Women, The (1967)
Vampire's Ghost, The (1945)
Vampiri, I (1956)
Vampiro, El (1957)
Vampyr (1932)
Vampyros Lesbos (Heritage of Dracula) (1970)
Van Nuys Blvd. (1979)
Vanda Teres (1975)
Vanessa, Her Love Story (1935)
Vanishing Frontier, The (1932)
Vanishing Virginian, The (1942)
Vauxhall, Bedford, England (1965)
Vengeance (1968)
Venial Sin (1974)
Venus Planet (1972)
Vera (1973)
Vera Romeyke Is Not Acceptable (1976)
Vera's Training (1979)
Verdict (1974)
Verdict, The (1977)
Verdun (1928)
Veridiquement Votre (1968)
Very Happy Alexander (1970)

Very Natural Thing, A (1974)
Vessel of Wrath (see The Beachcomber)
Veuve Couderc, La (see Widow Couderc)
Vicar of Vejlby, The (1972)
Vice Squad (1978)
Vicious Breed, The (1957)
Victim of Passion (1975)
Victor Frankenstein (1977)
Victoria the Great (1937)
Victory at Sea (1952)
Victory March (1976)
Vie de Jesus (Life of Jesus) (1914)
Vietnam (1972)
Vigil in the Night (1939)
Vigilante Force (1975)
Vigilantes of Dodge City (1944)
Villa Zone (1975)
Village Barn Dance (1940)
Village Head at the Border, The (1977)
Village of the Eight Tombs (1977)
Village Performance of Hamlet, A (1973)
Village Tale (1935)
Villain, The (1979)
Villain Still Pursued Her, The (1940)
Vincent, Francois, Paul ... and the Others (1974)
Vincent Puts the Ass in a Field (1975)
Violanta (1977)
Violated Love (1977)
Violation of Claudia, The (1977)
Violent Life, A (1962)
Violent Saturday (1955)
Violets Are Blue (1975)
Violette and Francois (1977)
Virgin Named Mary, A (1975)
Virgin of Stamboul, The (1920)
Virgin Witch, The (1978)
Virginian, The (1968)
Virility (1976)
Visions of Eight (1973)
Visit, The (1964)
Visit to a Chief's Son (1974)
Visitor, The (1973)
Vita Agra, La (1964)
Vitrine Sous la Mer (1960)
Viva Italia (1978)
Viva Knievel! (1977)
Viva la France (1974)
Viva Zapata! (1952)
Vivre la Nuit (1967)
Vixen (1968)
Vogues of 1938 (1937)
Voice of the Turtle, The (1948)
Voices (1979)
Voici le Ski (1961)
Voodo (1933)
Vormittagspuk (1928)
Vote for Gundisalvo (1978)
Voyage de Noces, Le (1975)
Voyage into the Whirlpool Has Begun, The (1977)
Voyage of Khonostrov, The (1962)
Voyage of the Damned (1976)
Voyage to Next (1974)
Voyage to the Center of the Earth (1977)
Voyage Vers la Lumiere (1969)
Voyage with Jacob (1973)
Vultures, The (1978)

W (1974)
W. C. Fields and Me (1976)
W. W. and the Dixie Dancekings (1975)
Wackey World of Numberrs, The (1970)
Wagon Train (1940)
Wagons Roll at Night, The (1941)
Wagons Westward (1940)
Wait a Minute! (1974)
Wake Up and Die (1966)
Walk Fory, The (1975)
Walk on Clear Water if You Can (1979)
Walk Proud (1979)
Walk the Proud Land (1956)
Walking Tall (1973)
Walking Tall (Part 2) (1975)
Walking Upright (1976)
Wall, The (1978)
Wall Street Cowboy (1939)
Walls of Jericho, The (1948)
Walpurgis Night (1970)
Waltzers, The (1974)
Wanda Nevada (1979)

Wanderers, The (1973)
Wandering (1979)
Wandering Jew, The (1935)
War Between Men and Women, The (1972)
War Between the Tates, The (1977)
War Is War (1972)
War Lord, The (1965)
Warlords of Atlantis (1978)
Warm December, A (1973)
Warmth of Your Hands, The (1972)
Warrior Within, The (1977)
Warriors, The (1979)
Warriors 5 (1961)
Wash Out My Faults (1976)
Washington Masquerade (1932)
Washington Melodrama (1941)
Wasp Woman, The (1959)
Watchmaker of Saint-Paul, The (1974)
Water Birds (1952)
Water It and Dew for the Thir sty Soil (1975)
Watership Down (1978)
Watts Monster, The (1979)
Way Down East (1920)
Way Down South (1939)
Way of the Wind, The (1976)
Way Out (1973)
Way to the Gold, The (1957)
Way We Were, The (1973)
We Are Arab Jews in Israel (1977)
We Are the Lambeth Boys (1959)
We Are Young (1967)
We Sail at Midnight (1943)
We Still Kill the Old Way (1968)
We Want the Colonels (1973)
We Will All Go to Heaven (1977)
Weak Spot, The (1975)
Wedding (1974)
Wedding, The (1973)
Wedding in White (1972)
Wedding Night, The (1935)
Wedding of Zein, The (1978)
Wedding Trough (1975)
Wedding Without Rings (1972)
Wednesday Children, The (1973)
Wednesday's Child (1934)
Wee Willie Winkie (1937)
Weekend for Three (1941)
Weekend Marriage (1932)
Weekend Murders, The (1972)
Weekend of Shadows (1978)
Weird Woman (1944)
Welcome (1978)
Welcome Home, Soldier Boys (1972)
Welcome to Blood City (1977)
Welcome to L. A. (1976)
We'll Call Him Andreas (1972)
We'll Grow Thin Together (1979)
Weltkrieg, Der (1927)
We're Going to Be Rich (1938)
We're Not Married (1952)
We're Only Human (1935)
We're Rich Again (1934)
Werewolf of Washington (1973)
West (1963)
West of Cimarron (1941)
West of the Brazos (1950)
West of the Pecos (1934)
West Point of the Air (1935)
West Point Widow (1941)
Western Daze (1941)
Westerner, The (1940)
Westward Passage (1932)
Westworld (1973)
Wet Parade, The (1932)
Wetbacks (1955)
We've Never Been Licked (1943)
What a Flash (1972)
What a Woman (1943)
What Do You Want, Julie? (1977)
What Is to Be Done? (1972)
What Max Said (1978)
What Price Glory? (1926)
What Price Hollywood? (1932)
Whatever Happened to Uncle Fred? (1967)
What's Autumn? (1977)
What's Next? (1975)
What's Up, Doc? (1972)
When a Stranger Calls (1979)
When Roobard Made a Spike (1973)
When Svante Disappeared (1975)
When the Heavens Fell (1972)
When the Legends Die (1972)
When the Mad Aunts Are Coming (1970)
When the Poppies Bloom Again (1976)

When the Sun Rises (1978)
When There Wasn't Treasure (1974)
When Willie Comes Marching Home (1950)
When You Comin' Back, Red Ryder? (1979)
Where Are You Going? (1976)
Where Are You Going on Your Vacation? (1979)
Where Did You Get That Girl? (1941)
Where Does It Hurt? (1972)
Where Eagles Dare (1968)
Where the Bullets Fly (1966)
Where the Lilies Bloom (1974)
Where the Pavement Ends (1923)
Where the Red Fern Grows (1974)
Where the Sidewalk Ends (1950)
Wherever You Are, Mr. President (1979)
Which Way Is Up? (1977)
Whiffs (1975)
While There's War There's Hope (1975)
Whispering Death (1976)
Whispering Ghosts (1942)
Whispering Shadow, The (1933)
Whispering Smith (1949)
Whispering Winds (1929)
White Buffalo, The (1977)
White Collar Blues (1975)
White Dawn, The (1974)
White Fang (1936)
White Feather (1955)
White Gloves of the Devil (1973)
White Grass (1976)
White Hunter (1936)
White Legion (1936)
White Lightning (1973)
White Line Fever (1975)
White Parade, The (1934)
White Pongo (1945)
White Rat, The (1972)
White Rock (1976)
White Rose, The (1923)
White Rose, The (1972)
White Shop, The (1976)
White Sister (1973)
White, Yellow, Black (1975)
White Zombie (1932)
Whity (1971)
Whizzer (1979)
Who Are the DeBolts? (and Where Did They Get 19 Kids?) (1977)
Who Can Kill a Child? (1976)
Who Done It? (1942)
Who Fears the Devil? (1972)
Who Has Seen the Wind? (1977)
Who Is Hope Schuyler? (1942)
Who Is Killing the Great Chefs of Europe? (1978)
Who Killed Aunt Maggie? (1940)
Who Leaves in the Rain (1976)
Who Saw Her Die? (1972)
Who'll Stop the Rain? (1978)
Who's Crazy? (1965)
Who's Guilty? (1945)
Why Does One Kill a Magistrate? (1975)
Why Girls Leave Home (1945)
Why Not? (1977)
Why Rock the Boat? (1974)
Why Shoot the Teacher? (1977)
Wicked, Wicked (1973)
Wicked Woman, A (1934)
Wicket Gate, The (1974)
Wide Open Faces (1938)
Wide Open Town (1941)
Widow Couderc, The (1971)
Widower, The (1978)
Widow's Nest (1977)
Wife vs. Secretary (1936)
Wilby Conspiracy, The (1975)
Wild Country (1947)
Wild for Kicks (1959)
Wild Geese, The (1978)
Wild Geese Calling (1941)
Wild Hare Census, The (see Hare Census, The)
Wild Horse Hank (1979)
Wild Horse Rodeo (1937)
Wild Living (1962)
Wild Pack, The (1972)
Wild Party, The (1975)
Wild Rose, The (1923)
Wild Weed (1949)
Willa (1979)
Willi and the Comrades (1979)
Willi Busch Report, The (1979)
Willi Manages the Whole Thing (1972)
Williamsburg: The Story of a

Patriot (1957)
Willie and the Chinese Cat (1977)
Willie Dynamite (1973)
Willie the Kid (1952)
Winchell Affair, The (1979)
Wind, The (1974)
Wind and the Lion, The (1975)
Wind and the Oak, The (1979)
Wind Blows Under Your Feet, The (1976)
Wind, Cloud and Rainbow (1976)
Winged Idol, The (1915)
Wings (1927)
Wings (1978)
Wings over Honolulu (1937)
Winner Take All (1932)
Winning of Freedom (1979)
Winning Ticket, The (1935)
Winter Kills (1979)
Winterborn (1978)
Winterhawk (1976)
Winterspelt (1978)
Wise Guys, The (1977)
Wise Monkey, The (1978)
Witchcraft Through the Ages (Haxan) (1921)
With Clean Hands (1978)
With Lots of Love (1979)
With Love and Tenderness (1978)
With Nobody (1975)
With Shared Love (1979)
With the Blood of Others (1974)
With You and Without You (1974)
Within the Law (1939)
Without Anaesthetic (1979)
Without Family (1972)
Witness, The (1978)
Witness Chair, The (1936)
Witness in the City (1959)
Wizards (1977)
Wolf and the Dove, The (1974)
Wolf Man, The (1941)
Wolf of New York (1940)
Wolfpen Principle, The (1974)
Wolves, The (1972)
Woman, A (1975)
Woman Across the Way (1978)
Woman Between Dog and Wolf, A (1979)
Woman Doctor (1939)
Woman from Headquarters (1950)
Woman from the Torrid Land (1978)
Woman in Green, The (1945)
Woman in the Window (1944)
Woman Is a Marvelous Thing, A (1964)
Woman, Man, City (1978)
Woman Needs Loving, A (1968)
Woman of Everyone, The (1969)
Woman Under the Influence, A (1974)
Woman Wanted (1935)
Woman, You Should Not Have Been Created (1975)
Women Are Trouble (1936)
Women Buried Alive (1973)
Women Duelling (1976)
Women in Cell Block 7 (1974)
Women in the Sun (1974)
Women of Doom (1972)
Women Without Names (1940)
Women, Women (1974)
Won Ton Ton, the Dog Who Saved Hollywood (1976)
Wonder Man (1945)
Wonder of It All, The (1973)
Wonderful Life, A (1951)
Wood Nymph, The (1916)
Word Is Out (1978)
Working Class Goes to Heaven, The (1972)
Works of Calder (1950)
World at Three, The (1965)
World Is Full of Married Men, The (1979)
World Moves On, The (1934)
World of Love, A (1975)
World of the Vampire (1961)
World's Greatest Athlete, The (1973)
World's Greatest Lover, The (1977)
Wrath of God, The (1972)
Wrestling Women vs. the Aztec Mummy, The (1965)
Written-Off Return, The (1977)
Wrong Arm of the Law, The (1962)
Wrong Door, The (1915)
Wrong Movement (1975)
Wrong Number (1979)
Wrong Road, The (1937)

Wyoming (1940)
Wyoming (1947)
Wyoming Outlaw (1939)
Wyoming Wildcat (1941)

X, Y and Zee (1972)
Xica de Silva (1976)

Yakuza, The (1975)
Yank in London, A (1946)
Yank in the R. A. F., A (1941)
Yankee Girl, The (1915)
Yankee Pasha (1954)
Yanks (1979)
Yanks Ahoy (1943)
Yaqui, The (1916)
Year of School, A (1977)
Year of the Caribou (1974)
Year of the Hare, The (1979)
Year One (1974)
Yellow Dust (1936)
Yellow Handkerchief of Happiness (1978)
Yellow Sky (1948)
Yes, But... (1972)
Yes, Sir, That's My Baby (1949)
Yesterday's Hero (1979)
Yesterday's Tomorrow (1978)
Yeti, Il Gigante del 20o Secolo (1977)
You and Me (1938)
You and Me (1972)
You Are Not Alone (1978)
You Are Weighed but Found Lacking (1974)
You Can't Buy Everything (1934)
You Can't Fool Your Wife (1940)
You Can't Get Away with Murder (1939)
You Light Up My Life (1977)
You Only Love Once (1969)
You'll Like My Mother (1972)
Young and the Restless, The (1973)
Young Animals, The (1968)
Young Bill Hickok (1940)
Young Frankenstein (1974)
Young Fugitives (1938)
Young Joe, the Forgotten Kennedy (1977)
Young Ladies of Wilko, The (1979)
Young Man and Moby Dick, The (1979)
Young Rebel--Cervantes, The (1967)
Young Sinner, The (1962)
Young Winston (1972)
Your Child, the Unknown Creature (1970)
Your Husband Is My Lover (1975)
Your Husband, the Unknown Creature (1970)
Your Son and Brother (1976)
Your Three Minutes Are Up (1973)
You're in the Army Now (1941)
You're Not So Tough (1940)
You're Out of Your Mind, Maggie (1979)
Youth Killer, The (1977)
Youth on Parole (1937)
Yukinojo's Revenge (1978)
Yuppi Du (1975)

Zapped by a Strange Destiny in a Blue August Sea (see Swept Away)
Zardoz (1974)
Zeami (1974)
Zero Hour (1977)
Zero Hour, The (1939)
Zeta One (1969)
Zigzag (1973)
Zig-Zig (1975)
Zita (1968)
Zones (1979)
Zorro (1975)
Zorro Rides Again (1937)
Zorro's Fighting Legion (1939)
Zulu Dawn (1979)

FILMS AND THEIR COMPOSERS/ADAPTORS

Key to Abbreviations

AA Allied Artists
ABC American Broadcasting Corp.
AFR Africa
AI or AIP American International
ALB Albania
ALL Allied
AMB Ambassador
ARG Argentina
AST Astor
AUS Austria
AUT Australia
BAN Bangladesh
BAR Barr
BEL Belgium
BIO Biograph
BLU Bluebird
BRA Brazil
BRI Great Britain
BUL Bulgaria
CAN Canada
CBC Canadian Broadcasting Corp.
CBS Columbia Broadcasting System
CC Cinema Center
CEY Ceylon (Sri Lanka)
CHE Chesterfield
CHL Chile
CHN China
CIN Cinerama
CIV Cinema 5
COL Columbia
CRO Crown International
CUB Cuba
CZE Czechoslovakia
DCA Distributors Corp. of America
DEN Denmark
DIS Disney (Buena Vista)
EGY Egypt
EL Eagle-Lion
EMB Avco Embassy
EPC Epoch
EST Estonia
FAM Famous Players/Lasky
FIL Filmmakers
FIN Finland
FN First National
FOR Formosa
FOX or TCF Twentieth Century-Fox
FRA France
GAM Gamma
GER Germany
GHA Ghana
GN Grand National
GOL Goldwyn
GRA Graphic
GRE Greece
GRI D. W. Griffith
HK Hong Kong
HOL Holland/Netherlands
HOW Howco
HUN Hungary
IN India
INC Ince
IND independent release

INO Indochina
INV Invincible
IRAN Iran
IRE Ireland
ISR Israel
ITA Italy
JAM Jamaica
JAP Japan
KAL Kalem
KLE Kleine/Edward F. Klein
KOR Korea
LAS Lasky
LEB Lebanon
LIB Liberty
LIBYA Libya
LIP Lippert
MAJ Majestic
MAL Malaysia
MAS Mascot
MAY Mayfair
MET Metro
MEX Mexico
MGM Metro-Goldwyn-Mayer
MON Monogram
MOR Morocco
NBC National Broadcasting Co.
NET National Educational TV
NGP National General
NIG Nigeria
NOR Norway
NWP New World
NZ New Zealand
OLI Oliver Morosco
PAR Paramount
PHI Philippine Islands
PIC Pictorial Clubs/Ohio Film
POL Poland
POR Portugal
PRC Producers Releasing Corp.
PRI Principal
PUR Puritan
RAN Rankin/Bass
REP Republic
RKO Radio Pictures/RKO Radio Pictures
RUM or ROU Rumania
RUS Russia
SA South America
SEN Senegal
SIG Sigma 3
SPA Spain
SWE Sweden
SWI Switzerland
TAH Tahiti
TAI Thailand/Taipei
TCF Fox/Twentieth Century-Fox (see also FOX)
TIF Tiffany
TIM Time/Life
TRI Triangle
TUR Turkey
TV television production
UA United Artists
UMC Universal Marion
UN Universal
URU Uruguay
VIT Vitagraph
WB Warner Brothers
WNP World Northal
WOL Wolper
YUG Yugoslavia

1908

Empreinte, L'	FRA	Fernand LeBorne

1909

Retour d'Ulysse, Le	FRA	Georges Hue

1911

Arrah-na-Pough (short)	KAL	Walter Cleveland Simon

1912

Arabian Tragedy, An	KAL	Walter Cleveland Simon
Bugler of Battery B., The	KAL	Walter Cleveland Simon
Captured by Bedouins	KAL	Walter Cleveland Simon

Confederate Ironclad, The	KAL	Walter Cleveland Simon
Drummer Girl of Vicksburg, The	KAL	Walter Cleveland Simon
Egyptian Sports (short)	KAL	Walter Cleveland Simon
Fighting Dan McCool	KAL	N. Komroff
Fighting Dervishes of the Desert, The	KAL	Walter Cleveland Simon
Hungry Hank's Hallucination (short)	KAL	Walter Cleveland Simon
Odyssey, The	MOL	Edgar Selden
Prisoner of the Harem	KAL	Walter Cleveland Simon
Queen Elizabeth	FAM	Joseph Carl Breil
Siege of Petersburg, The (short)	KAL	Walter Cleveland Simon
Soldier Brothers of Susanna, The	KAL	Walter Cleveland Simon
Spanish Revolt of 1836, Thc	KAL	Walter Cleveland Simon
Spartan Mother, A	KAL	Walter Cleveland Simon
Tragedy of the Desert	KAL	Walter Cleveland Simon
Under a Flag of Truce	KAL	Walter Cleveland Simon

1913

Cabiria	ITA	Joseph Carl Breil
Comtesse Ursel	GER	Giuseppe Becce
Drake's Love Story	BRI	Victor Montefiore
Last Days of Pompeii, The	KLE	Palmer Clark
Prisoner of Zenda, The	FAM	Joseph Carl Breil
Richard Wagner	GER	Giuseppe Becce
Schuldig	GER	Giuseppe Becce
Student von Prag, Der	GER	Joseph Weiss
Tragedy of Big Eagle Mine, The (short)	KAL	Walter Cleveland Simon

1914

Ach wie ist's Moglich Dann	GER	Bruno Mueller
America	ALL	Manuel Klein
Antony and Cleopatra	KLE	George Colburn
Bismarck	GER	Ferdinand Hummel
Dan	ALL	Manuel Klein
Germania	ITA	Alberto Franchetti/R. Tenaglia
In Mizzoura	ALL	Manuel Klein
Jungle, The	ALL	Manuel Klein
Paid in Full	ALL	Manuel Klein
Patchwork Girl of Oz, The	IND	Louis F. Gottschalk
Pierre of the Plains	ALL	Manuel Klein
Samson	FOX	Noble Kreider
Soldiers of Fortune	ALL	Manuel Klein
Vie de Jesus (Life of Jesus)	FRA	Charles Quef

1915

Aloha Oe	TRI	Wedgewood Nowell
Battle Cry of Peace, The	VIT	S. L. "Roxy" Rothapfel

Between Men	TRI	Joseph E. Nurnberger/ Victor Schertzinger/ Wedgewood Nowell
Birth of a Nation, The	EPC	Joseph Carl Breil
Corner, The	TRI	George W. Beynon
Cross Currents	TRI	J. A. Raynes
D'Artagnan	TRI	Victor Schertzinger/ Wedgewood Nowell
Daughter of the Gods, A	FOX	Robert Hood Bowers
Double Trouble	TRI	Joseph Carl Breil
Gentleman from Indiana, The	PAL	George W. Beynon
Golden Claw, The	TRI	Wedgewood Nowell/ Joseph E. Nurnberger/ Victor Schertzinger
Jane	PAL	George W. Beynon
Jordan Is a Hard Road	TRI	J. A. Raynes
Let Katie Do It	TRI	William Furst
Lily and the Rose, The	TRI	Joseph Carl Breil/J. A. Raynes
Martyrs of the Alamo, The	TRI	Joseph Carl Breil
Matrimony	TRI	Wedgewood Nowell/ Joseph Nurnberger
Peer Gynt	OLI	George W. Beynon
Penitentes, Los	TRI	Joseph Carl Breil
Reform Candidate, The	PAL	George W. Beynon
Sable Lorcha, The	TRI	J. A. Raynes
Winged Idol, The	TRI	Wedgewood Nowell/ Joseph E. Nurnberger/ Victor Schertzinger
Wrong Door, The	BLU	Max Winkler
Yankee Girl, The	OLI	George W. Beynon

1916

Black Crook, The	KAL	Walter Cleveland Simon
Conquerer, The	TRI	Victor Schertzinger/ Wedgewood Nowell
Crippled Hand, The	BLU	F. Rehsen/Max Winkler
Despoilers, The	TRI	Louis F. Gottschalk
Edge of the Abyss, The	TRI	Victor Schertzinger/ Joseph E. Nurnberger
Flirt, The	BLU	Max Winkler
Flying Torpedo, The	TRI	J. A. Raynes
Gay Lord Waring, The	BLU	R. Rehsen/Max Winkler
Gloria's Romance (serial)	KLE	Jerome Kern
Great Problem, The	BLU	R. Rehsen/Max Winkler
Green Swamp, The	TRI	William Furst/C. Herbert Kerr
Grip of Jealousy, The	BLU	Max Winkler
Honor's Altar	TRI	Louis F. Gottschalk
Hop, the Devil's Brew	BLU	Max Winkler
Intolerance	GRI	Joseph Carl Breil
Jeanne Dore	BLU	Max Winkler

John Needham's Double	BLU	R. Rehsen/Max Winkler
Price of Power, The	TRI	J. A. Raynes
Rupert of Hentzau	BLU	Max Winkler
Secret Love	BLU	Max Winkler
Strength of the Weak, The	BLU	Max Winkler
Tangled Hearts	BLU	F. Rehsen/Max Winkler
Tongues of Men, The	OLI	George W. Beynon
Undine	BLU	Max Winkler
Wood Nymph, The	TRI	Joseph Carl Breil
Yaqui, The	BLU	Max Winkler

1917

Joan the Woman	PAR	William Furst
Princess of the Dark, The	INC	Victor Schertzinger

1918

Great Love, The	GRI	Carli Elinor/Louis F. Gottschalk
Hearts of the World	GRI	Carli Elinor

1919

Echo of Youth, The	GRA	Walter Cleveland Simon
Greatest Question, The	GRI	Albert Pesce
Right to Happiness, The	UN	Sol P. Levy/Max Winkler
Romance of Happy Valley, A	GRI	Harley Hamilton

1920

In Old Kentucky	FN	George W. Beynon
Love Flower, The	GRI	Albert Pesce
Virgin of Stamboul, The	UN	Max Winkler
Way Down East	GRI	Louis Silvers/William F. Peters

1921

Mary Regan	FN	George W. Beynon
Old Nest, The	GOL	Firmin Swinnen
Three Musketeers, The	UA	Louis F. Gottschalk
Witchcraft Through the Ages (Haxan) (rereleased version of 1968)	SWE	Daniel Humair

1922

Fabiola	IND	Alexander Henneman
Fridericus Rex	GER	Marc Roland
Hearts Aflame	MAY	Ernst Luz
Jenseits des Stroms	GER	Ferdinand Hummel

One Exciting Night	GRI	Albert Pesce
Peg O' My Heart	MET	Ernst Luz
Prisoner of Zenda, The	MGM	Louis Breau/Ernst Luz
Quincy Adams Sawyer	MET	Ernst Luz
Robin Hood	UA	Victor Schertzinger
Toll of the Sea, The	MET	Ernst Luz
Trifling Women	MET	Ernst Luz

1923

Where the Pavement Ends	MET	Ernst Luz
White Rose, The	GRI	Joseph Carl Breil

1924

America	UA	Joseph Carl Breil/ Adolph Fink
Briere, La	FRA	Paul Ladmirault
Carlos und Elisabeth	GER	Willy Schmidt-Gentner
Iron Horse, The	FOX	Erno Rapee

1925

Baree, Son of Kazan	VIT	Michael Hoffman
Chronik von Grieshuus	GER	Gottfried Huppertz
Gold Rush, The	UA	Charles Chaplin/Carli Elinor/R. H. Bassett
Grass	PAR	Hugo Riesenfeld/Edward Kilenyi
Man Nobody Knows, The	PIC	Alexander Savine
Martin Luther	IND	Edward Rechlin/H. Spielter
Salammbo	FRA	Florent Schmitt

1926

As We Forgive	PAT	Alexander Savine
Barrier, The	MGM	Sol P. Levy/Frederick O. Hanks
Manon	VIT	Henry Hadley
Old Ironsides	PAR	Hugo Riesenfeld/J. S. Zamecnik
Ronde de Nuit, La	FRA	Charles Silver
Temptress, The	MGM	Ernst Luz
What Price Glory?	TCF	Carli Elinor/R. H. Bassett

1927

Chang	PAR	Hugo Riesenfeld
Joueur d'Echecs, Le	FRA	Henri Rabaud
Seventh Heaven	TCF	Carli Elinor/R. H. Bassett

Uncle Tom's Cabin	UN	Hugo Riesenfeld
Weltkrieg, Der	GER	Marc Roland
Wings	PAR	J. S. Zamecnik

1928

Abie's Irish Rose	PAR	J. S. Zamecnik/Edward Kilenyi/C. Rybner
Arsenal	RUS	Ivan Belza
Circus, The	UA	Charles Chaplin
Lebende Leichnam, Der	GER	Werner Schmidt-Boelcke
Lilac Time	FN	Nathaniel Shilkret
Passion de Jeanne d'Arc, La	FRA	Victor Allix/Leo Pouget
Ramona	UA	Hugo Riesenfeld
Sheherazade	GER	Victor Allix/Leo Pouget
Tonende Welle, Die	GER	Edmund Meisel
Verdun	FRA	Andre Petiot
Vormittagspuk (short)	GER	Paul Hindemith

1929

Betrayal	PAR	J. S. Zamecnik/Louis de Francesco
Fenne et le Pantin, La	FRA	Ed. Lavagne/Ph. Pares/ Georges van Parys
Flying Feet	MGM	Percy Grainger
Iron Mask, The	UA	Hugo Riesenfeld
King of the Congo (serial)	MAS	Lee Zahler
Kiss, The	MGM	William Axt
Looping the Loop	PAR	Hugo Riesenfeld
Lucky Boy	TIF	Hugo Riesenfeld
Midstream	TIF	Hugo Riesenfeld
Molly and Me	TIF	Hugo Riesenfeld
My Lady's Past	TIF	Hugo Riesenfeld
New Orleans	TIF	Hugo Riesenfeld
Our Modern Maidens	MGM	William Axt
Redskin	PAR	Louis de Francesco/ J. S. Zamecnik
Rhapsodie Hongroise	GER	Marcel Delannoy/ Jacques Brillouin
River, The	FOX	Maurice Baron/Erno Rapee
Single Standard, The	MGM	William Axt
Speedway	MGM	William Axt
Three Live Ghosts	UA	Hugo Riesenfeld
Thunder	MGM	William Axt
Two Men and a Maid	TIF	Hugo Riesenfeld
Whispering Winds	TIF	Erno Rapee

1930

Bad One, The	UA	Hugo Riesenfeld
Be Yourself	UA	Hugo Riesenfeld

Cain	FRA	Andre Petiot
Call of the Flesh	MGM	Herbert Stothart
Captain of the Guard	UN	Charles Wakefield Cadman
Devil May Care	MGM	Herbert Stothart
Devil to Pay, The	UA	Alfred Newman
Floradora Girl, The	MGM	Herbert Stothart
Half Shot at Sunrise	RKO	Max Steiner
Honey	PAR	W. Franke Harling
In Gay Madrid	MGM	Herbert Stothart
Lady's Morals, A	MGM	Herbert Stothart
Lottery Bride, The	UA	Hugo Riesenfeld
Madam Satan	MGM	Herbert Stothart
Mamba	TIF	James C. Bradford
Montana Moon	MGM	Herbert Stothart
Monte Carlo	PAR	W. Franke Harling
Pure and Simple (short)	RKO	Lee Zahler
Rogue Song	MGM	Herbert Stothart
Under Paris Skies	FRA	H. Giraud

1931

Age for Love	UA	Alfred Newman
Are These Our Children?	RKO	Max Steiner
Around the World in 80 Minutes	UA	Alfred Newman
Beau Ideal	RKO	Max Steiner
Chinatown After Dark	IND	Lee Zahler
Consolation Marriage	RKO	Max Steiner
Corsair	UA	Alfred Newman
Cuban Love Song, The	MGM	Charles Maxwell/Herbert Stothart
Drums of Jeopardy	TIF	Val Burton
Frankenstein	UN	David Broekman/Bernhard Kaun
Gay Diplomat, The	RKO	Max Steiner
Hamlet	RUS	Dmitri Shostakovich
Indiscreet	UA	Alfred Newman
Kept Husbands	RKO	Max Steiner
King of the Wild (serial)	MAS	Lee Zahler
Murder at Midnight	TIF	Val Burton
New Moon	MGM	Herbert Stothart
Phantom of the West (serial)	MAS	Lee Zahler
Private Scandal, A	IND	Lee Zahler
Prodigal, The	MGM	Herbert Stothart
Rango	PAR	W. Franke Harling
Resurrection	UN	Dmitri Tiomkin
Tabu	PAR	Hugo Riesenfeld
Tonight or Never	UA	Alfred Newman
Transgression	RKO	Max Steiner
Traveling Husbands	RKO	Max Steiner
Unholy Garden	UA	Alfred Newman

1932

Animal Kingdom, The	RKO	Max Steiner
Bird of Paradise	RKO	Max Steiner
Broken Lullaby	PAR	W. Franke Harling
Chandu the Magician	TCF	Louis de Francesco
Cock of the Air	UA	Alfred Newman
Conquerers, The	RKO	Max Steiner
Death Kiss, The	WW	Val Burton
Expert, The	WB	W. Franke Harling
Farewell to Arms, A	PAR	Bernhard Kaun
Fireman, Save My Child	WB	W. Frank Harling
Greeks Had a Word for Them, The	UA	Alfred Newman
Half-Naked Truth, The	RKO	Max Steiner
Hurricane Express, The (serial)	MAS	Lee Zahler
Hypnotized	WW	Edward Ward
I Am a Fugitive from a Chain Gang	WB	Bernhard Kaun
Is My Face Red?	RKO	Max Steiner
Little Orphan Annie	RKO	Max Steiner
Lost Squadron, The	RKO	Max Steiner
Madame Butterfly	PAR	W. Franke Harling
Men Are Such Fools	RKO	W. Franke Harling
Midnight Warning	MAY	Lee Zahler
Miracle Man, The	PAR	W. Franke Harling
Monster Walks, The	IND	Lee Zahler
Most Dangerous Game, The	RKO	Max Steiner
One Hour with You	PAR	W. Franke Harling
One-Way Passage	WB	W. Franke Harling
Play Girl	WB	W. Franke Harling
Polly of the Circus	MGM	William Axt
Rain	UA	Alfred Newman
Rich Are Always with Us, The	WB	W. Franke Harling
Roar of the Dragon	RKO	Max Steiner
Rockabye	RKO	Max Steiner
Sea Spiders (short)	MGM	William Axt
Shadow of the Eagle (serial)	MAS	Lee Zahler
Silver Dollar	WB	Milan Roder
Silver Lining	UA	Lee Zahler
Sky Devils	UA	Alfred Newman
Smilin' Through	MGM	William Axt
Son-Daughter, The	MGM	Herbert Stothart
Sport Parade, The	RKO	Max Steiner
Strangers of the Evening	TIF	Val Burton
Street of Women	WB	W. Franke Harling
Symphony of Six Million	RKO	Max Steiner
Tangled Destinies	MAY	Lee Zahler
Thirteen Women	RKO	Max Steiner
This Is the Night	PAR	W. Franke Harling
Tombstone Canyon	WW	Val Burton
Trouble in Paradise	PAR	W. Franke Harling
Two Seconds	WB	W. Franke Harling
Vampyr (Strange Adventures of David Grey, The)	FRA	Wolfgang Zeller

Vanishing Frontier, The	PAR	Lee Zahler
Washington Masquerade	MGM	William Axt
Week-End Marriage	WB	W. Franke Harling
Westward Passage	RKO	Max Steiner
Wet Parade, The	MGM	William Axt
What Price Hollywood?	RKO	Max Steiner
White Zombie	IND	Xavier Cugat/Hugo Riesenfeld/Guy Bevier Williams *et al.*
Winner Take All	WB	W. Franke Harling

1933

Ace of Aces	RKO	Max Steiner
Adorable	TCF	Werner Heymann
After Tonight	RKO	Max Steiner
Aggie Appleby, Maker of Men	RKO	Max Steiner
As Husbands Go	TCF	Louis de Francesco
Avenger, The	MON	Abe Meyer
Barbarian, The	MGM	Herbert Stothart
Before Dawn	RKO	Max Steiner
Bitter Tea of General Yen, The	COL	W. Franke Harling
Blood Money	TCF	Alfred Newman
Bowery, The	TCF	Alfred Newman
Broadway to Hollywood	MGM	William Axt
Chance at Heaven, A	RKO	Max Steiner
Cheyenne Kid, The	RKO	Max Steiner
Christopher Strong	RKO	Max Steiner
Deluge, The	IND	Val Burton
Diplomaniacs	RKO	Max Steiner
Double Harness	RKO	Max Steiner
Eight Girls in a Boat	PAR	Howard Jackson
Emperor Jones, The	IND	Rosamond Johnson/Frank Tours
Flaming Signal, The	IND	Abe Meyer
Flying Devils	RKO	Max Steiner
Gabriel over the White House	MGM	William Axt
Golden Harvest	PAR	Heinz Roemheld
Great Jaspar, The	RKO	Max Steiner
Headline Shooter	RKO	Max Steiner
Hoopla	TCF	Louis de Francesco
Horror, The	IND	William David
I Cover the Waterfront	UA	Alfred Newman
I Loved You Wednesday	TCF	Louis de Francesco
Kiss Before the Mirror, A	UN	W. Franke Harling
Laughing at Life	MAS	Lee Zahler
Lucky Devils	RKO	Max Steiner
Man's Castle, A	COL	W. Franke Harling
Masquerader, The	UA	Alfred Newman
Midnight Mary	MGM	William Axt
Midshipman Jack	RKO	Max Steiner
Mr. Skitch	TCF	Louis de Francesco
Monkey's Paw, The	RKO	Max Steiner

No Marriage Ties	RKO	Max Steiner
No Other Woman	RKO	Max Steiner
Penthouse	MGM	William Axt
Pleasure Cruise	TCF	Louis de Francesco
Power and the Glory, The	TCF	Louis de Francesco
Rafter Romance	RKO	Max Steiner
Reunion in Vienna	MGM	William Axt
Right to Romance, The	RKO	Max Steiner
Samarang	UA	Sam K. Wineland
Savage Gold	IND	James C. Bradford
Secret of Madame Blanche, The	MGM	William Axt
Secrets	UA	Alfred Newman
Shriek in the Night, A	ALL	Abe Meyer
Sphinx, The	MON	Abe Meyer
State Fair	TCF	Louis de Francesco
Storm at Daybreak	MGM	William Axt
Strange People	CHE	Abe Meyer
Tarzan the Fearless (serial)	PRI	Sam K. Wineland
Three Musketeers, The (serial)	MAS	Lee Zahler
Turn Back the Clock	MGM	Herbert Stothart
20, 000 Years in Sing Sing	WB	Bernhard Kaun
Voodo	IND	Brown and Spencer
Whispering Shadow, The (serial)	MAS	Abe Meyer

1934

Age of Innocence, The	RKO	Max Steiner
All Men Are Enemies	TCF	Louis de Francesco
Anne of Green Gables	RKO	Max Steiner
Bachelor Bait	RKO	Max Steiner
Band Played On, The	MGM	Oscar Radin
Belle of the Nineties	PAR	Andrea Setaro
Bolero	PAR	Andrea Setaro
Born to Be Bad	TCF	Alfred Newman
Bulldog Drummond Strikes Back	UA	Alfred Newman
By Your Leave	RKO	Max Steiner
Caravan	TCF	Werner Heymann
Carolina	TCF	Louis de Francesco
Catherine the Great	UA	Ernst Toch
Chained	MGM	Herbert Stothart
Change of Heart	TCF	Louis de Francesco
Cheating Cheaters	UN	Edward Ward
Chloe	IND	Erno Rapee
Church Mouse, The	WB	W. Franke Harling
Cockeyed Cavaliers	RKO	Roy Webb
Coming Out Party	TCF	Louis de Francesco
Count of Monte Cristo, The	UA	Alfred Newman
Crime Without Passion	PAR	Oscar Levant/Frank Tours
Dangerous Corner	RKO	Max Steiner
Death Takes a Holiday	PAR	Bernhard Kaun/Sigmund Krumgold
Embarrassing Moments	UN	Edward Ward

Evelyn Prentice	MGM	Oscar Radin
Finishing School	RKO	Max Steiner
Forsaking All Others	MGM	William Axt
Gambling	TCF	Frank Tours
Ghost Walks, The	INV	Abe Meyer
Gift of Gab, The	UN	Edward Ward
Girl o' My Dreams	MON	Edward Ward
Glamour	UN	Howard Jackson
Grand Canary	TCF	Louis de Francesco
Green Eyes	CHE	Abe Meyer
Gridiron Flash	RKO	Max Steiner
Helldorado	TCF	Louis de Francesco
Here Is My Heart	PAR	Rudolph G. Kopp
Hide-Out	MGM	William Axt
His Greatest Gamble	RKO	Max Steiner
House of Mystery, The	MON	Abe Meyer
I Am Suzanne	TCF	Frederick Hollander
I Like It That Way	UN	Edward Ward
Jane Eyre	MON	Abe Meyer
Kentucky Kernels	RKO	Roy Webb
Kid Millions	UA	Alfred Newman
Last Gentleman, The	UA	Alfred Newman
Laughing Boy	MGM	Herbert Stothart
Lazy River	MGM	William Axt
Lightning Strikes Twice	RKO	Roy Webb
Little Friend	BRI	Ernst Toch
Little Men	MAS	Hugo Riesenfeld
Little Minister, The	RKO	Max Steiner
Long Lost Father, The	RKO	Max Steiner
Lost Jungle, The (serial)	MAS	Hal Chasnoff
Man Who Knew Too Much, The	BRI	Sir Arthur Benjamin
Man Who Reclaimed His Head, The	UN	Heinz Roemheld
Manhattan Melodrama	MGM	William Axt
Meanest Gal in Town, The	RKO	Max Steiner
Mighty Barnum, The	TCF	Alfred Newman
Moonstone, The	MON	Abe Meyer
Murder at the Vanities	PAR	Rudolph G. Kopp
Mystery Liner	MON	Abe Meyer
Mystery Mountain (serial)	MAS	Abe Meyer
Old-Fashioned Way, The	PAR	Andrea Setaro
Peck's Bad Boy	TCF	Hugo Riesenfeld
Picture Brides	ALL	Abe Meyer
Private Life of Don Juan, The	UA	Ernst Toch
Red Morning	RKO	Alberto Colombo
Return of Chandu, The	PRI	Abe Meyer
Romance in the Rain	UN	Edward Ward
Sadie McKee	MGM	William Axt
Scarlet Empress, The	PAR	W. Frank Harling/John Leipold
Silver Streak, The	RKO	Max Steiner
Sing and Like It	RKO	Max Steiner
Springtime for Henry	TCF	Louis de Francesco
Star Packer	MON	Abe Meyer

Straight Is the Way	MGM	William Axt
Such Women Are Dangerous	TCF	Louis de Francesco
Their Big Moment	RKO	Max Steiner
This Side of Heaven	MGM	William Axt
Transatlantic Merry-Go-Round	UA	Alfred Newman
Two Alone	RKO	Max Steiner
Wednesday's Child	RKO	Max Steiner
We're Rich Again	RKO	Max Steiner
White Parade, The	TCF	Louis de Francesco
Wicked Woman, A	MGM	William Axt
World Moves On, The	TCF	Louis de Francesco
You Can't Buy Everything	MGM	William Axt

1935

Affair of Susan, The	UN	Franz Waxman
Age of Indiscretion	MGM	Edward Ward
Alice Adams	RKO	Max Steiner
All the King's Horses	PAR	Rudolph G. Kopp
Annie Oakley	RKO	Alberto Colombo
Another Face	RKO	Roy Webb
Arizonian, The	RKO	Roy Webb
Becky Sharp	RKO	Roy Webb
Biography of a Bachelor Girl, The	MGM	Herbert Stothart
Break of Hearts	RKO	Max Steiner
Bride of Frankenstein	UN	Franz Waxman
Calm Yourself	MGM	Charles Maxwell
Captain Hurricane	RKO	Roy Webb
Casino Murder Case, The	MGM	Dimitri Tiomkin
Chasing Yesterday	RKO	Alberto Colombo
Circumstantial Evidence	CHE	Abe Meyer
Clive of India	TCF	Alfred Newman
College Scandal	PAR	Andrea Setaro
Condemned to Live	INV	David Broekman
Crime of Dr. Crespi, The	REP	Milton Schwartzwald
David Copperfield	MGM	Charles Maxwell/Herbert Stothart
Diamond Jim	UN	Franz Waxman
Dizzy Dames	LIB	Howard Jackson
Dog of Flanders, A	RKO	Alberto Colombo
Enchanted April	RKO	Roy Webb
Fighting Marines, The (serial)	MAS	Arthur Kay
Fire Trap, The	IND	Lee Zahler
Freckles	RKO	Alberto Colombo
Goin' to Town	PAR	Andrea Setaro
Grand Old Girl	RKO	Alberto Colombo
Here Comes the Band	MGM	Edward Ward
Here's to Romance	TCF	Louis de Francesco
Hi, Gaucho	RKO	Albert Hay Malotte
His Family Tree	RKO	Alberto Colombo
Hooray for Love	RKO	Alberto Colombo
Hot Tip	RKO	Alberto Colombo
Jalna	RKO	Alberto Colombo

Just My Luck	IND	Lee Zahler
Kind Lady	MGM	Edward Ward
Kliou, the Tiger	RKO	Heinz Roemheld
Laddie	RKO	Roy Webb
Last Days of Pompeii, The	RKO	Roy Webb
Last of the Pagans, The	MGM	Milan Roder
Lives of a Bengal Lancer, The	PAR	Milan Roder
Lone Wolf Returns, The	COL	Howard Jackson
Lost City, The (serial)	IND	Lee Zahler
Mad Love	MGM	Dimitri Tiomkin
Melody Lingers On, The	UA	Alfred Newman
Motive for Revenge	MAJ	Lee Zahler
Murder by Television	IND	Oliver Wallace
Murder on a Honeymoon	RKO	Alberto Colombo
Murder on the Campus	CHE	Abe Meyer
Mutiny on the Bounty	MGM	Herbert Stothart
Mysterious Mr. Wong	MON	Abe Meyer
Night at the Opera, A	MGM	Herbert Stothart
Night Life of the Gods	UN	Arthur Morton
Nitwits, The	RKO	Roy Webb
No More Yesterdays	COL	Howard Jackson
Old Homestead, The	LIB	Howard Jackson
Old Man Rhythm	RKO	Roy Webb
Once in a Blue Moon	PAR	George Antheil
One Frightened Night	MAS	Arthur Kay
Perfect Gentleman, The	MGM	William Axt
Phantom Empire (serial)	MAS	Henry Hadley/Arthur Kay/ Hugo Riesenfeld
Powdersmoke Range	RKO	Alberto Colombo
President Vanishes, The	PAR	Hugo Riesenfeld
Princess O'Hara	UN	Arthur Morton
Public Opinion	INV	Lee Zahler
Pursuit	MGM	William Axt
Queen of the Jungle	IND	Hal Chasnoff
Rainmakers, The	RKO	Roy Webb
Reckless	MGM	Edward Ward
Remember Last Night?	UN	Franz Waxman
Rendezvous	MGM	William Axt
Return of Peter Grimm, The	RKO	Alberto Colombo
Romance in Manhattan	RKO	Alberto Colombo
Sequoia	MGM	Herbert Stothart
Shadow of Doubt	MGM	Oscar Radin
She	RKO	Max Steiner
Shot in the Dark, A	CHE	Abe Meyer
Society Doctor	MGM	Oscar Radin
Star of Midnight	RKO	Max Steiner
Story of Louis Pasteur, The	WB	Heinz Roemheld/Bern- hard Kaun
Strangers All	RKO	Roy Webb
Symphony of Living	INV	Lee Zahler
Times Square Lady	MGM	Edward Ward
To Beat the Band	RKO	Alberto Colombo
Unknown Ranger, The	COL	Lee Zahler

Vanessa, Her Love Story	MGM	Herbert Stothart
Village Tale, A	RKO	Alberto Colombo
Wandering Jew, The	IND	Hugo Riesenfeld
Wedding Night, The	UA	Alfred Newman
We're Only Human	RKO	Roy Webb
West of the Pecos	RKO	Max Steiner
West Point of the Air	MGM	Charles Maxwell
Winning Ticket, The	MGM	Charles Maxwell
Woman Wanted	MGM	William Axt

1936

After the Thin Man	MGM	Edward Ward
All-American Chump	MGM	William Axt
Amazing Exploits of the Clutching Hand, The (serial)	IND	Lee Zahler
Banjo on My Knee	TCF	Arthur Lange/Charles Maxwell
Big Game, The	RKO	Nathaniel Shilkret
Case Against Mrs. Ames, The	PAR	Gerard Carbonara
Counterfeit	COL	Howard Jackson
Daniel Boone	RKO	Hugo Riesenfeld
Darkest Africa (serial)	REP	Arthur Kay
Death from a Distance	INV	Abe Meyer
Devil on Horseback, The	GN	Hugo Riesenfeld
Devil's Squadron, The	COL	Howard Jackson
Dracula's Daughter	UN	Heinz Roemheld
Easy to Take	PAR	Gregory Stone
Exclusive Story	MGM	Edward Ward
Fatal Lady	PAR	Gerard Carbonara/Victor Young
Follow Your Heart	REP	Hugo Riesenfeld
Forgotten Faces	PAR	Gerard Carbonara
Garden Murder Case, The	MGM	William Axt
Girl of the Ozarks	PAR	Gerard Carbonara
Girl's Dormitory	TCF	Arthur Lange/Charles Maxwell
Give Us This Night	PAR	Erich Wolfgang Korngold
Grand Jury	RKO	Alberto Colombo
Great Ziegfeld, The	MGM	Arthur Lange/Charles Maxwell
Hearts in Bondage	REP	Hugo Riesenfeld
House of a Thousand Candles, The	REP	Arthur Kay
I Cover Chinatown	IND	Abe Meyer
Invisible Ray, The	UN	Franz Waxman
Kelly the Second	MGM	Marvin Hatley
Lady Consents, The	RKO	Roy Webb
Lady of Secrets	COL	Howard Jackson/William Grant Still
Last of the Mohicans, The	UA	Roy Webb
Mad Holiday	MGM	William Axt
Magnificent Brute, The	UN	Arthur Lange/Charles Maxwell

Mary of Scotland	RKO	Nathaniel Shilkret
Mine with the Iron Door, The	COL	Abe Meyer
Mister Cinderella	MGM	Marvin Hatley
Moonlight Murder	MGM	Herbert Stothart/Edward Ward
Moon's Our Home, The	PAR	Gerard Carbonara
Mummy's Boys	RKO	Roy Webb
Murder on a Bridle Path	RKO	Roy Webb
Muss 'Em Up	RKO	Roy Webb
New Adventures of Tarzan, The (serial)	IND	Abe Meyer
North of Nome	COL	Lee Zahler
Palm Springs	PAR	Gerard Carbonara
Penitente Murder Case, The	IND	Lee Zahler
Pennies from Heaven	COL	William Grant Still
President's Mystery, The	REP	Hugo Riesenfeld
Rainbow on the River	RKO	Hugo Riesenfeld
Revolt of the Zombies	IND	Abe Meyer
Rogue's Tavern	PUR	Abe Meyer
Second Wife	RKO	Roy Webb
Shadows of the Orient	IND	Lee Zahler
Silly Billies	RKO	Roy Webb
Sky Parade, The	PAR	Gerard Carbonara
Slander House	IND	Lee Zahler
Small Town Girl	MGM	Edward Ward
Smartest Girl in Town, The	RKO	Nathaniel Shilkret
Speed	MGM	Edward Ward
Star for a Night	TCF	Charles Maxwell
Theodora Goes Wild	COL	William Grant Still
Three Godfathers, The	MGM	William Axt
Three Live Ghosts	MGM	William Axt
Three Smart Girls	UN	Heinz Roemheld
Tough Guy	MGM	William Axt
Two in the Dark	RKO	Alberto Colombo
Under Your Spell	TCF	Arthur Lange/Charles Maxwell
Undersea Kingdom, The (serial)	REP	Arthur Kay
Valiant Is the Word for Carrie	PAR	Frederick Hollander
White Fang	TCF	Arthur Lange/Charles Maxwell
White Hunter	TCF	Charles Maxwell
White Legion	GN	Hugo Riesenfeld
Wife vs. Secretary	MGM	Herbert Stothart/Edward Ward
Witness Chair, The	RKO	Roy Webb
Women Are Trouble	MGM	Edward Ward
Yellow Dust	RKO	Alberto Colombo

1937

Affairs of Cappy Ricks, The	REP	Alberto Colombo
All Over Town	REP	Alberto Colombo
Bad Guy	MGM	Edward Ward

Big City	MGM	William Axt
Border Cafe	RKO	Nathaniel Shilkret
Boy Who Saved a Nation, The (short)	COL	Lee Zahler
Bride Wore Red, The	MGM	Franz Waxman
Champagne Waltz	PAR	Victor Young
Charlie Chan at the Opera	TCF	Charles Maxwell
Conquest	MGM	Herbert Stothart
Dangerous Holiday	REP	Alberto Colombo
Dark Journey	BRI	Richard Addinsell
Day at the Races, A	MGM	Bronislau Kaper
Dead End	UA	Alfred Newman
Dead March, The	IND	Erno Rapee
Dick Tracy (serial)	REP	Alberto Colombo
Double Wedding	MGM	Edward Ward
Duke Comes Back, The	REP	Alberto Colombo
Emperor's Candlesticks, The	MGM	Franz Waxman
Escape by Night	REP	Alberto Colombo
Espionage	MGM	William Axt
Exclusive	PAR	Milan Roder
Exiled to Shanghai	REP	Alberto Colombo
Family Affair, A	MGM	David Snell
Farewell Again	BRI	Richard Addinsell
Fifty-Year Barter, The (short)	COL	Lee Zahler
Fight for Your Lady	RKO	Frank Tours
First Lady	RKO	Max Steiner
Fit for a King	RKO	Arthur Morton
Green Cockatoo, The (Four Dark Hours)	UA	Miklos Rozsa
Headin' East	COL	Edward Kilenyi
Herald of the Skies, The (short)	COL	Lee Zahler
High Flyers	RKO	Roy Webb
Hurricane, The	UA	Alfred Newman
I Met Him in Paris	PAR	John Leipold
It Could Happen to You	REP	Alberto Colombo
King and the Chorus Girl, The	WB	Werner Heymann
Knight Without Armor	UA	Miklos Rozsa
Lancer Spy	TCF	Arthur Lange/Charles Maxwell
Let Them Live	UA	Lou Forte
Life of Emile Zola, The	WB	Max Steiner
Life of the Party, The	RKO	Roy Webb
Live, Love and Learn	MGM	Edward Ward
Love Under Fire	TCF	Arthur Lange/Charles Maxwell
Mama Steps Out	MGM	Edward Ward
Manhattan Merry-Go-Round	REP	Alberto Colombo
Married Before Breakfast	MGM	David Snell
Marry the Girl	WB	David Raksin
Meet the Boy Friend	REP	Alberto Colombo
Michael O'Halloran	REP	Alberto Colombo
Midnight Court	WB	David Raksin
Mighty Treve, The	UN	David Raksin

Mr. Dodd Takes the Air	WB	Adolph Deutsch
Murder on Diamond Row (The Squeaker)	UA	Miklos Rozsa
My Dear Miss Aldrich	MGM	David Snell
Nothing Sacred	UA	Oscar Levant
Pick a Star	MGM	Marvin Hatley/Arthur Morton
Portia on Trial	REP	Alberto Colombo
Prisoner of Zenda, The	UA	Alfred Newman
Rhythm in the Clouds	REP	Alberto Colombo
Riding on Air	RKO	Arthur Morton
Road Back, The	UN	Dimitri Tiomkin
San Quentin	WB	David Raksin
Sea Racketeers	REP	Alberto Colombo
Sheik Steps Out, The	REP	Alberto Colombo
She's Dangerous	UN	David Raksin
She's Got Everything	RKO	Frank Tours
Silver Threads (short)	COL	Lee Zahler
Slave Ship	TCF	Alfred Newman
Slim	WB	Max Steiner
Song of the City	MGM	William Axt
Souls at Sea	PAR	W. Franke Harling/Milan Roder/Ralph Rainger
Springtime in the Rockies	REP	Alberto Colombo
Stage Door	RKO	Roy Webb
Stella Dallas	UA	Alfred Newman
Submarine D-1	WB	Max Steiner
Swing High, Swing Low	PAR	Victor Young
That Certain Woman	WB	Max Steiner
This Is My Affair	TCF	Arthur Lange/Charles Maxwell
Thoroughbreds Don't Cry	MGM	William Axt
Toast of New York, The	RKO	Nathaniel Shilkret
Tovarich	RKO	Max Steiner
True Confession	PAR	Frederick Hollander
Victoria the Great	RKO	Anthony Collins
Vogues of 1938	UA	Victor Young
Wee Willie Winkie	TCF	Alfred Newman
Wild Horse Rodeo	REP	Alberto Colombo
Wings over Honolulu	UN	David Raksin
Wrong Road, The	REP	Alberto Colombo
Youth on Parole	REP	Alberto Colombo
Zorro Rides Again (serial)	REP	Alberto Colombo

1938

Adventures of Chico	MON	Edward Kilenyi
Adventures of Marco Polo, The	UA	Hugo Friedhofer
Arkansas Traveler, The	PAR	Gerard Carbonara
Arson Gang Busters	REP	Alberto Colombo
Artists and Models Abroad	PAR	Gerard Carbonara/Leo Shuken
Barnabe	FRA	R. Dumas

Billy the Kid Returns	REP	Cy Feuer
Blonde Cheat	RKO	Roy Webb
Bluebeard's Eighth Wife	PAR	Werner Heymann/Frederick Hollander
Border G-Man	RKO	Roy Webb
Born to Be Wild	REP	Alberto Colombo
Bulldog Drummond in Africa	PAR	Milan Roder
Call of the Yukon	REP	Alberto Colombo
Call the Mesquiteers	REP	Alberto Colombo
Condemned Women	RKO	Roy Webb
Cowboy and the Lady, The	UA	Alfred Newman
Crime Ring	RKO	Roy Webb
Crime School	WB	Max Steiner
Down in "Arkansaw"	REP	Cy Feuer
Dramatic School	MGM	Franz Waxman
Everybody's Doing It	RKO	Frank Tours
Fighting Devil Dogs (serial)	REP	Alberto Colombo
Flirting with Fate	MGM	Victor Young
Four's a Crowd	WB	Heinz Roemheld
Gangs of New York	REP	Alberto Colombo
Gateway	TCF	Arthur Lange/Charles Maxwell
Go Chase Yourself	RKO	Roy Webb
Gold Mine in the Sky	REP	Alberto Colombo
Gun Law	RKO	Roy Webb
Having Wonderful Time	RKO	Roy Webb
Hawaii Calls	RKO	Hugo Riesenfeld
Hawk of the Wilderness (serial)	REP	William Lava
Higgins Family, The	REP	Cy Feuer
Hollywood Stadium Mystery	REP	Alberto Colombo
I Met My Love Again	UA	Heinz Roemheld
Invisible Enemy	REP	Alberto Colombo
Jezebel	WB	Max Steiner
Judge Hardy's Children	MGM	David Snell
Kid Comes Back, The	WB	David Raksin
Kidnapped	TCF	Charles Maxwell
King of the Newsboys	REP	Alberto Colombo
Ladies in Distress	REP	Alberto Colombo
Lady, Behave!	REP	Alberto Colombo
Lawless Valley	RKO	Roy Webb
Lone Ranger, The (serial)	REP	Alberto Colombo
Love Finds Andy Hardy	MGM	David Snell
Mama Runs Wild	REP	Alberto Colombo
Meet the Mayor	IND	Edward Ward
Mr. Doodle Kicks Off	RKO	Roy Webb
Mother Carey's Chickens	RKO	Frank Tours
Mysterious Mr. Moto	TCF	Charles Maxwell
Mysterious Rider	PAR	Gerard Carbonara
Next Time I Marry	RKO	Roy Webb
Old Barn Dance, The	REP	Alberto Colombo
Orphans of the Street	REP	Cy Feuer
Out West with the Hardys	MGM	David Snell
Outlaws of Sonora	REP	Alberto Colombo

Outside of Paradise	REP	Alberto Colombo
Pals of the Saddle	REP	Cy Feuer
Pioneer Trail	COL	Lee Zahler
Port of Seven Seas	MGM	Franz Waxman
Prison Nurse	REP	Alberto Colombo
Promissi Sposi, I	ITA	Carlo Rustichelli
Purple Vigilantes, The	REP	Alberto Colombo
Racket Busters	WB	Adolph Deutsch
Rat, The	RKO	Anthony Collins
Red River Range	REP	William Lava
Renegade Ranger, The	RKO	Roy Webb
Ride a Crooked Mile	PAR	Gregory Stone
Romance on the Run	REP	Alberto Colombo
Room Service	RKO	Roy Webb
Rose of the Rio Grande	MON	Hugo Riesenfeld
Royal Divorce, A	PAR	Anthony Collins
Santa Fe Stampede	REP	William Lava
Sky Giant	RKO	Roy Webb
Smashing the Rackets	RKO	Frank Tours
Stagecoach Days	COL	Lee Zahler
Storm over Bengal	REP	Cy Feuer
Submarine Patrol	TCF	Charles Maxwell
Sunset Murder Case, The	GN	Hugo Riesenfeld
Sunset Trail	PAR	Gerard Carbonara
Three Blind Mice	TCF	Charles Maxwell
Tom Sawyer, Detective	PAR	Gerard Carbonara
Two-Gun Justice	MON	Edward Kilenyi
Under Western Stars	REP	Alberto Colombo
We're Going to Be Rich	TCF	Arthur Lange/Charles Maxwell
Wide Open Faces	COL	Hugo Riesenfeld
You and Me	PAR	Kurt Weill
Young Fugitives	UN	Hans J. Salter

1939

Adventures of Sherlock Holmes, The	FOX	David Raksin/David Buttolph/Cyril Mockridge
Almost a Gentleman	RKO	Frank Tours
Arizona Legion	RKO	Roy Webb
Bachelor Mother	RKO	Roy Webb
Beachcomber, The (Vessel of Wrath)	BRI	Richard Addinsell
Beauty for the Asking	RKO	Frank Tours
Big Guy	UN	Hans J. Salter
Blackmail	MGM	David Snell/Edward Ward
Boy Slaves	RKO	Frank Tours
Conspiracy	RKO	Frank Tours
Cowboys from Texas	REP	William Lava
Dancing Co-Ed	MGM	David Snell/Edward Ward
Daredevils of the Red Circle (serial)	REP	William Lava

Dick Tracy's G-Men (serial)	REP	William Lava
Exile Express	GN	George Parrish
Fisherman's Wharf	RKO	Victor Young
Frontier Marshal	TCF	Charles Maxwell
Full Confession	RKO	Roy Webb
Geronimo	PAR	Gerard Carbonara/John Leipold
Girl and the Gambler, The	RKO	Roy Webb
Hardys Ride High, The	MGM	David Snell
Henry Goes Arizona	MGM	David Snell/Edward Ward
Heritage of the Desert	PAR	Victor Young
Hidden Power	COL	Lee Zahler
Hollywood Cavalcade	TCF	David Raksin/David Buttolph/Cyril Mockridge
Honolulu	MGM	Franz Waxman
I Was a Convict	REP	Cy Feuer
Idiot's Delight	MGM	Herbert Stothart
In Old Caliente	REP	Cy Feuer
Invisible Stripes	WB	Heinz Roemheld
It's a Wonderful World	MGM	Edward Ward
Jeepers Creepers	REP	Cy Feuer
Judge Hardy and Son	MGM	David Snell
Kansas Terrors, The	REP	William Lava
Kid from Kokomo, The	WB	Adolph Deutsch
King of Chinatown	PAR	Gerard Carbonara
King of the Turf	UA	Frank Tours
Lady from Kentucky, The	UA	Leo Shuken
Law Comes to Texas, The	COL	Lee Zahler
Let Us Live	COL	Karol Rathaus
Light That Failed, The	PAR	Victor Young
Llano Kid, The	PAR	Victor Young
Lone Ranger Rides Again, The (serial)	REP	William Lava
Love Affair	RKO	Roy Webb
Lucky Night	MGM	Franz Waxman
Made for Each Other	UA	Oscar Levant
Main Street Lawyer	REP	Cy Feuer
Man of Conquest	REP	Victor Young
Mexican Spitfire	RKO	Paul Sawtell
Mickey the Kid	REP	Cy Feuer
Midnight	PAR	Frederick Hollander
Missing Ten Days (Ten Days in Paris)	COL	Miklos Rozsa
Mr. Moto's Last Warning	TCF	David Raksin/David Buttolph/Cyril Mockridge
My Wife's Relatives	REP	Cy Feuer
Mysterious Miss X, The	REP	Cy Feuer
Nancy Drew, Reporter	WB	Heinz Roemheld
Never Say Die	PAR	Milan Roder
New Frontier, The	REP	William Lava
Nick Carter, Master Detective	MGM	Edward Ward
Night of Nights, The	PAR	Victor Young

Night Riders, The	REP	William Lava
Off the Record	WB	Adolph Deutsch
Oklahoma Kid, The	WB	Max Steiner
... One-Third of a Nation...	PAR	Nathaniel Shilkret
Our Neighbors, the Carters	PAR	Victor Young
Panama Lady	RKO	Roy Webb
Paris Honeymoon	PAR	Gerard Carbonara/Leo Shuken
Pete Roleum and His Cousins (short)	IND	Hanns Eisler
Pride of the Blue Grass	WB	Howard Jackson
Pride of the Navy	REP	Cy Feuer
Racketeers of the Range	RKO	Roy Webb
Remember?	MGM	Edward Ward
Rookie Cop, The	RKO	Roy Webb
Rough Riders Round-Up	REP	Cy Feuer
S. O. S. --Tidal Wave	REP	Cy Feuer
Saga of Death Valley	REP	Cy Feuer
Saint Strikes Back, The	RKO	Roy Webb
Secret of Dr. Kildare, The	MGM	David Snell/Edward Ward
Sergeant Madden	MGM	William Axt
She Married a Cop	REP	Cy Feuer
Should Husbands Work?	REP	Cy Feuer
6, 000 Enemies	MGM	Edward Ward
Smuggled Cargo	REP	Cy Feuer
Society Lawyer	MGM	Edward Ward
Soil	IND	Hanns Eisler
Son of Frankenstein	UN	Frank Skinner
Sorority House	RKO	Roy Webb
Southward Ho!	REP	Cy Feuer
Stagecoach	UA	Richard Hageman/Max Steiner/W. Franke Harling/Paul J. Smith/Leo Shuken/John Leipold
Stanley and Livingstone	FOX	David Raksin/David Buttolph/Cyril Mockridge
Street of Missing Men	REP	Cy Feuer
Stronger Than Desire	MGM	David Snell/Edward Ward
Sued for Libel	RKO	Roy Webb
Suez	TCF	David Raksin/David Buttolph/Cyril Mockridge
These Glamour Girls	MGM	David Snell/Edward Ward
They All Come Out	MGM	David Snell/Edward Ward
They Made Her a Spy	RKO	Roy Webb
They Made Me a Criminal	WB	Max Steiner
Thou Shalt Not Kill	REP	Cy Feuer
Three Sons	RKO	Roy Webb
Three Texas Steers	REP	William Lava

Timber Stampede	RKO	Roy Webb
Topper Takes a Trip	TCF	Hugo Friedhofer
Tower of London	UN	Frank Skinner
Trouble in Sundown	RKO	Roy Webb
Twelve Crowded Hours	RKO	Roy Webb
Two Thoroughbreds	RKO	Roy Webb
U-Boat 29 (The Spy in Black)	COL	Miklos Rozsa
Vigil in the Night	RKO	Alfred Newman
Wall Street Cowboy	REP	Cy Feuer
Way Down South	RKO	Victor Young
Within the Law	MGM	William Axt
Woman Doctor	REP	Cy Feuer
Wyoming Outlaw	REP	William Lava
You Can't Get Away with Murder	WB	Heinz Roemheld
Zero Hour, The	REP	Cy Feuer
Zorro's Fighting Legion (serial)	REP	William Lava

1940

Adventure in Diamonds	PAR	Leo Shuken
Alias the Deacon	UN	Hans J. Salter
And One Was Beautiful	MGM	Daniele Amfitheatrof
Angel from Texas, An	WB	Howard Jackson
Angels over Broadway	COL	George Antheil
Anne of Windy Poplars	RKO	Roy Webb
Barnyard Follies	REP	Cy Feuer
Behind the News	REP	Cy Feuer
Bill of Divorcement, A	RKO	Roy Webb
Black Diamonds	UN	Hans J. Salter
Black Friday	UN	Hans J. Salter/Frank Skinner/Charles Previn/Charles Henderson
Blondie Has Servant Trouble	COL	Leigh Harline
Blondie on a Budget	COL	Leigh Harline
Blondie Plays Cupid	COL	Leigh Harline
Border Legion	REP	Cy Feuer
Bowery Boy	REP	Cy Feuer
Britain at Bay (short)	BRI	Richard Addinsell
British Intelligence	WB	Heinz Roemheld
Brother Rat and a Baby	WB	Heinz Roemheld
Buck Benny Rides Again	PAR	Victor Young
Bullet Code	RKO	Paul Sawtell
Camouflage	BRI	Richard Addinsell
Captain Is a Lady, The	MGM	Bronislau Kaper
Carson City Kid, The	REP	Cy Feuer
Castle on the Hudson	WB	Adolph Deutsch
Child Is Born, A	WB	Heinz Roemheld
Chump at Oxford, A	UA	Marvin Hatley
Colorado	REP	Cy Feuer
Congo Maisie	MGM	Edward Ward
Contraband	BRI	Richard Addinsell
Courageous Dr. Christian	RKO	William Lava
Covered Wagon Days	REP	Cy Feuer

Crooked Road, The	REP	Cy Feuer
Curtain Call	RKO	Roy Webb
Devil's Pipeline, The	UN	Hans J. Salter
Diamond Frontier	UN	Hans J. Salter
Dr. Cyclops	PAR	Gerard Carbonara/Ernst Toch/Alfred Hay Malotte
Dr. Kildare's Crisis	MGM	David Snell
Dr. Kildare's Strange Case	MGM	David Snell
Doctor Takes a Wife, The	COL	Frederick Hollander
Dreaming Out Loud	RKO	Lucien Moraweck
Dulcy	MGM	Bronislau Kaper
Earl of Puddlestone	REP	Cy Feuer
Earthbound	TCF	Alfred Newman
Ellery Queen, Master Detective	COL	Lee Zahler
Enemy Agent	UN	Hans J. Salter
Fargo Kid, The	RKO	John Leipold
Fighting 69th, The	WB	Adolph Deutsch
First Love	UN	Hans J. Salter/Frank Skinner
Forgotten Girls	REP	Cy Feuer
Framed	UN	Hans J. Salter
Friendly Neighbors	REP	Cy Feuer
Frontier Vengeance	REP	Cy Feuer
Fugitive, The (On the Night of the Fire)	UN	Miklos Rozsa
Gallant Song	MGM	David Snell
Gangs of Chicago	REP	Cy Feuer
Gay Caballero, The	TCF	Charles Maxwell
Ghost Comes Home, The	MGM	David Snell
Ghost Valley Raiders	REP	Cy Feuer
Girl from God's Country	REP	Cy Feuer
Girl from Havana, The	REP	Cy Feuer
Give Us Wings	UN	Hans J. Salter
Gold Rush Maisie	MGM	David Snell
Golden Fleecing, The	MGM	David Snell
Grand Ole Opry	REP	Cy Feuer
Grandpa Goes to Town	REP	Cy Feuer
Great Plane Robbery, The	COL	Lee Zahler
Her First Romance	MON	Gregory Stone
Heroes of the Saddle	REP	Cy Feuer
His Girl Friday	COL	Sidney Cutner
Hit Parade of 1941	REP	Cy Feuer
House of the Seven Gables, The	UN	Frank Skinner
Hudson's Bay	TCF	Alfred Newman
I Can't Give You Anything but Love, Baby	UN	Hans J. Salter
I Married Adventure	COL	Gerard Carbonara
I'm Nobody's Sweetheart Now	UN	Hans J. Salter
I'm Still Alive	RKO	Roy Webb
In Old Missouri	REP	Cy Feuer
Invisible Man Returns, The	UN	Hans J. Salter/Frank Skinner

Island of Doomed Men	COL	Gerard Carbonara
Keeping Company	MGM	Daniele Amfitheatrof
Knights of the Range	PAR	John Leipold/Victor Young
Knute Rockne, All-American	WB	Ferde Grofe
Lady in Question, The	COL	Lucien Moraweck
Law and Order	UN	Hans J. Salter
Leather Pushers, The	UN	Hans J. Salter
Legion of the Lawless	RKO	Paul Sawtell
Light of Western Stars, The	PAR	Victor Young
Little Old New York	TCF	Alfred Newman
Little Orvie	RKO	Paul Sawtell
Lone Star Raiders	REP	Cy Feuer
Love, Honor and Oh, Baby!	UN	Hans J. Salter
Love Thy Neighbor	PAR	Victor Young
Man from Dakota, The	MGM	Daniele Amfitheatrof
Margie	UN	Hans J. Salter
Married and in Love	RKO	Arthur Lange/Roy Webb
Meet the Missus	REP	Cy Feuer
Meet the Wildcats	UN	Hans J. Salter
Melody and Moonlight	REP	Cy Feuer
Men Against the Sky	RKO	Frank Tours
Mexican Spitfire Out West	RKO	Roy Webb
Millionaire Playboy	RKO	Paul Sawtell
Millionaires in Prison	RKO	Roy Webb
Miracle on Main Street	COL	Walter Jurmann/Hans J. Salter
Money to Burn	REP	Cy Feuer
Mummy's Hand, The	UN	Hans J. Salter/Frank Skinner
Mysterious Dr. Satan, The (serial)	REP	Cy Feuer
One Man's Law	REP	Cy Feuer
Outside the 3-Mile Limit	COL	Lee Zahler
Parole Fixer	PAR	Gerard Carbonara
Passport to Alcatraz	COL	Lee Zahler
Phantom Raiders	MGM	David Snell
Pioneers of the West	REP	Cy Feuer
Pop Always Pays	RKO	Paul Sawtell
Prairie Law	RKO	Paul Sawtell
Private Affairs	UN	Hans J. Salter
Quarterback, The	PAR	John Leipold
Rain (short)	IND	Hanns Eisler
Ranger and the Lady, The	REP	Cy Feuer
River's End	WB	Howard Jackson
Road to Singapore	PAR	Victor Young
Rocky Mountain Rangers	REP	Cy Feuer
Saint Takes Over, The	RKO	Roy Webb
Saint's Double Trouble, The	RKO	Roy Webb
Sandy Gets Her Man	UN	Hans J. Salter
Santa Fe Marshal	PAR	John Leipold
Saps at Sea	UA	Marvin Hatley
Scatterbrain	REP	Cy Feuer
Sea Hawk, The	WB	Erich Wolfgang Korngold

Seven Sinners	UN	Hans J. Salter/Frank Skinner
Showdown, The	PAR	John Leipold
Sing, Dance, Plenty Hot	REP	Cy Feuer
Ski Patrol	UN	Hans J. Salter
Sky Murder	MGM	David Snell
Slightly Tempted	UN	Hans J. Salter
So You Won't Talk?	COL	Leigh Harline
South of Suez	WB	Frederick Hollander
South to Karanga	UN	Hans J. Salter
Special Dispatch (short)	BRI	Richard Addinsell
Sporting Blood	MGM	Franz Waxman
Spring Parade	UN	Hans J. Salter
Stage to Chino	RKO	Paul Sawtell
Stagecoach War	PAR	John Leipold
Storm Warning	IND	David Raksin
This England	BRI	Richard Addinsell
Three Cheers for the Irish	WB	Adolph Deutsch
Three Men from Texas	PAR	Victor Young
Too Many Husbands	COL	Frederick Hollander
Trail Blazers, The	REP	Cy Feuer
Trail of the Vigilantes	UN	Hans J. Salter
Tugboat Annie Sails Again	WB	Adolph Deutsch
Tulsa Kid, The	REP	Cy Feuer
Turnabout	UA	Arthur Morton
20 Mule Team	MGM	David Snell
Typhoon	PAR	Frederick Hollander
Ulster (short)	BRI	Richard Addinsell
Under Texas Skies	REP	Cy Feuer
Village Barn Dance	REP	Cy Feuer
Villain Still Pursued Her, The	RKO	Frank Tours
Wagon Train	RKO	Paul Sawtell
Wagons Westward	REP	Cy Feuer
Westerner, The	UA	Alfred Newman
Who Killed Aunt Maggie?	REP	Cy Feuer
Wolf of New York	REP	Cy Feuer
Women Without Names	PAR	Gerard Carbonara
Wyoming	MGM	David Snell
You Can't Fool Your Wife	RKO	Roy Webb
Young Bill Hickok	REP	Cy Feuer
You're Not So Tough	UN	Hans J. Salter

1941

Adventure in Washington	COL	W. Franke Harling
Adventures of Captain Marvel (serial)	REP	Cy Feuer
All-American Co-Ed	UA	Edward Ward
Aloma of the South Seas	PAR	Victor Young
Along the Rio Grande	RKO	Paul Sawtell
Among the Living	PAR	Gerard Carbonara
Angels with Broken Wings	REP	Cy Feuer
Apache Kid, The	REP	Cy Feuer

Arizona Cyclone	UN	Hans J. Salter
Arkansas Judge	REP	Cy Feuer
Bachelor Daddy	UN	Hans J. Salter
Bad Man, The	MGM	Franz Waxman
Bad Men of Deadwood	REP	Cy Feuer
Bad Men of Missouri	WB	Howard Jackson
Badlands of Dakota	UN	Hans J. Salter
Bahama Passage	PAR	David Buttolph
Bandit Trail, The	RKO	Paul Sawtell
Barnacle Bill	MGM	Bronislau Kaper
Bedtime Story	COL	Werner Heymann
Big Blockade, The (short)	BRI	Richard Addinsell
Black Cat, The	UN	Hans J. Salter/Frank Skinner/Charles Previn/Charles Henderson
Blonde Inspiration	MGM	Bronislau Kaper
Body Disappears, The	WB	Howard Jackson
Border Vigilantes	PAR	John Leipold
Burma Convoy	UN	Hans J. Salter
Charley's Aunt	TCF	Alfred Newman
Citadel of Crime	REP	Cy Feuer
Dance of the Weed (short)	MGM	Scott Bradley
Dangerous Game, A	UN	Hans J. Salter
Dark Streets of Cairo	UN	Hans J. Salter
Dead Men Tell	FOX	David Raksin/David Buttolph/Cyril Mockridge
Death Valley Outlaws	REP	Cy Feuer
Desert Bandit	REP	Cy Feuer
Design for Scandal	MGM	Franz Waxman
Devil and Miss Jones, The	RKO	Roy Webb
Devil Pays Off, The	REP	Cy Feuer
Dipsy Gypsy (short)	PAR	David Raksin
Dr. Jekyll and Mr. Hyde	MGM	Franz Waxman
Dr. Kildare's Wedding Day	MGM	Bronislau Kaper
Doctors Don't Tell	REP	Cy Feuer
Double Date	UN	Hans J. Salter
Down in San Diego	MGM	David Snell
Ellery Queen and the Murder Ring	COL	Lee Zahler
Ellery Queen and the Perfect Crime	COL	Lee Zahler
Ellery Queen's Penthouse Mystery	COL	Lee Zahler
Fair Today (short)	UN	Darrell Calker
Flame of New Orleans, The	PAR	Frank Skinner
Flying Blind	PAR	Dimitri Tiomkin
Flying Cadets	UN	Hans J. Salter
Forced Landing	PAR	Dimitri Tiomkin
Four Mothers	WB	Heinz Roemheld
Frank Buck's Jungle Cavalcade	RKO	Nathaniel Shilkret
Gauchos of Eldorado	REP	Cy Feuer
Gay Vagabond, The	REP	Cy Feuer
Get-Away, The	MGM	Daniele Amfitheatrof
Great Mr. Nobody, The	WB	Adolph Deutsch
Great Swindle, The	COL	Lee Zahler
Great Train Robbery, The	REP	Cy Feuer

Green Belt, The (short)	BRI	Richard Addinsell
H. M. Pulham, Esq.	MGM	Bronislau Kaper
Hello Sucker	UN	Hans J. Salter
Hellzapoppin'	UN	Frank Skinner
Here Comes Mr. Jordan	COL	Frederick Hollander
Hit the Road	UN	Hans J. Salter
Hold That Ghost	UN	Hans J. Salter/Frank Skinner/Charles Previn/Charles Henderson
Honeymoon for Three	WB	Heinz Roemheld
Horror Island	UN	Hans J. Salter/Frank Skinner/Charles Previn/Charles Henderson
Hurricane Smith	REP	Cy Feuer
Hurry, Charlie, Hurry	RKO	Roy Webb
Ice-Capades	REP	Cy Feuer
I'll Wait for You	MGM	Bronislau Kaper
In Old Cheyenne	REP	Cy Feuer
In Old Colorado	PAR	John Leipold
It Started with Eve	UN	Hans J. Salter
Jesse James at Bay	REP	Cy Feuer
Kansas Cyclone	REP	Cy Feuer
Keep 'Em Flying	UN	Frank Skinner
Kings Row	WB	Erich Wolfgang Korngold
Kisses for Breakfast	WB	Adolph Deutsch
Lady Has Plans, The	PAR	Leo Shuken/Leigh Harline
Law of the Tropics	WB	Howard Jackson
Life with Henry	PAR	Frederick Hollander
Little Men	RKO	Roy Webb
Look Who's Laughing	RKO	Roy Webb
Lucky Devils	UN	Hans J. Salter
Mad Doctor, The	PAR	Victor Young
Maisie Was a Lady	MGM	David Snell
Man Betrayed, A	REP	Cy Feuer
Man-Made Monster	UN	Hans J. Salter/Frank Skinner/Charles Henderson
Man Who Lost Himself, The	UN	Hans J. Salter
Man's Best Friend (short)	UN	Darrell Calker
Married Bachelor	MGM	Lennie Hayton
Maryland	TCF	Alfred Newman
Meet the Chump	UN	Hans J. Salter
Men in Her Life, The	COL	David Raksin
Men of the Timberland	UN	Hans J. Salter
Mercy Island	REP	Cy Feuer
Mexican Spitfire Sees a Ghost	RKO	Roy Webb
Miss Polly	UA	Edward Ward
Mr. Bug Goes to Town (Hoppity Goes to Town)	PAR	Leigh Harline
Mr. District Attorney	REP	Cy Feuer
Mr. District Attorney in the Carter Case	REP	Cy Feuer
Mr. Dynamite	UN	Hans J. Salter

Mob Town	UN	Hans J. Salter
Model Wife	UN	Hans J. Salter
Mountain Moonlight	REP	Cy Feuer
Mutiny in the Arctic	UN	Hans J. Salter
Nevada City	REP	Cy Feuer
Never Give a Sucker an Even Break	UN	Frank Skinner
New York Town	PAR	Leo Shuken
Niagara Falls	UA	Edward Ward
Night of January 16th, The	PAR	Gerard Carbonara
No Hands on the Clock	PAR	Paul Sawtell
On the Sunny Side	TCF	Cyril Mockridge/Leigh Harline
Our Wife	COL	Leo Shuken
Outlaws of the Cherokee Trail	REP	Cy Feuer
Parachute Battalion	RKO	Roy Webb
Penalty, The	MGM	David Snell
Penny Serenade	COL	W. Franke Harling
People vs. Dr. Kildare, The	MGM	David Snell
Petticoat Politics	REP	Cy Feuer
Phantom Cowboy, The	REP	Cy Feuer
Pirates on Horseback	PAR	John Leipold
Pittsburgh Kid, The	REP	Cy Feuer
Prairie Pioneers	REP	Cy Feuer
Public Enemies	REP	Cy Feuer
Puddin' Head	REP	Cy Feuer
Rage in Heaven	MGM	Bronislau Kaper
Rags to Riches	REP	Cy Feuer
Raiders of the Desert	UN	Hans J. Salter
Red River Valley	REP	Cy Feuer
Redhead	MON	Paul Sawtell
Remember the Day	TCF	Alfred Newman
Ride On, Vaquero	TCF	David Raksin/David Buttolph/Cyril Mockridge
Riders of the Timberline	PAR	John Leipold
Ringside Maisie	MGM	David Snell
Road Agent	UN	Hans J. Salter
Road to Zanzibar	PAR	Victor Young
Robbers of the Range	RKO	Paul Sawtell
Robin Hood of the Pecos	REP	Cy Feuer
Romance of the Rio Grande	TCF	Charles Maxwell/Cyril Mockridge
Rookies on Parade	REP	Cy Feuer
Round-Up, The	PAR	Gerard Carbonara
Saddlemates	REP	Cy Feuer
Sailors on Leave	REP	Cy Feuer
Saint in Palm Springs, The	RKO	Roy Webb
San Francisco Docks	UN	Hans J. Salter
Scattergood Meets Broadway	RKO	Dimitri Tiomkin
Screw Driver, The (short)	UN	Darrell Calker
Sealed Lips	UN	Hans J. Salter
Secrets of the Wasteland	PAR	John Leipold
Shepherd of the Hills	PAR	Gerard Carbonara

Sheriff of Tombstone	REP	Cy Feuer
Singapore Woman	WB	Adolph Deutsch
Sis Hopkins	REP	Cy Feuer
Six-Gun Gold	RKO	Paul Sawtell
Son of Monte Cristo, The	UA	Edward Ward
Spooks Run Wild	MON	Johnny Lange/Louis Porter
Stolen Paradise	RKO	Nathaniel Shilkret
Swamp Water	TCF	David Buttolph
Tanks a Million	UA	Edward Ward
Tarzan's Secret Treasure	MGM	David Snell
They Met in Bombay	MGM	Herbert Stothart
This Is Colour (short)	BRI	Richard Addinsell
This Thing Called Love	COL	Werner Heymann
This Woman Is Mine	UN	Richard Hageman
Three Sons O'Guns	WB	Howard Jackson
Tight Shoes	UN	Hans J. Salter
Tom, Dick and Harry	RKO	Roy Webb
Topper Returns	UA	Werner Heymann
Tuxedo Junction	REP	Cy Feuer
Twilight on the Trail	PAR	John Leipold
Two-Gun Sheriff	REP	Cy Feuer
Unexpected Uncle	RKO	Anthony Collins
Unholy Partners	MGM	David Snell
Wagons Roll at Night, The	WB	Heinz Roemheld
Washington Melodrama	MGM	David Snell
Weekend for Three	RKO	Roy Webb
West of Cimarron	REP	Cy Feuer
West Point Widow	PAR	Leo Shuken
Western Daze (short)	PAR	David Raksin
Where Did You Get That Girl?	UN	Hans J. Salter
Wide Open Town	PAR	John Leipold
Wild Geese Calling	TCF	Alfred Newman
Wolf Man, The	UN	Hans J. Salter/Frank Skinner/Charles Previn
Wyoming Wildcat	REP	Cy Feuer
Yank in the R. A. F., A	TCF	Alfred Newman
You're in the Army Now	WB	Howard Jackson

1942

Affairs of Jimmy Valentine, The	REP	Cy Feuer
Affairs of Martha, The	MGM	Bronislau Kaper
Arizona Terrors	REP	Cy Feuer
Ball of Fire	RKO	Alfred Newman
Battle of Midway, The	IND	Alfred Newman
Blondie for Victory	COL	John Leipold
Bombs over Burma	PRC	Lee Zahler
Brooklyn Orchid	UA	Edward Ward
Captain Midnight (serial)	COL	Lee Zahler
Careful, Soft Shoulder	TCF	Leigh Harline
Close Fall for Ellery Queen, A	COL	Lee Zahler

Colleges at War (short)	IND	Gail Kubik
Come on, Danger	RKO	Paul Sawtell
Commandos Strike at Dawn	COL	Louis Gruenberg
Courtship of Andy Hardy, The	MGM	David Snell
Date with the Falcon, A	RKO	Paul Sawtell
Day Will Dawn, The	BRI	Richard Addinsell
Desperate Chance for Ellery Queen, A	COL	Lee Zahler
Desperate Journey	WB	Max Steiner
Destination Unknown	UN	Hans J. Salter
Dr. Kildare's Victory	MGM	Lennie Hayton
Dr. Renault's Secret	TCF	David Raksin/David Buttolph/Cyril Mockridge
Dover (short)	IND	Gail Kubik
Enemy Agents Meet Ellery Queen	COL	Lee Zahler
Falcon's Brother, The	RKO	Roy Webb
Flying Tigers	REP	Victor Young
Flying with Music	UA	Edward Ward
Forest Rangers, The	PAR	Victor Young
Frisco Lil	UN	Hans J. Salter
G-Men vs. the Black Dragon (serial)	REP	Mort Glickman
Gallant Lady	PRC	Lee Zahler
Half Way to Shanghai	UN	Hans J. Salter
Hay Foot	UA	Edward Ward
Henry Aldrich, Editor	PAR	Leo Shuken
Hi, Neighbor	REP	Cy Feuer
Highways by Night	RKO	Roy Webb
I Live on Danger	PAR	Freddie Rich
I Married a Witch	UA	Roy Webb
Iceland	TCF	David Buttolph
Invisible Agent	UN	Hans J. Salter
Jacare	UA	Miklos Rozsa
Jaguar	IND	Karol Rathaus
Jail House Blues	UN	Frank Skinner
Jesse James Jr.	REP	Cy Feuer
Joan of Ozark	REP	Cy Feuer
Johnny Eager	MGM	Bronislau Kaper
Just Off Broadway	TCF	David Raksin/David Buttolph/Cyril Mockridge
King of the Mounties (serial)	REP	Mort Glickman
Land of the Open Range	RKO	Paul Sawtell
McGuerins from Brooklyn, The	UA	Edward Ward
Mad Doctor of Market Street, The	UN	Hans J. Salter
Madame Spy	UN	Hans J. Salter
Magnificent Dope, The	TCF	David Raksin/David Buttolph/Cyril Mockridge/Leigh Harline
Man from Cheyenne	REP	Cy Feuer
Man Who Came to Dinner, The	WB	Frederick Hollander
Man Who Wouldn't Die, The	TCF	David Raksin/David Buttolph/Cyril Mockridge
Manila Calling	TCF	David Raksin/David Buttolph/Cyril Mockridge

Manpower (short)	IND	Gail Kubik
Men of Texas	UN	Edward Ward
Mexican Spitfire Sees a Ghost	RKO	Roy Webb
Mexican Spitfire's Elephant	RKO	Roy Webb
Miss V from Moscow	PRC	Lee Zahler
Mr. and Mrs. North	MGM	David Snell
Moonlight Masquerade	REP	Cy Feuer
Moontide	TCF	Alfred Newman
Moscow Strikes Back	REP	Dimitri Tiomkin
My Gal Sal	TCF	Cyril Mockridge/Leigh Harline
Night Before the Divorce, The	TCF	Leigh Harline
Obliging Young Lady, An	RKO	Roy Webb
Old Chisholm Trail, The	UN	Hans J. Salter
Pacific Rendezvous	MGM	David Snell
Perils of Nyoka (serial)	REP	Mort Glickman
Perils of the Royal Mounted (serial)	COL	Lee Zahler
Pittsburgh	UN	Hans J. Salter/Frank Skinner
Postman Didn't Ring, The	TCF	David Raksin/David Buttolph/Cyril Mockridge/Leigh Harline
Powder Town	RKO	Roy Webb
Prelude to War	IND	Alfred Newman/Leigh Harline
Ravaged Earth	IND	Edward Kilenyi
Red River Robin Hood	RKO	Paul Sawtell
Right to the Heart	TCF	Leigh Harline
Rings on Her Fingers	TCF	Cyril Mockridge/Leigh Harline
Secret Agent of Japan	TCF	Cyril Mockridge/Leigh Harline
Sherlock Holmes and the Secret Weapon	UN	Hans J. Salter
Siege of Tobruk, The (short)	BRI	Richard Addinsell
Snuffy Smith, Yard Bird	MON	Rudy Schrager
Spy Smasher (serial)	REP	Mort Glickman
Syncopation	RKO	Leith Stevens
They Died with Their Boots On	WB	Max Steiner
Through Different Eyes	TCF	David Raksin/David Buttolph/Cyril Mockridge
Thundering Hoofs	RKO	Paul Sawtell
Undying Monster, The	TCF	David Raksin/David Buttolph/Cyril Mockridge
Vanishing Virginian, The	MGM	David Snell
Whispering Ghosts	TCF	David Raksin/David Buttolph/Cyril Mockridge/Leigh Harline
Who Done It?	UN	Hans J. Salter
Who Is Hope Schuyler?	TCF	David Raksin/David Buttolph/Cyril Mockridge

1943

A. T. S. (short)	BRI	Richard Addinsell
Amazing Mrs. Holliday, The	UN	Hans J. Salter/Frank Skinner
Appointment in Berlin	COL	Werner Heymann
Arizona Trail	UN	Hans J. Salter
At the Front in North America	IND	Alfred Newman
Batman (serial)	COL	Lee Zahler
Calaboose	UA	Edward Ward
Calling Dr. Death	UN	Hans J. Salter/Paul Saw-tell/Frank Skinner
City Without Men	COL	David Raksin
Corbeau, Le	FRA	Toni Aubain
Dead Man's Gulch	REP	Mort Glickman
Dead Men Walk	PRC	Leo Erdody
December Seventh	IND	Alfred Newman
Dixie Dugan	TCF	Arthur Lange/Charles Maxwell
Drums of Fu Manchu	REP	Cy Feuer
Earthquakers (short)	IND	Gail Kubik
Eyes of the Underworld	UN	Hans J. Salter
Fall In	UA	Edward Ward
Frankenstein Meets the Wolf Man	UN	Hans J. Salter/Frank Skinner/Charles Pre-vin
Frontier Badmen	UN	Hans J. Salter
Fugitive of the Plains	PRC	Leo Erdody
Gentle Gangster, A	REP	Lee Zahler
Girl from Monterey, The	PRC	Mahlon Merrick
Great Gildersleeve, The	RKO	Paul Sawtell
Heat's On, The	COL	John Leipold
Henry Aldrich Haunts a House	PAR	Gerard Carbonara
He's My Guy	UN	Milton Rosen
Hitler's Children	RKO	Roy Webb
Jitterbugs	TCF	Leigh Harline
Journey into Fear	RKO	Roy Webb
Man from the Rio Grande, The	REP	Mort Glickman
Man of Courage	PRC	Lee Zahler
My Kingdom for a Cook	COL	John Leipold
New Lot, The (short)	BRI	Richard Addinsell
Night Plane from Chunking	PAR	Gerard Carbonara
Northwest Rangers	MGM	Daniel Amfitheatrof/ David Snell
Over My Dead Body	TCF	Cyril Mockridge
Petticoat Larceny	RKO	Roy Webb
Phantom, The (serial)	COL	Lee Zahler
Quiet Please, Murder	TCF	Arthur Lange/Charles Maxwell
Return of the Vampire, The	COL	Mario Castelnuovo-Tedes-co
Sagebrush Law	RKO	Paul Sawtell
Seven Miles from Alcatraz	RKO	Roy Webb

Silver Skates	MON	Mahlon Merrick
Son of Dracula	UN	Hans J. Salter/Charles Previn/Frank Skinner
Stranger in Town, A	MGM	Daniele Amfitheatrof/ Nathaniel Shilkret
That Nazty Nuisance	UA	Edward Ward
Thousands Cheer	MGM	Ferde Grofe/Herbert Stothart
Thundering Trails	REP	Mort Glickman
Tonight We Raid Calais	TCF	Cyril Mockridge
We Sail at Midnight (short)	BRI	Richard Addinsell
We've Never Been Licked	UN	Frank Skinner
What a Woman	COL	John Leipold
Yanks Ahoy	UA	Edward Ward

1944

Air Pattern--Pacific (short)	IND	Gail Kubik
Allergic to Love	UN	Hans J. Salter
Beneath Western Skies	REP	Mort Glickman
Black Arrow (serial)	COL	Lee Zahler
Bordertown Trail	REP	Joseph Dubin
Boss of Boomtown	UN	Hans J. Salter
Call of the Rockies	REP	Joseph Dubin
Can't Help Singing	UN	Hans J. Salter
Career Girl	PRC	Rudy Schrager
Christmas Holiday	UN	Hans J. Salter
Climax, The	UN	Edward Ward
Code of the Prairie	REP	Joseph Dubin
Destination Tokyo	WB	Franz Waxman
Destiny	UN	Frank Skinner/Alexandre Tansman
Dixie Jamboree	PRC	Rudy Schrager
Firebrands of Arizona	REP	Joseph Dubin
Follow the Boys	UN	Frank Skinner/Oliver Wallace
Gildersleeve's Ghost	RKO	Paul Sawtell
Hat Check Honey	UN	Hans J. Salter
Haunted Harbor (serial)	REP	Joseph Dubin
House I Live In, The (short)	IND	Earl Robinson
House of Fear	UN	Hans J. Salter
House of Frankenstein	UN	Hans J. Salter/Paul Dessau/Frank Skinner/ Charles Previn
Invisible Man's Revenge, The	UN	Hans J. Salter/William Lava/Eric Zeisl
Jungle Captive	UN	Hans J. Salter/Paul Sawtell
Jungle Woman	UN	Hans J. Salter
Laramie Trail, The	REP	Mort Glickman
Marked for Murder	PRC	Lee Zahler
Merry Monahans, The	UN	Hans J. Salter
Mummy's Ghost, The	UN	Hans J. Salter/Charles Previn/Frank Skinner

No Time for Love	PAR	Victor Young
Oklahoma Raiders	UN	Paul Sawtell
Old Texas Trail, The	UN	Paul Sawtell
Outlaws of Santa Fe	REP	Mort Glickman
Pearl of Death, The	UN	Hans J. Salter
Rationing	MGM	David Snell
Riders of the Santa Fe	UN	Paul Sawtell
Rogue's Gallery	PRC	Lee Zahler
San Antonio Kid, The	REP	Joseph Dubin
Scarlet Claw, The	UN	Hans J. Salter
Secrets of Scotland Yard	REP	Charles Maxwell
See Here, Private Hargrove	MGM	David Snell
Seventh Cross, The	MGM	Roy Webb
Sheriff of Sundown	REP	Joseph Dubin
She's a Soldier, Too	COL	Mario Castelnuovo-Tedesco
Something for the Boys	TCF	Cyril Mockridge
Stagecoach to Monterey	REP	Joseph Dubin
Tiger Woman, The (serial)	REP	Joseph Dubin
Town Went Wild, The	PRC	Gerard Carbonara
Trail to Gunsight	UN	Paul Sawtell
Twilight on the Prairie	UN	Hans J. Salter
Two-Man Submarine	COL	Mario Castelnuovo-Tedesco
Vigilantes of Dodge City	REP	Joseph Dubin
Weird Woman	UN	Hans J. Salter
Woman in the Window, The	RKO	Hugo Friedhofer

1945

Along the Navajo Trail	REP	Dale Butts
Angel Comes to Brooklyn, An	REP	Dale Butts
Attack in the Pacific	IND	David Raksin
Club Havana	PRC	Howard Jackson
Corn Is Green, The	WB	Max Steiner
Crime Doctor's Courage, The	COL	Mario Castelnuovo-Tedesco
Don't Fence Me In	REP	Dale Butts
Enchanted Forest, The	PRC	Lucien Cailliet/Albert Hay Malotte
Enemy of the Law	PRC	Lee Zahler
Flame of the Barbary Coast	REP	Dale Butts
Forever Yours	MON	Dimitri Tiomkin
Histadruth	IND	Karol Rathaus
House of Dracula	UN	Hans J. Salter/Frank Skinner/William Lava/Charles Previn/Paul Sawtell/Edgar Fairchild/Paul Desseau/Charles Henderson
I Love a Mystery	COL	Mario Castelnuovo-Tedesco
Jeep Herders	IND	Lee Zahler

Jungle Raiders (serial)	COL	Lee Zahler
Man from Oklahoma	REP	Dale Butts
Monster and the Ape, The (serial)	COL	Lee Zahler
Mummy's Curse, The	UN	Paul Sawtell
Navajo Kid, The	PRC	Lee Zahler
Nob Hill	TCF	David Buttolph
On Stage Everybody	UN	Milton Rosen
Phantom Speaks, The	REP	Edward Plumb
Power of the Whistler, The	COL	Paul Sawtell
Prison Ship	COL	Mario Castelnuovo-Tedesco
Pursuit to Algiers	UN	Hans J. Salter
Renegades of the Rio Grande	UN	Paul Sawtell
Roughly Speaking	WB	Max Steiner
San Antonio	WB	Max Steiner
Strange Affair of Uncle Harry, The	UN	Hans J. Salter
Sunset in El Dorado	REP	Dale Butts
Swing Out, Sister	UN	Milton Rosen
Tell It to a Star	REP	Dale Butts
To Have and Have Not	WB	Franz Waxman
Utah	REP	Dale Butts
Vampire's Ghost, The	REP	Richard Cherwin
White Pongo	PRC	Leo Erdody
Who's Guilty?	COL	Lee Zahler
Why Girls Leave Home	PRC	Walter Greene
Woman in Green, The	UN	Hans J. Salter
Wonder Man	UA	Louis Forbes

1946

Abilene Town	UA	Gerard Carbonara
Alias Mr. Twilight	COL	Paul Sawtell
Bachelor's Daughters, The	UA	W. Franke Harling
Blondie Knows Best	COL	Alexander Steinert
Brute Man, The	UN	Hans J. Salter
Courage of Lassie	MGM	Scott Bradley/Bronislau Kaper
Cuban Pete	UN	Milton Rosen
Dangerous Business	COL	Mario Castelnuovo-Tedesco
Detour to Danger	IND	Lee Zahler
Don Ricardo Returns	PRC	Alexander Steinert
Dressed to Kill	UN	Hans J. Salter
Gay Blades	REP	Dale Butts
Gung Ho!	UN	Hans J. Salter/Frank Skinner
Home on the Range	REP	Dale Butts
Hop Harrigan (serial)	COL	Lee Zahler
In Old Sacramento	REP	Charles Maxwell
Madonna's Secret, The	REP	Joseph Dubin
Magnificent Doll, The	UN	Hans J. Salter
My Pal Trigger	REP	Dale Butts
Night Editor	COL	Mario Castelnuovo-Tedesco

O. S. S.	PAR	Daniele Amfitheatrof/ Heinz Roemheld
Out California Way	REP	Nathan Scott
People Are Funny	PAR	Rudy Schrager
Perilous Holiday	COL	Paul Sawtell
Personality Kid, The	COL	Alexander Steinert
Piccadilly Incident	BRI	Anthony Collins
Rainbow over Texas	REP	Dale Butts
Rendezvous with Annie	REP	Nathan Scott/Joseph Dubin
Slightly Scandalous	UN	Milton Rosen
Son of the Guardsman (serial)	COL	Lee Zahler
Spider Woman Strikes Back, The	UN	Milton Rosen
Terror by Night	UN	Hans J. Salter
That Brennan Girl	REP	George Anthiel
Thrill of Brazil, The	COL	Leo Arnaud
Thunder Town	PRC	Lee Zahler
Utamaro's World	JAP	Ryohei Hirose
Yank in London, A	TCF	Anthony Collins

1947

Actualities Prehistoriques (short)	FRA	Claude Luter
Actualities Romaines (short)	FRA	Claude Luter
Blonde Savage	PRC	Leo Erdody
Christmas Eve	UA	Heinz Roemheld
Courtneys of Curzon Street, The	BRI	Anthony Collins
Croisiere pour l'Inconnu	FRA	Hubert Rostaing
Fighting Vigilantes, The	PRC	Walter Greene
Flame, The	REP	Heinz Roemheld
Gas House Kids in Hollywood, The	PRC	Albert Glasser
Hight Conquest	MON	Lucien Moraweck/Lyn Murray
It Had to Be You	COL	Heinz Roemheld
Jack Armstrong (serial)	COL	Lee Zahler
Life in Bloom (see Michurin)		
Love from a Stranger	EL	Hans Salter
Millie's Daughter	COL	Arthur Morton
Swell Guy	UN	Frank Skinner
Time Out of Mind	UN	Mario Castelnuevo-Tedesco/Ferde Grofe/Miklos Rozsa
Trouble with Women, The	PAR	Robert Emmett Dolan/ Victor Young
Wild Country	PRC	Walter Greene
Wyoming	REP	Ernest Gold/Nathan Scott

1948

Abraham and Isaac	IND	Milton Rosen
Begone Dull Care (short)	CAN	Oscar Peterson
Call Northside 777	TCF	Alfred Newman
Cass Timberlane	MGM	Roy Webb

Cat That Hated People, The (short)	MGM	Scott Bradley
Dangerous Years, The	TCF	Rudy Schrager
Daniel in the Lion's Den	IND	Milton Rosen
Five Days and Five Nights	RUS	Dimitri Shostakovich
For You I Die	FC	Paul Sawtell
Frontier Revenge	IND	Walter Greene
Fury at Furnace Creek	TCF	David Raksin
Girl from Manhattan, The	UA	Heinz Roemheld
He Walked by Night	EL	Leonid Raab
Hollow Triumph	EL	Sol Kaplan
Luck of the Irish, The	TCF	Cyril Mockridge
Muscle Beach (short)	IND	Earl Robinson
Of Such Is the Kingdom	IND	Milton Rosen
Opus 1 (short)	DEN	Bent Fabricius-Bjerre
Paradine Case, The	SRO	Franz Waxman
Raising of Lazarus, The	IND	Milton Rosen
Ruthless	EL	Werner Janssen
16 Fathoms Deep	MON	Rene Garriguene
So Evil My Love	PAR	William Alwyn/Victor Young
So Well Remembered	RKO	Hanns Eisler
Song Is Born, A	RKO	Hugo Friedhofer
That Lady in Ermine	TCF	Alfred Newman
They Live by Night	RKO	Leigh Harline
Trouble Preferred	TCF	Lucien Cailliet
Tumbleweed Trail	PRC	Karl Hajos
Voice of the Turtle, The	WB	Max Steiner
Walls of Jericho, The	TCF	Alfred Newman
Yellow Sky	TCF	Alfred Newman

1949

Autour d'un Recif (short)	FRA	Andre Hodeir
Best Years, The	MGM	Leo Shuken
Big Wheel, The	UA	Gerard Carbonara/Nat Finston/John Leipold
Dark Past, The	COL	George Duning
Deputy Marshal	LIP	Mahlon Merrick
Everybody Does It	TCF	Alfred Newman
Family Honeymoon	UN	Frank Skinner
Farewell to Youth	ITA	S. Blanc
Father Was a Fullback	TCF	Cyril Mockridge
Lust for Gold	COL	George Duning
Massacre River	AA	John Leipold/Lucien Moraweck
My Own True Love	PAR	Robert Emmett Dolan
Powder River Rustlers	REP	Stanley Wilson
Red Desert	LIP	Walter Greene
Saint-Paul-de-Vence (short)	FRA	Henri Crolla
Shamrock Hill	EL	Herschel Burke Gilbert
Slightly French	COL	George Duning
Sun Comes Up, The	MGM	Andre Previn

Whispering Smith	WB	Adolph Deutsch
Wild Weed	IND	Raoul Kraushaar
Yes, Sir, That's My Baby	UN	Walter Scharf

1950

American Guerrilla in the Philippines, An	TCF	Cyril Mockridge
Bee at the Beach (short)	DIS	Joseph Dubin
Between Midnight and Dawn	COL	George Duning
Cheaper by the Dozen	TCF	Cyril Mockridge
Chicken in the Rough (short)	DIS	Joseph Dubin
Cold Storage (short)	DIS	Joseph Dubin
DuPont Story, The	IND	Mahlon Merrick
Farewell to Yesterday	TCF	Louis Applebaum
Francis	UN	Frank Skinner
Giddyap (short)	COL	David Raksin
Girl from San Lorenzo, The	UA	Albert Glasser
Guilty of Treason	EL	Hugo Friedhofer
Gunfire	LIP	Albert Glasser
Hills of Oklahoma	REP	Stanley Wilson
I Killed Geronimo	EL	Darrell Calker
If You Don't Watch Out (short)	IND	Joseph Dubin
Killer That Stalked New York, The	COL	Hans J. Salter
Man Who Cheated Himself, The	TCF	Louis Forbes
Miner's Daughter, The (short)	COL	Gail Kubik
Mister 880	TCF	Sol Kaplan
Mother Didn't Tell Me	TCF	Cyril Mockridge
Petty Girl, The	COL	George Duning
Please Believe Me	MGM	Hans J. Salter
Plutopia (short)	DIS	Joseph Dubin
Return of Jesse James, The	LIP	Ferde Grofe/Albert Glasser
Ring Around the Moon	BRI	Richard Addinsell
Rio Grande	REP	Victor Young
Rocketship X-M	LIP	Ferde Grofe/Albert Glasser
Rogues of Sherwood Forest	COL	Arthur Morton/Heinz Roemheld
Roll, Thunder, Roll	EL	Ralph Stanley
Salt Lake Raiders	REP	Stanley Wilson
Sampan Boy (short)	ITA	Piero Piccioni
There's a Girl in My Heart	EL	Herschel Burke Gilbert
Tripoli	PAR	Lucien Cailliet
UCLA Story, The	IND	Mahlon Merrick
Underworld Story, The	UA	David Rose
Union Station	PAR	Heinz Roemheld/Leigh Harline
West of the Brazos	LIP	Walter Greene
When Willie Comes Marching Home	TCF	Alfred Newman
Where the Sidewalk Ends	TCF	Cyril Mockridge
Woman from Headquarters, The	REP	Dale Butts

Works of Calder, The (short)	IND	John Cage

1951

Abbott & Costello Meet the Invisible Man	UN	Hans J. Salter
African Queen, The	UA	Allan Gray
Big Carnival, The (Ace in the Hole)	PAR	Hugo Friedhofer
Big Lie, The (short)	IND	Gerald Fried
Cattle Queen	UA	Darrell Calker
Day of the Fight (short)	IND	Gerald Fried
Elephant Stampede	MON	Raoul Kraushaar
Family Circus (short)	COL	Ernest Gold
Family Secret, The	COL	George Duning
Frenchie	UN	Hans J. Salter
Georgie and the Dragon (short)	COL	Ernest Gold
Goodbye, My Fancy	WB	Daniele Amfitheatrof
High and Dry (The Maggie)	BRI	John Addison
Home Town Story	MGM	Louis Forbes
Icebreaker (short)	IND	Gerald Fried
Lady and the Bandit, The	COL	George Duning
Lady with the Lamp, The	BRI	Anthony Collins
M	COL	Michel Michelet
Maggie, The (see High and Dry)		
Man in the Saddle	COL	George Duning
Molly	PAR	Nathan Van Cleave
Never Trust a Gambler	COL	Arthur Morton
New Mexico	UA	Rene Garriguene
Oklahoma Justice	MON	Raoul Kraushaar
One Man's Lifetime	IND	Mahlon Merrick
Prowler, The	UA	Lyn Murray
Quebec	PAR	Edward Plumb/Nathan Van Cleave
Return of Gilbert and Sullivan, The	UA	Lyn Murray
Skipalong Rosenbloom	UA	Irving Gertz
Storm over Tibet	COL	Leith Stevens
Strange Door, The	UN	Hans J. Salter
Terres et Flammes (short)	FRA	Henri Crolla/Andre Hodeir
13th Letter, The	TCF	Alex North
This Is Korea	REP	Victor Young
Wonderful Life, A	IND	Louis Forbes

1952

Actualities Gauloises (short)	FRA	Claude Luter
Affair in Monte Carlo (Twenty-Four Hours in the Life of a Woman)	AA	Robert Gill/Philip Green
Antipolis (short)	FRA	Claude Luter
At Sword's Point	RKO	Roy Webb
Belles on Their Toes	TCF	Cyril Mockridge
Bielles des Sables (short)	FRA	Andre Hodeir

Big Jim McLain	WB	Paul Dunlap
Big Trees, The	WB	Heinz Roemheld
Black Castle, The	UN	Hans J. Salter
Black Lash, The	REA	Walter Greene
Bloodhounds of Broadway	TCF	David Raksin
Brigand, The	COL	Mario Castelnuovo-Tedesco
Bugles in the Afternoon	WB	Dimitri Tiomkin
Captive City	UA	Jerome Moross
Clash by Night	RKO	Roy Webb
Deadline--U. S. A.	TCF	Cyril Mockridge
Death of a Salesman	COL	Alex North
Diplomatic Courier	TCF	Sol Kaplan
Fargo	MON	Raoul Kraushaar
Finders Keepers	UN	Hans J. Salter
First Time, The	COL	Frederick Hollander
5,000 Fingers of Dr. T, The	COL	Hans J. Salter/Frederick Hollander/Heinz Roemheld
Geisha Girl	LIP	Albert Glasser
Hellgate	LIP	Paul Dunlap
Hotsy Footsy (short)	UPA	Shorty Rogers
Iron Mistress, The	WB	Max Steiner
Japanese War Bride	TCF	Arthur Lange
Jour en Suede, Un (short)	FRA	Claude Luter
Just for You	PAR	Hugo Friedhofer
Kangaroo	TCF	Sol Kaplan
Las Vegas Story, The	RKO	Leigh Harline
Life Goes On (short)	FRA	Claude Luter
Lion and the Horse, The	WB	Max Steiner
Lydia Bailey	TCF	Hugo Friedhofer
Macao	RKO	Anthony Collins
Madeline (short)	UPA	David Raksin
Marrying Kind, The	COL	Hugo Friedhofer
Navajo	LIP	Leith Stevens
O. Henry's Full House	TCF	Cyril Mockridge
One Big Affair	SPA	Luis Hernandez Breton
Opus 65 (short)	BRI	Richard Arnell
Outcasts of Poker Flat, The	TCF	Hugo Friedhofer
Paula	COL	George Duning
Pride of St. Louis, The	TCF	Arthur Lange
Rancho Notorious	RKO	Hugo Friedhofer
Red Planet Mars	UA	Mahlon Merrick
Red Skies of Montana	TCF	Sol Kaplan
Return of the Texan	TCF	Sol Kaplan
Route de Suede, La (short)	FRA	Claude Luter
Saint-Tropez, Devoir de Vacances (short)	FRA	Andre Hodeir
San Francisco Story, The	WB	Paul Dunlap
Scandal Sheet	COL	George Duning
Sloppy Jalopy (short)	UPA	David Raksin
Sniper, The	COL	George Antheil
Sound Off	COL	George Duning

Tarzan and the She-Devil (Tarzan Meets the Vampire)	IND	Paul Sawtell
This Is Cinerama	CIN	Howard Jackson
Victory at Sea (series)	TV	Richard Rodgers
Viva Zapata!	TCF	Alex North
Water Birds (short)	DIS	Paul Smith
We're Not Married	TCF	Cyril Mockridge
Willie the Kid (short)	UPA	Ernest Gold

1953

Abbott & Costello Meet Dr. Jekyll and Mr. Hyde	UN	Hans J. Salter
All Ashore	COL	George Duning
Bigamist, The	DCA	Leith Stevens
Black Vampire, The (Vampire Negro, El)	ARG	Juan Ehler
Blueprint for Murder	TCF	David Raksin
Cat Women of the Moon	AST	Elmer Bernstein
Chasseur de Chez Maxim's, Le	FRA	Paul Misraki
City of Bad Men	TCF	Lionel Newman
Fantasie au Vieux-Colombier (short)	FRA	Claude Luter
Fear and Desire	IND	Gerald Fried
Gerald McBoing Boing (short)	UPA	Ernest Gold
Gerald McBoing Boing's Symphony (short)	UPA	Ernest Gold
Glory Brigade, The	TCF	Lionel Newman
How to Marry a Millionaire	TCF	Alfred Newman/Cyril Mockridge
Island in the Sky	WB	Hugo Friedhofer
Last of the Comanches	COL	George Duning
Man Behind the Gun, The	WB	David Buttolph
Pickup on South Street	TCF	David Raksin
Robot Monster	AST	Elmer Bernstein
Saint-Germaine-des-Pres (short)	FRA	Claude Luter
Salome	COL	George Duning
Story of Bicycles, The (short)	FRA	Hubert Rostaing
Tanga Tika	IND	Les Baxter
Taxi	TCF	Leigh Harline/David Raksin
Thunder in the East	PAR	Hugo Friedhofer

1954

Bengal Brigade	UN	Hans J. Salter
Black Horse Canyon	UN	Hans J. Salter/Frank Skinner
Black Shield of Falworth, The	UN	Hans J. Salter/Herman Stein
Blood Money	IND	Gerald Fried
Creature from the Black Lagoon, The	UN	Hans J. Salter/Herman Stein/Henry Mancini/Milt Rosen/Robert Emmett Dolan

Desiree	TCF	Alex North
Dixieland Droopy (short)	MGM	Scott Bradley
End of the Road	BRI	John Addison
Far Country, The	UN	Hans J. Salter
Four Guns to the Border	UN	Hans J. Salter/Frank Skinner/Henry Mancini
Johnny Dark	UN	Hans J. Salter
Kiss of Fire	UN	Hans J. Salter
Money from Home	PAR	David Raksin
Naked Alibi	UN	Hans J. Salter
One Good Turn	BRI	John Addison
Paratrooper	COL	John Addison
Red Beret, The (see Paratrooper)		
River of No Return	TCF	David Raksin/Cyril Mock-ridge
Saskatchewan	UN	Hans J. Salter
Sign of the Pagan	UN	Hans J. Salter/Frank Skinner
Silent Raiders	LIP	Elmer Bernstein
Tanganyika	UN	Hans J. Salter
Yankee Pasha	UN	Hans J. Salter

1955

A Propos d'Une Riviere (short)	FRA	Henri Crolla/Andre Ho-deir
Abbott & Costello Meet the Mummy	UN	Hans J. Salter
Bras de la Seine, Les (short)	FRA	Henri Crolla
Captain Lightfoot	UN	Hans J. Salter
Creeping Unknown, The (Quater-mass Experiment, The)	BRI	James Bernard
Dementia	IND	George Anthiel
Enrico Cuisinier (short)	FRA	Henri Crolla
Etoiles en Croisette (short)	FRA	Sidney Bechet
Gas-Oil	FRA	Henri Crolla
House of Bamboo	TCF	David Raksin
Hunters of the Deep	DCA	George Anthiel
Jay Walker, The (short)	UPA	Billy May
Kentuckian, The	UA	Bernard Herrmann
Key Man, The	UA	Les Baxter
Mad at the World	FIL	Leith Stevens
Man Without a Star	UN	Hans J. Salter
My Dog (short)	FRA	Henri Crolla
Neiges (short)	FRA	Henri Crolla
Picnic	COL	George Duning
Private War of Major Benson, The	UN	Henry Mancini/Herman Stein
Quatermass Experiment, The (see Creeping Unknown, The)		
Racers, The	TCF	Alex North
Special Delivery	COL	Bernhard Kaun
This Island Earth	UN	Hans J. Salter/Herman Stein/Henry Mancini

This Strange Passion (El)	SPA	Luis Hernandez Breton
Touch and Go	BRI	John Addison
Violent Saturday	TCF	Hugo Friedhofer
Wetbacks	IND	Les Baxter
White Feather	TCF	Hugo Friedhofer

1956

Atlantic Salmon, The (short)	FRA	Henri Crolla
Battle of Algiers, The	FRA	Gillo Pontecorvo/Ennio Morricone
Blues Pattern (short)	IND	Shorty Rogers
Brave One, The	RKO	Victor Young
Case of the Mukkinese Battlehorn, The (short)	BRI	Edwin Astley
Charley Moon	BRI	Leslie Bricusse
Ciel est par Dessus le Toit, Le (short)	FRA	Henri Crolla
Donna che Venne del Mare, La	ITA	Piero Piccioni
Edge of the City	MGM	Leonard Rosenman
Finestra sul Luna Park, La	ITA	Piero Piccioni
Flying Carpet, The	RUS	Nadeshda Simonyan
Forbidden Planet	MGM	David Rose/Louis and Bebe Barron
Fresh Air (short)	FRA	Henri Crolla
Girl Can't Help It, The	TCF	David Raksin/Lionel Newman
Great Day in the Morning	RKO	Leith Stevens
Helen Keller in Her Story	IND	Morgan Lewis
I'll Cry Tomorrow	MGM	Alex North
Immortal Garrison, The	RUS	V. Basner
Josephine and Men	BRI	John Addison
Lady Godiva	UN	Hans J. Salter
Leon la Lune (short)	FRA	Henri Crolla
Mademoiselle Mosquito	GER	Peter Kreuder
Mole People, The	UN	Hans J. Salter/Herman Stein/Heinz Roemheld
Plan Nine from Outer Space (Grave Robbers from Outer Space)	DCA	Gordon Zahler
Poor but Handsome (Girl in a Bikini/Poveri ma Belli)	ITA	Piero Piccioni
Raw Edge, The	UN	Hans J. Salter
Rawhide Years, The	UN	Hans J. Salter
Rendez-vous a Melbourne	FRA	Christian Chevallier
Shiralee, The	AUT	Matyas Seiber
Somebody Up There Likes Me	MGM	Bronislau Kaper
Super-Giant 2 (Spacemen Against the Vampires from Space)	JAP	Chumei Watanabe
Terre Fleurie (short)	FRA	Henri Crolla/Andre Hodeir
There's Always Tomorrow	UN	Heinz Roemheld/Herman Stein
Three Little Bops (short)	WB	Shorty Rogers

Vampiri, I	ITA	Franco Mannino/Roman Vlad
Walk the Proud Land	UN	Hans J. Salter

1957

All at Sea (Barnacle Bill)	BRI	John Addison
Bachelor Party, The	UA	Alex North
Barnacle Bill (see All at Sea)		
Bayou	UA	Gerald Fried
China Gate	TCF	Max Steiner/Victor Young
Dangerous Age, A	CAN	Phil Nimmons
Desire Takes the Men	FRA	Hubert Rostaing
Dino	AA	Gerald Fried
End of an Era, The (short)	IND	David Amram
Incredible Shrinking Man, The	UN	Hans J. Salter
Joe Dakota	UN	Hans J. Salter
Kid, The (Monello, Il) (reissue)	UA	Piero Piccioni
Land Unknown, The	UN	Hans J. Salter
M Squad (series)	TV	Gerald Fried
Man in the Shadow, The	UN	Hans J. Salter
Midnight Story, The	UN	Hans J. Salter
Nata di Marzo	ITA	Piero Piccioni
Secret of the Sierra Dorada, The	ITA	Piero Piccioni
Simple Histoire, Une	FRA	Philippe Sarde
Simple Story, A (see Simple Histoire, Une)		
Susanna tutta Panna	ITA	Piero Piccioni
Sweet Smell of Success, The	UA	Elmer Bernstein/Chico Hamilton/Fred Katz
3:10 to Yuma	COL	George Duning
Vampiro, El	MEX	Gustavo C. Carreon
Vicious Breed, The	SWE	Les Baxter
Way to the Gold, The	TCF	Lionel Newman
Williamsburg: The Story of a Patriot	IND	Bernard Herrmann

1958

Anthology of Italian Cinema, The	ITA	Piero Piccioni
Appointment with a Shadow	UN	Hans J. Salter
Ballerina ed il Buon Dio, La	ITA	Piero Piccioni
Bons Amis, Les (short)	FRA	Christian Chevallier
Boss, The	ARG	Lalo Schifrin
Bravados, The	TCF	Hugo Friedhofer/Alfred Newman
Castles Through the Ages (short)	FRA	Andre Hodeir
Cette Nuit-la	FRA	Claude Bolling
Chemins de Lumiere	FRA	Christian Chevallier
Cinerama: South Seas Adventure	CIN	Alex North
Curse of the Faceless Man, The	UA	Gerald Fried
Deux Hommes dans Manhattan	FRA	Christian Chevallier/Martial Solal

Deux Plumes, Les (short)	FRA	Henri Crolla
Fantasticna Balada	YUG	Bojan Adamic
Flame Barrier, The	UA	Gerald Fried
Girls for the Summer (Racconti d'Estate)	ITA	Piero Piccioni
Glass (short)	HOL	Pim Jacobs
Harlem Wednesday (short)	IND	Benny Carter
Horror of Dracula	BRI	James Bernard/John Hollingsworth
Hot Car Girl	IND	Cal Tjader
I, Mobster	TCF	Gerald Fried
Indiscreet	WB	Richard Rodney Bennett/ Ken Jones
Life Together	FRA	Hubert Rostaing
Lost Missile, The	UA	Gerald Fried
Machine Gun Kelly	AI	Gerald Fried
Me and the Colonel	COL	George Duning
No Time for Sergeants	WB	Ray Heindorf
Operation Time Bomb	FRA/ ITA	Henri Crolla/Andre Hodeir
Parisienne, La	FRA	Henri Crolla/Andre Hodeir/Hubert Rostaing
Ragazzi del Parioli, I	ITA	Piero Piccioni
Rosemary	GER	Norbert Schultze
Sins of Youth	FRA	Henri Crolla/Andre Hodeir
Summer Love	UN	Hans J. Salter
T-Bird Gang, The	IND	Shelly Manne
Tempest, The	ITA	Piero Piccioni
Terror in the Haunted House	HOW	Darrell Calker
Three Rooms in Manhattan	IND	Mal Waldron
Tripes au Soleil, Les	FRA/ ITA	Andre Hodeir

1959

Adventure in Capri	ITA	Piero Piccioni
Ataud del Vampiro, El (Vampire's Coffin, The)	MEX	Gustavo C. Carreon
Attack of the Giant Leeches	AI	Alexander Laszlo
Battle of the Volga, The (Battellieri del Volga, I)	ITA	Piero Piccioni
Beat Girl (see Wild for Kicks)		
Black Orpheus (Orfeo Negro)	BRA	Luis Bonfa/Antonio Carlos Jobim
Blind Date	BRI	Richard Rodney Bennett
Breathless (A Bout de Souffle)	FRA	Martial Solal
Breve Amori a Palma di Majorca	ITA	Piero Piccioni
Chaplin Revue, The	UA	Charles Chaplin
Cool Sound from Hell, A	CAN	Phil Nimmons
Get Outta Town	IND	Bill Holman
Golden Fish, The (short)	FRA	Henri Crolla/Andre Hodeir

Goliath and the Barbarians	AI	Les Baxter
Holiday for Lovers	TCF	David Raksin
Ideal Palace, The (short)	FRA	Andre Hodeir
Impiegato, L'	ITA	Piero Piccioni
Liaisons Dangereuses, Les	FRA	Thelonius Monk/Jack Murray/Duke Jordan
Mighty Jungle, The	IND	Les Baxter
Night Train (Pociag)	POL	Andrzej Trzaskowski
On n'Enterre pas le Dimanche	FRA	Eric Dixon/Kenny Clarke
Race for Space, The	IND	Elmer Bernstein
Run with the Devil (Via Margutta)	ITA	Piero Piccioni
Sacred Idol, The	IND	Les Baxter
Skyscraper (short)	IND	Teo Macero
Slippery When Wet	IND	Bud Shank
Tempi Duri per I Vampiri (Hard Times for Vampires)	ITA	Armando Trovajoli
Three Worlds of Gulliver, The	COL	Bernard Herrmann
Wasp Woman, The	AI	Fred Katz
We Are the Lambeth Boys	BRI	John Dankworth
Wild for Kicks (Beat Girl)	BRI	John Barry
Witness in the City	FRA/ ITA	Barney Willen

1960

Adolescents, The (Dolci Inganni, I)	ITA	Piero Piccioni
Adventures of a Photographer, The (short)	FRA	Martial Solal
Atom Age Vampire (Seddock, l'Erede di Satana)	ITA	Armando Trovajoli
Bonanza (series)	TV	David Rose/Harry Sukman
Candide	FRA	Hubert Rostaing
Criminal, The	BRI	John Dankworth
Curse of the Vampire (Last Victim of the Vampire, The/Playgirls and the Vampire)	ITA	Aldo Piga
Femme Image, La (short)	CAN	Bobby Jaspar/Renc Thomas
Flight	IND	Laurindo Almeida
From a Roman Balcony (Day of Sin, A/Giornata Balorda, Una)	ITA	Piero Piccioni
Glass Mountain, The	POL	Krzystof Komeda
Hands of Orlac, The	BRI/ FRA	Claude Bolling
Hunchback of Rome (Gobbo, Il)	ITA	Piero Piccioni
Innocent Sorcerers	POL	Kryzstof Komeda
Israel	WB	Elmer Bernstein
It Happened All Night	FRA	Martial Solal
Lady with the Dog, The	RUS	Nadeshda Simonyan
Lawbreakers, The	IND	Johnny Mandel
Little Red Riding Hood and Tom Thumb vs. The Monsters	MEX	Raul Lavista

Love a la Carte (Hungry for Love/ Adua e le Compagne)	ITA	Piero Piccioni
Magnificent Seven, The	UA	Elmer Bernstein
Mani in Alto	ITA	Piero Piccioni
Men and Women	FRA	Claude Bolling
My Friend Pierrot	FRA	Henri Crolla
Never Let Go	BRI	John Barry
Night Is a Sorcerer (short)	FRA	Sidney Bechet
On Friday at Eleven	FRA/ GER/ ITA	Claude Bolling
Photo Souvenir (short)	FRA	Henri Crolla
Portes Claquent, Les	FRA	Michel Legrand
Primitifs du XIIIe, Les (short)	FRA	Henri Crolla/Andre Hodeir
Rooftops of New York (short)	IND	Joseph Liebman
Saint-Tropez Blues	FRA/ ITA	Henri Crolla
See You Tomorrow	POL	Kryzstof Komeda
Si le Vent te Faire Peur	BEL	Martial Solal
Ski Troop Attack	IND	Fred Katz
Sundowners, The	WB	Dimitri Tiomkin
Sunrise at Campobello	WB	Franz Waxman
Swedish Girls in Paris	SWE	Martial Solal
Vitrine Sous la Mer (short)	FRA	Henri Crolla/Andre Hodeir

1961

A Toute Heure en Tour Saison (short)	FRA	Martial Solal
Assassin, The	ITA	Piero Piccioni
Barefoot Adventure	IND	Bud Shank
Bloody Vampire, The (Vampiro Sangriento, El)	MEX	Luis Hernandez Breton
Boy in the Tree	SWE	Quincy Jones
Crimebusters, The (series)	TV	Jerry Goldsmith
Due Marescialli, I	ITA	Piero Piccioni
Duel of the Titans (Romulus and Remus)	ITA	Piero Piccioni
Eruption (Congo Vivo)	ITA	Piero Piccioni
Explosive Generation, The	UA	Hal Borne
Falling in Love	BRI	John Barry
Fat and the Lean, The (short)	FRA	Kryzstof Komeda
Gioventu di Notte	ITA	Piero Piccioni
Guns of the Black Witch	AI	Les Baxter
Hamilton in the Musical Festival (short)	BRI	John Dankworth
Hamilton, the Musical Elephant (short)	BRI	John Dankworth
Hercules at the Center of the Earth (Hercules in the Haunted World/ Hercules Against the Vampires)	ITA	Armando Trovajoli

Imprevisto, L'	ITA	Piero Piccioni
King of the Roaring Twenties	AA	Franz Waxman
Lisette	IND	Les Baxter
Love of the Vampire, The (Amante del Vampiro, L')	ITA	Aldo Piga
Lovemakers, The (Viaccia, La)	ITA	Piero Piccioni
Night Tide	IND	David Raksin
Nostradamus and the Destroyer of Monsters	MEX	George Perez
Nuda ogni Sera	ITA	Piero Piccioni
Orlak, the Hell of Frankenstein	MEX	George Perez
Portrait Robot	FRA	Bill Byers
Ragazze Bruciate Verdi, Le	ITA	Piero Piccioni
Reptilicus	AI	Les Baxter
Sad Young Men, The	ARG	Sergio Mihanovich
Svedesi, Le	ITA	Piero Piccioni
Tant Qu'il y Aura des Capricornes (short)	FRA	Martial Solal
Voici le Ski (short)	FRA	Andre Hodeir
Warriors 5	AI	Les Baxter/Ronald Stein
World of the Vampire	MEX	Gustavo C. Carreon

1962

Alibi per Morire, Un	ITA	Piero Piccioni
Ambulance (short)	POL	Kryzstof Komeda
Amorous Prawn, The (see Playgirl and the War Minister, The)		
Anima Nera	ITA	Piero Piccioni
Anni Ruggenti	ITA	Piero Piccioni
Beauty and the Beast	UA	Hugo Friedhofer
Betrayers, The	BRI	John Barry
Bidone, Il (Swindle, The)	ITA	Nino Rota
Birdman of Alcatraz	UA	Elmer Bernstein
Bread of the Sky, The (short)	FRA	Hubert Rostaing
Commare Secca, La	ITA	Piero Piccioni
Conquered City (Captive City, The/ Citta Prigioniera, La)	ITA	Piero Piccioni
Cuccagna, La	ITA	Ennio Morricone
D-Day Seen Through American Eyes	IND	Elmer Bernstein
Daughter of the Sun God	IND	Les Baxter
Dilemma	DEN	Gideon Nxomalo/Max Roach
Doucement les Basses	FRA/ ITA	Claude Bolling
Doulos, Le	FRA/ ITA	Jacques Loussier
Due Colonnelli, I	ITA	Piero Piccioni
Erik the Conqueror	AI	Les Baxter
Evil Eye, The	AI	Les Baxter
Giorno piu Corto, Il	ITA	Piero Piccioni
Giustiziere, Il	ITA	Piero Piccioni

Goliath and the Vampires	AI	Les Baxter
House of Sand, A	IND	Les Baxter
House on Bare Mountain	IND	Pierre Martel
In Capo al Mondo	ITA	Piero Piccioni
Invasion of the Vampires, The	MEX	Luis Hernandez Breton
Janine (short)	FRA	Rene Urtreger
Jeu 1 (short)	FRA	Jacques Loussier
Laurence (short)	FRA	Lou Bennett
Lost Battalion, The	AI	Les Baxter
Mamma Roma	ITA	Carlo Rustichelli
Mammals (short)	POL	Kryzstof Komeda
Marcia su Roma, La	ITA	Piero Piccioni
Matter of WHO, A	BRI	Edwin Astley
Opening Tomorrow (1962)	POL	Kryzstof Komeda
Operation Heartbeat	TV	Lalo Schifrin
Parallels (short)	FRA	Pierre Michelot
Playgirl and the War Minister, The (Amorous Prawn, The)	BRI	John Barry
Saint vs. the Vampire Women, The (Santo Contro los Mujeres Vampiros)	MEX	Raul Lavista
Salvatore Giuliano	ITA	Piero Piccioni
Samson and the Seven Miracles of the World	AI	Les Baxter
Samson and the Slave Queen	AI	Les Baxter
Senilita	ITA	Piero Piccioni
Ski Total (short)	FRA	Andre Hodeir
Slaughter of the Vampires, The (Stragi dei Vampiri, La)	ITA	Aldo Piga
Slave, The (Son of Spartacus)	ITA	Piero Piccioni
Small World of Sammy Lee, The	BRI	Kenny Graham
Smemorato di Collegno, Lo	ITA	Piero Piccioni
Sorpasso, Il	ITA	Riz Ortolani
Tales of Terror	AI	Les Baxter
Toto Diabolicus	ITA	Piero Piccioni
Trauma	IND	Buddy Collette
Violent Life, A (Vita Violenta, Una)	ITA	Piero Piccioni
Voyage of Khonostrov, The (short)	FRA	Jacques Loussier
Wild Living	FRA/ ITA	Andre Hodeir/Hubert Rostaing
Wrong Arm of the Law, The	BRI	Richard Rodney Bennett
Young Sinner, The	IND	Shelly Manne

1963

A ... Is for Apple (short)	BRI	Jacques Loussier
Apache Gold	GER	Martin Boettcher
Attico, L'	ITA	Piero Piccioni
Battle Beyond the Sun	AI	Les Baxter
Bird Life in Mauritania (short)	FRA	Jacques Loussier
Black Sabbath	AI	Piero Piccioni
Boom, Il	ITA	Piero Piccioni
Carpetbaggers, The	PAR	Elmer Bernstein

Chicken, The (short)	FRA	Rene Urtreger
Commando	AI	Francesco Lavagnino
Contrechant	FRA	Maxim Saury
Cool World, The	IND	Mal Waldron
Curse of the Karnsteins, The (Maldicion de los Karnsteins, La)	ITA/ SPA	Carlo Savina
Day and the Hour, The	FRA/ ITA	Claude Bolling
Demon, The (Demonio, Il)	ITA	Piero Piccioni
Department 66 (short)	FRA	Jacques Loussier
Dr. No	UA	John Barry
Elizabeth Taylor in London	TV	John Barry
Epilogue	DEN	Kryzstof Komeda
Erotikon--Karussell der Leidenschaften	YUG	Bojan Adamic
Etudes (short)	FRA	Jacques Loussier
Goliath and the Sins of Babylon	ITA	Francesco de Masi
Great Rights, The (short)	IND	Gerald Fried
High and Low	JAP	Masaru Sato
McLintock!	UA	Frank de Vol
Maestro di Vigevano, Il	ITA	Piero Piccioni
Mani sulla Citta, Le	ITA	Piero Piccioni
Mepris, Le (Disprezzo, Il)	FRA	Georges Delerue
Mondo Cane	ITA	Riz Ortolani/Nino Oliviero
New Clothes	POL	Kryzstof Komeda
Ore dell'amore, Le	ITA	Ennio Morricone
Paris des Mannequins, Le (short)	FRA	Jacques Loussier
Parmigiana, La	ITA	Piero Piccioni
Refugees (short)	FRA	Jacques Loussier
Scale in Hi-Fi (Escala en Hi-Fi)	SPA	Waldo de los Rios
Successo, Il	ITA	Ennio Morricone
Sud-Express (short)	FRA	Jacques Loussier
Suleiman the Conqueror	ITA	Francesco de Masi
Ten Seconds That Shook the World	TV	Gerald Fried
Tentativo Sentimentale, Un	ITA	Piero Piccioni
Terrorist, The (Terrorista, Il)	ITA	Piero Piccioni
West (short)	FRA	Jacques Loussier
Winnetou I (see Apache Gold)		

1964

American Tragedy, An (Tragedia Americana, Una)	ITA	Piero Piccioni
Anges Gardiens (short)	FRA	Jacques Loussier
Backfire	FRA/ ITA/ SPA	Martial Solal
Before the Revolution	ITA	Leandro "Gato" Barbieri
Beyond the Great Wall	IND	traditional
Bikini Beach	AI	Les Baxter
Castle of the Living Dead, The	FRA/ ITA	Francesco Lavagnino

Cats (Kattorna)	SWE	Kryzstof Komeda
CirCarC Gear, The (short)	BRI	Johnny Hawksworth
Day of Infamy	TV	Gerald Fried
Disco Volante, Il	ITA	Piero Piccioni
Empty Canvas, The	EMB	Luis Enrique Bacalov
Fall of the Roman Empire, The	PAR	Dimitri Tiomkin
Fuga, La	ITA	Piero Piccioni
Good Life, The	FRA	Henri Lanoe
Help! My Snowman's Burning Down (short)	IND	Gerry Mulligan
Io la Conoscevo Bene	ITA	Piero Piccioni
Jolly Bad Fellow, A (They All Died Laughing)	BRI	Alan Haven/John Barry
Joy House	FRA	Lalo Schifrin
Last Man on Earth, The (Night Creatures)	LIP	Paul Sawtell/Bert Shefter
Longest Night, The	FRA	Chet Baker
Making of a President--1960, The	TV	Lalo Schifrin
Man Called Gringo, The	ITA	Piero Piccioni
Man in the Middle	TCF	John Barry/Lionel Bart
Muscle Beach Party	AI	Les Baxter
Naturally, It's Rubber (short)	BRI	Kenneth Graham
100 Horsemen (Cento Cavalieri, I)	ITA	Piero Piccioni
Pajama Party	AI	Les Baxter
Par un Beau Matin d'Ete	FRA	Michel Magne
Paris des Scandinaves, Le (short)	FRA	Jacques Loussier
Polyolefins (short)	BRI	Johnny Hawksworth
Rig Move (short)	BRI	Johnny Hawksworth
Sallah	ISR	Yohanan Zarai
Scene Nun, Take One (short)	BRI	Kenneth Graham
Sexy Probitissimo	ITA	Lallo Gori
Six Faces of Terylene (short)	BRI	Johnny Hawksworth
Snow (short)	BRI	Johnny Hawksworth/Daphne Oram
Space Monster	IND	Les Baxter
Three Nights of Love (Tre Notti d'Amore)	ITA	Giovanni Fusco/Piero Piccioni/Carlo Rustichelli
Time of Violence (Tiempo de Violencia)	SPA	Piero Piccioni
To Love	SWE	Bo Nilsson
Top Flight (short)	BRI	John Dankworth
Tre per una Rapina	ITA	Piero Piccioni
Tre Volti, I	ITA	Piero Piccioni
Visit, The	TCF	Hans-Martin Majewski
Vita Agra, La	ITA	Piero Piccioni
Woman Is a Marvelous Thing, A (Donna e una Cosa Meravigliosa, La)	ITA	Piero Piccioni

1965

Au Guadalquivir (short)	FRA	Jacques Loussier

Avatar Botanique de Melle Flora, L' (short)	FRA	Jacques Loussier
Billy the Kid vs. Dracula	EMB	Raoul Kraushaar
Bird, The (short)	IND	Paul Horn
Boy Ten Feet Tall, A	PAR	Les Baxter/Tristram Cary
Carousella (short)	BRI	Kenneth Graham
Crocodile Tears (short)	FRA	Dave Brubeck
Cuckoo Patrol	BRI	Kenneth Graham
Curse of the Green Eyes, The (Night of the Vampire/Fluch der Grunen Augen, Der)	GER/ YUG	Herbert Jarczyk
Deux Uraniums, Les (short)	FRA	Martial Solal
Devils of Darkness	TCF	Bernie Fenton
Dingaka	BRI	Basil Gary
Dr. Who and the Daleks	BRI	Malcolm Lockyer
Eva	FRA	Michel Legrand
Fanny Hill	IND	Erwin Halletz
Figlia del Capitano, La	ITA	Piero Piccioni
Four in the Morning	BRI	John Barry
From the Orient with Fury (Agente 077--dall'Oriente con Furore)	ITA	Piero Piccioni
Fumo di Londra	ITA	Piero Piccioni
Game Called Scruggs, A	BRI	John Dankworth
Harmony Abroad (short)	BRI	Johnny Hawksworth
I Salute the Mafia	FRA/ ITA	Hubert Rostaing
Italiani Brava Gente	ITA/ RUS	Armando Trovajoli
Jail Keys Made Here (short)	IND	Dave Brubeck
Journal of Combat, The (short)	FRA	Jacques Loussier
Life of the Locusts (short)	FRA	Jacques Loussier
Linesman, The (short)	BRI	Johnny Hawksworth
Love in Four Dimensions	ITA	Franco Mannino
M. M. M. 83--Missione Mortale Molo 83	ITA	Piero Piccioni
Metamorphosis of Cloportes, The	FRA	Jimmy Smith
Myth, The	ITA	Armando Trovajoli
Naked World of Harrison Marks, The	BRI	Johnny Hawksworth
Neutron and Fission, The (short)	FRA	Martial Solal
Nightmare Castle (Faceless Monster/Night of the Doomed/ Amanti d'Oltretomba, L')	ITA	Ennio Morricone
One Man and His Bank (short)	BRI	John Barry
Operation MJC (short)	FRA	Andre Hodeir
Penguin, The	POL	Kryzstof Komeda
Pierrot le Fou (Crazy Peter)	FRA/ ITA	Antoine Duhamel
Saharan Venture (short)	BRI	Kenneth Graham
Sal-a-Malle-Ek (short)	FRA	Mal Waldron
Sister of Satan, The	ITA/ YUG	Ralph Ferraro

Sophia Loren in Rome	TV	John Barry
Story of Taikoh, The	JAP	Yoshio Irino
Timber Move (short)	BRI	Kenneth Graham
Time Objectives (short)	FRA	Andre Hodeir
Up to His Ears	FRA/ ITA	Georges Delerue
Vauxhall, Bedford, England (short)	BRI	Johnny Hawksworth
War Lord, The	UN	Hans J. Salter/Jerome Moross
Who's Crazy?	IND	Ornette Coleman
World at Three, The (short)	BRI	John Dankworth
Wrestling Women vs. the Aztec Mummy, The	MEX	Antonio Diaz Conde

1966

Ballad of Emile, The (short)	FRA	Martial Solal
Barrier	POL	Kryzstof Komeda
Beast of Morocco (Hand of Night)	BRI	John Shakespeare
A Belles Dents	FRA/ GER	Jacques Loussier
Blood Drinkers, The (Vampire People, The)	PHI	Tito Arevalo
Blood Fiend (Female Fiend/Theater of Death, The)	BRI	Elizabeth Lutyens
Bougnats, Les (short)	FRA	Martial Solal
Can I Help You? (short)	BRI	Kenneth Graham
Carry On Screaming	BRI	Eric Rogers
Chaplin's Art of Comedy	IND	Elias Breeskin
Depart, Le	BEL	Kryzstof Komeda
Devil's Mistress, The	IND	Billy Allen/Doug Warren
Do You Like Girls?	FRA	Ward Swingle
Doomsday Flight	TV	Lalo Schifrin
Excuse Me, Are You For or Against? (Scusi, Lei e Favorevole o Contrario?)	ITA	Piero Piccioni
Fireball 500	AI	Les Baxter
Hunger (short)	DEN/ NOR/ SWE	Kryzstof Komeda
I Killed Rasputin	FRA	Andre Hossein
Island of Aphrodite, The	GRE	Mikis Theodorakis
Khartoum	UA	Frank Cordell
Lollipop Cover	IND	Ruby Raskin
Matchless	ITA	Gino Marinuzzi/Ennio Morricone
Matter of Honor, A	FRA/ ITA	Luis Enrique Bacalov
Minatomo Yoshitune	JAP	Toru Takemitsu
Naked Hearts	FRA	Serge Gainsbourg/Henri Renaud
Nostri Mariti, I	ITA	Piero Piccioni/Armando Trovajoli

Nuclear Reactor, The (short)	FRA	Martial Solal
Ohanahan	JAP	Noriyoshi Ogawa
Once Before I Die	WB	Gerald Fried
One of Our Spies Is Missing	MGM	Gerald Fried
Orpheon (short)	FRA	Martial Solal
Pistol for Ringo, A	ITA/ SPA	Ennio Morricone
Paranoia	ITA	Luis Enrique Bacalov/ Nino Rota/Teo Usuelli
Plainsman, The	UN	John Williams
Qualcono ha Tradito	ITA	Piero Piccioni
Queen of Blood (Planet of Blood)	AI	Leonard Moreland
Red Beard	JAP	Masaru Sato
Redeemer, The	IND	David Raksin
Second Truth, The	FRA/ ITA	Jacques Loussier
Secret Agent Superdragon	FRA/ GER/ ITA	Benedetto Ghiglia
Signalet (short)	DEN	Bill Evans
Streghe, Le	ITA	Ennio Morricone/Piero Piccioni
Study in Terror, A	COL	Patrick John Scott
Tant Qu'il Aura de l'Angoisse (short)	FRA	Martial Solal
This Property Is Condemned	WB	Kenyon Hopkins
Thunderbirds Are Go	BRI	Barry Gray
Tiko and the Shark	MGM	Francesco de Masi
Trap, The	BRI	Ron Goodwin
Vampire for Two, A	SPA	Anton Garcia Abril
Wake Up and Die	FRA/ ITA	Ennio Morricone
Where the Bullets Fly	BRI	Kenneth Graham

1967

Adios Gringo	FRA/ ITA/ SPA	Benedetto Ghiglia
Africa	IND	Alex North
Albert Peckingpaw's Revenge	IND	Harley Hatcher
Any Gun Can Play	ITA	Francesco de Masi
Birds, the Bees and the Italians, The	ITA	Carlo Rustichelli
Blood of Dracula's Castle, The	CRO	Lincoln Mayorage
Born Losers	AI	Mike Curb
Caio	IND	Ed Summerlin
Chimes at Midnight (Falstaff)	SPA/ SWI	Francesco Lavagnino
Come Impari ad Amare le Donne	ITA	Ennio Morricone
Dreamers	DEN	Erik Moseholm
Eric Soya's 17	DEN	Ole Hoeyer
Frontiers of Power (short)	BRI	Kenneth Graham

Galia	FRA	Ward Swingle
Glass Sphinx, The	EGY/ ITA/ SPA	Les Baxter/Roberto Pregadio
Gromaire (short)	FRA	Michel Portal
Island of the Lost	IND	George Bruns
Journey, A (Tabiji)	JAP	Mitsutada Ida
Just Routine (short)	BRI	Kenneth Graham
Karate Killers, The	IND	Gerald Fried
King of Hearts	UA	Georges Delerue
Labyrinthe	CAN	Eldon Rathburn
Lecon Particuliere, Le (see Tender Moment, The--1968)		
Marat/Sade (see Persecution of ...)		
Mercenaries, The	BRI	Jacques Loussier
More Than a Miracle (Cinderella--Italian Style/C'era una Volta)	ITA	Piero Piccioni
Navajo Joe	IND	Ennio Morricone
Our Time No. 1 (short)	BRI	Kenneth Graham
Peacemeal (short)	IND	Chico Hamilton
People Meet and Sweet Music Fills the Air	DEN/ SWE	Kryzstof Komeda
Persecution and Assassination of Jean-Paul Marat as Performed by the Inmates of the Asylum of Charenton under the Direction of the Marquis de Sade	BRI	Richard Peaslee
Population Explosion (short)	CAN	Ornette Coleman
Producers, The	EMB	John Morris
Question of Rape, A (Viol, Le)	FRA/ SWE	Michel Portal
Return of the Gunfighter, The	TV	Hans J. Salter
Rose for Everyone, A	ITA	Luis Enrique Bacalov
Rover, The	ITA	Ennio Morricone
Search and Research (short)	BRI	Johnny Hawksworth
Ski on the Wild Side	SIG	Billy Allen
Sky over Holland (short)	HOL	Robert Heppener
Small Propeller, The (short)	BRI	Johnny Hawksworth
Snake Pit and the Pendulum, The (Blood Demon, The)	GER	Peter Thomas
Soleil de Pierre (short)	FRA	Michel Portal
Something Nice to Eat (short)	BRI	Johnny Hawksworth
Sons and Daughters	IND	Virgil Gonsalves/Jon Hendricks
Sullivan's Empire	UN	Lalo Schifrin
Taste of Blood, A (Secret of Dr. Alucard, The)	IND	Larry Wellington
Temptation	ITA	Piero Piccioni
Three Sisters	JAP	Masaru Sato
Ti Ho Sposato per Allegria	ITA	Piero Piccioni
Timber (short)	DEN	Martial Solal
Triple Cross	WB	Georges Garvarentz
Tu Seras Terriblement Gentille	FRA	Jacques Loussier

Urbanissimo (short)	IND	Benny Carter
Vampire-Beast Craves Blood, The (Blood Beast Terror)	BRI	Paul Ferris
Vampire Women, The (Femmes Vampires, Les)	IND	Yvon Gerault
Vivre la Nuit	FRA/ ITA	Claude Bolling
We Are Young (short)	CAN	David Amram
Whatever Happened to Uncle Fred? (short)	BRI	Johnny Hawksworth
Young Rebel--Cervantes, The	AI	Les Baxter/Jean Ledrut/ Angel Arteaga

1968

Absolutely, Tomorrow (Ashita Koso)	JAP	Norio Kuwabara
All the Loving Couples	IND	Les Baxter
And for a Roof, a Sky Full of Stars	ITA	Ennio Morricone
Ant and the Aardvark, The (short)	IND	Doug Goodwin
Ant from U. N. C. L. E., The (short)	IND	Doug Goodwin
Beau Militaire, Le (short)	FRA	Jacques Loussier
Biches, Les	FRA/ ITA	Pierre Jansen
Black Sheep, The	ITA	Luis Enrique Bacalov
Born to Buck	IND	Dick Stabile
Boston Strangler, The	TCF	Lionel Newman
Bride Wore Black, The	FRA	Bernard Herrmann
Bullet for the General, A	ITA	Luis Enrique Bacalov
Challengers, The	IND	Pete Rugolo
Comandementi per un Gangster	ITA	Ennio Morricone
Detective, The	TCF	Jerry Goldsmith
Dirty Angels, The	ITA	Ennio Morricone
5, 000, 000 Years to Earth (Quatermass and the Pit)	BRI	Tristram Cary
Five Steps (short)	BRI	Johnny Hawksworth
Girls in the Sun	GRE	Stavros Xarchakos
Goke, Body Snatcher from Hell	JAP	Shunsuke Kikuchi
Grande Silenzio, Il	ITA	Ennio Morricone
Greek Pearls, The	GRE	Mimis Plessas
How to Make It	IND	Les Baxter
I Love You, I Hate You	BRI	John Dankworth
If He Hollers, Let Him Go	CIN	Coleridge-Taylor Perkinson
Istanbul Express	UN	Oliver Nelson
Jazzoo (short)	IND	Oliver Lake
Killing Game, The (Comic Strip Hero)	FRA	Jacques Loussier
Kuroneko (Black Cat)	JAP	Hikaru Hayashi
Mark of the Wolfman, The	SPA	Angel Arteaga
Mission: Stardust (Orbita Mortal)	SPA	Anton Garcia Abril
Mondo Balordo (Mondo Keyhole)	ITA	Lallo Gori

Orbita Mortal (see Mission: Stardust)		
Pick-Up (short)	FRA	Leandro "Gato" Barbieri
Quatermass and the Pit (see 5,000,000 Years to Earth)		
Racing World (short)	IND	Duke Ellington
Romeo and Juliet	PAR	Nino Rota
Ruma Is Going	JAP	Yoshio Mamiya
Santo and Blue Demon vs. the Monsters	MEX	Gustavo Cesar Carreon
Santo in the Revenge of the Vampire Women	MEX	Gustavo Cesar Carreon
Saul and David	ITA/ SPA	Teo Usuelli
Sebastian	PAR	Jerry Goldsmith
Seducers, The	ITA	Santa Romitelli
Take One Baby (short)	BRI	Johnny Hawksworth
Teacher Nansen (short)	DEN	Erik Moseholm
Tender Moment, The	FRA	Francis Lai
13 Days in France	FRA	Francis Lai
Track of Thunder	UA	John Caper Jr.
Vampire (Upior)	POL	Wojiech Kilar
Vampire and Sex, The (Vampiro y el Sexo, El)	MEX	Sergio Guerrero
Vampire Girls, The	MEX	Gustavo Cesar Carreon
Vengeance	ITA	Carlo Savina
Veridiquement Votre (short)	FRA	Martial Solal
Virginian, The (series)	TV	Percy Faith/Bernard Herrmann
Vixen	IND	William Loose
We Still Kill the Old Way	ITA	Luis Enrique Bacalov
Where Eagles Dare	MGM	Ron Goodwin
Woman Needs Loving, A	GER	Jacques Loussier
Young Animals, The	AI	Les Baxter
Zita	FRA	Francois de Roubaix

1969

Absolutely Natural (Assoluto Naturale, L'/He and She)	ITA	Ennio Morricone
Ace High (Quattro dell'Ave Maria, I)	ITA	Carlo Rustichelli
Battle of Britain, The	BRI	Ron Goodwin
Battle of Neretva	AI	Bernard Herrmann
Bequest for a Village (short)	BRI	Richard Arnell
Bicyclettes de Belsize, Les	BRI	Les Reed
Bomb, The	HOL	Robert Heppener
Brief Season	ITA	Ennio Morricone
Cantagallo (short)	BRI	Kenneth Graham
Che Guevara, El	ITA	Nico Fidenco
Cherry, Harry and Raquel	IND	Igo Kantor/William Loose
Decline and Fall of a Birdwatcher, The	BRI	Ron Goodwin
Dossier Prostitution	FRA	Jacques Loussier

Fangs of the Living Dead (see Malenka, Niece of the Vampire)		
Fanny Hill	IND	Clay Pitts
Figures in a Landscape	BRI	Richard Rodney Bennett
Follow Me	IND	Stu Phillips
Fraulein Doktor	ITA/ YUG	Ennio Morricone
Guess What Happened to Count Dracula? (Master of the Dungeon)	IND	Des Roberts
Heavens and the Earth, The	JAP	Isao Tomita
High Chaparral, The (series)	TV	Harry Sukman/David Rose
Hoa-Binh	FRA	Michel Portal
How, When and With Whom?	ITA	Armando Trovajoli
In the Year of the Lord	ITA	Armando Trovajoli
Mafia	ITA	Giovanni Fusco
Magic Christian, The	BRI	Ken Thorne
Malenka, Niece of the Vampire (Fangs of the Living Dead)	ITA/ SPA	Carlo Savina
Man from Nowhere, The	IND	Francesco de Masi
Master of the Dragon (see Guess What Happened to Count Dracula?)		
Murder Clinic, The	FRA/ ITA	Francesco de Masi
Naked Angels	IND	Jeffrey Simmons/Randy Steirling
Naked Vampire	FRA	Yvon Gerauld/Francis Tusques
Necropolis	ITA	Gavin Bryars
Picasso Summer	WB	Michel Legrand
Race for the Golden Flag (short)	BRI	Johnny Hawksworth
Sabata	ITA	Marcello Giombini
Scratch a Tiger (short)	IND	Doug Goodwin
Season of the Senses (Stagione dei Sensi)	ITA	Ennio Morricone
Second Chance (short)	IND	Bill Russo
Sette Baschi Rossi	ITA	Gianni Marchetti
Support Your Local Sheriff	UA	Jeff Alexander
Tower of the Devil	PHI	Pablo Vergara
Transit Supervan (short)	BRI	Johnny Hawksworth
Valley of Gwangi, The	WB	Jerome Moross
Voyage Vers la Lumiere (short)	FRA	Martial Solal
Woman of Everyone, The (Mulher de Todes, A)	BRA	Ana Soralina
You Only Love Once	SIG	Jacques Loussier
Zeta One	BRI	Johnny Hawksworth

1970

Absent-Minded	FRA	Vladimir Cosma
Alechinsky After Nature (short)	BEL/ FRA	Michel Portal
Anatomy of a Motor Oil (short)	BRI	Johnny Hawksworth
Antiseptics in Hospital (short)	BRI	Johnny Hawksworth

Bora Bora	AI	Les Baxter
Burn! (Queimada)	UA	Ennio Morricone
C. C. and Company	EMB	Lenny Stack
Charlie Brown Christmas, A (short)	CBS	Vince Guaraldi
Cities (short)	TV	Gerald Fried
Countess Dracula	BRI	Harry Robinson
Curse of the Vampires (Creatures of Evil)	PHI	Tito Arevalo
Daughters of Darkness (Promise of Red Lips/Erzebeth)	BEL/ FRA/ GER/ ITA	Francois de Roubaix
David Copperfield	BRI	Malcolm Arnold
Diamant, Le	FRA	Jacques Loussier
Dramma della Gelosia (Pizza Triangle, The)	ITA	Armando Trovajoli
Du Soleil Plein les Yeux	FRA	Francis Lai
Eggs (short)	IND	Quincy Jones
Elephant Called Slowly, An	BRI	Howard Blake
Engagement, The (short)	BRI	John Dankworth
Equinox	IND	John Caper Jr.
Eyewitness	BRI	Fairfield Parloer/Van der Graaf Generator
Fir Is Left, A	JAP	Mitsutada Ida
Fire (Feu) (short)	FRA	Michel Portal
Five-Man Army, The	ITA	Ennio Morricone
Frisson des Vampires, Le (Vampire Thrills/Sex and the Vampire)	FRA	Georges Acanthus
Great White Hope, The	TCF	Lionel Newman
Groupie Girl	BRI	John Fiddy
Hamlet	BRI	Patrick Gowers
Hawaii Five-O (series)	TV	Morton Stevens
Hawaiians, The	UA	Henry Mancini
Henry 9 Till 5 (short)	BRI	Johnny Hawksworth
Heritage of Dracula (see Vampyros Lesbos)		
His Land	IND	Ralph Carmichael
Horrible Sexy Vampire, The	SPA	Angel Arteaga
Horror of the Blood Monsters	IND	Mike Velerde
How Did a Nice Girl Like You Get into This Business?	GER	Klaus Doldinger
Jane Eyre	BRI	John Williams
Joe	IND	Bobby Scott
Jonathan	GER	Roland Kovac
Just Another War	ITA	Piero Piccioni
Kill Them All and Come Back Alone	ITA	Francesco de Masi
Klute	WB	Michael Small
Kongi's Harvest	NIG/ SWE	Chris McGregor
Lady in the Car with Glasses and a Gun	FRA	Michel Legrand

Laughing Woman, The	ITA	Stelvio Cipriani
Lonely Hearts	ITA	Luis Enrique Bacalov
Love by Rape	GER	Irmen Schmidt
Machine Gun McCain	ITA	Ennio Morricone
Madly	FRA	Francis Lai
Man Who Came from Ummo, The (Dracula Hunts Frankenstein/ Monsters of Terror)	GER/ ITA/ SPA	Rafael Ferrer
Memories of the Future (see Chariots of the Gods)		
Moment	BRI	Gavin Bryars
Myra Breckinridge	TCF	Lionel Newman/John Philips
Ned Kelly	BRI	Shel Silverstein
Night of Counting the Years	EGY	Mario Nascimbene
Nini Tirabuschio, la Donna che Invento la Mossa	ITA	Carlo Rustichelli
Notes for an African Orestes	ITA	Leandro "Gato" Barbieri
Of Men and Demons (short)	IND	Quincy Jones
Once Before I Die	TV	Gerald Fried
Peau d'Ane	FRA	Michel Legrand
Pizza Triangle, The (see Dramma Della Gelosia)		
Qui (Cadavere Dagli Artigli d'Acciaio, Il)	FRA/ ITA	Claude Bolling
Rainbow, The	JAP	Ryohei Hirose
Savage Wild, The	AI	Jaime Mendoza-Nava
Sex and the Vampire	FRA	Georges Acanthus
Sonho de Vampiros, Um	BRA	Joao Silverio Tevisan
Swedish Love Story, A	SWE	Bjoern Isfaelt
Teresa	FRA	Vladimir Cosma
That Little Difference	FRA/ ITA	Benedetto Ghiglia
3 in the Cellar	AI	Don Randi
Three into a Thousand	ITA	Ennio Morricone
Time of the Vampires, The (short)	YUG	Vojislav Kostic
Times Four	BRI	Gavin Bryars
Tora! Tora! Tora!	FOX	Jerry Goldsmith
Valerie and Her Week of Wonders	CZE	Lubos Fiser
Vampyros Lesbos (Heritage of Dracula)	GER/ SPA	Paul Grasel
Very Happy Alexander	FRA	Vladimir Cosma
Wackey World of Numberrs, The (short)	IND	Shorty Rogers
Walpurgis Night	GER/ SPA	Anton Garcia Abril
When the Mad Aunts Are Coming	GER	Gerhard Heinz
Your Child, the Unknown Creature	GER	Heinz Keissling/Peter Schirmann
Your Husband, the Unknown Creature	GER	Heinz Keissling

1971

Title	Country	Composer
Big Doll House, The	NWP	Les Baxter
Blood on Satan's Claw, The	BRI	Marc Wilkinson
Blood Pie (Pastel de Sangre)	SPA	Juan Pineda
Blood Sabbath	IND	Les Baxter
Bloodsuckers (Incense for the Damned)	BRI	Bobby Richards
Burglars, The	FRA	Ennio Morricone
Califfa, La	ITA	Ennio Morricone
Cometogether	AA	Stelvio Cipriani
Cross-Eyed Saint, The	ITA	Guido and Maurizio de Angelis
Cup Glory	BRI	Johnny Hawksworth
Dagmar's Hot Pants Inc.	IND	Les Baxter
Deathmaster, The (Khorda)	IND	Bill Marx
Delusions of Grandeur	FRA	Michel Polnareff
Devil in the Brain	ITA	Ennio Morricone
Devils, The	WB	Peter Maxwell Davies
Dr. Phibes (see Abominable Dr. Phibes, The)		
Dracula in the Castle of Terror (see In the Grip of the Spider)		
Dracula vs. Frankenstein	FRA/ SPA	Bruno Nicolai/Daniel White/William Lava
Earth 11	IND	Lalo Schifrin
Encounter	ITA	Ennio Morricone
Endless Night	IND	Bernard Herrmann
Esercito di 5 Uomini	ITA	Ennio Morricone
Fellini Satyricon	ITA	Nino Rota
Getting There First	TV	Gerald Fried
Honky	IND	Quincy Jones
Horsemen, The	COL	Georges Delerue
House That Dripped Blood, The	BRI	Michael Dress
Imputazione di Omicidio per uno Studente	ITA	Ennio Morricone
In the Grip of the Spider (Dracula in the Castle of Terror)	FRA/ GER/ ITA	Riz Ortolani
In the Name of the Father	ITA	Nicola Piovani
Incense for the Damned (see Bloodsuckers)		
It Only Happens to Others	FRA/ ITA	Michel Polnareff
Khorda (see Deathmaster, The)		
Kidnapped	BRI	Roy Budd
Lake of Dracula (Bloodthirsty Eyes/Japula)	JAP	Ruchiro Manabe
Last Run	MGM	Jerry Goldsmith
Let's Scare Jessica to Death	IND	Orville Stoeber
Lucky Luke	BEL/ FRA	Claude Bolling

Lust for a Vampire	BRI	Philip Martell
Man and Boy	IND	J. J. Johnson
Mandarine, La	FRA	Claude Bolling
Mayuko, the Only One	JAP	Go Yanagisawa
N. P.	ITA	Nicola Piovani
Night Digger, The	MGM	Bernard Herrmann
Night of the Devils, The	ITA/ SPA	Giorgio Gaslini
Noi Donne Siamo Fatte Cosi	ITA	Armando Trovajoli
Oceano	ITA	Ennio Morricone
Per Grazia Ricevuta (Between Miracles)	ITA	Guido and Maurizio de Angelis
Percy	BRI	Ray Davies
Permette, Rocco Papaleo	ITA	Armando Trovajoli
Present, The (short)	BRI	Johnny Hawksworth
Private Parts	MGM	Hugo Friedhofer
Raga	BRI	Ravi Shankar/Colin Walcott
Red Sun	FRA/ ITA	Maurice Jarre
Roma Bene	FRA/ GER/ ITA	Luis Enrique Bacalov
Sadist with Red Teeth, The	FRA	Raymond Legrand
Ski Raiders (see Snow Job)		
Slope in Spring, The	JAP	Akira Miyoshi
Snow Job (Ski Raiders)	IND	Jacques Loussier
Sudden Wealth of the Poor People of Kombach, The	GER	Klaus Doldinger
Sugar Is a Business (short)	BRI	Johnny Hawksworth
Time for Loving, A	BRI	Michel Legrand
Topo, El	IND	Alejandro Jodorowsky
Vampire Circus	BRI	David Whittaker
Vampire Happening, The	GER	Jerry van Rooyen
Whity	GER	Peer Raben
Widow Couderc, The (Escape/ Veuve Couderc/Evaso, Le)	FRA/ ITA	Caruso

1972

Amico, Stammi Lontano Almeno un Palmo	ITA	Gianni Ferrio
Anche se Volessi Lavovare, Che Cosa Faccio?	ITA	Ennio Morricone
Antony and Cleopatra	BRI	Patrick John Scott
Baby, The	IND	Gerald Fried
Beau Masque	FRA/ ITA	Andre Hodeir
Black Bunch, The (Jungle Sex)	IND	Jack Millman
Black Girl	CIN	Ed Bogas/Ray Shanklin/ Jesse Osborne/Mort Saunders
Blaise Pascal	ITA	Mario Nascimbene

Brother Sun, Sister Moon	PAR	Riz Ortolani
Captain Kronos--Vampire Hunter	BRI	Laurie Johnson
Cesar and Rosalie	FRA/GER/ITA	Hubert Rostaing
Cosa Buffa, La	ITA	Ennio Morricone
Course du Lievre a Travers les Champs, La	FRA	Francis Lai
Cry of the Black Wolves, The	GER	Gerhard Heinz
Daughter-in-Law, The	RUS	Redjep Redjepov
Deep Throat	IND	unlisted
Deux Saisons de la Vie, Les	FRA/ITA	Ennio Morricone
Devil and Leroy Bassett, The	IND	Les Baxter
Dig	IND	Quincy Jones
Directions (short)	BRI	Philip Green
Dracula A. D. 1972	BRI	Philip Martell
Dyn Amo	BRI	Gavin Bryars
Erotic Adventures of Zorro, The	FRA/GER	Billy Allen/William Loose
Everybody He Is Nice ... Everybody He Is Beautiful	FRA	Michel Legrand
Fear Is the Key	PAR	Roy Budd
Fellini Roma	FRA/ITA	Nino Rota
5 Dolls for an August Moon	ITA	Piero Umiliani
Fritz the Cat	IND	Ed Bogas/Ray Shanklin
Girl in Australia, A	ITA	Berto Pisano
Hearts and Minds	GER/ITA	Ennio Morricone
Hot Parts	IND	Michael Brown/Bert Sommer
Junior Bonner	CIN	Jerry Fielding
Justine de Sade	FRA	Francoise and Roger Cotte
Kronos (see Captain Kronos--Vampire Hunter)		
Kung Fu (series)	TV	Jim Helms
Last Tango in Paris	UA	Leandro "Gato" Barbieri
Madame Sin	BRI	Michael Gibbs
Main Thing Holiday	GER	Heinz Kiessling
Man from the East, A	ITA	Guido and Maurizio de Angelis
Minx, The	IND	Tom Dawes/Don Dannermann
Mio	FRA/ITA/JAP	Jean Guillou
More Blue than Blue Color	JAP	Johji Yuasa
Night Stalker, The (Kolchak Papers, The)	ABC	Robert Cobert
Nocturne	GER	Eugen Thomass
Outside In	IND	Randy Edelman
Pacifist, The	ITA	Giorgio Gaslini

Pebbles of Etretat	FRA	Georges Garvarentz
Pinocchio	FRA/ GER/ ITA	Fiorenzo Carpi
Piu Bella Serata della Mia Vita, A	ITA	Armando Trovajoli
... Piu Forte Ragazzi	ITA	Guido and Maurizio de Angelis
Plod (short)	BRI	Johnny Hawksworth
Prima Notte di Quiete, La	FRA/ ITA	Mario Nascimbene
Questa Specie d'Amore	ITA	Ennio Morricone
Rak	FRA	Andre Hodeir
Rebel Jesus, The	IND	Alex North
Santo and the Blue Demon vs. Dracula and the Wolf Man	MEX	Gustavo Carreon
Scoumoune, La	FRA/ ITA	Francois de Roubaix
Scoundrel, The	FRA	Michel Legrand
Second Best (short)	BRI	Richard Arnell
Seven Samurai	JAP	Fumio Hayasaka
Sex of Their Bodies	ITA	Piero Umiliani
Slap the Monster on Page One	FRA/ ITA	Nicola Piovani
Stadium Nuts	FRA	Four Charlots
Stone Killer, The	COL	Roy Budd
Story of the Taira Family, The	JAP	Isao Tomita
Summertime Killer	ITA	Luis E. Bacalov
Sun on the Skin	ITA	Gianni Marchetti
T. R. Baskin	PAR	Jack Elliott
Take Care, France	FRA	Francis Lai
Tom Thumb (Petit Poucet, Le)	FRA	Francis Lai
Top of the Heap	IND	J. J. Johnson
Traitement de Choc	FRA/ ITA	Rene Koering/Alain Jessua
Trastevere	ITA	Guido and Maurizio de Angelis
Trial of the Catonsville Nine, The	IND	Shelly Manne
Trinity Is Still My Name	ITA	Guido and Maurizio de Angelis
Tutti i Colori del Buio	ITA/ SPA	Bruno Nicolai
Twins of Evil	BRI	Harry Robinson
War Is War	FRA	Gerard Calvi
Who Saw Her Die?	ITA	Ennio Morricone
You and Me	RUS	Alfred Schnittke

1973

Ace Eli and Rodger of the Skies	TCF	Jerry Goldsmith
Across 110th Street	UA	J. J. Johnson/Bobby Womack
Affection	BUL	Simeon Pironkov
Agony of Mr. Boroka, The	HUN	Gyorgy Vukan

Aguirre, the Wrath of God	GER	Florian Fricke
Alfredo, Alfredo	ITA	Carlo Rustichelli
All Nudity Will Be Punished	BRA	Astor Piazzola
All People Will Be Brothers	GER	Erich Ferstl
Allonsanfan	ITA	Ennio Morricone
Alvin Purple	AUT	Brian Cadd
Amazons, The	FRA/ ITA	Riz Ortolani
And the Rain Blots Out All the Traces	GER	Erich Ferstl
Angela	BEL/ HOL	Georges Delerue
Anna and the Wolves	SPA	Luis de Pablo
Antoine and Sebastien	FRA	Claude Luter
Ape and Superape	HOL	Otto Ketting
Apocalypse des Animaux, L'	FRA	Vangelis Papathanassiou
Arnold	CIN	George Duning
Ash Wednesday	PAR	Maurice Jarre
Assassin of Rome, The	ITA	Riz Ortolani
Assassination of Metteotti, The	ITA	Egisto Macchi
August and July	CAN	Bruce Nyznik
Baba Yaga	ITA	Piero Umiliani
Bad Charleston Charlie	IND	Luchi de Jesus
Badge 373	PAR	J. J. Jackson
Badlands	IND	George Aliceson Tipton/ James Taylor
Bang the Drum Slowly	PAR	Stephen Lawrence
Battle of the Amazons	AI	Franco Micalizzi
Battle of the Planet of the Apes	TCF	Leonard Rosenman
Baxter!	NGP	Michael J. Lewis
Because of the Cats	BEL/ HOL	Ruud Bos
Bedside Romance	DEN	Ole Hoeyer
Bell, The	SPA	Adolfo Waitzman
Belladonna	JAP	Masashiko Sato
Belstone Fox, The	BRI	Laurie Johnson
Benjamin	GER	Gary Wright
Big Sentiments Make for Good Sports	FRA	Vladimir Cosma
Billy Two Hats	UA	John Scott
Black Caesar	AI	James Brown
Black Jack	AI	Jerry Styner
Black Mama, White Mama	AI	Harry Betts
Blade	IND	John Cacavas
Blockhouse, The	BRI	Stanley Myers
Blue Summer	IND	Richard Billay
Body, The	BRI	Ron Geeson
Book of Numbers	EMB	Al Schackman
Borrowers, The	TV	Rod McKuen
Boy Who Cried Werewolf, The	UN	Ted Stovall
Breezy	UN	Michel Legrand
Bride, The	IND	Peter Bernstein
Cahill, United States Marshal	WB	Elmer Bernstein

Call of the Wild	GER	Carlo Rustichelli
Cannibal Girls	AI	Doug Riley
Caroline Cherie	FRA	Georges Garvarentz
Case of the Full-Moon Murders, The	IND	Bud Fanton/Jacques Urbont
Chariots of the Gods	GER	Peter Thomas
Charley and the Angel	DIS	Buddy Baker
Charley One-Eye	BRI	John Cameron
Charley Varrick	UN	Lalo Schifrin
Charlie and His Two Birds	FRA	Philippe Sarde
Cheerleaders, The	IND	Dave Herman
Chetan, Indian Boy	GER	Peer Raben
Child Is Ours, The	SPA	Antonio Perez Olea
Cinderella Liberty	TCF	John Williams
Class of '44	WB	David Shire
Cleopatra Jones	WB	J. J. Johnson/Carl Brandt/Brad Shapiro
Coffy	AI	Roy Ayers
Confessions of a Police Inspector to the District Attorney	ITA	Riz Ortolani
Confessor, The	IND	Chico Hamilton
Contact	GHA/ ITA	Riz Ortolani
Cops and Robbers	UA	Michel Legrand
Corruption of Chris Miller, The	SPA	Waldo de los Rios
Counsellor, The (Consigliore, Il)	ITA	Riz Ortolani
Crazies, The	IND	Bruce Roberts
Creeping Flesh	BRI	Paul Ferris
Dangerous Kisses	DEN	Patrick Gowers
Daughters, Daughters	ISR	Alex Kagan
Dawn Has Not Broken Yet	SWI	Thierry Fervant
Day for Night	FRA	Georges Delerue
Day of the Dolphin	EMB	Georges Delerue
Day of the Jackal	UN	Georges Delerue
Deadly Fathoms	IND	Paul La Valle
Deaf Smith and Johnny Ears	ITA	Daniele Patucchi
Deep Sleep	IND	Butch Taylor
Detroit 9000	IND	Luchi de Jesus
Devil in Miss Jones, The	IND	Alden Shuman
Diary of a Cloistered Nun, The (Nun and the Devil, The)	FRA/ GER/ ITA	Piero Piccioni
Dillinger	AI	Barry de Vorzon
Dirty Weekend	ITA	Carlo Rustichelli
Distant Thunder	IN	Satyajit Ray
Doctor Death: Seeker of Souls	CIN	Richard La Salle
Doll's House, A	PAR	John Barry
Doll's House, A	BRI	Michel Legrand
Don Is Dead, The	UN	Jerry Goldsmith
Don Juan (If Don Juan Were a Woman)	FRA	Michel Magne
Don Quixote	AUT	Ludwig Minkus
Don Ramiro	SPA	Luis de Pablo

Don't Know Anything but I'll Tell All	FRA	Michel Fugain
Don't Look Now	ITA	Pino Donaggio
Eakins	IND	J. K. Randall
Edifying and Joyous Story of Colinot, the Skirt-Puller-Upper, The	FRA	Guy Bontempelli
Elektra Glide in Blue	UA	James William Guercio
Emperor of the North (Pole), The	TCF	Frank de Vol
England Made Me	BRI	Patrick John Scott
Enter the Dragon	WB	Lalo Schifrin
Escape, The	DEN	Soeren Christensen
Executive Action	NGP	Randy Edelman
Exorcist, The	WB	Jack Nitzsche
Experts, The	GER	Janis Joplin
Extreme Close-Up	NGP	Basil Poledouris
Family of North Country, The	JAP	Nariaki Mitsueda
Far-West, The	BEL/FRA	Jacques Brel
Fed Up	BEL/FRA	Andre Burton
Feminin-Feminin	FRA	Jean Weiner
First Circle, The	PAR	Roman Palester
Five on the Black Hand Side	UA	H. B. Bornum
Flower of Holiness	SPA	Carmelo Bernaola
For Love One Dies	ITA	Ennio Morricone
40 Carats	COL	Michel Legrand
14, The	BRI	Kenny Clayton
Foxy Brown	AI	Willie Hutch
Frank and Eva--Living Apart Together	HOL	Antoine Duhamel
Frankenstein: The True Story	BRI	Gil Melle
Frasier, the Sensuous Lion	IND	Robert Emenegger
Free Man, A	FRA	Francis Lai
Friends of Eddie Coyle, The	PAR	Dave Grusin
From the Mixed-Up Files of Mrs. Basil E. Frankweiler	CIV	Donald Devor
Ganja and Hess	IND	Sam Waymon
George Who?	FRA	J. J. Debout
Get Carter	MGM	Roy Budd
Giordano Bruno	ITA	Ennio Morricone
Giorno del Furore, Il (Fury)	ITA	Riz Ortolani
Girl with the Cello, The	FRA/SWI	Jean-Pierre Doering
Girls Are for Loving	IND	Robert G. Orpin
Glass Menagerie, The	TV	John Barry
Goddesses, The	BRA	Rogerio Deprat
Going Places (short)	BRI	Mike Westbrook
Good Year, The (see Happy New Year)		
Gordon's War	TCF	Al Alias/Andy Badale/Horace Ott
Grand Bouffe, Le	FRA	Philippe Sarde
Hail the Artist	FRA	Vladimir Cosma
Hail, Thieves	FRA	Areski

Hannibal	SWI	Jonas C. Haefeli
Happy as the Grass Was Green	IND	Gordon Zahler
Happy Mother's Day ... Love, George	CIV	Don Vincent
Happy New Year	FRA	Francis Lai
Hard Part Begins, The	CAN	Jan Guenther
Harrad Experiment, The	CIN	Artie Butler
Harry in Your Pocket	UA	Lalo Schifrin
Heavenly Bodies, The	CAN	Philippe Sarde
Heavy Traffic	AI	Ray Shanklin/Ed Bogas
Hell Up in Harlem	AI	Freddie Perren/Fonce Mizell
Hex	TCF	Charles Bernstein
High Plains Drifter	UA	Dee Barton
High Rise	IND	Jacques Urbont
Hireling, The	BRI	Marc Wilkinson
Hit	PAR	Lalo Schifrin
Hitler: The Last Ten Days	PAR	Mischa Spoliansky
Holiday, The	ITA	Christian de Sica
Holy Mountain, The	MEX	Alexandro Jodorowsky/Ron Frangipane/Don Cherry
Home, Sweet Home	BEL/FRA	Walter Heymen
Homeland	FRA	Gilles Servat
Horror Express	BRI	John Cacavas
Hospitals: The White Mafia	ITA	Riz Ortolani
Hot-Blooded Paolo (Paolo il Caldo)	ITA	Armando Trovajoli
Hot Channels	IND	Gilly
Hour-Glass Sanatorium, The	POL	Jerzy Maksymiuk
Hour of Parting, The	DEN	Henning Christiansen
Hunchback of the Morgue, The	SPA	Carmelo Bernaola
Hungry Wives	IND	Steve Gorn
Hurry Up, or I'll Be 30	EMB	Stephen Laurence
I Am Looking for My Own	RUS	Eugeni Krylatov
I Could Never Have Sex with Any Man Who Has So Little Regard for My Husband	IND	Joseph Liebman
I Did It	ITA	Armando Trovajoli
I Escaped from Devil's Island	UA	Les Baxter
Idaho Transfer	IND	Bruce Langehorne
If Don Juan Were a Woman (see Don Juan)		
Impossible Object	FRA	Michel Legrand
In the Driver's Seat	ARG	Horacio Malvicino
In Your Dad's Pocket	DEN	Bent Fabricius-Bjerre
Inheritor, The	FRA	Michel Colombier
Innocent Bystanders	PAR	John Keating
Inside Job	IND	Oliver Nelson
Interval	EMB	Armando Manzanero/Ruben Fuentes
Invitation, The	FRA/SWI	Patrick Moraz

It Happened in Hollywood	IND	Ron Frangipane/Al Steckles
Italian Connection, The	ITA	Armando Trovajoli
J'ai Mon Voyage	CAN/ FRA	Claude Bolling
Jeremy	UA	Lee Holdridge
Johnny Vik	IND	Bill Marx
Jonathan Livingston Seagull	PAR	Neil Diamond/Lee Holdridge
Journey Through the Past	IND	Neil Young
Juan Moreira	ARG	Pocho Leyes
Kaigenieri	JAP	Toshi Ichiyanagi
Kashima Paradise	FRA	Hiroshi Hara
Keep All Doors Open	SWE	Berndt Egerbladh
Kid Blue	TCF	John Rubenstein/Tim Mc-Intire
Kill!	ITA	Berto Pisano
Killing Kind	IND	Andrew Belling
Lady Ice	NGP	Perry Botkin Jr.
Last American Hero, The	TCF	Charles Fox
Last Detail, The	COL	Johnny Mandel
Last of Sheila, The	WB	Billy Goldenberg
Last Snows of Spring, The	ITA	Franco Micalizzi
Laughing Policeman, The	TCF	Charles Fox
Legend of Hell House, The	TCF	Brian Hodgson/Delia Derbyshire
Lialeh	IND	Bernard Purdie
Life Study	IND	Emmanuel Vardi
Light at the Edge of the World, The	BRI	Piero Piccioni
Little Cigars	AI	Harry Betts
Live and Let Die	UA	George Martin
Lolly Madonna XXX	MGM	Fred Myrow
Lonely Heart, The	FRA/ SPA	Carmelo Bernaola
Loner, The	FRA	Claude Bolling
Long Goodbye, The	UA	John Williams
Long Live the Island Frogs	KOR	Sangki Han
Lost Horizon	COL	Burt Bacharach
Love Among the Ruins	TV	John Barry
Love and Pain and the Whole Damn Thing	COL	Michael Small
Loveland	IND	Gardner Olson
Lucky Luciano	FRA/ ITA	Piero Piccioni
Mack, The	CIN	Willie Hutch
Mackintosh Man, The	WB	Maurice Jarre
Mad Bomber, The	IND	Michel Mention
Magic Adventure, The	SPA	Antonio Oreta
Magnificent One, The (Magnifique, Le)	FRA	Claude Bolling
Magnum Force	WB	Lalo Schifrin
Malizia	ITA	Fred Bongusto

Man Called Noon, The	BRI	Luis Enrique Bacalov
Man from Swan Farm, The	DEN	Sven Gyldmark
Man Is Dead, A	FRA	Michel Legrand
Man Who Loved Cat Dancing, The	MGM	John Williams
Marriage a la Mode	FRA	Philippe Sarde
Massacre in Rome	ITA	Ennio Morricone
Me and the Mafia	DEN	Ib Glindemann
Metamorphosis	GRE	Sophia Mihalitsi
Michael, the Brave	FRA/ RUM	Tiberu Olah
Moi y'En a Vouloir des Sous	FRA	Michel Magne
Money! Money! Money!	ITA	Francis Lai
Monk, The	FRA	Ennio Morricone
Monolog	RUS	Oleg Karavaitchouk
Morning Schedule, The	JAP	Ichiro Araki
Most Important Event Since Man First Set Foot on the Moon, The	FRA	Michel Legrand
My Brother Anastasia	ITA	Piero Piccioni
My Name Is Nobody	FRA/ GER/ ITA	Ennio Morricone
Naked Ape, The	UN	Jimmy Webb
National Health, or Nurse Norton's Affair, The	BRI	Carl Davis
Natives of Planet Earth	CHILE	Raul Trujillo
Nelson Affair, The	BRI	Michel Legrand
Neptune Factor, The	TCF	Lalo Schifrin/William McCauley
New Ones, The	PERU	Kabul
Newcomers, The	IND	Milford Kulhagen
Night Before, The	IND	David Earnest
Night Watch	EMB	John Cameron
No, the Case Is Happily Resolved	ITA	Riz Ortolani
No Way Out	FRA/ ITA	Gianni Ferrio
Norliss Tapes, The	NBC	Robert Cobert
Number One	ITA	Giancarlo Chiaramello
Nun and the Devil, The (see Diary of a Cloistered Nun, The)		
Nuns of Sant'Archangelo	FRA/ ITA	Piero Piccioni
O Lucky Man	BRI	Alan Price
Oh, Jonathan, Oh, Jonathan	GER	Horst Jankowski
Oklahoma Crude	COL	Henry Mancini
Olsen Gang Runs Amok, The	DEN	Bent Fabricius-Bjerre
Once	IND	Aminadav Aloni
Once Upon a Scoundrel	IND	Alex North
One Day More, One Day Less	HUN	Emil Petrovics
One Hamlet Less	ITA	Carmelo Bene
One Little Indian	DIS	Jerry Goldsmith
Operation Bororo	CZE	Petr Hapka
Optimists, The	PAR	Lionel Bart
Ordinary Tenderness	FRA	Plume and Jocelyn Barube

Title	Company	Composer
Outfit, The	MGM	Jerry Fielding
Pain in the Neck, The	FRA	Jacques Brel/Francois Gabuber
Paolo il Caldo (see Hot-Blooded Paolo)		
Paper Chase, The	TCF	John Williams
Paperback Hero	CAN	Ron Collier
Papillon	AA	Jerry Goldsmith
Pat Garrett and Billy the Kid	MGM	Bob Dylan
Petofi '73	HUN	Leventi Szorenyi
Pianorama (short)	BRI	John Dankworth
Piedone lo Sbirro	ITA	Guido and Maurizio de Angelis
Pistol, The	SWE	Ture Rangstreom
Plot, The	FRA	Michel Magne
Police Story (series)	TV	Jerry Goldsmith
Polizia Incrimina, la Legge Assolve, La	ITA	Guido and Maurizio de Angelis
Prince and the Pauper, The	IND	George Fischoff
Private Projection	FRA	Serge Gainsbourg
Property Is No Longer a Theft (Proprieta non Piu un Furto, La)	FRA/ITA	Ennio Morricone
Pyx, The	CAN	Harry Freedman
Question Mark	FRA	Michel Legrand
Rainbow Boys, The	CAN	Howard Blake
Rare Bird, The	FRA	Laurent Petitgirard
Red Mantle, The	FIN	Marc Fredericks
Red Rose, The	ITA	Luis Enrique Bacalov
Reflection of Fear	COL	Fred Myrow
Resurrection of Eve	IND	Richard Wynkoop
Return	ITA	Astor Piazzola
Revolution of the Seven Madmen, The	ARG	Mariano Etkin/Osvaldo Requena
Revolver	ITA	Ennio Morricone
Right of the Maddest, The	FRA	Vladimir Cosma
Robin Hood	DIS	George Bruns
Rough Day for the Queen	FRA	Philippe Arthuys
Sacred Knives of Vengeance, The	CHN	Chen Yung-Yu
Salut l'Artiste (Hail the Artist)	FRA	Vladimir Cosma
Salvation	POL	Andrze Korzynski
Sannikov's Land	RUS	A. Zapin
Santee	IND	Don Randi
Savage Planet, The	CZE/FRA	Alain Goraguer
Save the Tiger	PAR	Marvin Hamlisch
Scalawag	PAR	John Cameron
Scarecrow	WB	Fred Myrow
Scarlet Letter, The	GER/SPA	Jurgen Knieper
Schiava Io ce l'Ho e Tu No, La	ITA	Piero Umiliani
Schlock	IND	David Gibson
Scorpio	UA	Jerry Fielding
Scream, Blacula, Scream	AI	Bill Marx

Sea Gull, The	RUS	Alfred Schnitke
Seduction	ITA	Luis Enrique Bacalov
Serpent, The	FRA/GER	Ennio Morricone
Serpents of the Pirate Moon, The	IND	Judith Bell
Serpico	PAR	Mikis Theodorakis
Seven Ups, The	TCF	Don Ellis
Sex Crazy	ITA	Armando Trovajoli
Shaft in Africa	MGM	Johnny Pate
Shamus	COL	Jerry Goldsmith
Showdown	UN	David Shire
Silent One, The	FRA	Jacques Datin/Alain Goraguer
Sinful Dwarf, The	IND	Ole Arnfred
Sisters	AI	Bernard Herrmann
Slams, The	MGM	Luther Henderson
Slaughter's Big Rip-Off	AI	James Brown/Fred Wesley
Slave, The	ITA	Piero Umiliani
Sleeper	UA	Woody Allen
Slither	MGM	Tom McIntosh
So Long, Blue Boy	IND	Bruce Buckingham
Some Arpents of Snow	CAN	Francois Cousineau
Some Call It Loving	IND	Richard Hazard
Son, The	FRA	Philippe Sarde
Soul Hustler, The	MGM	Harley Hatcher
Soul of Nigger Charley, The	PAR	Don Costa
Soylent Green	MGM	Gerald Fried/Fred Myrow
Spirit of the Beehive, The	SPA	Luis de Pablo
Spook Who Sat by the Door, The	UA	Herbie Hancock
S-s-s-s-s-s	UN	Patrick Williams
State of Siege	FRA	Mikis Theodorakis
Steel Arena	IND	Don Tweedy
Steelyard Blues	WB	Mike Bloomfield/Paul Butterfield/Nick Gravenites/David Shire
Sting, The	UN	Marvin Hamlisch
Story of the Age of Wars, The	JAP	Hikaru Hayashi
Summer Wishes, Winter Dreams	COL	Johnny Mandel
Superfly T. N. T.	PAR	Osibisa
Sutjeska	YUG	Mikis Theodorakis
Sweet Jesus, Preacher Man	MGM	Horace Tapscott
Sweet Suzy	IND	William Loose
Tales That Witness Madness	PAR	Bernard Ebbinghouse
Tall Blond Man with One Black Shoe, The	FRA	Vladimir Cosma
Temptations in the Summer Wind	GER	Peter Thomas
Tenderness of Wolves, The	GER	Peer Raben
Teresa the Thief	ITA	Riz Ortolani
Terror in the Wax Museum	CIN	George Duning
That Man Bolt	UN	Charles Bernstein
Theater of Blood	BRI	Michael J. Lewis

There's Always a Way to Find a Way	CAN	Marcel Lefebvre
Thief Who Came to Dinner, The	WB	Henry Mancini
Third After the Sun, The	BUL	Kiril Dontchev
This Is a Hijack	IND	Charles Alden
This Kind of Love	ITA	Ennio Morricone
Three Musketeers, The	TCF	Michel Legrand
Time Within Memory	JAP	Toru Takemitsu
Torndal Cousins, The	DEN/SWE	Sven Gyldmark
Tosca, La	ITA	Armando Trovajoli
Touch of Class, A	EMB	John Cameron
Trader Horn	MGM	Shelly Manne
Train, The	FRA	Philippe Sarde
Train Robbers, The	WB	Dominic Frontiere
Trick Baby	UN	James Bond
Triple Echo, The	BRI	Denis Lewiston
Triple Irons	NGP	Chen Yung-Huang
Turkish Delight	HOL	Rogier van Otterloo
Two People	UN	David Shire
U-Turn	CAN	Neil Chotem
Up 'n' at 'em, Amalie	DEN	Ib Glindemann
Upkeep (short)	IND	Benny Carter
VD	HOL	Antoine Duhamel
Valdez the Halfbreed	ITA	Guido and Maurizio de Angelis
Valise, The	FRA	Philippe Sarde/Hubert Rostaing
Vera	SPA	Roman Alix
Village Performance of Hamlet, A	YUG	Delo Jusic
Visions of Eight	IND	Henry Mancini
Visitor, The	CAN	Luigi Zaninelli
Voyage with Jacob	HUN	Janos Conda
Walking Tall	CIN	Walter Scharf
Wanderers, The	JAP	Shitei Kuri/Yukio Asame
Warm December, A	NGP	Coleridge-Taylor Perkinson
Way Out	BEL/HOL	Walter Heymen
Way We Were, The	COL	Marvin Hamlisch
We Want the Colonels	ITA	Carlo Rustichelli
Wedding, The	POL	Stanislaw Radwan
Wednesday Children, The	IND	Tom Baker/Dene Bays
Werewolf of Washington	IND	Arnold Freed
Westworld	MGM	Fred Karlin
When Roobard Made a Spike (short)	BRI	Johnny Hawksworth
White Gloves of the Devil	FRA	Karl Heinz Schaeffer
White Lightning	UA	Charles Bernstein
White Sister	ITA	Fred Bongusto
Wicked, Wicked	MGM	Philip Springer
Willie Dynamite	UN	J. J. Johnson
Women Buried Alive	ITA	Ennio Morricone

Wonder of It All, The	IND	William Loose
World's Greatest Athlete, The	DIS	Marvin Hamlisch
Young and the Restless, The (serial)	TV	Don McGinnis/Barry de Vorzon/Jerry Winn/ Bob Todd/Perry Botkin Jr.
Your Three Minutes Are Up	CIN	Perry Botkin Jr.
Zigzag	BEL/ HOL	Arsene Souffriau

1974

Abby	AI	Robert O. Ragland
Abdication, The	WB	Nino Rota
About Seven Girls	SWE	Lars Faernloef
Act of Vengeance	AI	Bill Marx
Airport 1975	UN	John Cacavas
Alice Doesn't Live Here Anymore	WB	Richard LaSalle
Alvin Rides Again	AUT	Brian Cadd
Always a New Beginning	IND	Herb Pilhofer
Amarcord	ITA	Nino Rota
Amazing Grace	UA	Coleridge-Taylor Perkinson
Amlash Enchanted Forest, The	ISR	Alex Kagan/Yehuda Rotman
Amore de Pluie, Un	FRA	Francis Lai
Antonio and Sebastian	FRA	Jacques Dutronc
Antonio Gaudi: An Unfinished Vision	SPA	Jean Pineda
Appassionata	ITA	Piero Piccioni
Apple, the Stem and the Seeds, The	CAN	Cyril Beaulieu
Apprenticeship of Duddy Kravitz, The	CAN	Stanley Myers
Arabian Nights, The	FRA/ ITA	Ennio Morricone
At Home Among Strangers	RUS	E. Artemyev
Bamboo Gods and Iron Men	PHI	Tito Scotto
Bank Shot	UA	John Morris
Barry McKenzie Rides Again	AUT	Peter Best
Basketball Stars	PHI	Pablo Vergara
Bat People, The	IND	Artie Kane
Batingaw	PHI	Restie Umali
Bears and I, The	DIS	Buddy Baker
Beast, The	FRA/ ITA	Guido and Maurizio de Angelis
Beast Must Die, The	CIN	Douglas Gamley
Benji	IND	Euel Box
Best Friends	THAI	Prasit Payomyong
Beyond the Door	ITA	Franco Micalizzi
Beyond Time	HUN	Zsolt Durko
Big Bad Mama	IND	The Great American Music Band

Film	Source	Composer
Birds Do It ... Bees Do It ...	COL/WB	Gerald Fried
Bitter Love	ITA	Armando Trovajoli
Black Belt Jones	WB	Luchi de Jesus
Black Christmas	CAN	Carl Zittrer
Black Eye, The	WB	Mort Garson
Black Godfather	IND	Martin Yarbrough
Black Samson	WB	Allen Toussaint
Black Six, The	IND	David Moscie
Black Thursday	FRA	Mort Schuman
Black Windmill, The	UN	Roy Budd
Blazing Saddles	WB	John Morris
Blood for Dracula	FRA/ITA	Claudio Gizzi
Bobby's War	NOR	Egie Monn-Iversen
Bootleggers (5 Sons of Dogs)	ITA	Riz Ortolani
Bootleggers, The	IND	Jaime Mendoza-Nava
Boquitas Pintadas	ARG	Waldo de los Rios
Borsalino and Co.	FRA	Claude Bolling
Bread and Chocolate	ITA	Daniele Patucchi
Bring Me the Head of Alfredo Garcia	UA	Jerry Fielding
Brother on the Run	IND	Johnny Pate
Buque Maldito, El (see The Ghost Galleon)		
Burn, Samar, Burn!	PHI	Jose Reyes Jr.
Buster and Billie	COL	Al de Lory
Busting	UA	Billy Goldenberg
But Where Is Daniel Vax?	ISR	Ariel Zilber
California Split	COL	Phyllis Shotwell
Calzonin Inspector	MEX	Leonardo Velasquez
Captain Mikula, the Kid	YUG	Nikica Kalodera
Caravan to Vaccares	BRI/FRA	Stanley Myers
Cars That Ate Paris, The	AUT	Bruce Smeaton
Castaway Cowboy, The	DIS	Robert F. Brunner
Castle of Purity	MEX	Joaquin Gutierrez Heras
Catch My Soul	CIN	Tony Joe White
Cat's Play	HUN	Peter Eotvos
Chance and Violence	FRA	Michel Colombier
Cheap	IND	Mark Volman/Howard Kaylin
China Behind	CHN	Doming Lam
Chinatown	PAR	Jerry Goldsmith
Choca, La	MEX	Antonio Diaz Conde
Chosen Survivors	COL	Fred Karlin
Christina	CAN	Cyril Ornadel
Cities and Years	GER/RUS	Alfred Schnitke
Citizen Rebels, A	ITA	Guido and Maurizio de Angelis
Claudine	TCF	Curtis Mayfield
Clockmaker, The	FRA	Hubert Rostaing

Colors of the Rainbow, The	GRE	Stamatis Spanoudakis
Come Home and Meet My Wife	ITA	Enzo Jannacci
Confessions of a Window Cleaner	BRI	Sam Sklair
Conrack	TCF	John Williams
Conversation, The	PAR	David Shire
Crazy	WB	John Scott
Crazy Joe	COL	Giancarlo Chiaramello
Crazy World of Julius Vrooder, The	TCF	Bob Alcivar
Criminal Records	POL	Jerzy Maksymiuk
Cry of the Heart	FRA	Pierre Jansen
Curio Lake, The	POL	Wanda Warska
Dakota	HOL	Antoine Duhamel
Dark Places	BRI	Wilfred Josephs
Darshan	IN	Ghatnagar
Day Does Not Die	CZE	Svetozar Stracina
Days of Betrayal	CZE	Zdenek Liska
Death Wish	PAR	Herbie Hancock
Deep Throat II	IND	Tony Bruno/Michael Colicchio
Deer, The	IRAN	Esfandiyar Monfaredzedeh
Defiance	IND	Alex Allen
Deluge, The	POL	Kasimierz Serocki
Deps	YUG	Alfi Kablijo
Deranged	AI	Carl Zittrer
Dervish and Death, The	YUG	Zoran Hristic
Destructors, The	BRI	Roy Budd
Deux Grandes Filles dans un Pyjama	FRA	Claude Bolling
Digby, the Biggest Dog in the World	CIN	Edwin Astley
Dirty O'Neill	AI	Raoul Kraushaar
Don't Touch White Women	FRA	Philippe Sarde
Don't Turn the Other Cheek	GER/ ITA/ SPA	Gianni Ferrio
Dove, The	PAR	John Barry
Dream Town	GER	Eberhard Schoener
Dreaming Youth	HUN	Gyorgy Ranki
Driver's Seat, The	ITA	Franco Mannino
Duel, The	RUS	Nadeshda Simonyan
Dunderklumpen (Thundering Fatty)	SWE	Toots Thielemans
Earthquake	UN	John Williams
Ebon Lundin	SWE	Arne Olsson
Education of Sonny Carson, The	PAR	Coleridge-Taylor Perkinson
11 Harrowhouse	TCF	Michael J. Lewis
Eleventh Hour, The	POL	Marian Ziminski
"Elite" Group, The	FRA	Philippe Sarde
Emmanuelle	FRA	Pierre Bachelet/Herve Roy
Empty Chair, The	FRA	Maxime le Forestier
Escapade	FRA/ SWI	Guy Bonet

Everything's Ready, Nothing Works	ITA	Piero Piccioni
Family, The	HOL	Louis Andriessen
Father Heart Wants to Get Married	ARG	Tito Ribero
Ferocious One, The	RUS	D. Botbaev
Fighters, The	CON	David Matthews
5 Sons of Dogs (see Bootleggers, The)		
Flesh Gordon	IND	Ralph Ferraro
For an Unimportant Reason	GRE	Domna Samiou
Forgotten Island of Santosha	IND	Carlos Pardeiro
Frankenstein	FRA/ITA	Carlo Grizzi
Frankenstein and the Monster from Hell	PAR	James Bernard
Freebie and the Bean	WB	Dominic Frontiere
Fringe Benefits	IND	Reese and Steve Ziplow
Front Page, The	UN	Billy May
Gambler, The	PAR	Jerry Fielding
Game of Love, A	IND	John Yow
Gangster Movie, The	SWE	Bengt Ernryd
Gaspards, Les	FRA	Gerard Calvi
Gatefold Girl, The	DEN	Sebastien
Gazoros, Serres	GRE	George Papadakis
George Hauser's Happy Minutes	AUS	Ingrid Fessler
Ghost Galleon, The (Buque Maldito, El)	SPA	Anton Garcia Abril
Girl and the Dream Castle, The	DEN	Ole Hoeyer
Girl from Petrovka, The	UN	Henry Mancini
Girl Who Liked Purple Flowers	HUN	Szavoles Fenyes/Pal Abraham
Giron	CUB	Sergio Vitier
Godfather II	PAR	Nino Rota/Carmine Coppola
Gold	AA	Elmer Bernstein
Golden Needles	AI	Lalo Schifrin
Golden Voyage of Sinbad	COL	Miklos Rozsa
Gone in 60 Seconds	IND	Ronald Halicki/Philip Kachaturian
Gosh	IND	Vic Caesar
Got It Made	BRI	James Kenelm Clark
Gravy Train, The	COL	Fred Karlin
Great Adventure, The	ARG	Pocho Leyes/Luis Maria Serra
Great American Cowboy, The	IND	Harold Farberman
Great Gatsby, The	PAR	Nelson Riddle
Greetings and a Living	BEL/HOL	Roger Mores
Guest Workers	DEN	Povl Dissing
Hand to Cut Off, A	FRA	Paul Misraki
Happy Days	IND	Marcus Anthony
Hare Census, The	BUL	Kiril Dontchev
Harrad Summer, The	CIN	Patrick Williams

Harry and Tonto	TCF	Bill Conti
Hatoko's Sea, The	JAP	Toru Huyuki
Herbie Rides Again	DIS	George Bruns
Himiko	JAP	Toru Takemitsu
History of Postwar Japan as Told by a Bar Hostess, The	JAP	Harumi Ibe
Holy Office, The	MEX	Joaquin Gutierrez Heras
Homebodies	EMB	Bernardo Segall
Honeybaby, Honeybaby	IND	Michael Tschudin
Hot Rabbit, The	FRA	Vladimir Cosma
Hottest Show in Town, The	DEN	Ole Hoeyer
House on Skull Mountain, The	TCF	Jerrold Immel
How Low Can You Fall?	ITA	Fiorenzo Carpi
How to Seduce a Woman	CIN	Stu Phillips
Huckleberry Finn	UA	Fred Werner
Human Revolution, The	JAP	Akira Ifukubi
I Fix America and Return	ITA	Luis Enrique Bacalov
I Love You	CAN	Frank Dervieux
I Want a Solution	EGY	Gamal Salama
Icy Breasts	FRA	Philippe Sarde
If I Had a Million Rubles	RUS	Georgy Firtich
I'll Take Her Like a Father	ITA	Fred Bongusto
Illusions of a Lady	IND	Arlow Ober/Vern Carlson
Immoral Tales	FRA	Maurice la Roux
Impossible Is Not French	FRA	Henri Bourtayre
In the Sign of the Taurus	DEN	Bertrand Bech
Inbreaker, The	CAN	Grant Herrocks
Inn of the Damned	AUT	Bob Young
Inside the Great Pyramid	DEN	Ben Lorentzen
Internecine Project, The	AA	Roy Budd
Island at the Top of the World	DIS	Maurice Jarre
Italian Graffiti	ITA	Guido and Maurizio de Angelis
It's Alive!	WB	Bernard Herrmann
It's Not the Size That Counts	BRI	Tony Macaulay
Jezebels, The	IND	Les Baxter
John and Marsha	PHI	Dominic Salistra
Jongara	JAP	Gunhachiro Shirakawa
Journey into Fear	TV	Alex North
Juggernaut	UA	Ken Thorne
Justine	ITA	Bruno Nicolai
Katsu Taiheiki	JAP	Isao Tomita
Keyhole	DEN	Moirana
Kill Barbara with Panic	PHI	Ernani Cuenco
Kisses Till Monday	FRA	Gerard Calvi
Klansman, The	PAR	Dale O. Warren/Stu Gardner
Lancelot of the Lake	FRA	Philippe Sarde
Lars Ole, 5c	DEN	Gunnar Moeller Pedersen
Last Days of Mussolini	ITA	Ennio Morricone
Last Exploits of the Olsen Gang, The	DEN	Bent Fabricius-Bjerre
Last Word, The	BUL	Simeon Pironkov

Legend of Frenchie King, The	FRA	Francis Lai
Lenny	UA	Ralph Burns
Lickety Split	IND	Head
Life Size	FRA/ ITA/ SPA	Maurice Jarre
Lifetime, A	FRA/ ITA	Francis Lai
Little Malcolm	BRI	Stanley Myers
Live a Little, Steal a Lot (Murph the Surf)	AI	Phillip Lambro
Living Dead at the Manchester Morgue, The	ITA	Giuliano Sorgini
Longest Yard, The	PAR	Frank de Vol
Lords of Flatbush, The	COL	Joe Brooks
Lost Boy, The (Huckleberry Finn)	RUS	Andrey Petrov
Love	FRA	Vangelis Papathanassiou
Love of Captain Brando, The	SPA	Jose Nieto
Lovers in the Year I	CZE	Karel Mares
Lovin' Molly	COL	Fred Hefferman
Macon County Line	AI	Stu Phillips
McQ	WB	Elmer Bernstein
Mad Adventures of Rabbi Jacob, The	FRA	Vladimir Cosma
Madhouse	AI	Douglas Gamley
Mai 68	FRA	Philippe Arthuys
Mama's Dirty Girls	IND	Don Bagley/Steve Michaels
Man and War (Part 3)	JAP	Masaru Sato
Man on a Swing	PAR	Lalo Schifrin
Man with the Golden Gun, The	UA	John Barry
Mary, La	ARG	Luis Maria Serra
Master Touch, The	GER/ ITA	Ennio Morricone
Me, Too, I'm the Mafia	DEN	Ib Glindermann
Melodies of Veruski District	RUS	Tsabadze
Memories Within Miss Aggie	IND	Rupert Holmes
Midnight Man, The	UN	Dave Grusin
Milano Calibro 9	ITA	Luis Enrique Bacalov/ Osanna
Milarepa	ITA	Daniele Paris
Miss O'Gynie and the Flower Men	BEL	Gabriel Yared
Mr. Majestyk	UA	Charles Bernstein
Mixed Company	UA	Fred Karlin
Moments	BRI	John Cameron
Montreal Main	CAN	Beverly Glenn-Copelann
Morel's Invention	ITA	Nicola Piovani
Murder on the Orient Express	PAR	Richard Rodney Bennett
Murdered House, The	BRA	Antonio Carlos Jobim
Murderess, The	GRE	Stavros Logarides
Murph the Surf (see Live a Little, Steal a Lot)		
Mutation, The	COL	Basil Kirchin

My Little Loves	FRA	Theodore Botrel
My Way	AFR	Robin Netcher
Mysterious Island of Captain Nemo, The	ITA	Gianni Ferrio
Nashville Coyote	IND	Buddy Baker
Neither the Sea nor the Sand	BRI	Nachum Heiman
Newman's Law	UN	Robert Prince
Nickel Ride, The	TCF	Dave Grusin
Night of the Scarecrow, The	BRA	Ricardo
Night Porter, The	UA	Daniele Paris
19 Red Roses	DEN	Thomas Koppen
99 and 44/100% Dead	TCF	Henry Mancini
Noldebo Vicarage	DEN	Sven Gyldmark
Not Just Another Woman	IND	Harold Ousley
Oddballs, The	RUS	Giya Kancheli
Odessa File, The	COL	Andrew Lloyd Webber
Office Picnic, The	AUT	Don Mow
Old-Fashioned Woman, An	IND	Lucy Coolidge
One by One (East Wind)	IND	Stomu Yamashita
One Who Came from Heaven, The	MEX	Hector Sanchez
Only God Knows	CAN	Ben McPeek
Open Season	COL	Ruggero Cini
Operation Rose Rose	ARG	Sandro
Our Time	WB	Michel Legrand
Parade	FRA	Charles Dumont
Parallax View, The	PAR	Michael Small
Partisans	YUG	Mikis Theodrakis
Paul and Michelle	PAR	Michel Colombier
Pavlinka	CZE	Zdenek Liska
Pedestrian, The	CIN	Manos Hadjidakis
People from the Subway	CZE	Lubos Fiser
People in Buenos Aires	ARG	Camaleon Rodriguez
Petersen	AUT	Peter Best
Phantastic World of Matthew Madson, The	GER	Nicholas Busch/Anthony Moore
Phantom of the Paradise	TCF	Paul Williams/George Aliceson Tipton
Phase VI	PAR	Brian Gascoigne
Photography	HUN	Ferenc Sabo
Pippi in the South Seas	GER/SWE	Georg Riedel
Pirosmani	RUS	M. Gabunia
Police Inspector Accuses, A	RUM	Richard Oschanitzky
Policewoman (series)	TV	Gerald Fried
Porno at the School of Scandal	SWE	Marcus Oesterdahl
Prince Ehtejab	IRAN	Ahmad Pezhman
Prisoner of Second Avenue, The	WB	Marvin Hamlisch
Profiteer, The	ITA	Sante Maria Romitelli
Promised Land, The	CHILE	Luis Advis
Purgatory	SWE	Pink Floyd
QB VII	TV	Jerry Goldsmith
Quebracho	ARG	Francisco Kropfl/Gustavo Beytelmann

Race in the Head, The	FRA	David Munrow
Rainy Love, A	FRA	Francis Lai
Reason to Live, a Reason to Die, A	IND	Riz Ortolani
Rebel Patagonia, The	ARG	Oscar Cardozo Ocampo
Red-Haired Revolver	BEL/ FRA	Armand Seggian
Red Snowball Tree, The	RUS	Pavel Chekalov
Republic of Uzice, The	YUG	Zoran Hristic
Return of the Big Blond, The (see Return of the Tall Blond, The)		
Return of the Dragon	HK	Ku Chia Hui
Return of the Tall Blond, The	FRA	Vladimir Cosma
Rhinoceros	AFT	Galt MacDermot
Rise, Fair Sun	JAP	Teizo Matsumara
Roland Rivas, Cab Driver	ARG	Alain Debray
Romance of Lovers	RUS	Alexander Gradsky
Rome Wants Another Caesar	ITA	Uberta Bertacca
Routine Has to Be Broken	ARG	Buddy McClusky
Ruslan and Ludmila	RUS	Tikon Krennikov
S*P*Y*S	TCF	Jerry Goldsmith
Sagarana Duel, The	BRA	Antonio Carlos Jobim
Savage Is Loose, The	IND	Gil Melle
Savage Sisters	AI	Les Baxter
Say It with Flowers (Dites-le Avec des Fleurs)	FRA	Claude Bolling
Scent of Woman	ITA	Armando Trovajoli
Second Coming of Suzanne, The	IND	Don Caverhill
Secret, The	FRA	Ennio Morricone
Seduction of Mimi, The	ITA	Piero Piccione
Seed, The	NOR	Karl Kolberg
Seedling, The	IN	Vanraj Bhatia
Seizure	AI	Lee Gagnon
Sex Thief, The	BRI	Mike Vickers
Shanghai Joe	ITA	Bruno Nicolai
Shanks	PAR	Alex North
Shoot It: Black, Shoot It: Blue	IND	Terry Stockdale
Shut Up, Gulls	FRA	Gerard Calvi
Simple Melody, A	SWE	Bjoern Jason Lindh
Skipper and Co.	IND	Lars Jensen
Sky High	IND	Mariano Moreno
Slipstream	CAN	Brian Ahern/Van Morrison/Eric Clapton
Snowfall	HUN	Zsolt Durko
Solomon King	IND	Jimmy Lewis
Sometime Sweet Susan	IND	Scott Mansfield
Somewhere Beyond Love	ITA	Carlo Rustichelli
Son of Dracula	IND	Harry Nilsson/Paul Buckmaster
Sonny and Jed	ITA	Ennio Morricone
Spectre of Edgar Allan Poe, The	CIN	Allen D. Allen
Spikes Gang, The	UA	Fred Karlin
Stardust	ITA	Piero Piccioni

Stars and the Water Carrier, The	DEN	Gunnar Moeller
Stavisky	FRA/ ITA	Stephen Sondheim
Steppenwolf	IND	George Gruntz
Stone	AUT	Billy Green
Stranger's Gundown, The	ITA	Mancuso
Street Gangs of Hong Kong	CIN	Chen Yung-Yu
Submersion of Japan (Tidal Wave)	JAP	Masaru Sato
Successive Slidings of Pleasure	FRA	Michel Fano
Sugar Hill	AI	Nick Zesses
Sugarland Express, The	UN	John Williams
Super Cops, The	MGM	Jerry Fielding
Superb Trip, The	FRA	Vladimir Cosma
Superdad	DIS	Buddy Baker
Supermarket	GER	Peter Hesslein
Swallows and Amazons	BRI	Wilfred Josephs
Sweet Movie	CAN/ YUG	Manos Hadjidakis
Swept Away (by a Strange Destiny in a Blue August Sea)	ITA	Piero Piccioni
Take It Easy	POL	Andrzej Korzynski
Takiji Kobayashi	JAP	Taku Izumi
Taking of Pelham 1, 2, 3, The	UA	David Shire
Tamarind Seed, The	EMB	John Barry
Tangsir	IRAN	Loris Chcknavarian
Tears of Happiness	IND	Jaime Mendoza-Nava
Tell Me You Love Me (Dis-moi que Tu m'Aimes)	FRA	Claude Bolling
Tempter, The (Devil Is a Woman, The)	ITA	Ennio Morricone
That's Enough, Man	PHI	Ernani Cuenco
There Is No 13	IND	Riz Ortolani
They Shall Overcome	IND	Bruce Roberts
Thomasine and Bushrod	COL	Coleridge-Taylor Perkinson
Those Dirty Dogs	IND	Nico Fidenco
Three the Hard Way	AA	Richard Tufo
Three Tough Guys	PAR	Isaac Hayes
Thunderbolt and Lightfoot	UA	Dee Barton
Tidal Wave (see Submersion of Japan)		
Tipchang	THAI	Sanga Arampi
To Love Ophelia	ITA	Riz Ortolani
Together Brothers, The	TCF	Barry White
Too Skinny for Love?	GER	Illest Ensemble
Torment	SPA	Carmelo Bernaola
Towering Inferno, The	TCF/ WB	John Williams
Tree Without Roots, A	BUL	Kassimir Kyurkchiyski
Trial of Billy Jack, The	IND	Elmer Bernstein
Trial of the Judges, The	GRE	Christos Leontis
Trio Infernal, Le	FRA/ GER/ ITA	Ennio Morricone

Trip, The (Viaggio, El)	ITA	Manuel de Sica
Trip Through Purgatory	FRA	Gerard Anfosso
Truce, The	ARG	Julian Plaza
Truck Turner	AI	Isaac Hayes
23 Fireman's Street	HUN	Zdenko Tamassy
27A	AUT	Winsome Evans
Two	IND	Akira Talmi
Two Men of Karamoja	IND	Charles Randolph Grean
Uptown Saturday Night	WB	Tom Scott
Venial Sin	ITA	Fred Bongusto
Verdict	FRA	Louiguy
Very Natural Thing, A	NLC	Bert Lucarelli/Gordon Gottlieb
Vincent, Francois, Paul ... and the Others	FRA	Philippe Sarde
Visit to a Chief's Son	UA	Francis Lai
Vive la France	FRA	Eddie Vartan
Voyage to Next (short)	IND	Dizzy Gillespie
W	CIN	Johnny Mandel
Wait a Minute!	HUN	Gabor Presser
Waltzers, The	FRA	Stephane Grappelli
Watchmaker of Saint-Paul, The	FRA	Philippe Sarde
Wedding	RUS/YUG	Cvetko Slilepcevic
When There Wasn't Treasure (short)	BRI	Johnny Hawksworth
Where the Lilies Bloom	UA	Earl Scruggs
Where the Red Fern Grows	IND	Lex de Azevedo
White Dawn, The	PAR	Henry Mancini
Why Rock the Boat?	CAN	John Howe
Wicket Gate, The	POL	Wojiech Kilar
Wild Hare Census, The (see Hare Census, The)		
Wind, The	YUG	Arsen Dedic
With the Blood of Others	FRA	Francis Lai
With You and Without You	RUS	Bigdan Trozjuk
Wolf and the Dove, The	SPA	Malcolm Lockyer
Wolfpen Principle, The	CAN	Don Druick
Woman Under the Influence, A	IND	Bo Harwood
Women in Cell Block 7	ITA/USA	George Craig
Women in the Sun	FRA	Bookie Brinkley
Women, Women	FRA	Roland Vincent
Year of the Caribou	IND	John Anderson
Year One	ITA	Mario Nascimbene
You Are Weighed but Found Lacking	PHI	Lutgardo Labad
Young Frankenstein	TCF	John Morris
Zapped by a Strange Destiny in a Blue August Sea (see Swept Away)		
Zardoz	TCF	David Munrow
Zeami	JAP	Toshiro Mayazumi

1975

Aaron Loves Angela	COL	Jose Feliciano
Abduction	IND	Ron Frangipane/Robbie Farrow
Actors and the Savages, The	RUM	George Grigoriu
Adoption, The	HUN	Gyorgy Kovacs
Adventures of Sherlock Holmes' Smarter Brother, The	TCF	John Morris
Against a Crooked Sky	IND	Lex de Azevedo
Aggression	FRA	Robert Charlebois
Akenfield	BRI	Sir Michael Tippett
Aldevaran	GRE	Demetris Poulicacos
Alfie Darling	BRI	Alan Price
Ali the Man: Ali the Fighter	IND	Simon Stokes
Amelie's Trip	FRA	Maurice Vander
American Surplus, The	THAI	Prasit Payomyong
Amici Miei	ITA	Armando Trovajoli
Amulet of Ogum, The	BRA	Jards Macale
And Now My Love (Tout une Vie)	FRA/ ITA	Francis Lai
Anna Karenina	RUS	Rodion Shchedrin
Ante Up	ITA	Franco Micalizzi
Apple Dumpling Gang, The	DIS	Buddy Baker
Apple Pie	IND	Brad Fiedel
Attenti al Buffone	ITA	Ennio Morricone
Attila '74	GRE	Michel Christodoulides
Autobiography of a Princess	BRI	Vic Flick
Babe	TV	Jerry Goldsmith
Baby Sitter, The	FRA/ GER/ ITA	Francis Lai
Barry Lyndon	WB	Leonard Rosenman
Bay of Marbles, A	FRA	Philippe Sarde
Beloved Elektra	HUN	Tomas Cseh
Best Friends	IND	Richard Cunha
Between Night and Day	GER	Karl-Ernst Sasse
Beware: When a Widow Falls in Love	PHI	Totoy Nuke
Beyond Fear	FRA/ ITA	Alain Goraguer
Beyond the Door	IND	Riz Ortolani
Beyond the Sun	ARG	Victor Proncet
Big Brother Ching	HK	Lo Pao-Sheng
Bio-Graphia	GRE	Stamatis Spanoudakis
Bite the Bullet	COL	Alex North
Black Bird, The	COL	Jerry Fielding
Blondy	FRA/ GER	Stelvio Cipriani
Blood Stains in a New Car	SPA	Teddy Bautista
Bokyo	JAP	Akira Ikufube
Book of Good Love, The	SPA	Patxi Andion
Born to Kill	IND	Michael Franks

Born to Raise Hell	IND	Rod Riker
Boss and the Worker, The	ITA	Gianni Ferrio
Boy and His Dog, A	IND	Tim McIntire
Brannigan	UA	Dominic Frontiere
Breakout	COL	Jerry Goldsmith
Brutalization of Franz Blum, The	GER	Michael J. Lewis
Bucktown	AI	Johnny Pate
Bug	PAR	Charles Fox
Burned Bridge	BEL/ FRA	Alain Pierre
Butcher, the Star and the Orphan, The	FRA	Jacques Coutureau
Cagliostro	ITA	Manuel de Sica
Caone	TCF	David Grisman
Cat and the Mouse, The	FRA	Francis Lai
Catherine Inc.	FRA	Vladimir Cosma
Ce Cher Victor (That Dear Victor)	FRA	Bernard Gerard
Cecilia, La	FRA/ ITA	Michel Portal
Cell Zero, The	GRE	Nicos Kanakis
Chain of Life	THAI	Kangwan Cholakul
Challenge to Be Free	IND	Ian Bernard
Children of Rage	BRI/ ISR	Patrick Gowers
Chorus	IN	Ananda Shankar
Chronicle of the Years of Fire	ALG	Philippe Arthuys
Cleopatra Jones and the Casino of Gold	WB	Dominic Frontiere
Cold Journey	CAN	Eldon Rathburn
Cold Soup, The	FRA	Jean-Pierre Pouret
Colour (short)	BRI	Tony Kinsey
Common Man, The	SWI	Arthur Paul Huber
Companero	BRI	Victor Jara
Conquistadores, Les	FRA	Daniel Humair/Joachim Kuhn/Michel Portal
Constabulary, The	PHI	Tito Arevalo
Conversation Piece	ITA	Franco Mannino
Cookbook of Birth Control, The	CHN	Lau Ka Cheong
Cooley High	AI	Freddie Perren
Coonskin	BRY	Chico Hamilton
Cop Story (Flic Story, The)	FRA	Claude Bolling
Cornbread, Earl and Me	AI	Donald Byrd
Corruption in the Halls of Justice	ITA	Pino Donaggio
Counter Kill	PHI	Ernani Cuenco
Country Inc.	SPA	Victor and Diego
Cousin, Cousine	FRA	Gerard Anfasso
Cubs, The	MEX	Joaquin Gutierrez Heras
Daosawan, I Love You	THAI	Eddie Wong
Dark Lady	THAI	Prasert Churaketr
Day of the Locust	PAR	John Barry
Dead One, The	ARG/ SPA	Ariel Ramirez
Death of a Nun	BEL/ HOL	Pierre Verlinden

Death Race 2000	NWP	Paul Chikara
Devil Queen, The	BRA	Gilhermo Vaz
Devil's Rain, The	IND	Al de Lory
Diamonds	EMB	Roy Budd
Dirty Western, A	IND	Steve Jason/Lee O'Donnell
Do You Hear the Dogs Barking?	FRA/MEX	Vangelos Papathanasiou
Doc Savage ... The Man of Bronze	WB	Frank de Vol
Dr. Francoise Gailland	FRA	Catherine Lara
Dolemite	IND	Arthur Wright
Don't Be Weak with Life	ARG	Tito Ribero
Doomed Souls	BUL	Mitko Shterev
Down the Ancient Staircase	ITA	Ennio Morricone
Dracula and the 7 Golden Vampires	BRI/CHN	Wang Fu-Ling
Drama of the Rich	FRA/ITA	Ennio Morricone
Dreyfus, or the Unbearable Truth	FRA	Jean-Pierre Doering
Drowning Pool, The	WB	Michael Small/Charles Fox
Earthly Body, The	PHI	Demet Velasquez
Education in Love of Valentin, The	FRA	Jean Prodromides
Eiger Sanction, The	UN	John Williams
81st Flow, The	ISR	Josef Mar-Haim
Elective Affinities	GER	Karl-Ernst Sasse
Entertainer, The	AUT	Marvin Hamlisch
Escape to Witch Mountain	DIS	Johnny Mandel
Espy	JAP	Masaki Hirao
Eternal Times	BUL	Kiril Dontchev
Everlasting Glory, The	THAI	Yang Ping-Chung
Every Inch a Lady	IND	Firth de Mule
Everybody Rides the Carousel	IND	Bill Russo
Eye of the Cat	ITA	Ennio Morricone
Fantasies Behind the Pearly Curtain	CHN	Lui Cha Chang
Fantastic Comedy	RUM	C. Capoinu
Farewell My Lovely	EMB	David Shire
Fear on the City	FRA	Ennio Morricone
Fete Sauvage, La	FRA	Vangelis Papathanassiou
Fight to the Death	SPA	Stelvio Cipriani/M. Molino/D. Patucchi/Dusan Radic/Carlo Rustichelli
Film, The	ARG	Gustavo Beytelman
Fireworks Woman	IND	Jacques Urbont
First Step, The	RUS	Djansuch Kachidze
First Time, on the Grass, The	ITA	Fiorenzo Carpi
Flame	BRI	Noddy Holder/Jimmy Lea
Flesh of the Orchid, The	FRA	Fiorenzo Carpi
For Better or Worse	CAN	Pierre Brault
Foreplay	IND	Stan Vincent
Forever Young, Forever Free	UN	Lee Holdridge
Fortune, The	COL	David Shire

Four Musketeers, The	TCF	Lalo Schifrin
Framed	PAR	Patrick Williams
French Connection II	TCF	Don Ellis
Friday Foster	AI	Luchi de Jesus
Galileo	AFT	Hanns Eisler
Garden That Tilts, The	FRA	Marc Hilman/Jean-Pierre Stora
Gaucho Jews, The	ARG	Gustavo Beytelman
Ghoul, The	BRI	Harry Robinson
Gifts of an Eagle	IND	Clark Gassman
Giliap	SWE	Bjoern Isafelt
Girl with the Long Hair	CHN	Chen Yung-Yu
Girls at Arms	DEN	Ole Hoeyer
Gloria Mundi	FRA	Barbaud Brown Klein
Glorious Dust	YUG	Darijian Bozic
Goin' Surfin'	IND	Richard Henn
Golden Fortress, The	IN	Satyajit Ray
Golden Mass, The	FRA	Severino Gazzellino
Golden Ophelia	BEL	Etienne Verschueren
Good and the Bad, The	DEN	Gunnar Moeller Pedersen
Good Morning (Ohayosan)	JAP	Mitsugu Okumura
Goodbye Singing, The	FRA	Elisabeth Wiener
Grande Bourgeoisie, La	FRA/ ITA	Ennio Morricone
Great House, The	SPA	Emilio de Diego
Great MacArthy, The	AUT	Bruce Smeaton
Great McGonagall, The	BRI	John Shakespeare/Derek Warne
Great Waldo Pepper, The	UN	Henry Mancini
Grotze Farmer, The	SWI	Pepe Solbach
Guttersnipes	SWE	Charles Redland
Guy and a Gal, A	SWE	Berndt Egerblad
Gypsy, The	FRA	Django Reinhardt/Claude Bolling
Hajduk	HUN	Levente Szorenyi
Happy Divorce, The	DEN/ FRA	Philippe Sarde
Happy Hooker, The	IND	Don Elliott
Hard Times	COL	Barry de Vorzon
Have a Nice Weekend	IND	Charles Gross
Headless Horseman, The	RUS	Nikita Bugoslovski
Hearts of the West	MGM	Ken Lauber
Hedda	BRI	Laurie Johnson
Hello, Goodnight, Goodbye	PHI	George Canseco
He's Quite a Man	BUL	Alexandre Brazitzov
Hester Street	IND	William Bolcom
Hiding Place, The	IND	Tedd Smith
Hindenburg, The	UN	David Shire
Hitler Around the Corner	YUG	Zivan Cvitkovic
Home for Christmas	FIN	Otto Donner
Homo Eroticus	ITA	Armando Trovajoli
Hotel Pacific	CZE/ POL	Jerzy Matuszkiewicz

Film	Country	Composer
House, The	YUG	Tomica Simobovic
House in the South, The	MEX	Gustavo C. Carreon
How Wonderful to Die Assassinated	ITA	Roberto de Simone
Hu-Man	FRA	David Horowitz/Jean Guillou/Patrick Vian
Human Factor, The	IND	Ennio Morricone
Hundred Days After Childhood, A	RUS	Isaak Schwarz
Husbands Vacationing	ARG	Buddy McCluskey
Hustle	PAR	Frank de Vol
I Did Kill Facundo	ARG	Oscar Cardozo Ocampo
I Had a Feeling I Was Dead	GER	Peter Schirmann
I Never Cried Like This Before	HOL	Pieter Verlinden
I Saw Her First	SPA	Carlos Vizziello
I Will Fight No More Forever	TV	Gerald Fried
Ice-Age	GER/NOR	Peer Raben
Ice Continent, The	ITA	Giuliano Sorgini
I'd Like to Have My Troubles	GER	Roderick Melvin/Franz Hummel/Robert Schumann
I'm a Woman Already	SPA	Carlos Vizziello
In Search of Dracula	FRA	Calvin Floyd
In the Sign of Gemini	DEN/SWE	Bertrand Bech
Incorrigible	FRA	Georges Delerue
India Song	FRA	Carlos D'Alessio
Inki	GER	Wilfried Schroepfer
Innocents with Dirty Hands, The	FRA/GER/ITA	Pierre Jansen
Inside Amy	IND	Jack Preisner
Inside Out	BRI	Konrad Elfers
Isabelle Devant le Desir	BEL/FRA	Claude Luter/Yannick Singery
It Seemed Like a Good Idea at the Time	CAN	William McCauley
Jacob the Liar	GER	Joachim Wetzlau
Jaws	UN	John Williams
John Glueckstadt	GER	Eberhard Schoener
Juan Vicente Gomez and His Era	SA	Luis T. Laffer
Jungle in the City, The	PHI	Ernani Cuenco
Kettje Tippel	HOL	Rogier van Otterloo
Kid Head	ARG	Pocho Leyes
Killer Elite, The	UA	Jerry Fielding
Killer Force	AI	Georges Garvarentz
Land of Promise	POL	Wojiech Kilar
Land That Time Forgot, The	BRI	Douglas Gamley
Last Days of Man on Earth, The	BRI	Paul Beaver/Bernard Krause/Gerry Mulligan
Last Love, The	THAI	Ading Dila
Leave Us Alone	DEN	Lasse Lunderskov
Legacy	IND	Roger Kellaway

Leonor	FRA/ ITA/ SPA	Ennio Morricone
Let Go of My Beard	HUN	Gyorgy Vukan
Let Joy Reign Supreme	FRA	Philippe d'Orleans
Let's Do It Again	WB	Curtis Mayfield
Libera, My Love	ITA	Ennio Morricone
Lies My Father Told Me	CAN	Sol Kaplan
Lifespan	IND	Terry Riley
Lily, Love Me	FRA	Edgardo Canton
Lina Braake--The Bank's Interests Can't Be the Interests Lina Braake Has	GER	Joe Haider
Lion and the Virgin, The	SWE	Bjoern Jason Lindh
Lisztomania	BRI	Rick Wakeman
Lit--Ze Bawdy Bed, Le	CAN	Charles Dumont
Live Coal in the East	PHI	Demet Velasquez
Long Returning, A (Largo Retorno, Un)	SPA	Anton Garcia Abril
Looping	GER	Peter Rabenalt
Loose Ends	IND	John Paul Hammond
Lord Shango	IND	Howard Roberts
Lost Honor of Katharine Blum, The	GER	Hans-Werner Henze
Lotte in Weimar	GER	Karl-Ernst Sasse
Love and Anarchy	ITA	Nino Rota
Love and Energy	ITA	Fred Bongusto
Lucky Lady	TCF	Ralph Burns
McCullochs, The	AI	Ernest Gold
Mackintosh and T. J.	IND	Waylon Jennings
Madame Kitty (Salon Kitty)	AI	Fiorenzo Carpi
Mahogany	PAR	Michael Masser
Maids, The	AFT	Laurie Johnson
Main Thing Is to Love, The	FRA/ ITA	Georges Delerue
Male of the Century	FRA	Claude Morgan
Man Friday	BRI	Carl Davis
Man Who Would Be King, The	AA	Maurice Jarre
Manchu Eagle Murder Caper Mystery, The	UA	Dick de Benedictus
Mandingo	PAR	Maurice Jarre
Maria	SWE	Kjell Andersson
Marilyn and the Senator	IND	Santos Moroyoqui
Marriage	FRA	Francis Lai
Marriage Revolution, The	SPA	Juan Pardo
Mary, Mary, Bloody Mary	IND	Tom Bahler
Master Gunfighter, The	IND	Lalo Schifrin
Me	CAN	Noel Elson
Meal, The	IND	Stu Phillips
Memories	BUL	Kiril Tseboulka/Kiril Dontchev
Messiah of Evil	IND	Phillan Bishop
Metamorphosis	SWE	Eric Ericson

Midnight Pleasures	ITA	Guido and Maurizio de Angelis
Might Makes Right	GER	Peer Raben
Miss Maliwan	THAI	Kangwan Cholakul
Mr. Ricco	MGM	Chico Hamilton
Mr. Sycamore	IND	Maurice Jarre
Mitchell	AA	Larry Brown
Mondo Candido	ITA	Riz Ortolani
Monty Python and the Holy Grail	BRI	De Wolfe
Most Beautiful Animal in the World, The	PHI	Ernani Cuenco
Mother and Daughter	PHI	Tito Arevalo
Murder on the Bridge	GER/ ITA	Ennio Morricone
My Brother Has a Cute Brother	CZE	Jiri Malasek
My Fiance, the Transvestite	ARG	Buddy McCluskey
My Friends	ITA	Carlo Rustichelli
My Lady	THAI	Servasan Group
My Michael	ISR	Alex Cogan
My Sexy Girl Friend	PHI	Jose Mari Chan
Nail of Brightness, The	PHI	Max Jooson
Naked Came the Stranger	IND	George Craig
National Mechanics	MEX	Ruben Fuentes
Nazarene Cross and the Wolf	ARG	Juan Garcia Caffi
New Parthenon, The	GRE	Loukianos Kalaidonis
New Spaniards, The	SPA	Carmelo Bernaola
New Teacher, The	THAI	Montri Ong-lam
Night Caller, The	FRA	Ennio Morricone
Night Moves	WB	Michael Small
Night of Orange Fires	CZE	Jiri Stenvald
Nights and Days	POL	Waldemar Kazanecki
92 in the Shade	UA	Michael J. Lewis
Nitra Sayan	THAI	Prasert Churaketr
No Pockets in a Shroud	PAR	Paul de Senneville
Not as Wicked as All That ...	FRA/ SWI	Arie Szirlatka
Nothing but the Truth	DEN	Palle Mikkelsborg
Nothing by Chance	IND	Lee Holdridge
Off Bedside Limits	DEN	Ole Hoeyer
Oh, America	FRA	Jack Treese
Old Dracula	BRI	David Whittaker
Olsen Gang on the Track, The	DEN	Bent Fabricius-Bjerre
On Top of All	PHI	Danny Subido
Once Is Not Enough	PAR	Henry Mancini
One-Armed Boxer vs. the Flying Guillotine	CHN	Chan Fung Ki
One Flew Over the Cuckoo's Nest	UA	Jack Nitzsche
One Must Live Dangerously (Il Faut Vivre Dangereusement)	FRA	Claude Bolling
One Night, Three Women	PHI	O. Velasquez
One of Our Dinosaurs Is Missing	DIS	Ron Goodwin
One Silver Dollar	FRA/ ITA	Gianni Ferrio

Onion Chase, The	FRA	Vladimir Cosma
Orders, The	CAN	Philippe Gagnon
Other Francisco, The	CUB	Leo Brouwer
Other Side of the Mountain, The	UN	Charles Fox
Out of Season	BRI	John Cameron
Overlord	BRI	Paul Glass
Pacific Challenge	IND	Bill Conti
Paco	SA	Mariano and Mauro Bruno
Paolo Barca, Schoolteacher and Weekend Nudist	ITA	Riz Ortolani
Paper Tiger	EMB	Boy Budd
Passion According to Matthew	YUG	Vladimir Kraus
Pastorale Hide and Seek	JAP	J. A. Seazar
Peasant on a Bicycle	BUL	Boris Karadimchev
Peeper	TCF	Richard Clements
People, People, People (short)	IND	Benny Carter
Pepita Jimenez	SPA	Stelvio Cipriani
Per	DEN	Gunnar Moeller
Permission to Kill	EMB	Richard Rodney Bennett
Picnic at Hanging Rock	AUT	Bruce Smeaton
Pig's War, The	ARG	Leandro "Gato" Barbieri
Pim, Pam, Pum ... Fire!	SPA	Carmelo Bernaola
Poachers	SPA	Vainica Doble
Polemonta	GRE	Eleni Karaendrou
Policewoman	ITA	Gianni Ferrio
Posse	PAR	Maurice Jarre
Pregnant by a Ghost	THAI	Sakat Tuchinda
Premonition, The	EMB	Ennio Morricone
Private Enterprise, A	BRI	Ram Narayan
Prometheus' Second Person	GRE	Stamatis Spanoudakis
Psychic Killer	EMB	William Kraft
Pussy Talk	FRA	Mike Steitheson
Quarterly Balance-Taking	GER	Vojiech Kilar
Race with the Devil	TCF	Leonard Rosenman
Rafferty and the Gold Dust Twins	WB	Artie Butler
Raging Fists	FRA	Eric Demarsan
Rancho DeLuxe	UA	Jimmy Buffet
Ransom (see Terrorists, The)		
Recommendation for Mercy	CAN	Don Gillis
Red Earth	YUG	Zoran Hristic
Red Sun	HOL	Ruud Bos
Regent's Wife, The	SPA	Francesco Lavagnino/ Carmello Bernaola
Reincarnation of Peter Proud, The	AI	Jerry Goldsmith
Release the Prisoners, It's Spring	SWE	Rune Gustafsson
Report to the Commissioner	UA	Elmer Bernstein
Return of the Pink Panther	UA	Henry Mancini
Return to Campus	IND	Gordon Zahler/Harry Fields
Return to Macon County	AI	Robert O. Ragland/ Roger Christian
Ride a Wild Pony	AUT	John Addison
Road, The	LIBYA	Atiyah Mohamed

Romantic Englishwoman, The	BRI/ FRA	Richard Hartley
Rooster Cogburn	UN	Laurence Rosenthal
Root, The	PHI	Luigi
Rose-Colored Telephone, The	FRA	Vladimir Cosma
Rosebud	UA	Laurent Petitgirard
Royal Flash	TCF	Ken Thorne
Rufus	HOL	Clous van Mechelen
Russian Roulette	EMB	Michael J. Lewis
S. O. S.	IND	Ron Frangipane
Salo or 120 Days of Sodom	ITA	Ennio Morricone
Salon Kitty (see Madame Kitty)		
Sauvage, Le (see Savage, The)		
Savage, The	FRA	Michel Legrand
Scobie Malone	AUT	Peter Clark/Alan Johnston
Scorched Triangle, The	FRA	Humbert Ibach-Romuald
Scorpion Sea	PHI	Ernani Cuenco
Section Speciale	FRA	Eric Demarsan
Sensations	HOL	Richard Moore
7 Morts sur Ordonnance (7 Deaths by Subscription)	FRA	Philippe Sarde
Serail	FRA	Michel Portal
Serious as Pleasure	FRA	Michel Berger
Seven Alone	IND	Robert O. Ragland
7 Deaths by Subscription	FRA/ GER/ SPA	Philippe Sarde
Sextool	IND	Donald Geoffreys/Eric Satie
Shampoo	COL	Paul Simon
Shark's Treasure	UA	Robert O. Ragland
Sheba Baby	AI	Monk Higgins/Alex Brown
Sheila Levine Is Dead and Living in New York	PAR	Michel Legrand
Sherlock Jones	HOL	"Toots" Thielemans
Show Business	FRA	Jean Yanne
Sidecar Racers	UN	Tom Scott
Sins in the Family	ITA	Guido and Maurizio de Angelis
Six Pack Annie	AI	Raoul Kraushaar
67 Days	YUG	Zoran Hristic
Sleep, Sleep My Love	SPA	F. Campuzano
Sleeping Dragon	CHN/ PHI	Lucio San Pedro
Slip-Up	IND	S. Ziplow/Slim Pickens
Smile	UA	Danile Osborn/Leroy Holmes/Charles Chaplin
Softening of the Egg, The	SWE	Alfred Janson
Son from Bergaarden, The	DEN	Sven Gyldmark
Sons of Fire	HUN	Zoltan Jeney
Soup du Jour	IND	Kenny Armstrong/Joseph Gallello

Souvenir of Gibraltar	BEL	Tucker Zimmerman
Speak to Me of Love	FRA	Alan Reeves
Stepford Wives, The	COL	Michael Small
Stepmother, The	MEX/ SPA	Jose Salcedo
Story of Adele H., The	FRA	Maurice Jaubert
Story of Joanna, The	IND	Edward Earle
Story of "O," The	FRA	Pierre Bachelet
Story of Peaceful Genroku Era, The	JAP	Johji Yuasa
Strongest Man in the World, The	DIS	Robert F. Brunner
Struggle	GRE	Phoebus Economides
Student Body, The	IND	Don Bagley
Sudden Fury	CAN	Matthew McCauley
Sunday Chronicle	GRE	Eleni Karaendrou
Sunday in the Country	CAN	Paul Hoffert
Sup Sap Bup Dap	CHN	Fu Ka Fang
Super Super Adventure, The	ARG	Pocho Leyes
Survive!	PAR	Gerald Fried
TNT Jackson	IND	Tito Scotto
Take a Hard Ride	TCF	Jerry Goldsmith
Tarzoon, the Snake of the Jungle	BEL/ FRA	Marc Moulin
Ten Little Indians	EMB	Bruno Nicolai
Terrorists, The (Ransom)	BRI	Jerry Goldsmith
Testament	YUG	Kornelije Kovac
Thai Tiger's Roar	THAI	Prasert Churaketr
That Lucky Touch	BRI	John Scott
That's the Way of the World	UA	Philip Bailey/Larry Dunn/Maurice White
They Fought for Their Country	RUS	Vyecheslav Ovchinnikov
Thomas	FRA	Marie-Paule Belle
Those Were the Years	ITA	Armando Trovajoli
Three Days of the Condor	PAR	David Grusin
Three, Two, One	PHI	Minda Azarcon
Time of Blue, The	JAP	Norio Kuwabara
To Search for a Golden Earth	CZE	J. Sust/A. Michajlov
Tomorrow, Pheasant	HUN	Janos Gonda
Track, The	FRA	Giancarlo Chiaramello
Train Ride to Hollywood	IND	Pip Williams
Triangle of Four	ARG	Sergio Mihanovich
Trompe d'Oeil	FRA	Alain Pierre
Trop c'est Trop	FRA	Jean Bouchety/Christian Chevallier
True Story of Eskimo Nell, The	AUT	Brian May
Turn the Other Cheek	FRA/ ITA	Guido and Maurizio de Angelis
$2 Haircut, The (Coupe a Dix)	FRA	Anthony Brazlon/Antoine Duhamel
Two Women	SWE	Sven-Olaf Waldorf/Bengt Ernryd
Ultimate Warrior, The	IND	Gil Melle

Undercovers Hero	UA	Neil Rhoden
Unfinished Sentence in 141 Minutes, The	HUN	Gyorgy Vukan
Vanda Teres	FRA/ SWI	Francois Rabbath
Victim of Passion	THAI	Kang Wangchorakul
Vigilante Force	UA	Gerard Fried
Villa Zone	BUL	Kiril Dontchev
Vincent Puts the Ass in a Field	FRA	Francois Rabbath
Violets Are Blue	DEN	Bent Fabricius-Bjerre
Virgin Named Mary, A	ITA	Sante Maria Romitelli
Voyage de Noces, Le	FRA	Christian Chevallier/ Michel Legrand
W. W. and the Dixie Dancekings	TCF	Dave Grusin
Walk Fory, The	HUN	Ferenc Gyulai-Gaal
Walking Tall (Part 2)	AI	Walter Scharf
Water It and Dew for the Thirsty Soil	PHI	Ernani Cuenco
Weak Spot, The	FRA/ GER/ ITA	Ennio Morricone
Wedding Trough	BEL	Alain Pierre
What's Next?	BRI	Carl Davis
When Svante Disappeared	DEN	Benny Andersen
Whiffs	TCF	John Cameron
While There's War There's Hope	ITA	Piero Piccioni
White Collar Blues	ITA	Fabio Frizzi
White Line Fever	COL	David Nicktern
White, Yellow, Black	ITA	Guido and Maurizio de Angelis
Why Does One Kill a Magistrate?	ITA	Riz Ortolani
Wilby Conspiracy, The	UA	Stanley Myers
Wild Party, The	AI	Laurence Rosenthal
Wind and the Lion, The	MGM	Jerry Goldsmith
With Nobody	BUL	Simeon Pironkov
Woman, A	ARG	Luis Maria Serra
Woman, You Should Not Have Been Created	PHI	Danny Holmes
World of Love, A	ARG	Victor Proncet
Wow (Women of the World)	CAN	Bill Russo
Wrong Movement	GER	Jurgen Knieper
Yakuza, The	WB	Dave Grusin
Your Husband Is My Lover	PHI	Ernani Cuenco
Yuppi Du	ITA	Adriano Celentato
Zig-Zig	FRA	Carl Hans Sachafer
Zorro	FRA/ ITA	Guido and Maurizio de Angelis

1976

Aces High	BRI	Richard Hartley
Across the Great Divide	IND	Gene Kauer/Douglas Lackey

Film	Studio	Composer
Adios Amigo	IND	Luchi de Jesus
Adolescents, The	SPA	Juan Carlos Calderon
Adventures of a Wilderness Family, The	IND	Gene Kauer/Douglas Lackey
Agaton Sax and the Bykoebing Village Festival	SWE	Charles Redland
Alex and the Gypsy	TCF	Henry Mancini
All the President's Men	WB	David Shire
Alone	ARG	Jorge Calandrell
Amazing Dobermans, The	IND	Alan Silvestri
Amendment to the Law for the Defense of the State	BUL	Simeon Pironkov
American Dream, The	SWE	David Clayton-Thomas/ Doug Riley
America's Fat	ARG	Buddy McCluskey
Amorous Adventures of Don Quixote and Sancho Panza, The	IND	Don Great
And They Lived Happily Ever After	SPA	Victor Manuel
Andes Odyssey, The	MEX	Angel Parra
Angels	IND	Olubji Adetoye
Anguish	NOR	Peter Lowdwick
Anno Domini 1573	YUG	Alfi Kabiljo
Aphonyo	RUS	Moises Vainberg
Assassination in Sarajevo	CZE/ YUG	Ljubos Fiser
Assault on Agathon	IND	Ken Thorne
At the Earth's Core	AI	Mike Vickers
Babatu	NIG	Dyeliba Badye/Daouda Kante
Baby Blue Marine	COL	Fred Karlin
Bad News Bears, The	PAR	Jerry Fielding
Bad Starters, The	FRA	Eric Demarsan
Barefooten Gen	JAP	Takeshi Shibuya
Barocco	FRA	Philippe Sarde
Beach Guard in Winter, The	YUG	Zoran Hristic
Bedside Sailors	DEN	Ole Hoeyer
Berlinger	GER	Joe Haider
Bernice Bobs Her Hair	IND	Dick Hyman
Between Heaven and Hell	PHI	Danny Holmsen
Beyond the Bridge	RUM	Romeo Chelaru
Big Bus, The	PAR	David Shire
Bim	IND	Andre Tanker
Bingo Long Traveling All-Stars and Motor Kings, The	UN	William Goldstein
Birch Interval	IND	Leonard Rosenman
Birds of Baden-Baden, The	SPA	Anton Garcia Abril
Bittersweet Love	EMB	Ken Wannberg
Black and White in Color	AA	Pierre Bachelet
Black Shampoo	IND	Gerald Lee
Black Victory	FRA	Pierre Bachelet
Blazing Magnum	ITA	Armando Trovajoli
Blood in the Streets	FRA/ GER/ ITA	Ennio Morricone

Blowdry	IND	Bill Dern/Joel Mofsenson
Blue Bird, The	RUS/ TCF	Irwin Kostal/Lionel Newman
Bobbie Jo and the Outlaw	AI	Barry de Vorzon
Body of My Enemy, The	FRA	Francis Lai
Boscop Diagram, The	FRA	Sotha
Bound for Glory	UA	Leonard Rosenman
Breakheart Pass	UA	Jerry Goldsmith
Breaking Point	CAN	David McLey
Breaking with Old Ideas	CHN	Lu Yuan Tang
Brothers, The	GER	Guido and Maurizio de Angelis
Bruce Lee--True Story	CHN	Chow Fu Liang
Brutus	PHI	Dominic Salustiano
Bubble, The	SWI	Paul Misraki
Buddies	SWE	Lalla Hansson
Buffalo Bill and the Indians, or Sitting Bull's History Lesson	UA	Richard Baskin
Bugsy Malone	PAR	Paul Williams
Burned City, The	SPA	Manuel Valls Gorina
Burnt Offerings	UA	Robert Cobert
Bus, The	SWE	Omar Zulfu
By Hook or By Crook	GER	Jurgen Knieper
Caddie	AUT	Patrick Flynn
California Reich, The	IND	Craig Sofan
Call Him Mr. Shatter	EMB	David Lundup
Calm, Cool and Collected (see Femmes Fatales)		
Calmos (see Femmes Fatales)		
Cannonball	NWP	David A. Axelrod
Car Wash	UN	Norman Whitfield
Carpet on the Cloud, The	JAP	Kochi Sakata
Carrie	UA	Pino Donaggio
Casanova	ITA	Nino Rota
Castaways of Turtle Island, The	FRA	Dorival Caymi/Nana Vasconellos
Cat Murkil and the Silks	IND	Bernie Kaai Lewis
Celestina	MEX	Marcos Lipschitz
Challenge of Greatness, The	IND	Michel Michelet
Child in the Crowd, A	FRA	Jean Schwarz
Child Is a Wild Thing, A	IND	Derek Wadsworth
Chin, Chin, the Drunken Bum	MEX	Manuel Esperon
Chinese Roulette	GER	Peer Raben
Choice, The	BEL/ FRA	Guy Boulanger
Chronicle of a Latin-American Subversive	VEN	Miguel Angel Fuster
Clown, The	GER	Eberhard Schoener
Commitment, The	IND	Dobie Gray/John D'Andrea
Context, The	ITA	Piero Piccioni
Cop	DEN	Kaspar Winding
Corrida of Love	FRA/ JAP	Minoru Miki

Could We Maybe	DEN	Sebastian (Knud Joergensen)
Count of Monte Cristo, The	BRI	Allyn Ferguson
Count the Ways	IND	Dan Samuels
Countdown at Kusini	COL	Manu Dibango
Country Is Calm, The	GER	Angel Parra
Coup de Grace, The	FRA/ GER	Stanley Myers
Crazy Sex	HK	Chen Yung Yu
Cricket in the Ear	BUL	Kiril Dontchev
Cyclops	BUL	Kiril Chiboulka
Dandy, the All-American Girl (see Sweet Revenge)		
Daughter-in-Law	BUL	Kiril Chiboulka
Day of Glory, The	FRA	Darry Cowl
Deadly Hero	EMB	Brad Fiedel/Tommy Mandel
Dear Fatherland, Be at Peace	GER	Jurgen Knieper
Dear Michael	ITA	Nino Rota
Death at an Old Mansion	JAP	Nobichiko Obayashi
Deathcheaters	AUT	Peter J. Martin
Deep Jaws	IND	Jack Millman
Deep Red	ITA	Giorgio Gaslini
Desert of the Tartars, The	FRA/ ITA	Ennio Morricone
Devil Within Her, The	AI	Ron Grainer
Devil's Island	GER	Sergio Ortega
Devil's Playground, The	AUT	Bruce Smeaton
Divine Plan, The	IN	Edgard Varese
Do You Know Pavla Plesa?	YUG	Djordje Karaklajic
Dr. Black and Mr. Hyde	IND	Johnny Pate
Doctor Judym	POL	Amdrzej Korzynski
Dog's Heart, The	ITA	Piero Piccioni
Don't Go Away	BUL	Boris Karadimchev
Double Exposure of Holly, The	IND	Stan Free
Double Man, The	DEN	"Fuzzy"
Dracula Father and Son	FRA	Vladimir Cosma
Drum	UA	Charlie Smalls
Duchess and the Dirtwater Fox, The	TCF	Charles Fox
Duck in Orange Sauce	ITA	Armando Trovajoli
Dulscy	POL	Piotr Figiel
Eat My Dust	NWP	David Grisman
Echoes of a Summer	IND	Terry James
Edweard Muybridge, Zoopraxographer	IND	Michael Cohen
800 Heroes	CHN	Huang Mou-Shan
Eleanor and Franklin	TV	John Barry
Eleanor and Franklin--The White House Years	TV	John Barry
Elephant Can Be Extremely Deceptive, An (Elephant ca Trompe Enormement, Un)	FRA	Vladimir Cosma
Eliza Fraser	AUT	Bruce Smeaton

Embryo	IND	Gil Melle
Emily	BRI	Rod McKuen
Emma Mae	IND	H. B. Bornum
Emmanuelle II--Joys of a Woman	FRA	Francis Lai
End of Night	PERU/ VEN	Arturo Ruis del Pozo
Enforcer, The	WB	Jerry Fielding
Entire Days in the Trees	FRA	Carlo d'Alessio
Executive Suite (series)	TV	Gerald Fried
F Is for Fairbanks	FRA	Patrick Dequaere
Fairy Dance	BUL	Simeon Pironkov
Faithful Woman, A	FRA	Mort Schuman/Pierre Porte
False Face	IND	Robert Cobert
Family Plot	UN	John Williams
Family Portrait	SPA	Carmelo Bernaola
Fantastic Balloon Trip, The	MEX	Jose Antonio Zavala
Far Shore, The	CAN	Douglas Pringle
Faux Pas de Deux	GER	Jan Berger
Fear of Fear	GER	Peer Raben
Felines, Les	FRA	Vladimir Cosma
Femmes Fatales (Calmos)	FRA	Georges Delerue
Fever	VEN	Freddy Reina
Fighting Mad	TCF	Bruce Langehorne
First Time, The (Premiere Fois, La)	FRA	Rene Urtreger
Flannagan	HOL	Juriaan Andriessen
Food of the Gods, The	AI	Elliot Kaplan
Four Days to Death	YUG	Radomir Petrovic
Foxtrot	NWP	Pete Rugolo
Francis Gary Powers: The True Story of the U-2 Spy Incident	TV	Gerald Fried
Freaky Friday	DIS	Johnny Mandel
Free for All	ARG	Roberto Lar
Freewheelin'	IND	Stephen Freud
From Noon Till Three	UA	Elmer Bernstein
Front, The	COL	Dave Grusin
Futureworld	AI	Fred Karlin
Gable and Lombard	UN	Michel Legrand
Game Pass	GER	Peer Raben
Gangster's Apprentice, The	DEN	Aske Bentzon
Garden of Torture, The	FRA	Jean-Pierre Doering
Gator	UA	Charles Bernstein
Genius, The	FRA/ GER/ ITA	Ennio Morricone
Get Charlie Tully	BRI	Christopher Gunning
Getting Together	IND	Tony Camillo
Ghost Train	DEN	Soeren Christensen
Girl Fit to Be Killed, The	CZE	Bohuslav Ondracek
Girls at Arms, Part 2	DEN	Ole Hoeyer
Go for It	IND	Dennis Dragon
God Told Me To	NWP	Frank Cordell

Goin' Home	IND	Lee Holdridge
Golden Nights	FRA	Pierre Jansen
Good Evening to Everybody	PHI	Ryan Cayabyah
Good Guys and the Bad Guys, The	FRA	Francis Lai
Goodbye Norma Jean	IND	Joe Beck
Great Saturday, The	THAI	Pramual Lab
Great Scout and Cathouse Thursday, The	NWP	Craig Safan
Griffin and Phoenix	IND	George Aliceson Tipton
Grizzly	IND	Robert O. Ragland
Gumball Rally	WB	Dominic Frontiere
Gus	DIS	Robert F. Brunner
Guy Like Me Should Never Die, A	FRA	Mort Schuman
Gypsies Go to Heaven	RUS	Eugeni Doga
Hamlet	BRI	Carlos Miranda
Happy Days	GRE	Dionyssios Savopoulos
Harry and Walter Go to New York	COL	David Shire
Hawmps	IND	Euel Box
Hearts High	DEN	Hans Erik Philip
Heat of Normandie St.-Onge, The	CAN	Lewis Furey
Hello, Baby	SWE	Julius Jacobson
Herz aus Glas	GER	Florian Fricke
Hey, Mister, I Am Your Wife	PHI	Ernani Cuenco
Hide and Seek	PHI	Demet Velasquez
High Street	BEL/FRA	Mort Schuman
Hollywood Boulevard	NWP	Andrew Stein
Honeymoon Trip, The	FRA	Michel Legrand
Hornet's Nest, The	FRA	Giancarlo Chiaramello
Hot Potato	WB	Christopher Trussel
Hour of Mary and the Bird of Gold, The	ARG	Oscar Lopez Ruiz
Hugo the Hippo	TCF	Burt Keyes
I Love You No Longer	FRA	Serge Gainsbourg
I Need You So Much, Love	ARG	Tito Ribero
I, Tintin	BEL/FRA	Alain Pierre
I Will ... I Will ... For Now	TCF	John Cameron
Idealist, The	YUG	Bojan Adamic
If I Had a Girl	CZE	Stepan Konicek
If I Were to Do It Over Again	FRA	Francis Lai
Illuminations	AUT	Norman Kaye/Alex Berry
Image, L'	FRA	George Craig
In the Fire Land	JAP	Masahi Tanaka
In the Realm of the Senses	FRA/JAP	Toru Takemitsu
In the Sign of the Lion	DEN	Ole Hoeyer
Independence	TCF	Jack Cortner
Independence Day	IND	Mauro Bruno
Inheritance, The (Eredita Ferramonti)	ITA	Ennio Morricone
Innocent, The	ITA	Franco Mannino
Intruder, The	ITA	Franco Mannino

Investigator and the Woods, The	BUL	Kiril Dontchev
It All Adds Up	DEN	George Quincy
It Shouldn't Happen to a Vet	BRI	Laurie Johnson
It's Showtime	UA	Artie Butler
J. D. 's Revenge	AI	Robert Prince
Jackson County Jail	NWP	Loren Newkirk
Jim, the World's Greatest	UN	Fred Myrow
Joe Panther	IND	Fred Karlin
Jonah--Who Will be 25 in the Year 2000	FRA/ SWI	Jean-Marie Senia
Joy of Letting Go, The	IND	Bob Maser
Judge and the Assassin, The	FRA	Philippe Sarde
Julie	GER	Gerhard Heinz
Juliette and the Feel of the Times	FRA	Bernard Gilson
Jumpin' at the Bedside	DEN	Ole Hoeyer
Jumping Ash	BRI/ HK	Joseph and Michael Lai
Jungle Adventure Campa Campa	SWE	Sven Olaf Waldoff
Justine	BRI	Johnny Hawksworth
Kansas City Trucking Co.	IND	Al Steinman
Keeper, The	CAN	Eric Hoyt
Kenny and Co.	TCF	Fred Myrow
Killer Inside Me, The	WB	Tim McIntire/John Rubenstein
Killing of a Chinese Bookie, The	IND	Bo Harwood
King Kong	PAR	John Barry
Las Vegas Lady	IND	Alan Silvestri
Last Affair, The	IND	Sooren Alexander
Last Hard Men, The	TCF	Jerry Goldsmith
Last Plantation, The	BRA	Quinteto Armorial/Pedro Santos
Last Tycoon, The	PAR	Maurice Jarre
Last Woman, The	FRA	Philippe Sarde/Hubert Rostaing
Leadbelly	PAR	Fred Karlin
Left ... Right ... Sickness of the Body	PHI	D'Amarillo
Legend of the Ubirajara	BRI	Tuze de Abreu
Let the Balloon Go	AUT	George Dreyfus
Let's Get Those English Girls	FRA	Mort Schuman
Letters from Mausia	MEX	Mikis Theodorakis
Life Changes	MEX	Gustavo Cesar Carreon
Lifeguard	PAR	Dale Menten
Light	FRA	Astor Piazzola
Lion and the Rat, The	PHI	Ernani Cuenco
Lipstick	PAR	Michel Polnareff/Jimmie Haskell
Little Marcel	FRA	Gaeme Allwight
Little Mermaid, The	RUS	Eugeni Krylatov
Logan's Run	MGM	Jerry Goldsmith
Lola's Lolos	FRA	Jean-Claude Wannier
Long Live Progress	POL	Adam Slawinski
Long Vacations of '36, The	SPA	Javier Montsalvage

Longest Journey, The	YUG	Tomislaw Zografski
Lost Life, A	GER	Hans Martin Majewski
Love and Cool Water	FRA	Michel Bernhloc
Loves and Times of Scaramouche, The	EMB	Dammico Bixio
Loving Cousins	ITA	Claudio Narrone
Mad Dog	AUT	Patrick Flynn
Mado	FRA	Philippe Sarde
Man Against Man	GER	Gerhard Wohlgemuth
Man on the Bridge	MEX	Oscar Carrillon
Man on the Roof, The	SWE	Bjoern Jason Lindh
Man Who Fell to Earth, The	BRI	John Phillips
Man Who Knew Love, The	SPA	Antonio Perez Olea
Man Without a Name, The	HUN	Emil Petrovics
Marathon Man	PAR	Michael Small
Marco Polo	CHN	Chen Yung-Yu
Marie the Doll	FRA	Philippe Sarde
Massacre at Central High	IND	Tony Leonetti
Matter of Time, A	AI	Nino Oliviero
Mauahovsky Laughs	RUS	Yuri Dashkovich
May	GRE	Loukianos Kalaidonis
May I Have the Floor?	RUS	Cadim Bigergan
Medical Story (series)	TV	Gerald Fried
Message, The	BRI	Maurice Jarre
Midway	UN	John Williams
Mikey and Nicky	PAR	John Strauss
Minister and Me, The	MEX	Gustavo C. Carreon
Miracles of the Gods	GER	Peter Thomas
Missouri Breaks, The	UA	John Williams
Mr. Klein	FRA	Egisto Macchi
Mrs. Abad, I Am Bing	PHI	Willie Cruz
Mistress	FRA	Carlos D'Alessio
Mistress, The	SPA	Manuel Alejandro
Monkey Bridge, The	FRA	Jacques Delaporte
Monkey Hustle, The	AI	Jack Conrad
Moses	EMB	Ennio Morricone
Moving Violation	TCF	Don Peake
Murder by Death	COL	Dave Grusin
Mushroom Eater, The	MEX	Raul Lavista
Mustang Country	UN	Lee Holdridge
Mustang: The House That Joe Built	IND	Carmine Coppola
Mute, The	SWI	Jonas C. Haefeli
My War--My Love	POL	Piotr Figiel
Mysterious Monsters, The	IND	Ruby Raskin
Nasty Habits	BRI	John Cameron
Network	UA	Elliott Lawrence
Next Man, The	AA	Michael Kamen
Next Stop, Greenwich Village	TCF	Bill Conti
Nickelodeon	COL	Richard Hazard
1900	ITA	Ennio Morricone
No Deposit, No Return	DIS	Buddy Baker
No Man's Daughter	HUN	Rudolf Maros

Norman ... Is That You?	MGM	William Goldstein
Normans, The	DEN	Henning Christiansen
North Sea Is Dead Sea	GER	Udo Lindenberg
Obsession	COL	Bernard Hermann
Ode to Billy Joe	WB	Michel Legrand
Office Party, The	DEN	Ole Hoeyer
Olsen Gang Sees Red, The	DEN	Bent Fabricius-Bjerre
Omen, The	TCF	Jerry Goldsmith
On the Tip of the Tongue	BEL	Frederic DeVreese
Once Upon a Time	GER/ ITA	Peter Thomas
One Night in Life with One Woman	PHI	Freddy Dandan
One Silver Piece	CZE	Karel Mares
Only One, The	RUS	Nadeshda Simonyan
Opening of Misty Beethoven, The	IND	George Craig
Operation Daybreak	WB	David Hentschel
Ordinateur des Pompes Funebres, L'	FRA/ ITA	Claude Bolling
Otalia de Bahia	BRA/ FRA	Antonio Carlos Jobim
Out on Parole	SPA	Paxti Andion
Outlaw Josey Wales, The	WB	Jerry Fielding
Outlaw Morality	GER	Uve Schikora
Oz	AUT	Ross Wilson
Paradise	GER	Predrag/Vranesevic/ Sparifankal
Part 2, Sounder	GAM	Taj Mahal
Partners	CAN	Murray McLauchlan
Pascual Duarte	SPA	Luis de Pablo
Pasquelino: Seven Beauties (see Seven Beauties)		
Passover Plot, The	ISR/ USA	Alex North
Peaks of Zelengore, The	YUG	Zoran Hristic
People of the Wind	IND	G. T. Moore/Shusha
Per Amore	ITA	Ennio Morricone
Personnel	POL	Michal Zarnecki
Pink Panther Strikes Again, The	UA	Henry Mancini
Pipe Dreams	EMB	Dominic Frontiere
Pleasantville	IND	Michael Riesman
Police Python 357	FRA	Georges Delerue
Pom Pom Girls, The	IND	Michael Lloyd
Potato Fritz	GER	Udo Juergens
Predator, The	FRA	Michel Colombier
Private Vices, Public Virtues	ITA/ YUG	Francesco de Masi
Proceedings	GRE	Christodoulas Halaris
Prostitution	FRA	Alan Reeves
Pure S	AUT	Red Symons
Rabbi and the Shikse, The	ISR	Dov Seltzer
Red Zone	MEX	Manuel Esperon
Request, The	SPA	Roman Alix
Requiem for a Village	BRI	David Fanshawe

Return of a Man Called Horse, The	UA	Laurence Rosenthal
Revenge of the Cheerleaders	IND	John Sterling
Ritz, The	WB	Ken Thorne
Robin and Marian	COL	John Barry
Rocky	UA	Bill Conti
Rome: Armed to the Teeth	ITA	Franco Micalizzi
Roots (series)	TV	Gerald Fried
S. T. A. B.	CHN	Noel Quinlan
Sailor Who Fell from Grace with the Sea, The	EMB	Johnny Mandel
Saint Anne (Annee Sainte, L')	FRA/ ITA	Claude Bolling
St. Ives	WB	Lalo Schifrin
Santi and Veena	THAI	Seksan
Satan's Brew	GER	Peer Raben
Savage Party, The	FRA	V. Papaloussia
Scorchy	AI	Igo Cantor
Scorpion Woods	PHI	Ernani Cuenco
Scrambled Eggs, The	FRA	Vladimir Cosma
Sebastian	BRI	Brian Eno/Andrew Wilson
Seclusion Near a Forest	CAE	Jiri Sust
Second Chance--Sea (short)	PYR	Dizzy Gillespie
Second Wind	CAN	Hagood Hardy
Secret Rivals, The	HK	Chou Fu-liang
Sell-Out, The	BRI	Mick Green/Colin Frichter
Seven Beauties	ITA	Enzo Jannicci
Seven-Man Army	CHN	Chen Yung-Yu
Seven Nights in Japan	PAR	David Hentschel
Seven Per Cent Solution	UN	John Addison
Shadow of the Castles	FRA	Maurice Vander
Shadow of the Hawk	CAN	Robert McMullin
Shaggy D. A., The	DIS	Buddy Baker
Shoot	CAN	Doug Riley
Shootist, The	PAR	Elmer Bernstein
Short and Sweet	FRA	Francois de Roubaix
Shout at the Devil	BRI	Maurice Jarre
Silent Movie	TCF	John Morris
Silk Worms	SPA	Emilio de Diego
Silver Streak	TCF	Henry Mancini
Six Bears and a Clown	CZE	Vlastimil Hala
Six O'Clock USA	FRA	Mort Schuman/Claude Gaubert
Sky Riders	TCF	Lalo Schifrin
Sleeping Car, The	YUG	Vojislav Simic
Slum Boy	ITA	Carlo Savina/Nino Rota
Small Insect	PHI	Demet Velasquez
Small Town in Texas, A	AI	Charles Bernstein
Smile Orange	JAM	Melba Liston
Snake Prince, The	HK	Wang Fu-ling
Sodom and Gomorrah	IND	Mike Bloomfield/Barry Goldberg

Sorrows of Young Werther, The	GER	Siegfried Matthus
Sparkle	WB	Curtis Mayfield
Special Delivery	AI	Lalo Schifrin
Spending Money	FRA	Maurice Jaubert
Spiral, The	FRA	Jean-Claude Elyo
Squirm	AI	Robert Prince
Stay Hungry	UA	Bruce Langhorne/Byron Berline
Sternstein Manor, The	GER	Eugen Thomass
Storm Boy	AUT	Michael Carlos
Stormy Wine	CZE	Karel Svoboda
Story of Chinese Gods, The	CHN	Woy Koy Shin
Story of the Dragon, The	CHN	Chou Fu-liang
Strange People	RUS	Karen Khachaturian
Street People	AI	Luis Enriquez Bacalov
Strongest Karate, The	JAP	Keisuke Hidaka
Stupid Boy Friend, The	PHI	Demet Velasquez
Sudden Loneliness of Konrad Steiner, The	SWI	Peter Jacques
Summer Guests	GER	Peter Fischer
Summer of Secrets	AUT	Cameron Allen
Sunday Woman	FRA/ITA	Ennio Morricone
Supply Column Soldier, The	BUL/RUS	Yan Frenckel
Supreme Kid, The	CAN	Howie Vickers
Swashbuckler	UN	John Addison
Sweet Punkin'	IND	Harold Hindgrind/Slim Pickens
Sweet Revenge	MGM	Paul Chihara
Taking of Christina, The	IND	Jack Malken
Tanner Steel Mill, The	GER	Peter Fischer
Taxi Driver	COL	Bernard Herrmann
Tenant, The	FRA	Philippe Sarde
Tenants, The	PHI	Lucio D. San Pedro
That Brief Summer	DEN	Ole Hoeyer
There Is No Forgetting	CAN	Alberto Sendra/Denis Larochelle
Third Door, The	SPA	Carlos Vizziello
Three Wise Men, The	MEX	Jose Antonio Zavala
Through the Ashes of the Empire	RUM	Radu Serban
Through the Looking Glass	IND	Arlon Ober
Tidal Wave and West Wind	PHI	Ernani Cuenco
Tiger and Crane Fists	HK	Wong Mao-shan
Tomorrow's Children	FRA	Eric Demarsan
Touchy	BRA	Eduardo Gudin
Toy, The	FRA	Vladimir Cosma
Trackdown	UA	Charles Bernstein
Train in the Snow	YUG	Arsen Dedic
Traveling Companions	RUS	Pavel Chekalov
Treasure of Matecumbe	DIS	Buddy Baker
Trespassers, The	AUT	Bruce Smeaton
Trial by Combat	BRI	Frank Cordell

Tunnelvision	IND	Dennis Lambert/Brian Potter
Two-Minute Warning	UN	Charles Fox
Ugly, Dirty and Bad	ITA	Armando Trovajoli
Up	IND	William Loose/Paul Ruhland
Vera Romeyke Is Not Acceptable	GER	Wilhelm Dieter Siebert
Victory March	FRA/GER/ITA	Nicola Piovani
Virility	ITA	Daniele Patucchi
Voyage of the Damned	EMB	Lalo Schifrin
W. C. Fields and Me	UN	Henry Mancini
Walking Upright	GER	Erhard Grosskopf
Wash Out My Faults	PHI	George Canseco
Way of the Wind, The	IND	John Bilezikjian
Welcome to L. A.	UA	Richard Baskin
When the Poppies Bloom Again	HOL	Otto Ketting
Where Are You Going?	PHI	George Canseco
Whispering Death	AFR/GER	Erich Ferstl
White Grass	YUG	Bojan Adamic
White Rock	BRI	Rick Wakeman
White Shop, The	RUS	Alfred Schnitke
Who Can Kill a Child?	SPA	Waldo de los Rios
Who Leaves in the Rain	CZE	Zdenek Liska
Wind Blows Under Your Feet, The	HUN	Ferenc Sabo
Wind, Cloud and Rainbow	JAP	Naozumi Yamamoto
Winterhawk	IND	Lee Holdridge
Women Duelling	FRA	Jean Weiher
Won Ton Ton, the Dog Who Saved Hollywood	PAR	Neal Hefti
Xica de Silva	BRA	Roberto Menescal
Your Son and Brother	RUS	Pavel Chekalov

1977

Accuser, The (Imprecateur, L')	FRA	Richard Rodney Bennett
Agent 69 Jensen in the Sign of Scorpio	DEN	Bertrand Bech
Airport '77	UN	John Cacavas
Ajuricaba	BRA	Airton Barbosa
Al Kautsar	INDONESIA	Thoifur
Alice, or the Last Escapade	FRA	Pierre Jansen
American Friend, The	FRA/GER	Jurgen Knieper
Anima Persa	ITA	Francis Lai
Animal, The	FRA	Vladimir Cosma
Another Man, Another Chance	FRA	Francis Lai
Anschi and Michael	GER	Joerg Evers
Antti the Treebranch	FIN	Kari Ryudman
Antonio Gramsci--The Days of Prison	ITA	Egisto Macchi

Apprentice Sorcerers, The	FRA	Edgardo Canton
Armaguedon	FRA/ ITA	Astor Piazzola
As the Moon	FRA	Philippe Sarde
Ascent, The	RUS	A. Schnitke
At Night All Cats Are Gray	FRA	Jean-Claude Vannier
Audrey Rose	UA	Michael Small
Autostop Sosso Sangue	ITA	Ennio Morricone
Average Man, An	ITA	Giancarlo Chiaramello
Bad	NWP	Mike Bloomfield
Bad News Bears in Breaking Training, The	PAR	Craig Safan
Baker's Hawk	IND	Lex de Azevedo
Barney	AUT	Tommy Tucho
Base of the Air Is Red, The	FRA	Luciano Berio
Battleflag	GER	Hans-Martin Majewski
Baxter, Vera Baxter	FRA	Carlos D'Alessio
Beasts	YUG	Boro Tamindzic
Before the Day Breaks	POL	Maciej Malecki
Bel Paseo, Il ...	ITA	Gianni Boncompagni
Beloved Love	YUG	Malovaj Markovic
Ben and Benedict	FRA	Larry Martin
Between the Lines	IND	Michael Kamen
Beyond Good and Evil	FRA/ GER/ ITA	Daniele Paris
Big Thumbs	IND	Roger Joyce
Bilitis	FRA/ ITA	Francis Lai
Billy Jack Goes to Washington	IND	Elmer Bernstein
Bishop's Bedroom, The	ITA	Armando Trovajoli
Black Banana, The	ISR	P. C. Usherovici
Black Diamond, The	HUN	Emil Petrovics
Black Litter	SPA	Jose Nieto
Black Magic 2	HK	Chan Yang-Yu
Black Oak Conspiracy	NWP	Don Peake
Black Panther, The	BRI	Richard Arnell
Black Pirate, The (Corsaro Nero, Il)	ITA	Guido and Maurizio de Angelis
Black Sunday	PAR	John Williams
Blue Country	FRA	Gerard Anfosso
Blue Ferns, The	FRA	Frederic Bottom
Bobby Deerfield	COL	Dave Grusin
Bomber and Paganini	GER	Nicos Mamangakis
Boxer, The	JAP	J. A. Seazer
Boys	DEN	Gunnar Moeller Pedersen
Breaker, Breaker	AI	Don Hulette
Bricklayers, The	MEX	Gustavo C. Carreon
Bridge Too Far, A	UA	John Addison
Brothers	WB	Taj Mahal
Budapest Tales	HUN	Zdenko Tamassy
Budding Love	FRA	Maxime le Forestier
Camouflage	POL	Wojiech Kilar

Can I Do It ... Till I Need Glasses?	IND	Bob Jung
Candleshoe	DIS	Ron Goodwin
Captain Lust	IND	Fred Schminke
Car, The	UN	Leonard Rosenman
Casanova and Company	AUS/ FRA/ GER/ ITA	Riz Ortolani
Cassandra Crossing, The	EMB	Jerry Goldsmith
Catastrophe 1999	NWP	Isao Tomita
Chatter-Box	AI	Fred Karger
Chess Players, The	IN	Satyajit Ray
Children of Agony	DEN	Gunnar Moeller Pedersen
Choirboys, The	UN	Frank de Vol
Christiania	DEN	Soeren Christensen
Citizen's Band	PAR	Bill Conte
Clark	DEN	Gunnar Moeller Pedersen
Close Encounters of the Third Kind	COL	John Williams
Cold Heart, The	FRA	Guy Boulanger
Comme un Boomerang	FRA	Georges Delerue
Communion	AA	Stephen Laurence
Conquest of the Citadel, The	GER	George Gruntz
Consequence, The	GER	Nils Sustrate
Crab Drum, The	FRA	Philippe Sarde
Cracking Up	AI	Ward Jewel
Crazy Days	YUG	Branislav Zivkovic
Crazy Horse Paris--France	FRA	Jacques Morali
Cross of Iron	EMB	Ernest Gold
Crossed Swords (Prince and the Pauper, The)	BRI	Maurice Jarre
Dagny	NOR/ POL	Arne Nordheim
Damnation Alley	TCF	Jerry Goldsmith
Daredevil's Time	YUG	Zivan Cvitkovick
Day for My Love	CZE	Petr Hapka
Day of the Animals	IND	Lalo Schifrin
Dear Wife	ITA	Stelvio Cipriani
Dearest Executioners	SPA	Antonio Camero
Death at Dawn	PERU/ VEN	Arturo Pinto
Death Game	IND	Jimmie Haskell
Death of a Corrupt Man, The	FRA	Philippe Sarde
Death of the Water Carrier	EGY/ TUN	Fouad El Zaheri
Deep, The	COL	John Barry
Defense Takes the Floor, The	RUS	V. Martynov
Demon Seed	MGM	Jerry Fielding
Desperate Living	NLC	Chris Lobinger/Allen Yarus
Devil in the Box, The	FRA	Jean-Claude Dequeant
Devil, Probably, The	FRA	Philippe Sarde

Diablo Menthe (Peppermint Soda)	FRA	Yves Simone
Diary of a Lover, The	GER	Rolf Bauer
Dishonest Profit, The	GER	Erhard Grosskopf
Disturbance	RUS	M. Gabunia
Dog, The	SPA	Anton Garcia Abril
Domino Principle, The	EMB	Billy Goldenberg
Don of Japan--Big Schemes, The	JAP	Toshiro Mayazumi
Dona Flora and Her Two Husbands	BRA	Chico Buarque/Francis Hime
Dona Perfecta	SPA	Angel Orteaga
Don't Lean Out the Window	YUG	Oaren Depolo
Doom, The	RUM	Tiberu Olah
Eagle and the Dove, The	FRA	Alain Goraguer
Eagle Has Landed, The	COL	Lalo Schifrin
Earth Is Flat, The	DEN	Jurij Moskvitin
Elixirs of the Devil, The	GER	Hans-Martin Majewski
Elvis! Elvis!	SWE	Ralph Lundsten
Emergency! (series)	TV	Gerald Fried
Empire of the Ants	AI	Dana Kaproff
Enfants Gates, Des (see Spoiled Children)		
Entanglement	HUN	Gyorgy Selmeczi/Tomas Cseh
Equus	UA	Richard Rodney Bennett
Evening Land	DEN	Anders Koppel
Evolution of Snuff, The	GER	Gerhard Heinz
Exorcist II: The Heretic	WB	Ennio Morricone
F. J. Holden, The	AUT	Jim Manzie
Family Honor, The	TUR	Melik Kibar
Farmer, The	COL	Hugo Montenegro
Father Master (see Padre Padrone)		
Feelings	IND	Selma Marks
Fifth Seal, The	HUN	Gyorgy Vukan
Final Chapter--Walking Tall	AI	Walter Scharf
Fire Sale	TCF	Dave Grusin
First Love	PAR	John Barry
First Star, The	JAP	Akihiro Komori
Flunking Out	SPA	Jesus Gluck
Flyers of the Open Skies	YUG	Alfi Kabiljo
Focal Point	FRA	Georges Delerue
For Clemence	FRA	Michel Portal/Jean Schwarz
For the Love of Benji	IND	Euel Box
Forbidden Room, The (see Anima Persa)		
Foul Play	POL	Piotr Figiel
Foxbat	HK	Roy Budd
Frankenstein--Italian Style	ITA	Stelvio Cipriani
Fruit Is Ripe, The	GER	Gerhard Heinz
Full Circle	CAN	Colin Towns
Fun with Dick and Jane	COL	Ernest Gold
Funny Note	JAP	Masao Yagi
Fuses	GER	Franz Josef Degenhardt

Game of the Apple	CZE	Miroslav Korinek
Games of the XXI Olympiad Montreal 1976	CAN	Andre Gagnon
Garden, The	ISR	Noham Schaif
Gathering, The	TV	John Barry
Gauntlet, The	WB	Jerry Fielding
Girl Named Poo Lom, A	THAI	Siam Pattana
Girls at Sea	DEN	Ole Hoeyer
Gloria	FRA	Bernard Gerard
God Bless Each Corner of This House	SPA	Carlos Vizziello
God of Flower, The (Hanagami)	JAP	Hikaru Hayashi
Going for Broke	DEN	Joern Grauengaard
Golden Swan	THAI	Uan Singyao
Goldencauliflower Family Gets the Vote, The	DEN	Ole Hoeyer
Goodbye Alicia	VAN	Vytas Brenner
Goodbye Girl, The	MGM/WB	Dave Grusin
Goodnight, Ladies and Gentlemen	ITA	Lucio Dalla/Antonello Venditti/Giuseppe Mazzuca/Nicola Samale
Grand Theft Auto	NWP	Peter Ivers
Grandma Schulz	GER	Neils Frederick Hoffmann
Grayeagle	AI	Jaime Mendoza-Nava
Greased Lightning	WB	Fred Karlin
Great Day, The	ITA	Armando Trovajoli
Great Escape from Dien Pien Phu, The	THAI	Lek Kitiparaporn
Great Gundown, The	IND	Alan Caddy
Greatest, The	COL	Michael Masser
Greedy People, The	THAI	Montri Ong-iyam
Grete Minde	AUS/GER	Niels Jannette Walen
Growing Up Suddenly	ARG	Rodolfo Mederos
Guardian of the Wilderness	IND	Robert Summers
Guinea Pig Couple, The	FRA	Michel Colombier
Ham from the Ardennes	BEL/FRA	Peter Verlinden
Hazing, The	IND	Ian Freebairn-Smith
Heavy Trouble	BRA	Edu Lobo
Hempas Bar	SWE	Bjoern Isfaelt
Hennessy	AI	Patrick John Scott
Herbie Goes to Monte Carlo	DIS	Frank de Vol
Hero Ain't Nothin' But a Sandwich, A	NWP	Tom McIntosh
Heroes	UN	Jack Nitzsche/Richard Hazard
High Anxiety	TCF	John Morris
High Velocity	IND	Jerry Goldsmith
Hitler, a Career	GER	Hans Posegga
Holocaust 2000	BRI/ITA	Ennio Morricone
Homage to Chagall--The Colors of Love	CAN	Louis Appelbaum

Home and Refuge	SWE	Heikki Valpola
Homeward in the Night	FIN/ SWE	Heikki Valpola
House	JAP	Asei Kobayashi/Miki Yoshino
Hunters, The	GRE	Loukianos Kalaidonis
Hyena's Sun (Soleil des Hyenes/ Sun of the Hyenes)	HOL/ TUN	Nicola Piovani
I Am a Delinquent	VEN	Miguel Angel Fuster
I Never Promised You a Rose Garden	NWP	Paul Chihara
I Want to Be a Woman	SPA	Ricardo Miralles
If Pigs Had Wings	ITA	Giovanna Marini
In a Wild Moment	FRA	Michel Stelio
In MacArthur Park	IND	Rocky Davis
In Memoriam	SPA	Luis Eduardo Aute
Inside Looking Out	AUT	Norman Kaye
Iphighenia	GRE	Mikis Theodorakis
Iron Buffalo, The	THAI	Seksan Sonimasat
Iron Prefect, The	ITA	Ennio Morricone
Island of Dr. Moreau, The	AI	Lawrence Rosenthal
Island of the Silver Herons, The	CZE/ GER	Lubos Fiser
Islands in the Stream	PAR	Jerry Goldsmith
It's Never Too Late	SPA	Jose Nieto
J. A. Martin, Photographer	CAN	Maurice Blackburn
Jabberwocky	BRI	DeWolfe
Jack	SWE	Ulf Lundell
Jacub	CZE	Stepan Lucky
Joseph Andrews	PAR	John Addison
Journey Among Women	AUT	Roy Ritchie
Joy	IND	Martin Lewinter
Joyride	AI	Jimmie Haskell
Juan Perez Jolote	MEX	Richard Alderson
Judge Fayard Called the Sheriff	FRA	Philippe Sarde
Judgment of an Assassin	HK	Chen Yung-Yu
Julia	TCF	Georges Delerue
Julie Glue Pot	FRA	Georges Delerue
Just the Beginning	KOR	Jung Soung Jo
Key That Should Not Be Handed On, The	RUS	Eugeni Krylatov
Kneeler Peak	HUN	Geza Berki
Lacemaker, The	FRA/ SWI	Pierre Jansen
Last Exit Before Roissy	FRA	Eric Demarsan
Last of the Cowboys, The	IND	Craig Safan
Last Remake of Beau Geste, The	UN	John Morris
Last Three Days, The	ITA	Nicola Piovani
Last Wave, The	AUT	Charles Wain
Late Blossom, The	CAN	Beau Dommage
Late Show, The	WB	Kenn Wannberg
Legacy of L. S. B. Leakey, The	TV	Gerald Fried
Leper	POL	Wojiech Kilar

Let's Leave the War in Peace	SPA	Antonio Garcia Abril
Life Before Him	FRA	Philippe Sarde
Life of Chikuzan, The	JAP	Hikaru Hayashi
Light on the Gallows, The	GER	Karl-Ernst Sasse
Lincoln Conspiracy, The	SUN	Robert Summers
Little Mermaid, The	CZE	Zdenek Liska
Location Hunting	FRA/ SWI	Aric Dzierlatka
Long Weekend, The (Puente, La)	SPA	Jose Nieto
Looking for Mr. Goodbar	PAR	Artie Kane
Looking Up	IND	Brad Fiedel
Louis	THAI	Prasert Churaketr
Love at First Sight	CAN	Roy Payne
Love Follows Pain	KOR	Sung Jo Chung
Love Is Blue	THAI	Thaweepong Mainin
Lover, Wife	ITA	Armando Trovajoli
Lumiere	FRA	Astor Piazzola
MacArthur	UN	Jerry Goldsmith
Machine, The	FRA	Roland Vincent
Madame Claude	FRA	Serge Gainsbourg
Maiden's War, The	GER	Nicos Mamangakis
Main Actor, The	GER	Klaus Doldinger
Mama, I'm Alive	GER/ RUS	Rainer Boehm
Man of Marble	POL	Andrzej Korzynski
Man Who Loved Women, The	FRA	Maurice Jaubert
Mango Tree, The	AUT	Marc Wilkinson
Manthan	IN	Vanraj Bhatia
March or Die	COL	Maurice Jarre
Mina, Wind of Freedom	CUBA/ MEX	Leo Brouwer
Mind Your Back, Professor	DEN	Steen Holkenow
Misfire	AUS/ GER	Alexander Steffen
Mr. Billion	TCF	Dave Grusin
Mohammad, the Messenger of God	IND	Maurice Jarre
Monsieur Papa	FRA	Mort Schuman
Moods of Love	HK	Wu Hsu-ching
Moonshine County Express	NWP	Fred Werner
More It Goes, the Less It Goes, The	FRA	Mort Schuman
Mount Hakkoda	JAP	Yasushi Akutagawa
My Daughter Hildegart	SPA	Luis Eduardo Aute
My Dear Friend	THAI	Prasert Churaketr
My First Sin	SPA	Carlos Vizzielo
My Heart Is Red	FRA	Keith Jarrett
Nene	ITA	Francesco Guccini
New York, New York	UA	Ralph Burns
Night of St.-Germain des Pres, The	FRA	Mort Schuman/Christian Gaubert
Nine Months	HUN	Gyorgy Kovacs
9/30/55	UN	Leonard Rosenman
Noelleby Affair, The	DEN	Bent Fabricius-Bjerre

O, Madda	THAI	Seksan Sonimsat
Oedipus Orca	ITA	James Dashow
Off the Edge	IND	Richard Clements
Oh, God!	WB	Jack Elliott
Old Country Where Rimbaud Died, The	CAN/FRA	Claude Fonfrede
Old House, The	KOR	Choi Chang Kwon
Olsen Gang Outta Sight, The	DEN	Bent Fabricius-Bjerre
Omar Gallato	ALG	Malek Ahmed
On the Sideline	HUN	Gabor Presser
One Can Say It Without Getting Angry	FRA	Michel Legrand
One Man	CAN	Ben Low
One on One	WB	Charles Fox
One Sings, the Other Doesn't	FRA	Francois Wertheimer
1 2 3 Monster Express	THAI	Seksan Sonimsat
Only 16 (Part 2)	THAI	Pairath Theptiam
Opening Night	IND	Bo Harwood
Operation Black Panther	THAI	Chalie Intravijit
Operation Stadium	YUG	Tomica Simobovic
Operation Thunderbolt	ISR	Dov Seltzer
Orca, the Killer Whale	PAR	Ennio Morricone
Other Side of Midnight, The	TCF	Michel Legrand
Outlaw Blues	WB	Charles Bernstein/Bruce Langhorne
Outrageous!	CAN	Paul Hoffert
Outsiders	SEN	Manu Dibango
Over-Under, Sideways-Down	IND	Ozzie Ahlers
Padre Padrone (Father Master)	ITA	Egisto Macchi
Page of Love, A	BEL/FRA	Marc Herouet
Paradise Square	SWE	Georg Riedel
Park, The	WB	Lee Holdridge
Passengers, The	FRA	Claude Bolling
Pedro Paramo	MEX	Ennio Morricone
Pele	FRA/MEX	Arantes do Nascimento
People That Time Forgot, The	AI	John Scott
Peppermint Soda (see Diablo Menthe)		
Personal Opinion, A	RUS	Boris Tchaikovski
Petty Thieves	GER	Juergen Knieper
Phantom on Horseback, The	HUN	Emil Petrovics
Piano in Midair, A	HUN	Gyorgy Vukan
Picture Show Man, The	AUT	Peter Best
Piece of the Action, A	WB	Curtis Mayfield
Pioneers, The	CHN	Chin Yung-Cheng
Platanov	RUS	Eduard Artemyev
Portrait of Shunkin, A	JAP	Masaru Sato
Private Eyes, The	HK	Samuel Hui
Private Files of J. Edgar Hoover, The	AI	Miklos Rozsa
Providence	FRA	Miklos Rozsa

Pumping Iron	CIV	Michael Small
Purple Taxi, The	FRA/ IRE/ ITA	Philippe Sarde
Question, The	FRA	Antoine Duhamel
Race for Your Life, Charlie Brown	PAR	Ed Bogas
Raggedy Ann and Andy	TCF	Joe Raposo
Raw Deal	AUT	Ron Edgeworth
Redeemer, The	YUG	Brane Zivkovic
Reluctant Gunfighter, The	THAI	Prasert Churaketr
Rene the Cane	FRA	Ennio Morricone
Rescuers, The	DIS	Artie Butler
Rich Man, Poor Man	TV	Alex North
Rollercoaster	UN	Lalo Schifrin
Rolling Thunder	AI	Barry de Vorzon
Roots: One Year Later	TV	Gerald Fried
Rose-Tinted Dreams	CZE	Petr Hapka
Roseland	IND	Michael Gibson
Royal Hunt, The	IN	Salil Chaudhury
Rubber Gun, The	CAN	Lewis Furey
Ruby	IND	Don Ellis
Sandstone	IND	Darryl and Dennis Dragon
Saturday Night Fever	PAR	David Shire
Save the City	POL/ RUS	Piotr Hertel
Scar, The	POL	Stanislaw Radwan
Schoolmaster Hober	GER	Robert Eliscu
Scott Joplin	UN	Scott Joplin
Scrounged Meals	GER	Stefan Melbinger
Sea Gull, The	ITA	Nicola Piovani
Sea Urchin in the Pocket, A	FRA	Vladimir Cosma
Seabo	IND	David Allan Coe/Clay Smith/Arthur Smith
Second Power, The	SPA	Adolfo Waitzman
Semi-Tough	UA	Jerry Fielding
Sentimental Story, A	RUS	Viktor Dareshevich
Sentinel, The	UN	Gil Melle
Serpent's Egg, The	UA	Rolf Wilhelm
Servant and Mistress	FRA	Jean-Marie Benjamin
Sex and the Married Woman	TV	Gerald Fried
Shenanigans	IND	Arthur B. Rubenstein
Short Eyes (Slammer)	IND	Curtis Mayfield
Sidewinder 1	EMB	Mundell Lowe
Silent Cry, The	BRI/ FRA/ GER	Benedict Mason/Stephen Dwoskin/Roger Oller-head
Silver Bears	COL	Claude Bolling
Sinbad and the Eye of the Tiger	COL	Roy Budd
Singer and the Dancer, The	AUT	Robert Murphy
Sixth and Main	IND	Robert Summers
Slap Shot	UN	Elmer Bernstein
Slavers	GER	Eberhard Schoener
Sleeping Dogs	AUT	Murray Findlay/David Calber/Matthew Brown

Slumber Party '57	IND	Miles Goodman
Small Change	FRA	Maurice Jaubert
Smoke on the Potato Fields	CZE	Zdenek Liska
Smokey and the Bandit	UN	Bill Justis/Jerry Reed/ Rich Feller
Snowstorm	YUG	Pero Gotovac
Solaris	RUS	Eduard Artemyev
Solemn Communion	FRA	Sergio Ortaga
Something Beautiful	INDONESIA	Idris Sardi
Sonata over the Lake	RUS	Imant Kalnynsh
Sophie	POL	Caeslaw-Niemen
Sorcerer	PAR/ UN	Tangerine Dream/Charlie Parker/Keith Jarrett
Sourdough	IND	Jerrold Immel
Space Cruiser Yamato	JAP	Hiroshi Miyagawa
Special Education	YUG	Zoran Simjanovic
Spell, The	TV	Gerald Fried
Spider Football	HUN	Janos Brody
Spiral of Mist, A	FRA/ ITA	Ivan Vandor
Spoiled Children (Enfants Gates, Des)	FRA	Philippe Sarde
Spring Day in Hell	DEN	Gunnar Moeller Pedersen
Spy Who Loved Me, The	UA	Marvin Hamlisch
Squeeze, The	BRI	David Hentschel
Stand Up Straight, Delfina	YUG	Slave Dimitrov
Stand Up, Virgin Soldiers	BRI	Ed Welch
Star Wars	TCF	John Williams
Starship Invasions	WB	Gil Melle
Stop Calling Me Baby!	FRA	Francois D'Aime
Stormtroopers	ITA	Enzo Janacci
Strait-Laced Girl, A	FRA	Oliver Dassault
Strange Events	ITA	Piero Piccione
Strange Letters	RUS	Oleg Karavaitchouk
Strange Role, A	HUN	Zdenko Tamassy
Strange Shadows in an Empty Room	ITA	Armando Trovajoli
Stunts	NLC	Michael Kamen
Stupid Life	THAI	Seksan Sonimsat
Submission	ITA	Riz Ortolani
Summerfield	AUT	Bruce Smeaton
Sun of the Hyenes (see Hyena's Sun)		
Super Van	IND	Andy de Martino/Mark Gibbons/Bob Stone
Suspiria	ITA	Goblin/Dario Argento
Swami	IN	Rejesh Roshan
Sweeney	BRI	Denis King
Sweet Woman	RUS	Soloview-Sedoi
Swimming Pool, The	BUL	Simeon Pironkov
Sword, The	HUN	Zdenko Tamassy
Take Me to the Ritz	FRA	Claude Bolling
Take One	IND	Tommy Tally
Tanasse Scatiu	RUM	Adrian Enescu
Telefon	MGM	Lalo Schifrin

Tell Him I Love Him	FRA	Alain Jonny
10 Per Cent of Hope	CZE	Tibor Andrasovan
Tender Cop	FRA	Georges Delerue
Tent of Miracles, The	BRA	Gilberto Gil
Tentacles	AI	Stelvio Cipriani
Terror	DEN	Palle Nikkelsborg
Testimony of Two Men	TV	Gerald Fried
Thaw	GER/ SWI	Bruno Spoerri
Thieves	PAR	Jule Styne/Mike Miller/ Shel Silverstein
Threat, The	CAN/ FRA	Gerry Mulligan
Three Tigers Against Three Tigers	ITA	Guido and Maurizio de Angelis
Thunder and Lightning	TCF	Andrew Stein
Ti-Cul Tougas	CAN	Georges Langford
Ties for the Olympics	GER	Wilhelm Dieter Siebert
Tiger's Way, The	THAI	Maitree Janjaraskul
Tiina	EST/ FIN	Taavo Virkhaus
Till Divorce Us Do Part	SPA	Antonio Garcia Abril
To an Unknown God	SPA	Luis de Pablo
Town That Dreaded Sundown, The	AI	Jaime Mendoza-Nava
Truster, The	BEL/ FRA	Ennio Morricone
Turning Point, The	TCF	John Lanchbery
Twilight's Last Gleaming	AA	Jerry Goldsmith
Two of Them, The	HUN	Gyorgy Kovacs
2076 Olympiad	IND	Lawrence J. Ponzak
Valentino	UA	Stanley Black/Ferde Grofe
Verdict, The	YUG	Tomislav Zografski
Victor Frankenstein	IRE/ SWE	Gerard Victor
Village Head at the Border, The	THAI	Chonati Tanlong
Village of the Eight Tombs	JAP	Yashiski Akutagawa
Violanta	SWI	Peer Raben
Violated Love	FRA	Aram Sedefian
Violation of Claudia, The	IND	Michael Karp
Violette and Francois	FRA	Philippe Sarde
Viva Knievel!	WB	Charles Bernstein
Voyage into the Whirlpool Has Begun, The	ITA	Egisto Macchi
Voyage to the Center of the Earth	SPA	Juan Garcia Caffi
War Between the Tates, The	TV	John Barry
Warrior Within, The	IND	Robert Lee
We Are Arab Jews in Israel	SWI	Moshe Habalo
We Will All Go to Heaven	FRA	Vladimir Cosma
Welcome to Blood City	BRI/ CAN	Roy Budd
What Do You Want, Julie?	FRA	Janez Matcic
What's Autumn?	ARG	Astor Piazzola

Which Way Is Up?	UN	Paul Riser
White Buffalo, The	UA	John Barry
Who Are the De Bolts? (and Where Did They Get 19 Kids?)	IND	Ed Bogas
Who Has Seen the Wind?	CAN	Eldon Rathburn
Why Not?	FRA	Jean-Pierre Mas
Why Shoot the Teacher?	CAN	Ricky Hyslop
Widow's Nest	IND	Francis Lai
Willie and the Chinese Cat	AUS/GER	Heinz Loenhardsberger
Wise Guys, The	FRA	Elizabeth Wiener/Horacio Vaggione
Wizards	TCF	Andrew Belling
World's Greatest Lover, The	TCF	John Morris
Written-Off Return, The	YUG	Malovaj Markovic
Year of School, A	ITA	Luis Enrique Bacalov
Yeti, Il Gigante del 20º Secolo	ITA	Santa Maria Comitelli
You Light Up My Life	COL	Joe Brooks
Young Joe, the Forgotten Kennedy	TV	John Barry
Youth Killer, The	JAP	Goddigo
Zero Hour	GER	Nicos Mamangakis

1978

Adele Hasn't Had Her Supper Yet	CZE	Lubos Fiser
Adoption, The	FRA	Michel Portal
Advantage, The	BUL	Bozhidar Petkov
Adventures of a Dentist	RUS	Alfred Schnitke
Adventures of Picasso, The	SWE	Gunnar Svensson
After the Rain	THAI	Movala Vorskul
Afyon Oppio	ITA	Guido and Maurizio de Angelis
Agent 69 Jensen in the Sign of Sagittarius	DEN	Bent Fabricius-Bjerre
Alice in Spanish Wonderland	SPA	Juan Pineda
Almost Summer	UN	Charles Lloyd/Ron Altbach
Alone at Daybreak	SPA	Jesus Gluck
Angel and Woman	CAN	Lewis Furey
Angel Mine	NZ	Mark Nicholas
Anton the Magician	E. GER.	Wolfram Heicking
Arrive Before Daybreak	YUG	Mladen and Predrag Vransevic
Art of Killing, The	JAP	Stomu Yamashita
Asya's Happiness	RUS	Vyecheslav Ovchinnikov
At the Service of Spanish Womanhood	SPA	Mari Carmen Santoja
Avalanche	NWP	William Kraft
Bad News Bears Go to Japan, The	PAR	Paul Chihara
Bad Spirits of the Euphrates, The	TUR	Cahit Berkay
Ballad of the Daltons, The	FRA	Claude Bolling
Banished	JAP	Toru Takemitsu
Bare Knuckles	IND	Vic Caesar

Barricade at Pont du Jour, The	FRA	Antoine Duhamel/Pascal Auberson
Battle for the Railway	YUG	Zoran Hristic
Be Blessed	BUL	Dimiter Griva
Beasts Are on the Streets, The	TV	Gerald Fried
Belfer	ISR	Roni Weiss
Betsy, The	AA	John Barry
Beyond and Back	SUN	Robert Summers
Big Fix, The	UN	Bill Conti
Big Sleep, The	UA	Jerry Fielding
Big Wednesday	WB	Basil Poledouris
Bilbao	SPA	Iceberg
Billion Dollar Hobo	IND	Michael Leonard
Black and White Lite Days and Nights	GER	Klaus Doldinger
Black Sun	SWE/YUG	Wilfred Josephs
Blackout	CAN/FRA	Didier Vasseur
Blood and Guts	CAN	Milton Barnes
Blood Relatives	CAN/FRA	Paul Jensen
Bloodbrothers	WB	Elmer Bernstein
Blue Collar	UN	Jack Nitzsche
Blue Fin	AUT	Michael Carlos
Born Again	EMB	Les Baxter
Boss' Son, The	IND	Richard Markowitz
Boys from Brazil, The	TCF	Jerry Goldsmith
Boys in Company C, The	COL	Jaime Mendoza-Nava
Brass Target	MGM	Laurence Rosenthal
Bravo Maestro	YUG	Branislav Zivkovic
Breakfast in Bed	IND	Tom Grant
Brink's Job, The	UN	Richard Rodney Bennett
Bronzes, Les	FRA	Serge Gainsbourg
Bruce Lee's Game of Death	HK	John Barry
Brutes and Savages	IND	Riz Ortolani
But Aren't You Ever Going to Change, Margarita?	SPA	Carlos A. Vizziello
Bye Bye Monkey	FRA/ITA	Philippe Sarde
Cage aux Folles, La	FRA/ITA	Ennio Morricone
Calamity	RUM	Adrian Enescu
California Suite	COL	Claude Bolling
Call Me from Afar	RUS	Yuri Butcko
Call of Spring, The	YUG	Alojz Srebotnjak
Capricorn One	WB	Jerry Goldsmith
Caravans	UN	Mike Batt
Carrot Queen, The	SPA	Luis de Pablo
Carry On, Emmanuelle	BRI	Eric Rogers
Casey's Shadow	COL	Patrick Williams
Cat, The	ITA	Ennio Morricone
Cat from Outer Space, The	DIS	Lalo Schifrin

Film	Code	Composer
Charleston	ITA	Maurizio and Guido de Angelis
Child of the Night	FRA/ ITA	Stelvio Cipriani
Children of Sanchez, The	IND	Chuck Mangione
Class of Miss MacMichael, The	BRI	Stanley Myers
Coach	IND	Anthony Harris
Cold Homeland	GER	Juergen Knieper
Coma	MGM	Jerry Goldsmith
Comes a Horseman	UA	Michael Small
Confidences for Confidences	FRA	Vladimir Cosma
Contract, The	HK	Samuel Hui
Convoy	UA	Chip Davis
Coquito, La	SPA	Gregorio Garcia Segura
Corleone (Father of the Godfather)	ITA	Ennio Morricone
Corn Is Green, The	TV	John Barry
Corvette Summer	MGM	Craig Safan
Count Dracula and His Vampire Bride	BRI	John Cacavas
Covert Action	ITA	Stelvio Cipriani
Creature, The	SPA	Victor Aute
Cruel Love	CZE	Svetozar Stracina
Cruise into Terror	TV	Gerald Fried
Damien--Omen II	TCF	Jerry Goldsmith
Dance Class on Vacation, The	TUR	Melik Kibar
Dante, Mind the Shark	SWE	Bjoern Jason Lindh/ Lasse Borghagen
Days of Heaven	PAR	Ennio Morricone
Days of the Past	SPA	Anton Garcia Abril
Dear Comrades	CHILE/ VEN	Jesus Sanoja Jr.
Death at Work	ITA	Bernard Herrmann
Death of the President	POL	Adam Walacinski
Death on the Nile	PAR	Nino Rota
Deathsport	NWP	Andrew Stein
Deer Hunter, The	UN	Stanley Myers
Despair	GER	Peer Raben
Different Story, A	EMB	David Frank
Dirty Dreamer	FRA	Jacques Dutronc
Discover Turquoise Mountain	CZE	L. Mordordzh
Doctor Polnaru	RUM	Adrian Enescu
Doctor Vlimmen	BEL/ HOL	Pim Koopman
Dog Soldiers (see Who'll Stop the Rain?)		
Dog That Liked Trains, The	YUG	Zoran Hristic
Don't Count on Us	ITA	Maurizio Rota
Don't Lean Out the Window	HUN	Gabor Presser
Dora and the Magic Lantern	FRA	Daniel Vangarde
Doramundo	BRA	Alemdo Prado
Dossier 51, Le	FRA	Jean Schwarz
Double Murder	FRA/ ITA	Riz Ortolani

Film		Composer
Double Suicide of Sonezaki	JAP	Ryudo Uzaki
Doubles	IND	Jim Bredouw/Martin Lund
Dracula's Dog	CRO	Andrew Belling
Dream of Passion, A	GRE	Iannis Markopoulos
Driver, The	TCF	Michael Small
Earth and the Sky, The	CUB	Sergio Vitier
Ecco Bombo	ITA	Franco Piersanti
80 Hussars	HUN	Andras Szollosy
El Paso Wrecking Co.	IND	Al Steinman
Elective Affinities	ITA	Nicola Samale/Giuseppe Mazzuca
Enclosure, The	BEL	Koen de Bruyne
End, The	UA	Paul Williams
End of Autumn	JAP	Kojan Saito
End of the World in Our Usual Bed in a Night Full of Rain, The	WB	Roberto de Simone
Enemy of the People, An	WB	Leonard Rosenman
Evil, The	NWP	Johnny Harris
Explosion	RUM	Theodor Grigoriu
Extras, The	HK	Joseph Koo/James Wong
Eyes of Laura Mars, The	COL	Artie Kane
F. I. S. T.	UA	Bill Conti
Factory Outing, The	DEN	Ole Hoeyer
Fall, The	BRA	Milton Nascimento/Ruy Guerra
Far Road, The	JAP	Minoru Miki
Father Sergius	RUS	Alfred Schnitke
Fedora	FRA/GER	Miklos Rozsa
Feedback	RUS	A. Rybnikov
Fifty-Fifty	GER	Peer Raben/J. J. Cale/Munich Factory
Filming "Othello"	IND	Francesco Lavagnino/Alberto Barbaris
Fire in the Middle	IND	William Harkleroad
Fire's Share, The	FRA	Paul Misraki
First Love	ITA	Riz Ortolani
Five Days from Home	UN	Bill Conti
Flight, The	E. GER.	Guenther Fischer
Foolish Years	YUG	Kornelije Kovac
Force 10 from Navarone	AI	Ron Goodwin
Foreigner, The	IND	Ivan Kral
Foul Play	PAR	Charles Fox
Fox in the Chicken Coop, The	ISR	Nurit Hirsch
Further Adventures of the Wilderness Family--Part 2	IND	Douglas Lackey/Gene Kauer
Fury, The	TCF	John Williams
Game of Death (see Bruce Lee's Game of Death)		
Gamin (Waif)	FRA	Francisco Zumaque
Get Out Your Handkerchiefs	FRA	Georges Delerue
Girl Friends	WB	Michael Small

Girl in Yellow Pajamas, The	ITA	Riz Ortolani
Girl with the Red Scarf, The	TUR	Cahit Berkay
Glass Cell, The	GER	Niels Walen
Go On Mama	FRA	Marie-Paule Belle
Go See Mother ... Father Is Working	FRA	Georges Delerue
Go Tell the Spartans	EMB	Dick Halligan
Goin' South	PAR	Van Dyke Parks
Good-for-Nothings	GER	Hans Werner Henze
Good Guys Wear Black	IND	Craig Safan
Goodbye Emmanuelle	FRA	Serge Gainsbourg
Gray Lady Down	UN	Jerry Fielding
Great Train Robbery, The	BRI	Jerry Goldsmith
Great Waves Purify the Sand	CAN	Che Ming
Greek Tycoon, The	UN	Stanley Myers
Green Room, The	FRA	Maurice Jaubert
Gun, The	ITA	Tullio de Piscopo
Halloween	IND	John Carpenter
Happiness Is So Near	RUM	Radu Goldis
Happy Confusion	THAI	Chariat Tiaptiam
Hark to the Cock	BUL	Georgi Genkov
Harper Valley P. T. A.	IND	Nelson Riddle
Heave Up	E. GER.	Gert Natschinski
Heaven and Hell	THAI	Chalie Intravijit/Sanga Arampi
Heaven Can Wait	PAR	David Grusin
Here Come the Tigers	AI	Harry Manfredini
Heritage, The	DEN	Kasper Winding
Hills Have Eyes, The	IND	Don Peake
Hole in the Wall, A	MOR	Jil Jilala
Holy Alliance, The	POR	Pedro Osorio
Hooper	WB	Bill Justis
Hope	TUR	Arif Erkin
Hot Lead and Cold Feet	DIS	Buddy Baker
Hound of the Baskervilles, The	BRI	Dudley Moore
House Calls	UN	Henry Mancini
Houses in This Alley	IRAN	Abdel Amir Alsarraf
How to Lose a Wife and Find a Lover	ITA	Gianni Ferrio
Hue and Cry	FRA	Jean-Michel Cayre
Hungarians, The	HUN	Gyorgy Vukan
Hunting Accident, A	RUS	Yevgeni Doga
Hurricane	CHN	Li Huan-Chi
I Belong to Me	GER/ ITA/ SPA	Giovana Marini
I, Maureen	CAN	Hagood Hardy
I Miss You, Hugs and Kisses	CAN	Howard Shore
Ice Castles	COL	Marvin Hamlisch
If Ever I See You Again	COL	Joe Brooks
I'll Force You to Leave	E. GER.	Siegfried Mattus
Immigrants, The	TV	Gerald Fried
In Praise of Older Women	CAN	Tibar Polgar

Film	Country/Studio	Composer
In the Name of the Pope King	ITA	Armando Trovajoli
Incredible Melting Man, The	AI	Arlon Ober
Insiang	PHI	Minda Azarcon
Institution, The	GER	Andi Brauer
Interior of a Convent	ITA	Sergio Monetori
International Velvet	MGM	Francis Lai
Invasion of the Body Snatchers	UA	Denny Zeitlin
Irishman, The	AUT	Charles Marawood
It's Alive II (It Lives Again)	WB	Bernard Herrmann/ Laurie Johnson
Jaws II	UN	John Williams
Jennifer	AI	Jerry Styner
Joerg Ratgeb, Painter	E. GER.	Andrzej Korzynski
Just Crazy About Horses	IND	Sam Wayman
Key Is in the Door, The	FRA	Philippe Sarde
Key to Love, The	THAI	Jonrak Jankanna
King of the Gypsies	PAR	David Grisman
Kingdom of Naples, The	GER/ ITA	M. Tregadio
Kirlian Witness, The	IND	Harry Manfredini
Kneuss	GER/ SWI	Tangerine Dream
Knife in the Head	GER	Irmin Schmidt
Lady on the Bus	BRA	Caetano Velloso
Last Challenge of the Dragon, The	HK	Frankie Chan
Last Mission of Demolitions Man Cloud, The	YUG	Martijan Makar
Last Romantic Lover, The	FRA	Pierre Bachelet
Last Supper, The	CUB	Leo Brouwer
Last Winter, The	ALB	Aleksander Lalo
Lawyer, The	CZE	Svetozar Stracina
Lebanon--Why?	LEB	Hussein Nazek
Legato	HUN	Andras Szollosy
Let's Go, Barbara	SPA	Carlos Laporta
Ligabue	ITA	Armando Trovajoli
Little Girl in Blue Velvet, The	FRA	Georges Delerue
Little Man	ISR	Shem-tov Levi
Little Town of Anara, The	RUS	T. Bakourdaze
Lone Wolf	RUS	V. Guba
Long Drive, The	RUM	Lucian Metianu
Long Live Hazana	SPA	Luis Eduardo Aute
Long Shot	BRI	Terry Dougherty
Long Weekend	AUT	Michael Carlos
Lord of the Rings	UA	Leonard Rosenman
Lost Paradise	BEL	Roger Mores
Love and Rage	YUG	Zoran Hristic
Love and the Midnight Auto Supply (see Midnight Auto Supply)		
Love in Question	FRA	Oliver Dassault
Love Lesson	BRA	Frances Hime
Lovers, The	THAI	Prachin Songpow
Mackan	SWE	Jan Lindell
Mad Cage, The (see Cage aux Folles, La)		

Madame Rosa	FRA	Philippe Sarde
Mafu Cage, The	IND	Roger Kellaway
Magic	TCF	Jerry Goldsmith
Man Called Autumn Flower, A	SPA	Carmelo Bernaola
Maneaters Are Loose, The	TV	Gerald Fried
Manitou, The	EMB	Lalo Schifrin
Manly Times	BUL	Kiril Dontchev
Manrape	SWE	Heikki Valpola
March on Paris 1914, The	IND	Jessie Holladay Duane
Marginal Ones, The	IN	Vijay Raghava Rao
Marie-Ann	CAN	Maurice Marshall
Martin	IND	Donald Rubinstein
Maternale	ITA	Stelvio Cipriani
Matriarchy	BUL	Boris Karadimchev
Me and Charley	DEN	Kaspar Winding
Mean Dog Blues	AI	Fred Karlin
Message from Space, A	JAP	Ken-Ichiro Morioka
Messiah, The	ITA	Mario Nascimbene
Metamorphoses	COL	Bob Randles
Midnight Auto Supply	IND	Ed Bogas
Midnight Express	COL	Giorgio Moroder
Millionaire in Trouble	ISR	Dov Seltzer
Mine, The	TUR	C. Zulfu Livaneli
Miracle Tree, The	RUS	Bidsina Kvernadze
Mirror Mirror	DEN	Ole Hoeyer
Misfire	SWE	Kaj Chydenius
Moliere	FRA	Rene Clemencie
Moment by Moment	UN	Lee Holdridge
Moritz, Dear Moritz	GER	Klaus Doldinger
Mountain Pass	FRA	Philippe Sarde
Mouth to Mouth	AUT	Roy Ritchie
Movie Movie	WB	Ralph Burns
My Father's Happy Years	HUN	Zdenko Tamassy
National Lampoon's Animal House	UN	Elmer Bernstein
New Beaujolais Wine Has Arrived, The	FRA	Carlo Rustichelli
Newsfront	AUT	William Motzing
Night Before Christmas, The	ITA	Steve Powder
Night, the Prowler, The	AUT	Alan Cameron
Nighthawks	BRI	David Graham Ellis
92 Minutes of Yesterday	DEN	Henrick Blichmann
No Longer Alone	IND	Tedd Smith
No Trespassing	RUM	Tiberiu Olah
Norseman, The	AI	Jaime Mendoza-Nava
Northern Lights	IND	Ozzie Ahlers
Nunzio	UN	Lalo Schifrin
Occupation in 26 Pictures	YUG	Alfi Kabiljo
Odd Job, The	BRI	Howard Blake
Oh the Days	MOR	Nass El Ghiwane
Old Woman, An	THAI	Nopadol Busapaketr
Oliver's Story	PAR	Lee Holdridge/Francis Lai
Olly, Olly, Oxen Free	IND	Bob Alcivar

Olsen Gang Goes to War, The	DEN	Bent Fabricius-Bjerre
On the Yard	IND	Charles Gross
Once in Paris	IND	Mitch Leigh
One and Only, The	PAR	Patrick Williams
122 Rue de Provence	FRA	Ennio Morricone
Only 15	THAI	Seksan Sonimsat
Order and Security of the World	FRA	Claude Mougaro/Maurice Vander
Other People's Money	FRA	Patrice Mestral
Other Side of the Mountain, Part 2, The	UN	Lee Holdridge
Ottokar, the World Reformer	E. GER.	Guenther Fischer
Our Winning Season	AI	Charles Fox
Outside Chance	IND	Murphy Dunne/Lou Levy
Pablo	CUB	Silvio Rodriguez
Pantelei	BUL	Bozhidar Petkov
Paper Flowers	MEX	Mario Lavista/Raul Lavista/Javier Mateos
Paradise Alley	UN	Bill Conti
Passion	POL	Piotr Mosy
Passion Flower Hotel	GER	Francis Lai
Patrick	AUT	Brian May
Payoff, The	ITA	Pino Daniele
Perceval la Gallois	FRA	Guy Robert
Phantom Love	FRA/ JAP	Toru Takemitsu
Photo Souvenir	FRA	Georges Delerue
Piranha	NWP	Pino Donaggio
Place Without Limits, The	MEX	Joaquin Gutierrez Heras
Pocket Lover, The	FRA	Laurent Petigirard
Porter, The	AFR	Lamin Konte
Portrait in the Rain	RUS	Alexei Mashukov
Preparation for the Festival	JAP	Teizo Matsumura
Pretty Good for a Human	FIN	Harri Tuominen
Promise, The	UN	David Shire
Proof of the Wild	JAP	Kuji Ono
Puppets Under Starry Skies	JAP	Ryoichi Kuniyoshi
Queen Bee	JAP	Shinichi Tanabe
Rabbit Test	EMB	Mike Post
Raomi	BEL/ FRA	Egberto Gismonti
Recollections	POL	Helmut Nadolski
Recourse to the Method, The	CUB/ FRA/ MEX	Leo Brouwer
Red Gold	MEX/ SPA	Carmelo Bernaola
Red Midnight	GER	Gunter Hampel/Galaxie Dream Band
Remains of the Shipwreck	SPA	David Thomas
Rembrandt--Fecit 1669	HOL	Laurens van Rooyen
Remember My Name	COL	Alberta Hunter
Rescue from Gilligan's Island	TV	Gerald Fried

Return from Witch Mountain	DIS	Lalo Schifrin
Return of Casanova	ITA	Riz Ortolani
Revenge of the Pink Panther, The	UA	Henry Mancini
Rheingold	GER	Eberhard Schoener
Roads of the South	FRA	Michel Legrand
Robert and Robert	FRA	Francis Lai
Roberte	FRA	Eric Demarsan
Rock 'n' Roll Wolf	FRA/ RUM/ RUS	Temistode Popa/Gerald Bourgeois
Roof, The	BUL	Georgi Genkov
Roots 2	TV	Gerald Fried
Round Trip	YUG	Kornelije Kovac
Run for the Roses	IND	Raul Lavista
Room with a View on the Sea, A	POL	Adam Stawinski
Running Fence	IND	Jim Dickinson
Rural Teacher, The	THAI	Phet Pingtong/Titsch Lampreun
Saen Saeb Canal	THAI	Seksan Somisat
Sailor's Return, The	BRI	Carl Davis
Same Time Next Year	UN	Marvin Hamlisch
Savage State, The	FRA	Pierre Jensen
Saxophone	ITA	Enzo Jannacci
Scar, The	THAI	Samarn Karnchanapalin
Scenes of Fires	E. GER.	Peter Gotthardt
Scent of Earth, The	YUG	Szeslaw Nieman
Score, The	SWE	Robert Cornford
Sea Gypsies, The	WB	Fred Steiner
Second Awakening of Christa Klages, The	GER	Klaus Doldinger
Second Wind, A	FRA	Jean-Pierre Stora
Secret Life of Plants, The	PAR	Stevie Wonder
Secrets	IND	Mike Gibbs
September Love	THAI	Prachin Songpao
Seven Freckles	E. GER.	Guenter Erdmann
Sextette	CRO	Artie Butler
Shadows of a Hot Summer	CZE	Zdenek Liska
Shout, The	BRI	Rupert Hine/Anthony Banks/Michael Rutherford
Simple Heart, A	ITA	Franco Mannino
Singer, The	E. GER.	Karel Svoboda
Sita's Wedding	IN	K. V. Mahadevan
Slave of Love, A	RUS	Eduard Artemyev
Slow Dancing in the Big City	UA	Bill Conti
Small Timers, The	FRA	Francis Lai
Smell of Wildflowers, The	YUG	Zoran Simjanovic
Smile Hello	THAI	Prachin Songpow
Somebody Killed Her Husband	COL	Alex North
Somnabulists	SPA	Jose Nieto
Song of Roland, The	FRA	Antoine Duhamel
Special Edition	RUM	Lucian Metianu
Speed Fever	ITA	Guido and Maurizio de Angelis

Spiral	POL	Wojiech Kilar
Sport, Sport, Sport	RUS	Alfred Schnitke
Squadron Antigangster	ITA	Goblin
Stars in the Hair, Tears in the Eyes	BUL	Kiril Tseboulka
State Reasons	FRA/ ITA	Vladimir Cosma
Stay As You Are	ITA	Ennio Morricone
Steam Mare, The	FRA	Jean-Marie Senia
Steppe, The	RUS	Vyecheslav Ovchinnikov
Stevie	BRI	Patrick Young
Stick-Up, The	BRI	Michael J. Lewis
Stony Island	IND	David Matthews
Straight Time	WB	David Shire
Strauberg Is Here	GER	Stefan Melbinger
Sugar, The	FRA	Philippe Sarde/Hubert Rostaing
Sun over the Swamp	TUR	Hursit Yenigun
Sunstroke	BUL	Kiril Dontchev
Superman	WB	John Williams
Surgeons	BUL	Kiril Tseboulka
Surprise Sock	FRA	Marie-Paule Belle
Swarm, The	WB	Jerry Goldsmith
Sweeney 2	BRI	Tony Hatch
Swiss Affair, The	FRA/ ITA/ SWI	Giancarlo Chiaramello
Swissmakers, The	SWI	Jonas C. Haefeli
Take All of Me	ITA	Stelvio Cipriani
Talisman	BUL	Alexander Yosifov
Teacher, The	CUB	Sergio Vitier
Terror	BRI	Ivor Slaney
There Was a Lad	RUS	Pavel Chekalov
They Went That-a-Way and That-a-Way	IND	Michael Leonard
Third Base	JAP	Michi Tanaka
Third Walker, The	CAN	Paul Hoffert
39 Steps, The	BRI	Ed Welch
Three Card Monte	CAN	Jim Caverhill
Tiger, The	YUG	Vojislav Kostic
Times of the Constitution	SPA	Fernando Brunet/Luiz Fernandez Soria
Tit for Tat	YUG	Kornelije Kovac
Toolbox Murders, The	IND	George Deaton
Top Dog	POL	Jan Kanty-Pawluskiewicz
Towing	IND	Martin Rubenstein
Trocadero Lemon Blue (Trocadero Blue and Yellow)	FRA	Alec R. Costandinos
Trout	SPA	Victor Manuel
Two Solitudes	CAN	Maurice Jarre
Two Super Cops	ITA	Maurizio and Guido de Angelis
Uncle Joe Shannon	UA	Bill Conti
Unmarried Woman, An	TCF	Bill Conti

Untypical Story, An	RUS	M. Ziv
Utopia	FRA	Henri Raschle/Patrice Holiner
Vice Squad (Brigade Mondaine--La Secte de Marrakech)	FRA	Carrone
Virgin Witch, The	BRI	Ted Dicks
Viva Italia	ITA	Armando Trovajoli
Vote for Gundisalvo	SPA	Antonio Garcia Abril
Vultures, The	CAN	Dominique Tremblay
Wall, The	RUM	Cornelia Tantu
Warlords of Atlantis	BRI	Mike Vickers
Watership Down	BRI	Angela Morley/Malcolm Williamson/Mike Batt
Wedding of Zein, The	IND	Siddik/Souleiman Jamil
Weekend of Shadows	AUT	Charles Marawood
Welcome	RUS	M. Tariverdiev
What Max Said	SPA	Luis de Pablo
When the Sun Rises	TUR	Tum Ata Grubu
Who Is Killing the Great Chefs of Europe?	WB	Henry Mancini
Who'll Stop the Rain? (Dog Soldiers)	UA	Laurence Rosenthal
Widower, The	THAI	Prasert Chulaketr
Wild Geese, The	BRI	Roy Budd
Wings	RUS	Roman Ledenov
Winterborn	DEN	Hans Erik Phillip
Winterspelt	GER	Gyorgy Ligeti
Wise Monkey, The	SPA	Jose Nieto
With Clean Hands	RUM	Richard Oschanitzky
With Love and Tenderness	BUL	Kiril Dontchev
Witness, The	FRA/ITA	Piero Piccioni
Woman Across the Way	GER	Robert Eliscu
Woman from the Torrid Land	ITA/SPA	Carlo Savina
Woman, Man, City	CUB	Sergio Vitier
Word Is Out	IND	Trish Nugent/Buena Vista
Yellow Handkerchief of Happiness	JAP	Masaru Sato
Yesterday's Tomorrow	GER	Eugen Illin
You Are Not Alone	DEN	Sebastian (Knud Christensen)
Yukinojo's Revenge	JAP	Yasushi Akutagawa

1979

Acrobat, The	FRA	Antoine Duhamel
Adolescent, The	FRA/GER	Philippe Sarde
Affairs	HK	Joseph Koo
Agatha	WB	Johnny Mandel
Ah, Si! ... E Io Lo Dico a Zorro!	ITA	Gianfranco Plenizio
Alexandria ... Why?	ALG/EGY	Fouad El Zaheri

Film	Country/Studio	Composer
Alien	TCF	Jerry Goldsmith
Alison's Birthday	AUT	Brian King
All That Jazz	TCF	Ralph Burns
Alle Origini Della Mafia	ITA	Nino Rota
Almost Perfect Pair, An	PAR	Georges Delerue
American Nitro	IND	Art Twain
American Success Company, The	COL	Maurice Jarre
Americathon	UA	Tom Scott
Amityville Horror, The	AI	Lalo Schifrin
Among People	RUS	Rumil Vildanov
... And Justice for All	COL	Dave Grusin
Angry Man, The	CAN/ FRA	Claude Bolling
Apocalypse Now	UA	Francis Ford Coppola/ Carmine Coppola
Arabian Adventure	BRI	Ken Thorne
Ashanti	WB	Michael Melvoin Carrere
Associate, The	FRA/ GER	Mort Schuman
At the Beginning of Summer	ALB	Kujtim Laro
At the Brink of the Brink of the Bench	FRA	Georges Moustaki
Attack of the Killer Tomatoes	IND	Gordon Goodwin/Paul Sundfor
Avalanche Express	TCF	Allyn Ferguson
Baara	AFR	Lamin Konte
Baby Snakes	IND	Frank Zappa
Bad Guys, The	HUN	Ferenc Sabo
Bailiff of Griefensee, The	SWI	Arie Dzierlatka
Barrier	BUL	Kiril Tseboulka
Battlestar Galactica	UN	Stu Phillips
Being There	UA	Johnny Mandel
Bell Jar, The	EMB	Gerald Fried
Beloved Lover	BRA	Guto Graca Mello
Beyond the Poseidon Adventure	WB	Jerry Fielding
Big Mama	ITA	Eduardo Alfieri
Billy in the Lowlands	IND	The Nighthawks
Bit Between the Teeth, The	FRA	Antoine Duhamel
Black Hole, The	DIS	John Barry
Black Jack	BRI	Bog Pegg
Black Sheep, The	FRA	Georges Delerue
Black Stallion, The	UA	Carmine Coppola
Blood of the Railroad Workers	NOR	Gunnar Germeten
Bloodline	PAR	Ennio Morricone
Bobo, Jacco	BEL/ FRA/ TAH	Jacques Revaux
Boomerang	BUL	Kiril Tseboulka
Boon, The	IN	Vanraj Bhatia
Border Crossing, The	E. GER.	Ivan Pequeno
Bosko Buha	YUG	Zoran Simjanovic
Bottleneck (Ingorgo, L')	FRA/GER/ ITA/SPA	Fiorenzo Carpi

Boulevard Nights	WB	Lalo Schifrin
Bread and Stones	SWI	Martin Boettcher
Breaking Away	TCF	Patrick Williams
Breakthrough	GER	Peter Thomas
Broken Flag	MEX	Raul Lavista
Bronte Sisters, The	FRA	Philippe Sarde
Buck Rogers	UN	Stu Phillips
Burgos Trial, The	SPA	Hibai Rekondo
Burning	YUG	Arhivska
Butch and Sundance: The Early Days	COL	Patrick Williams
California Dreaming	AI	Fred Karlin
Caligula	ITA	Paul Clemente
Call-Up, The	SWE	Janne Schaffer
Camera Buff (Amator)	POL	Krzysztof Knittel
Canal, The (Kanal)	TUR	Arif Erkin
Castaways on Gilligan's Island, The	TV	Gerald Fried
Champ, The	MGM	Dave Grusin
Chapter Two	COL	Marvin Hamlisch
Charles and Lucie	FRA	Pierre Perret
Charlotte Lionshield	SWE	Eskil Hemberg
Charly and Steffen	DEN	Jacob Groth
Chi l'Ha Vista Morire?	ITA	Ennio Morricone
Children of Oblivion, The	BEL	G. Soccio
Chocolate Eclair	CAN	Richard Gregoire
Chomps	AI	Hoyt Curtin
Christ Stopped at Eboli	FRA/ ITA	Piero Piccioni
Ciao, You Guys	FRA	Paul-Jean Borowsky
Cinema Cinema	FRA	Vijay Raghava Rao
Circus Tent, The	IN	M. G. Radakrishnan
City on Fire	CAN	William McCauley/ Matthew McCauley
Clair de Femme (Womanlight)	FRA/ GER/ ITA	Jean Musy
Clear Horizons	ALB	Limos Dizdari
Coco la Fleur, Candidate	FRA	Experience 7
Collina dei Comali, La	ITA	Angela Morley
Colonel and the Werewolf, The	BRA	Helvius Vilela/Marco Versiani
Concorde--Airport '79, The	UN	Lalo Schifrin
Confederation--The People Make History, The	POR	Sergio Godinho-Fausto/ Jose Maria Branco
Cop or Hood	FRA	Philippe Sarde
Corpus	GRE	George Kouroupos/Stefanos Vassilliades/ Vaguelis Katsoulis/ Demetris Lecas/ Theodre Katelanos
Cramp	YUG	Tomaz Pengov
Cuba	UA	Patrick Williams

Dark, The	IND	Roger Kellaway
David	GER	Wojiech Kilar
Dawn of the Dead	IND	Goblin/Dario Argento
Days Are Passing, The	YUG	Zoran Simjanovic
Dear Papa	ITA	Manuel de Sica
Death Has No Mercy	PHI	Ernani Cuenco
Delirium	IND	David Williams
Deliver Us from Evil	HUN	Gabor Presser
Difficult Transport, A	ALB	Sh. Kosha
Dimboola	AUT	George Dreyfus
Dirt	IND	Dick Halligan
Distance	IN	Ain Rasheed
Divorcement, Le	FRA	Barouh
Dizengoff 99	ISR	Koby Oshrath
Dr. Norman Bethune	CHN	Liu Qiming
Dr. Plern	THAI	Prasit Payomyong
Dogs, The	FRA	Rene Koering
Dolphin	IND	Basil Poledouris
Donkey in a Brahmin Village	IN	M. B. Srinivasan
Don't Ever Ask Me if I Love	ISR	Nurit Hirsch
Double McGuffin, The	IND	Euel Box
Dracula	UN	John Williams
Dramma Borghese, Un (Mimi)	ITA	Riz Ortolani
Dreamer	TCF	Bill Conti
Driller Killer	IND	Joseph Delia
Eagle's Wing, The	BRI	Marc Wilkinson
Easy Road	GRE	Mikis Theodorakis/ George Theodorakis
Eighth Day, The	SWE	Keith Jarrett
Electric Horseman, The	COL	Dave Grusin
Elephant God, The	IN	Satyajit Ray
Emperor, The	SWE	Ragnar Grippe
Endless Trail, The	BAN	Alauddin Ali
Ernesto	ITA	Carmelo Bernaola
Escape from Athena	BRI	Lalo Schifrin
Europeans, The	BRI	Richard Robbins
Evictors, The	AI	Jaime Mendoza-Nava
Exiled in a Central Avenue	GRE	Nicos Zervos
Fabulous Adventures of the Legendary Baron Munchausen, The	FRA	Michel Legrand
Fall, The	GER	Klaus Doldinger
Family Nest	HUN	Janos Brody
Fast Break	COL	David Shire
Fast Charlie ... The Moonbeam Rider	UN	Stu Phillips
Fatal Comma, The	BUL	Bozhidar Petkov
Feedback	IND	Jake Stern
Felicite	FRA	Antoine Duhamel
Fifth Commandment, The	GER	Armando Trovajoli
5th Musketeer, The	COL	Riz Ortolani
Fight for Freedom	NIG	Duro Ladipe
Firepower	BRI	Leandro "Gato" Barbieri
First False Step, The	CHN	Ma Hwa

First Polka, The	GER	Edward Aniol
Fish That Saved Pittsburgh, The	UA	Thom Bell
Fist in the Pocket	GER	"Satin Whale"
Force of One, A	IND	Dick Halligan
Foretold by Fate	THAI	Pim Patiphan Poontama-jitr
40 Years Without Sex	SPA	Soto
Four Seasons, The	YUG	Arsen Dedic
French Postcards	FRA/GER	Lee Holdridge
Friday the 13th ... The Orphan	WNP	Teo Macero
Frisco Kid, The	WB	Frank de Vol
From Hell to Victory	FRA/ITA/SPA	Riz Ortolani
Gal Young Un	IND	Charles Engstrom
Gendarme and the Creatures from Outer Space, The	FRA	Raymond Lefevre
Getaway, The (Derobade, La)	FRA	Vladimir Cosma
Glacier Fox, The	JAP	Masaru Sato
God, Why Is There a Border in Love?	JAP	Miki Yoshino
Going	IN	Jaidev
Going in Style	WB	Michael Small
Golden Girl	EMB	Bill Conti
Golden Lady, The	BRI	Georges Garvarentz
Good Luck, Miss Wyckoff	IND	Ernest Gold
Good News (Buene Notizie)	ITA	Ennio Morricone
Goodbye, Flickmania (see So Long, Movie Friend)		
Goodbye ... See You Monday	CAN/FRA	Lewis Furey
Grand Piano, The (Royalut)	BUL	Simeon Pironkov
Grandmother, The (La Nona)	ARG	Oscar Cardozo Ocampo
Great American Bugs Bunny - Road Runner Chase, The	WB	Dean Elliott
Great Santini, The	WB	Elmer Bernstein
Green Jacket, The	ITA	Luis Bacalov
Guappi, I	ITA	Franco and Gigi Campanino
Guardian Angel, The	CAN/FRA	Marcel Napoleoni
H. C. Andersen in Italy	DEN/ITA	Steven Schlacks/Lars Fjeldmose
H. O. T. S.	IND	David Davis
Hamburg Syndrome, The	FRA/GER	Erich Ferstl
Hanover Street	COL	John Barry
He Never Gives Up	TAI	Tang Wong
Head over Heels	UA	Ken Lauber
Heart Beat	WB	Jack Nitzsche
Heartbreak People	THAI	Chintanart Wacharasathien
Heroes Are Not Wet Behind the Ears, The	FRA	Jacques Delaporte

Heroines of Evil, The	FRA	Oliver Dassault
Hit Song (Schlager)	ISR	Zvika Pik
Hitchhiker, The	CZE	Ferdinand Havlik
Hitter, The	IND	Garfeel Ruff
Home Movies	IND	Pino Donaggio
Honeymoon (Taxidi Toy Melitos)	GRE	Manos Hadjidakis
Hot-Head	FRA	Pierre Bachelet
Hot Stuff	COL	Patrick Williams
Hour of the Wolf, The	GRE	Sakis Tsilikis
House of the Lute	HK	John Thompson
Hullabaloo over Georgie and Bonnie's Pictures	BRI	Vic Flick
Human Factor, The	MGM	Richard and Gary Logan
Hurricane	PAR	Nino Rota
Hypochondriac, The	ITA	Piero Piccioni
Hypothesis of the Stolen Painting, The	FRA	Jose Arriagada
I Love You, I Love You Not (see Together?)		
I Sing I Cry	TAI	Wu Meg Lin
Ikarus	E. GER.	Peter Gotthardt
I'm Expecting	SWE	Bengt Palmers
In Search of Justice (short)	BAR	Charles Bernstein
In the Mouth of the World	BRA	Jorge Ben
In the Name of the Fuhrer	BEL	Arsene Souffriau
Incident, The (Jiken)	JAP	Yasushi Akutagawa
Incredible Journey of Dr. Meg Laurel, The	TV	Gerald Fried
In-Laws, The	WB	John Morris
Invito allo Sport	ITA	Ennio Morricone
Island, The	ARG	Victor Proncet
Itchy Fingers	HK	Frankie Chan/Ricky Fung
It's a Long Time I've Loved You	FRA	Gerard Anfosso
It's Me	HOL	Lodewijk de Boer
I've Got You, You've Got Me by the Hairs of My Chinny Chin Chin	FRA	Jacques Morali
Jacob Two-Two Meets the Hooded Fang	CAN	Lewis Furey
Jaguar Lives!	AI	Robert O. Ragland
Jealousy	THAI	Menrat Srikanond
Jerk, The	UN	Jack Elliott
Johnny Larsen	DEN	Toots Thielmans/Kaspar Winding/Ole Arnfred
Journalist	YUG	Alfi Kabiljo
Judge's Friend, The	BEL/HOL	Georges Delerue
Jules Starts with Jules	CHILE	Luis Advis
Jun	JAP	Toshi Ichiyanagi
Just a Gigolo	GER	Guenther Fischer
Just Out of Reach	AUT	William Motzing
Just You and Me, Kid	COL	Jack Elliott
Kaleidoscope: Valeska Gert, For Fun--For Pleasure	GER	Friedrich Meyer

Kasper in the Underworld	BEL	Francois Glorieux
Kassbach	AUS	Peter Zwetkoff
Keiko	JAP	Jun Fukamachi
Ken Murray Shooting Stars	IND	Richard LaSalle
Kids Are Alright, The	BRI	Peter Townshend
Killer Fish	BRA/ ITA	Guido and Maurizio de Angelis
Kindaich Kosue no Boken (Adventure of Kindaich, The)	JAP	Asei Kobayashi
Kristoffer's House	SWE	Lars Dahlberg
Lady from the Town, The	ALB	Agim Krajka
Lady in Red, The	NWP	James Horner
Lady Oscar	FRA/ JAP	Michel Legrand
Lady Vanishes, The	BRI	Richard Hartley
Lamore	GRE	Loukianos Kalaidonis
Lantern Festival Adventure	TAI	Tony Wong
Last Embrace	UA	Miklos Rozsa
Last Tasmanian, The	AUT	William Davies
Last Word, The	IND	Carol Lees
Last Year of Childhood, The	GER	Markus Urchs
Legacy, The	UN	Michael J. Lewis
Legend of the Mountain	HK	Ng Tai Kong
Life of Brian	BRI	Geoffrey Burgeon
Linus and the Mysterious Red Brick House	SWE	Bengt Ernryd
Little Archimedes, The	ITA	Roman Vlad
Little Escapes	FRA/ SWI	Leon Francioli
Little Romance, A	WB	Georges Delerue
Long Live Ghosts!	CZE	Jarislav Uhlis
Lost and Found	COL	John Cameron
Louvre Museum, The	JAP	Toru Takemitsu
Love and Bullets	BRI	Lalo Schifrin
Love and Faith: Lady Ogin	JAP	Akira Ikufube
Love at First Bite	AI	Charles Bernstein
Love of a Little Girl, The	THAI	Prachim Songpow
Love on the Run	FRA	Georges Delerue
Lovers' Wind, The	IRAN	Hosein Dehlavi
Lucie	NOR	Terje Rypdal
Lumiere des Justes, La (Light of Justice)	FRA	Georges Garvarentz
Machine Gun Stein	ITA	Stelvio Cipriani/Carlo Rustichelli
Mad Max	AUT	Brian May
Magician of Lublin, The	GER/ ISR	Maurice Jarre
Mais ou et Donc Ornicar	FRA	Antoine Duhamel
Man to Kill, The	YUG	Jose Privsek
Man with the Axe	IN	B. V. Karanth
Man You Love to Hate, The	BRI	Herbert Deutsch
Management Forgives a Moment of Madness, The	VEN	Alberto Slewynger

Marriage, Tel Aviv Style	ISR	Yannis Petritsis
Martian Chronicles, The	TV	Stanley Myers
Meadow, The (Prato, Il)	ITA	Ennio Morricone
Meat (Fleisch)	GER	Eugen Thomass
Meatballs	PAR	Elmer Bernstein
Medic, The (Toubib, Le)	FRA	Philippe Sarde
Meetings with Remarkable Men	BRI	Thomas de Hartman/ Laurence Rosenthal
Megalomaniac, The (Rai Saneh Ha)	THAI	Seksan Sonimsat
Melancholy Baby	BEL/ FRA/ SWI	Serge Gainsbourg
Memories of Leticia Valle	SPA	Alberto Bourbon
Messidor	FRA/ SWI	Arie Dzierlatka
Meteor	AI	Laurence Rosenthal
Michael Kohlhaas	GER	Peter Sandloff
Middle Age Spread	NZ	Stephen McCurdy
Milk War in Bavaria	GER	Birger Heymann
Mimi (see Dramma Borghese, Un)		
Miss Salak Jitr	THAI	Piac
Missing Prisoners	CUB/ SWE	Juanito Rodriguez/Chem- bo
Mistletoes	HUN	Zsolt Dome
Moments	FRA/ ISR	Hubert Rostaing
Moments in a Matchbox	BUL	Simeon Pironkov
Mool-Dori Village	KOR	Choi Yon Dong
Moonlight Serenade	SPA	Juan Pineda/Albert Moraleda
Moonraker	UA	John Barry
Mountain Family Robinson	IND	Robert O. Ragland
Mountain Man, The	THAI	Knit Kounavuhdi
Muppet Movie, The	BRI	Paul Williams
My Asylum (Chiedo Asilo)	ITA	Philippe Sarde
My Brilliant Career	AUT	Nathan Waks
My Mother, the General	ISR	Nurit Hirsch
Mysteries	HOL	Laurens van Rooyen
Nahia	ALG	Ziad Rahbani
National Class	YUG	Zoran Simjanovic
Natural Enemies	CIV	Don Ellis
Nest of Vipers (Ritratto di Borghesia in Nero)	ITA	Vincenzo Tempera
Night Creature	IND	Jim Helms
Night Flowers	IND	Harry Manfredini
Nightmares	POL	Zigmunt Konicezny
Nightwing	COL	Henry Mancini
1941	UN	John Williams
Nocturnal Uproar	FRA	Serge Gainsbourg
Norma Rae	TCF	David Shire
North Avenue Irregulars, The	DIS	Robert F. Brunner
North Dallas Forty	PAR	John Scott
Nosferatu, Phantom of the Night	FRA/ GER	Popol Vuk/Florian Fricke

Not Everything That Flies Is a Bird	GER	Rolf Adrian
November 1828	INO	Frankie Raden
Obsession	IN	Vanraj Bhatia
Of Death and Corpses	BEL/FRA	Alain Pierre
Ogro	FRA/ITA/SPA	Ennio Morricone
Oh! The Nomugi Pass	JAP	Masaru Sato
Old Comedy, The	RUS	M. Tariverdiev
Olsen Gang Never Surrenders, The	DEN	Bent Fabricius-Bjerre
On the Tracks of the Missing	BUL	Kiril Dontchev
Once Upon a Time	IN	Bhaskar Chandvarkar
1 + 1 = 3	GER	Andreas Kobner
Onion Field, The	EMB	Eumir Deodato
Only Once in a Lifetime	IND	Robert O. Ragland
Orchestra Rehearsal	FRA/GER/ITA	Nino Rota
Oscar, Kina and the Laser	SPA	Castro Dario
Out of Whack (Rien ne va plus)	FRA	Michel Rivard
Outsider, The	PAR	Ken Thorne
Over the Edge	WB	Sol Kaplan
Palm Beach	AUT	Terry Hannigan
Pals, The	YUG	Vojislav Kostic
Parts, the Clonus Horror	IND	Hod David Schudson
Passage, The	UA	Michael J. Lewis
Paths of War	ALB	Kujtim Laro
Pearl	TV	John Addison
Penitentiary	IND	Frankie Gaye
Pentecost Outing, The	GER	Hans-Martin Majewski
Perfect Couple, A	TCF	Allan Nicholls
Personal Affairs	YUG	Goran Bregovic
Phantasm	EMB	Fred Myrow
Players	PAR	Jerry Goldsmith
Plutonium	GER	Eugen Thomass
Police War, The	FRA	Jean-Marie Senia
Poor Lucas	BUL	Kiril Tseboulka
Portable Country	VEN	Chuchito Sanoja
Portrait of Teresa	CUB	Carlos Farinas
Portrait of the Artist as a Young Man, A	IND	Stanley Myers
Prisoner of Zenda, The	UN	Henry Mancini
Private Collections	FRA/JAP	Pierre Bachelet/J. A. Seazer
Prize Fighter, The	NWP	Peter Matz
Promise, The	UN	David Shire
Promises in the Dark	WB	Leonard Rosenman
Prophecy	PAR	Leonard Rosenman
Proud Twins, The	HK	Eddie Wang
Quadrophenia	BRI	The Who
Quiet Is the Night	POL	Jerzy Matuszkiewicz

Quintet	TCF	Tom Pierson
Rage	SPA	J. Vidal
Raining in the Mountain	HK	Ng Tai Kong
Ratataplan	ITA	Detto Mariano
Ray of Sunlight, A	BUL	Boris Karadimchev
Real Life	PAR	Mort Lindsey
Rebels, The	TV	Gerald Fried
Red Poppies on the Wall	ALB	Kujtim Laro
Red Seedlings	IN	Devera Jan
Red Sweater, The (Pull-Over Rouge, Le)	FRA	Jean-Louis D'Onorio
Restless Corpse, The	IN	G. K. Venkstesh
Resurrection of the Golden Wolf	JAP	Casey Rankin
Return, The	YUG	Miljenko Prohaska
Return to the Beloved	FRA	Antoine Duhamel
Revenge	ITA	Dangio and Nando de Luca
Revolt of the Thralls	DEN	Benny Holst
Rich Kids	UA	Craig Doerge
Riddle of the Sands, The	BRI	Howard Blake
Rites of May, The	PHI	Max Jocson
River, The	IRAQ	Faiq Hanna
Rocky II	UA	Bill Conti
Roller Boogie	UA	Bob Esty
Roots of Blood	MEX	Sergio Guerrero
Roses of Danzig, The	ITA	Luis Enrique Bacalov
Run Away, I Love You	BUL	Peter Yossifov
Runner Stumbles, The	IND	Ernest Gold
Running	CAN	Andre Gagnon
Sabina, The	SPA/ SWE	Paco de Lucia
Sai Thip	THAI	Panthip Virayaphanit
Scavenger Hunt	TCF	Billy Goldenberg
Scream of Silence, A	CAN	Maurice Blackburn
Screams of a Winter Night	IND	Don Zimmers
Search for Solutions, The	IND	Pat Metheny/Lyle Meyers
Secret, The	HK	Violet Lam
Seduction of Joe Tynan, The	UN	Bill Conti
Seekers, The	TV	Gerald Fried
Sgt. Buntung	THAI	Montri Ong-Lam
Servants, The	HK	Joseph Koo
7 Days in January	SPA	Nicholas Peyrac
Sewers of Paradise, The	FRA	Jean-Pierre Doering
Shades of Silk	CAN	Alain Leroux
Shaolin Abbot	HK	Chen Yung-Yu
Shaolin Rescuers	HK	Chen Yung-Yu
Shape of Things to Come, The	CAN	Paul Hoffert
Short Memory	FRA	Eric Simon
Siberiade	RUS	Eduard Artemyev
Silent Partner, The	CAN	Oscar Peterson
Sirocco Blow, The	FRA	Serge Franklin
Sisters, or the Balance of Happiness	GER	Konstantin Wecker

Sitting Ducks	IND	Richard Romanus
Sitting on the Edge of Tomorrow with the Feet Hanging	SPA	Carlos Vizziello
Skatetown, U. S. A.	COL	Miles Goodman
Skirt Chaser, The	FRA	Georges Delerue
Slow Motion	YUG	Alfi Kabiljo
Slum People in the Sun	THAI	Prat Suwannasorn
Snap-Shot	AUT	Brian May
Snapshots as Souvenirs	BUL	Bozhidar Petkov
So Long, Movie Friend (Goodbye, Flickmania)	JAP	Ryudo Uzaki
Soldier of Orange	HOL	Rogier van Otterloo
Soldiers Never Cry	RUM	Stefan Zorzar
Some Kind of Saint	GER	Lothar Meid
Something Short of Paradise	AI	Mark Snow
Something's Rotten	CAN	John Kuipers
Son-Rise	TV	Gerald Fried
Song of the Canary	IND	Doug McKechnie/Si Kahn
Sons for the Return Home	NZ	Malcolm Smith
Sorriso del Grande Tentatore, Il	ITA	Ennio Morricone
Spirit of the Wind	IND	Buffy Sainte-Marie
Stalker	GER/RUS	Eduard Artemyev
Star Trek--The Motion Picture	PAR	Jerry Goldsmith
Starcrash	NWP	John Barry
Starting Over	PAR	Marvin Hamlisch
Strangler's Melody	MAL	Kasem Masdoor
Street of the Crane's Foot (Rue du Pied-de-Grue)	BEL/FRA	Andre Georget
Such a Lovely Town ...	FRA	Paul Misraki
Summer Camp	IND	Sparky Sugarman
Summer of Love, A	SWE	Terje Rypdal
Sunburn	PAR	John Cameron
Supersonic Man	SPA	Gino Peguri/Juan Luis Izaguirre/Carlos Attias
Swap Meet	IND	Hemlock
Sweet Creek County War, The	IND	Richard Bowden
Sweet Revenge	JAP	Nobumasa Fukushima
Sweetheart	THAI	Prasert Churaketr
Tachi and Her Fathers	CHN	Lei Chen-pang
Tailor from Ulm, The	GER	Nicos Mamangakis
Take Down	DIS	Merrill B. Jensen
Takeoff, The	RUS	Oleg Karavaitchouk
Tall Shadows of the Wind	IRAN	Ahmad Pejamn
Tempest, The	BRI	Wavemaker
10	WB	Henry Mancini
Tess	BRI/FRA	Philippe Sarde
Test Pilot Pirx	POL	Arvo Part
That Long Night	CUB	Carlos Farinas
That Sinking Feeling	BRI	Colin Tully
That Summer	COL	Ray Russell
They Are Their Own Gifts	IND	Susanna Nason

Third Generation, The	GER	Peer Raben
Thirst	AUT	Brian May
This Is Love, Isn't It?	GER	Heiner Goebels
Those Wonderful Men with a Crank	CZE	Jiri Sust
Tic Tac Toe (Tres en Raya)	SPA	Pedro Luis Domingo
Tilt	WB	Lee Holdridge
Time After Time	WB	Miklos Rozsa
Tin Drum, The	FRA/ GER/ POL/ YUG	Friedrich Meyer
Title Shot	CAN	Paul James Zaza
To Forget Venice	FRA/ ITA	Benedetto Ghiglia
Together? (Amo Non Amo/I Love You, I Love You Not)	ITA	Burt Bacharach/Goblin/ Dammico Bixio
Top Secret--The History of German Resistance Against Hitler	GER	Wolfgang de Gelmini
Torch High	GER	Gaby Mueller-Blattau
Tourist Trap, The	IND	Pino Donaggio
Traditions, My Behind	DEN	Ole Hoeyer
Tragedy of Love	CHN	Lua Ming Toh
Travels with Anita	ITA	Ennio Morricone
Triple Death of the Third Personage, The	BEL/ FRA/ SPA	Juan Jose Mosalini
Tristan et Iseult	FRA	Christian Vander
Trophy	YUG	Mladen and Predrag Vransevic
True Life of Dracula, The	RUM	Tiberiu Olah
Trumpeter, The	HUN	Leventi Szorenyi
Tutti a Squola	ITA	Gianni Ferrio
Twice a Woman	HOL	Willem Breuker
Two Pieces of Bread	FRA/ ITA	Alessandro Alessandroni
Uncompromising Man, An	GRE	George Theodorakis
Unidentified Flying Oddball, The	DIS	Ron Goodwin
Unknown Soldier's Patent Leather Shoes, The	BUL	Kiril Dontchev
Up from the Depths	PHI	Russell O'Malley
Up Wind	GER	Charles Orieux
Us Two	FRA	Francis Lai
Van Nuys Blvd.	CRO	Ron Wright/Ken Mansfield
Vera's Training	HUN	Gyorgy Selmeczi
Villain, The	COL	Bill Justis
Voices	MGM	Jimmy Webb
Walk on Clear Water if You Can	SWE	Berndt Egerbladh
Walk Proud	UN	Robby Benson
Wanda Nevada	UA	Ken Lauber
Wandering	GRE	Eleni Karaendrou
Warriors, The	PAR	Barry De Vorzon
Watts Monster, The	IND	Johnny Pate

We'll Grow Thin Together	FRA	Pierre Perret
When a Stranger Calls	COL	Dana Kaproff
When You Comin' Back, Red Ryder?	COL	Jack Nitzsche
Where Are You Going on Your Vacation? (Dove Vai in Vacanza?)	ITA	Dammico Bixio/Fabio Frizzi/Ennio Morricone/Piero Piccioni/Vincenzo Tempera
Wherever You Are, Mr. President	POL	Jerzy Maksymiuck
Whizzer	GER	Joerg Evers
Wild Horse Hank	CAN	Paul and Brenda Hoffert
Willa	TV	John Barry
Willi and the Comrades	GER	Rio Raiser
Willi Busch Report, The	GER	Patchwork
Winchell Affair, The	ISR	Naomi Shemer
Wind and the Oak, The	YUG	Rexho Mulioi
Winning of Freedom	YUG	Vojkan Borisavljevic
Winter Kills	EMB	Maurice Jarre
With Lots of Love	SPA	Fermin Gurbindo
With Shared Love	BUL/RUS	Kiril Tseboulka
Without Anaesthetic	POL	Jerzy Derfal
Woman Between Dog and Wolf, A	BEL/FRA	Etienne Verschueren
World Is Full of Married Men, The	BRI	Frank Musker/Dominic Bugatti
Wrong Number	ISR	Yoel Sher
Yanks	UN	Richard Rodney Bennett
Year of the Hare, The	FIN	Markku Kopisto
Yesterday's Hero	BRI	Stanley Myers
Young Ladies of Wilko, The	FRA/POL	Karol Szymanowski
Young Man and Moby Dick, The	CZE	Ladislav Staidl
You're Out of Your Mind, Maggie	SWE	Bengt Hallberg
Zones	SWI	Mario Beretta
Zulu Dawn	BRI	Elmer Bernstein

COMPOSERS AND THEIR FILMS

ABRAHAM, PAL
- Girl Who Liked Purple Flowers, The (1974)

ABRIL, ANTONIO GARCIA
- Vampire for Two (1966)
- Mission: Stardust (Orbita Mortal) (1968)
- Walpurgis Night (1970)
- Ghost Galleon, The (Buque Maldito, El) (1974)
- Long Returning, A (Largo Retorno, Un) (1975)
- Birds of Baden-Baden, The (1976)
- Dog, The (1977)
- Let's Leave the War in Peace (1977)
- Till Divorce Us Do Part (1977)
- Vote for Gundisalvo (1978)
- Days of the Past (1978)

ACANTHUS, GEORGE
- Sex and the Vampire (1970)

ADAMIC, BOJAN
- Fantasticna Balada (1958)
- Erotikon--Karussell der Leidenschaften (1963)
- Idealist, The (1976)
- White Grass (1976)

ADDINSELL, RICHARD
- Dark Journey (1937)
- Farewell Again (1937)
- Beachcomber, The (Vessel of Wrath) (1939)
- Britain at Bay (1940)
- Contraband (1940)
- This England (1940)
- Camouflage (1940)
- Special Dispatch (1940)
- Ulster (1940)
- Big Blockade, The (1941)
- Green Belt, The (1941)
- This Is Colour (1941)
- Siege of Tobruk, The (1942)
- Day Will Dawn, The (1942)
- We Sail at Midnight (1943)
- A. T. S. (1943)
- New Lot, The (1943)
- Ring Around the Moon (1950)

ADDISON, JOHN
- High and Dry (Maggie, The) (1951)
- Paratrooper (Red Beret, The) (1954)
- End of the Road (1954)
- One Good Turn (1954)
- Touch and Go (1955)
- Josephine and Men (1956)
- All at Sea (Barnacle Bill) (1957)
- Hamlet (1970)
- Ride a Wild Pony (1975)
- Seven Per Cent Solution, The (1976)
- Swashbuckler (1976)
- Bridge Too Far, A (1977)
- Joseph Andrews (1977)

Pearl (1979)

ADETOYE, OLUBJI
Angels (1976)

ADRIAN, ROLF
Not Everything That Flies Is a Bird (1979)

ADRIESSEN, LOUIS
Family, The (1974)

ADVIS, LUIS
Promised Land, The (1974)
Jules Starts with Jules (1979)

AHERN, BRIAN
Slipstream (1974)

AHMED, MALEK
Omar Gallato (1977)

AHLERS, OZZIE
Over-Under, Sideways-Down (1977)
Northern Lights (1978)

AKUTAGAWA, YASUSHI
Mount Hakkoda (1977)
Village of the Eight Tombs (1977)
Yukinojo's Revenge (1978)
Incident, The (Jiken) (1979)

ALCIVAR, BOB
Crazy World of Julius Vrooder, The (1974)
Olly, Olly, Oxen Free (1978)

ALDEN, CHARLES
This Is a Hijack (1973)

ALDERSON, RICHARD
Juan Perez Jolote (1977)

ALEJANDRO, MANUEL
Mistress, The (1976)

ALESSANDRONI, ALESSANDRO
Two Pieces of Bread (1979)

ALEXANDER, JEFF
Support Your Local Sheriff (1969)

ALEXANDER, SOOREN
Last Affair, The (1976)

ALFIERI, EDUARDO
Big Mama (1979)

ALI, ALAUDDIN
Endless Trail, The (1979)

ALIAS, AL
Gordon's War (1973)

ALIX, ROMAN
Vera (1973)
Request, The (1975)

ALLEN, ALEX
Defiance (1974)

ALLEN, ALLEN D.
Spectre of Edgar Allan Poe, The (1974)

ALLEN, BETTY
delete

ALLEN, BILLY
Devil's Mistress, The (1966)
Ski on the Wild Side (1967)
Erotic Adventures of Zorro, The (1972)

ALLEN, CAMERON
Summer of Secrets (1976)

ALLEN, WOODY
Sleeper (1973)

ALLIX, VICTOR
Passion de Jeanne d'Arc, La (1928)
Sheherazade (1928)

ALLWIGHT, GAEME
Little Marcel (1976)

ALMEIDA, LAURINDO
Flight (1960)

ALONI, AMINADAV
Once (1973)

ALSARRAF, ABDEL AMIR
Houses in This Alley (1978)

ALTBACH, RON
Almost Summer (1978)

ALWYN, WILLIAM
So Evil My Love (1948)

AMFITHEATROF, DANIELE
Man from Dakota, The (1940)
And One Was Beautiful (1940)
Keeping Company (1940)
Get-Away, The (1941)
Northwest Rangers (1943)
Stranger in Town, A (1943)
O. S. S. (1946)
Goodbye My Fancy (1951)

AMRAM, DAVID
Echo of an Era, The (1957)
We Are Young (1967)

ANDERSEN, BENNY
When Svante Disappeared (1975)

ANDERSON, JOHN
Year of the Caribou (1974)

ANDERSSON, KJELL
Maria (1975)

ANDION, PATXI
Book of Good Love, The (1975)
Out on Parole (1976)

ANDRASOVAN, TIBOR
10 Per Cent of Hope (1977)

ANDRIESSEN, JURIAAN
Flannagan (1976)

ANDRIESSEN, LOUIS
Family, The (1974)

ANFOSSO, GERARD
Trip Through Purgatory (1974)

Cousin, Cousine (1975)
Blue Country (1977)
It's a Long Time I've Loved You (1979)

ANIOL, EDWARD
First Polka, The (1979)

ANTHEIL, GEORGE
Once in a Blue Moon (1935)
Angels over Broadway (1940)
That Brennan Girl (1946)
Sniper, The (1952)
Dementia (1955)
Hunters of the Deep (1955)

ANTHONY, MARCUS
Happy Days (1974)

APPLEBAUM, LOUIS
Farewell to Yesterday (1950)
Homage to Chagall--The Colors of Love (1977)

ARAKI, ICHIRO
Morning Schedule, The (1973)

ARAMPI, SANGA
Tipchang (1974)
Heaven and Hell (1978)

ARESKI
Hail, Thieves (1973)

AREVALO, TITO
Blood Drinkers, The (1966)
Curse of the Vampires (1970)
Constabulary, The (1975)
Mother and Daughter (1975)

ARGENTO, DARIO
Suspiria (1977)
Dawn of the Dead (1979)

ARHIVSKA
Burning (1979)

ARMSTRONG, KENNY
Soup de Jour (1975)

ARNAUD, LEO
Thrill of Brazil, The (1946)

ARNELL, RICHARD
Opus 65 (1952)
Bequest for a Village (1969)
Second Best (1972)
Black Panther, The (1977)

ARNFRED, OLE
Sinful Dwarf, The (1973)
Johnny Larsen (1979)

ARNOLD, MALCOLM
David Copperfield (1970)

ARRIAGADA, JOSE
Hypothesis of the Stolen Painting, The (1979)

ARTEAGA, ANGEL
Young Rebel--Cervantes, The (1967)
Mark of the Wolfman, The (1968)
Horrible Sexy Vampire, The (1970)

ARTEMYEV, EDUARD
At Home Among Strangers (1974)
Platanov (1977)
Solaris (1977)
Slave of Love (1978)
Stalker (1979)
Siberiade (1979)

ARTHUYS, PHILIPPE
Rough Day for the Queen (1973)
Mai 68 (1974)
Chronicle of the Years of Fire (1975)

ASAMI, YUKIO
Wanderers, The (1973)

ASTLEY, EDWIN
Case of the Mukkinese Battlehorn, The (1956)
Matter of WHO, A (1962)
Digby, the Biggest Dog in the World (1974)

ATTIAS, CARLOS
Supersonic Man (1979)

AUBERSON, PASCAL
Barricade at Pont du Jour, The (1978)

AUBIN, TONI
Courbeau, Le (1943)

AUTE, LUIS EDUARDO
In Memoriam (1977)
My Daughter Hildegart (1977)
Long Live Hazana (1978)

AUTE, VICTOR
Creature, The (1978)

AXELROD, DAVID A.
Cannonball (1976)

AXT, WILLIAM
Kiss, The (1929)
Our Modern Maidens (1929)
Speedway (1929)
Single Standard, The (1929)
Thunder (1929)
Polly of the Circus (1932)
Sea Spiders (1932)
Smilin' Through (1932)
Washington Masquerade (1932)
Wet Parade, The (1932)
Broadway to Hollywood (1933)
Gabriel over the White House (1933)
Midnight Mary (1933)
Penthouse (1933)
Secret of Madame Blanche, The (1933)
Reunion in Vienna (1933)
Storm at Daybreak (1933)
Forsaking All Others (1934)
Lazy River (1934)
Hide-Out (1934)
Manhattan Melodrama (1934)
Sadie McKee (1934)
Straight Is the Way (1934)
This Side of Heaven (1934)
Wicked Woman, A (1934)
You Can't Buy Everything (1934)
Perfect Gentleman, The (1935)
Pursuit (1935)
Rendezvous (1935)
Woman Wanted (1935)
All-American Chump (1936)

Garden Murder Case, The (1936)
Three Godfathers, The (1936)
Three Live Ghosts (1936)
Mad Holiday (1936)
Tough Guy (1936)
Big City (1937)
Espionage (1937)
Song of the City (1937)
Thoroughbreds Don't Cry (1937)
Sergeant Madden (1939)
Within the Law (1939)

AYERS, ROY
Coffy (1973)

AZARCON, MINDA
Three, Two, One (1975)
Insiang (1978)

BACALOV, LUIS ENRIQUE
Empty Canvas, The (1964)
Paranoia (1966)
Matter of Honor, A (1966)
Rose for Everyone, A (1967)
Who Knows? (1967)
Catch as Catch Can (1968)
Black Sheep, The (1968)
Bullet for the General, A (1968)
We Still Kill the Old Way (1968)
Kiss the Other Sheik (1968)
Protagonists, The (1968)
Big Baby Doll (1969)
Ghosts--Italian Style (1969)
Lonely Hearts (1970)
Roma Bene (1971)
Summertime Killer (1972)
Man Called Noon, The (1973)
Red Rose, The (1973)
Seduction (1973)
I Fix America and Return (1974)
Milano Calibro 9 (1974)
Street People (1976)
Year of School, A (1977)
Green Jacket, The (1979)
Roses of Danzig, The (1979)

BACHARACH, BURT
Lost Horizon (1973)
Together? (1979)

BACHELET, PIERRE
Emmanuelle (1974)
Story of "O," The (1975)
Black and White in Color (1976)
Black Victory (1976)
Last Romantic Lover, The (1978)
Hot-Head (1979)
Private Collections (1979)

BADALE, ANDY
Gordon's War (1973)

BADYE, DYELIBA
Babatu (1976)

BAGLEY, DON
Mama's Dirty Girls (1974)
Student Body, The (1975)

BAHLER, TOM
Mary, Mary, Bloody Mary (1975)

BAILEY, PHILIP
That's the Way of the World (1975)

BAKER, BUDDY
Charley and the Angel (1973)
Bears and I, The (1974)
Nashville Coyote (1974)
Superdad (1974)
Apple Dumpling Gang (1975)
No Deposit, No Return (1976)
Shaggy D. A., The (1976)
Treasure of Matecumbe (1976)
Hot Lead and Cold Feet (1978)

BAKER, CHET
Longest Night, The (1964)

BAKER, TOM
Wednesday Children, The (1973)

BAKOURDAZE, T.
Little Town of Anara, The (1978)

BANKS, ANTHONY
Shout, The (1978)

BARAGLI, ENNIO
delete

BARBARIS, ALBERTO
Filming "Othello" (1978)

BARBIERI, LEANDRO "GATO"
Before the Revolution (1964)
Pick-Up (1968)
Notes for an African Orestes (1970)
Last Tango in Paris (1972)
Pig's War, The (1975)
Firepower (1979)

BARBOSA, AIRTON
Ajuricaba (1977)

BARNES, MILTON
Blood and Guts (1978)

BARON, MAURICE
River, The (1929)

BAROUH
Divorcement, Le (1979)

BARRON, LOUIS and BEBE
Forbidden Planet (1956)

BARRY, JOHN
Wild for Kicks (Beat Girl) (1959)
Never Let Go (1960)
Falling in Love (1961)
Betrayers, The (1962)
Playgirl and the War Minister, The (Amorous Prawn, The) (1962)
Dr. No (1963)
Elizabeth Taylor in London (1963)
Man in the Middle (1963)
Jolly Bad Fellow, A (They All Died Laughing) (1964)
Four in the Morning (1965)
Sophia Loren in Rome (1965)
One Man and His Bank (1965)
They Might Be Giants (1971)
Love Among the Ruins (1973)
Glass Menagerie, The (1973)
Doll's House, A (1973)
Dove, The (1974)
Man with the Golden Gun, The (1974)
Tamarind Seed, The (1974)
Day of the Locust, The (1975)
Eleanor and Franklin (1976)
Eleanor and Franklin--The White House Years (1976)
Robin and Marian (1976)
King Kong (1976)
War Between the Tates, The (1977)
Gathering, The (1977)
Young Joe, the Forgotten Kennedy (1977)
Deep, The (1977)
White Buffalo, The (1977)
First Love (1977)
Betsy, The (1978)
Corn Is Green, The (1978)
Bruce Lee's Game of Death (1978)
Hanover Street (1979)
Black Hole, The (1979)
Moonraker (1979)
Starcrash (1979)
Willa (1979)

BART, LIONEL
Man in the Middle (1964)
Optimists, The (1973)

BARTON, DEE
High Plains Drifter (1973)
Thunderbolt and Lightfoot (1974)

BARUBE, PLUME AND JOCELYN
Ordinary Tenderness (1973)

BASKIN, RICHARD
Buffalo Bill and the Indians, or Sitting Bull's History Lesson (1976)
Welcome to L.A. (1976)

BASNER, V.
Immortal Garrison, The (1956)

BASSETT, R. H.
Gold Rush, The (1925)
What Price Glory? (1926)
Seventh Heaven (1927)

BATT, MIKE
Caravans (1978)
Watership Down (1978)

BAUER, ROLF
Diary of a Lover, The (1977)

BAUTISTA, TEDDY
Blood Stains in a New Car (1975)

BAXTER, LES
Tanga Tika (1953)
Key Man, The (1955)
Wetbacks (1955)
Vicious Breed, The (1957)
Sacred Idol, The (1959)
Mighty Jungle, The (1959)
Goliath and the Barbarians (1959)
Lisette (1961)
Guns of the Black Witch (1961)
Warriors 5 (1961)
Reptilicus (1961)
Daughter of the Sun God (1962)
Lost Battalion, The (1962)
Tales of Terror (1962)
Erik the Conqueror (1962)
Samson and the Seven Miracles of the World (1962)
Evil Eye, The (1962)
House of Sand, A (1962)
Goliath and the Vampires (1962)
Samson and the Slave Queen (1962)
Battle Beyond the Sun (1963)
Pajama Party (1964)
Muscle Beach Party (1964)
Bikini Beach (1964)
Space Monster (1964)
Boy Ten Feet Tall, A (1965)
Fireball 500 (1966)
Glass Sphinx, The (1967)
Young Rebel, The (1967)
Young Animals, The (1968)
How to Make It (1968)
All the Loving Couples (1968)
Bora Bora (1968)
Dagmar's Hot Pants Inc. (1971)
Big Doll House, The (1971)
Blood Sabbath (1971)
Devil and LeRoy Bassett, The (1972)
I Escaped from Devil's Island (1973)
Savage Sisters (1974)
Jezebels (1974)
Born Again (1978)

BAYS, DENE
Wednesday Children, The (1973)

BEAULIEU, CYRIL
Apple, the Stem and the Seeds, The (1974)

BEAVER, PAUL
Last Days of Man on Earth, The (1975)

BECCE, GIUSEPPE
Comtesse Ursel (1913)
Richard Wagner (1913)
Schuldig (1913)

BECH, BERTRAND
In the Sign of the Taurus (1974)
In the Sign of Gemini (1975)
Agent 69 Jensen in the Sign of Scorpio (1977)

BECHET, SIDNEY
Etoiles en Croisette (1955)
Night Is a Sorcerer (1960)

BECK, JOE
Goodbye Norma Jean (1976)

BELL, JUDITH
Serpents of the Pirate Moon, The (1973)

BELL, THOM
Fish That Saved Pittsburgh, The (1979)

BELLE, MARIE-PAULE
Thomas (1975)
Go to Mama (1978)
Surprise Sock (1978)

BELLING, ANDREW
Killing Kind (1973)
Wizards (1977)
Dracula's Dog (1978)

BELZA, IVAN
Arsenal (1928)

BEN, JORGE
In the Mouth of the World (1979)

BENE, CARMELO
One Hamlet Less (1973)

BENJAMIN, SIR ARTHUR
Man Who Knew Too Much, The (1934)

BENJAMIN, JEAN-MARIE
Servant and Mistress (1977)

BENNETT, LOU
Laurence (1962)

BENNETT, RICHARD RODNEY
Indiscreet (1958)
Blind Date (1959)
Wrong Arm of the Law, The (1962)
Figures in a Landscape (1969)
Murder on the Orient Express (1974)
Permission to Kill (1975)
Accuser, The (1977)
Equus (1977)
Brinks' Job, The (1978)
Yanks (1979)

BENSON, ROBBY
Walk Proud (1979)

BENTZON, ASKE
Gangster's Apprentice, The (1976)

BERETTA, MARIO
Zones (1979)

BERGER, JAN
Faux Pas de Deux (1976)

BERGER, MICHEL
Serious as Pleasure (1975)

BERGHAGEN, LASSE
Dante, Mind the Shark (1978)

BERIO, LUCIANO
Base of the Air Is Red, The (1977)

BERKAY, CAHIT
Bad Spirits of the Euphrates, The (1978)
Girl with the Red Scarf, The (1978)

BERKI, GEZA
Kneeler Peak (1977)

BERLINE, BYRON
Stay Hungry (1976)

BERNAOLA, CARMELO
Flower of Holiness (1973)
Hunchback of the Morgue, The (1973)
Lonely Heart, The (1973)
Torment (1974)
New Spaniards, The (1975)
Pim, Pam, Pum ... Fire! (1975)
Regent's Wife, The (1975)
Family Portrait (1976)
Man Called Autumn Flower, A (1978)
Red Gold (1978)
Ernesto (1979)

BERNARD, IAN
Challenge to the Free (1975)

BERNARD, JAMES
Creeping Unknown, The (Quatermass Experiment, The) (1955)

Horror of Dracula (1958)
Frankenstein and the Monster from Hell (1974)

BERNHLOC, MICKEL
Love and Cool Water (1976)

BERNSTEIN, CHARLES
Hex (1973)
That Man Bolt (1973)
White Lightning (1973)
Mr. Majestyk (1974)
Gator (1976)
Small Town in Texas, A (1976)
Trackdown (1976)
Outlaw Blues (1977)
Viva Knievel! (1977)
In Search of Justice (1979)
Love at First Bite (1979)

BERNSTEIN, ELMER
Cat Women of the Moon (1953)
Robot Monster (1953)
Silent Raiders (1954)
Race for Space, The (1959)
Israel (1960)
Magnificent Seven, The (1960)
Birdman of Alcatraz (1962)
D-Day Seen Through American Eyes (1962)
Carpetbaggers, The (1963)
Cahill, United States Marshal (1973)
Gold (1974)
McQ (1974)
Trial of Billy Jack, The (1974)
Report to the Commissioner (1975)
From Noon Till Three (1976)
Shootist, The (1976)
Billy Jack Goes to Washington (1977)
Slap Shot (1977)
Bloodbrothers (1978)
National Lampoon's Animal House (1978)
Great Santini, The (1979)
Meatballs (1979)
Zulu Dawn (1979)

BERNSTEIN, PETER
Bride, The (1973)

BERRY, ALEX
Illuminations (1976)

BERTACCA, UBERTA
Rome Wants Another Caesar (1974)

BEST, PETER
Barry McKenzie Rides Again (1974)
Petersen (1974)
Picture Show Man, The (1977)

BETTS, HARRY
Black Mama, White Mama (1973)
Little Cigars (1973)

BEYNON, GEORGE W.
Corner, The (1915)
Gentleman from Indiana, The (1915)
Jane (1915)
Peer Gynt (1915)
Reform Candidate, The (1915)
Yankee Girl, The (1915)
Tongues of Men, The (1916)
In Old Kentucky (1920)
Mary Regan (1921)

BEYTELMAN, GUSTAVO
Quebracho (1974)
Film, The (1975)
Gaucho Jews, The (1975)

BHATIA, VANRAJ
Seedling, The (1974)
Manthan (1977)
Boon, The (1979)
Obsession (1979)

BIGERGAN, CADIM
May I Have the Floor? (1976)

BILEZIKJIAN, JOHN
Way of the Wind, The (1976)

BILLAY, RICHARD
Blue Summer (1973)

BISHOP, PHILLAN
Messiah of Evil (1975)

BIXIO, DAMMICO
Loves and Times of Scaramouche, The (1976)
Together? (1979)
Where Are You Going on Your Vacation? (1979)

BLACK, STANLEY
Valentino (1977)

BLACKBURN, MAURICE
J. A. Martin, Photographer (1977)
Scream of Silence, A (1979)

BLAKE, HOWARD
Elephant Called Slowly, An (1970)
Rainbow Boys, The (1973)
Odd Job, The (1978)
Riddle of the Sands, The (1979)

BLANC, S.
Farewell to Youth (1949)

BLICHMANN, HENRICK
92 Minutes of Yesterday (1978)

BLOOMFIELD, MIKE
Steelyard Blues (1973)
Sodom and Gomorrah (1976)
Bad (1977)

BOEHM, RAINER
Mama, I'm Alive (1977)

BOETTCHER, MARTIN
(corrected spelling)
Apache Gold (1963)
Bread and Stones (1979)

BOGAS, ED
Black Girl (1972)
Fritz the Cat (1972)
Heavy Traffic (1973)
Race for Your Life, Charlie Brown (1977)
Who Are the DeBolts? (and Where Did They Get 19 Kids?) (1977)
Midnight Auto Supply (1978)

BOGGS, ED
delete

BOLCOM, WILLIAM
Hester Street (1975)

BOLLING, CLAUDE
Cette Nuit-La (1958)
Hands of Orlac, The (1960)
Men and Women (1960)
On Friday at Eleven (1960)
Doucement les Basses (1962)
Day and the Hour, The (1963)
Vivre la Nuit (1967)
Qui (1970)
Lucky Luke (1971)
Mandarine, La (1971)
J'ai Mon Voyage (1973)
Loner, The (1973)
Magnificent One, The (1973)
Borsalino and Co. (1974)
Deux Grandes Filles dans un Pyjamas (1974)
Say It with Flowers (Dites-le Avec des Fleurs) (1974)
Tell Me You Love Me (Dis-moi Que Tu m'Aimes) (1974)
Cop Story (Flic Story, The) (1975)
Gypsy, The (1975)
One Must Live Dangerously (Il Faut Vivre Dangereusement) (1975)
Ordinateur de Pompes Funebres, L' (1976)
Saint Anne (Anne Sainte, L') (1976)
Passengers, The (1977)
Silver Bears (1977)
Take Me to the Ritz (1977)
Ballad of the Daltons, The (1978)
California Suite (1978)
Angry Man, The (1979)

BONCOMPAGNI, GIANNI
Bell Paseo, Il ... (1977)

BOND, JAMES
Trick Baby (1973)

BONET, GUY
Escapade (1974)

BONFA, LUIS
Black Orpheus (Orfeo Negro) (1959)

BONGUSTO, FRED
Malizia (1973)
White Sister (1974)
I'll Take Her Like a Father (1974)
Venial Sin (1974)
Love and Energy (1975)

BONTEMPELLI, GUY
Edifying and Joyous Story of Colinot, the Skirt-Puller-Upper (1973)

BORGHAGEN, LASSE
Dante, Mind the Shark (1978)

BORISAVLJEVIC, VOJKAN
Winning of Freedom (1979)

BORNE, HAL
Explosive Generation, The (1961)

BORNUM, H. B.
Five on the Black Hand Side (1973)
Emma Mae (1976)

BOROWSKY, PAUL-JEAN
Ciao, You Guys (1979)

BOS, RUUD
Because of the Cats (1973)
Red Sun (1975)

BOTBAEV, D.
Ferocious One, The (1974)

BOTKIN, PERRY JR.
Lady Ice (1973)
Young and the Restless, The (1973)
Your Three Minutes Are Up (1973)

BOTREL, THEODORE
My Little Loves (1974)

BOTTOM, FREDERIC
Blue Ferns, The (1977)

BOUCHETY, JEAN
Trop C'est Trop (1975)

BOULANGER, GUY
Choice, The (1976)
Cold Heart, The (1977)

BOURBON, ALBERTO
Memories of Leticia Valle (1979)

BOURGEOIS, GERALD
Rock 'n' Roll Wolf (1978)

BOURTAYRE, HENRI
Impossible Is Not French (1974)

BOWDEN, RICHARD
Sweet Creek County War, The (1979)

BOWERS, ROBERT HOOD
Daughter of the Gods, A (1915)

BOX, EUEL
Benji (1974)
Hawmps (1976)
For the Love of Benji (1977)
Double McGuffin, The (1979)

BOZIC, DARIJAN
Glorious Dust (1975)

BRADFORD, JAMES C.
Mamba (1930)
Savage Gold (1933)

BRADLEY, SCOTT
Dance of the Weed (1941)
Courage of Lassie (1946)
Cat That Hated People, The (1948)

Dixieland Droopy (1954)

BRANCO, JOSE MARIA
Confederation--The People Make History, The (1979)

BRANDT, CARL
Cleopatra Jones (1973)

BRAUER, ANDI
Institution, The (1978)

BRAULT, PIERRE
For Better or Worse (1975)

BRAZITZOV, ALEXANDER
He's Quite a Man (1975)

BRAZLON, ANTHONY
$2 Haircut, The (Coupe a Dix Francs, Le) (1975)

BREAU, LOUIS
Prisoner of Zenda, The (1922)

BREDOUW, JIM
Doubles (1978)

BREESKIN, ELIAS
Chaplin's Art of Comedy (1966)

BREGOVIC, GORAN
Personal Affairs (1979)

BREIL, JOSEPH CARL
Queen Elizabeth (1912)
Cabiria (1913)
Prisoner of Zenda, The (1913)
Birth of a Nation, The (1915)
Double Trouble (1915)
Lily and the Rose, The (1915)
Martyrs of the Alamo, The (1915)
Penitentes, Los (1915)
Intolerance (1916)
Wood Nymph, The (1916)
White Rose, The (1923)
America (1924)

BREL, JACQUES
Far-West, The (1973)
Pain in the Neck, The (1973)

BRENNER, VYTAS
Goodbye Alicia (1977)

BRETON, L. HERNANDEZ
delete

BRETON, LUIS HERNANDEZ
One Big Affair (1952)
This Strange Passion (El) (1955)
Bloody Vampire, The (1961)
Invasion of the Vampires, The (1962)

BREUKER, WILLEM
Twice a Woman (1979)

BRICUSSE, LESLIE
Charley Moon (1956)

BRIEL, JOSEPH CARL (see BREIL, JOSEPH CARL)

BRILLOUIN, JACQUES
Rhapsodie Hongroise (1929)

BRINKLEY, BOOKIE
Women in the Sun (1974)

DRODY, JANOS
Spider Football (1977)
Family Nest (1979)

BROEKMAN, DAVID
Condemned to Live (1935)

BROOKS, JOE
Lords of Flatbush, The (1974)
You Light Up My Life (1977)
If Ever I See You Again (1978)

BROUWER, LEO
Other Francisco, The (1975)
Mina, Wind of Freedom (1977)
Last Supper, The (1978)
Recourse to the Method, The (1978)

BROWN, ALEX
Sheba Baby (1975)

BROWN, JAMES
Black Caesar (1973)
Slaughter's Big Rip-Off (1973)

BROWN, LARRY
Mitchell (1975)

BROWN, MATTHEW
Sleeping Dogs (1977)

BROWN, MICHAEL
Hot Parts (1972)

BROWN AND SPENCER
Voodo (1933)

BRUBECK, DAVE
Crocodile Tears (1965)
Jail Keys Made Here (1965)

BRUNET, FERNANDO
Times of the Constitution (1978)

BRUNNER, ROBERT F.
Castaway Cowboy, The (1974)
Strongest Man in the World (1975)
Gus (1976)
North Avenue Irregulars, The (1979)

BRUNO, MARIANO
Paco (1975)

BRUNO, MAURO
Paco (1975)
Independence Day (1976)

BRUNO, TONY
Deep Throat II (1974)

BRUNS, GEORGE
Island of the Lost (1967)
Robin Hood (1973)
Herbie Rides Again (1974)

BRYARS, GAVIN
Necropolis (1969)
Moment (1970)
Times Four (1970)
Dyn Amo (1972)

BUARQUE, CHICO
Dona Flor and Her Two Husbands (1977)

BUCKINGHAM, BRUCE
So Long, Blue Boy (1973)

BUCKMASTER, PAUL
Son of Dracula (1974)

BUDD, ROY
Kidnapped (1971)
Fear is the Key (1972)
Stone Killer, The (1972)
Get Carter (1973)
Black Windmill, The (1974)
Destructors, The (1974)
Internecine Project, The (1974)
Diamonds (1975)
Paper Tiger (1975)
Foxbat (1977)
Sinbad and the Eye of the Tiger (1977)
Welcome to Blood City (1977)
Wild Geese, The (1978)

BUENA VISTA
Word Is Out (1978)

BUFFET, JIMMY
Rancho DeLuxe (1975)

BUGATTI, DOMINIC
World Is Full of Married Men, The (1979)

BUGOSLOVSKI, NIKITA
Headless Horseman, The (1975)

BYRD, DONALD
Cornbread, Earl and Me (1975)

BURGEON, GEOFFREY
Life of Brian (1979)

BURNS, RALPH
Lenny (1974)
Lucky Lady (1975)
New York, New York (1977)
Movie Movie (1978)
All That Jazz (1979)

BURTON, ANDRE
Fed Up (1973)

BURTON, VAL
Drums of Jeopardy (1931)
Murder at Midnight (1931)
Death Kiss, The (1932)
Strangers of the Evening (1932)
Tombstone Canyon (1932)
Deluge, The (1933)

BUSAPAKETR, NOPADOL
Old Woman, An (1978)

BUSCH, NICHOLAS
Phantastic World of Matthew Madson, The (1974)

BUTCKO, YURI
Call Me from Afar (1978)

BUTLER, ARTIE
Harrad Experiment, The (1973)
Rafferty and the Gold Dust Twins (1975)
It's Showtime (1976)
Rescuers, The (1977)
Sextette (1978)

BUTTERFIELD, PAUL
Steelyard Blues (1973)

BUTTOLPH, DAVID
Adventures of Sherlock Holmes, The (1939)
Hollywood Cavalcade (1939)
Mr. Moto's Last Warning (1939)
Stanley and Livingstone (1939)
Suez (1939)
Bahama Passage (1941)
Dead Men Tell (1941)
Ride On, Vaquero (1941)
Swamp Water (1941)
Dr. Renault's Secret (1942)
Iceland (1942)
Just Off Broadway (1942)
Magnificent Dope, The (1942)
Man Who Wouldn't Die, The (1942)
Manila Calling (1942)
Postman Didn't Ring, The (1942)
Through Different Eyes (1942)
Undying Monster, The (1942)
Whispering Ghosts (1942)
Who Is Hope Schuyler? (1942)
Nob Hill (1945)
Man Behind the Gun, The (1953)

BUTTS, DALE
Along the Navajo Trail (1945)
Angel Comes to Brooklyn, An (1945)
Don't Fence Me In (1945)
Flame of the Barbary Coast, The (1945)
Man from Oklahoma (1945)
Sunset in El Dorado (1945)
Tell It to a Star (1945)
Utah (1945)
Gay Blades (1946)
Home on the Range (1946)
My Pal Trigger (1946)
Rainbow over Texas (1946)
Woman from Headquarters (1950)

BYARS, GAVIN
delete

BYERS, BILL
Portrait Robot (1961)

CACAVAS, JOHN
Blade (1973)
Horror Express (1973)
Airport 1975 (1974)
Airport '77 (1977)
Count Dracula and His Vampire Bride (1978)

CADD, BRIAN
Alvin Purple (1973)
Alvin Rides Again (1974)

CADDY, ALAN
Great Gundown, The (1977)

CADMAN, CHARLES WAKEFIELD
Captain of the Guard (1930)

CAESAR, VIC
Gosh (1974)
Bare Knuckles (1978)

CAESLAW-NIEMEN
Sophie (1977)

CAFFI, JUAN GARCIA
Nazarene Cross and the Wolf (1975)
Voyage to the Center of the Earth (1977)

CAGE, JOHN
Works of Calder (short) (1950)

CAILLIET, LUCIEN
Enchanted Forest, The (1945)
Trouble Preferred (1948)
Tripoli (1950)

CALANDRELL, JORGE
Alone (1976)

CALBER, DAVID
Sleeping Dogs (1977)

CALDERON, JUAN CARLOS
Adolescents, The (1976)

CALE, J. J.
Fifty-Fifty (1978)

CALKER, DARRELL
Fair Today (1941)
Man's Best Friend (1941)
Screw Driver, The (1941)
I Killed Geronimo (1950)
Cattle Queen
Terror in the Haunted House (1958)

CALVI, GERARD
War Is War (1972)
Gaspards, Les (1974)
Kisses Till Monday (1974)
Shut Up, Gulls (1974)

CAMERO, ANTONIO
Dearest Executioners (1977)

CAMERON, ALAN
Night, The Prowler, The (1978)

CAMERON, JOHN
Charley One-Eye (1973)
Night Watch (1973)
Scalawag (1973)
Touch of Class, A (1973)
Moments (1974)
Out of Season (1975)
Whiffs (1975)
I Will ... I Will ... For Now (1976)
Nasty Habits (1976)
Lost and Found (1979)
Sunburn (1979)

CAMILLO, TONY
Getting Together (1976)

CAMPANINO, FRANCO AND GIGI
Guiappi, I (1979)

CAMPUZANO, F.
Sleep, Sleep, My Love (1975)

CANSECO, GEORGE
Hello Goodnight Goodbye (1975)
Wash Out My Faults (1976)
Where Are You Going? (1976)

CANTON, EDGARDO
Lily, Love Me (1975)
Apprentice Sorcerers, The (1977)

CANTOR, IGO
Scorchy (1976)

CAPE, JOHN
delete

CAPER, JOHN JR.
Track of Thunder (1968)
Equinox (1970)

CAPOINU, C.
Fantastic Comedy (1975)

CARBONARA, GERARD
Case Against Mrs. Ames,

The (1936)
Fatal Lady (1936)
Forgotten Faces (1936)
Girl of the Ozarks (1936)
Moon's Our Home, The (1936)
Palm Springs (1936)
Sky Parade, The (1936)
Arkansas Traveler, The (1938)
Artists and Models Abroad (1938)
Mysterious Rider (1938)
Sunset Trail (1938)
Tom Sawyer, Detective (1938)
Geronimo (1939)
King of Chinatown (1939)
Paris Honeymoon (1939)
Dr. Cyclops (1940)
I Married Adventure (1940)
Island of Doomed Men (1940)
Parole Fixer (1940)
Women Without Names (1940)
Among the Living (1941)
Night of January 16th, The (1941)
Round-Up, The (1941)
Shepherd of the Hills (1941)
Henry Aldrich Haunts a House (1943)
Night Plane from Chunking (1943)
Town Went Wild, The (1944)
Abilene Town (1946)
Big Wheel, The (1949)

CARLOS, ANTONIO
Otalia da Bahia (1976)

CARLOS, MICHAEL
Storm Boy (1976)
Blue Fin (1978)
Long Weekend (1978)

CARLSON, VERN
Illusions of a Lady (1974)

CARMICHAEL, RALPH
His Land (1970)

CARPENTER, JOHN
Halloween (1978)

CARPI, FIORENZO
Pinocchio (1972)
How Low Can You Fall? (1974)
First Time, on the Grass, The (1975)
Flesh of the Orchid, The (1975)
Madam Kitty (Salon Kitty) (1975)
Bottleneck (1979)

CARREON, GUSTAVO C.
Vampiro, El (1957)
Ataud del Vampiro, El (1959)
World of the Vampire (1961)
Santo and Blue Demon vs. the Monsters (1968)
Santo in the Revenge of the Vampire Women (1968)
Vampire Girls, The (1968)
Santo and the Blue Demon vs. Dracula and the Wolf Man (1972)
House in the South, The (1975)
Life Changes (1976)
Minister and Me, The (1976)
Bricklayers, The (1977)

CARRERE, MICHAEL MELVOIN
Ashanti (1979)

CARILLON, OSCAR
Man on the Bridge (1976)

CARRONE
Vice Squad (1978)

CARTER, BENNY
Harlem Wednesday (1958)
Urbanissimo (1967)
Upkeep (1973)
People, People, People (1975)

CARUSO
Widow Couderc, The (1971)

CARY, TRISTRAM
Boy Ten Feet Tall, A (1965)
5,000,000 Years to Earth (Quatermass and the Pit) (1968)

CASANOVA (see BAXTER, LES)

CASTELNUEVO-TEDESCO, MARIO
Return of the Vampire (1943)
She's a Soldier, Too (1944)
Two-Man Submarine (1944)
Crime Doctor's Courage (1945)
I Love a Mystery (1945)
Prison Ship (1945)
Dangerous Business (1946)
Night Editor (1946)
Time Out of Mind (1947)
Brigand, The (1952)

CAVERHILL, DON
Second Coming of Suzanne, The (1974)

CAVERHILL, JIM
Three Card Monte (1978)

CAYABYAH, RYAN
Good Evening to Everybody (1976)

CAYMI, DORIVAL
Castaways of Turtle Island, The (1976)

CAYRE, JEAN-MICHEL
Hue and Cry (1978)

CELENTATO, ANDRIANO
Yuppi Du (1975)

CHAN, FRANKIE
Last Challenge of the Dragon, The (1978)
Itchy Fingers (1979)

CHAN, JOSE MARI
My Sexy Girl Friend (1975)

CHANDVARKAR, BHASKAR
Once Upon a Time (1979)

CHANG, LUI CHA
Fantasies Behind the Pearly Curtain (1975)

CHAPLIN, CHARLES
Gold Rush, The (1925)
Circus, The (1928)
Chaplin Revue, The (1959)
Smile (1975)

CHARLEBOIS, ROBERT
Aggression (1975)

CHARLOT
delete

CHASNOFF, HAL
Lost Jungle, The (1934)
Queen of the Jungle (1935)

CHAUDHURY, SALIL
Royal Hunt, The (1977)

CHEKALOV, PAVEL
Red Snowball Tree, The (1974)
Traveling Companions (1976)
Your Son and Brother (1976)
There Was a Lady (1978)

CHEKVAVARIAN, LORIS
Tangsir (1974)

CHELARU, ROMEO
Beyond the Bridge (1976)

"CHEMBO"
Missing Prisoners (1979)

CHEN-PANG, LEI
Tachi and Her Fathers (1979)

CHEONG, LAU KA
Cookbook of Birth Control, The (1975)

CHERRY, DON
Holy Mountain, The (1973)

CHERWIN, RICHARD
Vampire's Ghost, The (1945)

CHEVALLIER, CHRISTIAN
Rendez-vous a Melbourne (1956)
Bons Amis, Les (1958)
Chemins de Lumiere (1958)
Deux Hommes dans Manhattan (1958)
Trop C'est Trop (1975)
Voyage de Noces, Le (1975)

CHIARAMELLO, GIANCARLO
Number One (1973)
Crazy Joe (1974)
Track, The (1975)
Hornet's Nest, The (1976)
Average Man, An (1977)
Swiss Affair, The (1978)

CHIBOULKA, KIRIL
Cyclops (1976)
Daughter-in-Law (1976)

CHIHARA, PAUL
Death Race 2000 (1975)
Sweet Revenge (1976)
I Never Promised You a Rose Garden (1977)
Bad News Bears Go to Japan, The (1978)

CHOLAKUL, KANGWAN
Chain of Life (1975)
Miss Maliwan (1975)

CHOPIN, FREDERIC
delete

CHOTEM, NEIL
U-Turn (1973)

CHRISTENSEN, SOEREN
Escape, The (1973)
Ghost Train (1976)
Christiania (1977)

CHRISTIAN, ROGER
Return to Macon County (1975)

CHRISTIANSEN, HENNING
Hour of Parting, The (1973)
Normans, The (1976)

CHRISTODOULIDES, MICHEL
Attila 74 (1975)

CHUNG, SUNG JO
Love Follows Rain (1977)

CHURAKETR, PRASERT
Dark Lady (1975)
Nitra Sayan (1975)
Thai Tiger's Roar (1975)
Louis (1977)
My Dear Friend (1977)
Reluctant Gunfighter, The (1977)
Widower, The (1978)
Sweetheart (1979)

CHYDENIUS, KAJ
Misfire (1978)

CINI, RUGGERO
Open Season (1974)

CIPRIANI, STELVIO
Laughing Woman, The (1970)
Cometogether (1971)
Blondy (1975)
Fight to the Death (1975)
Pepita Jimenez (1975)
Dear Wife (1977)
Frankenstein--Italian Style (1977)
Tentacles (1977)
Child of the Night (1978)
Covert Action (1978)
Maternale (1978)
Take All of Me (1978)
Machine Gun Stein (1979)

CLAPTON, ERIC
Slipstream (1974)

CLARK, PALMER
Last Days of Pompeii, The (1913)

CLARK, PETER
Scobie Malone (1975)

CLARKE, JAMES KENELM
Got It Made (1974)

CLARKE, KENNY
On n'Enterre pas le Dimanche (1959)

CLAYTON, KENNY
14, The (1973)

CLAYTON-THOMAS, DAVID
American Dream, The (1976)

CLEMENCIE, RENE
Moliere (1978)

CLEMENTE, PAUL
Caligula (1979)

CLEMENTS, RICHARD
Peeper (1975)
Off the Edge (1977)

COBERT, ROBERT
Night Stalker, The (1972)
Burnt Offerings (1976)
False Face (1976)

COE, DAVID ALLAN
Seabo (1977)

COGAN, ALEX
My Michael (1975)

COHEN, MICHAEL
Eadweard Muybridge, Zoopraxographer (1976)

COLBURN, GEORGE
Antony and Cleopatra (1914)

COLEMAN, ORNETTE
Who's Crazy? (1965)
Population Explosion (1967)

COLICCHIO, MICHAEL
Deep Throat II (1974)

COLLETTE, BUDDY
Trauma (1962)

COLLIER, RON
Paperback Hero (1973)

COLLINS, ANTHONY
Victoria the Great (1937)
Rat, The (1938)
Royal Divorce, A (1938)
Unexpected Uncle (1943)
Yank in London, A (1946)
Piccadilly Incident (1946)
Courtneys of Curzon Street, The (1947)
Lady with the Lamp, The (1951)
Macao (1952)

COLOMBIER, MICHEL
Inheritor, The (1973)
Chance and Violence (1974)
Paul and Michelle (1974)
Predator, The (1976)
Guinea Pig Couple, The (1977)

COLOMBO, ALBERTO
Red Morning (1934)
Annie Oakley (1935)
Chasing Yesterday (1935)
Dog of Flanders, A (1935)
Freckles (1935)
Grand Old Girl (1935)
His Family Tree (1935)
Hooray for Love (1935)
Hot Tip (1935)
Jalna (1935)
Murder on a Honeymoon (1935)
Powdersmoke Range (1935)
Return of Peter Grimm, The (1935)
Romance in Manhattan (1935)
To Beat the Band (1935)
Village Tale (1935)
Grand Jury (1936)
Two in the Dark (1936)
Yellow Dust (1936)
Affairs of Cappy Ricks (1937)
All over Town (1937)
Call of the Mesquiteers (1937)
Dick Tracy (1937)
Dangerous Holiday (1937)
Duke Comes Back, The (1937)
Escape by Night (1937)
Exiled to Shanghai (1937)
It Could Happen to You (1937)
Manhattan Merry-Go-Round (1937)
Michael O'Halloran (1937)
Meet the Boy Friend (1937)
Portia on Trial (1937)
Rhythm in the Clouds (1937)
Sea Racketeers (1937)
Sheik Steps Out, The (1937)
Springtime in the Rockies (1937)
Wild Horse Rodeo (1937)
Wrong Road, The (1937)
Youth on Parole (1937)
Zorro Rides Again (serial) (1937)
Arson Gang Busters (1938)

Born to Be Wild (1938)
Call of the Yukon (1938)
Fighting Devil Dogs (1938)
Gangs of New York (1938)
Gold Mine in the Sky (1938)
Hollywood Stadium Mystery (1938)
Invisible Enemy (1938)
King of the Newsboys (1938)
Ladies in Distress (1938)
Lady, Behave! (1938)
Lone Ranger, The (1938)
Mama Runs Wild (1938)
Old Barn Dance, The (1938)
Outlaws of Sonora (1938)
Outside of Paradise (1938)
Prison Nurse (1938)
Purple Vigilantes, The (1938)
Romance on the Run (1938)
Under Western Stars (1938)

COMITELLI, SANTA MARIA
Yeti, Il Gigante del 20o Secolo (1977)

CONDA, JANOS
Voyage with Jacob (1973)

CONDE, ANTONIO DIAS
Wrestling Women vs. the Aztec Mummy, The (1965)
Choca, La (1974)

CONRAD, JACK
Monkey Hustle, The (1976)

CONTI, BILL
Harry and Tonto (1974)
Pacific Challenge (1975)
Next Stop, Greenwich Village (1976)
Rocky (1976)
Citizens' Band (1977)
Big Fix, The (1978)
F. I. S. T. (1978)
Five Days from Home (1978)
Paradise Alley (1978)
Slow Dancing in the Big City (1978)
Uncle Joe Shannon (1978)
Unmarried Woman, An (1978)
Dreamer (1979)
Goldengirl (1979)
Rocky II (1979)
Seduction of Joe Tynan, The (1979)

COOLIDGE, LUCY
Old Fashioned Woman (1974)

COPPOLA, CARMINE
Godfather II (1974)
Mustang: The House That Joe Built (1976)
Apocalypse Now (1979)
Black Stallion, The (1979)

COPPOLA, FRANCIS FORD
Apocalypse Now (1979)

CORDELL, FRANK
Khartoum (1966)
God Told Me To (1976)
Trial by Combat (1976)

CORNFORD, ROBERT
Score, The (1978)

CORTNER, JACK
Independence (1976)

COSMA, VLADIMIR
Absent-Minded (1970)
Teresa (1970)
Very Happy Alexander (1970)
Neither by Day Nor by Night (1972)
Big Sentiments Make for Good Sports (1973)
Hail the Artist (1973)
Right of the Maddest, The (1973)
Tall Blond Man with One Black Shoe, The (1973)
Hot Rabbit, The (1974)
Mad Adventures of Rabbi Jacob, The (1974)
Return of the Tall Blond, The (1974)
Superb Trip, The (1974)
Catherine Inc. (1975)
Onion Chase, The (1975)
Rose-Colored Telephone, The (1975)

Dracula Father and Son (1976)
Elephant Can Be Extremely Deceptive, An (1976)
Felines, Les (1976)
Scrambled Eggs, The (1976)
Toy, The (1976)
Animal, The (1977)
Sea Urchin in the Pocket, A (1977)
We Will All Go to Heaven (1977)
Confidences for Confidences (1978)
State Reasons (1978)
Getaway, The (Derobade, La) (1979)

COSTA, DON
Soul of Nigger Charlie, The (1973)

COSTANDINOS, ALEC
Trocadero Lemon Blue (Trocadero Blue and Yellow) (1978)

COTTE, FRANCOISE and ROGER
Justine de Sade (1972)

COTTS, FRANCOISE and ROGER
delete

COUSINEAU, FRANCOIS
Some Arpents of Snow (1973)

COUTUREAU, JACQUES
Butcher, the Star and the Orphan, The (1975)

COWL, DARRY
Day of Glory, The (1976)

CRAIG, GEORGE
Women in Cell Block 7 (1974)
Naked Came the Stranger (1975)
Image, L' (1976)
Opening of Misty Beethoven, The (1976)

CROLLA, HENRI
Saint-Paul-de-Vence (1949)
Terres et Flammes (1951)
A Propos d'Une Riviere (1955)
Bras de la Seine, Les (1955)
Enrico Cuisinier (1955)
Gas-Oil (1955)
My Dog (1955)
Neiges (1955)
Atlantic Salmon, The (1956)
Ciel des par Dessus le Toit, Le (1956)
Fresh Air (1956)
Leon la Lune (1956)
Terre Fleurie (1956)
Deux Plumes, Les (1958)
Operation Time Bomb (1958)
Parisienne, La (1958)
Sins of Youth (1958)
Golden Fish, The (1959)
My Friend Pierrot (1960)
Photo Souvenir (1960)
Primitifs du XIIIe, Les (1960)
Saint-Tropez Blues (1960)
Vitrine Sous la Mer (1960)

CRUZ, WILLIE
Mrs. Abad, I Am Bing (1976)

CSEH, TOMAS
Beloved Elecktra (1975)
Entanglement (1977)

CUENCO, ERNANI
Kill Barbara with Panic (1974)
That's Enough, Man (1974)
Counter Kill (1975)
Jungle in the City, The (1975)
Most Beautiful Animal in the World, The (1975)
Scorpion Sea (1975)
Water It and Dew for the Thirsty Soil (1975)
Your Husband Is My Lover (1975)
Hey, Mister, I Am Your Wife (1976)
Lion and the Rat, The (1976)
Scorpion Woods (1976)
Tidal Wave and West Wind (1976)
Death Has No Mercy (1979)

CUGAT, XAVIER
White Zombie (1932)

CUNHA, RICHARD
Best Friends (1975)

CURB, MIKE
Born Losers (1967)

CURTIN, HOYT
Chomps (1979)

CUTNER, SIDNEY
His Girl Friday (1940)

CVITKOVIC, ZIVAN
Hitler Around the Corner (1975)
Daredevils' Time (1977)

DAHLBERG, LARS
Kristoffer's House (1979)

D'AIME, FRANCOIS
Stop Calling Me Baby! (1977)

D'ALESSIO, CARLOS
India Song (1975)
Entire Days in the Trees (1976)
Mistress (1976)
Baxter, Vera Baxter (1977)

DALLA, LUCIO
Goodnight, Ladies and Gentlemen (1977)

d'AMARILLO
Left, Right ... Sickness of the Body (1976)

DANDAN, FREDDY
One Night in Life with One Woman (1976)

d'ANDREA, JOHN
Commitment, The (1976)

DANIELE, PINO
Payoff, The (1978)

DANKWORTH, JOHN
We Are the Lambeth Boys (1959)
Criminal, The (1960)
Hamilton at the Musical Festival (1961)
Hamilton, the Musical Elephant (1961)
Top Flight (1964)
Game Called Scruggs, A (1965)
World at Three, The (1965)
I Love You, I Hate You (1968)
Engagement, The (1970)
Pianorama (1973)

DANNERMAN, DON
Minx, The (1972)

DARESHEVICH, VIKTOR
Sentimental Story, A (1977)

DARIO, CASTRO
Oscar, Kina and the Laser (1979)

DASHKOVICH, YURI
Mauahovsky Laughs (1976)

DASHOW, JAMES
Oedipus Orca (1977)

DASSAULT, OLIVER
Strait-Laced Girl, A (1977)
Love in Question (1978)
Heroines of Evil, The (1979)

DATIN, JACQUES
Silent One, The (1973)

DAVID, WILLIAM
Horror, The (1933)

DAVIES, PETER MAXWELL
Devils, The (1971)

DAVIES, RAY
Percy (1971)

DAVIES, ROY
delete

DAVIES, WILLIAM
Last Tasmanian, The (1979)

DAVIS, CARL
National Health, or Nurse Norton's Affair, The (1973)

Man Friday (1975)
What's Next? (1975)
Sailor's Return, The (1978)

DAVIS, CHIP
Convoy (1978)

DAVIS, DAVID
H. O. T. S. (1979)

DAVIS, PETER MAXWELL
delete

DAVIS, ROCKY
In MacArthur Park (1977)

DAWES, TOM
Minx, The (1972)

DE ABREU, TUZE
Legend of the Ubirajara (1976)

DE ANGELIS, GUIDO and MAURIZIO
Cross-Eyed Saint, The (1971)
Per Grazia Ricevuta (1971)
Man from the East, A (1972)
... Piu Forte Ragazzi (1972)
Trastevere (1972)
Trinity Is Still My Name (1972)
Piedone lo Sbirro (1973)
Polizia Incrimina, le Legge Assolve, La (1973)
Valdez the Halfbreed (1973)
Beast, The (1974)
Citizen Rebels, A (1974)
Italian Graffiti (1974)
Midnight Pleasures (1975)
Sins in the Family (1975)
Turn the Other Cheek (1975)
White, Yellow, Black (1975)
Zorro (1975)
Brothers, The (1976)
Black Pirate, The (1977)
Three Tigers Against Three Tigers (1977)
Afyon Oppio (1978)
Charleston (1978)
Speed Fever (1978)
Two Super Cops (1978)
Killer Fish (1979)

DE AZEVDO, LEX
Where the Red Fern Grows (1974)
Against a Crooked Sky (1975)
Baker's Hawk (1977)

DE BENEDICTUS, DICK
Manchu Eagle Murder Caper Mystery, The (1975)

DE BOER, LODEWIJK
It's Me (1979)

DE BRUYNE, KOEN
Enclosure, The (1978)

DE DIEGO, EMILIO
Great House, The (1975)
Silk Worms (1976)

DE FRANCESCO, LOUIS
Betrayal (1929)
Redskin (1929)
Chandu the Magician (1932)
As Husbands Go (1933)
Hoopla (1933)
I Loved You Wednesday (1933)
Mr. Skitch (1933)
Pleasure Cruise (1933)
Power and the Glory, The (1933)
State Fair (1933)
All Men Are Enemies (1934)
Carolina (1934)
Change of Heart (1934)
Coming Out Party (1934)
Grand Canary (1934)
Helldorado (1934)
Springtime for Henry (1934)
Such Women Are Dangerous (1934)
White Parade, The (1934)
World Moves On, The (1934)
Here's to Romance (1935)

DE GELMINI, WOLFGANG
Top Secret--The History of the German Resistance Against Hitler (1979)

DE HARTMAN, THOMAS
Meetings with Remarkable Men (1979)

DE JESUS, LUCHI
Bad Charleston Charlie (1973)
Detroit 9000 (1973)
Black Belt Jones (1974)
Friday Foster (1975)
Adios Amigo (1976)

DE LORY, AL
Buster and Billie (1974)
Devil's Rain, The (1975)

DE LOS RIOS, WALDO
Scale in Hi-Fi (1963)
Corruption of Chris Miller, The (1973)
Boquitas Pintadas (1974)
Who Can Kill a Child? (1976)

DE LUCA, DANGIO
Revenge (1979)

DE LUCA, NANDO
Revenge (1979)

DE LUCIA, PACO
Sabina, The (1979)

DE MARTINO, ANDY
Super Van (1977)

DE MASI, FRANCESCO
Goliath and the Sins of Babylon (1963)
Suleiman the Conqueror (1963)
Tiko and the Shark (1966)
Any Gun Can Play (1967)
Man from Nowhere, The (1969)
Murder Clinic, The (1969)
Kill Them All and Come Back Alone (1970)
Private Vices, Public Virtues (1976)

DE MULE, FIRTH
Every Inch a Lady (1975)

DE PABLO, LUIS
Anna and the Wolves (1973)
Don Ramiro (1973)
Spirit of the Bee-Hive, The (1973)
Pascual Duarte (1976)
To an Unknown God (1977)
Carrot Queen, The (1978)
What Max Said (1978)

DE PISCOPO, TULLIO
Gun, The (1978)

DE ROUBAIX, FRANCOIS
Zita (1968)
Daughters of Darkness (1970)
Short and Sweet (1976)

DE SENNEVILLE, PAUL
No Pockets in a Shroud (1975)

DE SICA, CHRISTIAN
Holiday, The (1973)

DE SICA, MANUEL
Trip, The (1974)
Cagliostro (1975)
Dear Papa (1979)

DE SIMONE, ROBERTO
How Wonderful to Die Assassinated (1975)
End of the World in Our Usual Bed in a Night Full of Rain, The (1978)

DE VOL, FRANK
McLintock! (1963)
Emperor of the North (Pole), The (1973)
Longest Yard, The (1974)
Doc Savage ... The Man of Bronze (1975)
Hustle (1975)
Choirboys, The (1977)
Herbie Goes to Monte Carlo (1977)
Frisco Kid, The (1979)

DE VORZON, BARRY
Young and the Restless, The (1973)
Dillinger (1973)
Hard Times (1975)
Bobbie Joe and the Outlaw (1976)
Rolling Thunder (1977)
Warriors, The (1979)

DE VREESE, FREDERIC
On the Tip of the Tongue (1976)

DE WOLFE
Monty Python and the Holy Grail (1975)
Jabberwocky (1977)

DEATON, GEORGE
Toolbox Murders, The (1978)

DEBOUT, J. J.
George Who? (1973)

DEBRAY, ALAIN
Rolando Rivas, Cab Driver (1974)

DEDIC, ARSEN
Wind, The (1974)
Train in the Snow (1976)
Four Seasons, The (1979)

DEGENHARDT, FRANZ JOSEF
Fuses (1977)

DEHLAVI, HOSEIN
Lovers' Wind, The (1979)

DEL POZO, ARTURO RUIS
End of Night (1976)

DELANNOY, MARCEL
Rhapsodie Hongroise (1929)

DELAPORTE, JACQUES
Monkey Bridge, The (1976)
Heroes Are Not Wet Behind the Ears, The (1979)

DELERUE, GEORGES
Mepris, Le (1963)
Up to His Ears (1965)
King of Hearts (1967)
Horsemen, The (1971)
Angela (1973)
Day for Night (1973)
Day of the Dolphin (1973)
Day of the Jackal (1973)
Incorrigible (1975)
Main Thing Is to Love, The (1975)
Femmes Fatales (1976)
Police Python 357 (1976)
Comme un Boomerang (1977)
Julia (1977)
Julie Glue Pot (1977)
Tender Cop (1977)
Get Out Your Handkerchiefs (1978)
Go See Mother ... Father Is Working (1978)
Little Girl in Blue Velvet, The (1978)
Photo Souvenir (1978)
Almost Perfect Pair, An (1979)
Black Sheep, The (1979)
Judge's Friend, The (1979)
Little Romance, A (1979)
Love on the Run (1979)
Skirt Chaser, The (1979)

DELIA, JOSEPH
Driller Killer (1979)

DEMARSAN, ERIC
Raging Fists (1975)
Section Speciale (1975)
Bad Starters, The (1976)
Tomorrow's Children (1976)
Last Exit Before Roissy (1977)
Roberte (1978)

DEODATO, EUMIR
Onion Field, The (1979)

DEPOLO, OAREN
Don't Lean Out the Window (1977)

DEPRAT, ROGERIO
Goddesses, The (1973)

DEQUAERE, PATRICK
F Is for Fairbanks (1976)

DEQUEANT, JEAN-CLAUDE
Devil in the Box, The (1977)

DER GRAFF, GENERATOR VAN
delete

DERBYSHIRE, DELIA
Legend of Hell House, The (1973)

DERFAL, JERZY
Without Anaesthetic (1979)

DERN, BILL
Blowdry (1976)

DERVIEUX, FRANK
I Love You (1974)

DESSEAU, PAUL
House of Frankenstein (1944)
House of Dracula (1945)

DEUTSCH, ADOLPH
Tovarich (delete)
Mr. Dodd Takes the Air (1937)
Racket Busters (1938)
Kid from Kokomo, The (1939)
Off the Record (1939)
Castle on the Hudson (1940)
Fighting 69th, The (1940)
Three Cheers for the Irish (1940)
Tugboat Annie Sails Again (1940)
Great Mr. Nobody, The (1941)
Kisses for Breakfast (1941)
Singapore Woman (1941)
Whispering Smith (1949)

DEUTSCH, HERBERT
Man You Love to Hate, The (1979)

DEVOR, DONALD
From the Mixed-Up Files of Mrs. Basil E. Frankweiler (1973)

DIAMOND, NEIL
Jonathan Livingston Seagull (1973)

DIBANGO, MANU
Countdown at Kusini (1976)
Outsiders (1977)

DICKINSON, JIM
Running Fence (1978)

DICKS, TED
Virgin Witch, The (1978)

DILA, ADING
Last Love, The (1975)

DIMITROV, SLAVE
Stand Up Straight, Delfina (1977)

DISSING, POVL
Guest Workers (1974)

DIXON, ERIC
On n'Enterre pas le Dimanche (1959)

DIZDARI, LIMOS
Clear Horizons (1979)

DO NASCIMENTO, ARANTES
Pele (1977)

DOBLE, VAINICA
Poachers (1975)

DOERGE, CRAIG
Rich Kids (1979)

DOERING, JEAN-PIERRE
Girl with the Cello, The (1973)
Dreyfus, or the Unbearable Truth (1975)
Garden of Torture, The (1976)
Sewers of Paradise, The (1979)

DOGA, YEVGENI
Gypsies Go to Heaven (1976)
Hunting Accident, A (1978)

DOLAN, ROBERT EMMETT
Trouble with Women, The (1947)
My Own True Love (1949)
Creature from the Black Lagoon, The (1954)

DOLDINGER, KLAUS
How Did a Nice Girl Like You Get into This Business? (1970)
Sudden Wealth of the Poor People of Kombach, The (1971)

Main Actor, The (1977)
Black and White Lite Days and Nights (1978)
Moritz, Dear Moritz (1978)
Second Awakening of Christa Klages, The (1978)
Fall, The (1979)

DOME, ZSOLT
Mistletoes (1979)

DOMINGO, PEDRO LUIS
Tic Tac Toe (1979)

DOMMAGE, BEAU
Late Blossom, The (1977)

DONAGGIO, PINO
Don't Look Now (1973)
Corruption in the Halls of Justice (1975)
Carrie (1976)
Piranha (1978)
Home Movies (1979)
Tourist Trap (1979)

DONG, CHOI YON
Mool-Dori Village (1979)

DONNER, OTTO
Home for Christmas (1975)

D'ONORIO, JEAN-LOUIS
Red Sweater, The (1979)

DONTCHEV, KIRIL
Third After the Sun, The (1973)
Hare Census, The (1974)
Eternal Times (1975)
Memories (1975)
Villa Zone (1975)
Cricket in the Ear (1976)
Investigator and the Woods, The (1976)
Manly Times (1978)
Sunstroke (1978)
With Love and Tenderness (1978)
On the Tracks of the Missing (1979)
Unknown Soldier's Patent Leather Shoes, The (1979)

D'ORLEANS, PHILIPPE
Let Joy Reign Supreme (1975)

DOUGHERTY, TERRY
Long Shot (1978)

DRAGON, DARRYL
Sandstone (1977)

DRAGON, DENNIS
Go for It (1976)
Sandstone (1977)

DRESS, MICHAEL
House That Dripped Blood, The (1971)

DREYFUS, GEORGE
Let the Balloon Go (1976)
Dimboola (1979)

DRUICK, DON
Wolfpen Principle, The (1974)

DUANE, JESSIE HOLLADAY
March of Paris 1914, The (1978)

DUBIN, JOSEPH
Bordertown Trail (1944)
Call of the Rockies (1944)
Code of the Prairie (1944)
Firebrands of Arizona (1944)
Haunted Harbor (1944)
San Antonio Kid, The (1944)
Sheriff of Sundown (1944)
Stagecoach to Monterey (1944)
Tiger Woman, The (1944)
Vigilantes of Dodge City (1944)
Madonna's Secret, The (1946)
Rendezvous with Annie (1946)
Bee at the Beach (1950)
Chicken in the Rough (1950)
Cold Storage (1950)
If You Don't Watch Out (1950)
Plutopia (1950)

DUHAMEL, ANTOINE
Pierrot le Fou (1965)
Frank and Eva--Living Apart Together (1973)
VD (1973)
Dakota (1974)
$2 Haircut, The (Coupe a Dix

Francs, La) (1975)
Question, The (1977)
Barricade at Pont du Jour, The (1978)
Song of Roland, The (1978)
Acrobat, The (1979)
Bit Between the Teeth (1979)
Felicite (1979)
Mais ou et Donc Ornicar (1979)
Return to the Beloved (1979)

DUMAS, R.
Barnabe (1938)

DUMONT, CHARLES
Parade (1974)
Lit--Ze Bawdy Bed, Le (1975)

DUNING, GEORGE
Dark Past, The (1949)
Lust for Gold (1949)
Slightly French (1949)
Between Midnight and Dawn (1950)
Petty Girl, The (1950)
Family Secret, The (1951)
Lady and the Bandit, The (1951)
Man in the Saddle (1951)
Paula (1952)
Scandal Sheet (1952)
Sound Off (1952)
All Ashore (1953)
Last of the Comanches (1953)
Salome (1953)
Picnic (1955)
3:10 to Yuma (1957)
Me and the Colonel (1958)
Arnold (1973)
Terror in the Wax Museum (1973)
Three Worlds of Gulliver, The (delete)

DUNLAP, PAUL
Big Jim McLain (1952)
Hellgate (1952)
San Francisco Story, The (1952)

DUNN, LARRY
That's the Way of the World (1975)

DUNNE, MURPHY
Outside Chance (1978)

DURKO, ZSOLT
Beyond Time (1974)
Snowfall (1974)

DUTRONC, JACQUES
Antonio and Sebastien (1974)
Dirty Dreamer (1978)

DWOSKIN, STEPHEN
Silent Cry, The (1977)

DYLAN, BOB
Pat Garrett and Billy the Kid (1973)

DZIERLATKA, ARIE
Location Hunting (1977)
Bailiff of Griefensee, The (1979)
Messidor (1979)

EARLE, EDWARD
Story of Joanna, The (1975)

EARNEST, DAVID
Night Before, The (1973)

EBBINGHOUSE, BERNARD
Tales That Witness Madness (1973)

ECONOMIDES, PHOEBUS
Struggle (1975)

EDELMAN, RANDY
Outside In (1972)
Executive Action (1973)

EDGEWORTH, RON
Raw Deal (1977)

EGERBLADH, BERNDT (BERNDT EGER)
Keep All Doors Open (1973)
Guy and a Gal, A (1975)
Walk on Clear Water if You Can (1979)

EHLER, JUAN
Black Vampire, The (1953)

EISLER, HANNS
Pete Roleum and His Cousins (1939)
Soil (1939)
Rain (1940)
So Well Remembered (1948)
Galileo (1975)

EL GHIWANE, NASS (see GHIWANE, NASS EL)

EL ZAHERI, FOUAD (see ZAHERI, FOUAD EL)

ELFERS, KONRAD
Inside Out (1975)

ELINOR, CARLI
Great Love, The (1918)
Hearts of the World (1918)
Gold Rush, The (1925)
What Price Glory? (1926)
Seventh Heaven (1927)

ELISCU, ROBERT
Schoolmaster Hober (1977)
Woman Across the Way (1978)

ELLINGTON, DUKE
Racing World (1968)

ELLIOTT, DEAN
Great American Bugs Bunny - Road Runner Chase, The (1979)

ELLIOTT, DON
Happy Hooker, The (1975)

ELLIOTT, JACK
T. R. Baskin (1972)
Oh, God! (1977)
Jerk, The (1979)
Just You and Me, Kid (1979)

ELLIS, DAVID GRAHAM
Nighthawks (1978)

ELLIS, DON
Seven Ups, The (1973)
French Connection II (1975)
Ruby (1977)
Natural Enemies (1979)

ELSON, NOEL
Me (1975)

ELYO, JEAN-CLAUDE
Spiral, The (1976)

EMENEGGER, ROBERT
Frasier, the Sensuous Lion (1973)

ENESCU, ADRIAN
Tanasse Scatiu (1977)
Calamity (1978)
Doctor Polnaru (1978)

ENGSTROM, CHARLES
Gal Young Un (1979)

ENO, BRIAN
Sebastian (1976)

ENRIQUEZ, LUIS
delete

EOTVOS, PETER
Cat's Play (1974)

ERDMANN, GUENTER
Seven Freckles (1978)

ERDODY, LEO
Dead Men Walk (1943)
Fugitive of the Plains (1943)
White Pongo (1945)
Blonde Savage (1947)

ERICSON, ERIC
Metamorphosis (1975)

ERKIN, ARIF
Hope (1978)
Canal, The (Kanal) (1979)

ERNRYD, BENGT
Gangster Movie, The (1974)
Two Women (1975)
Linus and the Mysterious Red Brick House (1979)

ESPERON, MANUEL
Chin, Chin, the Drunken Bum (1976)
Red Zone (1976)

ESTY, BOB
Roller Boogie (1979)

ETKIN, MARIANO
Revolution of the Seven Madmen, The (1973)

EVANS, BILL
Signalet (1966)

EVANS, WINSOME
27A (1974)

EVERS, JOERG
Anschi and Michael (1977)
Whizzer (1979)

EXPERIENCE 7
Coco la Fleur, Candidate (1979)

FABRICIUS-BJERRE, BENT
Opus 1 (1948)
In Your Dad's Pocket (1973)
Olsen Gang Runs Amok, The (1973)
Last Exploits of the Olsen Gang, The (1974)
Olsen Gang on the Track, The (1975)
Violets Are Blue (1975)
Olsen Gang Sees Red, The (1976)
Noelleby Affair, The (1977)
Olsen Gang Outta Sight, The (1977)
Agent 69 Jensen in the Sign of Sagittarius (1978)
Olsen Gang Goes to War, The (1978)
Olsen Gang Never Surrenders, The (1979)

FAERNLOEF, LARS
About Seven Girls (1974)

FAIRCHILD, EDGAR
House of Dracula (1945)

FAITH, PERCY
Virginian, The (1968)

FANG, FU KA
Sup Sap Bup Dap (1975)

FANO, MICHEL
Successive Slidings of Pleasure (1974)

FANSHAWE, DAVID
Requiem for a Village (1976)

FANTON, BUD
Case of the Full-Moon Murders, The (1973)

FARBERMAN, HAROLD
Great American Cowboy, The (1974)

FARINAS, CARLOS
Portrait of Teresa (1979)
That Long Night (1979)

FARROW, ROBBIE
Abduction (1975)

FELICIANO, JOSE
Aaron Loves Angela (1975)

FELLER, RICH
Smokey and the Bandit (1977)

FELTON, BERNIE
delete

FENTON, BERNIE
Devils of Darkness (1965)

FENYES, SZABOLES
Girl Who Liked Purple Flowers, The (1974)

FERGUSON, ALLYN
Count of Monte Cristo, The (1976)
Avalanche Express (1979)

FERRARO, RALPH
Sister of Satan, The (1965)
Flesh Gordon (1974)

FERRER, RAFAEL
Man Who Came from Ummo, The (1970)

FERRIO, GIANNI
Amico, Stammi Lontano Almeno un Palmo (1972)
No Way Out (1973)
Don't Turn the Other Cheek (1974)
Mysterious Island of Captain Nemo, The (1974)
Boss and the Worker, The (1975)
One Silver Dollar (1975)
Policewoman (1975)
How to Lose a Wife and Find a Lover (1978)
Tutti a Squola (1979)

FERRIS, PAUL
Vampire-Beast Craves Blood, The (1967)
Creeping Flesh (1973)

FERSTL, ERICH
All People Will Be Brothers (1973)
And the Rain Blots Out All Traces (1973)
Whispering Death (1976)
Hamburg Syndrome, The (1979)

FERVANT, THIERRY
Dawn Has Not Broken Yet (1973)

FESSLER, INGRID
Georg Hauser's Happy Minutes (1974)

FEUER, CY
Billy the Kid Returns (1938)
Down in "Arkansaw" (1938)
Higgins Family, The (1938)
Orphans of the Street (1938)
Pals of the Saddle (1938)
Storm over Bengal (1938)
I Was a Convict (1939)
In Old Caliente (1939)
Jeepers Creepers (1939)
Main Street Lawyer (1939)
Mickey the Kid (1939)
My Wife's Relatives (1939)
Mysterious Miss X, The (1939)
Pride of the Navy (1939)
Rough Riders Round-Up (1939)
S. O. S. Tidal Wave (1939)
Saga of Death Valley (1939)
She Married a Cop (1939)
Should Husbands Work? (1939)
Smuggled Cargo (1939)
Southward Ho! (1939)
Street of Missing Men (1939)
Thou Shalt Not Kill (1939)
Wall Street Cowboy (1939)
Woman Doctor (1939)
Zero Hour, The (1939)
Barnyard Follies (1940)
Behind the News (1940)
Border Legion (1940)
Bowery Boy (1940)
Carson City Kid, The (1940)
Colorado (1940)
Covered Wagon Days (1940)
Crooked Road, The (1940)
Earl of Puddlestone, The (1940)
Forgotten Girls (1940)
Friendly Neighbors (1940)
Frontier Vengeance (1940)
Gangs of Chicago (1940)
Ghost Valley Raiders (1940)
Girl from God's Country (1940)
Girl from Havana (1940)
Grand Ole Opry (1940)
Grandpa Goes to Town (1940)
Heroes of the Saddle (1940)
Hit Parade of 1941 (1940)
In Old Missouri (1940)
Lone Star Raiders (1940)
Meet the Missus (1940)
Melody and Moonlight (1940)
Money to Burn (1940)
Mysterious Dr. Satan, The (1940)
One Man's Law (1940)
Pioneers of the West (1940)
Ranger and the Lady, The (1940)
Rocky Mountain Rangers (1940)
Scatterbrain (1940)
Sing, Dance, Plenty Hot (1940)
Trail Blazers, The (1940)
Tulsa Kid, The (1940)
Under Texas Skies (1940)
Village Barn Dance (1940)
Wagons Westward (1940)

Who Killed Aunt Maggie? (1940)
Wolf of New York (1940)
Young Bill Hickok (1940)
Adventures of Captain Marvel (1941)
Angels with Broken Wings (1941)
Apache Kid, The (1941)
Arkansas Judge (1941)
Bad Man of Deadwood (1941)
Citadel of Crime (1941)
Death Valley Outlaws (1941)
Desert Bandit (1941)
Devil Pays Off, The (1941)
Doctors Don't Tell (1941)
Gauchos of Eldorado (1941)
Gay Vagabond, The (1941)
Great Train Robbery, The (1941)
Hurricane Smith (1941)
Ice-Capades (1941)
In Old Cheyenne (1941)
Jesse James at Bay (1941)
Kansas Cyclone (1941)
Man Betrayed, A (1941)
Mercy Island (1941)
Mr. District Attorney (1941)
Mr. District Attorney in the Carter Case (1941)
Mountain Moonlight (1941)
Nevada City (1941)
Outlaws of the Cherokee Trail (1941)
Petticoat Politics (1941)
Phantom Cowboy, The (1941)
Pittsburgh Kid, The (1941)
Prairie Pioneers (1941)
Public Enemies (1941)
Puddin' Head (1941)
Rags to Riches (1941)
Red River Valley (1941)
Robin Hood of the Pecos (1941)
Rookies on Parade (1941)
Saddlemates (1941)
Sailors on Leave (1941)
Sheriff of Tombstone (1941)
Sis Hopkins (1941)
Tuxedo Junction (1941)
Two-Gun Sheriff (1941)
West of Cimarron (1941)
Wyoming Wildcat (1941)
Affairs of Jimmy Valentine (1942)
Arizona Terrors (1942)
Hi, Neighbor! (1942)
Jesse James Jr. (1942)
Joan of Ozark (1942)
Man from Cheyenne (1942)
Moonlight Masquerade (1942)
Drums of Fu Manchu (1943)

FIDDY, JOHN
Groupie Girl (1970)

FIDENCO, NICO
Che Guevara, El (1969)
Those Dirty Dogs (1974)

FIEDEL, BRAD
Apple Pie (1975)
Deadly Hero (1976)
Looking Up (1977)

FIELDING, JERRY
Junior Bonner (1972)
Outfit, The (1973)
Scorpio (1973)
Bring Me the Head of Alfredo Garcia (1974)
Gambler, The (1974)
Super Cops, The (1974)
Black Bird, The (1975)
Killer Elite, The (1975)
Bad News Bears, The (1976)
Enforcer, The (1976)
Outlaw Josey Wales, The (1976)
Demon Seed (1977)
Gauntlet, The (1977)
Semi-Tough (1977)
Big Sleep, The (1978)
Gray Lady Down (1978)
Beyond the Poseidon Adventure (1979)

FIELDS, HARRY
Return to Campus (1975)

FIGIEL, PIOTR
Dulscy (1976)
My Way ... My Love (1976)
Foul Play (1977)

FINDLAY, MURRAY
Sleeping Dogs (1977)

FINK, ADOLPH
America (1924)

FINSTON, NAT
Big Wheel, The (1949)

FIRTICH, GEORGY
If I Had a Million Rubles (1974)

FISCHER, GUENTHER
Flight, The (1978)
Ottokar, the World Reformer (1978)
Just a Gigolo (1979)

FISCHER, PETER
Summer Guests (1976)
Tanner Steel Mill, The (1976)

FISCHOFF, GEORGE
Prince and the Pauper, The (1973)

FISER, LUBOS
Valerie and Her Week of Wonders (1970)
People from the Subway (1974)
Assassination in Sarajevo (1976)
Island of the Silver Herons, The (1977)
Adele Hasn't Had Her Supper Yet (1978)

FJELDMOSE, LARS
H. C. Andersen in Italy (1979)

FLICK, VIC
Autobiography of a Princess (1975)
Hullabaloo over Georgie and Bonnie's Pictures (1979)

FLOYD, CALVIN
In Search of Dracula (1975)

FLYNN, PATRICK
Caddie (1976)
Mad Dog (1976)

FONFREDE, CLAUDE
Old Country Where Rimbaud Died, The (1977)

FORBES, LOUIS
Wonder Man (1945)
Man Who Cheated Himself, The (1950)
Home Town Story (1951)
Wonderful Life, A (1951)

FORTE, LOU
Let Them Live (1937)

FOUR CHARLOTS
Stadium Nuts (1972)

FOX, CHARLES
Last American Hero, The (1973)
Laughing Policeman, The (1973)
Bug (1975)
Drowning Pool, The (1975)
Other Side of the Mountain, The (1975)
Duchess and the Dirtwater Fox, The (1976)
Two-Minute Warning (1976)
One on One (1977)
Foul Play (1978)
Our Winning Season (1978)

FRANCHETTI, ALBERTO
Germania (1914)

FRANCIOLI, LEON
Little Escapes (1979)

FRANGIPANE, RON
Holy Mountain (1973)
It Happened in Hollywood (1973)
Abduction (1975)
S. O. S. (1975)

FRANK, DAVID
Different Story, A (1978)

FRANKLIN, SERGE
Sirocco Blow, The (1979)

FRANKS, MICHAEL
Born to Kill (1975)

FREDERICKS, MARC
Red Mantle, The (1973)

FREE, STAN
Double Exposure of Holly, The (1976)

FREEBAIRN-SMITH, IAN
Hazing, The (1977)

FREED, ARNOLD
Werewolf of Washington (1973)

FREEDMAN, HARRY
Pyx, The (1973)

FRENCKEL, YAN
Supply Column Soldier, The (1976)

FREUD, STEPHEN
Freewheelin' (1976)

FRICHTER, COLIN
Sell-Out, The (1976)

FRICKE, FLORIAN
Aguirre, the Wrath of God (1973)
Herz aus Glas (1976)
Nosferatu--Phantom of the Night (1979)

FRIED, GERALD
Day of the Fight (1951)
Icebreaker (1951)
Big Lie, The (1951)
Fear and Desire (1953)
Blood Money (1954)
Bayou (1957)
Dino (1957)
M Squad (1957)
Curse of the Faceless Man, The (1958)
Flame Barrier, The (1958)
I, Mobster (1958)
Lost Missile, The (1958)
Machine Gun Kelly (1958)
Rawhide (1958)
Johnny Midnight (1959)
Riverboat (1959)
Shotgun Slade (1959)
Whispering Smith (1959)
Ben Casey (1960)
My Three Sons (1960)
Wagon Train (1960)
Gunsmoke (1962)
Story of ..., The (1962)
Breaking Point (1963)
Great Rights, The (1963)
Ten Seconds That Shook the World (1963)
Day of Infamy (1964)
Slattery's People (1964)
Gilligan's Island (1965)
Lost in Space (1965)
Man from U. N. C. L. E., The (1965)
Wackiest Ship in the Army, The (1965)
Family Affair, A (1966)
Felony Squad (1966)
Girl from U. N. C. L. E., The (1966)
Iron Horse, The (1966)
It's About Time (1966)
Jericho (1966)
Man Who Never Was, The (1966)
Mission: Impossible (1966)
Once Before I Die (1966)
One of Our Spies Is Missing (1966)
Star Trek (1966)
T. H. E. Cat (1966)
Dundee and the Culhane (1967)
Gauguin in Tahiti (1967)
Karate Killers, The (1967)
Mannix (1967)
Mr. Terrific (1967)
Cities (1970)
Childhood: The Enchanted Years (1971)
Getting There First (1971)
Sixth Sense (1971)
Baby, The (1972)
Police Story (1973)
Soylent Green (1973)

Policewoman (1974)
Birds Do It, Bees Do It (1975)
I Will Fight No More Forever (1975)
Survive! (1975)
Vigilante Force (1975)
Executive Suite (1976)
Francis Gary Powers: The True Story of the U-2 Spy Incident (1976)
Medical Story (1976)
Roots (1976)
Emergency! (1977)
Legacy of L. S. B. Leakey, The (1977)
Roots: One Year Later (1977)
Sex and the Married Woman (1977)
Spell, The (1977)
Testimony of Two Men (1977)
Beasts Are on the Streets, The (1978)
Cruise into Terror (1978)
Immigrants, The (1978)
Maneaters Are Loose, The (1978)
Rescue from Gilligan's Island (1978)
Roots 2 (1978)
Bell Jar, The (1979)
Castaways on Gilligan's Island, The (1979)
Incredible Journey of Dr. Meg Laurel, The (1979)
Rebels, The (1979)
Seekers, The (1979)
Son-Rise (1979)
I, Monster (delete)
Last Missile, The (delete)

FRIEDHOFER, HUGO
Adventures of Marco Polo, The (1938)
Topper Takes a Trip (1939)
Woman in the Window (1944)
Song Is Born, A (1948)
Guilty of Treason (1950)
Big Carnival, The (1951)
Just for You (1952)
Lydia Bailey (1952)
Marrying Kind, The (1952)
Outcasts of Poker Flat, The (1952)
Rancho Notorious (1952)
Island in the Sky (1953)
Thunder in the East (1953)
Violent Saturday (1955)
White Feather (1955)
Bravados, The (1958)
Beauty and the Beast (1962)
Private Parts (1971)

FRIZZI, FABIO
Where Are You Going on Your Vacation? (1979)
White Collar Blues (1975)

FRONTIERE, DOMINIC
Train Robbers, The (1973)
Freebie and the Bean (1974)
Brannigan (1975)
Cleopatra Jones and the Casino of Gold (1975)
Gumball Rally (1976)
Pipe Dream (1976)

FU-LIANG, CHOU
Secret Rivals, The (1976)
Story of the Dragon, The (1976)

FU-LING, WANG
Dracula and the Golden Vampires (1975)
Snake Prince, The (1976)

FUENTES, RUBEN
Interval (1973)
National Mechanics (1975)

FUGAIN, MICHEL
Don't Know Anything but I'll Tell All (1973)

FUKAMACHI, JUN
Keiko (1979)

FUKUSHIMA, NOBUMASA
Sweet Revenge (1979)

FUNG, RICKY
Itchy Fingers (1979)

FUREY, LEWIS
Heat of Normandie St.-Onge, The (1976)
Rubber Gun, The (1977)
Angel and Woman (1978)
Goodbye ... See You Monday (1979)
Jacob Two-Two Meets the Hooded Fang (1979)

FURST, WILLIAM
Let Katie Do It (1915)
Green Swamp, The (1916)
Joan the Woman (1917)

FUSCO, GIOVANNI
Three Nights of Love (1964)
Mafia (1969)

FUSTER, MIGUEL ANGEL
Chronicle of a Latin-American Subversive (1976)
I Am a Delinquent (1977)

"FUZZY"
Double Man, The (1976)

GABUBER, FRANCOIS
Pain in the Neck, The (1973)

GABUNIA, M.
Pirosmani (1974)
Disturbance (Poloh) (1977)

GAGNON, ANDRE
Games of the XXI Olympiad Montreal 1976 (1977)
Running (1979)

GAGNON, LEE
Seizure (1974)

GAGNON, PHILIPPE
Orders, The (1975)

GAINSBOURG, SERGE
Naked Hearts (1966)
Private Projection (1973)
I Love You No Longer (1976)
Madame Claude (1977)
Bronzes, Les (1978)
Goodbye Emmanuelle (1978)
Melancholy Baby (1979)
Nocturnal Uproar (1979)

GALAXIE DREAM BAND
Red Midnight (1978)

GALLELLO, JOSEPH
Soup du Jour (1975)

GAMLEY, DOUGLAS
Beast Must Die, The (1974)
Madhouse (1974)
Land That Time Forgot, The (1975)

GARDNER, STU
Klansman, The (1974)

GARRIGUENE, RENE
16 Fathoms Deep (1948)
New Mexico (1951)

GARSON, MORT
Black Eye, The (1974)

GARVARENTZ, GEORGES
Triple Cross (1967)
Pebbles of Etretat (1972)
Caroline Cherie (1973)
Killer Force (1975)
Golden Lady, The (1979)
Lumiere des Justes, La (1979)

GASCOIGNE, BRIAN
Phase VI (1974)

GASLINI, GIORGIO
Night of the Devils, The (1971)
Pacifist, The (1972)
Deep Red (1976)

GASSMAN, CLARK
Gifts of an Eagle (1975)

GAUBERT, CHRISTIAN
Night of St. Germain de Pres, The (1977)

GAUBERT, CLAUDE
Six O'Clock USA (1976)

GAYE, FRANKIE
Penitentiary (1979)

GAZZELLINO, SEVERINO
Golden Mass, The (1975)

GEESON, RON
Body, The (1973)

GENKOV, GEORGI
Hark to the Cock (1978)
Roof, The (1978)

GEOFFREYS, DONALD
Sextool (1975)

GEORGET, ANDRE
Street of the Crane's Foot (1979)

GERARD, BERNARD
Ce Cher Victor (1975)
Gloria (1977)

GERAULT, YVON
Vampire Women, The (1967)
Naked Vampire (1969)

GERMETEN, GUNNAR
Blood of the Railroad Workers (1979)

GERTZ, IRVING
Skipalong Rosenbloom (1951)

GHATNAGAR
Darshan (1974)

GHIGLIA, BENEDETTO
Secret Agent Superdragon (1966)
Adios Gringo (1967)
That Little Difference (1970)
To Forget Venice (1979)

GHIGLIA, MAESTRO
delete

GHIWANE, NASS EL
Oh the Days (1978)

GIBBONS, MARK
Super Van (1977)

GIBBS, MICHAEL
Madame Sin (1972)
Secrets (1978)

GIBSON, DAVID
Schlock (1973)

GIBSON, MICHAEL
Roseland (1977)

GIL, GILBERTO
Tent of Miracles, The (1977)

GILBERT, HERSCHEL BURKE
Shamrock Hill (1949)
There's a Girl in My Heart (1950)

GILL, ROBERT
Affair in Monte Carlo (1952)

GILLESPIE, DIZZY
Voyage to Next (1974)
Second Chance--Sea (1976)

GILLIS, DON
Recommendation for Mercy (1975)

GILLY
Hot Channels (1973)

GILSON, BERNARD
Juliette and the Feel of the Times (1976)

GIRAUD, H.
Under Paris Skies (1930)

GISMONTI, EGBERTO
Raomi (1978)

GIZZI, CLAUDIO
Blood for Dracula (1974)

GLASS, PAUL
Overlord (1975)

GLASSER, ALBERT
Gas House Kids in Hollywood (1947)
Girl from San Lorenzo, The (1950)

Gunfire (1950)
Return of Jesse James, The (1950)
Rocketship X-M (1950)
Geisha Girl (1952)

GLENN-COPELANN, BEVERLY
Montreal Main (1974)

GLICKMAN, MORT
G-Men vs. the Black Dragon (1942)
King of the Mounties (1942)
Perils of Nyoka (1942)
Spy Smasher (1942)
Dead Man's Gulch (1943)
Man from the Rio Grande, The (1943)
Thundering Trails (1943)
Beneath Western Skies (1944)
Laramie Trail, The (1944)
Outlaws of Santa Fe (1944)

GLINDEMANN, IB
Me and the Mafia (1973)
Up 'n' at 'em, Amalie (1973)
Me, Too, I'm the Mafia (1974)

GLORIEUX, FRANCOIS
Kasper in the Underworld (1979)

GLUCK, JESUS
Flunking Out (1977)
Alone at Daybreak (1978)

"GOBLIN"
Suspiria (1977)
Squadron Antigangster (1978)
Dawn of the Dead (1979)
I Love You, I Love You Not (1979)
Together? (1979)

GODDIGO
Youth Killer, The (1977)

GODHINO-FAUSTO, SERGIO
Confederation--The People Make History, The (1979)

GOEBELS, HEINER
This Is Love, Isn't It? (1979)

GOLD, ERNEST
Wyoming (1947)
Family Circus, The (1951)
Georgie and the Dragon (1951)
Willie the Kid (1952)
Gerald McBoing Boing (1953)
Gerald McBoing Boing's Symphony (1953)
McCullochs, The (1975)
Cross of Iron (1977)
Fun with Dick and Jane (1977)
Good Luck, Miss Wyckoff (1979)
Runner Stumbles, The (1979)

GOLDBERG, BARRY
Sodom and Gomorrah (1976)

GOLDENBERG, BILLY
Last of Sheila, The (1973)
Busting (1974)
Domino Principle, The (1977)
Scavenger Hunt (1979)

GOLDIS, RADU
Happiness Is So Near (1978)

GOLDSMITH, JERRY
Crimebusters, The (1961)
Detective, The (1968)
Sebastian (1968)
Tora! Tora! Tora! (1970)
Last Run (1971)
Ace Eli and Rodger of the Skies (1973)
Don Is Dead, The (1973)
One Little Indian (1973)
Papillon (1973)
Police Story (1973)
Shamus (1973)
Chinatown (1974)
QB VII (1974)
S*P*Y*S (1974)
Babe (1975)
Breakout (1975)
Reincarnation of Peter Proud, The (1975)
Take a Hard Ride (1975)
Terrorists, The (Ransom) (1975)
Wind and the Lion, The (1975)
Breakheart Pass (1976)
Last Hard Man, The (1976)

Logan's Run (1976)
Omen, The (1976)
Cassandra Crossing, The (1977)
Damnation Alley (1977)
High Velocity (1977)
Islands in the Stream (1977)
MacArthur (1977)
Twilight's Last Gleaming (1977)
Boys from Brazil, The (1978)
Capricorn One (1978)
Coma (1978)
Damien--Omen II (1978)
Great Train Robbery, The (1978)
Magic (1978)
Swarm, The (1978)
Alien (1979)
Players (1979)
Star Trek--The Motion Picture (1979)

GOLDSTEIN, WILLIAM
Bingo Long Traveling All-Stars and Motor Kings, The (1976)
Norman ... Is That You? (1976)

GONDA, JANOS
Voyage with Jacob (1973)
Tomorrow, Pleasant (1975)

GONSALVES, VIRGIL
Sons and Daughters (1967)

GOODMAN, MILES
Slumber Party '57 (1977)
Skatetown, U. S. A. (1979)

GOODWIN, DOUG
Ant and the Aardvark, The (1968)
Ant from U. N. C. L. E., The (1968)
Scratch a Tiger (1969)

GOODWIN, GORDON
Attack of the Killer Tomatoes (1979)

GOODWIN, RON
Trap, The (1966)
Where Eagles Dare (1968)
Battle of Britain, The (1969)
Decline and Fall of a Bird-watcher, The (1969)
One of Our Dinosaurs Is Missing (1975)
Candleshoe (1977)
Force 10 from Navarrone (1977)
Unidentified Flying Oddball, The (1979)

GORAGUER, ALAIN
Savage Planet, The (1973)
Silent One, The (1973)
Beyond Fear (1975)
Eagle and the Dove, The (1977)

GORI, LALLO
Sexy Probitissimo (1964)
Mondo Balordo (Mondo Keyhole) (1968)

GORINA, MANUEL VALLS
Burned City, The (1976)

GORN, STEVE
Hungry Wives (1973)

GOTOVAC, PERO
Snowstorm (1977)

GOTTHARDT, PETER
Scenes of Fires (1978)
Ikarus (1979)

GOTTLIEB, GORDON
Very Natural Thing, A (1974)

GOTTSCHALK, LOUIS F.
Patchwork Girl of Oz, The (1914)
Despoilers, The (1916)
Honor's Altar (1916)
Great Love, The (1918)
Three Musketeers, The (1921)

GOWERS, PATRICK
Hamlet (1970)
Dangerous Kisses (1973)
Children of Rage (1975)

GRADSKY, ALEXANDER
Romance of Lovers (1974)

GRAHAM, KENNETH
Small World of Sammy Lee, The (1962)
Naturally, It's Rubber (1964)
Scene Nun, Take One (1964)
Carousella (1965)
Cuckoo Patrol (1965)
Saharan Venture (1965)
Timber Move (1965)
Can I Help You? (1966)
Where the Bullets Fly (1966)
Frontiers of Power (1967)
Just Routine (1967)
Our Time No. 1 (1967)
Cantagallo (1969)

GRAINER, RON
Trap, The (delete)
Devil Within Her, The (1976)

GRAINGER, PERCY
Flying Feet (1929)

GRANT, TOM
Breakfast in Bed (1978)

GRAPPELLI, STEPHANE
Waltzers, The (1974)

GRASEL, PAUL
Vampyros Lesbos (1970)

GRAUENGAARD, JOERN
Going for Broke (1977)

GRAVENITES, NICK
Steelyard Blues (1973)

GRAY, ALLAN
African Queen, The (1951)

GRAY, BARRY
Thunderbirds Are Go (1966)

GRAY, BASIL
Dingaka (1965)

GRAY, DOBIE
Commitment, The (1976)

GREAN, CHARLES RANDOLPH
Two Men of Karamoja (1974)

THE GREAT AMERICAN MUSIC BAND
Big Bad Mama (1974)

GREAT, DON
Amorous Adventures of Don Quixote and Sancho Panza, The (1976)

GREEN, BILLY
Stone (1974)

GREEN, MICK
Sell-Out, The (1976)

GREEN, PHILIP
Directions (1972)

GREENE, WALTER
Why Girls Leave Home (1945)
Fighting Vigilantes (1947)
Wild Country (1947)
Frontier Revenge (1948)
Red Desert (1949)
West of the Brazos (1950)
Affair in Monte Carlo (1952)
Black Lash, The (1952)

GREGOIRE, RICHARD
Chocolate Eclair (1979)

GRIGORIU, GEORGE
Actors and the Savages, The (1975)

GRIGORIU, THEODOR
Explosion (1978)

GRIPPE, RAGNAR
Emperor, The (1979)

GRISMAN, DAVID
Capone (1975)
Eat My Dust (1976)
King of the Gypsies (1978)

GRIVA, DIMITER
Be Blessed (1978)

GRIZZI, CARLO
Frankenstein (1974)

GROFE, FERDE
King of Jazz (1930)
Knute Rockne, All-American (1940)
Thousands Cheer (1943)
Time Out of Mind (1947)
Return of Jesse James (1950)
Rocketship X-M (1950)
Valentino (1977)

GROSS, CHARLES
Have a Nice Weekend (1975)
On the Yard (1978)

GROSSKOPF, ERHARD
Walking Upright (1976)
Dishonest Profit, The (1977)

GROTH, JACOB
Charly and Steffen (1979)

GRUBU, TUM ATA
When the Sun Rises (1978)

GRUENBERG, LOUIS
Commandos Strike at Dawn (1942)

GRUNTZ, GEORGE
Steppenwolf (1974)
Conquests of the Citadel, The (1977)

GRUSIN, DAVID
Waterhole #3 (1967)
Friends of Eddie Coyle, The (1973)
Midnight Man, The (1974)
Nickel Ride, The (1974)
Three Days of the Condor (1975)
W. W. and the Dixie Dance Kings (1975)
Yakuza, The (1975)
Front, The (1976)
Murder by Death (1976)
Bobby Deerfield (1977)
Fire Sale (1977)
Goodbye Girl, The (1977)
Mr. Billion (1977)
Heaven Can Wait (1978)
... And Justice for All (1979)
Champ, The (1979)
Electric Horseman, The (1979)

GUARALDI, VINCE
Charlie Brown Christmas, A (1970)

GUBA, V.
Lone Wolf (1978)

GUCCINI, FRANCESCO
Nene (1977)

GUDIN, EDUARDO
Touchy (1976)

GUENTHER, JAN
Hard Part Begins, The (1973)

GUERCIO, JAMES WILLIAM
Elektra Glide in Blue (1973)

GUERRA, RUY
Fall, The (1978)

GUERRERO, SERGIO
Vampire and Sex, The (1968)
Roots of Blood (1979)

GUILLOU, JEAN
Mio (1972)
Hu-Man (1975)

GUNNING, CHRISTOPHER
Get Charlie Tully (1976)

GURBINDO, FERMIN
With Lots of Love (1979)

GUSTAFSSON, RUNE
Release the Prisoners, It's Spring (1975)

GYLDMARK, SVEN
Man from Swan Farm, The (1973)
Torndal Cousins, The (1973)
Noldebo Vicarage (1974)
Son from Bergaarden, The (1975)

GYULAI-GAAL, FERENC
Walk Fory, The (1975)

HABALO, MOSHE
We Are Arab Jews in Israel (1977)

HADJIDAKIS, MANOS
Pedestrian, The (1974)
Sweet Movie (1974)
Honeymoon (1979)

HADLEY, HENRY
Manon (1926)
Phantom Empire (1935)

HAEFELI, JONAS C.
Hannibal (1973)
Mute, The (1976)
Swissmakers, The (1978)

HAGEMAN, RICHARD
Stagecoach (1939)
This Woman Is Mine (1941)

HAIDER, JOE
Lina Braake--The Bank's Interests Can't Be the Interests Lina Braake Has (1975)
Berlinger (1976)

HAJOS, KARL
Tumbleweed Trail (1948)

HALA, VLASTIMIL
Six Bears and a Clown (1976)

HALARIS, CHRISTODOULAS
Proceedings (1976)

HALICKI, RONALD
Gone in 60 Seconds (1974)

HALLBERG, BENGT
You're Out of Your Mind, Maggie (1979)

HALLETZ, ERWIN
Fanny Hill (1965)

HALLIGAN, DICK
Go Tell the Spartans (1978)
Dirt (1979)
Force of One, A (1979)

HAMILTON, CHICO
Sweet Smell of Success, The (1957)
Peacemeal (1967)
Confessor, The (1973)
Coonskin (1975)
Mr. Ricco (1975)

HAMILTON, HARLEY
Romance of Happy Valley, A (1919)

HAMLISCH, MARVIN
Save the Tiger (1973)
Sting, The (1973)
Way We Were, The (1973)
World's Greatest Athlete, The (1973)
Prisoner of Second Avenue, The (1974)
Entertainer, The (1975)
Spy Who Loved Me, The (1977)
Ice Castles (1978)
Same Time, Next Year (1978)
Chapter Two (1979)
Starting Over (1979)

HAMMOND, JOHN PAUL
Loose Ends (1975)

HAMPEL, GUNTER
Red Midnight (1978)

HAN, SANGKI
Long Live the Island Frogs (1973)

HANCOCK, HERBIE
Spook Who Sat by the Door, The (1973)
Death Wish (1974)

HANKS, FREDERICK O.
Barrier, The (1926)

HANNA, FAIQ
River, The (1979)

HANNIGAN, TERRY
Palm Beach (1979)

HANSSON, LALLA
Buddies (1976)

HAPKA, PETR
Operation Bororo (1973)
Day for My Love (1977)
Rose-Tinted Dreams (1977)

HARA, HIROSHI
Kashima Paradise (1973)

HARDY, HAGOOD
Second Wind (1976)
I, Maureen (1978)

HARKLEROAD, WILLIAM
Fire in the Middle (1978)

HARLINE, LEIGH
Blondie Has Servant Trouble (1940)
Blondie on a Budget (1940)
Blondie Plays Cupid (1940)
So You Won't Talk (1940)
Lady Has Plans, The (1941)
Mr. Bug Goes to Town (1941)
On the Sunny Side (1941)
Careful, Soft Shoulder (1942)
Magnificent Dope, The (1942)
My Gal Sal (1942)
Night Before the Divorce, The (1942)
Postman Didn't Ring, The (1942)
Prelude to War (1942)
Right to the Heart (1942)
Rings on Her Fingers (1942)
Secret Agent of Japan (1942)
Whispering Ghosts (1942)
Jitterbugs (1943)
They Live by Night (1948)
Union Station (1950)
Las Vegas Story, The (1952)
Taxi (1953)

HARLING, W. FRANKE
Honey (1930)
Monte Carlo (1930)
Rango (1931)
Broken Lullaby (1932)
Expert, The (1932)
Fireman, Save My Child (1932)
Madame Butterfly (1932)
Men Are Such Fools (1932)
Miracle Man, The (1932)
One Hour with You (1932)
One-Way Passage (1932)
Play Girl (1932)
Rich Are Always with Us, The (1932)
Street of Woman (1932)
This Is the Night (1932)
Trouble in Paradise (1932)
Two Seconds (1932)
Week-End Marriage (1932)
Winner Take All (1932)
Bitter Tea of General Yen, The (1933)
Kiss Before the Mirror, A (1933)
Man's Castle, A (1933)
Church Mouse, The (1934)
Scarlet Empress, The (1934)
Souls at Sea (1937)
Stagecoach (1939)
Adventure in Washington (1941)
Penny Serenade (1941)
Bachelor's Daughters, The (1946)

HARRIS, ANTHONY
Coach (1978)

HARRIS, JOHNNY
Evil, The (1978)

HARTLEY, RICHARD
Romantic Englishwoman, The (1975)
Aces High (1976)
Lady Vanishes, The (1979)

HARWOOD, BO
Woman Under the Influence, A (1974)
Killing of a Chinese Bookie, The (1976)
Opening Night (1977)

HASKELL, JIMMIE
Lipstick (1976)

Death Game (1977)
Joyride (1977)

HATCH, TONY
Sweeney 2 (1978)

HATCHER, HARLEY
Albert Peckingpaw's Revenge (1967)
Soul Hustler (1973)

HATLEY, MARVIN
Kelly the Second (1936)
Mister Cinderella (1936)
Pick a Star (1937)
Chump at Oxford, A (1940)
Saps at Sea (1940)

HAVEN, ALAN
Jolly Bad Fellow, A (1964)

HAVLIK, FERDINAND
Hitchhiker, The (1979)

HAWKSWORTH, JOHNNY
CirCarC Gear, The (1964)
Polyolefins (1964)
Rig Move (1964)
Six Faces of Terylene (1964)
Snow (1964)
Harmony Abroad (1965)
Linesman, The (1965)
Naked World of Harrison Marks, The (1965)
Vauxhall, Bedford, England (1965)
Search and Research (1967)
Small Propeller, The (1967)
Something Nice to Eat (1967)
Whatever Happened to Uncle Fred? (1967)
Five Steps (1968)
Take One Baby (1968)
Race for the Golden Flag (1969)
Transit Supervan (1969)
Zeta One (1969)
Anatomy of a Motor Oil (1970)
Antiseptics in Hospital (1970)
Henry 9 Till 5 (1970)
Cup Glory (1971)
Present, The (1971)
Sugar Is a Business (1971)
Plod (1972)
When Roobard Made a Spike (1973)
When There Wasn't Treasure (1974)
Justine (1976)

HAYASHI, HIKARU
Kuroneko (Black Cat) (1968)
Story of the Age of Wars, The (1973)
God of Flower, The (Hanagami) (1977)
Life of Chukuzan, The (1977)

HAYES, ISAAC
Three Tough Guys (1974)
Truck Turner (1974)

HAYTON, LENNIE
Married Bachelor (1941)
Dr. Kildare's Victory (1942)

HAZARD, RICHARD
Some Call It Loving (1973)
Nickelodeon (1976)
Heroes (1977)

HEAD
Lickity Split (1974)

HEFFERMAN, FRED
Lovin' Molly (1974)

HEFTI, NEAL
Won Ton Ton, the Dog Who Saved Hollywood (1976)

HEICKING, WOLFRAM
Anton the Magician (1978)

HEIMAN, NACHUM
Neither the Sea Nor the Sand (1974)

HEINDORF, RAY
No Time for Sergeants (1958)

HEINZ, GERHARD
When the Mad Aunts Are Coming (1970)
Cry of the Black Wolves, The

(1972)
Julie (1976)
Evolution of Snuff, The (1977)
Fruit Is Ripe, The (1977)

HELMS, JIM
Kung Fu (1972)
Night Creature (1979)

HEMBERG, ESKIL
Charlotte Lionshield (1979)

"HEMLOCK"
Swap Meet (1979)

HENDERSON, CHARLES
Black Friday (1940)
Black Cat, The (1941)
Hold That Ghost (1941)
Horror Island (1941)
Man-Made Monster (1941)
House of Dracula (1945)

HENDERSON, LUTHER
Slams, The (1973)

HENDRICKS, JON
Sons and Daughters (1967)

HENN, RICHARD
Goin' Surfin' (1975)

HENNEMAN, ALEXANDER
Fabiola (1922)

HENTSCHEL, DAVID
Operation Daybreak (1976)
Seven Nights in Japan (1976)
Squeeze, The (1977)

HENZE, HANS-WERNER
Lost Honor of Katharine Blum, The (1975)
Good-for-Nothing (1978)

HEPPENER, ROBERT
Sky over Holland (1967)
Bomb, The (1969)

HERAS, JOAQUIN GUTIERREZ
Castle of Purity (1974)
Holy Office, The (1974)
Cubs, The (1975)
Place Without Limits, The (1978)

HERMAN, DAVE
Cheerleaders, The (1973)

HEROUET, MARC
Page of Love, A (1977)

HERRMANN, BERNARD
Kentuckian, The (1955)
Williamsburg: The Story of A Patriot (1957)
Three Worlds of Gulliver, The (1959)
Bride Wore Black, The (1968)
Virginian, The (1968)
Battle of Neretva (1969)
Endless Night (1971)
Night Digger, The (1971)
Sisters (1973)
It's Alive! (1974)
Obsession (1976)
Taxi Driver (1976)
Death at Work (1978)
It's Alive II (It Lives Again) (1978)
Christmas Carol, A (delete)

HERROCKS, GRANT
Inbreaker, The (1974)

HERTEL, PIOTR
Save the City (1977)

HESSLEIN, PETER
Supermarket (1974)

HEYMANN, BIRGER
Milk War in Bavaria (1979)

HEYMANN, WERNER
Adorable (1933)
Caravan (1934)
King and the Chorus Girl, The (1937)
Bluebeard's Eighth Wife (1938)
Bedtime Story (1941)
This Thing Called Love (1941)
Topper Returns (1941)
Appointment in Berlin (1943)

HEYMEN, WALTER
Home, Sweet, Home (1973)
Way Out (1973)

HIDAKA, KEISUKE
Strongest Karate, The (1976)

HIGGINS, MONK
Sheba Baby (1975)

HILMAN, MARC
Garden That Tilts, The (1975)

HIME, FRANCES
Dona Flor and Her Two Husbands (1977)
Love Lesson (1978)

HINDEMITH, PAUL
Vormittagspuk (1928)

HINDGRIND, HAROLD
Sweet Punkin' (1976)

HINE, RUPERT
Shout, The (1978)

HIRAO, MASAKI
Espy (1975)

HIROSE, RYOHEI
Utamaro's World (1946)
Rainbow, The (1970)

HIRSCH, NURIT
Fox in the Chicken Coop, The (1978)
Don't Ever Ask Me If I Love (1979)
My Mother, the General (1979)

HODEIR, ANDRE
Autour d'un Recif (1949)
Terres et Flammes (1951)
Bielles des Sables (1952)
Saint-Tropez, Devoir de Vacances (1952)
A Propos d'une Riviere (1955)
Terre Fleurie (1956)
Castles Through the Ages (1958)
Operation Time Bomb (1958)
Parisienne, La (1958)
Sins of Youth (1958)
Tripes au Soleil, Les (1958)
Golden Fish, The (1959)
Ideal Palace, The (1959)
Primitifs du XIIIe, Les (1960)
Vitrine Sous la Mer (1960)
Voici le Ski (1961)
Ski Total (1962)
Wild Living (1962)
Operation MJC (1965)
Time Objectives (1965)
Beau Masque (1972)
Rak (1972)

HODGSON, BRIAN
Legend of Hell House, The (1973)

HOEYER, OLE
Beside Romance (1973)
Girl and the Dream Castle, The (1974)
Hottest Show in Town, The (1974)
Girls at Arms (1975)
Off Beside Limits (1975)
Bedside Sailors (1976)
Flamin' Fire-Chief (1976)
Girls At Arms, Part 2 (1976)
In the Sign of the Lion (1976)
Jumpin' at the Bedside (1976)
Office Party, The (1976)
That Brief Summer (1976)
Girls at Sea (1977)
Goldencauliflower Family Gets the Vote, The (1977)
Factory Outing, The (1978)
Mirror Mirror (1978)
Traditions, My Behind (1979)

HOFFERT, BRENDA
Wild Horse Hank (1979)

HOFFERT, PAUL
Sunday in the Country (1975)
Outrageous! (1977)
Third Walker, The (1978)
Shape of Things to Come, The (1979)
Wild Horse Hank (1979)

HOFFMAN, MICHAEL
Baree, Son of Kazan (1925)

HOFFMANN, NEILS FREDERICK
Grandma Schulz (1977)

HOLDER, NODDY
Flame (1975)

HOLDRIDGE, LEE
Jeremy (1973)
Jonathan Livingston Seagull (1973)
Forever Young, Forever Free (1975)
Nothing by Chance (1975)
Goin' Home (1976)
Mustang Country (1976)
Winterhawk (1976)
Park, The (1977)
Moment by Moment (1978)
Oliver's Story (1978)
Other Side of the Mountain, The (Part 2) (1978)
French Postcards (1979)
Tilt (1979)

HOLINER, PATRICE
Utopia (1978)

HOLKENOW, STEEN
Mind Your Back, Professor (1977)

HOLLANDER, FREDERICK
I Am Suzanne (1934)
Valiant Is the Word for Carrie (1936)
True Confession (1937)
Bluebeard's Eighth Wife (1938)
Midnight (1939)
Doctor Takes a Wife, The (1940)
South of Suez (1940)
Too Many Husbands (1940)
Typhoon (1940)
Here Comes Mr. Jordan (1941)
Life with Henry (1941)
Man Who Came to Dinner, The (1942)
First Time, The (1952)
5, 000 Fingers of Dr. T, The (1952)

HOLLINGSWORTH, JOHN
Horror of Dracula (1958)
Wrong Arm of the Law, The (delete)

HOLMAN, BILL
Get Outta Town (1959)

HOLMES, DANNY
Woman, You Should Not Have Been Created (1975)

HOLMES, LEROY
Smile (1975)

HOLMES, RUPERT
Memories Within Miss Aggie (1974)

HOLMSEN, DANNY
Between Heaven and Hell (1976)

HOLST, BENNY
Revolt of the Thralls (1979)

HOPKINS, KENYON
This Property Is Condemned (1966)

HORN, PAUL
Bird, The (1965)

HORNER, JAMES
Lady in Red, The (1979)

HOROWITZ, DAVID
Hu-Man (1975)

HOSSEIN, ANDRE
I Killed Rasputin (1966)

HOWE, JOHN
Why Rock the Boat? (1974)

HOYT, ERIC
Keeper, The (1976)

HRISTIC, ZORAN
Dervish and Death, The (1974)
Republic of Uzice, The (1974)
Red Earth (1975)
67 Days (1975)

Beach Guard in Winter, The (1976)
Peaks of Zelengore, The (1976)
Battle for the Railway (1978)
Dog that Liked Trains, The (1978)
Love and Rage (1978)

HSU-CHING, WU
Moods of Love (1977)

HUAN-CHI, LI
Hurricane (1978)

HUBER, ARTHUR PAUL
Common Man, The (1975)

HUE, GEORGES
Retour d'Ulysse, Le (1909)

HUI, KU CHIA
Return of the Dragon (1974)

HUI, SAMUEL
Private Eyes, The (1977)
Contract, The (1978)

HULETTE, DON
Breaker, Breaker (1977)

HUMAIR, DANIEL
Witchcraft Through the Ages (Haxan) (1921)
Conquistadores, Les (1975)

HUMMEL, FERDINAND
Bismarck (1914)
Jenseits des Stroms (1922)

HUMMEL, FRANZ
I'd Like to Have My Troubles (1975)

HUNTER, ALBERTA
Remember My Name (1978)

HUPPERTZ, GOTTFRIED
Chronik von Grieshuus (1925)

HUTCH, WILLIE
Foxy Brown (1973)
Mack, The (1973)

HUYUKI, TORU
Hatoko's Sea, The (1974)

HWA, MA
First False Step, The (1979)

HYMAN, DICK
Bernice Bobs Her Hair (1976)

HYSLOP, RICKY
Why Shoot the Teacher? (1977)

IBACH-ROMUALD, HUMBERT
Scorched Triangle, The (1975)

IBE, HARUMI
History of Postwar Japan as Told by a Bar Hostess (1974)

"ICEBERG"
Bilbao (1978)

ICHIYANAGI, TOSHI
Kaigenieri (1973)
Jun (1979)

IDA, MITSUTADA
Journey, A (Tabiji) (1967)
Fir Is Left, A (1970)

IKUFUBE, AKIRA
Human Revolution, The (1974)
Bokyo (1975)
Love and Faith: Lady Ogin (1979)

ILLEST ENSEMBLE
Too Skinny for Love? (1974)

ILLIN, EUGEN
Yesterday's Tomorrow (1978)

IMMEL, JERROLD
House on Skull Mountain, The (1974)
Sourdough (1977)

INTRAVIJIT, CHALIE
Operation Black Panther (1977)
Heaven and Hell (1978)

IRINO, YOSHIO
Story of Taikoh, The (1965)

ISFAELT, BJOERN
Swedish Love Story, A (1970)
Giliap (1975)
Hempas Bar (1977)

ISFALT, BJORN
delete

IVERS, PETER
Grand Theft Auto (1977)

IZAGUIRRE, JUAN LUIS
Supersonic Man (1979)

IZUMI, TAKU
Takiji Kobayashi (1974)

JACKSON, HOWARD
Eight Girls in a Boat (1933)
Glamour (1934)
Dizzy Dames (1935)
Lone Wolf Returns, The (1935)
No More Yesterdays (1935)
Old Homestead, The (1935)
Counterfeit (1936)
Devil's Squadron, The (1936)
Lady of Secrets (1936)
Pride of the Blue Grass (1939)
Angel from Texas, An (1940)
River's End (1940)
Bad Men of Missouri (1941)
Body Disappears, The (1941)
Law of the Tropics (1941)
Three Sons O' Guns (1941)
You're in the Army Now (1941)
Club Havana (1945)
This Is Cinerama (1952)

JACKSON, J. J.
Badge 373 (1973)

JACOBS, PIM
Glass (1958)

JACOBSON, JULIUS
Hello, Baby (1976)

JACQUES, PETER
Sudden Loneliness of Konrad Steiner, The (1976)

JAIDEV
Going (1979)

JAMES, TERRY
Echoes of a Summer (1976)

JAMIL, SOULEIMAN
Wedding of Zein, The (1978)

JAN, DEVERA
Red Seedlings (1979)

JANJARASKUL, MAITRE
Tiger's Way, The (1977)

JANKANNA, JONRAK
Key to Love, The (1978)

JANKOWSKI, HORST
Oh, Jonathan, Oh, Jonathan (1973)

JANNACCI, ENZO
Come Home and Meet My Wife (1974)
Seven Beauties (1976)
Stormtroopers (1977)
Saxophone (1978)

JANSEN, PIERRE
Birches, Les (1968)
Cry of the Heart (1974)
Innocents with Dirty Hands, The (1975)
Golden Nights (1976)
Alice, or the Last Escapade (1977)
Lacemaker, The (1977)

JANSON, ALFRED
Softening of the Egg, The (1975)

JANSSEN, WERNER
Ruthless (1948)

JARA, VICTOR
Companero (1975)

JARCZYK, HERBERT
Curse of the Green Eyes, The (1965)

JARRE, MAURICE
Red Sun (1971)
Ash Wednesday (1973)
Mackintosh Man, The (1973)
Island at the Top of the World (1974)
Life Size (1974)
Man Who Would Be King, The (1975)
Mandingo (1975)
Mr. Sycamore (1975)
Posse (1975)
Last Tycoon, The (1976)
Message, The (1976)
Shout at the Devil (1976)
Crossed Swords (1977)
March or Die (1977)
Mohammad, the Messenger of God (1977)
Two Solitudes (1978)
American Success Company, The (1979)
Magician of Lublin, The (1979)
Winter Kills (1979)

JARRETT, KEITH
My Heart Is Red (1977)
Sorcerer (1977)
Eighth Day, The (1979)

JASON, STEVE
Dirty Western, A (1975)

JASPAR, BOBBY
Femme Image, La (1960)

JAUBERT, MAURICE
Story of Adele H., The (1975)
Spending Money (1976)
Man Who Loved Women, The (1977)
Small Change (1977)
Green Room, The (1978)

JENEY, ZOLTAN
Sons of Fire (1975)

JENNINGS, WAYLON
Mackintosh & T. J. (1975)

JENSEN, LARS
Skipper and Co. (1974)

JENSEN, MERRILL B.
Take Down (1979)

JENSEN, PAUL
Blood Relatives (1978)

JENSEN, PIERRE
Savage State, The (1978)

JESSUA, ALAIN
Traitement de Choc (1972)

JEWEL, WARD
Cracking Up (1977)

JILALA, JIL
Hole in the Wall, A (1978)

JO, JUNG SOUNG
Just the Beginning (1977)

JOBIM, ANTONIO CARLOS
Black Orpheus (Orfeo Negro) (1959)
Murdered House, The (1974)
Sagarana Duel, The (1974)
Otalia de Bahia (1976)

JOCAFI
Otalia da Bahia (1977)

JOCSON, MAX
Rites of May, The (1979)

JODOROWSKY, ALEJANDRO
Topo, El (1971)
Holy Mountain, The (1973)

JOHNSON, J. J.
Man and Boy (1971)
Top of the Heap (1972)
Across 110th St. (1973)
Cleopatra Jones (1973)
Willie Dynamite (1973)

JOHNSON, LAURIE
Captain Kronos: Vampire

Hunter (1972)
Belstone Fox, The (1973)
Hedda (1975)
Maids, The (1975)
It Shouldn't Happen to a Vet (1976)
It's Alive II (It Lives Again) (1978)

JOHNSON, ROSAMOND
Emperor Jones, The (1933)

JOHNSTON, ALAN
Scobie Malone (1975)

JONES, KEN
Indiscreet (1958)
Room 43 (1958)
tom thumb (1958)
Green Helmet, The (1961)
Two-Way Stretch (1961)
Nearly a Nasty Accident (1962)
Operation Snatch (1962)
Tarzan Goes to India (1962)
Horror Hotel (1963)
Dr. Crippen (1964)
Battle Beneath the Earth (1968)

JONES, KENNETH V.
How to Murder a Rich Uncle (1957)
High Flight (1958)
Horse's Mouth, The (1958)
Intent to Kill (1958)
Task Force (No Time to Die) (1958)
Bandit of Zhobe, The (1959)
Ten Seconds to Hell (1959)
Jazz Boat (1960)
Oscar Wilde (1960)
Tarzan the Magnificent (1960)
Ferry to Hong Kong (1961)
Cairo (1963)
Psyche '59 (1964)
Maroc 7 (1967)
Projected Man, The (1967)
Who Slew Auntie Roo? (1971)

JONES, QUINCY
Boy in the Tree (1961)
Eggs (1970)
Of Men and Demons (1970)
Honky (1971)
Dig (1972)

JONNY, ALAIN
Tell Him I Love Him (1977)

JOOSON, MAX
Nail of Brightness, The (1975)

JOPLIN, JANIS
Experts, The (1973)

JOPLIN, SCOTT
Scott Joplin (1977)

JORDAN, DUKE
Liaisons Dangereuses, Les (1959)

JOSEPHS, WILFRED
Dark Places (1974)
Swallows and Amazons (1974)
Black Sun (1978)

JOYCE, ROGER
Big Thumbs (1977)

JUERGENS, UDO
Potato Fritz (1976)

JUNG, BOB
Can I Do It ... Til I Need Glasses? (1977)

JURMANN, WALTER
Miracle on Main Street (1940)

JUSIC, DELO
Village Performance of Hamlet, A (1973)

JUSTIS, BILL
Smokey and the Bandit (1977)
Hooper (1978)
Villain, The (1979)

KABILJO, ALFI
Deps (1974)
Anno Domini 1573 (1976)
Flyers of the Open Skies (1977)
Occupation in 26 Pictures (1978)

Journalist (1979)
Slow Motion (1979)

KABUL
New Ones, The (1973)

KACHATURIAN, PHILIP
Gone in 60 Seconds (1974)

KACHIDZE, DJANSUCK
First Step, The (1975)

KAGAN, ALEX
Daughters, Daughters (1973)
Amlash Enchanted Forest, The (1974)

KAHN, SI
Song of the Canary (1979)

KALAIDONIS, LOUKIANOS
New Parthenon, The (1975)
May (1976)
Hunters, The (1977)
Lamore (1979)

KALNYNSH, IMANT
Sonata over the Lake (1977)

KALODERA, NIKICA
Captain Mikula, The Kid (1974)

KAMEN, MICHAEL
Next Man, The (1976)
Ben and Benedict (1977)
Stunts (1977)

KANAKIS, NICOS
Cell Zero, The (1975)

KANCHELI, GIYA
Oddballs, The (1974)

KANE, ARTIE
Bat People, The (1974)
Looking for Mr. Goodbar (1977)
Eyes of Laura Mars, The (1978)

KANTE, DAOUDA
Babatu (1976)

KANTOR, IGO
Cherry, Harry and Raquel (1969)

KANTY-PAWLUSKIEWICZ, JAN
Top Dog (1978)

KAPER, BRONISLAU
Day at the Races, A (1937)
Captain Is a Lady, The (1940)
Dulcy (1940)
Barnacle Bill (1941)
Blonde Inspiration (1941)
Dr. Kildare's Wedding Day (1941)
H. M. Pulham, Esq. (1941)
I'll Wait for You (1941)
Rage in Heaven (1941)
Affairs of Martha, The (1942)
Johnny Eager (1942)
Somebody Up There Likes Me (1956)

KAPLAN, ELLIOT
Food of the Gods, The (1976)

KAPLAN, SOL
Hollow Triumph (1948)
Mister 880 (1950)
Diplomatic Courier (1952)
Kangaroo (1952)
Red Skies of Montana (1952)
Return of the Texan (1952)
Lies My Father Told Me (1975)
Over the Edge (1979)

KAPROFF, DANA
Empire of the Ants (1977)
When a Stranger Calls (1979)

KARADIMCHEV, BORIS
Peasant on a Bicycle (1975)
Don't Go Away! (1976)
Matriarchy (1978)
Ray of Sunlight, A (1979)

KARAENDROU, ELENI
Polemonta (1975)
Sunday Chronicle (1975)
Wandering (1979)

KARAKLAJIC, DJORDJE
Do You Know Pavla Plesa? (1976)

KARANTH, B. V.
Man with the Axe (1979)

KARAVAITCHOUK, OLEG
Monolog (1973)
Strange Letters (1977)
Takeoff, The (1979)

KARGER, FRED
Chatter-Box (1977)

KARLIN, FRED
Westworld (1973)
Chosen Survivors (1974)
Gravy Train, The (1974)
Mixed Company (1974)
Spikes Gang, The (1974)
Baby Blue Marine (1976)
Futureworld (1976)
Joe Panther (1976)
Leadbelly (1976)
Greased Lightning (1977)
Mean Dog Blues (1978)
California Dreaming (1979)

KARNCHANAPALIN, SAMARN
Scar, The (1978)

KARP, MICHAEL
Violation of Claudia, The (1977)

KATELANOS, THEODORE
Corpus (1979)

KATSOULIS, VAGUELIS
Corpus (1979)

KATZ, FRED
Sweet Smell of Success, The (1957)
Wasp Woman, The (1959)
Ski Troop Attack (1960)

KAUER, GENE
Across the Great Divide (1976)
Adventures of a Wilderness Family, The (1976)
Further Adventures of the Wilderness Family--Part 2 (1978)

KAUN, BERNHARD
Frankenstein (1931)
Farewell to Arms, A (1932)
I Am a Fugitive from a Chain Gang (1932)
20, 000 Years in Sing Sing (1933)
Death Takes a Holiday (1934)
Story of Louis Pasteur, The (1935)
Special Delivery (1955)

KAY, ARTHUR
Fighting Marines, The (1935)
One Frightened Night (1935)
Phantom Empire (1935)
Darkest Africa (1936)
House of a Thousand Candles, The (1936)
Undersea Kingdom, The (1936)

KAYE, NORMAN
Illuminations (1976)
Inside Looking Out (1977)

KAYLAN, HOWARD
Cheap (1974)

KAZANECKI, WALDEMAR
Nights and Days (1975)

KEATING, JOHN
Innocent Bystanders (1973)

KEISSLING, HEINZ
Main Thing Holiday (1972)
Your Child, the Unknown Creature (1970)
Your Husband, the Unknown Creature (1970)

KELLAWAY, ROGER
Legacy (1975)
Mafu Cage, The (1978)
Dark, The (1979)

KENSEN, LARS
Skipper and Co. (1974)

KERN, JEROME
Gloria's Romance (1916)

KERR, C. HERBERT
Green Swamp, The (1916)

KETTING, OTTO
Ape and Superape (1973)
When the Poppies Bloom Again (1976)

KEYES, BURT
Hugo the Hippo (1976)

KHACHATURIAN, KAREN
Strange People (1976)

KI, CHAN FUNG
One-Armed Boxer vs. the Flying Guillotine (1975)

KIBAR, MELIK
Family Honor, The (1977)
Dunce Class on Vacation, The (1978)

KIESSLING, HEINZ
Main Thing Holiday (1972)

KIKUCHI, SHUNSUKE
Goke, Body Snatcher from Hell (1968)

KILAR, WOJIECH
Vampire (Upior) (1968)
Wicket Gate, The (1974)
Land of Promise (1975)
Quarterly Balance-Taking (1975)
Camouflage (1977)
Leper (1977)
Spiral (1978)
David (1979)

KILENYI, EDWARD
Grass (1925)
Abie's Irish Rose (1928)
Headin' East (1937)
Adventures of Chico (1938)
Two-Gun Justice (1938)
Ravaged Earth (1942)

KING, BRIAN
Alison's Birthday (1979)

KING, DENIS
Sweeney (1977)

KINSEY, TONY
Colour (1975)

KIRCHIN, BASIL
Mutation, The (1974)

KITIPARAPORN, LEK
Great Escape from Dien Pien Phu, The (1977)

KLEIN, BARBAUD BROWN
Gloria Mundi (1975)

KLEIN, MANUEL
America (1914)
Dan (1914)
In Mizzoura (1914)
Jungle, The (1914)
Paid in Full (1914)
Pierre of the Plains (1914)
Soldiers of Fortune (1914)

KNIEPER, JURGEN
Scarlet Letter, The (1973)
Wrong Movement (1975)
By Hook or By Crook (1976)
Dear Fatherland, Be at Peace (1976)
American Friend, The (1977)
Petty Thieves (1977)
Cold Homeland (1978)

KNITTEL, KRZYSZTOF
Camera Buff (Amator) (1979)

KOBAYASHI, ASEI
House (1977)
Kindaich Kosue no Boken (1979)

KOBNER, ANDREAS
1 + 1 = 3 (1979)

KOERING, RENE
Traitement de Choc (1972)
Dogs, The (1979)

KOLBERG, KARL
Seed, The (1974)

KOMEDA, KRYZSTOF
Glass Mountain, The (1960)
Innocent Sorcerers (1960)
See You Tomorrow (1960)
Fat and the Lean, The (1961)
Ambulance (1962)
Mammals (1962)
Opening Tomorrow (1962)
Epilogue (1963)
New Clothes (1963)
Cats (Kattorna) (1964)
Penguin, The (1965)
Barrier (1966)
Depart, Le (1966)
Hunger (1966)
People Meet and Sweet Music Fills the Air (1967)

KOMORI, AKIHIRO
First Star, The (1977)

KOMROFF, N.
Fighting Dan McCool (1912)

KONG, NG TAI
Legend of the Mountain (1979)
Raining in the Mountain (1979)

KONICEK, STEPAN
If I Had a Girl (1976)

KONICEZNY, ZIGMUNT
Nightmares (1979)

KONTE, LAMIN
Porter, The (1978)
Baara (1979)

KOO, JOSEPH
Extras, The (1978)
Affairs (1979)
Servants, The (1979)

KOOPMAN, PIM
Doctor Vlimmen (1978)

KOPISTO, MARKKU
Year of the Hare, The (1979)

KOPP, RUDOLPH
Here Is My Heart (1934)
Murder at the Vanities (1934)
All the King's Horses (1935)

KOPPEL, ANDERS
Evening Land (1977)

KOPPEN, THOMAS
19 Red Roses (1974)

KORINEK, MIROSLAV
Game of the Apple (1977)

KORNGOLD, ERICH WOLFGANG
Give Us This Night (1936)
Sea Hawk, The (1940)
Kings Row (1941)

KORZYNSKI, ANDRZEJ
Salvation (1973)
Take It Easy (1974)
Doctor Judym (1976)
Man of Marble (1977)
Joerg Ratgeb, Painter (1978)

KOSHA, SH.
Difficult Transport, A (1979)

KOSMA, JOSEPH
Katia (n. d.)

KOSTAL, IRWIN
Blue Bird, The (1976)

KOSTIC, VOJISLAV
Time of the Vampires, The (1970)
Tiger, The (1978)
Pals, The (1979)

KOUNAVUHDI, KNIT
Mountain Man, The (1979)

KOUROUPOS, GEORGE
Corpus (1979)

KOVAC, KORNELIJE
Testament (1975)
Foolish Years (1978)
Round Trip (1978)
Tit for Tat (1978)

KOVAC, ROLAND
Jonathan (1970)

KOVACS, GYORGY
Adoption, The (1975)
Nine Months (1977)
Two of Them, The (1977)

KRAFT, WILLIAM
Psychic Killer (1975)
Avalanche (1978)

KRAJKA, AGIM
Lady from the Town, The (1979)

KRAL, IVAN
Foreigner, The (1978)

KRAUS, VLADIMIR
Passion According to Matthew (1975)

KRAUSE, BERNARD
Last Days of Man on Earth, The (1975)

KRAUSHAAR, RAOUL
Wild Weed (1949)
Elephant Stempede (1951)
Oklahoma Justice (1951)
Fargo (1952)
Billy the Kid vs. Dracula (1965)
Dirty O'Neill (1974)
Six-Pack Annie (1975)

KREIDER, NOBLE
Samson (1914)

KRENNIKOV, TIKON
Ruslan and Ludmila (1974)

KREUDER, PETER
Mademoiselle Mosquito (1956)

KROPFL, FRANCISCO
Quebracho (1974)

KRYLATOV, EUGENI
I Am Looking for My Own (1973)
Little Mermaid, The (1976)
Key That Should Not Be Handed On, The (1977)

KUBIK, GAIL
Colleges at War (1942)
Dover (1942)
Manpower (1942)
Earthquakers (1943)
Air Pattern--Pacific (1944)
Miner's Daughter, The (1950)

KUHN, JOACHIM
Conquistadores, Les (1975)

KUIPERS, JOHN
Something's Rotten (1979)

KUKHIANIDZE, V.
Pirosmani (1974)

KULHAGEN, MILFORD
Newcomers, The (1973)

KUNIYOSHI, RYOICHI
Puppets Under Starry Skies (1978)

KURI, SHITEI
Wanderers, The (1973)

KUWABARA, NORIO
Absolutely, Tomorrow (Ashita Koso) (1968)
Time of Blue, The (1975)

KVERNADZE, BIDSINA
Miracle Tree, The (1978)

KWON, CHOI CHANG
Old House, The (1977)

KYURKCHIYSKI, KASSIMIR
Tree Without Roots, A (1974)

LA ROUX, MAURICE
Immoral Tales (1974)

LA SALLE, RICHARD
Doctor Death: Seeker of Souls (1973)

Alice Doesn't Live Here Anymore (1974)
Ken Murray Shooting Stars (1979)

LA VALLE, PAUL
Deadly Fathoms (1973)

LAB, PRAMUAL
Great Saturday, The (1976)

LABAD, LUTGARDO
You Are Weighed but Found Lacking (1974)

LACKEY, DOUGLAS
Across the Great Divide (1976)
Adventures of a Wilderness Family, The (1976)
Further Adventures of the Wilderness Family--Part 2 (1978)

LADIPE, DURO
Fight for Freedom (1979)

LADMIRAULT, PAUL
Briere, La (1924)

LAFFER, LUIS T.
Juan Vicente Gomez and His Era (1975)

LAI, FRANCIS
Tender Moment, The (1968)
13 Days in France (1968)
Du Soleil Plein les Yeux (1970)
Madly (1970)
Course du Lievre a Travers les Champs, La (1972)
Take Care, France (1972)
Tom Thumb (Petit Poucet, Le) (1972)
Free Man, A (1973)
Happy New Year (1973)
Money! Money! Money! (1973)
Amore de Pluie, Un (1974)
Legend of Frenchie King, The (1974)
Lifetime, A (1974)
Rainy Love, A (1974)
Visit to a Chief's Son (1974)
With the Blood of Others (1974)
And Now My Love (1975)
Baby Sitter, The (1975)
Cat and Mouse (1975)
Marriage (1975)
Body of My Enemy, The (1976)
Emmanuelle II--Joys of a Woman (1976)
Good Guys and the Bad Guys, The (1976)
If I Were to Do It All Over Again (1976)
Anima Persa (1977)
Another Man, Another Chance (1977)
Bilitis (1977)
Widow's Nest (1977)
International Velvet (1978)
Oliver's Story (1978)
Passion Flower Hotel (1978)
Robert and Robert (1978)
Small Timers, The (1978)
Us Two (1979)

LAI, JOSEPH and MICHAEL
Jumping Ash (1976)

LAKE, OLIVER
Jazzoo (1968)

LALO, ALEKSANDER
Last Winter, The (1978)

LAM, DOMING
China Behind (1974)

LAM, VIOLET
Secret, The (1979)

LAMBERT, DENNIS
Tunnelvision (1976)

LAMBRO, PHILIP
Live a Little, Steal a Lot (1974)

LAMPREUN, TITSOH
Rural Teacher, The (1978)

LANCHBERY, JOHN
Turning Point, The (1977)

LANGE, ARTHUR
Banjo on My Knee (1936)
Girl's Dormitory (1936)
Great Ziegfeld, The (1936)
Magnificent Brute, The (1936)
Under Your Spell (1936)
White Fang (1936)
Lancer Spy (1937)
Love Under Fire (1937)
This Is My Affair (1937)
Gateway (1938)
We're Going to Be Rich (1938)
Married and in Love (1940)
Dixie Dugan (1943)
Quiet Please, Murder (1943)
Japanese War Bride (1952)
Pride of St. Louis, The (1952)

LANGE, JOHNNY
Spooks Run Wild (1941)

LANGEHORNE, BRUCE
Outlaw Blues (1971)
Idaho Transfer (1973)
Fighting Mad (1976)
Stay Hungry (1976)

LANGFORD, GEORGES
Ti-Cul Tougas (1977)

LANOE, HENRI
Good Life, The (1964)

LAPORTA, CARLOS
Let's Go, Barbara (1978)

LAR, ROBERTO
Free for All (1976)

LARA, CATHERINE
Dr. Francoise Gailland (1975)

LARO, KUJTIM
At the Beginning of Summer (1979)
Paths of War (1979)
Red Poppies on the Wall (1979)

LAROCHELLE, DENIS
There Is No Forgetting (1976)

LASZLO, ALEXANDER
Attack of the Giant Leeches (1959)

LAUBER, KEN
Hearts of the West (1975)
Wanda Nevada (1979)
Head over Heels (1979)

LAURENCE, STEPHEN
Bang the Drum Slowly (1973)
Hurry Up, or I'll Be 30 (1973)
Communion (1977)

LAVA, WILLIAM
Hawk of the Wilderness (1938)
Red River Range (1938)
Santa Fe Stampede (1938)
Cowboys from Texas (1939)
Daredevils of the Red Circle (1939)
Dick Tracy's G-Men (1939)
Kansas Terrors, The (1939)
Lone Ranger Rides Again, The (1939)
New Frontier, The (1939)
Night Riders, The (1939)
Three Texas Steers (1939)
Wyoming Outlaw (1939)
Zorro's Fighting Legion (1939)
Courageous Dr. Christian (1940)
Invisible Man's Revenge, The (1944)
House of Dracula (1945)
Dracula vs. Frankenstein (1971)

LAVAGNE, ED.
Femme et le Pantin, La (1929)

LAVAGNINO, FRANCESCO
Commando (1963)
Castle of the Living Dead, The (1964)
Chimes at Midnight (Falstaff) (1967)
Regent's Wife, The (1975)
Filming "Othello" (1978)

LAVISTA, MARIO
Paper Flowers (1978)

LAVISTA, RAUL
Little Red Riding Hood and Tom Thumb vs. the Monsters (1960)
Saint vs. the Vampire Women, The (1962)
Mushroom Eater, The (1976)
Paper Flowers (1978)
Run for the Roses (1978)
Broken Flag (1979)

LAWRENCE, ELLIOTT
Network (1976)

LAWRENCE, STEPHEN
Bang the Drum Slowly (1973)

LE BORNE, FERNAND
Empreinte, L' (1908)

LE FORESTIER, MAXIME
Empty Chair, The (1974)
Budding Love (1977)

LEA, JIMMY
Flame (1975)

LECAS, DEMETRIS
Corpus (1979)

LEDENOV, ROMAN
Wings (1978)

LEDRUT, JEAN
Young Rebel--Cervantes, The (1967)

LEE, GERALD
Black Shampoo (1976)

LEE, ROBERT
Warrior Within, The (1977)

LEES, CAROL
Last Word, The (1979)

LEFEBVRE, MARCEL
There's Always a Way to Find a Way (1973)

LEFEVRE, RAYMOND
Gendarme and the Creatures from Outer Space, The (1979)

LEGRAND, MICHEL
Portes Claquent, Les (1960)
Eva (1965)
Picasso Summer (1969)
Lady in a Car with Glasses and a Gun (1970)
Peau d'Ane (1970)
Time for Loving, A (1971)
Everybody He Is Nice ... Everybody He Is Beautiful (1972)
Breezy (1973)
Cops and Robbers (1973)
Doll's House, A (1973)
40 Carats (1973)
Impossible Object (1973)
Man Is Dead, A (1973)
Most Important Event Since Man First Set Foot on the Moon, The (1973)
Nelson Affair, The (1973)
Question Mark (1973)
Our Time (1974)
Three Musketeers, The (1974)
Savage, The (1975)
Sheila Levine Is Dead and Living in New York (1975)
Voyage de Noces, Le (1975)
Gable and Lombard (1976)
Honeymoon Trip, The (1976)
Ode to Billy Joe (1976)
One Can Say It Without Getting Angry (1977)
Other Side of Midnight, The (1977)
Roads of the South, The (1978)
Fabulous Adventures of the Legendary Baron Munchausen, The (1979)
Lady Oscar (1979)

LEGRAND, RAYMOND
Sadist with Red Teeth, The (1971)

LEIGH, MITCH
Once in Paris (1978)

LEIPOLD, JOHN
Scarlet Empress, The (1934)
I Met Him in Paris (1937)
Geronimo (1939)
Stagecoach (1939)
Fargo Kid, The (1940)
Knights of the Range (1940)
Quarterback, The (1940)
Sante Fe Marshall (1940)
Showdown, The (1940)
Stagecoach War (1940)
Border Vigilantes (1941)
In Old Colorado (1941)
Pirates on Horseback (1941)
Riders of the Timberline (1941)
Secrets of the Wasteland (1941)
Twilight on the Trail (1941)
Wide Open Town (1941)
Blondie for Victory (1942)
Heat's On, The (1943)
My Kingdom for a Cook (1943)
What a Woman (1943)
Big Wheel, The (1949)
Massacre River (1949)

LEONARD, MICHAEL
Billion Dollar Hobo (1978)
They Went That-a-Way and That-a-Way (1978)

LEONETTI, TONY
Massacre at Central High (1976)

LEONTIS, CHRISTOS
Trial of the Judges, The (1974)

LEROUX, ALAIN
Shades of Silk (1979)

LEVANT, OSCAR
Crime Without Passion (1934)
Nothing Sacred (1937)
Made for Each Other (1939)

LEVI, SHEM-TOV
Little Man (1978)

LEVY, LOU
Outside Chance (1978)

LEVY, SOL P.
Right to Happiness, The (1919)
Barrier, The (1926)

LEWINTER, MARTIN
Joy (1977)

LEWIS, BERNIE KAAI
Cat Murkil and the Silks (1976)

LEWIS, JIMMY
Solomon King (1974)

LEWIS, MICHAEL J.
Baxter! (1973)
Theater of Blood (1973)
11 Harrowhouse (1974)
Brutalization of Franz Blum, The (1975)
92 in the Shade (1975)
Russian Roulette (1975)
Stick-Up, The (1978)
Legacy, The (1979)
Passage, The (1979)

LEWIS, MORGAN
Helen Keller in Her Story (1956)

LEWISTON, DENIS
Triple Echo, The (1973)

LEYES, POCHO
Juan Moreira (1973)
Great Adventure, The (1974)
Kid Head (1975)
Super Super Adventure, The (1975)

LIANG, CHOW FU
Bruce Lee--True Story (1976)

LIEBMAN, JOSEPH
Rooftops of New York (1960)
I Could Never Have Sex with Any Man Who Has So Little Regard for My Husband (1973)

LIGETI, GYORGY
Winterspelt (1978)

LIN, WU MEG
I Sing I Cry (1979)

LINDELL, JAN
Mackan (1978)

LINDENBERG, UDO
North Sea Is Dead Sea (1976)

LINDH, BJOERN JASON
Simple Melody, A (1974)
Lion and the Virgin, The (1975)
Man on the Roof, The (1976)
Dante, Mind the Shark (1978)

LINDSEY, MORT
Real Life (1979)

LIPSHITZ, MARCOS
Celestina (1976)

LISKA, ZDENEK
Days of Betrayal (1974)
Pavlinka (1974)
Who Leaves in the Rain (1976)
Little Mermaid, The (1977)
Smoke on the Potato Fields (1977)
Shadows of a Hot Summer (1978)

LISTON, MELBA
Smile Orange (1976)

LIVANELI, C. ZULFU
Mine, The (1978)

LLOYD, CHARLES
Almost Summer (1978)

LLOYD, MICHAEL
Pom Pom Girls, The (1976)

LOBINGER, CHRIS
Desperate Living (1977)

LOBO, EDU
Heavy Trouble (1977)

LOCKYER, MALCOLM
Dr. Who and the Daleks (1965)
Wolf and the Dove, The (1974)

LOENHARDSBERGER, HEINZ
Willie and the Chinese Cat (1977)

LOGAN, RICHARD and GARY
Human Factor, The (1979)

LOGARIDES, STAVROS
Murderess, The (1974)

LOOSE, WILLIAM
Vixen (1968)
Cherry, Harry and Raquel (1969)
Erotic Adventures of Zorro, The (1972)
Sweet Suzy (1973)
Wonder of It All (1973)
Up (1976)

LORENTZEN, BEN
Inside the Great Pyramid (1974)

LOUIGUY
Verdict (1974)

LOUSSIER, JACQUES
Doulos, Le (1962)
Jeu 1 (1962)
Voyage of Khonostrov, The (1962)
A ... Is for Apple (1963)
Bird Life in Mauritania (1963)
Department 66 (1963)
Etudes (1963)
Paris des Mannequins, Le (1963)
Refuges (1963)
Sud-Express (1973)
West (1963)
Anges Gardiens (1964)
Paris des Scandinaves, Le (1964)
Au Guadalquivir (1965)
Avatar Botanique de Melle Flora, L' (1965)
Journal of Combat, The (1965)

Life of the Locusts (1965)
A Belles Dents (1966)
Second Truth, The (1966)
Mercenaries, The (1967)
Tu Seras Terriblement Gentille (1967)
Beau Militaire, Le (1968)
Killing Game, The (Comic Strip Hero) (1968)
Woman Needs Loving, A (1968)
Dossier Prostitution (1969)
You Only Love Once (1969)
Diamant, Le (1970)
Snow Job (1971)

LOW, BEN
One Man (1977)

LOWDWICK, PETER
Anguish (1970)

LOWE, MUNDELL
Sidewinder 1 (1977)

LUCARELLI, BERT
Very Natural Thing, A (1974)

LUCKY, STEPAN
Jacub (1977)

LUIGI
Root, The (1975)

LUND, MARTIN
Doubles (1978)

LUNDELL, ULF
Jack (1977)

LUNDERSKOV, LASSE
Leave Us Alone (1975)

LUNDSTEN, RALPH
Elvis! Elvis! (1977)

LUNDUP, DAVID
Call Him Mr. Shatter (1976)

LUTER, CLAUDE
Actualities Prehistoriques (1947)
Actualities Romaines (1947)
Actualities Gauloises (1952)
Antipolis (1952)
Jour en Suede, Un (1952)
Life Goes On (1952)
Route de Suede, La (1952)
Fantasie au Vieux-Colombier (1953)
Saint-Germaine-des-Pres (1953)
Antoine and Sebastien (1973)
Isabelle Devant le Desir (1975)

LUTYENS, ELIZABETH
Blood Fiends (1966)

LUZ, ERNST
Hearts Aflame (1922)
Peg O' My Heart (1922)
Prisoner of Zenda, The (1922)
Quincy Adams Sawyer (1922)
Toll of the Sea (1922)
Trifling Women (1922)
Where the Pavement Ends (1923)
Temptress, The (1926)

MACALE, JARDS
Amulet of Ogum, The (1975)

MACAULAY, TONY
It's Not the Size That Counts (1974)

McCAULEY, MATTHEW
Sudden Fury (1975)
City on Fire (1979)

McCAULEY, WILLIAM
Neptune Factor, The (1973)
It Seemed Like a Good Idea at the Time (1975)
City on Fire (1979)

McCLUSKEY, BUDDY
Routine Has to Be Broken (1974)
Husbands Vacationing (1975)
My Fiance, The Transvestite (1975)
America's Fat (1976)

McCURDY, STEPHEN
Middle Age Spread (1979)

MACCHI, EGISTO
Assassination of Metteotti, The (1973)
Mr. Klein (1976)
Antonio Gramsci--The Days of Prison (1977)
Padre Padrone (1977)
Voyage into the Whirlpool Has Begun, The (1977)

MacDERMONT, GALT
Rhinoceros (1974)

MACERO, TEO
Skyscraper (1959)
Friday the 13th ... The Orphan (1979)

McGINNIS, DON
Young and the Restless, The (1973)

McGREGOR, CHRIS
Kongi's Harvest (1970)

McINTIRE, TIM
Kid Blue (1973)
Boy and His Dog, A (1975)
Killer Inside Me, The (1976)

McINTOSH, TOM
Slither (1973)
Hero Ain't Nothin' but a Sandwich, A (1977)

McKECHNIE, DOUG
Song of the Canary (1979)

McKUEN, ROD
Borrowers, The (1973)
Emily (1976)

McLAUCHLAN, MURRAY
Partners (1976)

McLEY, DAVID
Breaking Point (1976)

McMULLIN, ROBERT
Shadow of the Hawk (1976)

McPEEK, BEN
Only God Knows (1974)

MAGNE, MICHEL
Par un Beau Matin d'Ete (1964)
Don Juan (1973)
Moi y'En a Vouloir des Sous (1973)
Plot, The (1973)

MAHADEVAN, K. V.
Sita's Wedding (1978)

MAHAL, TAJ
Part 2, Sounder (1976)
Brothers (1977)

MAININ, THAWEEPONG
Love Is Blue (1977)

MAJEWSKI, HANS-MARTIN
Visit, The (1964)
Lost Life, A (1976)
Battleflag (1977)
Elixirs of the Devil, The (1977)
Pentecost Outing, The (1979)

MAKAR, MARTIJAN
Last Mission of Demolitions Man Cloud, The (1978)

MAKSYMIUCK, JERZY
Hour-Glass Sanatorium, The (1973)
Criminal Records (1974)
Wherever You Are, Mr. President (1979)

MALASEK, JIRI
My Brother Has a Cute Brother (1975)

MALECKI, MACIEJ
Before the Day Breaks (1977)

MALKEN, JACK
Taking of Christina, The (1976)

MALOTTE, ALBERT HAY
Hi, Gaucho (1935)

Dr. Cyclops (1940)
Enchanted Forest, The (1944)

MALVICINO, HORACIO
In the Driver's Seat (1973)

MAMANGAKIS, NICOS
Bomber and Paganini (1977)
Maiden's War, The (1977)
Zero Hour (1977)
Tailor from Ulm, The (1979)

MAMIYA, YOSHIO
Ruma Is Going (1968)

MANABE, RUCHIRO
Lake of Dracula (1971)

MANCINI, HENRY
Creature from the Black Lagoon, The (1954)
Four Guns to the Border (1954)
Private War of Major Benson, The (1955)
This Island Earth (1955)
Hawaiians, The (1970)
Oklahoma Crude (1973)
Thief Who Came to Dinner, The (1973)
Visions of Eight (1973)
Girl from Petrovka, The (1974)
99 and 44/100% Dead (1974)
White Dawn, The (1974)
Great Waldo Pepper, The (1975)
Once Is Not Enough (1975)
Return of the Pink Panther, The (1975)
Alex and the Gypsy (1976)
Pink Panther Strikes Again, The (1976)
Silver Streak (1976)
W. C. Fields and Me (1976)
House Calls (1978)
Revenge of the Pink Panther, The (1978)
Who Is Killing the Great Chefs of Europe? (1978)
Nightwing (1979)
Prisoner of Zenda, The (1979)
10 (1979)

MANCUSO
Stranger's Gundown, The (1974)

MANDEL, JOHNNY
Lawbreakers, The (1960)
Last Detail, The (1973)
Summer Wishes, Winter Dreams (1973)
W (1974)
Escape to Witch Mountain (1975)
Freaky Friday (1976)
Sailor Who Fell from Grace with the Sea, The (1976)
Agatha (1979)
Being There (1979)

MANDEL, TOMMY
Deadly Hero (1976)

MANFREDINI, HARRY
Here Come the Tigers (1978)
Kirlian Witness, The (1978)
Night Flowers (1979)

MANGIONE, CHUCK
Children of Sanchez, The (1978)

MANNE, SHELLY
T-Bird Gang, The (1958)
Young Sinner, The (1962)
Trial of the Catonsville Nine, The (1972)
Trader Horn (1973)

MANNINO, FRANCO
Vampiri, I (1956)
Love in Four Dimensions (1965)
Driver's Seat, The (1974)
Conversation Piece (1975)
Innocent, The (1976)
Intruder, The (1976)
Simple Heart, A (1978)

MANSFIELD, KEN
Van Nuys Blvd. (1979)

MANSFIELD, SCOTT
Sometime Sweet Susan (1974)

MANUEL, VICTOR
And They Lived Happily Ever After (1976)
Trout (1978)

MANZANERO, ARMANDO
Interval (1973)

MANZIE, JIM
F. J. Holden, The (1977)

MAO-SHAN, WONG
Tiger and Crane Fists (1976)

MAR, DEL
delete

MAR-HAIM, JOSEF
81st Flow, The (1975)

MARAWOOD, CHARLES
Irishman, The (1978)
Weekend of Shadows (1978)

MARCHETTI, GIANNI
Sun on the Skin (1972)

MARES, KAREL
Lovers in the Year I (1974)
One Silver Piece (1976)

MARIANO, DETTO
Ratataplan (1979)

MARINI, GIOVANNA
If Pigs Had Wings (1977)
I Belong to Me (1978)

MARINUZZI, GINO
Matchless (1966)

MARKOPOULOS, IANNIS
Dream of Passion, A (1978)

MARKOVIC, MALOVAJ
Beloved Love (1977)
Written-Off Return, The (1977)

MARKOWITZ, RICHARD
Boss' Son, The (1978)

MARKS, SELMA
Feelings (1977)

MAROS, RUDOLF
No Man's Daughter (1976)

MARSHALL, MAURICE
Marie-Ann (1978)

MARTEL, PIERRE
House on Bare Mountain (1962)

MARTELL, PHILIP
Lust for a Vampire (1971)
Dracula A. D. 1972 (1972)

MARTIN, GEORGE
Live and Let Die (1973)

MARTIN, LARRY
Ben and Benedict (1977)

MARTIN, PETER J.
Deathcheaters (1976)

MARTYNOV, V.
Defense Takes the Floor, The (1977)

MARX, BILL
Deathmaster, The (Khorda) (1971)
Johnny Vik (1973)
Scream, Blacula, Scream (1973)
Act of Vengeance (1974)

MAS, JEAN-PIERRE
Why Not? (1977)

MASDOOR, KASEM
Strangler's Melody (1979)

MASER, BOB
Joy of Letting Go, The (1976)

MASHUKOV, ALEXEI
Portrait in the Rain (1978)

MASON, BENEDICT
Silent Cry, The (1977)

MASON, FRANK
see DE MASI, FRANCESCO

MASSER, MICHAEL
Mahogany (1975)
Greatest, The (1977)

MATCIC, JANEZ
What Do You Want, Julie? (1977)

MATEOS, JAVIER
Paper Flowers (1978)

MATSUMURA, TEIZO
Rise, Fair Sun (1974)
Preparation for the Festival (1978)

MATTHEWS, DAVID
Fighters, The (1974)
Stony Island (1978)

MATTHUS, SIEGFRIED
Sorrows of Young Werther, The (1976)
I'll Force You to Leave (1978)

MATUSZIEWICZ, JERZY
Hotel Pacific (1975)
Quiet Is the Night (1979)

MATZ, PETER
Prize Fighter, The (1979)

MAXWELL, CHARLES
Cuban Love Song (1931)
Calm Yourself (1935)
David Copperfield (1935)
West Point of the Air (1935)
Winning Ticket, The (1935)
Banjo on My Knee (1936)
Girl's Dormitory (1936)
Great Ziegfeld, The (1936)
Magnificent Brute, The (1936)
Star for a Night (1936)
Under Your Spell (1936)
White Fang (1936)
White Hunter (1936)
Charlie Chan at the Opera (1937)
Lancer Spy (1937)
Love Under Fire (1937)
This Is My Affair (1937)
Gateway (1938)
Kidnapped (1938)
Mysterious Mr. Moto (1938)
Submarine Patrol (1938)
Three Blind Mice (1938)
We're Going to Be Rich (1938)
Frontier Marshal (1939)
Gay Caballero, The (1940)
Romance of the Rio Grande (1941)
Dixie Dugan (1943)
Quiet Please, Murder (1943)
Secrets of Scotland Yard (1944)
In Old Sacramento (1946)

MAY, BILLY
Jay Walker, The (1955)
Front Page, The (1974)

MAY, BRIAN
True Story of Eskimo Nell, The (1975)
Patrick (1978)
Mad Max (1979)
Snap-Shot (1979)
Thirst (1979)

MAYAZUMI, TOSHIRO
Zeami (1974)
Don of Japan--Big Schemes, The (1977)

MAYERS, LYLE
Search for Solutions, The (1979)

MAYFIELD, CURTIS
Claudine (1974)
Let's Do It Again (1975)
Sparkle (1976)
Piece of the Action, The (1977)
Short Eyes (1977)

MAYORAGE, LINCOLN
Blood of Dracula's Castle, The (1967)

MAZZUCA, GIUSEPPE
Goodnight, Ladies and Gentlemen (1977)
Elective Affinities (1978)

MEDEROS, RODOLFO
Growing Up Suddenly (1977)

MEID, LOTHAR
Some Kind of Saint (1979)

MEISEL, EDMUND
Tonende Walle, Die (1928)

MELBINGER, STEFAN
Scrounged Meals (1977)
Strauberg Is Here (1978)

MELLE, GIL
Frankenstein: The True Story (1973)
Savage Is Loose, The (1974)
Ultimate Warrior, The (1975)
Embryo (1976)
Sentinel, The (1977)
Starship Invasions (1977)

MELLO, GUTO GRACA
Beloved Lover (1979)

MELVIN, RODERICK
I'd Like to Have My Troubles (1975)

MENDOZA-NAVA, JAIME
Bootleggers, The (1974)
Tears of Happiness (1974)
Grayeagle (1977)
Town That Dreaded Sundown, The (1977)
Boys in Company C, The (1978)
Norseman, The (1978)
Evictors, The (1979)

MENESCAL, ROBERTO
Xica de Silva (1976)

MENTEN, DALE
Lifeguard (1976)

MENTION, MICHEL
Mad Bomber, The (1973)

MERRICK, MAHLON
Girl from Monterey, The (1943)
Silver Skates (1943)
Deputy Marshal (1949)
Dupont Story, The (1950)
U. C. L. A. Story, The (1950)
One Man's Lifetime (1951)
Red Planet Mars (1952)

MESTRAL, PATRICE
Other People's Money (1978)

METHENY, PAT
Search for Solutions, The (1979)

METIANU, LUCIAN
Long Drive, The (1978)
Special Edition (1978)

MEYER, ABE
Avenger, The (1933)
Flaming Signal, The (1933)
Shriek in the Night, A (1933)
Sphinx, The (1933)
Strange People (1933)
Whispering Shadow, The (1933)
Ghost Walks, The (1934)
Green Eyes (1934)
House of Mystery, The (1934)
Jane Eyre (1934)
Moonstone, The (1934)
Mystery Liner (1934)
Mystery Mountain (1934)
Picture Brides (1934)
Return of Chandu, The (1934)
Star Packer (1934)
Circumstantial Evidence (1935)
Murder on the Campus (1935)
Mysterious Mr. Wong (1935)
Shot in the Dark, A (1935)
Death from a Distance (1936)
I Cover Chinatown (1936)
New Adventures of Tarzan, The (1936)
Mine with the Iron Door, The (1936)
Revolt of the Zombies (1936)
Rogue's Tavern (1936)

MEYER, FRIEDRICH
Kaleidoscope: Valeska Gert, For Fun--For Pleasure (1979)
Tin Drum, The (1979)

MEYERBEER, JACOB
delete

MICALIZZI, FRANCO
Last Snows of Spring, The (1973)
Battle of the Amazons (1973)
Beyond the Door (1974)
Ante Up (1975)
Rome: Armed to the Teeth (1976)

MICHAELS, STEVE
Mama's Dirty Girls (1974)

MICHAJLOV, A.
To Search for a Golden Earth (1975)

MICHELET, MICHEL
M (1951)
Challenge of Greatness, The (1976)

MICHELOT, PIERRE
Parallels (1962)

MIHALITSI, SOPHIA
Metamorphosis (1973)

MIHANOVICH, SERGIO
Sad Young Men, The (1961)
Triangle of Four (1975)

MIKI, MINORU
Corrida of Love (1976)
Far Road, The (1978)

MIKKELSBORG, PALLE
Nothing but the Truth (1975)
Terror (1977)

MILLER, MIKE
Thieves (1977)

MILLMAN, JACK
Black Bunch, The (Jungle Sex) (1972)
Deep Jaws (1976)

MING, CHE
Great Waves Purify the Sand (1978)

MINKUS, LUDWIG
Don Quixote (1973)

MIRALLES, RICARDO
I Want to Be a Woman (1977)

MIRANDA, CARLOS
Hamlet (1976)

MISRAKI, PAUL
Chasseur de Chez Maxim's, Le (1953)
Hand to Cut Off, A (1974)
Bubble, The (1976)
Fire's Share, The (1978)
Such a Lovely Town... (1979)

MITSUEDA, NARIAKI
Family of North Country, The (1973)

MIYAGAWA, HIROSHI
Space Cruiser Yamato (1977)

MIYOSHI, AKIRA
Slope in Spring, The (1971)

MIZELL, FONCE
Hell up in Harlem (1973)

MOCKRIDGE, CYRIL
Adventures of Sherlock Holmes, The (1939)
Hollywood Cavalcade (1939)
Mr. Moto's Last Warning (1939)
Stanley and Livingstone (1939)
Suez (1939)
Dead Men Tell (1941)
On the Sunny Side (1941)
Ride On, Vaquero (1941)
Romance of the Rio Grande (1941)
Dr. Renault's Secret (1942)
Just Off Broadway (1942)
Magnificent Dope, The (1942)

Man Who Wouldn't Die, The (1942)
Manila Calling (1942)
My Gal Sal (1942)
Postman Didn't Ring, The (1942)
Rings on Her Fingers (1942)
Secret Agent of Japan (1942)
Through Different Eyes (1942)
Undying Monster, The (1942)
Whispering Ghosts (1942)
Who Is Hope Schuyler? (1942)
Over My Dead Body (1943)
Tonight We Raid Calais (1943)
Something for the Boys (1944)
Luck of the Irish, The (1948)
Father Was a Fullback (1949)
American Guerilla in the Philippines, An (1950)
Cheaper by the Dozen (1950)
Mother Didn't Tell Me (1950)
Where the Sidewalk Ends (1950)
Belles on Their Toes (1952)
Deadline--U. S. A. (1952)
O. Henry's Full House (1952)
We're Not Married (1952)
How to Marry a Millionaire (1953)
River of No Return (1954)

MOELLER, GUNNAR
Stars and the Water Carrier, The (1974)
Per (1975)

MOFSENSON, JOEL
Blowdry (1976)

MOHAMED, ATIYAH
Road, The (1975)

MOIRANA
Keyhole (1974)

MOLINO, M.
Fight to the Death (1975)

MONETORI, SERGIO
Interior of a Convent (1978)

MONFAREDZEDEH, ESFANDIYAR
Deer, The (1974)

MONK, THELONIUS
Liaisons Dangereuses, Les (1959)

MONN-IVERSEN, EGIE
Bobby's War (1974)

MONTEFIORE, VICTOR
Drake's Love Story (1913)

MONTENEGRO, HUGO
Farmer, The (1977)

MONTSALVAGE, JAVIER
Long Vacation of '36, The (1976)

MOORE, ANTHONY
Phantastic World of Matthew Madson, The (1974)

MOORE, DUDLEY
Hound of the Baskervilles, The (1978)

MOORE, G. T.
People of the Wind (1976)

MOORE, RICHARD
Sensations (1975)

MORALEDA, ALBERTO
Moonlight Serenade (1979)

MORALI, JACQUES
Crazy Horse Paris--France (1977)
I've Got You, You've Got Me by the Hairs of My Chinny Chin Chin (1979)

MORAWECK, LUCIEN
Dreaming Out Loud (1940)
Lady in Question, The (1940)
High Conquest (1947)
Massacre River (1949)

MORAZ, PATRICK
Invitation, The (1973)

MORDORDZH, L.
Discover Turquoise Mountain (1978)

MORELAND, LEONARD
Queen of Blood (1966)

MORENO, MARIANO
Sky High (1974)

MORES, ROGER
Greetings and a Living (1974)
Lost Paradise (1978)

MORGAN, CLAUDE
Male of the Century (1975)

MORIOKA, KEN-ICHIRO
Message from Space (1978)

MORLEY, ANGELA
Watership Down (1978)
Collina dei Comali, La (1979)

MORODER, GIORGIO
Midnight Express (1978)

MOROSS, JEROME
Captive City (1952)
War Lord, The (1965)
Valley of the Gwangi, The (1969)

MOROYOQUI, SANTOS
Marilyn and the Senator (1975)

MORRICONE, ENNIO
Battle of Algiers, The (1956)
Cuccagna, La (1962)
Ore dell'amore, Le (1963)
Successo, Il (1963)
Nightmare Castle (1965)
Matchless (1966)
Pistol for Ringo, A (1966)
Streghe, Le (1966)
Wake Up and Die (1966)
Come Impari ad Amare le Donne (1967)
Navajo Joe (1967)
Rover, The (1967)
And for a Roof, a Sky Full of Stars (1968)
Comandementi per un Gangster (1968)
Dirty Angels, The (1968)
Grand Silenzio, Il (1968)
Absolutely Natural (1969)
Brief Season (1969)
Fraulein Doktor (1969)
Burn! (Queimada) (1970)
Five-Man Army (1970)
Machine Gun McCain (1970)
Three into a Thousand (1970)
Burglars, The (1971)
Califfa, La (1971)
Devil in the Brain (1971)
Encounter (1971)
Esercito di 5 Uomini (1971)
Inputazione di Omicidio per uno Studente (1971)
Oceano (1971)
Anche se Volessi Lavovare, Che Cosa Faccio? (1972)
Cosa Buffa, La (1972)
Deux Saisons de la Vie, Les (1972)
Hearts and Minds (1972)
Questa Specie d'Amore (1972)
Who Saw Her Die? (1972)
Allonsanfan (1973)
For Love One Dies (1973)
Giordano Bruno (1973)
Massacre in Rome (1973)
Monk, The (1973)
My Name Is Nobody (1973)
Property Is No Longer a Theft (1973)
Revolver (1973)
Serpent, The (1973)
This Kind of Love (1973)
Women Buried Alive (1973)
Arabian Nights, The (1974)
Last Days of Mussolini (1974)
Master Touch, The (1974)
Secret, The (1974)
Sonny and Jed (1974)
Tempter, The (1974)
Trio Infernal, Le (1974)
Attenti al Buffone (1975)
Down the Ancient Staircase (1975)
Drama of the Rich (1975)
Eye of the Cat (1975)
Fear on the City (1975)
Grand Bourgeoisie, La (1975)
Human Factor, The (1975)
Leonor (1975)
Libera, My Love (1975)
Murder on the Bridge (1975)

Night Caller, The (1975)
Premonition, The (1975)
Salo or 120 Days of Sodom (1975)
Weak Spot, The (1975)
Blood in the Streets (1976)
Desert of the Tartars, The (1976)
Genius, The (1976)
Inheritance, The (1976)
Moses (1976)
1900 (1976)
Per Amore (1976)
Sunday Woman (1976)
Autostop Sosso Sangue (1977)
Exorcist II: The Heretic (1977)
Holocaust 2000 (1977)
Iron Prefect, The (1977)
Orca, the Killer Whale (1977)
Pedro Paramo (1977)
Rene the Cane (1977)
Truster, The (1977)
Cage aux Folles, La (1978)
Cat, The (1978)
Corleone (Father of the Godfather) (1978)
Days of Heaven (1978)
122 Rue de Provence (1978)
Stay as You Are (1978)
Bloodline (1979)
Chi l'Ha Vista Morire? (1979)
Good News (1979)
Invito allo Sport (1979)
Meadow, The (Prato, Il) (1979)
Ogro (1979)
Sorriso del Grande Tentatore, Il (1979)
Travels with Anita (1979)
Where Are You Going on Your Vacation? (1979)
(see also PIOVANI, NICOLA)

MORRIS, JOHN
Producers, The (1967)
Bank Shot (1974)
Blazing Saddles (1974)
Young Frankenstein (1974)
Adventures of Sherlock Holmes' Smarter Brother, The (1975)
Silent Movie (1976)
High Anxiety (1977)
Last Remake of Beau Geste, The (1977)
World's Greatest Lover, The (1977)
In-Laws, The (1979)

MORRISON, VAN
Slipstream (1974)

MORTON, ARTHUR
Night Life of the Gods (1935)
Princess O'Hara (1935)
Fit for a King (1937)
Pick a Star (1937)
Riding on Air (1937)
Turnabout (1940)
Millie's Daughter (1947)
Rogues of Sherwood Forest (1950)
Never Trust a Gambler (1951)

MOSALINI, JUAN JOSE
Triple Death of the Third Personage, The (1979)

MOSCIE, DAVID
Black Six, The (1974)

MOSEHOLM, ERIK
Dreamers (1967)
Teacher Nansen (1968)

MOSKVITIN, JURIJ
Earth Is Flat, The (1977)

MOSY, PIOTR
Passion (1978)

MOTZING, WILLIAM
Newsfront (1978)
Just Out of Reach (1979)

MOU-SHAN, HUANT
800 Heroes (1976)

MOUGARO, CLAUDE
Order and Security of the World (1978)

MOULIN, MARC
Tarzoon, The Snake of the Jungle (1975)

MOUSTAKI, GEORGES
At the Brink of the Brink of the Bench (1979)

MOW, DON
Office Picnic, The (1974)

MUELLER, BRUNO
Ach wie ist's Moglich Dann (1914)

MUELLER-BLATTAU, GABY
Torch High (1979)

MULIOI, REXHO
Wind and the Oak, The (1979)

MULLIGAN, GERRY
Help! My Snowman's Burning Down (1964)
Last Days of Man on Earth, The (1975)
Threat, The (1977)

"MUNICH FACTORY"
Fifty-Fifty (1978)

MUNROW, DAVID
Race in the Head, A (1974)
Zardoz (1974)

MURPHY, ROBERT
Singer and the Dancer, The (1977)

MURRAY, JACK
Liaisons Dangereuses, Les (1959)

MURRAY, LYN
High Conquest (1947)
Prowler, The (1951)
Return of Gilbert and Sullivan, The (1951)

MUSKER, FRANK
World Is Full of Married Men, The (1979)

MUSY, JEAN
Clair de Femme (1979)

MYERS, STANLEY
Blockhouse, The (1973)
Apprenticeship of Duddy Kravitz, The (1974)
Caravan to Vaccares (1974)
Little Malcolm (1974)
Wilby Conspiracy, The (1975)
Coup de Grace, The (1976)
Class of Miss MacMichael, The (1978)
Deer Hunter, The (1978)
Greek Tycoon, The (1978)
Martian Chronicles, The (1979)
Portrait of the Artist as a Young Man, A (1979)
Yesterday's Hero (1979)

MYROW, FRED
Lolly Madonna XXX (1973)
Reflection of Fear (1973)
Scarecrow (1973)
Soylent Green (1973)
Jim, The World's Greatest (1976)
Kenny and Co. (1976)
Phantasm (1979)

NADOLSKI, HELMUT
Recollections (1978)

NAPOLEONI, MARCEL
Guardian Angel, The (1979)

NARAYAN, RAM
Private Enterprise, A (1975)

NARRONE, CLAUDIA
Loving Cousins (1976)

NASCIMBENE, MARIO
Night of Counting the Years (1970)
Blaise Pascal (1972)
Prima Notte di Quiete, La (1972)
Year One (1974)
Messiah, The (1978)

NASCIMENTO, ARANTES DO
(see DO NASCIMENTO, ARANTES)

NASCIMENTO, MILTON
Fall, The (1978)

NASON, SUSANNA
They Are Their Own Gifts (1979)

NATSCHINSKI, GERT
Heavy Up (1978)

NAZEK, HUSSEIN
Lebanon ... Why? (1978)

NELSON, OLIVER
Istanbul Express (1968)
Inside Job (1973)

NETCHER, ROBIN
My Way (1974)

NEWKIRK, LOREN
Jackson County Jail (1976)

NEWMAN, ALFRED
Devil to Pay, The (1930)
Age for Love, The (1931)
Around the World in 80 Minutes (1931)
Corsair (1931)
Indiscreet (1931)
Tonight or Never (1931)
Unholy Garden, The (1931)
Cock of the Air (1932)
Greeks Had a Word for Them, The (1932)
Rain (1932)
Sky Devils (1932)
Blood Money (1933)
Bowery, The (1933)
I Cover the Waterfront (1933)
Masquerader, The (1933)
Secrets (1933)
Born to Be Bad (1934)
Bulldog Drummond Strikes Back (1934)
Count of Monte Cristo, The (1934)
Kid Millions (1934)
Last Gentleman, The (1934)
Mighty Barnum, The (1934)
Transatlantic Merry-Go-Round (1934)
Clive of India (1935)
Melody Lingers On, The (1936)
Wedding Night, The (1936)
Dead End (1937)
Hurricane (1937)
Prisoner of Zenda, The (1937)
Slave Ship (1937)
Stella Dallas (1937)
Wee Willie Winkie (1937)
Cowboy and the Lady, The (1938)
Vigil in the Night (1939)
Earthbound (1940)
Little Old New York (1940)
Hudson's Bay (1940)
Westerner, The (1940)
Charley's Aunt (1941)
Maryland (1941)
Remember the Day (1941)
Wild Geese Calling (1941)
Yank in the R.A.F., A (1941)
Ball of Fire (1942)
Battle of Midway, The (1942)
Moontide (1942)
Prelude to War (1942)
At the Front in North Africa (1943)
December Seventh (1943)
Call Northside 777 (1948)
That Lady in Ermine (1948)
Walls of Jericho, The (1948)
Yellow Sky (1948)
Everybody Does It (1949)
When Willie Comes Marching Home (1950)
How to Marry a Millionaire (1953)
Bravados, The (1958)
Adventures of Marco Polo (delete)
She (delete)

NEWMAN, EMIL
Seven Wonders of the World (1956)

NEWMAN, LIONEL
City of Bad Men (1953)
Girl Can't Help It, The (1953)
Glory Brigade, The (1953)
Way to the Gold, The (1957)
Boston Strangler, The (1968)
Great White Hope, The (1970)

Myra Breckinridge (1970)
Blue Bird, The (1976)

NICHOLAS, MARK
Angel Mine (1978)

NICHOLLS, ALLAN
Perfect Couple, A (1979)

NICHOLS, LEO
(see MORRICONE, ENNIO)

NICKTERN, DAVID
White Line Fever (1975)

NICOLAI, BRUNO
Dracula vs. Frankenstein (1971)
Tutti i Colori del Buio (1972)
Justine (1974)
Shanghai Joe (1974)
Ten Little Indians (1975)

NIEMAN, SZESLAW
Scent of Earth, The (1978)

NIETO, JOSE
Love of Captain Brando, The (1974)
Black Litter (1977)
It's Never Too Late (1977)
Long Weekend, The (Puente, La) (1977)
Somnabulists, The (1978)
Wise Monkey, The (1978)

NIGHTHAWKS, THE
Billy in the Lowlands (1979)

NILSSON, BO
To Love (1964)

NILSSON, HARRY
Son of Dracula (1974)

NIMMONS, PHIL
Dangerous Age, A (1957)
Cool Sound from Hell, A (1959)

NITZSCHE, JACK
Exorcist, The (1973)
One Flew over the Cuckoo's Nest (1975)
Heroes (1977)
Blue Collar (1978)
Heart Beat (1979)
When You Comin' Back, Red Ryder? (1979)

NORDHEIM, ARNE
Dagny (1977)

NORTH, ALEX
13th Letter, The (1951)
Viva Zapata! (1952)
Death of a Salesman (1952)
Desiree (1954)
Racers, The (1955)
I'll Cry Tomorrow (1956)
Bachelor Party, The (1957)
Cinerama: South Seas Adventure (1958)
Africa (1967)
Once Upon a Scoundrel (1972)
Rebel Jesus (1972)
Shanks (1973)
Journey into Fear (1974)
Bite the Bullet (1975)
Passover Plot, The (1976)
Rich Man, Poor Man (1977)
Somebody Killed Her Husband (1978)

NOWELL, WEDGEWOOD
Aloha Oe (1915)
Between Men (1915)
D'Artagnan (1915)
Golden Claw, The (1915)
Matrimony (1915)
Winged Idol, The (1915)
Conqueror, The (1916)

NUGENT, TRISH
Word Is Out (1978)

NUKE, TOTOY
Beware: When a Widow Falls in Love (1975)

NURNBERGER, JOSEPH E.
Between Men (1915)
Golden Claw, The (1915)
Matrimony (1915)
Winged Idol, The (1915)
Edge of the Abyss, The (1916)

NXOMALO, GIDEON
Dilemma (1962)

NYZNIK, BRUCE
August and July (1973)

OBAYASHI, NOBICHIKO
Death at an Old Mansion (1976)

OBER, ARLON
Illusions of a Lady (1974)
Through the Looking Glass (1976)
Incredible Melting Man, The (1978)

OCAMPO, OSCAR CARDOZO
Rebel Patagonia, The (1974)
I Did Kill Facundo (1975)
Grandmother, The (1979)

O'DONNELL, LEE
Dirty Western, A (1975)

OESTERDAHL, MARCUS
Porno at the School of Scandal (1974)

OGAWA, NORIYOSHI
Ohanahan (1966)

OKUMURA, MITSUGU
Good Morning (Ohayosan) (1975)

OLAH, TIBERIU
Michael the Brave (1973)
Doom, The (1977)
No Trespassing (1978)
True Life of Dracula, The (1979)

OLEA, ANTONIO PEREZ
Child Is Ours, The (1973)
Men Who Knew Love, The (1976)

OLIVIERO, NINO
Mondo Cane (1963)
Matter of Time, A (1976)

OLLERHEAD, ROGER
Silent Cry, The (1977)

OLSON, GARDNER
Loveland (1973)

OLSSON, ARNE
Ebon Lundin (1974)

O'MALLEY, RUSSELL
Up from the Depths (1979)

ONDRACEK, BOHUSLAV
Girl Fit to Be Killed, The (1976)

ONG-LAM, MONTRI
New Teacher, The (1975)
Greedy People, The (1977)
Sgt. Buntung (1979)

ONO, KUJI
Proof of the Wild (1978)

ORAM, DAPHNE
Snow (1964)

ORETA, ANTONIO
Magic Adventure, The (1973)

ORIEUX, CHARLES
Up Wind (1979)

ORNADEL, CYRIL
Christina (1974)

ORPIN, ROBERT G.
Girls Are for Loving (1973)

ORTEAGA, ANGEL
Dona Perfecta (1977)

ORTEGA, SERGIO
Devil's Island (1976)
Solemn Communion (1977)

ORTOLANI, RIZ
Sorpasso, Il (1962)
Mondo Cane (1963)
In the Grip of the Spider (1971)
Brother Sun, Sister Moon (1972)
Amazons, The (1973)

Assassin of Rome, The (1973)
Confessions of a Police Inspector to the District Attorney (1973)
Counsellor, The (Consigliore, Le) (1973)
Contact (1973)
Giorno de Furore, Il (1973)
Hospitals: The White Mafia (1973)
No, the Case Is Happily Resolved (1973)
Teresa the Thief (1973)
Bootleggers, The (5 Sons of Dogs) (1974)
Reason to Live, a Reason to Die, A (1974)
There Is No 13 (1974)
To Love Ophelia (1974)
Beyond the Door (1975)
Mondo Candido (1975)
Paolo Barca, Schoolteacher and Weekend Nudist (1975)
Why Does One Kill a Magistrate? (1975)
Casanova and Company (1977)
Submission (1977)
Brutes and Savages (1978)
Double Murder (1978)
First Love (1978)
Girl in Yellow Pajamas, The (1978)
Return of Casanova, The (1978)
Dramma Borghese, Un (Mimi) (1979)
5th Musketeer, The (1979)
From Hell to Victory (1979)

OSANNA
Milano Calibro 9 (1974)

OSBORN, DANILE
Smile (1975)

OSBORNE, JESSE
Black Girl (1972)

OSCHANITZKY, RICHARD
Police Inspector Accuses, A (1974)
With Clean Hands (1978)

OSHRATH, KOBY
Dizengoff 99 (1979)

OSIBISA
Superfly T. N. T. (1973)

OSORIO, PEDRO
Holy Alliance, The (1978)

OTT, HORACE
Gordon's War (1973)

OUSLEY, HAROLD
Not Just Another Woman (1974)

OVCHINNIKOV, VYECHESLAV
They Fought for Their Country (1975)
Asya's Happiness (1978)
Steppe, The (1978)

PALESTER, ROMAN
First Circle, The (1973)

PALMERS, BENGT
I'm Expecting (1979)

PAO-SHENG, LO
Big Brother Ching (1975)

PAPADAKIS, GEORGE
Gazoros, Serres (1974)

PAPALOUSSIA, V.
Savage Party, The (1976)

PAPATHANASSIOU, VANGELIS
Apocalypse des Animaux, L' (1973)
Love (1974)
Do You Hear the Dogs Barking? (1975)
Fete Sauvage, La (1975)

PARDEIRO, CARLOS
Forgotten Island of Santosha (1974)

PARDO, JUAN
Marriage Revolution, The (1975)

PARES, PH.
Femme et le Pantin, La (1929)

PARIS, DANIELE
Milarepa (1974)
Night Porter, The (1974)
Beyond Good and Evil (1977)

PARKER, CHARLIE
Sorcerer (1977)

PARKS, VAN DYKE
Goin' South (1978)

PARLOER, FAIRFIELD
Eyewitness (1970)

PARRA, ANGEL
Andes Odyssey, The (1976)
Country Is Calm, The (1976)

PARRISH, GEORGE
Exile Express (1939)

PART, ARVO
Test Pilot Pirx (1979)

"PATCHWORK"
Willi Busch Report, The (1979)

PATE, JOHNNY
Shaft in Africa (1973)
Brother on the Run (1974)
Bucktown (1975)
Dr. Black and Mr. Hyde (1976)
Watts Monster, The (1979)

PATTANA, SIAM
Girl Named Poo Lom, A (1977)

PATUCCHI, DANIELE
Deaf Smith and Johnny Ears (1973)
Bread and Chocolate (1974)
Fight to the Death (1975)
Virility (1976)

PAYNE, ROY
Love at First Sight (1977)

PAYOMYONG, PRASIT
Best Friends (1974)
American Surplus, The (1975)
Dr. Plern (1979)

PEAKE, DON
Moving Violation (1976)
Black Oak Conspiracy (1977)
Hills Have Eyes, The (1978)

PEASLEE, RICHARD
Marat/Sade (1967)

PEDERSEN, GUNNAR MOELLER
Lars Ole, 5c (1974)
Good and the Bad, The (1975)
Boys (1977)
Children of Agony (1977)
Clark (1977)
Spring Day in Hell (1977)

PEGG, BOG
Black Jack (1979)

PEGURI, GINO
Supersonic Man (1979)

PEJAMN, AHMAD
Tall Shadows of the Wind (1979)

PENGOV, TOMAZ
Cramp (1979)

PEQUENO, IVAN
Border Crossing, The (1979)

PEREZ, GEORGE (FONDO JORGE)
Nostradamus and the Destroyer of Monsters (1961)
Orlak, the Hall of Frankenstein (1961)

PERKINSON, COLERIDGE-TAYLOR
If He Hollers, Let Him Go (1968)

Warm December, A (1973)
Amazing Grace (1974)
Education of Sonny Carson, The (1974)
Thomasine and Bushrod (1974)

PERREN, FREDDIE
Hell up in Harlem (1973)
Cooley High (1975)

PERRET, PIERRE
Charles and Lucie (1979)
We'll Grow Thin Together (1979)

PESCE, ALBERT
Greatest Question, The (1919)
Love Flower, The (1920)
One Exciting Night (1922)

PETERS, WILLIAM F.
Way Down East (1920)

PETERSON, OSCAR
Begone Dull Care (1948)
Silent Partner, The (1979)

PETIOT, ANDRE
Verdun (1928)
Cain (1930)

PETITGIRARD, LAURENT
Rare Bird, The (1973)
Rosebud (1975)
Pocket Lover, The (1978)

PETKOV, BOZHIDAR
Advantage, The (1978)
Pantelei (1978)
Fatal Comma, The (1979)
Snapshots as Souvenirs (1979)

PETRITSIS, YANNIS
Marriage, Tel Aviv Style (1979)

PETROV, ANDREY
Lost Boy, The (Huckleberry Finn) (1974)

PETROVIC, RADOMIR
Four Days to Death (1976)

PETROVICS, EMIL
One Day More, One Day Less (1973)
Man Without a Name, The (1976)
Black Diamond, The (1977)
Phantom on Horseback, The (1977)

PEYRAC, NICOLAS
7 Days in January (1979)

PEZHMAN, AHMAD
Prince Ehtejab (1974)

PHILIP, HANS ERIK
Hearts High (1976)
Winterborn (1978)

PHILLIPS, JOHN
Myra Breckinridge (1970)
Man Who Fell to Earth, The (1976)

PHILLIPS, STU
Follow Me (1969)
How to Seduce a Woman (1974)
Macon County Line (1974)
Meal, The (1975)
Battlestar Galactica (1979)
Buck Rogers (1979)
Fast Charlie ... The Moonbeam Rider (1979)

PIAC
Miss Salak Jitr (1979)

PIAZZOLA, ASTOR
All Nudity Will Be Punished (1973)
Return (1973)
Light (1976)
Armaguedon (1977)
Lumiere (1977)
What's Autumn? (1977)

PICCIONI, PIERO
Sampan Boy (1950)
Donna che Venne del Mare, La (1956)
Finestra sul Luna Park, La (1956)
Poor but Handsome (1956)

Kid, The (1957)
Nata di Marzo (1957)
Secret of the Sierra Dorada, The (1957)
Susanna tutta Panna (1957)
Anthology of Italian Cinema, The (1958)
Ballerina ed il Buon Dio, La (1958)
Girls for the Summer (1958)
Ragazzi del Parioli, I (1958)
Tempest, The (1958)
Adventure in Capri (1959)
Battle of the Volga, The (1959)
Breve Amori a Palma di Majorca (1959)
Impiegato, L' (1959)
Run with the Devil (1959)
Adolescents, The (1960)
From a Roman Balcony (1960)
Hunchback of Rome (1960)
Love a la Carte (1960)
Mani in Alto (1960)
Assassin, The (1961)
Due Marescialli, I (1961)
Duel of the Titans (1961)
Eruption (1961)
Gioventu di Notte (1961)
Imprevisto, L' (1961)
Lovemakers, The (1961)
Nuda ogni Sera (1961)
Razagge Bruciate Verdi, Le (1961)
Svedesi, Le (1961)
Alibi per Morire, Un (1962)
Anima Nera (1962)
Anni Ruggenti (1962)
Commare Secca, La (1962)
Conquered City (1962)
Due Colonnelli, I (1962)
Giorno piu Corto, Il (1962)
Giustiziere, Il (1962)
In Capo al Mondo (1962)
Marcia su Roma, La (1962)
Salvatore Giuliano (1962)
Senilita (1962)
Slave, The (1962)
Smemorato di Collegno, Lo (1962)
Toto Diabolicus (1962)
Violent Life, A (1962)
Attico, L' (1963)
Boom, Il (1963)
Demon, The (1963)
Maestro di Vigevano, Il (1963)
Mani sulla Citta, Le (1963)
Parmigiana, La (1963)
Tentativo Sentimentale, Un (1963)
Terrorist, The (1963)
American Tragedy, An (1964)
Black Sabbath (1964)
Disco Volante, Il (1964)
Fuga, La (1964)
Il la Conoscevo Bene (1964)
Man Called Gringo, The (1964)
100 Horsemen (1964)
Three Nights of Love (1964)
Time of Violence (1964)
Tre per una Rapina (1964)
Tre Volti, I (1964)
Vita Agra, La (1964)
Woman Is a Marvelous Thing, A (1964)
Figlia del Capitano, La (1965)
From the Orient with Fury (1965)
Fumo di Londra (1965)
M. M. M. 83--Missione Mortale Molo 83 (1965)
Excuse Me, Are You For or Against? (1966)
Nostri Mariti, I (1966)
Qualcono ha Tradito (1966)
Streghe, Le (1966)
More Than a Miracle (1967)
Temptation (1967)
To Ho Sposato per Allegria (1967)
Just Another War (1970)
Girl in Australia, A (1972)
Diary of a Cloistered Nun, The (1973)
Light at the Edge of the World, The (1973)
Lucky Luciano (1973)
My Brother Anastasia (1973)
Nuns of Sant'Archangelo (1973)
Appassionata (1974)
Everything Ready, Nothing Works (1974)
Star Dust (1974)
Swept Away (by a Strange Destiny in a Blue August Sea) (1974)

While There's War There's Hope (1975)
Context, The (1976)
Dog's Heart, The (1976)
Strange Events (1977)
Witness, The (1978)
Christ Stopped at Eboli (1979)
Hypochondriac, The (1979)
Where Are You Going on Your Vacation? (1979)

PICKENS, SLIM
Slipup (1975)
Sweet Punkin' (1976)

PIERRE, ALAIN
Burned Bridge (1975)
Trompe d'Oeil (1975)
Wedding Trough (1975)
I, Tin Tin (1976)
Of Death and Corpses (1979)

PIERSANTI, FRANCO
Ecce Bombo (1978)

PIERSON, TOM
Quintet (1979)

PIGA, ALDO
Curse of the Vampire (1960)
Love of the Vampire, The (1961)
Slaughter of the Vampires, The (1962)

PIK, ZVIKA
Hit Song (Schlager) (1979)

PILHOFER, HERB
Always a New Beginning (1974)

PINEDA, JUAN
Blood Pie (1971)
Antonio Gaudi: An Unfinished Vision (1974)
Alice in Spanish Wonderland (1978)
Moonlight Serenade (1979)

PING-CHUNG, YANG
Everlasting Glory, The (1975)

PINGTONG, PHET
Rural Teacher, The (1978)

PINK FLOYD
Purgatory (1974)

PINTO, ARTURO
Death at Dawn (1977)

PIOVANI, NICOLA
In the Name of the Father (1971)
N. P. (1971)
Slap the Monster on Page One (1972)
Morel's Invention (1974)
Victory March (1976)
Hyena's Sun (1977)
Last Three Days, The (1977)
Sea Gull, The (1977)
(see also MORRICONE, ENNIO)

PIRONKOV, SIMEON
Affection (1973)
Last Word, The (1974)
With Nobody (1975)
Amendment to the Law for the Defense of the State (1976)
Fairy Dance (1976)
Swimming Pool, The (1977)
Grand Piano, The (1979)
Moments in a Matchbox (1979)

PISANO, BERTO
Girl in Australia, A (1972)
Kill! (1973)

PITTS, CLAY
Fanny Hill (1969)

PLAZA, JULIAN
Truce, The (1974)

PLENIZIO, GIANFRANCO
Ah, Si! ... E Io Lo Dico a Zorro! (1979)

PLESSAS, MIMIS
Greek Pearls, The (1968)

PLUMB, EDWARD
Phantom Speaks, The (1945)
Quebec (1951)

POLEDOURIS, BASIL
Extreme Close-Up (1973)
Big Wednesday (1978)
Dolphin (1979)

POLGAR, TIBAR
In Praise of Older Women (1978)

POLNAREFF, MICHEL
Delusions of Grandeur (1971)
It Only Happens to Others (1971)
Lipstick (1976)

PONTECORVO, GILLO
Battle of Algiers, The (1956)

PONZAK, LAWRENCE J.
2076 Olympiad (1977)

POONTAMAJITR, PIM PATIPHAN
Foretold by Fate (1979)

POPA, TEMISTODE
Rock 'n' Roll Wolf (1978)

PORTAL, MICHEL
Gromaire (1967)
Soleil de Pierre (1967)
Question of Rape, A (Le Viol) (1967)
Hoa-Binh (1969)
Alechinsky After Nature (1970)
Fire (Feu) (1970)
Cecilia, La (1975)
Conquistadores, Les (1975)
Serail (1975)
For Clemence (1977)
Adoption, The (1978)

PORTE, PIERRE
Faithful Woman, A (1976)

PORTER, LOUIS
Spooks Run Wild (1941)

POSEGGA, HANS
Hitler, a Career (1977)

POST, MIKE
Rabbit Test (1978)

POTTER, BRIAN
Tunnelvision (1976)

POUFET, LEO
(delete)

POUGET, LEO
Passion de Jeanne d'Arc, La (1928)
Sheherazade (1928)

POULICACOS, DEMETRIS
Aldevaran (1975)

POURET, JEAN-PIERRE
Cold Soup, The (1975)

POWDER, STEVE
Night Before Christmas, The (1978)

PRADO, ALEMDO
Doramundo (1978)

PREGADIO, ROBERTO
Glass Sphinx, The (1967)

PREISNER, JACK
Inside Amy (1975)

PRESSER, GABOR
Wait a Minute! (1974)
On the Sideline (1977)
Don't Lean Out the Window (1978)
Deliver Us from Evil (1979)

PREVIN, ANDRE
Sun Comes Up, The (1949)

PREVIN, CHARLES
Black Friday (1940)
Black Cat, The (1941)
Hold That Ghost (1941)
Horror Island (1941)
Wolf Man, The (1941)
Frankenstein Meets the Wolf Man (1943)
Son of Dracula (1943)
House of Frankenstein (1944)

Mummy's Ghost, The (1944)
House of Dracula (1945)

PRICE, ALAN
Oh, Lucky Man! (1973)
Alfie Darling (1975)

PRINCE, ROBERT
Newman's Law (1974)
J. D.'s Revenge (1976)
Squirm (1976)

PRINGLE, DOUGLAS
Far Shore, The (1976)

PRIVSEK, JOSE
Man to Kill, The (1979)

PRODROMIDES, JEAN
Education in Love of Valentin, The (1975)

PROHASKA, MILJENKO
Return, The (1979)

PROKOFIEV, SERGEI
Ballet of Romeo and Juliet, The (delete)

PRONCET, VICTOR
Beyond the Sun (1975)
World of Love, A (1975)
Island, The (1979)

PURDIE, BERNARD
Lialeh (1973)

QIMING, LIU
Dr. Norman Bethune (1979)

QUEF, CHARLES
Vie de Jesus (Life of Jesus) (1914)

QUINCY, GEORGE
It All Adds Up (1976)

QUINLAN, NOEL
S. T. A. B. (1976)

"QUINTETO ARMORIAL"
Last Plantation, The (1976)

RAAB, LEONID
He Walked by Night (1948)

RABAUD, HENRI
Joueur d'Echecs, Le (1927)

RABBATH, FRANCOIS
Vanda Teres (1975)
Vincent Puts the Ass in a Field (1975)

RABEN, PEER
Whity (1971)
Chetan, Indian Boy (1973)
Tenderness of Wolves, The (1973)
Ice-Age (1975)
Might Makes Right (1975)
Chinese Roulette (1976)
Fear of Fear (1976)
Game Pass (1976)
Satan's Brew (1976)
Violanta (1977)
Despair (1978)
Fifty-Fifty (1978)
Third Generation, The (1979)

RABENALT, PETER
Looping (1975)

RACHMANINOFF, SERGE
(delete)

RADAKRISHNAN, M. G.
Circus Tent, The (1979)

RADEN, FRANKIE
November 1828 (1979)

RADIC, DUSAN
Fight to the Death (1975)

RADIN, OSCAR
Band Played on, The (1934)
Evelyn Prentice (1934)
Shadow of Doubt (1935)
Society Doctor (1935)

RADWAN, STANISLAW
Wedding, The (1973)
Scar, The (1977)

RAGLAND, ROBERT O.
Abby (1974)
Return to Macon County (1975)
Seven Alone (1975)
Shark's Treasure (1975)
Grizzly (1976)
Jaguar Lives! (1979)
Mountain Family Robinson (1979)
Only Once in a Lifetime (1979)

RAHBANI, ZIAD
Nahia (1979)

RAINGER, RALPH
Souls at Sea (1937)

RAISER, RIO
Willi and the Comrades (1979)

RAJTERIC-KRAUS, VLADIMIR
delete

RAKSIN, DAVID
Marry the Girl (1937)
Midnight Court (1937)
Mighty Treve, The (1937)
San Quentin (1937)
She's Dangerous (1937)
Wings Over Honolulu (1937)
Kid Comes Back, The (1938)
Adventures of Sherlock Holmes, The (1939)
Hollywood Cavalcade (1939)
Mr. Moto's Last Warning (1939)
Stanley and Livingstone (1939)
Suez (1939)
Storm Warning (1940)
Dead Men Tell (1941)
Dipsy Gypsy (1941)
Men in Her Life, The (1941)
Ride On, Vaquero (1941)
Western Daze (1941)
Dr. Renault's Secret (1942)
Just Off Broadway (1942)
Man Who Wouldn't Die, The (1942)
Magnificent Dope, The (1942)
Manila Calling (1942)
Postman Didn't Ring, The (1942)
Through Different Eyes (1942)
Undying Monster, The (1942)
Whispering Ghosts (1942)
Who Is Hope Schuyler? (1942)
City Without Men (1943)
Attack in the Pacific (1945)
Fury at Furnace Creek (1948)
Giddyap (1950)
Bloodhounds of Broadway (1952)
Madeline (1952)
Sloppy Jalopy (1952)
Blueprint for Murder (1953)
Pickup on South Street (1953)
Taxi (1953)
Money from Home (1954)
River of No Return (1954)
House of Bamboo (1955)
Girl Can't Help It, The (1956)
Holiday for Lovers (1959)
Night Tide (1961)
Redeemer, The (1966)

RAMIREZ, ARIEL
Dead One, The (1975)

RANDALL, J. K.
Eakins (1973)

RANDI, DON
3 in the Cellar (1970)
Santee (1973)

RANDLES, BOB
Metamorphoses (1978)

RANGSTREOM, TURE
Pistol, The (1973)

RANKI, GYORGY
Dreaming Youth (1974)

RANKIN, CASEY
Resurrection of the Golden Wolf (1979)

RAO, VIJAY RAGHAVA
Marginal Ones, The (1978)
Cinema Cinema (1979)

RAPEE, ERNO
Iron Horse, The (1924)
River, The (1929)

Whispering Winds (1929)
Chloe (1934)
Dead March, The (1937)

RAPOSO, JOE
Raggedy Ann and Andy (1977)

RASCHLE, HENRI
Utopia (1978)

RASHEED, AIN
Distance (1979)

RASKIN, RUBY
Lollipop Cover (1966)
Mysterious Monsters, The (1976)

RATHAUS, KAROL
Let Us Live (1939)
Jaguar (1942)
Histadruth (1945)

RATHBURN, ELDON
Labyrinthe (1967)
Cold Journey (1975)
Who Has Seen the Wind? (1977)

RAY, SATYAJIT
Distant Thunder (1973)
Golden Fortress, The (1975)
Chess Players, The (1977)
Elephant God, The (1979)

RAYNES, J. A.
Cross Currents (1915)
Jordan Is a Hard Road (1915)
Lily and the Rose, The (1915)
Sable Lorcha, The (1915)
Flying Torpedo, The (1916)
Price of Power, The (1916)

RECHLIN, EDWARD
Martin Luther (1925)

REDJEPOV, REDJEP
Daughter-in-Law, The (1972)

REDLAND, CHARLES
Guttersnipes (1975)
Agaton Sax and the Bykoebing Village Festival (1976)

REED, JERRY
Smokey and the Bandit (1977)

REED, LES
Bicyclettes de Belsize, Les (1969)

REEVES, ALAN
Speak to Me of Love (1975)
Prostitution (1976)

REHSEN, F.
Crippled Hand, The (1916)
Gay Lord Waring, The (1916)
Great Problem, The (1916)
John Needham's Double (1916)
Tangled Hearts (1916)

REINA, FREDDY
Fever (1976)

REINHARDT, DJANGO
Gypsy, The (1975)

REKONDO, HIBAI
Burgos Trial, The (1979)

RENAUD, HENRI
Naked Hearts (1966)

REQUENA, OSVALDO
Revolution of the Seven Madmen, The (1973)

REVAUX, JACQUES
Bobo, Jacco (1979)

REYES, JR., JOSE
Burn, Samar, Burn! (1974)

RHODEN, NEIL
Undercovers Hero (1975)

RIBERO, TITO
Father Heart Wants to Get Married (1974)
Don't Be Weak with Life (1975)
I Need You So Much, Love (1976)

RICARDO
Night of the Scarecrow, The (1974)

RICH, FREDDIE
I Live on Danger (1942)

RICHARDS, BOBBY
Bloodsuckers (1971)

RIDDLE, NELSON
Great Gatsby, The (1974)
Harper Valley P. T. A. (1978)

RIEDEL, GEORG
Pippi in the South Seas (1974)
Paradise Square (1977)

RIESENFELD, HUGO
Grass (1925)
Old Ironsides (1926)
Chang (1927)
Uncle Tom's Cabin (1927)
Ramona (1928)
Iron Mask, The (1929)
Looping the Loop (1929)
Lucky Boy (1929)
Midstream (1929)
Molly and Me (1929)
My Lady's Past (1929)
New Orleans (1929)
Three Live Ghosts (1929)
Two Men and a Maid (1929)
Bad One, The (1930)
Be Yourself (1930)
Lottery Bride, The (1930)
Tabu (1931)
White Zombie (1932)
Little Men (1934)
Peck's Bad Boy (1934)
Phantom Empire (1935)
President Vanishes, The (1935)
Wandering Jew, The (1935)
Daniel Boone (1936)
Devil on Horseback, The (1936)
Follow Your Heart (1936)
Hearts in Bondage (1936)
President's Mystery, The (1936)
Rainbow on the River (1936)
White Legion (1936)
Hawaii Calls (1938)
Rose of the Rio Grande (1938)
Sunset Murder Case, The (1938)
Wide Open Faces (1938)

RIESMAN, MICHAEL
Pleasantville (1976)

RIKER, ROD
Born to Raise Hell (1975)

RILEY, DOUG
Cannibal Girls (1973)
American Dream, The (1976)
Shoot (1976)

RILEY, TERRY
Lifespan (1975)

RISER, PAUL
Which Way Is Up? (1977)

RITCHIE, ROY
Journey Among Women (1977)
Mouth to Mouth (1978)

RIVARD, MICHEL
Out of Whack (1979)

ROACH, MAX
Dilemma (1962)

ROBBINS, RICHARD
Europeans, The (1979)

ROBERT, GUY
Perceval le Gallois (1978)

ROBERTS, BRUCE
Crazies, The (1973)
They Shall Overcome (1974)

ROBERTS, DES
Guess What Happened to Count Dracula? (1969)

ROBERTS, HOWARD
Lord Shango (1975)

ROBINSON, EARL
House I Live In, The (1944)
Muscle Beach (1948)

ROBINSON, HARRY
Countess Dracula (1970)
Twins of Evil (1972)
Ghoul, The (1975)

RODER, MILAN
Silver Dollar (1932)
Last of the Pagans, The (1935)
Lives of a Bengal Lancer, The (1935)
Exclusive (1937)
Souls at Sea (1937)
Bulldog Drummond in Africa (1938)
Never Say Die (1939)

RODGERS, RICHARD
Victory at Sea (1952)

RODRIGUEZ, CAMALEON
People in Buenos Aires (1974)

RODRIGUEZ, JUANITO
Missing Prisoners (1979)

RODRIGUEZ, SILVIO
Pablo (1978)

ROEMHELD, HEINZ
Golden Harvest (1933)
Man Who Reclaimed His Head, The (1934)
Kliou the Tiger (1935)
Story of Louis Pasteur, The (1935)
Dracula's Daughter (1936)
Three Smart Girls (1936)
Four's a Crowd (1938)
I Met My Love Again (1938)
Invisible Stripes (1939)
Nancy Drew, Reporter (1939)
You Can't Get Away with Murder (1939)
British Intelligence (1940)
Brother Rat and a Baby (1940)
Child Is Born, A (1940)
Four Mothers (1941)
Honeymoon for Three (1941)
Wagons Roll at Night (1941)
O. S. S. (1946)
Christmas Eve (1947)
Flame, The (1947)
It Had to Be You (1947)
Girl from Manhattan, The (1948)
Rogues of Sherwood Forest (1950)
Union Station (1950)
Big Trees, The (1952)
5, 000 Fingers of Dr. T, The (1952)
Mole People, The (1956)
There's Always Tomorrow (1956)

ROGERS, ERIC
Carry On Screaming (1966)
Carry On, Emmanuelle (1978)

ROGERS, SHORTY
Hotsy Footsy (1952)
Blues Pattern (1956)
Three Little Bops (1956)
Wackey World of Numberrs, The (1970)

ROLAND, MARC
Fridericus Rex (1922)
Weltkrieg, Der (1927)

ROMANUS, RICHARD
Sitting Ducks (1979)

ROMITELLI, SANTE MARIA
Profiteer, The (1974)
Virgin Named Mary, A (1975)

ROSE, DAVID
Underworld Story, The (1950)
Forbidden Planet (1956)
Bonanza (1960)
High Chaparral, The (1969)

ROSEN, MILTON
He's My Guy (1943)
On Stage Everybody (1945)
Swing Out, Sisters (1945)
Cuban Pete (1946)
Slightly Scandalous (1946)
Spider Woman Strikes Back, The (1946)
Abraham and Isaac (1948)
Daniel in the Lion's Den (1948)
Of Such Is the Kingdom (1948)
Raising of Lazarus, The (1948)
Creature from the Black

Lagoon, The (1954)

ROSENMAN, LEONARD
Edge of the City (1956)
Battle of the Planet of the Apes (1973)
Barry Lyndon (1975)
Race with the Devil (1975)
Birch Interval (1976)
Bound for Glory (1976)
Car, The (1977)
9/30/55 (1977)
Enemy of the People, An (1978)
Lord of the Rings (1978)
Promises in the Dark (1979)
Prophecy (1979)

ROSENTHAL, LAURENCE
Rooster Cogburn (1975)
Wild Party, The (1975)
Return of a Man Called Horse (1976)
Island of Dr. Moreau, The (1977)
Brass Target (1978)
Who'll Stop the Rain? (Dog Soldiers) (1978)
Meetings with Remarkable Men (1979)
Meteor (1979)

ROSHAN, REJESH
Swami (1977)

ROSTAING, HUBERT
Croisiere pour l'Inconnu (1947)
Story of Bicycles, The (1953)
Desire Takes the Men (1957)
Life Together (1958)
Parisienne, La (1958)
Candide (1960)
Bread of the Sky, The (1962)
Wild Living (1962)
I Salute the Mafia (1965)
Cesar and Rosalie (1972)
Valise, La (1973)
Clockmaker, The (1974)
Judge and the Assassin, The (1975)
Last Woman, The (1976)
Sugar, The (1978)

Moments (1979)

ROTA, MAURIZIO
Don't Count on Us (1978)

ROTA, NINO
Bidone, Il (Swindle, The) (1962)
Paranoia (1966)
Romeo and Juliet (1968)
Fellini Satyricon (1971)
Fellini Roma (1972)
Abdication, The (1974)
Amarcord (1974)
Godfather II, The (1974)
Love and Anarchy (1975)
Casanova (1976)
Dear Michael (1976)
Slum Boy (1976)
Death on the Nile (1978)
Alla Origini Della Mafia (1979)
Hurricane (1979)
Orchestra Rehearsal (1979)

ROTHAPFEL, S. L. "ROXY"
Battle Cry of Peace, The (1915)

ROTMAN, YEHUDA
Amlash Enchanted Forest, The (1974)

ROY, HERVE
Emmanuelle (1974)

ROZSA, MIKLOS
Knight Without Armor (1937)
Murder on Diamond Row (Squeaker, The) (1937)
Green Cockatoo, The (Four Dark Hours) (1937)
Missing Ten Days (Ten Days in Paris) (1939)
U-Boat 29 (Spy in Black, The) (1939)
Fugitive, The (On the Night of the Fire) (1940)
Jacare (1942)
Time Out of Mind (1947)
Golden Voyage of Sinbad, The (1974)
Private Files of J. Edgar

Hoover, The (1977)
Providence (1977)
Fedora (1978)
Last Embrace (1979)
Time After Time (1979)

RUBENSTEIN, ARTHUR B.
Shenanigans (1977)

RUBENSTEIN, JOHN
Kid Blue (1973)
Killer Inside Me, The (1976)

RUBENSTEIN, MARTIN
Towing (1978)

RUBINSTEIN, DONALD
Martin (1978)

RUFF, GARFEEL
Hitter, The (1979)

RUGOLO, PETE
Challengers, The (1968)
Foxtrot (1976)

RUHLAND, PAUL
Up (1976)

RUIZ, OSCAR LOPEZ
Hour of Mary and the Bird of Gold, The (1976)

RUSSELL, RAY
That Summer (1979)

RUSSO, BILL
Second Chance (1969)
Everybody Rides the Carousel (1975)
Wow (Women of the World) (1975)

RUSTICHELLI, CARLO
Promessi Sposi, I (1938)
Mamma Roma (1962)
Three Nights of Love (1964)
Birds, the Bees, and the Italians, The (1967)
Ace High (1969)
Nini Tirabuschio, le Donna che Invento la Mossa (1970)
Alfredo, Alfredo (1973)
Call of the Wild (1973)
Dirty Weekend (1973)
We Want the Colonels (1973)
Somewhere Beyond Love (1974)
Fight to the Death (1975)
My Friends (1975)
New Beaujolais Wine Has Arrived, The (1978)
Machine Gun Stein (1979)

RUTHERFORD, MICHAEL
Shout, The (1978)

RYBNER, C.
Abie's Irish Rose (1928)

RYBNIKOV, A.
Feedback (1978)

RYPDAL, TERJE
Lucie (1979)
Summer of Love, A (1979)

RYUDMAN, KARI
Antti the Treebranch (1977)

SABO, FERENC
Photography (1974)
Wind Blows Under Your Feet, The (1976)
Bad Guys, The (1979)

SACHAFER, CARL HANS
Zig-Zig (1975)

SAFAN, CRAIG
California Reich, The (1976)
Great Scout and Cathouse Thursday, The (1976)
Bad News Bears in Breaking Training, The (1977)
Last of the Cowboys, The (1977)
Corvette Summer (1978)
Good Guys Wear Black (1978)

SAINTE-MARIE, BUFFY
Spirit of the Wind (1979)

SAITO, KOJAN
End of Autumn (1978)

SAKATA, KOCHI
Carpet on the Cloud, The (1976)

SALAMA, GAMAL
I Want a Solution (1974)

SALCEDO, JOSE
Stepmother, The (1975)

SALISTRA, DOMINIC
John and Marsha (1974)

SALTER, HANS J.
Young Fugitives (1938)
Big Guy (1939)
Alias the Deacon (1940)
Black Diamonds (1940)
Black Friday (1940)
Devil's Pipeline, The (1940)
Diamond Frontier (1940)
Enemy Agent (1940)
First Love (1940)
Framed (1940)
Give Us Wings (1940)
I Can't Give You Anything but Love, Baby (1940)
I'm Nobody's Sweetheart Now (1940)
Invisible Man Returns, The (1940)
Law and Order (1940)
Leather Pushers, The (1940)
Love, Honor and Oh, Baby! (1940)
Margie (1940)
Meet the Wildcat (1940)
Miracle on Main Street (1940)
Mummy's Hand, The (1940)
Private Affairs (1940)
Sandy Gets Her Man (1940)
Seven Sinners (1940)
Ski Patrol (1940)
Slightly Tempted (1940)
South to Karanga (1940)
Spring Parade (1940)
Trail of the Vigilantes (1940)
You're Not So Tough (1940)
Arizona Cyclone (1941)
Bachelor Daddy (1941)
Badlands of Dakota (1941)
Black Cat, The (1941)
Burma Convoy (1941)
Dangerous Game, A (1941)
Dark Streets of Cairo (1941)
Double Date (1941)
Flying Cadets (1941)
Hello Sucker (1941)
Hit the Road (1941)
Hold That Ghost (1941)
Horror Island (1941)
It Started with Eve (1941)
Lucky Devils (1941)
Man-Made Monster (1941)
Man Who Lost Himself, The (1941)
Meet the Chump (1941)
Men of the Timberland (1941)
Mr. Dynamite (1941)
Mob Town (1941)
Model Wife (1941)
Mutiny in the Arctic (1941)
Raiders of the Desert (1941)
Road Agent (1941)
San Francisco Docks (1941)
Sealed Lips (1941)
Tight Shoes (1941)
Where Did You Get That Girl? (1941)
Wolf Man, The (1941)
Destination Unknown (1942)
Frisco Lil (1942)
Half Way to Shanghai (1942)
Invisible Agent (1942)
Mad Doctor of Market Street, The (1942)
Madame Spy (1942)
Old Chisholm Trail, The (1942)
Pittsburgh (1942)
Sherlock Holmes and the Secret Weapon (1942)
Who Done It? (1942)
Amazing Mrs. Holliday, The (1943)
Arizona Trail (1943)
Calling Dr. Death (1943)
Eyes of the Underworld (1943)
Frankenstein Meets the Wolf Man (1943)
Frontier Badmen (1943)
Son of Dracula (1943)
Allergic to Love (1944)
Boss of Boomtown (1944)
Can't Help Singing (1944)
Christmas Holiday (1944)

Hat Check Honey (1944)
House of Fear (1944)
House of Frankenstein (1944)
Invisible Man's Revenge, The (1944)
Jungle Captive (1944)
Jungle Woman (1944)
Merry Monahans, The (1944)
Mummy's Ghost, The (1944)
Pearl of Death, The (1944)
Scarlet Claw, The (1944)
Twilight on the Prairie (1944)
Weird Woman (1944)
House of Dracula (1945)
Pursuit to Algiers (1945)
Strange Affair of Uncle Harry, The (1945)
Woman in Green, The (1945)
Brute Man, The (1946)
Dressed to Kill (1946)
Gung Ho! (1946)
Magnificent Doll, The (1946)
Terror by Night (1946)
Love from a Stranger (1947)
Killer That Stalked New York, The (1950)
Please Believe Me (1950)
Abbott & Costello Meet the Invisible Man (1951)
Frenchie (1951)
Strange Door, The (1951)
Black Castle, The (1952)
Finders Keepers (1952)
5,000 Fingers of Dr. T, The (1952)
Abbott & Costello Meet Dr. Jekyll and Mr. Hyde (1953)
Bengal Brigade (1954)
Black Horse Canyon (1954)
Black Shield of Falworth, The (1954)
Creature from the Black Lagoon, The (1954)
Far Country, The (1954)
Four Guns to the Border (1954)
Johnny Dark (1954)
Kiss of Fire (1954)
Naked Alibi (1954)
Saskatchewan (1954)
Sign of the Pagan (1954)
Tanganyika (1954)
Yankee Pasha (1954)
Abbott & Costello Meet the Mummy (1955)
Captain Lightfoot (1955)
Man Without a Star (1955)
This Island Earth (1955)
Lady Godiva (1956)
Mole People, The (1956)
Raw Edge, The (1956)
Rawhide Years, The (1956)
Walk the Proud Land (1956)
Incredible Shrinking Man, The (1957)
Joe Dakota (1957)
Land Unknown, The (1957)
Man in the Shadow, The (1957)
Midnight Story, The (1957)
Appointment with a Shadow (1958)
Summer Love (1958)
War Lord, The (1965)
Return of the Gunfighter, The (1967)

SALUSTIANO, DOMINIC
Brutus (1976)

SAMALE, NICOLA
Goodnight, Ladies and Gentlemen (1977)
Elective Affinities (1978)

SAMIOU, DOMNA
For an Unimportant Reason (1974)

SAMUELS, DAN
Count the Ways (1976)

SAN PEDRO, LUCIO
Sleeping Dragon (1975)
Tenants, The (1976)

SANCHEZ, HECTOR
One Who Came from Heaven, The (1974)

SANDLOFF, PETER
Michael Kohlhaas (1979)

SANDRO
Operation Rose Rose (1974)

SANOJA, CHUCHITO
Portable Country (1979)

SANOJA, JESUS JR.
Dear Comrades (1978)

SANTOJA, MARI CARMEN
At the Service of Spanish Womanhood (1978)

SANTOS, PEDRO
Last Plantation, The (1976)

SARDE, PHILIPPE
Une Simple Histoire (1957)
Charlie and His Two Birds (1973)
Grande Bouffe, Le (1973)
Heavenly Bodies, The (1973)
Marriage a la Mode (1973)
Son, The (1973)
Train, The (1973)
Valise, The (1973)
Don't Touch White Women (1974)
"Elite" Group, The (1974)
Icy Breasts (1974)
Lancelot of the Lake (1974)
Vincent, Francois, Paul ... and the Others (1974)
Watchmaker of Saint-Paul, The (1974)
Bay of Marbles, A (1975)
Happy Divorce, The (1975)
7 Deaths by Subscription (1975)
Barocco (1976)
Judge and the Assassin, The (1976)
Last Woman, The (1976)
Mado (1976)
Marie the Doll (1976)
Tenant, The (1976)
As the Moon (1977)
Crab Drum, The (1977)
Death of a Corrupt Man, The (1977)
Devil, Probably, The (1977)
Judge Fayard Called the Sheriff (1977)
Life Before Him (1977)
Purple Taxi, The (1977)
Spoiled Children (1977)
Violette and Francois (1977)
Bye Bye Monkey (1978)
Key Is in the Door, The (1978)
Madame Rosa (1978)
Mountain Pass (1978)
Sugar, The (1978)
Adolescent, The (1979)
Bronte Sisters, The (1979)
Cop or Hood (1979)
Medic, The (Toubib, Le) (1979)
My Asylum (1979)
Tess (1979)

SARDI, IDRIS
Something Beautiful (1977)

SASSE, KARL-ERNST
Between Night and Day (1975)
Elective Affinities (1975)
Lotte in Weimar (1975)
Light on the Gallows, The (1977)

SATIE, ERIC
Sextool (1975)

"SATIN WHALE"
Fist in the Pocket (1979)

SATO, MASARU
High and Low (1963)
Red Beard (1966)
Three Sisters (1967)
Man and War (Part III) (1974)
Submersion of Japan (Tidal Wave) (1974)
Portrait of Shunkin, A (1977)
Yellow Handerchief of Happiness, The (1978)
Glacier Fox, The (1979)
Oh! The Nomugi Pass (1979)

SATO, MASASHIKO
Belladonna (1973)

SAUNDERS, MORT
Black Girl (1972)

SAURY, MAXIM
Contrechant (1963)

SAVINA, CARLO
Curse of the Karnsteins,

The (1963)
Vengeance (1968)
Malenka, Niece of the Vampire (1969)
Slum Boy (1976)
Woman from the Torrid Land (1978)

SAVINE, ALEXANDER
Man Nobody Knows, The (1925)
As We Forgive (1926)

SAVOPOULOS, DIONYSSIOS
Happy Days (1976)

SAWTELL, PAUL
Mexican Spitfire (1939)
Bullet Code (1940)
Legion of the Lawless (1940)
Little Orvie (1940)
Millionaire Playboy (1940)
Pop Always Pays (1940)
Prairie Law (1940)
Stage to Chino (1940)
Wagon Train (1940)
Along the Rio Grande (1941)
Bandit Trail, The (1941)
No Hands on the Clock (1941)
Redhead (1941)
Robbers of the Range (1941)
Six-Gun Gold (1941)
Come On, Danger (1942)
Date with the Falcon, A (1942)
Land of the Open Range (1942)
Red River Robin Hood (1942)
Thundering Hoofs (1942)
Calling Dr. Death (1943)
Great Gildersleeve, The (1943)
Sagebrush Law (1943)
Gildersleeve's Ghost (1944)
Jungle Captive (1944)
Oklahoma Raiders (1944)
Old Texas Trail, The (1944)
Riders of the Santa Fe (1944)
Trail to Gunsight (1944)
House of Dracula (1945)
Mummy's Curse, The (1945)
Power of the Whistler, The (1945)
Renegades of the Rio Grande (1945)
Alias Mr. Twilight (1946)
Perilous Holiday (1947)
For You I Die (1948)
Tarzan and the She-Devil (1952)
Last Man on Earth, The (1964)

SCHACKMAN, AL
Book of Numbers (1973)

SCHAEFFER, KARL HEINZ
White Gloves of the Devil (1973)

SCHAFFER, JANNE
Call-Up, The (1979)

SCHAIF, NOHAM
Garden, The (1977)

SCHARF, WALTER
Yes, Sir That's My Baby (1949)
Walking Tall (1973)
Walking Tall (Part II) (1975)
Final Chapter--Walking Tall (1977)

SCHERTZINGER, VICTOR
Between Men (1915)
D'Artagnan (1915)
Golden Claw, The (1915)
Winged Idol, The (1915)
Conqueror, The (1916)
Edge of the Abyss, The (1916)
Princess of the Dark, The (1917)
Robin Hood (1922)

SCHIFRIN, LALO
Boss, The (1958)
Operation Heartbeat (1962)
Joy House (1964)
Making of a President--1960, The (1964)
Doomsday Flight (1966)
Sullivan's Empire (1967)
Earth 11 (1971)
Charley Varrick (1973)
Enter the Dragon (1973)
Harry in Your Pocket (1973)
Hit (1973)
Magnum Force (1973)

Neptune Factor, The (1973)
Golden Needles (1974)
Man on a Swing (1974)
Four Musketeers, The (1975)
Master Gunfighter, The (1975)
St. Ives (1976)
Sky Riders (1976)
Special Delivery (1976)
Voyage of the Damned (1976)
Day of the Animals (1977)
Eagle Has Landed, The (1977)
Rollercoaster (1977)
Telefon (1977)
Cat from Outer Space, The (1978)
Manitou, The (1978)
Nunzio (1978)
Return from Witch Mountain (1978)
Amityville Horror, The (1979)
Boulevard Nights (1979)
Concorde--Airport '79, The (1979)
Escape from Athena (1979)
Love and Bullets (1979)

SCHIKORA, UVE
Outlaw Morality (1976)

SCHIRMANN, PETER
Your Child, the Unknown Creature (1970)
I Had a Feeling I Was Dead (1975)

SCHLACKS, STEVEN
H. C. Andersen in Italy (1979)

SCHMIDT, IRMIN
Love by Rape (1970)
Knife in the Head (1978)

SCHMIDT-BOELCKE, WERNER
Lebende Leichnam, Der (1928)

SCHMIDT-GENTNER, WILLY
Carlos and Elisabeth (1924)

SCHMINKE, FRED
Captain Lust (1977)

SCHMITT, FLORENT
Salammbo (1925)

SCHNITKE, ALFRED
You and Me (1972)
Sea Gull, The (1973)
Cities and Years (1974)
White Shop, The (1976)
Ascent, The (1977)
Adventures of a Dentist (1978)
Father Sergius (1978)
Sport, Sport, Sport (1978)

SCHOENER, EBERHARD
Dream Town (1974)
John Glueckstadt (1975)
Clown, The (1976)
Slavers (1977)
Rheingold (1978)

SCHRAGER, RUDY
Snuffy Smith, Yardbird (1942)
Career Girl (1944)
Dixie Jamboree (1944)
People Are Funny (1946)
Dangerous Years, The (1948)

SCHROEPFER, WILFRIED
Inki (1975)

SCHUDSON, HOD DAVID
Parts, the Clonus Horror (1979)

SCHULTZE, NORBERT
Rosemary (1958)

SCHUMAN, MORT
Black Thursday (1974)
Faithful Woman, A (1976)
Guy Like Me Should Never Die, A (1976)
High Street (1976)
Let's Get Those English Girls (1976)
Six O'Clock USA (1976)
Monsieur Papa (1977)
More It Goes, the Less It Goes, The (1977)
Night of St.-Germain des

Pres, The (1977)
Associate, The (1979)

SCHUMANN, ROBERT
I'd Like to Have My Troubles (1975)

SCHWARTZWALD, MILTON
Crime of Dr. Crespi, The (1935)

SCHWARZ, ISAAK
Hundred Days After Childhood, A (1975)

SCHWARZ, JEAN
Child in the Crowd, A (1976)
For Clemence (1977)
Dossier 51, Le (1978)

SCOTT, BOBBY
Joe (1970)

SCOTT, JOHN
Billy Two Hats (1973)
Craze (1974)
That Lucky Touch (1975)
People That Time Forgot, The (1977)
North Dallas Forty (1979)

SCOTT, NATHAN
Out California Way (1946)
Rendezvous with Annie (1946)
Wyoming (1947)

SCOTT, PATRICK JOHN
Study in Terror, A (1966)
Antony and Cleopatra (1972)
England Made Me (1973)
Hennessy (1975)

SCOTT, TOM
Uptown Saturday Night (1974)
Sidecar Racers (1975)
Americathon (1979)

SCOTTO, TITO
Bamboo Gods and Iron Men (1974)
TNT Jackson (1975)

SCRUGGS, EARL
Where the Lilies Bloom (1974)

SEAZER, J. A.
Pastorale Hide and Seek (1975)
Boxer, The (1977)
Private Collections (1979)

SEBASTIAN (KNUD CHRISTENSEN)
Gatefold Girl, The (1974)
Could We Maybe (1976)
You Are Not Alone (1978)

SEDEFIAN, ARAM
Violated Love (1977)

SEGALL, BERNARDO
Homebodies (1974)

SEGGIAN, ARMAND
Red-Haired Revolver (1974)

SEGURA, GREGORY
Coquito, La (1978)

SEIBER, MATYAS
Shiralee, The (1956)

SEKSAN
Santi and Veena (1976)

SELDEN, EDGAR
Odyssey, The (1912)

SELMECZI, GYORGY
Entanglement (1977)
Vera's Training (1979)

SELTZER, DOV
Rabbi and the Shikse, The (1976)
Operation Thunderbolt (1977)
Millionaire in Trouble (1978)

SENDRA, ALBERTO
There Is No Forgetting (1976)

SENIA, JEAN-MARIE
Jonas--Who Will Be 25 in the Year 2000 (1976)
Steam Mare, The (1978)
Police War, The (1979)

SERBAN, RADU
Through the Ashes of the Empire (1976)

SEROCKI, KASIMIERZ
Deluge, The (1974)

SERRA, LUIS MARIA
Great Adventure, The (1974)
Mary, La (1974)
Woman, A (1975)

SERVASAN GROUP
My Lady (1975)

SERVAT, GILLES
Homeland (1973)

SETARO, ANDREA
Belle of the Nineties (1934)
Bolero (1934)
Old-Fashioned Way, The (1934)
College Scandal (1935)
Goin' to Town (1935)

SHAKESPEARE, JOHN
Best of Morocco (1966)
Great McGonagall, The (1975)

SHANK, BUD
Slippery When Wet (1959)
Barefoot Adventure (1961)

SHANKAR, ANANDA
Chorus (1975)

SHANKAR, RAVI
Raga (1971)

SHANKLIN, RAY
Black Girl (1972)
Fritz the Cat (1972)
Heavy Traffic (1973)

SHAPIRO, BRAD
Cleopatra Jones (1973)

SHARIF, NOHAM
Garden, The (1977)

SHCHEDRIN, RODION
Anna Karenina (1975)

SHEFTER, BERT
Last Man on Earth, The (1964)

SHEMER, NAOMI
Winchell Affair, The (1979)

SHER, YOEL
Wrong Number (1979)

SHIBUYA, TAKESHI
Barefooten Gen (1976)

SHILKRET, NATHANIEL
Lilac Time (1928)
Big Game, The (1936)
Mary of Scotland (1936)
Smartest Girl in Town, The (1936)
Border Cafe (1937)
Toast of New York, The (1937)
... One Third of a Nation... (1939)
Frank Buck's Jungle Cavalcade (1941)
Stolen Paradise (1941)
Stranger in Town, A (1943)

SHIN, WOY KOY
Story of Chinese Gods, The (1976)

SHIRAKAWA, GUNHACHIRO
Jongara (1974)

SHIRE, DAVID
Class of '44 (1973)
Showdown (1973)
Steelyard Blues (1973)
Two People (1973)
Conversation, The (1974)
Taking of Pelham 1, 2, 3, The (1974)
Farewell My Lovely (1975)
Fortune, The (1975)
Hindenburg, The (1975)
All the President's Men (1976)
Big Bus, The (1976)
Harry and Walter Go to New York (1976)
Saturday Night Fever (1977)

Promise, The (1978)
Straight Time (1978)
Fast Break (1979)
Norma Rae (1979)
Promise, The (1979)

SHORE, HOWARD
I Miss You, Hugs and Kisses (1978)

SHOSTAKOVICH, DMITRI
Hamlet (1931)
Five Days and Five Nights (1948)

SHOTWELL, PHYLLIS
California Split (1974)

SHTEREV, MITKO
Doomed Souls (1975)

SHUKEN, LEO
Artists and Models Abroad (1938)
Lady from Kentucky, The (1939)
Paris Honeymoon (1939)
Stagecoach (1939)
Adventure in Diamonds (1940)
Lady Has Plans, The (1941)
New York Town (1941)
Our Wife (1941)
West Point Widow (1941)
Henry Aldrich, Editor (1942)
Best Years, The (1949)

SHUMAN, ALDEN
Devil in Miss Jones, The (1973)

SHUSHA
People of the Wind (1976)

SIDDIK
Wedding of Zein, The (1978)

SIEBERT, WILHELM DIETER
Vera Romeyke Is Not Acceptable (1976)
Ties for the Olympics (1977)

SILVER, CHARLES
Ronde de Nuit, La (1926)

SILVERS, LOUIS
Way Down East (1920)

SILVERSTEIN, SHEL
Ned Kelly (1970)
Thieves (1977)

SILVESTRI, ALAN
Amazing Dobermans, The (1976)
Las Vegas Lady (1976)

SIMIC, VOJISLAV
Sleeping Car, The (1976)

SIMJANOVIC, ZORAN
Special Education (1977)
Smell of Wildflowers, The (1978)
Bosko Buha (1979)
Days Are Passing, The (1979)
National Class (1979)

SIMMONS, JEFFREY
Naked Angels (1969)

SIMOBOVIC, TOMICA
House, The (1975)
Operation Stadium (1977)

SIMON, ERIC
Short Memory (1979)

SIMON, PAUL
Shampoo (1975)

SIMON, WALTER CLEVELAND
Arrah-na-Pough (1911)
Arabian Tragedy, An (1912)
Bugler of Battery B., The (1912)
Captured by Bedouins (1912)
Confederate Ironclad, The (1912)
Drummer Girl of Vicksburg, The (1912)
Egyptian Sports (1912)
Fighting Dervishes of the Desert (1912)
Hungry Hank's Hallucination (1912)
Prisoner of the Harem (1912)
Siege of Petersburg, The

(1912)
Soldier Brothers of Susanna, The (1912)
Spanish Revolt of 1836, The (1912)
Spartan Mother, A (1912)
Tragedy of the Desert (1912)
Under a Flag of Truce (1912)
Tragedy of Big Eagle Mine, The (1913)
Black Crook, The (1916)
Echo of Youth, The (1919)

SIMONE, YVES
Diablo Menthe (1977)

SIMONYAN, NADESHDA
Flying Carpet, The (1956)
Lady with the Dog, The (1960)
Duel, The (1974)
Only One, The (1976)

SINGERY, YANNICK
Isabelle Devant le Desir (1975)

SINGYAO, UAN
Golden Swan (1977)

SKINNER, FRANK
Son of Frankenstein (1939)
Tower of London (1939)
Black Friday (1940)
First Love (1940)
House of the Seven Gables, The (1940)
Invisible Man Returns, The (1940)
Mummy's Hand, The (1940)
Seven Sinners (1940)
Black Cat, The (1941)
Flame of New Orleans, The (1941)
Hellzapoppin' (1941)
Hold That Ghost (1941)
Horror Island (1941)
Keep 'Em Flying (1941)
Man-Made Monster (1941)
Never Give a Sucker an Even Break (1941)
Wolf Man, The (1941)
Jail House Blues (1942)
Pittsburgh (1942)
Amazing Mrs. Holliday, The (1943)
Calling Dr. Death (1943)
Frankenstein Meets the Wolf Man (1943)
Son of Dracula (1943)
We've Never Been Licked (1943)
Destiny (1944)
Follow the Boys (1944)
House of Frankenstein (1944)
Mummy's Ghost, The (1944)
House of Dracula (1945)
Gung Ho! (1946)
Swell Guy (1947)
Family Honeymoon (1949)
Francis (1950)
Black Horse Canyon (1954)
Four Guns to the Border (1954)
Sign of the Pagan (1954)

SKLAIR, SAM
Confessions of a Window Cleaner (1974)

SLANEY, IVOR
Terror (1978)

SLAWSINSKI, ADAM
Long Live Progress (1976)

SLEWYNGER, ALBERTO
Management Forgives a Moment of Madness, The (1979)

SLILEPCEVIC, CVETKO
Wedding (1974)

SMALL, MICHAEL
Klute (1970)
Love and Pain and the Whole Damn Thing (1973)
Parallax View, The (1974)
Drowning Pool, The (1975)
Night Moves (1975)
Stepford Wives, The (1975)
Marathon Man (1976)
Audrey Rose (1977)
Pumping Iron (1977)
Comes a Horseman (1978)

Driver, The (1978)
Girl Friends (1978)
Going in Style (1979)

SMALLS, CHARLIE
Drum (1976)

SMEATON, BRUCE
Cars That Ate Paris, The (1974)
Great MacArthy, The (1975)
Picnic at Hanging Rock (1975)
Devil's Playground, The (1976)
Eliza Fraser (1976)
Trespassers, The (1976)
Summerfield (1977)

SMITH, ARTHUR
Seabo (1977)

SMITH, CLAY
Seabo (1977)

SMITH, JIMMY
Metamorphosis of Cloportes, The (1967)

SMITH, MALCOLM
Sons for the Return Home (1979)

SMITH, PAUL
Stagecoach (1939)
Water Birds (1952)

SMITH, TEDD
Hiding Place, The (1975)
No Longer Alone (1978)

SNELL, DAVID
Family Affair, A (1937)
Married Before Breakfast (1937)
My Dear Miss Aldrich (1937)
Judge Hardy's Children (1938)
Love Finds Andy Hardy (1938)
Out West with the Hardys (1938)
Blackmail (1939)
Dancing Coed (1939)
Hardys Ride High, The (1939)
Henry Goes Arizona (1939)
Judge Hardy and Son (1939)
Secret of Dr. Kildare, The (1939)
Stronger Than Desire (1939)
These Glamour Girls (1939)
They All Come Out (1939)
Dr. Kildare's Crisis (1940)
Dr. Kildare's Strange Case (1940)
Gallant Sons (1940)
Ghost Comes Home, The (1940)
Gold Rush Maisie (1940)
Golden Fleecing, The (1940)
Phantom Raiders (1940)
Sky Murder (1940)
20 Mule Team (1940)
Wyoming (1940)
Down in San Diego (1941)
Maisie Was a Lady (1941)
Penalty, The (1941)
People vs. Dr. Kildare, The (1941)
Ringside Maisie (1941)
Tarzan's Secret Treasure (1941)
Unholy Partners (1941)
Washington Melodrama (1941)
Courtship of Andy Hardy, The (1942)
Mr. and Mrs. North (1942)
Pacific Rendezvous (1942)
Vanishing Virginian, The (1942)
Northwest Rangers (1943)
Rationing (1944)
See Here, Private Hargrove (1944)

SNOW, MARK
Something Short of Paradise (1979)

SOCCIO, G.
Children of Oblivion, The (1979)

SOFAN, CRAIG
California Reich, The (1976)

SOLAL, MARTIAL
Deux Hommes dans Manhat-

tan (1958)
Breathless (1959)
Adventures of a Photographer, The (1960)
It Happened All Night (1960)
Si le Vent te Faire Peur (1960)
Swedish Girls in Paris (1960)
A Toute Heure en Toute Saison (1961)
Tant Qu'il y Aura des Capricornes (1961)
Backfire (1964)
Deux Uraniums, Les (1965)
Neutron and Fission, The (1965)
Ballad of Emile, The (1966)
Bougnats, Les (1966)
Nuclear Reactor, The (1966)
Orpheon (1966)
Tant Qu'il y Aura de l'Angoisse (1966)
Timber (1967)
Veridiquement Votre (1968)
Voyage Vers la Lumiere (1969)

SOLBACH, PEPE
Grotze Farmer, The (1975)

SOLOVIEV-SEDOI
Sweet Woman (1977)

SOMMER, BERT
Hot Parts (1972)

SONDHEIM, STEPHEN
Stavisky (1974)

SONGPOW, PRACHIN
Lovers, The (1978)
September Love (1978)
Smile Hello (1978)
Love of a Little Girl, The (1979)

SONIMSAT, SEKSAN
Iron Buffalo, The (1977)
O, Madda (1977)
1 2 3 Monster Express (1977)
Stupid Life (1977)
Only 15 (1978)
Saen Saeh Canal (1978)
Megalomaniac, The (1979)

SORALINA, ANA
Woman of Everyone, The (1969)

SORGINI, GIULIANO
Living Dead at the Manchester Morgue, The (1974)
Ice Continent, The (1975)

SORIA, LUIZ FERNANDEZ
Times of the Constitution (1978)

SOTHA
Boscop Diagram, The (1976)

SOTO
40 Years Without Sex (1979)

SOUFFRIAU, ARSENE
Zigzag (1973)
In the Name of the Fuhrer (1979)

SPANOUDAKIS, STAMATIS
Colors of the Rainbow, The (1974)
Bio-Graphia (1975)
Prometheus' Second Person (1975)

SPARIFANKAL
Paradise (1976)

SPIELTER, H.
Martin Luther (1925)

SPOERRI, BRUNO
Thaw (1977)

SPOLIANSKY, MISCHA
Hitler: The Last Ten Days (1973)

SPRINGER, PHILIP
Wicked, Wicked (1973)

SREBOTNJAK, ALOJZ
Call of Spring, The (1978)

SRIKANOND, MENRAT
Jealousy (1979)

SRINIVASAN, M. B.
Donkey in a Brahmin Village (1979)

STABILE, DICK
Born to Buck (1968)

STACK, LENNY
C. C. and Company (1970)

STAIDL, LADISLAV
Young Man and Moby Dick, The (1979)

STANLEY, RALPH
Roll, Thunder, Roll (1950)

STAWINSKI, ADAM
Room with a View of the Sea, A (1978)

STECKLER, AL
It Happened in Hollywood (1973)

STEFFEN, ALEXANDER
Misfire (1977)

STEIN, ANDREW
Hollywood Boulevard (1976)
Thunder and Lightning (1977)
Deathsport (1978)

STEIN, HERMAN
Black Shield of Falworth, The (1954)
Creature from the Black Lagoon, The (1954)
Private War of Major Benson, The (1955)
This Island Earth (1955)
Mole People, The (1956)
There's Always Tomorrow (1956)

STEIN, RONALD
Warriors 5 (1961)

STEINER, FRED
Sea Gypsies, The (1978)

STEINER, MAX
Half Shot at Sunrise (1930)
Are These Our Children? (1931)
Beau Ideal (1931)
Consolation Marriage (1931)
Gay Diplomat, The (1931)
Kept Husbands (1931)
Transgression (1931)
Traveling Husbands (1931)
Animal Kingdom, The (1932)
Bird of Paradise (1932)
Conquerors, The (1932)
Half-Naked Truth, The (1932)
Is My Face Red? (1932)
Little Orphan Annie (1932)
Lost Squadron, The (1932)
Most Dangerous Game, The (1932)
Roar of the Dragon (1932)
Rockabye (1932)
Sport Parade, The (1932)
Symphony of Six Million (1932)
Thirteen Women (1932)
What Price Hollywood? (1932)
Westward Passage (1932)
Ace of Aces (1933)
After Tonight (1933)
Aggie Appleby, Maker of Men (1933)
Before Dawn (1933)
Chance at Heaven, A (1933)
Cheyenne Kid (1933)
Christopher Strong (1933)
Diplomaniacs (1933)
Double Harness (1933)
Flying Devils (1933)
Great Jaspar, The (1933)
Headline Shooter (1933)
Lucky Devils (1933)
Midshipman Jack (1933)
Monkey's Paw, The (1933)
No Marriage Ties (1933)
No Other Woman (1933)
Rafter Romance (1933)
Right to Romance, The (1933)
Age of Innocence, The (1934)
Anne of Green Gables (1934)
Bachelor Bait (1934)
By Your Leave (1934)

Dangerous Corner (1934)
Finishing School (1934)
Gridiron Flash (1934)
His Greatest Gamble (1934)
Little Minister, The (1934)
Long Lost Father (1934)
Meanest Gal in Town, The (1934)
Silver Streak (1934)
Sing and Like It (1934)
Their Big Moment (1934)
Two Alone (1934)
Wednesday's Child (1934)
We're Rich Again (1934)
Alice Adams (1935)
Break of Hearts (1935)
She (1935)
Star of Midnight (1935)
West of the Pecos (1935)
First Lady (1937)
Life of Emile Zola, The (1937)
Slim (1937)
Submarine D-1 (1937)
That Certain Woman (1937)
Tovarich (1937)
Crime School (1938)
Jezebel (1938)
Oklahoma Kid, The (1939)
Stagecoach (1939)
They Made Me a Criminal (1939)
Desperate Journey (1942)
They Died with Their Boots On (1942)
Corn Is Green, The (1945)
Roughly Speaking (1945)
San Antonio (1945)
Voice of the Turtle, The (1948)
Iron Mistress, The (1952)
Lion and the Horse, The (1952)
China Gate (1957)

STEINERT, ALEXANDER
Blondie Knows Best (1946)
Don Ricardo Returns (1946)
Personality Kid, The (1946)

STEINMAN, AL
Kansas City Trucking Co. (1976)
El Paso Wrecking Co. (1978)

STEIRLING, RANDY
Naked Angels (1969)

STEITHESON, MIKE
Pussy Talk (1975)

STELIO, MICHEL
In a Wild Moment (1977)

STENVALD, JIRI
Night of Orange Fires (1975)

STEOBER, ORVILLE
delete

STERLING, JOHN
Revenge of the Cheerleaders, The (1976)

STERN, JAKE
Feedback (1979)

STEVENS, LEITH
Syncopation (1942)
Navajo (1951)
Storm Over Tibet (1951)
The Bigamist (1953)
Mad at the World (1955)
Great Day in the Morning (1956)

STEVENS, MORTON
Hawaii Five-0 (1970)

STILL, WILLIAM GRANT
Lady of Secrets (1936)
Pennies from Heaven (1936)
Theodora Goes Wild (1936)

STOCKDALE, TERRY
Shoot It: Black, Shoot It: Blue (1974)

STOEBER, ORVILLE
Let's Scare Jessica to Death (1971)

STOKES, SIMON
Ali the Man: Ali the Fighter (1975)

STOLOFF, MORRIS
Marrying Kind, The (delete)

STONE, BOB
Super Van (1977)

STONE, GREGORY
Easy to Take (1936)
Ride a Crooked Mile (1938)
Her First Romance (1940)

STORA, JEAN-PIERRE
Garden That Tilts, The (1975)
Second Wind, A (1978)

STOTHART, HERBERT
Call of the Flesh (1930)
Devil May Care (1930)
Floradora Girl, The (1930)
In Gay Madrid (1930)
Lady's Morals, A (1930)
Madam Satan (1930)
Montana Moon (1930)
Rogue Song (1930)
Cuban Love Song, The (1931)
New Moon (1931)
Prodigal, The (1931)
Son-Daughter, The (1932)
Barbarian, The (1933)
Turn Back the Clock (1933)
Chained (1934)
Laughing Boy (1934)
Biography of a Bachelor Girl, The (1935)
David Copperfield (1935)
Mutiny on the Bounty (1935)
Night at the Opera, A (1935)
Sequoia (1935)
Vanessa, Her Love Story (1935)
Moonlight Murder (1936)
Wife vs. Secretary (1936)
Conquest (1937)
Idiot's Delight (1939)
They Met in Bombay (1941)
Thousands Cheer (1943)

STOVALL, TED
Boy Who Cried Werewolf, The (1973)

STRACINA, SVETOZAR
Day Does Not Die (1974)
Cruel Love (1978)
Lawyer, The (1978)

STRAUSS, JOHANN
delete

STRAUSS, JOHANN, JR.
delete

STRAUSS, JOHN
Mikey and Nicky (1976)

STRAUSS, RICHARD
delete

STRAVINSKY, IGOR
delete

STYNE, JULE
Thieves (1977)

STYNER, JERRY
Black Jack (1973)
Jennifer (1978)

SUBIDO, DANNY
On Top of All (1975)

SUGARMAN, SPARKY
Summer Camp (1979)

SUKMAN, HARRY
Bonanza (1960)
High Chaparral, The (1969)

SUMMERLIN, ED
Caio (1967)

SUMMERS, ROBERT
Guardian of the Wilderness (1977)
Lincoln Conspiracy, The (1977)
Sixth and Main (1977)
Beyond and Back (1978)

SUNDFOR, PAUL
Attack of the Killer Tomatoes (1979)

SUST, JIRI
To Search for a Golden Earth (1975)

Seclusion Near a Forest (1976)
Those Wonderful Men with a Crank (1979)

SUSTRATE, NILS
Consequence, The (1977)

SUWANNASORN, PRAT
Slum People in the Sun (1979)

SVENSSON, GUNNAR
Adventures of Picasso, The (1978)

SVOBODA, KAREL
Stormy Wine (1976)
Singer, The (1978)

SWINGLE, WARD
Do You Like Girls? (1966)
Galia (1967)

SWINNEN, FIRMIN
Old Nest, The (1921)

SYMONS, RED
Pure S (1976)

SZIRLATKA, ARIE
Not as Wicked as All That... (1975)

SZOLLOSY, ANDRAS
80 Hussars (1978)
Legato (1978)

SZORNEYI, LEVENTI
Petofi '73 (1973)
Hajduk (1975)
Trumpeter, The (1979)

SZYMANOWSKI, KAROL
Young Ladies of Wilko, The (1979)

TAKEMITSU, TORU
Minatomo Yoshitsune (1966)
Time Within Memory (1973)
Himiko (1974)
Banished (1978)
Phantom Love (1978)
Louvre Museum, The (1979)

TALLY, TOMMY
Take One (1977)

TALMI, AKIRA
Two (1974)

TAMASSY, ZDENKO
25 Fireman's Street (1974)
Budapest Tales (1977)
Strange Role, A (1977)
Sword, The (1977)
My Father's Happy Years (1978)

TAMINDZIC, BORO
Beasts (1977)

TANABE, SHINICHI
Queen Bee (1978)

TANAKA, MASASHI (MICHI)
In the Fire Land (1976)
Third Base (1978)

TANG, LU YUAN
Breaking with Old Ideas (1976)

"TANGERINE DREAM"
Sorcerer (1977)
Kneuss (1978)

TANKER, ANDRE
Bim (1976)

TANLONG, CHONATI
Village Head at the Border, The (1977)

TANSMAN, ALEXANDRE
Destiny (1944)

TANTU, CORNELIA
Wall, The (1978)

TAPSCOTT, HORACE
Sweet Jesus, Preacher Man (1973)

TARIVERDIEV, M.
Welcome (1978)
Old Comedy, The (1979)

TAYLOR, BUTCH
Deep Sleep (1973)

TAYLOR, JAMES
Badlands (1973)

TCHAIKOVSKI, BORIS
Personal Opinion, A (1977)

TEMPERA, VINCENZO
Nest of Vipers (1979)
Where Are You Going on Your Vacation? (1979)

TENAGLIA, R.
Germania (1914)

TEVISAN, JOAO SILVERIO
Sonho de Vampiros, Um (1970)

THEODORAKIS, GEORGE
Easy Road (1979)
Uncompromising Man, An (1979)

THEODORAKIS, MIKIS
Island of Aphrodite, The (1966)
Serpico (1973)
State of Siege (1973)
Sutjeska (1973)
Partisans (1974)
Letters from Marusia (1976)
Iphighenia (1977)
Easy Road (1979)

THEPTIAM, PAIRATH
Only 16 (Part II) (1977)

THIELEMANS, TOOTS
Thundering Fatty (Dunderklumpen) (1974)
Sherlock Jones (1975)
Johnny Larsen (1979)

THOIFUR
Al Kaustsar (1977)

THOMAS, DAVID
Remains of the Shipwreck (1978)

THOMAS, PETER
Snake Pit and the Pendulum, The (1967)
Chariots of the Gods (1973)
Temptations in the Summer Wind (1973)
Miracle of the Gods (1976)
Once Upon a Time (1976)
Breakthrough (1979)

THOMAS, RENE
Femme Image, La (1960)

THOMASS, EUGEN
Nocturne (1972)
Sternstein Manor, The (1976)
Meat (Fleisch) (1979)
Plutonium (1979)

THOMPSON, JOHN
House of the Lute (1979)

THORNE, KEN
Magic Christian, The (1969)
Juggernaut (1974)
Royal Flash (1975)
Assault on Agathon (1976)
Ritz, The (1976)
Arabian Adventure (1979)
Outsider, The (1979)

TIAPTIAM, CHAIRAT
Happy Confusion (1978)

TIOMKIN, DIMITRI
Resurrection (1931)
Casino Murder Case, The (1935)
Mad Love (1935)
Road Back, The (1937)
Flying Blind (1941)
Forced Landing (1941)
Scattergood Meets Broadway (1941)
Moscow Strikes Back (1942)
Forever Yours (1945)
Bugles in the Afternoon (1952)
Sundowners, The (1960)

TIPPETT, SIR MICHAEL
Akenfield (1975)

TIPTON, GEORGE ALICESON
Badlands (1973)
Phantom of the Paradise (1974)
Griffin and Phoenix (1976)

TJADER, CAL
Hot Car Girl (1958)

TOCH, ERNST
Catherine the Great (1934)
Little Friend (1934)
Private Life of Don Juan, The (1934)
Dr. Cyclops (1940)

TODD, BOB
Young and the Restless, The (1973)

TOH, LUA MING
Tragedy of Love (1979)

TOMITA, ISAO
Heavens and the Earth, The (1969)
Story of the Taira Family, The (1972)
Katsu Taiheiki (1974)
Catastrophe 1999 (1977)

TOURS, FRANK
Emperor Jones, The (1933)
Crime Without Passion (1934)
Gambling (1934)
Fight for Your Lady (1937)
She's Got Everything (1937)
Everybody's Doing It (1938)
Mother Carey's Chickens (1938)
Smashing the Rackets (1938)
Almost a Gentleman (1939)
Beauty for the Asking (1939)
Boy Slaves (1939)
Conspiracy (1939)
King of the Turf (1939)
Men Against the Sky (1940)
Villain Still Pursued Her, The (1940)

TOUSSAINT, ALLEN
Black Samson (1974)

TOWNS, COLIN
Full Circle (1977)

TOWNSHEND, PETER
Kids Are Alright, The (1979)

TREESE, JACK
Oh, America (1975)

TREGADIO, M.
Kingdom of Naples, The (1978)

TREMBLAY, DOMINIQUE
Vultures, The (1978)

TROVAJOLI, ARMANDO
Tempi Duri per I Vampiri (1959)
Atom Age Vampire (1960)
Hercules at the Center of the Earth (1961)
Italiani Brava Gente (1965)
Myth, The (1965)
Nostri Mariti, I (1966)
How, When and with Whom? (1969)
In the Year of the Lord (1969)
Dramma Della Gelosia (1970)
Noi Donne Siamo Fatte Cosi (1971)
Permette, Rocco Papaleo (1971)
Piu Bella Serata della Mia Vita, A (1972)
Hot-Blooded Paolo (1973)
I Did It (1973)
Italian Connection, The (1973)
Sex Crazy (1973)
Tosca, La (1973)
Bitter Love (1974)
Scent of Woman (1974)
Amici Miei (1975)
Homo Eroticus (1975)
Those Were the Years (1975)
Blazing Magnum (1976)
Duck in Orange Sauce (1976)
Ugly, Dirty and Bad (1976)
Bishop's Bedroom, The (1977)
Great Day, The (1977)
Lover, Wife (1977)
Strange Shadows in an Empty

Room (1977)
In the Name of the Pope King (1978)
Ligabue (1978)
Viva Italia (1978)
Fifth Commandment, The (1979)

TROZJUK, BIGDAN
With You and Without You (1974)

TRUJILLO, RAUL
Natives of Planet Earth (1973)

TRUSSEL, CHRISTOPHER
Hot Potato (1976)

TRZASKOWSKI, ANDRZEJ
Night Train (Pociag) (1959)

TSABADZE
Melodies of Veruski District (1974)

TSCHUDIN, MICHAEL
Honeybaby, Honeybaby (1974)

TSEBOULKA, KIRIL
Memories (1975)
Stars in the Hair, Tears in the Eyes (1978)
Surgeons (1978)
Barrier (1979)
Boomerang (1979)
Poor Lucas (1979)
With Shared Love (1979)

TSILIKIS, SAKIS
Hour of the Wolf, The (1979)

TUCHINDA, SAKAT
Pregnant by a Ghost (1975)

TUCHO, TOMMY
Barney (1977)

TUFO, RICHARD
Three the Hard Way (1974)

TULLY, COLIN
That Sinking Feeling (1979)

TUOMINEN, HARRI
Pretty Good for a Human (1978)

TUSQUES, FRANCIS
Naked Vampire (1969)

TWAIN, ART
American Nitro (1979)

TWEEDY, DON
Steel Arena (1973)

UHLIS, JARISLAV
Long Live Ghosts! (1979)

UMALI, RESTIE
Batingaw (1974)

UMILIANI, PIERO
5 Dolls for an August Moon (1972)
Baba Yaga (1973)
Slave, The (1973)

URBONT, JACQUES
Case of the Full-Moon Murders, The (1973)
High Rise (1973)
Fireworks Woman (1975)

URCHS, MARKUS
Last Years of Childhood, The (1979)

URTREGER, RENE
Janine (1962)
Chicken, The (1963)
First Time, The (1976)

USHEROVICI, P. C.
Black Banana, The (1977)

USUELLI, TEO
Paranoia (1966)

UZAKI, RYUDO
Double Suicide of Sonezaki (1978)
So Long, Movie Friend (Goodbye, Flickmania) (1979)

VAGGIONE, HORACIO
Wise Guys, The (1977)

VAINBERG, MOISES
Aphonyo (1976)

VALERDE, MIKE
Horror of the Blood Monsters (1970)

VALPOLA, HEIKKI
Home and Refuge (1977)
Homeward in the Night (1977)
Manrape (1978)

VAN CLEAVE, NATHAN
Sainted Sisters, The (1948)
Dear Wife (1949)
Fancy Pants (1950)
Dear Brat (1951)
Molly (1951)
Quebec (1951)
Rhubarb (1951)
Off Limits (1953)
Cinerama Holiday (1955)
Conquest of Space (1955)
Lucy Gallant (1955)
Devil's Hairpin, The (1957)
Lonely Man, The (1957)
Colossus of New York, The (1958)
Space Children, The (1958)
That Kind of Woman (1959)
Blueprint for Robbery (1961)
Robinson Crusoe on Mars (1964)
Project X (1968)

"VAN DER GRAAF GENERATOR"
Eyewitness (1970)

VAN MECHELEN, CLAUS
Rufus (1975)

VAN OTTERLOO, ROGIER
Turkish Delight (1973)
Keetje Tippel (1975)
Soldier of Orange (1979)

VAN PARYS, GEORGES
Femme et le Pantin, La (1929)

VAN ROOYEN, JERRY
Vampire Happening, The (1971)

VAN ROOYEN, LAURENS
Rembrandt--Fecit 1669 (1978)
Mysteries (1979)

VANDER, CHRISTIAN
Tristan et Iseult (1979)

VANDER, MAURICE
Amelie's Trip (1975)
Shadow of the Castles (1976)
Order and Security of the World (1978)

VANDOR, IVAN
Spiral of Mist, A (1977)

VANGARDE, DANIEL
Dora and the Magic Lantern (1978)

VANNIER, JEAN-CLAUDE
At Night All Cats Are Gray (1977)

VARDI, EMMANUEL
Life Study (1973)

VARESE, EDGARD
Divine Plan, The (1976)

VARTAN, EDDIE
Vive La France (1974)

VASCONELLOS, NANA
Castaways of Turtle Island, The (1976)

VASSEUR, DIDIER
Blackout (1978)

VASSILLIADES, STEFANOS
Corpus (1979)

VAZ, GILHERMO
Devil Queen, The (1975)

VELASQUEZ, DEMET
Earthly Body, The (1975)
Live Coal in the East (1975)
Hide and Seek (1976)
Small Insect (1976)
Stupid Boy Friend, The (1976)

VELASQUEZ, LEONARDO
Calzonin Inspector (1974)

VELASQUEZ, O.
One Night, Three Women (1975)

VELERDE, MIKE
Horror of the Blood Monsters (1970)

VELLOSO, CAETANO
Lady on the Bus (1978)

VENDITTI, ANTONELLO
Goodnight, Ladies and Gentlemen (1977)

VENKSTESH, G. K.
Restless Corpse, The (1979)

VERGARA, PABLO
Tower of the Devil (1969)
Basketball Stars (1974)

VERLINDEN, PETER
Death of a Nun (1975)
I Never Cried Like This Before (1975)
Ham from the Ardennes (1977)

VERSCHUEREN, ETIENNE
Golden Ophelia (1975)
Woman Between Dog and Wolf, A (1979)

VERSIANI, MARCO
Colonel and the Werewolf, The (1979)

VIAN, PATRICK
Hu-Man (1975)

VICKERS, HOWIE
Supreme Kid, The (1976)

VICKERS, MIKE
Sex Thief, The (1974)
At the Earth's Core (1976)
Warlords of Atlantis (1978)

VICTOR, GERARD
Victor Frankenstein (1977)

VICTOR AND DIEGO
Country Inc. (1975)

VIDAL, J.
Rage (1979)

VILDANOV, RUMIL
Among People (1979)

VILELA, HELVIUS
Colonel and the Werewolf, The (1979)

VINCENT, DON
Happy Mother's Day ... Love, George (1973)

VINCENT, ROLAND
Women, Women (1974)
Machine, The (1977)

VINCENT, STAN
Foreplay (1975)

VIRAYAPHANIT, PANTHIP
Sai Thip (1979)

VIRKHAUS, TAAVO
Tiina (1977)

VITIER, SERGIO
Giron (1974)
Earth and the Sky, The (1978)
Teacher, The (1978)
Woman, Man, City (1978)

VIZZIELLO, CARLOS
I Saw Her First (1975)
I'm a Woman Already (1975)
Third Door, The (1976)
God Bless Each Corner of This House (1977)
My First Sin (1977)
But Aren't You Ever Going to Change, Margarita? (1978)

Sitting on the Edge of Tomorrow with the Feet Hanging (1979)

VLAD, ROMAN
Vampiri, I (1956)
Little Archimedes, The (1979)

VOLMAN, MARK
Cheap (1974)

VORSKUL, MOVALA
After the Rain (1978)

VRANSEVIC, MLADEN
Arrive Before Daybreak (1978)
Trophy (1979)

VRANSEVIC, PREDRAG
Paradise (1976)
Arrive Before Daybreak (1978)
Trophy (1979)

VUH, POPOL
Nosferatu, Phantom of the Night (1979)

VUKAN, GYORGY
Agony of Mr. Boroka, The (1973)
Let Go of My Beard (1975)
Unfinished Sentence in 141 Minutes, The (1975)
Fifth Sea, The (1977)
Piano in Midair, A (1977)
Hungarians, The (1978)

WACHARASATHIEN, CHINTAN-ART
Heartbreak People (1979)

WAIN, CHARLES
Last Wave, The (1977)

WAITZMAN, ADOLFO
Bell, The (1973)
Second Power, The (1977)

WAKEMAN, RICK
Lisztomania (1975)
White Rock, The (1976)

WAKS, NATHAN
My Brilliant Career (1979)

WALACINSKI, ADAM
Death of the President (1978)

WALCOTT, COLIN
Raga (1971)

WALDORF, SVEN-OLAF
Two Women (1975)
Jungle Adventure Campa Campa (1976)

WALDRON, MAL
Three Rooms in Manhattan (1958)
Cool World, The (1963)
Sal-a-Malle-Ek (1965)

WALEN, NIELS
Grete Minde (1977)
Glass Cell, The (1978)

WALLACE, OLIVER
Murder by Television (1935)
Follow the Boys (1944)

WANG, EDDIE
Proud Twins, The (1979)

WANGCHORAKUL, KANG
Victim of Passion (1975)

WANNBERG, KENNETH
Bittersweet Love (1976)
Late Show, The (1977)

WANNIER, JEAN-CLAUDE
Lola's Lolos (1976)

WARD, EDWARD
Hypnotized (1932)
Age of Indiscretion (1934)
Cheating Cheaters (1934)
Embarrassing Moments (1934)
Gift of Gab, The (1934)
Girl o' My Dreams (1934)
I Like It That Way (1934)
Romance in the Rain (1934)
Here Comes the Band (1935)
Kind Lady (1935)
Reckless (1935)
Times Square Lady (1935)

After the Thin Man (1936)
Exclusive Story (1936)
Moonlight Murder (1936)
Small Town Girl (1936)
Speed (1936)
Wife vs. Secretary (1936)
Women Are Trouble (1936)
Bad Guy (1937)
Double Wedding (1937)
Live, Love and Learn (1937)
Mama Steps Out (1937)
Meet the Mayor (1938)
Blackmail (1939)
Dancing Co-Ed (1939)
Henry Goes Arizona (1939)
It's a Wonderful World (1939)
Nick Carter, Master Detective (1939)
Remember? (1939)
Secret of Dr. Kildare, The (1939)
6,000 Enemies (1939)
Society Lawyer (1939)
Stronger Than Desire (1939)
These Glamour Girls (1939)
They All Come Out (1939)
Congo Maisie (1940)
All-American Co-Ed (1941)
Miss Polly (1941)
Niagara Falls (1941)
Son of Monte Cristo, The (1941)
Tanks a Million (1941)
Brooklyn Orchid (1942)
Flying with Music (1942)
Hay Foot (1942)
McGuerins from Brooklyn, The (1942)
Men of Texas (1942)
Calaboose (1943)
Fall In (1943)
That Nazty Nuisance (1943)
Yanks Ahoy (1943)
Climax, The (1944)

WARNE, DEREK
Great McGonagall, The (1975)

WARREN, DALE O.
Klansman, The (1974)

WARREN, DOUG
Devil's Mistress, The (1966)

WARSKA, WANDA
Curio Lake, The (1974)

WATANABE, CHUMEI
Super-Giant 2 (1956)

"WAVEMAKER"
Tempest, The (1979)

WAXMAN, FRANZ
Affair of Susan (1935)
Bride of Frankenstein (1935)
Diamond Jim (1935)
Remember Last Night? (1935)
Invisible Ray, The (1936)
Bride Wore Red, The (1937)
Emperor's Candlesticks, The (1937)
Dramatic School (1938)
Port of Seven Seas (1938)
Honolulu (1939)
Lucky Night (1939)
Sporting Blood (1940)
Bad Man, The (1941)
Design for Scandal (1941)
Dr. Jekyll and Mr. Hyde (1941)
Destination Tokyo (1944)
To Have and Have Not (1945)
Paradine Case, The (1948)
Sunrise at Campobello (1960)
King of the Roaring Twenties (1961)

WAYMON, SAM
Ganja and Hess (1973)
Just Crazy About Horses (1978)

WEBB, JIMMY
Naked Ape, The (1973)
Voices (1979)

WEBB, ROY
Cockeyed Cavaliers (1934)
Kentucky Kernels (1934)
Lightning Strikes Twice (1934)
Another Face (1935)
Arizonian, The (1935)
Becky Sharp (1935)

Captain Hurricane (1935)
Enchanted April (1935)
Laddie (1935)
Last Days of Pompeii, The (1935)
Nitwits, The (1935)
Old Man Rhythm (1935)
Rainmakers, The (1935)
Strangers All (1935)
We're Only Human (1935)
Lady Consents, The (1936)
Last of the Mohicans, The (1936)
Mummy's Boys (1936)
Murder on a Bridle Path (1936)
Muss 'Em Up (1936)
Second Wife (1936)
Silly Billies (1936)
Witness Chair, The (1936)
High Flyers (1937)
Life of the Party, The (1937)
Stage Door (1937)
Blonde Cheat (1938)
Border G-Man (1938)
Condemned Women (1938)
Crime Ring (1938)
Go Chase Yourself (1938)
Gun Law (1938)
Having Wonderful Time (1938)
Lawless Valley (1938)
Mr. Doodle Kicks Off (1938)
Next Time I Marry (1938)
Renegade Ranger, The (1938)
Room Service (1938)
Sky Giant (1938)
Arizona Legion (1939)
Bachelor Mother (1939)
Full Confession (1939)
Girl and the Gambler, The (1939)
Love Affair (1939)
Panama Lady (1939)
Racketeers of the Range (1939)
Rookie Cop (1939)
Saint Strikes Back, The (1939)
Sorority House (1939)
Sued for Libel (1939)
They Made Her a Spy (1939)
Three Sons (1939)
Timber Stampede (1939)
Trouble in Sundown (1939)
Twelve Crowded Hours (1939)
Two Thoroughbreds (1939)
Anne of Windy Poplars (1940)
Bill of Divorcement, A (1940)
Curtain Call (1940)
I'm Still Alive (1940)
Married and in Love (1940)
Mexican Spitfire Out West (1940)
Millionaires in Prison (1940)
Saint Takes Over, The (1940)
Saint's Double Trouble, The (1940)
You Can't Fool Your Wife (1940)
Devil and Miss Jones, The (1941)
Hurry, Charlie, Hurry (1941)
Little Men (1941)
Look Who's Laughing (1941)
Mexican Spitfire Sees a Ghost (1941)
Parachute Battalion (1941)
Saint in Palm Springs, The (1941)
Tom, Dick and Harry (1941)
Weekend for Three (1941)
Falcon's Brother, The (1942)
Highways by Night (1942)
I Married a Witch (1942)
Mexican Spitfire Sees a Ghost (1942)
Mexican Spitfire's Elephant (1942)
Obliging Young Lady, An (1942)
Powder Town (1942)
Hitler's Children (1943)
Journey into Fear (1943)
Petticoat Larceny (1943)
Seven Miles from Alcatraz (1943)
Seventh Cross, The (1944)
Cass Timberlane (1948)
At Sword's Point (1952)
Clash by Night (1952)
Kentuckian, The (delete)

WEBBER, ANDREW LLOYD
Odessa File, The (1974)

WECKER, KONSTANTIN
Sisters, or the Balance of Happiness (1979)

WEILL, KURT
You and Me (1938)

WEINER, JEAN
Feminin-Feminin (1973)
Women Duelling (1976)

WEISS, JOSEPH
Student von Prag, Der (1913)

WEISS, RONI
Belfer (1978)

WELCH, ED
Stand Up, Virgin Soldiers (1977)
39 Steps, The (1978)

WELLINGTON, LARRY
Taste of Blood, A (1967)

WERNER, FRED
Huckleberry Finn (1974)
Moonshine County Express (1977)

WERTHEIMER, FRANCOIS
One Sings, the Other Doesn't (1977)

WESLEY, FRED
Slaughter's Big Rip-Off (1973)

WESTBROOK, MIKE
Going Places (1973)

WETZLAU, JOACHIM
Jacob the Liar (1975)

WHITE, BARRY
Together Brothers, The (1974)

WHITE, DANIEL
Dracula vs. Frankenstein (1971)

WHITE, MAURICE
That's the Way of the World (1975)

WHITE, TONY JOE
Catch My Soul (1974)

WHITFIELD, NORMAN
Car Wash (1976)

WHITTAKER, DAVID
Vampire Circus (1971)
Old Dracula (1975)

"WHO," THE
Quadrophenia (1979)

WIENER, ELISABETH
Goodbye Singing, The (1975)
Wise Guys, The (1977)

WILEN, BARNEY
Witness in the City (1959)

WILHELM, ROLF
Serpent's Egg, The (1977)

WILKINSON, MARC
Blood on Satan's Claw, The (1971)
Hireling, The (1973)
Mango Tree, The (1977)
Eagle's Wing, The (1979)

WILLIAMS, DAVID
Delirium (1979)

WILLIAMS, GUY BEVIER
White Zombie (1932)

WILLIAMS, JOHN
Plainsman, The (1966)
Jane Eyre (1970)
Cinderella Liberty (1973)
Long Goodbye, The (1973)
Man Who Loved Cat Dancing, The (1973)
Paper Chase, The (1973)
Conrack (1974)
Earthquake (1974)
Sugarland Express, The (1974)
Towering Inferno, The (1974)
Eiger Sanction, The (1975)
Jaws (1975)
Family Plot (1976)
Midway (1976)
Missouri Breaks, The (1976)
Black Sunday (1977)

Close Encounters of the Third Kind (1977)
Star Wars (1977)
Fury, The (1978)
Jaws II (1978)
Superman (1978)
Dracula (1979)
1941 (1979)

WILLIAMS, PATRICK
S-s-s-s-s-s (1973)
Harrad Summer, The (1974)
Framed (1975)
Casey's Shadow (1978)
One and Only, The (1978)
Breaking Away (1979)
Butch and Sundance: The Early Days (1979)
Cuba (1979)
Hot Stuff (1979)

WILLIAMS, PAUL
Phantom of the Paradise (1974)
Bugsy Malone (1976)
End, The (1978)
Muppet Movie, The (1979)

WILLIAMS, PIP
Train Ride to Hollywood (1975)

WILLIAMSON, MALCOLM
Watership Down (1978)

WILSON, ANDREW
Sebastian (1976)

WILSON, ROSS
Oz (1976)

WILSON, STANLEY
Powder River Rustlers (1949)
Hills of Oklahoma (1950)
Salt Lake Raiders (1950)

WINDING, KASPER
Cop (1976)
Heritage, The (1978)
Me and Charley (1978)
Johnny Larsen (1979)

WINELAND, SAM
Samarang (1933)
Tarzan the Fearless (1933)

WINKLER, MAX
Wrong Door, The (1915)
Crippled Hand, The (1916)
Flirt, The (1916)
Gay Lord Waring, The (1916)
Great Problem, The (1916)
Grip of Jealousy, The (1916)
Hop, the Devil's Brew (1916)
Jeanne Dore (1916)
John Needham's Double (1916)
Rupert of Hentzau (1916)
Secret Love (1916)
Strength of the Weak, The (1916)
Tangled Hearts (1916)
Undine (1916)
Yaqui, The (1916)
Right to Happiness, The (1919)
Virgin of Stamboul, The (1920)

WINN, JERRY
Young and the Restless, The (1973)

WOHLGEMUTH, GERHARD
Man Against Man (1976)

WOMACK, BOBBY
Across 110th St. (1973)

WONDER, STEVIE
Secret Life of Plants, The (1978)

WONG, EDDIE
Daosawan, I Love You (1975)

WONG, JAMES
Extras, The (1978)

WONG, TANG
He Never Gives Up (1979)

WONG, TONY
Lantern Festival Adventure (1979)

WRIGHT, ARTHUR
Dolemite (1975)

WRIGHT, GARY
Benjamin (1973)

WRIGHT, RON
Van Nuys Blvd. (1979)

WYNKOOP, RICHARD
Resurrection of Eve (1973)

XARCHAKOS, STAVROS
Girls in the Sun (1968)

YAGI, MASAO
Funny Note (1977)

YAMAMOTO, NAOZUMI
Wind, Cloud and Rainbow (1976)

YAMASHITA, STOMU
One by One (1974)
Art of Killing (1978)

YANAGISAWA, GO
Mayujo, the Only One (1971)

YANG-YU, CHAN
Black Magic 2 (1977)

YANNE, JEAN
Show Business (1975)

YARBROUGH, MARTIN
Black Godfather (1974)

YARED, GABRIEL
Miss O'Gynie and the Flower Man (1974)

YARUS, ALLEN
Desperate Living (1977)

YENIGUN, HURSIT
Sun over the Swamp (1978)

YOSHINO, MIKI
House (1977)
God, Why Is There a Border in Love? (1979)

YOSIFOV, ALEXANDER
Talisman (1978)

YOSSIFOV, PETER
Run Away, I Love You (1979)

YOUNG, BOB
Inn of the Damned (1974)

YOUNG, NEIL
Journey Through the Past (1973)

YOUNG, PATRICK
Stevie (1978)

YOUNG, VICTOR
Fatal Lady (1936)
Champagne Waltz (1937)
Swing High, Swing Low (1937)
Vogues of 1938 (1937)
Flirting with Fate (1938)
Fisherman's Wharf (1939)
Heritage of the Desert (1939)
Light That Failed, The (1939)
Llano Kid, The (1939)
Man of Conquest (1939)
Night of Nights, The (1939)
Our Neighbors the Carters (1939)
Way Down South (1939)
Buck Benny Rides Again (1940)
Knights of the Range (1940)
Light of Western Stars, The (1940)
Love Thy Neighbor (1940)
Road to Singapore (1940)
Three Men from Texas (1940)
Aloma of the South Seas (1941)
Mad Doctor, The (1941)
Road to Zanzibar (1941)
Flying Tigers (1942)
Forest Rangers, The (1942)
No Time for Love (1944)
Trouble with Women, The (1947)
So Evil My Love (1948)
Rio Grande (1950)
This Is Korea (1951)
Brave One, The (1956)
China Gate (1957)

YOW, JOHN
Game of Love, A (1974)

YUASA, JOHJI
More Blue than Blue Color (1972)
Story of Peaceful Genroku Era, The (1975)

YUNG-CHENG, CHIN
Pioneers, The (1977)

YUNG-HUANG, CHEN
Triple Irons (1973)

YUNG-YU, CHEN
Sacred Knives of Vengeance, The (1973)
Street Gangs of Hong Kong (1974)
Girl with Long Hair (1975)
Crazy Sex (1976)
Marco Polo (1976)
Seven-Man Army (1976)
Judgment of an Assassin (1977)
Shaolin Abbot (1979)
Shaolin Rescuers (1979)

ZAHERI, FOUAD EL
Death of the Water Carrier (1977)
Alexandria ... Why? (1979)

ZAHLER, GORDON
Plan 9 from Outer Space (1956)
Happy as the Grass Was Green (1973)
Return to Campus (1975)

ZAHLER, LEE
King of the Congo (1929)
Chinatown After Dark (1931)
King of the Wild (1931)
Phantom of the West (1931)
Private Scandal, A (1931)
Hurricane Express, The (1932)
Midnight Warning (1932)
Monster Walks, The (1932)
Shadow of the Eagle (1932)
Silver Lining (1932)
Tangled Destinies (1932)
Vanishing Frontier (1932)
Laughing at Life (1933)
Three Musketeers, The (1933)
Fire Trap, The (1935)
Just My Luck (1935)
Lost City, The (1935)
Motive for Revenge (1935)
Public Opinion (1935)
Symphony of Living (1935)
Unknown Ranger, The (1935)
Amazing Exploits of the Clutching Hand, The (1936)
North of Nome (1936)
Penitente Murder Case, The (1936)
Shadows of the Orient (1936)
Slander House (1936)
Boy Who Saved a Nation, The (1937)
Fifty-Year Barter, The (1937)
Herald of the Skies, The (1937)
Silver Threads (1937)
Pioneer Trail (1938)
Stagecoach Days (1938)
Hidden Power (1939)
Law Comes to Texas, The (1939)
Ellery Queen, Master Detective (1940)
Great Plane Robbery, The (1940)
Outside the 3-Mile Limit (1940)
Passport to Alcatraz (1940)
Ellery Queen and the Murder Ring (1941)
Ellery Queen and the Perfect Crime (1941)
Ellery Queen's Penthouse Mystery (1941)
Great Swindle, The (1941)
Bombs over Burma (1942)
Captain Midnight (1942)
Close Call for Ellery Queen, A (1942)
Desperate Chance for Ellery Queen, A (1942)
Enemy Agents Meet Ellery Queen (1942)
Gallant Lady (1942)
Miss V from Moscow (1942)
Perils of the Royal Mounted (1942)
Batman (1943)
Gentle Gangster (1943)
Man of Courage (1943)

Phantom, The (1943)
Black Arrow (1944)
Marked for Murder (1944)
Rogue's Gallery (1944)
Enemy of the Law (1945)
Jeep Herders (1945)
Jungle Raiders (1945)
Monster and the Ape, The (1945)
Navajo Kid (1945)
Who's Guilty? (1945)
Detour to Danger (1946)
Hop Harrigan (1946)
Son of the Guardsman (1946)
Thunder Town (1946)
Jack Armstrong (1947)

ZAMECNIK, J. S.
Old Ironsides (1926)
Wings (1927)
Abie's Irish Rose (1928)
Betrayal (1929)
Redskin (1929)

ZANINELLI, LUIGI
Visitor, The (1973)

ZAPIN, A.
Sannikov's Land (1973)

ZAPPA, FRANK
Baby Snakes (1979)

ZARNECKI, MICHAEL
Personnel (1976)

ZAVALA, JOSE ANTONIO
Fantastic Balloon Trip, The (1976)
Three Wise Men, The (1976)

ZAZA, PAUL JAMES
Title Shot (1979)

ZEISL, ERIC
Invisible Man's Revenge, The (1944)

ZEITLIN, DENNY
Invasion of the Body Snatchers (1978)

ZELLER, WOLFGANG
Vampyr (1932)

ZERVOS, NICOS
Exiled in a Central Avenue (1979)

ZESSES, NICK
Sugar Hill (1974)

ZILBER, ARIEL
But Where Is Daniel Vax? (1974)

ZIMINSKI, MARIAN
Eleventh Hour, The (1974)

ZIMMERMAN, TUCKER
Souvenir of Gilbraltar (1975)

ZIMMERS, DON
Screams of a Winter Night (1979)

ZIPLOW, REESE and STEVE
Fringe Benefits (1974)

ZIPLOW, STEVE
Slipup (1975)

ZITTRER, CARL
Black Christmas (1974)
Deranged (1974)

ZIV, M.
Untypical Story, An (1978)

ZIVKOVIC, BRANISLAV
Crazy Days (1977)
Redeemer, The (1977)
Bravo Maestro (1978)

ZOGRAFSKI, TOMISLAV
Longest Journey, The (1976)
Verdict, The (1977)

ZORZAR, STEFAN
Soldiers Never Cry (1979)

ZULFU, OMAR
Bus, The (1976)

ZUMAQUE, FRANCISCO
Gamin (1978)

ZWETKOFF, PETER
Kassbach (1979)

RECORDED MUSICAL SCORES
(A Discography)

This discography consists of a majority of film music on discs in 78, 45, and 33-1/3 r.p.m. Because soundtrack albums are usually commercially withdrawn a year or two after a film completes its first and second runs, most of the albums listed will no longer be generally available for sale, but may be purchased through record collectors or checked out from some public library record collections.

Complete scores and suites (or albums containing at least three themes from a film) are underlined. Other versions are usually single themes only. When two record numbers are given, the first is monaural and the second, a stereo version. Numbers or letters in parentheses before a record number indicate a stereo version.

Availability of tape, cartridge and cassette versions of these scores may be checked in the latest edition of the Schwann Record and Tape Guide and the Harrison Tape Catalog.

ABSENT-MINDED PROFESSOR, THE (Disney, 1961) George Bruns
Disneyland ST-1911 and DQ-1323

ABSOLUTELY NATURAL (ASSOLUTO NATURALE, L'/HE AND SHE) (Italy, 1969) Ennio Morricone
Cinevox MDF-33/23 (Italy)

ACCUSED, THE (Paramount, 1948) Victor Young
Decca 8466

ACCUSER, THE (IMPRECATEUR, L') (France, 1977) Richard Rodney Bennett
Barclay 900-543 (France)

ACE HIGH (QUATTRO DELL'AVE MARIA, I) (Italy, 1969) Carlo Rustichelli
Cinevox 33/9 (Italy)

ACROBAT, THE (ACROBATE, L') (France, 1979) Antoine Duhamel
Pathe Marconi/EMI 2C066-14282 (France)

ACROSS 110TH STREET (United Artists, 1973) J. J. Johnson, Bobby Womack
United Artists UAS-5225

ACROSS THE GREAT DIVIDE (Pacific International, 1976) Gene Kauer, Douglas Lackey
Bella Linda BLS-1001

AD OGNI COSTO see GRAND SLAM

ADA (MGM, 1961) Bronislau Kaper
MGM (S) 3988 and (S) 4064

ADDIO FRATELLO CRUDELE ('TIS A PITY SHE'S A WHORE) (Italy, 1971) Ennio Morricone
CAM 500 002 (France)

ADDIO GIOVINEZZA see FAREWELL TO YOUTH

ADIO GRINGO (France/Italy/Spain, 1967) Benedetto Ghiglia
CAM 33.15 (Italy)

ADOLESCENT, THE (France, 1979) Philippe Sarde
Pathe Marconi/EMI 2C068-14731 (France)

ADRIFT (Czechoslovakia, 1971) Zdenek Liska
MPO 1001

ADVANCE TO THE REAR (MGM, 1964) Randy Sparks
Columbia CL-2159/CS-8959

ADVENTURERS, THE (Paramount, 1970) Antonio Carlos Jobim
Symbolic SYS-9000

ADVENTURES OF ROBIN HOOD, THE (Warners, 1938) Erich Wolfgang Korngold
Delos DEL-F25409

AFFAIR IN MONTE CARLO (TWENTY-FOUR HOURS IN THE LIFE OF A WOMAN) (Allied Artists, 1953) Robert Gill, Philip Green
Coral 56062

AFRICA ADDIO (Italy, 1966) Riz Ortolani
United Artists 4141/5141

AFTER THE FOX (United Artists, 1966) Burt Bacharach
United Artists LA-286-G

AFYON OPPIO (Italy, 1978) Guido and Maurizio de Angelis
Cinevox 33/64 (Italy)

AGAINST A CROOKED SKY (Doty/Dayton, 1976) Lex de Azevedo
Embryo Music EM-1005-ST

AGAINST ALL FLAGS (Universal, 1952) Hans J. Salter
Citadel TT-HS-1/2

AGATHA (Warners, 1979) Johnny Mandel
Casablanca NBLP-7142

AH, SI! ... E IO LO DICO A ZORRO! (Italy, 1979) Gianfranco Plenizio
International ILS-9041

AIRPORT 1975 (Universal, 1974) John Cacavas
MCA 2082

AL DI LA' DEL BENE E DEL MALE (Italy, n. d.) Daniele Paris
CAM SAG-9082 (Italy)

ALASKA STORY, THE (ARUSAKA MONOGATARI) (Japan, n. d.) Masaru Sato
King SKD-428 (Japan)

ALBERO DALLE FOGLIE ROSA, L' (Italy, n. d.) Franco Micalizzi
Cinevox 33/80 (Italy)

ALBERT PECKINGPAW'S REVENGE (Independent, 1967) Harley Hatcher
Sidewalk (S)T-5907

ALEXANDER (France, 1970) Vladimir Cosma
Polydor 24-7001

ALFRED THE GREAT (MGM, 1969) Raymond Leppard
MGM 8112 (Britain)

ALFREDO, ALFREDO (Italy, 1973) Carlo Rustichelli
CAM 9044 (Italy)

ALICE'S ADVENTURES IN WONDERLAND (Britain, 1972) John Barry
Warners BS-2671

ALIEN (Fox, 1979) Jerry Goldsmith
Fox T-593

ALIKI--MY LOVE (Greece, 1962) Manos Hadjidakis
Capitol (S) 2527
Fontana 27523/67523

ALIVE BUT PREFERABLY DEAD (VIVI O PREFERIBILIMENTE MORTI) (Italy, n. d.) Gianni Ferrio
CAM 9023 (Italy)

ALL THE LOVING COUPLES (Cottage, 1968) Les Baxter
Crescendo 2051
United Artists 6742

ALL THE RIGHT NOISES (Britain, 1971) Melanie Safka
Buddah BDS-5132

ALLE ORIGINI DELLA MAFIA (Italy, 1979) Nino Rota
OR SMRL-6198

ALLONSANFAN (Italy, 1973) Ennio Morricone
RCA NL-30207 (Italy)

ALPIN L'E SEMPRE QUEL, L' (Italy, n.d.) Bruno Nicolai
Gemelli 10.012 (Italy)

ALTRA META DEL CIELO, L' (Italy, n.d.) Detto Mariano
Clan CLN-82014 (Italy)

AMARCORD (Italy, 1974) Nino Rota
RCA ARL1-0907

AMAZONES, LES see AMAZONS, THE

AMAZONS, THE (AMAZONES, LES/GUERRIER DAL SENO NUDA, LE) (France/Italy, 1973) Riz Ortolani
Cine-Disc 5010 (Italy)

AMERICATHON (United Artists, 1979) Tom Scott
Lorimar JS-36174

AMICI MIEI (Italy, 1975) Armando Trovajoli
CAM SAG-9096 (Italy)

AMICO, STAMMI LONTANO ALMENO UN PALMO (Italy, 1972) Gianni Ferrio
Cinevox 33/52 (Italy)

AMITYVILLE HORROR, THE (American International, 1979) Lalo Schifrin
American International AILP-3003

AMORE PIOMBO E FURORE (CHINA 9, LIBERTY 7) (Italy, n.d.) Pino Donaggio
Cinevox MDF-33-123 (Italy)

AMOUR DE PLUIE, UN (RAINY LOVE, A) (France, 1974) Francis Lai
Polydor 2393.078 (France)

AMOUR DESCEND DU CIEL, L' (France, n.d.) Guy Bernard
Dot 3120

ANCHE SE VOLESSI LAVOVARE, CHE COSA FACCIO? (Italy, 1972) Ennio Morricone
Cinevox MDF-33/56 (Italy)

AND FOR A ROOF, A SKY FULL OF STARS (E PER TETTO, UN CIELO DI STELLE) (Italy, 1968) Ennio Morricone
Cometa CMT-1003-11 (Italy)

AND GOD CREATED WOMAN (France, 1957) Paul Misraki
MCA-7147 (Japan)

AND HOPE TO DIE see COURSE DU LIEVRE A TRAVERS LES CHAMPS, LA

AND NOW MY LOVE (TOUT UNE VIE) (France/Italy, 1975) Francis Lai
Dart ARTS-65377 (Britain)
EMI-Pathe 2.156.12967/8 (France)

ANDREA DORIA (Italy, n.d.) Riz Ortolani
CAM 10024 (Italy)

ANGELI SENZA PARADISO (ANGELS WITHOUT PARADISE) (Italy, n.d.) Francesco Lavagnino
Cinevox 33/37 (Italy)

ANGELIQUE, MARQUISE DES ANGES (France, 1966) Michel Magne
Ducretet Thomson CO62-14204 (France)

ANIMA PERSA (FORBIDDEN ROOM, THE) (Italy, 1977) Frances Lai
CAM SAG-9074 (Italy)

ANOTHER MAN, ANOTHER CHANCE (AUTRE HOMME, UNE AUTRE CHANCE, UN) (France, 1979) Francis Lai
United Artists UAP-25017 (France) and FML-94 (Japan)

ANTONIO GRAMSCI (GIORNI DEL CARCERE, I) (Italy, 1977) Egisto Macchi
Feeling Record Italiana FR-69404 (Italy)

ANTONY AND CLEOPATRA (Britain, 1972) Patrick John Scott
Polydor 2383-109 (Britain)

ANY GUN CAN PLAY (VADO ... L'AMMAZZO E TORNO) (Italy, 1967) Francesco de Masi
Beat CDR 33-5 (Italy)

APARTMENT, THE (United Artists, 1960) Adolph Deutsch
United Artists 3105/6105

APOCALYPSE DES ANIMAUX, L' (France, 1973) Vangelis Papathanassiou
Polydor 2393-058 (France)

APOCALYPSE NOW (United Artists, 1979) Francis Ford Coppola, Carmine Coppola
Elektra DB-90001

APPASSIONATA (Italy, 1974) Piero Piccioni
Cinevox MDF-33/72 (Italy)

APRIL FOOLS, THE (National General, 1969) Marvin Hamlisch
Columbia 3340 and 9906

ARMA MERAVIGLIOSA, L' (Italy, n. d.) Bruno Nicolai
King Universal NLP 103-104 (Italy)

ARMAGUEDON (ARMAGEDDON) (France/Italy, 1977) Astor Piazzolla
Polydor 2393-154 (France)

ARRIVEDERCI, BABY! (Paramount, 1966) Dennis Farnon
RCA LOC/LSO-1132 and 7846 (Britain)

ARUSAKA MONOGATARI see ALASKA STORY, THE

ASHANTI (Warners, 1979) Michael Melvoin Carrere
Cobra 37022 (France)

ASSASSINATION, THE (FRENCH CONSPIRACY, THE/ATTENTAT, L'/PLOT, THE) (France/Italy, 1972) Ennio Morricone
Festival FLD-592 (France)
General Music ZSLGE-55121 (Italy)

ASSOLUTO NATURALE, L' see ABSOLUTELY NATURAL

ATHENA (MGM, 1954) George Stoll, Hugh Martin
Mercury 70465/25202

ATTENTAT, L' see ASSASSINATION, THE

ATTENTI AL BUFFONE (OPPOSITE ESPERIENZE) (Italy, 1975) Ennio Morricone
Cometa CMT-3 (Italy)

ATTI DEGLI APOSTOLI (Italy, n. d.) Mario Nascimbene
CAM 9025 (Italy)

ATTICO, L' (Italy, 1963) Piero Piccioni
CAM CEP-4593(45) (Italy)

ATTORE LO FUSTO (Italy, n. d.) Francesco di Masi
Music Parade-Cetra LEL-199 (Italy)

AUDIENCE, THE (UDIENZA, L') (Italy, 1972) Teo Usuelli
Cinevox 33/45 (Italy)

AUGUST WITHOUT EMPEROR (Japan, n. d.) Masaru Sato
Sony CBS 25-AH-552 (Japan)

AUTOSTOP SOSSO SANGUE (Italy, 1977) Ennio Morricone
Cometa CMT-1001-7 (Italy)

AUTRE HOMME, UNE AUTRE CHANCE, UN see ANOTHER MAN, ANOTHER CHANCE

AVALANCHE (New World, 1978) William Kraft
Delos DEL/F-25452

AVENTURES DE DAVID BALFOUR (KIDNAPPED) (France, n. d.) Vladimir Cosma
P. M. EMI 2CO68-14794 (France)

AVVENTURIERO, L' see ROVER, THE

BABY, THE RAIN MUST FALL (Columbia, 1965) Elmer Bernstein
Ava (S)A-53-ST

BAD AND THE BEAUTIFUL, THE (MGM, 1952) David Raksin
RCA 1205 and ARL1-1490

BAD SEED, THE (Warners, 1956) Alex North
Cinevox 33/25 (private)

BALERIC CAPER, THE (BALERI OPERAZIONE ORE) (Italy, 1966) Benedetto Ghiglia
Cinevox 33/13 (Italy)

BALI (Germany/Italy, 1971) Giorgio Gaslini
Cinevox 33/41 (Italy)

BANDIT OF SHERWOOD FOREST, THE (Columbia, 1946) Hugo Friedhofer
Premiere PR-1201 (private)

BANG THE DRUM SLOWLY (Paramount, 1973) Stephen Lawrence
Paramount PAS-1014

BARBABLU see BLUEBEARD

BARBARIAN AND THE GEISHA, THE (Fox, 1958) Hugo Friedhofer
Gemini CF-3384 (private)

BAREFOOT ADVENTURE (Independent, 1961) Bud Shank
Pacific Jazz 35

BAROCCO (France, 1977) Philippe Sarde
Barclay 930. 020 (France)

BARRY LYNDON (Warners, 1975) Leonard Rosenman
Warners BS-2903

BATTAGLIA DEL DESERTO, LA see BATTLE IN THE DESERT

BATTAGLIA DELL'ULTIMO PANZER (BATTLE OF THE LAST PANZER) (Italy, n. d.) Francesco Lavagnino
Cinevox 33/11 (Italy)

BATTLE IN THE DESERT (BATTAGLIA DEL DESERTO, LA) (Italy, n. d.) Bruno Nicolai
Gemelli 10.001 (Italy)

BATTLE OF ALGIERS, THE (France, 1966) Gillo Pontecorvo, Ennio Morricone
United Artists LA-293-G

BATTLE OF NERETVA (American International, 1969) Bernard Herrmann
Entr'acte ERS-6501

BATTLESTAR GALACTICA (Universal, 1979) Stu Phillips
MCA 3051

BECKET (Paramount, 1964) Laurence Rosenthal
MCA VIM-7237 (Japan)

BEHIND THE GREAT WALL (Italy, 1959) traditional
Monitor 525

BELL, BOOK AND CANDLE (Columbia, 1958) George Duning
Citadel CT-6006 and CT-7006

BELSTONE FOX, THE (Britain, 1979) Laurie Johnson
Ronco 2006 (Britain)

BEND OF THE RIVER (Universal, 1952) Hans J. Salter
Citadel TT-HS-1/2

BENEATH THE 12-MILE REEF (Fox, 1953) Bernard Herrmann
RCA ARL1-0707

BEN-HUR (MGM, 1926) David Mendoza, William Axt
Pelican LP-2001

BEN-HUR (MGM, 1959) Miklos Rozsa
London SPC-21166
MGM 2353-030 and 2353-075 (Britain)

BENJI (Mulberry Square, 1974) Euel Box
Epic KSE-33010

BEST YEARS OF OUR LIVES, THE (RKO, 1946) Hugo Friedhofer
Entr'acte EDP-8101

BETWEEN MIRACLES see PER GRAZIA RICEVUTA

BEYOND THE DOOR (CHI SEI?) (Italy, 1974) Franco Micalizzi
CAM 9062 (Italy)

BEYOND THE FOREST (Warners, 1949) Max Steiner
Citadel CT-MS-8

BEYOND THE GREAT WALL (Independent, 1964) traditional
Capitol T-10401

BIANCO VES TITO PER MARIALE, UN (Italy, n.d.) Fiorenzo Carpi
Gemelli 10-011 (Italy)

BICHES, LES (France/Italy, 1968) Pierre Jansen
Cinevox 33/15 (Italy)

BICYCLETTES DE BELSIZE, LES (Britain, 1969) Les Reed
Polydor 583728 (Britain)

BIDONE, IL (SWINDLE, THE) (Italy, 1962) Nino Rota
CAM 500-001 (France)

BIG BOSS PART II (Hong Kong, 1979) composer unlisted
Po Sing PSCP-1256 (Hong Kong)

BIG COUNTRY, THE (United Artists, 1958) Jerome Moross
Temple TLP-2001 (private)
United Artists 4004/5004 and LA-270-G

BIG GAME, THE (MACCHINA DELLA VIOLENZA, LA) (Italy, 1972) Francesco de Masi
Beat LPF-019 (Italy)

BIG GUNDOWN, THE (United Artists, 1968) Ennio Morricone
United Artists LA-297-G

BIG GUNS see NO WAY OUT

BIG RED (Disney, 1962) Oliver Wallace
Buena Vista 3319

BIG SLEEP, THE (Warners, 1946) Max Steiner
Cinema LP-8001 (private)

BILITIS (France/Italy, 1977) Francis Lai
Seven Seas FML-78 (Japan)

BILLY JACK (Warners, 1971) Mundell Lowe
Billy Jack 1001

BINGO LONG TRAVELING ALL-STARS AND MOTOR KINGS, THE (Universal, 1976) William Goldstein
MCA 2094

BIRDMAN OF ALCATRAZ (United Artists, 1962) Elmer Bernstein
BOA-101 (private)

BIRDS OF A FEATHER see CAGE AUX FOLLES, LA

BIRDS, THE BEES, AND THE ITALIANS, THE (SIGNORE AND SIGNORI) (Italy, 1967) Carlo Rustichelli
United Artists 4157/5157 and 3625/6625

BIRIBI (France, 1971) Mikis Theodorakis
Tuba 8500

BIT PLAYER, THE see SALUT L'ARTISTE

BITE THE BULLET (Columbia, 1975) Alex North
RFO 102 (private)

BLACK AND WHITE IN COLOR (BLACK VICTORY) (Allied Artists, 1976) Pierre Bachelet
Buddah BDS-5698-ST

BLACK GIRL (Cinerama, 1972) Ray Shanklin, Ed Bogas, et al.
Fantasy 9420

BLACK HOLE, THE (Disney, 1979) John Barry
Buena Vista 5008

BLACK ORCHID, THE (Paramount, 1959) Alessandro Cicognini
MCA VIM-7255 (Japan)

BLACK ORPHEUS (ORFEO NEGRO) (Brazil, 1960) Luis Bonfa
Epic LN-3672

BLACK VICTORY see BLACK AND WHITE IN COLOR

BLACULA (American International, 1972) Gene Page et al.
RCA LSP-4806

BLAST-OFF see THOSE FANTASTIC FLYING FOOLS

BLAZING MAGNUM (MAGNUM SPECIAL PER TONY SAITTA, UNA) (Italy, 1976) Armando Trovajoli
Beat LPF-033 (Italy)

BLAZING SADDLES (Warners, 1974) John Morris
Warners BS-2781 (Australia)

BLONDY (France/Germany, 1975) Stelvio Cipriani
Pathe-Marconi CO66-14269 (France)

BLOOD IN THE STREETS see REVOLVER

BLOOD ON THE SUN (United Artists, 1945) Miklos Rozsa
Citadel CT-6031

BLOODY MAMA (American International, 1970) Don Randi
AIR A-1041

BLUE ANGELS, THE (Independent, n. d.) Fred Myrow
TAM/CAM YX-5002 (Japan)

BLUE COLLAR (Universal, 1978) Jack Nitzsche
MCA 3034

BLUE MAX, THE (Fox, 1966) Jerry Goldsmith
Citadel CT-6008 and CT-7007

BLUEBEARD (BARBABLU) (Italy, 1972) Ennio Morricone
General Music ZSLGE-55122 (Italy)
Philips 6325-402

BOBBY DEERFIELD (Columbia, 1977) Dave Grusin
Casablanca NBLP-7071

BODY, THE (Britain, 1973) Ron Geeson
EMI 4008 (Britain)

BOOK OF NUMBERS (Embassy, 1973) Al Schackman
Brut 6002-ST

BOOM, IL (Italy, 1963) Piero Piccioni
CAM CMS-60065 and CA-2505 (45) (Italy)

BOOTLEGGERS, THE (5 SONS OF DOGS) (Italy, 1974) Riz Ortolani
Ariete 2004 (Italy)

BORA BORA (American International, 1968) Les Baxter (original score by Piero Piccioni)
American International 1029 (Baxter)
Cinevox 33/10 (Piccioni)

BORN AGAIN (Embassy, 1978) Les Baxter
Lamb & Lion LL-1041

BORN LOSERS (American International, 1967) Mike Curb
Tower (S)T-5082

BOSS AND THE WORKER, THE (PADRONE E L'OPERAIO, IL) (Italy, 1975) Gianni Ferrio
United Artists UAS-29906 (Italy)

BOTTLENECK (INGORGO, L') (France/Germany/Italy/Spain, 1979) Fiorenzo Carpi
Edipan CS-2008 (Italy)

BOULEVARD NIGHTS (Warners, 1979) Lalo Schifrin
Warners BSK-3328

BOY NAMED CHARLIE BROWN, A (National General, 1969) Vince Guaraldi
Fantasy 8430

BOYS FROM BRAZIL, THE (Fox, 1978) Jerry Goldsmith
A&M SP-4731

BRASS TARGET (MGM, 1978) Laurence Rosenthal
Varese Sarabande VC-81082

BRAVE ONE, THE (RKO, 1956) Victor Young
MCA 7135 (Japan)

BREAD AND CHOCOLATE (PAIN ET CHOCOLAT) (France/Italy, 1978) Daniele Patucchi
Barclay 900. 530 (France)

BREAKHEART PASS (United Artists, 1976) Jerry Goldsmith
POO LP-101 (private)

BREATH OF SCANDAL, A (Paramount, 1960) Alessandro Cicognini
Imperial 9132

BREEZY (Universal, 1973) Michel Legrand
MCA 384

BREVE STAGIONE, UNA see BRIEF SEASON

BRIDE WORE BLACK, THE (France, 1968) Bernard Herrmann
Cinema LP-8006 (private)

BRIDGE ON THE RIVER KWAI, THE (Columbia, 1957) Malcolm Arnold
Columbia CL-1100/CS-9426

BRIDGE TOO FAR, A (United Artists, 1977) John Addison
United Artists UA-LA762-H

BRIEF SEASON (BREVE STAGIONE, UNA) (Italy, 1969) Ennio Morricone
Sagittario ZMLS-55001 (Italy)

BRIGANTE, IL (BRIGAND, THE) (Italy, 1954) Nino Rota
CAM 30. 031 (Italy)

BROKEN ARROW (Fox, 1950) Hugo Friedhofer
Dot 3097/25097

BROTHER ON THE RUN (Independent, 1974) Johnny Pate
Perception PR-45

BROTHER SUN, SISTER MOON (FRATELLO SOLE, SORELLA LUNA) (Paramount, 1972) Riz Ortolani
Paramount 3C-064-93393 (Italy)

BRUCE LEE'S GAME OF DEATH (Hong Kong, 1978) John Barry
TAM CAM YX-7037 (Japan)

BUBU (Italy, n. d.) Carlo Rustichelli
Seven Seas 708 (Japan)

BUCCANEER, THE (Paramount, 1958) Elmer Bernstein
Columbia CL-1278/CS-8096

BUCK ROGERS (Universal, 1979) Stu Phillips
MCA 3097

BUGSY MALONE (Paramount, 1976) Paul Williams
RSO RS-1-3501

BULLET FOR THE GENERAL, A (QUIEN SABE?) (Italy, 1968) Luis Enrique Bacalov
FPR 312 (Italy)

BULLETS DON'T ARGUE (PISTOLE NON DISCUTONO, LE (Italy, 1965) Ennio Morricone
RCA INTI-1138 (Italy)

BULLITT (Warners, 1968) Lalo Schifrin
Warners WS-1777

BURGLARS, THE (France, 1971) Ennio Morricone
Bell 1105

BURN! (United Artists, 1970) Ennio Morricone
Foreign American LP-101 (private)
United Artists LA-303-G

C. C. AND COMPANY (Embassy, 1970) Lenny Stack
Avco Embassy AVE-O-11003

CACTUS IN THE SNOW (YOU CAN'T HAVE EVERYTHING) (Britain, 1972) Joe Parnello
Ember 5055 (Britain)

CAGE AUX FOLLES, LA (BIRDS OF A FEATHER/VIZIETTO, IL) (France, 1979) Ennio Morricone
CAM SAG-9090 (Italy)
General Music 803-003 (France)

CAGLIOSTRO (Italy, 1975) Manuel de Sica
CBS 69110 (Italy)

CALANDRIA, LA (Italy, n. d.) Gianni Ferrio
Cinevox 33/65 (Italy)

CALIFFA, LA (LADY CALIPH) (Italy, 1971) Ennio Morricone
CBS S-70090 (Italy)

CALIFORNIA SUITE (Columbia, 1978) Claude Bolling
Columbia JS-35727

CALM, COOL AND COLLECTED see CALMOS

CALMOS (FEMMES FATALES/CALM, COOL AND COLLECTED) (France, 1976) Georges Delerue
Black & Blue 33400 (France)

CANDIDATE, THE see PARTY GIRLS FOR THE CANDIDATE

CAPRICORN ONE (Warners, 1978) Jerry Goldsmith
Warners BSK-3201

CAPTAIN FROM CASTILE, THE (Fox, 1947) Alfred Newman
Delos DEL-F25411

CAPTAIN HORATIO HORNBLOWER (Warners, 1951) Robert Farnon
Citadel CT-7009
Delyse DS-6057

CARAVANS (Universal, 1978) Mike Batt
Epic SE-35787

CAROLINE CHERIE (France, 1973) Georges Garvarentz
Barclay 820.169 (France)

CARRIE (United Artists, 1976) Pino Donaggio
United Artists UA-LA716-H

CASANOVA (Italy, 1976) Nino Rota
CAM SAG-9075 (Italy)

CASEY'S SHADOW (Columbia, 1978) Patrick Williams
Columbia PS-35344

CASSANDRA CROSSING, THE (Embassy, 1977) Jerry Goldsmith
Citadel CT-6020

CASTRATTI, IL see VOICI BIANCHE, LE

CATASTROPHE 1999 (New World, 1977) Isao Tomita
TAM AX-8804 (Japan)

CATLOW (MGM, 1971) Roy Budd
EMI/Odeon 80544 (Britain)

CAVALIERI DELLA VENDETTA, I see RIDERS OF VENGEANCE

CESAR AND ROSALIE (SIMPATICO ME GLI ROMPEREI IL MUSO) (Italy, 1972) Philippe Sarde
CAM 9048 (Italy)

CHAMBRE VERTE, LA see GREEN ROOM, THE

CHAMP, THE (MGM, 1979) Dave Grusin
Planet P-9001

CHAPLIN REVUE, THE (United Artists, 1959) Charles Chaplin
MCA VIM-7238 (Japan)

CHAPLIN'S ART OF COMEDY (Independent, 1966) Elias Breeskin
Mainstream 56089/6089

CHARIOTS OF THE GODS? (Germany, 1973) Peter Thomas
Polydor 6504

CHASSEUR DE CHEZ MAXIM'S, LE (France, 1953) Paul Misraki
Pathe Marconi EMI CO66-14386 (France)

CHASTITY BELT, THE (CINTURA DI CASTITA/ON MY WAY TO THE CRUSADES, I MET A GIRL WHO ...) (Italy, 1968) Riz Ortolani
CAM 10006 (Italy)

CHATO'S LAND (United Artists, 1972) Jerry Fielding
Citadel CT-JF-2/3

CHE GUEVARA, EL (Italy, 1969) Nico Fidenco
CAM 9007 (Italy)

CHERRY, HARRY AND RAQUEL (Independent, 1969) William Loose
Beverly Hills BHS-23

CHI L'HA VISTA MORIRE? see WHO SAW HER DIE?

CHI SEI? see BEYOND THE DOOR

CHIMES AT MIDNIGHT (FALSTAFF) (Spain/Switzerland, 1967) Francesco Lavagnino
CAM 3 (Italy)

CHINA ARMED ESCORT (Hong Kong, 1979) composer unlisted
Po Sing PSCP-1256 (Hong Kong)

CHINA IS NEAR (CINE E VICINA, LA) (Italy, 1967) Ennio Morricone
Carrere 67066 (France)

CHINATOWN (Paramount, 1974) Jerry Goldsmith
ABC ABDP-848

CHINESE ADVENTURES IN CHINA see UP TO HIS EARS

CHOIRBOYS, THE (Universal, 1977) Frank de Vol
MCA 2326

CHRIST STOPPED AT EBOLI (CRISTO SI E FERMATO A EBOLI) (Italy, 1979) Piero Piccioni
CAM AMP-221 (45) (Italy)

CID, EL (Allied Artists, 1961) Miklos Rozsa
MGM Select 2353-046 (Britain)

CINDERELLA LIBERTY (Fox, 1973) John Williams
Fox ST-100

CINE E VICINA, LA see CHINA IS NEAR

CINQUE GIORNATE, LE (Italy, n. d.) Giorgio Gaslini
Det-MDG 71 (Italy)

CINTURA DI CASTITA see CHASTITY BELT, THE

CIRCUS, THE (United Artists, 1928) Charles Chaplin
United Artists 290571

CITIZEN KANE (RKO, 1941) Bernard Herrmann
RCA ARL1-0707
United Artists LA-372-G

CITTA PRIGIONIERA, LA see CONQUERED CITY, THE

CLASE OPERAIA VA IN PARADISO, LA see WORKING CLASS GOES TO HEAVEN, THE

CLAUDINE (Fox, 1974) Curtis Mayfield
Buddah BDS-5602

CLEOPATRA JONES (Warners, 1974) J. J. Johnson, Carl Brandt
Warners WS-2719

CLERAMBARD (France, n. d.) Vladimir Cosma
CBS S7. 63799 (France)

CLOCKWORK ORANGE, A (Warners, 1971) Walter (Wendy) Carlos
Columbia KC-31480

CLOSE ENCOUNTERS OF THE THIRD KIND (Columbia, 1977) John Williams
Arista AL-9500
London ZM-1001
RCA ARL1-2698

CLOWNS, THE (Italy, 1970) Nino Rota
Columbia KC-30772

COFFY (American International, 1973) Roy Ayers
Polydor 5048

COLLINA DEI COMALI, LA (Italy, 1979) Angela Morley
CBS 70161 (Italy)

COLPO DI MANO (Italy, n. d.) Gianni Marchetti
CAM 9028 (Italy)

COLPO DI STATO (Italy, n. d.) Gianni Marchetti
CAM 9019 (Italy)

COMA (MGM, 1978) Jerry Goldsmith
MGM MG-1-5403

COMANCHE (United Artists, 1956) Herschel Burke Gilbert
Coral 57046

COMANDEMENTI PER UN GANGSTER (Italy, 1968) Ennio Morricone
CAM MAG 10.014 (Italy)

COME BACK CHARLESTON BLUE (Warners, 1972) Donny Hathaway
Atco SD-7010

COME HAUNT WITH ME (Hong Kong, 1979) composer unlisted
Regal LPHX-891 (Hong Kong)

COME IMPARI AD AMARE LE DONNE (Italy, 1967) Ennio Morricone
RCA 8020 (Italy)

COME RUBARE LA CORONA D'INGHILTERRA (Italy, n. d.) Piero Umiliani
Beat 001 (Italy)
Beat 003 (Italy)

COMETOGETHER (Allied Artists, 1971) Stelvio Cipriani
Apple SW-3377

COMMANDO (Germany/Italy/Spain, 1964) Francesco Lavagnino
French Victor 430.667 (45)
RCA 10382 (Italy)
London 104

COMMANDOS (Italy, n. d.) Mario Nascimbene
Cinevox 33/11 (Italy)

COMMARE SECCA, LA (Italy, 1962) Piero Piccioni
CAM CA-2445(45) (Italy)

COMME UN BOOMERANG (France, 1977) Georges Delerue
Seven Seas (King) FML-65 (Japan)

CONCRETE JUNGLE, THE (Britain, 1962) John Dankworth
Cinema LP-8002 (private)

CONFESSIONS OF A POLICE COMMISSIONER TO THE DISTRICT ATTORNEY (Italy, 1973) Riz Ortolani
RCA 6 (Italy)

CONFORMIST, THE (France, 1970) Georges Delerue
Cinevox 33/43 (Italy)

CONGO HELL see SETTE BASCHI ROSSI

CONQUERED CITY (CAPTIVE CITY, THE/CITTA PRIGIONIERA, LA) (Italy, 1962) Piero Piccioni
CAM CMS-30050 and CA-2464(45) (Italy)

CONTRO QUATTRO BANDIERE (Italy, n. d.) Riz Ortolani
Duse ELP-063 (Italy)

CONTRORAPINA (AGAINST RAPE/RAPE) (Italy, n. d.) Vasile
Cinevox MDG-127 (Italy)

CONVERSATION PIECE (GRUPPO DI FAMIGLIA IN UN INTERNO) (Italy, 1975) Franco Mannino
Carosello CLN-25052 (Italy)

COOGAN'S BLUFF (Universal, 1968) Lalo Schifrin
Temple TLP-2001 (private)

COOL BREEZE (MGM, 1972) Solomon Burke
MGM 1SE-35-ST

COOL HAND LUKE (Warners, 1967) Lalo Schifrin
MCA VIM-7250 (Japan)

CORDE, UN COLT, UNE (CIMITERO SENZA CROCHE) (Italy, n. d.) Andre Hossein
FGS-5045 (Italy)

CORRI UOMO CORRI (Italy, n. d.) Bruno Nicolai
CAM 9006 (Italy)

CORRUPTION IN THE HALLS OF JUSTICE (CORRUZIONE AL PALAZZO DI GIUSTIZIA) (Italy, 1975) Pino Donaggio
Carosello CLN-25055 (Italy)

CORRUZIONE AL PALAZZO DI GIUSTIZIA see CORRUPTION IN THE HALLS OF JUSTICE

CORSARO NERO, IL (Italy, 1977) Guido and Maurizio de Angelis
Cinevox MDF 33-104 (Italy)

COSA BUFFA, LA (Italy, 1972) Ennio Morricone
Cinevox 33-60 (Italy)
Seven Seas FML-32 (Japan)

COSI COME SEI (Italy, n. d.) Ennio Morricone
Cinevox MDF-33. 122 (Italy)

COUNSELLOR, THE (IL CONSIGLIORI) (Italy, 1973) Riz Ortolani
Beat LPF-022 (Italy)

COURSE DU LIEVRE A TRAVERS LES CHAMPS, LA (AND HOPE TO DIE) (France, 1972) Francis Lai
Philips 6332. 095 (France)
Seven Seas 8 (Japan)

COWARDS DON'T PRAY see VIGLIACCHI NON PREGANO, I

COWBOY (Columbia, 1958) George Duning
MCA 7155 (Japan)

CRAZY JOE (Columbia, 1974) Giancarlo Chiaramello
Project 3 PR-5085-SD

CRISIS (MGM, 1950) Miklos Rozsa
Citadel CT-7004

CRIMINAL, THE see CONCRETE JUNGLE, THE

CRISTO DEL OCEANO, EL (Italy, n. d.) Bruno Nicolai
Gemelli CS-3002 (Italy)
Seven Seas 765 (Japan)

CROSS AND THE SWITCHBLADE, THE (Independent, 1970) Ralph Carmichael
Light LS-5550

CROSS OF IRON (Embassy, 1977) Ernest Gold
EMI EMA-782 (Britain)

CROSSED SWORDS (PRINCE AND THE PAUPER, THE) (Britain, 1977) Maurice Jarre
Warners BSK-3161

CRY OF THE GIANT, THE (URLO DEI GIGANTI, L') (Italy, n. d.) Armando Trovajoli
Beat CR-2 (Italy)

CUANDO LAS MUJERES SE LLAMAN SENORAS (Italy, n. d.) Giorgio Gaslini
Cinevox 1040 (Italy)

CUCURACHA, LA (Mexico, n. d.) Raul Lavista
Columbia WL-161
Musart 484

CULT OF THE DAMNED see ANGEL, ANGEL, DOWN WE GO

CYCLE SAVAGES (American International, 1970) Jerry Styner et al.
AIR ST-A-1033

DALLE ARDENNE AL'INFERNO see DIRTY HEROES, THE

DAME DANS L'AUTO, LA (WOMAN IN THE CAR WITH GLASSES AND A GUN, THE) see LADY IN THE CAR WITH GLASSES AND A GUN, THE

DAMIEN--OMEN II (Fox, 1978) Jerry Goldsmith
Fox T-563

DAMNED PISTOLS OF DALLAS (Italy, n. d.) Gioacchino Angelo
CAM 30.128 (Italy)

DANCING THE SIRTAKI (Greece, n. d.) Stavros Xarchakos
Lyra XLP-13001 (Greece)

DARLING LILI (Paramount, 1970) Henry Mancini
RCA LSPX-1000

DAVID AND BATHSHEBA (Fox, 1951) Alfred Newman
Sound of Hollywood 400-1 (private)

DAWN OF THE DEAD (ZOMBI) (United, 1979) Goblin, Dario Argento
Cinevox MDF 33-121 (Italy)
Varese Sarabande VC-81106

DAY OF THE DOLPHIN (Embassy, 1973) Georges Delerue
Avco Embassy AV-11014

DAY OF THE LOCUST (Paramount, 1975) John Barry
London PS-912

DAY THE EARTH STOOD STILL, THE (Fox, 1951) Bernard Herrmann
London SP-44207

DAYS OF HEAVEN (Paramount, 1978) Ennio Morricone
Pacific Arts PAC8-128

DEAF SMITH AND JOHNNY EARS (Italy, 1973) Daniele Patucchi
Columbia/EMI OC-062-94667 (Britain)

DEAR WIFE (CARA SPOSA) (Italy, 1977) Stelvio Cipriani
Cinevox MDF-33.115 (Italy)

DEATH OF A CORRUPT MAN, THE (MORT D'UN POURRI) (France, 1977) Philippe Sarde
Melba LDA-20314 (France)

DEATH OF A SALESMAN (Columbia, 1951) Alex North
Film Music Collection FMC-9

DEATH ON THE NILE (Paramount, 1978) Nino Rota
Capitol SW-11866

DEATH RIDES A HORSE (Italy, 1969) Ennio Morricone
Sunset SLS-50248 (Italy)

DEATH SENTENCE (SENTENCA DI MORTE) (Italy, n. d.) Gianni Ferrio
CAM 10. 009 (Italy)

DEATH TOOK PLACE LAST NIGHT (MORTE RISALE A IERI SERA, LA) (Italy, 1970) Gianni Ferrio
Cinevox MDF-33-35 (Italy)

DEATH WISH (Paramount, 1974) Herbie Hancock
Columbia PC-33199

DECLINE AND FALL OF A BIRDWATCHER, THE (Britain, 1969) Ron Goodwin
Fox 10259 (Britain)

DEDICATION TO TITO (SOUT KIESKA) (Greece, n. d.) Mikis Theodorakis
Delta GR-50025 (Greece)

DEDICATO AL MARE EGEO (Italy, n. d.) Ennio Morricone
Columbia LX-7062 (Japan)

DEEP, THE (Columbia, 1977) John Barry
Casablanca NBLP-7060

DEEP THROAT (Independent, 1972) composer unlisted
DT Music 1001 (private)

DEEP THROAT, PART II (Independent, 1974) Tony Bruno, Michael Colicchio
Bryan BRS-101

DEER HUNTER, THE (Universal, 1978) Stanley Myers
Capitol S00-11940

DEFENSE DE SAVIOR (Italy, n. d.) Bruno Nicolai
CAM 460-007 (Italy)

DEMON, THE (DEMONIO, IL) (Italy, 1963) Piero Piccioni
CAM CEP-45103(45) (Italy)

DENTELLIERE, LA see LACEMAKER, THE

DERNIER AMANT ROMANTIQUE, LE (France, n. d.) Pierre Bachelet
Pema Music 900-060 (France)

DESTINATION MOON (Eagle-Lion, 1950) Leith Stevens
Cinema LP-8005 (private)

DEUX SAISONS DE LA VIE, LES (France/Italy, 1972) Ennio Morricone
General Music ZSLGE-55079 (Italy)

DEVIL AND DANIEL WEBSTER, THE (RKO, 1941) Bernard Herrmann
Pye 13010 (Britain)
Unicorn UNS-237 (Britain)

DEVIL IN MISS JONES, THE (Independent, 1973) Alden Shuman
Janus JLS-3059

DEVIL IN THE BRAIN (DIABOLO NEL CERVELLO, IL) (Italy, 1971) Ennio Morricone
General Music ZSLGE-55076 (Italy)

DEVIL IS A WOMAN, THE see TEMPTER, THE

DEVIL'S ANGELS, THE (American International, 1967) Mike Curb
Tower (D)T-5074

DEVIL'S EIGHT, THE (American International, 1969) Mike Curb, Jerry Styner, et al.
Tower (S)T-5160

DIAMONDS ARE FOREVER (United Artists, 1971) John Barry
United Artists UAS-5220, LA-301-G and UXS-2-91

DIARIO SEGRETO DI UNA MINORENNE, IL (Italy, n. d.) Gianni Marchetti
CAM 9024 (Italy)

DIAVOLO, IL see TO BED OR NOT TO BED

DILLINGER (American International, 1973) Barry deVorzon
MCA 360

DINGAKA (Embassy, 1965) Bertha Egnos, Eddie Domingo, and Basil Gray
Mercury 21013/61013

DIRTY ANGELS, THE (VERGOGNA SCHIFOSI) (Italy, 1968) Ennio Morricone
Ariete ARLP-2003 (Italy)

DIRTY HEROES, THE (DALLE ARDENNE AL'INFERNO) (Italy, 1971) Ennio Morricone
Beat 001 (Italy)
Beat 003 (Italy)

DIRTY STORY OF THE WEST (QUELLA SPORCA STORIA NEL WEST) (Italy, n. d.) Francesco de Masi
CAM 10012 (Italy)

DISCO VOLANTE, IL (Italy, 1964) Piero Piccioni
Style STMS-602(45) (Italy)

DIVINE CREATURE (DIVINA CREATURA) (Italy, 1976) Cesare Andrea Bixio
Cinevox MDF-33-95 (Italy)

DR. FAUSTUS (Italy, 1967) Mario Nascimbene
CBS 63189 (Italy)

DR. NO (United Artists, 1963) Monty Norman
United Artists 4108/5108, LA-275-G, UXS-2-91 and 3303/6303

DOCTOR VLIMMEN (Belgium/Holland, 1978) Pim Koopman
EMI 5C-064-25829 (Holland)

DOLCI VIZI DELLA COSTA SUSANNA, I (Italy, n. d.) Gianni Ferrio
CAM 10. 008 (Italy)

DOLLARS ($) (Columbia, 1971) Quincy Jones
Reprise RS-2051

DOLL'S HOUSE, A (Britain, 1973) Michel Legrand
Bell 2308. 070 (France)

DON JUAN (DON JUAN 1973/IF DON JUAN WERE A WOMAN) (France, 1973) Michel Magne
Barclay 80. 485 (France)

DON JUAN IN SICILY (Italy, 1970) Bruno Nicolai
EDI-Pan CS-2005

DON QUIXOTE (Australia, 1973) Ludwig Minkus
Angel S-37008

DONA FLOR AND HER TWO HUSBANDS (Brazil, 1977) Chico Buarque, Francis Hime
Peters International PLD-1011

DONKEY SKIN see PEAU D'ANE

DON'T LOOK NOW (AVENEZIA ... UN DICEMBRE ROSSO SHOCKING) (Italy, 1973) Pino Donaggio
Carosello CLN-25030 (Italy)

DOUBLE LIFE, A (Universal, 1947) Miklos Rozsa
Premiere PR-1201 (private)

DOVE, THE (Paramount, 1974) John Barry
ABC ABDP-852

DOWN TO THE SEA IN SHIPS (Fox, 1949) Alfred Newman
Entr'acte ERS-6506

DRAMA OF THE RICH see GRANDE BOURGEOISIE, LA

DRAMMA DELLA GELOSIA (PIZZA TRIANGLE, THE) (Italy, 1970) Armando Trovajoli
RCA Italiana PSL-10457 (Italy)

DROP DEAD ... DARLING see ARRIVEDERCI, BABY!

DU SOLEIL PLEIN LES YEUX (France, 1970) Francis Lai
United Artists GXH-6014 (Japan)

DUCK, YOU SUCKER (FISTFUL OF DYNAMITE) (United Artists, 1972) Ennio Morricone
United Artists UAS-5221

DUEL AT DIABLO (United Artists, 1966) Neal Hefti
United Artists 4139/5139, LA-282-G, 3570/6570, and 3573/6573

DUEL IN THE SUN (Selznick, 1947) Dimitri Tiomkin
Cinema LP-8007 (private)
Sound Stage SS-2203 (private)

DUNWICH HORROR, THE (American International, 1970) Les Baxter
AIR A-1028
Varese Sarabande VC-81078

DYNAMITE BROTHERS, THE (Independent, 1974) Charles Earland
Prestige 10082

EAGLE HAS LANDED, THE (Columbia, 1977) Lalo Schifrin
Entr'acte ERS-6510

EARTHQUAKE (Universal, 1974) John Williams
MCA 2081

EAST OF EDEN (Warners, 1954) Leonard Rosenman
Columbia CL-941 and ACL-940

EAST WIND see ONE BY ONE

EDDY DUCHIN STORY, THE (Columbia, 1956) George Duning
MCA 2041

EDUCATION OF SONNY CARSON, THE (Paramount, 1974) Coleridge-Taylor Perkinson
Paramount PAS-1045

EGYPTIAN, THE (Fox, 1954) Alfred Newman, Bernard Herrmann
MCA 2029

EIGER SANCTION, THE (Universal, 1975) John Williams
MCA 2088

ELEANORA (Italy, n.d.) Bruno Nicolai
Gemelli 10.016 (Italy)

ELECTRA GLIDE IN BLUE (United Artists, 1973) James William Guercio
United Artists LA-062-H

ELEKTRA (Greece, 1963) Mikis Theodorakis
Philips 600508-PR (Greece)

ELEPHANT CA TROMPE ENORMEMENT, UN (France, 1978) Vladimir Cosma
Deesse DDLX-157 (France)

ELEPHANT CALLED SLOWLY, AN (Britain, 1971) Howard Blake
Bell 1202

ELMER GANTRY (United Artists, 1960) Andre Previn
United Artists UASF-5069 (France)

EMMANUELLE (France, 1974) Pierre Bachelet, Herve Roy
Arista AL-4036
CAM 9018 (Italy)

EMMANUELLE II--JOYS OF A WOMAN (France, 1976) Francis Lai
Warners K-56231 (Britain)

EMPIRE OF THE SENSES see IN THE REALM OF THE SENSES

ENCOUNTER (INCRONTRO) (Italy, 1971) Ennio Morricone
CAM 500 002 (France)
CAM SAG 9036 (Italy)

ENFANTS GATES, DES (SPOILED CHILDREN) (France, 1977) Philippe Sarde
Vogue LDA-20295 (France)

ENGLAND MADE ME (Britain, 1973) Patrick John Scott
DJM DJLPS-431 (Britain)
East Coast 1062

ENTER THE DRAGON (Warners, 1974) Lalo Schifrin
Warners BS-2727

EQUUS (United Artists, 1977) Richard Rodney Bennett
United Artists UA-LA839-H (with dialog)

ER PIU, STORIA D'AMORE E DI COLTELLO (Italy, n.d.) Carlo Rustichelli
Clan 602 (Italy)

ERIC SOYA'S 17 (Denmark, 1967) Ole Hoeyer
Mercury MG-21115/SR-61115

ESCALATION (Italy, 1968) Ennio Morricone
CAM MAG 10.010 (Italy)

ESCAPE TO WITCH MOUNTAIN (Disney, 1975) Johnny Mandel
Disneyland 3809

ESERCITO DI 5 UOMINI (Italy, 1971) Ennio Morricone
Ariete 2009

ETAT SAUVAGE, L' (France, n.d.) Pierre Jansen
Pema Music 900-059 (France)

ETTORE LO FUSTO (Italy, n.d.) Francesco de Masi
Beat-Music Parade 199 (Italy)

EVA (France, 1965) Michel Legrand
French Philips 432.821 (45)

EVERYBODY HE IS NICE ... EVERYBODY HE IS BEAUTIFUL (TOUT LE MONDE IL EST BEAU ... TOUT LE MONDE IL EST GENTIL) (France, 1972) Michel Legrand
Barclay 80.485 (France)

EVERYTHING'S READY, NOTHING WORKS (TUTTO A POSTO E NINENTE IN ORDINE) (Italy, 1974) Piero Piccioni
Beat 027 (Italy)

EXORCIST, THE (Warners, 1973) Jack Nitzsche
Warners WS-2774

EXORCIST II: THE HERETIC (Warners, 1977) Ennio Morricone
Warners BS-3068

EXPERIMENT IN TERROR (Columbia, 1962) Henry Mancini
Camden CAS-2158 and (S)736

EYES FULL OF SUN see DU SOLEIL PLAIN LES YEUX

EYES OF LAURA MARS, THE (Columbia, 1978) Artie Kane
Columbia JS-35487

F.I.S.T. (United Artists, 1978) Bill Conti
United Artists UA-LA897-H

FAHRENHEIT 451 (Universal, 1966) Bernard Herrmann
London SP-44207

FAILLE, LA see WEAK SPOT, THE

FAITHFUL WOMAN, A (FEMME FIDELE, UNE) (France, 1976)
Mort Schuman, Pierre Porte
Seven Seas FML-72 (Japan)

FALSTAFF see CHIMES AT MIDNIGHT

FANNY HILL (Independent, 1965) Erwin Halletz
Command (S) 887

FANNY HILL (Sweden, 1969) Clay Pitts
Canyon 7700
United Artists 6742

FAREWELL MY LOVELY (Embassy, 1975) David Shire
United Artists UA-LA556-G

FAREWELL TO YOUTH (ADDIO GIOVINEZZA) (Italy, 1949) S. Blanc
Epic 3593

FARFALLA CON LE ALI INSANGUINATE, UNA (Italy, n.d.) Gianni Ferrio
Carosello 25008 (Italy)

FAST BREAK (Columbia, 1979) David Shire et al.
Motown M7-915R1

FATTI DI GENTE PERBENE see GRANDE BOURGEOISIE, LA

FATTO DI SANGUE (Italy, n.d.) deLuca
RCA 31434 (Italy)

FEAR IS THE KEY (Paramount, 1972) Roy Budd
Pye 18398 (Britain)

FEDORA (United Artists, 1978) Miklos Rozsa
Varese Sarabande STV-81108

FELLINI CASANOVA see CASANOVA

FELLINI ROMA (France/Italy, 1972) Nino Rota
United Artists LA-052-F

FEMALE ANIMAL, THE (Italy/Spain, 1970) Clay Pitts
Canyon CAY-7702

FEMINA RIDENS see LAUGHING WOMAN, THE

FEMME FIDELE, UNE see FAITHFUL WOMAN, A

FEMMES FATALES see CALMOS

FEMMINE INSAZIABILI (INSATIABLES, THE) (Italy, n. d.) Bruno Nicolai
Ariete 2006 (Italy)

FETE SAUVAGE, LA (France, 1975) Vangelis Papathanassiou
Polydor 2421-100 (Greece)

FILS, LES (France, 1973) Philippe Sarde
RCA 443056 (France)

FIN DE SAMANA PARA LOS MUERTOS see LIVING DEAD AT THE MANCHESTER MORGUE, THE

FINAL COMEDOWN, THE (New World, 1972) Wade Marcus
Blue Note BST-84415

FIND A PLACE TO DIE (JOE, CERCATI UN POSTO PER MORIRE) (Italy, 1968) Gianni Ferrio
CAM 10. 018 (Italy)

FIVE DAYS AND FIVE NIGHTS (Russia, 1948) Dmitri Shostakovich
Cinema LP-8003
Melodiya 11327-28 (Russia)

FIVE DAYS FROM HOME (Universal, 1978) Bill Conti
MCA 2362

5 DOLLS FOR AN AUGUST MOON (5 BAMBOLE PER LA LUNA D'AGOSTO) (Italy, 1972) Piero Umiliani
Cinevox 33/33 (Italy)

FIVE-MAN ARMY, THE (UNESERCITO DI 5 UOMINI) (Italy, 1969) Ennio Morricone
Ariete ARLP-2009 (Italy)
Duse ELP-058 (Italy)

5 SONS OF DOGS see BOOTLEGGERS, THE

5, 000 DOLLARS ON THE ACE (5, 000 DOLLARI SULL'ASSO) (Italy, n. d.) Francesco Lavagnino
CAM 30. 129 (Italy)

FLOWER IN THE RAIN (Hong Kong, 1979) composer unlisted
Regal LPHX-891 (Hong Kong)

FOLLOW ME see PUBLIC EYE, THE

FOR THE LOVE OF BENJI (Mulberry Square, 1977) Euel Box
Epic KSE-34867

FOR WHOM THE BELL TOLLS (Paramount, 1943) Victor Young

Decca 8008, 8481 and (7)4362
MCA VIM-7212
Stanyan SRQ-4013

FORBIDDEN PLANET (MGM, 1956) theme by David Rose; electronic music by Louis and Bebe Barron
Planet PR-001 (private)

FORBIDDEN ROOM, THE see ANIMA PERSA

FOREVER AMBER (Fox, 1947) David Raksin
Cinema LP-8007
RCA ARLK-1490

FOREVER YOUNG, FOREVER FREE (Universal, 1975) Lee Holdridge
MCA 2093

FORNARETTO DI VENEZIA, IL (Italy, n. d.) Armando Trovajoli
CAM 30.106 (Italy)

FORTEZZA DI SAMOGRAD, LA see SULEIMAN THE CONQUERER

FORTUNE COOKIE, THE (United Artists, 1966) Andre Previn
United Artists 4145/5145 and 3570/6570

FORZA ITALIA (COME UN GIROTONDO) (Italy, n. d.) Ennio Morricone
CMT 1002-9 (Italy)

FOUL PLAY (Paramount, 1978) Charles Fox
Arista AL-9501

FOUR GIRLS IN TOWN (Universal, 1956) Alex North
Varese Sarabande VC-81074

FOUR MUSKETEERS, THE (Fox, 1975) Lalo Schifrin
Entr'acte ERS-6510

FOX, THE (Warners, 1967) Lalo Schifrin
Warners (S) 1738

FOX IN QUEST OF THE NORTHERN SUN, THE see GLACIER FOX, THE

FOXY BROWN (American International, 1973) Willie Hutch
Motown M-811

FRANCIS OF ASSISI (Fox, 1961) Mario Nascimbene
Capitol (S) 2627
Fox (S) 3053
London 3257/246

FRENCH CONSPIRACY, THE see ASSASSINATION, THE

FRESHMAN, THE (Pathe, 1925) Walter Scharf (reissue version)
Citadel CT-6018

FREUD (Universal, 1962) Jerry Goldsmith
Citadel CT-6019 and CT-7011

FROM RUSSIA WITH LOVE (United Artists, 1964) John Barry; theme by Lionel Bart
United Artists 4114/5114, UXS-2-91, 3376/6376 and 3424/6424

FROM THE TERRACE (Fox, 1960) Elmer Bernstein
Cinema LP-8009

FUGA, LA (Italy, 1964) Piero Piccioni
CAM CMS-30115 and CA-2592(45) (Italy)

FUMO DI LONDRA (Italy, 1965) Piero Piccioni
Parade FPR-310 (Italy)

FURY see GIORNO DEL FURORE, IL

FURY, THE (Fox, 1978) John Williams
Arista AB-4175

GABLE AND LOMBARD (Universal, 1976) Michel Legrand
MCA 2091

GALILEO (Italy, 1968) Ennio Morricone
CAM SAG 9010 (Italy)

GAMES, THE (Fox, 1970) Francis Lai
Viking LPS-105

GARIBALDI (Italy, n. d.) Carlo Rustichelli
CAM 9058 (Italy)

GATOR (United Artists, 1976) Charles Bernstein
United Artists UA-LA646-G

GATTO, IL (Italy, n. d.) Ennio Morricone
Cinevox MDF 33.117 (Italy)

GAUNTLET, THE (Warners, 1977) Jerry Fielding
Warners BSK-3144

GEGE BELLAVITA (Italy, n. d.) Riz Ortolani
CAM AMP-222 (Italy)

GEMINUS (Italy, n. d.) Bruno Nicolai
Gemelli 10.003 (Italy)

GENERAL WITH THE COCK-EYED I. D., THE (Independent, n. d.) (short) Jerry Goldsmith
Temple TLP-2001 (private)

GENIO, DUE COMPARI, UN POLLO, UN see GENIUS, THE

GENIUS, THE (GENIO, DUE COMPARI, UN POLLO, UN) (France/Germany/Italy, 1976) Ennio Morricone
CBS 69231 (Italy)

GET CARTER (MGM, 1973) Roy Budd
EMI/Odeon 80544 (Britain)

GET OUT YOUR HANDKERCHIEFS (PREPAREZ VOUS MOUCHOIRS) (France, 1978) Georges Delerue
Deesse DDLX-160 (France)

GETTING STRAIGHT (Columbia, 1970) Ronald Stein et al.
Colgems S-5010

GHOST AND MRS. MUIR, THE (Fox, 1947) Bernard Herrmann
Film Music Collection FMC-4
Unicorn 400-4 (Britain)

GHOST OF FRANKENSTEIN, THE (Universal, 1942) Hans J. Salter
Citadel TT-HS-1/2

GIANT (Warners, 1956) Dimitri Tiomkin
Columbia CL-940 and ACL-940

GIOCATTOLO, IL (Italy, n.d.) Ennio Morricone
Cinevox MDF 33.128 and MDG-128 (Italy)

GIORDANO BRUNO (Italy, 1973) Ennio Morricone
RCA OLS-21 (Italy)

GIORNATA SPESA BENE, UNA (Italy, n.d.) Bruno Nicolai
General Music 55494 (Italy)

GIORNO DEL FURORE, IL (FURY) (Italy, 1973) Riz Ortolani
CAM 9047 (Italy)

GIORNO DELLA CIVETTA, IL see MAFIA

GIRL IN AUSTRALIA, A (BELLO ONESTO EMIGRATO AUSTRALIA) (Italy, 1972) Berto Pisano
RCA 11 (Italy)

GIRLS IN THE SUN (Greece, 1968) Stavros Xarchakos
Odeon OMCGAS-95 (Greece)

GLACIER FOX, THE (FOX IN QUEST OF THE NORTHERN SUN, THE) (Japan, 1979) Masaru Sato, Yukihide Takekawa
Columbia YX-5003 (Japan)

GLENN MILLER STORY, THE (Universal, 1954) Henry Mancini
MCA 2036

GLOWING AUTUMN (MOERU AKI) (Japan, n. d.) Toru Takemitsu
Toho AX-5031 (Japan)

GOD WITH US (GOTT MIT UNS) (Italy, 1970) Ennio Morricone
Gemelli 10.016 (Italy)

GODFATHER, THE (Paramount, 1972) Nino Rota
Paramount PAS-1003

GODFATHER, PART II, THE (Paramount, 1974) Nino Rota, Carmine Coppola
ABC ABDP-856

GOD'S LITTLE ACRE (United Artists, 1958) Elmer Bernstein
Sonopr. United Artists 25068-82657

GOIN' SURFIN' (Independent, 1975) Richard Henn et al.
Cowabunga 1001

GOLD (Allied Artists, 1974) Elmer Bernstein
ABC ABCD-855

GOLDEN EARRINGS (Paramount, 1947) Victor Young
Decca 8008 and 8481

GOLDEN LADY, THE (France, n. d.) Georges Garvarentz
Ariola ARL-5019 (Britain)

GOLDEN VOYAGE OF SINBAD, THE (Columbia, 1974) Miklos Rozsa
United Artists LA-308-G

GOLDFINGER (United Artists, 1964) John Barry
United Artists 4117/5114, UXS-2-91, 3392/6392, and 3424/6424

GOLIATH AND THE BARBARIANS (American International, 1960) Les Baxter
AIR 1001
Varese Sarabande VC-81078

GOLIATH AND THE SINS OF BABYLON (MACISTE L'EROE PIU GRANDE DEL MONDO) (Italy, 1963) Francesco de Masi
CAM 30.094 (Italy)

GONE WITH THE WIND (MGM, 1939) Max Steiner
RCA ARL1-0452
Warners 1322

GOOD AGE (France, n. d.) Georges Delerue
Versailles 90M315(45) (France)

GOOD LIFE, THE (France, 1964) Henri Lanoe
Capitol (S) 8603

GOOD, THE BAD AND THE UGLY, THE (Italy, 1967) Ennio Morricone
Custom CS-1122

GOODBYE AGAIN (United Artists, 1961) Georges Auric
United Artists 4091/5091 and 3158/6158

GOODBYE, COLUMBUS (Paramount, 1969) The Association, Charles Fox
Warners 1786

GOODBYE GEMINI (Britain, 1970) Christopher Gunning
DJM 408

GOODBYE ... SEE YOU MONDAY (AU REVOIR A LUNDI) (Canada/France, 1979) Lewis Furey
RCA RSL-1077 (France)

GORDON'S WAR (Fox, 1973) Al Alias, Andy Badale
Buddah 0598

GRAND SLAM (AD OGNI COSTO) (Italy, 1967) Ennio Morricone
RCA SP-8021 (Italy)

GRANDE BOURGEOISIE, LA (FATTI DI GENTE PERBENE/DRAMA OF THE RICH) (France/Italy, 1975) Ennio Morricone
Polydor MP-2510 (Japan)

GRANDE SILENZIO, IL (Italy, 1968) Ennio Morricone
Beat CR-1 (Italy)
Parade FPR-317 (Italy)

GREAT GATSBY, THE (Paramount, 1974) Nelson Riddle
Paramount PAS-2-3001

GREAT TRAIN ROBBERY, THE (United Artists, 1978) Jerry Goldsmith
United Artists UA-LA962-I

GREAT WALDO PEPPER, THE (Universal, 1975) Henry Mancini
MCA 2085

GREATEST, THE (Columbia, 1977) Michael Masser
Arista AL-7000

GREATEST STORY EVER TOLD, THE (United Artists, 1965) Alfred Newman
United Artists 4120/5120, LA-277-G, and 3476/6476

GREECE, LAND OF DREAMS (LAND OF DREAMS) (Greece, 1966) Manos Hadjidakis
Fontana 680-241 (Greece)

GREEK PEARLS, THE (Greece, 1968) Mimis Plessas
MGM-Lyra (S)1008

GREEN ROOM, THE (CHAMBRE VERTE, LA) (France, 1979) Maurice Jaubert
EMI-Pathe 2CO66-14567 (France)

GRIZZLY (Independent, 1976) Robert O. Ragland
Truluv HWR-301 (private)

GROUNDS FOR MARRIAGE (MGM, 1950) David Raksin
MGM 30315 (78) and E-536

GROUPIE GIRL (Britain, 1970) John Fiddy
Polydor 2384.021 (Britain)

GUAPPI, I (Italy, 1979) Franco and Gigi Campanino
RCA TBL1-1040 (Italy)

GUARDAMI NUDA (Italy, n.d.) Bruno Zambrini
General Music 55053 (Italy)

GUERRIER DAL SENO NUDA, LE see AMAZONS, THE

GUNFIGHT AT THE O.K. CORRAL (Paramount, 1957) Dimitri Tiomkin
Film Music Collection FMC-13

GUNS FOR SAN SEBASTIAN (MGM, 1968) Ennio Morricone
MGM(S)E-4565

GYPSY MOTHS, THE (MGM, 1969) Elmer Bernstein
Cinema LP-8011 (private)

HAIL THE ARTIST see SALUT L'ARTISTE

HAKKODASAN (Japan, n.d.) Yasushi Akutagawa
Atlantic L-10075A (Japan)

HAMLET (Universal, 1948) Sir William Walton
Seraphim S-60205

HAMLET (Russia, 1964) Dmitri Shostakovich
Cinema LP-8003 (private)

HAMMERSMITH IS OUT (Britain, 1972) Dominic Frontiere
Capitol SW-861

HANGOVER SQUARE (Fox, 1945) Bernard Herrmann
RCA ARL1-0707

HAPPENING, THE (France, n.d.) Michel Colombier
Pathe 77201 (France)

HAROLD LLOYD'S WORLD OF COMEDY (Continental, 1962) Walter Scharf
Citadel CT-6018

HARRAD EXPERIMENT, THE (Cinerama, 1972) Artie Butler et al.
Capitol ST-11182

HARRAD SUMMER, THE (Cinerama, 1974) Pat Williams
Capitol ST-11338

HARRY AND TONTO (Fox, 1974) Bill Conti
Casablanca NBLP-7010

HAWAII (United Artists, 1966) Elmer Bernstein
United Artists 4143/5143, LA-283-G and 3570/6570

HAWAIIANS, THE (United Artists, 1970) Henry Mancini
United Artists UAS-5210

HE AND SHE see ABSOLUTELY NATURAL

HEART IS A REBEL, THE (World Wide, n. d.) Ralph Carmichael
Chancelor 2005(45)

HEARTBREAK KID, THE (Fox, 1972) Garry Sherman et al.
Columbia S-32155

HEARTS AND MINDS (UOMO DA RISPETTARE/MASTER TOUCH, THE/MAN TO RESPECT, A/ MASTER PLAN, THE) (Germany/Italy, 1972) Ennio Morricone
CBS 70117 (Italy)

HEAVY TRAFFIC (American International, 1973) Ray Shanklin, Ed Bogas
Fantasy 9436

HELEN OF TROY (Warners, 1955) Max Steiner
Film Music Collection FMC-1 (private)

HELL UP IN HARLEM (American International, 1974) Fonce Mizell, Freddie Perren
Motown M-802

HELLO, GOODBYE (Fox, 1970) Francis Lai
Fox S-4210

HELL'S ANGELS ON WHEELS (Independent, 1967) Stu Philips
Smash 27094/67094

HELP ME, MY LOVE (AMORE MIO AIUTARE) (Italy, 1969) Piero Piccioni
RCA 1007 (Italy)

HENRY V (United Artists, 1945) Sir William Walton
Seraphim S-60205

HENRY VIII AND HIS SIX WIVES (Britain, 1972) David Munrow et al.
Angel SFO-36895

HERE WE GO 'ROUND THE MULBERRY BUSH (Britain, 1968) various composers
United Artists 4175/5175 and LA-294-G

HERO AIN'T NOTHIN' BUT A SANDWICH, A (New World, 1977) Tom McIntosh
Columbia PS-35046

HEROES (Universal, 1977) Jack Nitzsche, Richard Hazard
MCA 2320

HIDING PLACE, THE (World Wide, 1975) Tedd Smith
Word WST-8697-LP

HIGH AND LOW (Japan, 1963) Masaru Sato
Toho 1001 (Japan)

HIGH AND THE MIGHTY, THE (Warners, 1954) Dimitri Tiomkin
Film Music Collection FMC-14 (private)

HIGH ANXIETY (Fox, 1977) John Morris
Asylum 5E-501

HIGH CRIME see POLIZIA INCRIMINA, LA LEGGE ASSOLVE, LA

HIGH TIME (Fox, 1960) Henry Mancini
RCA LPM-2314/LSP-2314

HILLS RUN RED, THE (United Artists, 1967) Ennio Morricone
POO LP-103 (private)

HINDENBERG, THE (Universal, 1975) David Shire
MCA 2090

HIS LAND (World Wide, 1970) Ralph Carmichael
EMI 6443 (Britain)

HISTOIRE D'O see STORY OF "O," THE

HITLER (Allied Artists, 1962) Hans J. Salter
Medallion ML-302

HITTER, THE (Independent, 1979) Garfeel Ruff
Capitol SW-11920

HOLOCAUST 2000 (Britain/Italy, 1977) Ennio Morricone
Beat LPF-040 (Italy)

HOMO EROTICUS (Italy, 1975) Armando Trovajoli
RCA 7 (Italy)

HONEY BABY, HONEY BABY (Kelly-Jordan, 1975) Michael Tschudin, Carl L. Maults-By
RCA APL1-0994

HONEY POT, THE (United Artists, 1967) John Addison
United Artists UAL-4159/UAS-5159

HONG KONG UN ADDIO (Italy, n. d.) Gino Marinuzzi
CAM 30.053 (Italy)

HOOK, THE (TO AGKISTRI) (Greece, n. d.) Giorgos Khatzenasios
Philips 6331-111 (Greece)

HOOPER (Warners, 1978) Bill Justis
Warners BSK-3234

HORIZONS GAGNES, LES (Japan, n. d.) Nobuyoshi Koshibe
Victor VIP-7203 (Japan)

HORNET'S NEST, THE (France, 1976) Giancarlo Chiaramello
POO LP-105 (private)
United Artists MAX-18 (Japan)

HORROR EXPRESS (Britain, 1973) John Cacavas
Citadel CT-6026

HORSE SOLDIERS, THE (United Artists, 1959) David Buttolph
United Artists GXH-6004 (Japan)

HORSEMEN, THE (Columbia, 1971) Georges Delerue
Sunflower-MGM SNF-5007

HOT MILLIONS (MGM, 1968) Laurie Johnson
MGM 8104 (Britain)

HOT PARTS (Independent, 1972) Michael Brown, Bert Sommer
Kama Sutra KSBS-2054

HOT ROCK, THE (Fox, 1972) Quincy Jones
Prophecy 6055

HOUR OF THE GUN (United Artists, 1967) Jerry Goldsmith
United Artists 4166/5166

HOW GREEN WAS MY VALLEY (Fox, 1941) Alfred Newman
Sound of Hollywood 400-1 (private)

HOW, WHEN AND WITH WHOM? (COME, CUANDO PERCHE) (Italy, 1969) Armando Trovajoli
RCA 1006 (Italy)

HUMANOID, THE (UMANOIDE, L') (Italy, n.d.) Ennio Morricone
RCA BL-31432 (Italy)

HUNCHBACK OF ROME (GOBBO, IL) (Italy, 1960) Piero Piccioni
RCA EPA-30 392(45) (Italy)

HURRICANE (Paramount, 1979) Nino Rota
Elektra 5E-504

HUSTLER, THE (Fox, 1961) Kenyon Hopkins
MCA 7133 (Japan)

HYENA'S SUN (SOLEIL DES HYENES) (Holland, 1979) Nicola Piovani
CBS 83206 (Holland)

I KILLED RASPUTIN (France, 1969) Andre Hossein
Philips 70.426 (France)

I LOVE YOU, ALICE B. TOKLAS (Warners, 1968) Elmer Bernstein
Cinema LP-8010 (private)

I NEVER SANG FOR MY FATHER (Columbia, 1970) Al Gorgoni, Barry Mann
Bell 1204

I WANT TO LIVE! (United Artists, 1958) Johnny Mandel
United Artists 4006/5006, LA-271-G, and 3122/6122

ICE CASTLES (Columbia, 1978) Marvin Hamlisch
Arista AL-9502

IERA, OGGA, DOMANI see YESTERDAY, TODAY AND TOMORROW

IF DON JUAN WERE A WOMAN see DON JUAN

IF EVER I SEE YOU AGAIN (Columbia, 1978) Joe Brooks
Warners 2WB-3199

IF HE HOLLERS, LET HIM GO (Cinerama, 1968) Coleridge-Taylor Perkinson
Tower (S) 5152

IMAGES (Britain, 1972) John Williams
C.I.F. 1002 (private)

IMMORALITA, L' (Italy, n.d.) Ennio Morricone
CAM SAG-9091 (Italy)

IMMORTAL GARRISON, THE (Russia, 1956) V. Basner
MK 022043/4 (Russia)

IMPERIAL VENUS (VENERE IMPERIALE) (Italy, n.d.) Francesco Lavagnino
CAM 30.052 (Italy)

IMPERIALE (Greece, n. d.) Theo Roybanis
Seagull 33/3E-SL-7 (Greece)

IMPUTAZIONE DI OMICIDIO PER UNO STUDENTE (Italy, 1971) Ennio Morricone
CBS/Sugar CGD-FG 5099 (Italy)

IN HARM'S WAY (Paramount, 1965) Jerry Goldsmith
RCA CR-10022 (Japan)

IN LOVE AND WAR (Fox, 1958) Hugo Friedhofer
Entr'acte ERS-6506

IN THE HEAT OF THE NIGHT (United Artists, 1967) Quincy Jones
United Artists 4160/5160 and LA-290-G

IN THE NAME OF THE ITALIAN PEOPLE (IN NOME DEL POPOLO ITALIANI) (Italy, 1971) Carlo Rustichelli
Music Parade-Cetra LEL-199 (Italy)

IN THE REALM OF THE SENSES (EMPIRE DE LA PASSION, L') (France/Japan, 1976) Toru Takemitsu
RCA RVC-2211 (Japan)

IN THE YEAR OF THE LORD (NELL'ANNO DEL SIGNORE) (Italy, 1969) Armando Trovajoli
Cinevox 33/26 (Italy)

IN TOCCABILI, GLI see MACHINE GUN McCAIN

INCORRIGIBLE, L' (France, 1975) Georges Delerue
EMI-Pathe 2CO66-14236 (France)

INDISCRETION OF AN AMERICAN WIFE (Columbia, 1954) Alessandro Cicognini
Cinema LP-8008 (private)

INFORMER, THE (RKO, 1935) Max Steiner
Angel S-36068

INHERITANCE, THE (EREDITA FERRAMONTI, IL) (Italy, 1976) Ennio Morricone
CAM SAG-9067 (Italy)

INHERITOR, THE (HERITIER, L') (France, 1973) Michel Colombier
A&M FML-12 (Japan)

INNOCENTE, L' see INTRUDER, THE

INSATIABLES, THE see FEMMINE INSAZIABILI

INSENSIBLEMENT (France, n. d.) Paul Misraki
Dot 3120

INTERNATIONAL VELVET (MGM, 1978) Francis Lai
MGM MG-1-5405

INTOUCHABLES, LES see MACHINE GUN McCAIN

INTRIGUE IN NYLONS (Hong Kong, 1979) composer unlisted
Regal LPHX-891 (Hong Kong)

INTRUDER, THE (INNOCENTE, L') (Italy, 1976) Franco Mannino
Cinevox MDF 33.100 (Italy)
Seven Seas FML-110 (Japan)

INVASION OF THE BODY SNATCHERS (United Artists, 1978) Denny Zeitlin
United Artists UA-LA940-H

INVITO ALLO SPORT (Italy, 1979) Ennio Morricone
General Music GML-10012 (Italy)

IO, IO, IO E GLI ALTRI see ME, ME, ME AND THE OTHERS

IO LA CONOSCEVO BENE (Italy, 1965) Piero Piccioni
CAM CE-10014 (Italy)

IP E LUI (Italy, n.d.) Bruno Zambrini
Cetra-Fonit 25 (Italy)

IPCRESS FILE, THE (Universal, 1965) John Barry
MCA VIM-7236 (Japan)

IRON PREFECT, THE (PREFETTO DI FERRO, IL) (Italy, 1977) Ennio Morricone
Beat LPF-041 (Italy)

ISLAND AT THE TOP OF THE WORLD, THE (Disney, 1974) Maurice Jarre
Disneyland 3814

ISLAND IN THE SKY (Warners, 1953) Hugo Friedhofer, Emil Newman
MCA VIM-7244 (Japan)

ISLAND OF APHRODITE, THE (CHRYSOPRASINO PHYLLO--THE SILVER LEAF) (Greece, 1966) Mikis Theodorakis
Odeon PGCLP-12 (Greece)

ISOLA DEGLI UOMINI PESCE, L' (Italy, n.d.) Luciano Michelini
Cometa 1009-21 (Italy)

ITALIANI BRAVA GENTE (Italy/Russia, 1965) Armando Trovajoli
RCA 10382 (Italy)

IT'S A MAD, MAD, MAD, MAD WORLD (United Artists, 1963)

Ernest Gold
United Artists 4110/5110, LA-276-G, and 3376/6376

IT'S ALIVE II (Warners, 1978) Bernard Herrmann, Laurie Johnson
Starlog SR-1002 (private)

IVANHOE (MGM, 1952) Miklos Rozsa
MGM 3507 and 2353-095 (Britain)

JAGUAR LIVES! (American International, 1979) Robert O. Ragland
Seven Seas FML-116 (Japan)

JAPANESE WIFE, THE (MOGLIE GIAPPONESE, LO) Nino Olivero
RCA 1001 (Italy)

JASON AND THE ARGONAUTS (Columbia, 1963) Bernard Herrmann
London SPC-21137 (Britain)

JAWS (Universal, 1975) John Williams
MCA 2087

JAWS 2 (Universal, 1978) John Williams
MCA 3045

JE SUIS TIMIDE, MAIS JE ME SOIGNE (France, n. d.) Georges Delerue
Deesse DDLX-176 (France)

JEREMIAH JOHNSON (Warners, 1971) John Rubenstein, Tim McIntire
Warners BS-2902

JEREMY (United Artists, 1974) Lee Holdridge
United Artists LA-145-G

JOE (Cannon, 1970) Bobby Scott
Mercury 605

JOE--CERCATO UN POSTO PER MORIRE (Italy, n. d.) Gianni Ferrio
CAM MAG-10. 018 (Italy)

JOHN THE BASTARD (Italy, n. d.) Nico Fidenco
CAM MAG 10. 015 (Italy)

JONATHAN LIVINGSTON SEAGULL (Paramount, 1973) Neil Diamond
Columbia KS-32550

JOURNEY, THE see VIAGGIO, IL

JOURNEY THROUGH THE PAST (Marvin, 1973) Neil Young
Reprise 2XS-6480

JOURNEY TO THE CENTER OF THE EARTH (Fox, 1959) Bernard Herrmann
London SP-44207

JUD (Independent, 1971) Stu Phillips et al.
Ampex A-50101

JULIA (Fox, 1977) Georges Delerue
King FML-99 (Japan)

JULIET OF THE SPIRITS (Italy, 1965) Nino Rota
CAM 500-001 (France)

JUNGLE BOOK (United Artists, 1942) Miklos Rozsa
RCA 2118
Sound Stage SS-2308 (private)
United Artists UAS-29725 (Britain)

JUST ANOTHER WAR (UOMINI CONTRO) (Italy, 1970) Piero Piccioni
RCA 10473 (Italy)

JUSTINE (Italy, 1974) Bruno Nicolai
Gemelli 10.013 (Italy)

KALI-YUG, LA DEA DELLA VENDETTA (KALI-YUG, THE GODDESS OF VENGEANCE) (Italy, n.d.) Francesco Lavagnino
CAM 30.093 (Italy)

KARATE AMAZONES (Italy, n.d.) Franco Micalizzi
TAM YX-8023 (Japan)

KATIA (KATIA AND THE EMPEROR) (France, 1963) Joseph Kosma
French Victor 440.138 (45)

KELLY'S HEROES (MGM, 1970) Lalo Schifrin
MGM 1SE-23ST

KENTUCKIAN, THE (United Artists, 1955) Bernard Herrmann
Entr'acte ERS-6506

KHARTOUM (United Artists, 1966) Frank Cordell
United Artists 4140/5140, 3526/6526, and 3570/6570

KID, THE (First National, 1921) Charles Chaplin
Camden CAS-2581

KILL! (Italy, 1973) Berto Pisano
General Music 55067 (Italy)

KILL THEM ALL AND COME BACK ALONE (AMMAZZALI TUTTI E TORNA SOLO) (Italy, 1970) Francesco de Masi
Beat CDR 33-5 (Italy)

KILLER, THE (Italy, 1972) Gianni Ferrio
CAM SAG-9012 (Italy)

KILLER FORCE (DIAMOND MERCENARIES) (American International, 1975)
Pye NSPL-28219 (Britain)

KINDAICH KOSUE NO BOKEN (ADVENTURE OF KINDAICH, THE) (Japan, 1979) Asei Kobayashi
Columbia YX-5014 (Japan)

KING KONG (RKO, 1933) Max Steiner
Entr'acte ERS-6504
United Artists LA-373-G

KING KONG (Paramount, 1976) John Barry
Reprise MS-2260

KING OF HEARTS (United Artists, 1967) Georges Delerue
United Artists 4150/5150 and LA-287-G

KING OF KINGS (MGM, 1961) Miklos Rozsa
MGM 2353-035 (Britain)

KISS, THE (BAISER, LE) (France, n. d.) Francis Lai
Polydor 2393. 068 (France)

KLUTE (Warners, 1970) Michael Small
(no label) WS-1940 (private)

KNACK--AND HOW TO GET IT, THE (United Artists, 1965) John Barry
United Artists 4129/5129, LA-279-G, and 3476/6476

LABYRINTHE (Canada, 1967) Eldon Rathburn
LAB 650-S (Canada)

LACEMAKER, THE (DENTELLIERE, LA) (France/Switzerland, 1977) Pierre Jansen
Barclay 900. 539 (France)

LADY CALIPH see CALIFFA, LA

LADY CAROLINE LAMB (United Artists, 1973) Richard Rodney Bennett
Angel S-36946

LADY IN THE CAR WITH GLASSES AND A GUN (France, 1970) Michel Legrand
Vogue 755 (France)

LADY OSCAR (France, 1979) Michel Legrand
Kitty MKF-1045 (Japan)

LADY SINGS THE BLUES (Paramount, 1972) Michel Legrand
Motown 2-758 (with dialog)

LAMA NEL CORPO, LE see MURDER CLINIC, THE

LAND OF THE PHARAOHS (Warners, 1955) Dimitri Tiomkin
Film Music Collection FMC-13

LAND RAIDERS (Columbia, 1969) Bruno Nicolai
Beverly Hills BHS-21

LAST CONCERT, THE (Italy, n. d.) Stelvio Cipriani
Seven Seas FML-64 (Japan)

LAST OF THE MOHICANS, THE (Germany, 1965) Peter Thomas
Telefunken 14390 (Germany)

LAST OF THE SKI BUMS, THE (Independent, 1969) The Sandals
World Pacific WPS-21884

LAST PICTURE SHOW, THE (Columbia, 1971) traditional popular music
Columbia S-31143
MGM 1SE-33-ST

LAST RUN, THE (MGM, 1971) Jerry Goldsmith
MGM 1SE-30-ST

LAST SNOWS OF SPRING, THE (ULTIMA NEVE DI PRIMAVERA, L') (Italy, 1973) Franco Micalizzi
RCA TBL1-1018 (Italy)

LAST TANGO IN PARIS, THE (Italy, 1973) Gato Barbieri
United Artists LA-045-F

LAUGHING WOMAN, THE (FEMINA RIDENS/WOMAN LAUGHS LAST) (Italy, 1970) Stelvio Cipriani
CAM 9017 (Italy)

LAURA (Fox, 1944) David Raksin
RCA ARL1-1490, LPM/LSP-2380, LPM/LSP-2895, and LPM/LSP-3887

LAWMAN (United Artists, 1971) Jerry Fielding
Citadel CT-JF-2/3

LAWRENCE OF ARABIA (Columbia, 1962) Maurice Jarre
Bell S-1205

LEGEND OF FRENCHIE KING, THE (France, 1974) Francis Lai
Music for Pleasure MFP-50034 (Britain)

LENNY (United Artists, 1974) Ralph Burns
United Artists LA-359-G (with dialog)

LEONARDO DA VINCI (LIFE OF LEONARDO DA VINCI, THE) (Italy, 1952) Roman Vlad
Ariston 12069 (Italy)

LESBOS (Italy, n. d.) Francesco de Masi, A. Alessandroni
CAM SAG-9014 (Italy)

LIAISONS DANGEREUSES, LES (DANGEROUS LOVE AFFAIRS) (France, 1959) Art Blakey, Duke Jordan
Fontana 27539/67539
Parker PLP(S)813

LIBERATION OF L. B. JONES, THE (Columbia, 1970) Elmer Bernstein
Cinema LP-8009 (private)

LIENS DE SANG, LES (France, n. d.) Pierre Jansen
Pema Music 900-062 (France)

LIFE AND TIMES OF JUDGE ROY BEAN, THE (National General, 1972) Maurice Jarre
Columbia S-31948

LIFE, LOVE AND DEATH (France, 1969) Francis Lai
United Artists 29007 (France)

LIFE OF BRIAN, THE (Britain, 1979) Geoffrey Burgeon
Warners 3396

LIFESPAN (SECRET DE LA VIE, LE) (France, 1975) Terry Riley
Stip ST-1011 (France)

LIGHT AT THE EDGE OF THE WORLD, THE (Britain, 1973) Piero Piccioni
General Music 55078 (Italy)

LILIES OF THE FIELD (United Artists, 1963) Jerry Goldsmith
Epic 24094/26094

LINGUA D'ARGENTO (Argentina, n. d.) Alberto Baldan Bembo
Aris Siae ANL-4007

LIPSTICK (Paramount, 1976) Michel Polnareff, Jimmie Haskell
Atlantic SD-18178

LISZTOMANIA (Britain, 1975) Rick Wakeman
A&M SP-4546

LITTLE, A LOT, PASSIONATELY, A (PEU, BEAUCOUP PASSIONNEMENT, UN) (France, 1971) Francois de Roubaix
Paramount 62.92217 (France)

LITTLE ROMANCE, A (Warners, 1979) Georges Delerue
Varese Sarabande STV-81109

LIVE A LITTLE, STEAL A LOT (MURPH THE SURF) (American International, 1974) Philip Lambro
Motown M6-839-S1

LIVE AND LET DIE (United Artists, 1973) George Martin
United Artists LA-100-G

LIVE FOR LIFE (France, 1967) Francis Lai
United Artists 4165/5165, LA-291-G, and 3633/6633

LIVING DEAD AT THE MANCHESTER MORGUE, THE (FIN DE SEMANA PARA LOS MUERTOS) (Italy, 1974) Giuliano Sorgini
Beat LPF-028 (Italy)

LIVING FREE (Britain, 1972) Sol Kaplan
RCA LSO-1172

LOGAN'S RUN (MGM, 1976) Jerry Goldsmith
MGM MG-1-5302

LOLLIPOP COVER (Independent, 1966) Ruby Raskin
Mainstream 56067/6067

LONG AGO TOMORROW (RAGING MOON, THE) (Britain, 1971) Stanley Myers
EMI 6447 (Britain)

LOOKING FOR MR. GOODBAR (Paramount, 1977) Artie Kane et al.
Columbia JS-35029

LOOT (Britain, 1971) Keith Mansfield
CBS 70073 (Britain)

LORD LOVE A DUCK (United Artists, 1966) Neal Hefti
United Artists 4137/5137 and 3573/6573

LORD OF THE RINGS (United Artists, 1978) Leonard Rosenman
Fantasy LOR-1

LORDS OF FLATBUSH, THE (Columbia, 1974) Joe Brooks
ABC ABCD-828

LOST COMMAND, THE (Columbia, 1966) Franz Waxman
Cinema LP-8017 (private)

LOVE A LA CARTE (HUNGRY FOR LOVE/ADUA E LE COMPAGNE) (Italy, 1960) Piero Piccioni
Cinevox CJO-1 (Italy)

LOVE AND ANARCHY (Italy, 1975) Nino Rota
Cinevox 33/67 (Italy)

LOVE AT FIRST BITE (American International, 1979) Charles Bernstein
Parachute RRLP-9016

LOVE CIRCLE see ONE NIGHT AT DINNER

LOVE IS A MANY-SPLENDORED THING (Fox, 1955) Alfred Newman
Cinema LP-8013 (private)

LOVE MACHINE, THE (Columbia, 1971) Artie Butler
Scepter 595

LOVE OF AN UNKNOWN WOMAN, THE (AMORI QUESTO SCONOSCIUTO, L') (Italy, n. d.) composer unlisted
CAM SAG-9014 (Italy)

LOVELY MONSTER, THE (BEAU MONSTRE, UN) (France, 1971) Georges Garvarentz
EMI-Pathe 62.11430 (France)

LUCKY LADY (Fox, 1976) Ralph Burns
Arista AL-4069

LUCKY LUCIANO (Italy, 1973) Piero Piccioni
CBS 70130 (Italy)

LUCKY LUKE (United Artists, 1971) Claude Bolling
United Artists 29290 (France)

LUDWIG (Germany, 1973) traditional classical
Philips S1-5401

LULU THE TOOL see WORKING CLASS GOES TO HEAVEN, THE

LUMIERE (France, 1977) Astor Piazzolla
Carosello CLN-25059 (Italy)

LUMIERE DES JUSTES, LA (LIGHT OF JUSTICE) (France, 1979) Georges Garvarentz
Barclay 910.008 (France)

LUTRING see WAKE UP AND DIE

M*A*S*H (Fox, 1970) Johnny Mandel
Columbia 3520 and S-32753

MacARTHUR (Universal, 1977) Jerry Goldsmith
MCA 2287

MACCHINA DELLA VIOLENZA, LA see BIG GAME, THE

MACHINE GUN McCAIN (INTOCCABILI, GLI/INTOUCHABLES, LES) (France/Italy, 1968) Ennio Morricone
Disc AZ LPO-32. 576 (France)
E. M. Records 1002 (private)
Jolly LPJ-5094 (Italy)

MACHINE GUN STEIN (METRALLETA STEIN) (Italy, 1979) Stelvio Cipriani, Carlo Rustichelli
CAM ZDL 1-7106 (Italy)

MACISTE L'EROE PIU GRANDE DEL MONDO see GOLIATH AND THE SINS OF BABYLON

MACK, THE (Cinerama, 1973) Willie Hutch
Motown M-766

MAD ADVENTURES OF RABBI JACOB, THE (France, 1974) Vladimir Cosma
London 652

MADAME BOVARY (MGM, 1949) Miklos Rozsa
Film Music Collection FMC-12
MGM 3507, 2353-095 (Britain), and (S)4112

MADAME ROSA (VIE DEVANT SOI, LA) (France, 1978) Philippe Sarde
Polydor 2393-182 (France)

MADDALENA (Italy, 1971) Ennio Morricone
General Music ZSLGE-55063 (Italy)

MADEMOISELLE DE MAUPIN (MADAMIGELLA DI MAUPIN) (Italy, 1966) Franco Mannino
CAM 13. 12 (Italy)

MADLY (France, 1970) Francis Lai
Barclay 920283 (France)

MAFIA (GIORNO DELLA CIVETTA, IL) (France/Italy, 1969) Giovanni Fusco
CAM 10013 (Italy)

MAGIC OF LASSIE, THE (International Picture Show, 1978) Richard and Robert Sherman
Durium 30-316 (Italy)

MAGNIFICENT DOLL, THE (Universal, 1946) Hans J. Salter
Citadel TT-HS-1/2

MAGNIFICENT ONE, THE (MAGNIFIQUE, LE) (France, 1973) Claude Bolling
Polydor 2393-075 (France)

MAGNIFICO TONY CARRERA, IL (Italy, n. d.) Gianni Marchetti
CAM 9011 (Italy)

MAGNUM PER TONY SAITTA, UNA see BLAZING MAGNUM

MAHOGANY (Paramount, 1975) Michael Masser
Motown M6-858S1

MAIN EVENT, THE (Warners, 1979) various composers
Columbia JS-36115

MALOMBRA (Italy, n. d.) Pino Calvi
Beat/Music Parade 228 (Italy)

MAMMA ROMA (Italy, 1962) Carlo Rustichelli
CAM 2446 (Italy)

MAN, A HORSE AND A GUN, A see STRANGER RETURNS, THE

MAN AND A WOMAN, A (France, 1966) Francis Lai
United Artists 4147/5147, 4184/5184 (Britain), 3570/6570, and 3625/6625

MAN AND BOY (Independent, 1972) J. J. Johnson
Sussex 7011

MAN CALLED ADAM, A (Embassy, 1966) Benny Carter et al.
Reprise R(S)-6180

MAN CALLED NOON, THE (LO CHIAMAVANO MEZZOGIORNO) (Italy, 1973) Luis Enrique Bacalov
General Music 55493 (Italy)

MAN FROM NOWHERE, THE (Independent, 1969) Francesco de Masi
United Artists 6710

MAN FROM THE EAST, A (E POI LO CHIAMARONO IL MAGNIFICO) (Italy, 1972) Guido and Maurizio de Angelis
SM 901 (Italy)

MAN IN THE FIFTH DIMENSION (World Wide, n. d.) Ralph Carmichael
RCA-Camden 5532

MAN IN THE MIDDLE (Fox, 1964) Lionel Bart, John Barry
Fox (S)4128

MAN IN THE WILDERNESS, THE (Warners, 1971) Johnny Harris
Warners K-46126

MAN TO RESPECT, A see HEARTS AND MINDS

MAN WHO LOVED WOMEN, THE (HOMME QUI AIMAIT LES

FEMMES, L') (France, 1977) Maurice Jaubert
EMI-Pathe 2CO66-14567

MAN WHO WOULD BE KING, THE (Allied Artists, 1975) Maurice Jarre
Capitol SW-11474

MAN WITH THE GOLDEN GUN, THE (United Artists, 1974) John Barry
United Artists LA-358-G

MANHATTAN (United Artists, 1979) music of George Gershwin
Columbia JS-36020

MANI SULLA CITTA, LE (Italy, 1963) Piero Piccioni
RCA PML-10353 and PME-30494 (Italy)

MANNAJA (Italy, n. d.) Guido and Maurizio de Angelis
Cometa CMT-1008-20 (Italy)

MARACAIBO (Paramount, 1958) Laurindo Almeida
MCA VIM-7239 (Japan)

MARAT/SADE see PERSECUTION AND ASSASSINATION OF JEAN-PAUL MARAT AS PERFORMED BY THE INMATES OF THE ASYLUM OF CHARENTON UNDER THE DIRECTION OF THE MARQUIS DE SADE

MARCIA TRIONFALE see VICTORY MARCH

MARNIE (Universal, 1964) Bernard Herrmann
Crimson CR-101 (private)
Sound Stage SS-2306 (private)

MARTIN (Independent, 1978) Donald Rubinstein
Varese Sarabande VC-81127

MARY QUEEN OF SCOTS (Universal, 1971) John Barry
Decca DL-79186

MASCHIO RUSPANTE, IL (Italy, n. d.) Gianni Ferrio
Cinevox 33/61 (Italy)

MASSACRE IN GRAND CANYON (Italy, 1965) Gianni Ferrio
CAM 30.097 (Italy)

MASTER PLAN, THE see HEARTS AND MINDS

MASTER TOUCH, THE see HEARTS AND MINDS

ME, ME, ME AND THE OTHERS (IO, IO, IO E GLI ALTRI) (Italy, 1966) Carlo Rustichelli
CAM 100.011 (Italy)

MEATBALLS (Paramount, 1979) Elmer Bernstein
RSO RS-1-3056

MECHANIC, THE (United Artists, 1972) Jerry Fielding
Citadel CT-JF-2/3

MEDICO DELLA MUTUA, IL (Italy, n.d.) Piero Piccioni
MSA 77242 (Italy)

MEETINGS WITH REMARKABLE MEN (Libra, 1979) Thomas de Hartmann, Laurence Rosenthal
Varese Sarabande STV-81129

MELINDA (MGM, 1972) Jerry Butler
Pride PRD-0006-ST

MENACE, LA see THREAT, THE

MENAGE ITALIAN STYLE (MENAGE ALL'ITALIANA) (Italy, 1966) Ennio Morricone
RCA SP-8013 (Italy)

MERCENARIO, IL see MERCENARY, THE

MERCENARY, THE (IL MERCENARIO/PROFESSIONAL GUN, A) (Italy, 1970) Ennio Morricone, Bruno Nicolai
United Artists SR-328 (Japan)
United Artists UAS-20995 (France)
United Artists UAS-29005-I (Germany)

MESSAGE, THE see MOHAMMAD, THE MESSENGER OF GOD

MESSALINA, MESSALINA (Italy, n.d.) Guido and Maurizio de Angelis
Cometa CMT 1007-19 (Italy)

METTI, UNA SERA A CENA see ONE NIGHT AT DINNER

MICKEY ONE (MGM, 1965) Eddie Sauter
MGM (S) 4312

MIDAS RUN (Cinerama, 1969) Elmer Bernstein
Citadel CT-6016

MIDNIGHT EXPRESS (Columbia, 1978) Giorgio Moroder
Casablanca NBLP-7114

MILANO CALIBRO 9 (Italy, 1974) Luis Enrique Bacalov, Osanna
PILPS-Cosmos 9001

MIMI METALLURGICO see SEDUCTION OF MIMI, THE

MIMI THE METAL-WORKER, WOUNDED IN HONOR see SEDUCTION OF MIMI, THE

MINNESOTA CLAY (Italy, 1966) Piero Piccioni
CAM CMS-30114 (Italy)
GW 167/168 (Italy)

MINX, THE (Independent, 1972) Tom Dawes, Don Dannermann
Amsterdam AMS-12007

MIO NOME E SHANGHAI JOE, IL see SHANGHAI JOE

MIO PADRE MONSIGNORE (Italy, n. d.) Franco Bixio
Cinevox 33/47 (Italy)

MIRACLE, THE (Warners, 1959) Elmer Bernstein
Film Music Collection FMC-2

MISFITS, THE (United Artists, 1961) Alex North
United Artists 3158/6158, 4087/5087, 4105/5105, and LA-273-G

MISSOURI BREAKS, THE (United Artists, 1976) John Williams
United Artists UA-LA623-G

MITO, IL see MYTH, THE

MOBY DICK (Warners, 1956) Philip Sainton
Movie Music MM-5146 (private)

MOBY DICK (Italy, n. d.) Fiorenzo Carpi
Gemelli 10-015 (Italy)

MODERN TIMES (United Artists, 1936) Charles Chaplin
United Artists UAS-5222

MOGLIE GIAPPONESE, LO see JAPANESE WIFE, THE

MOHAMMAD, THE MESSENGER OF GOD (MESSAGE, THE) (Birley/Tarik, 1977) Maurice Jarre
Namara EMI SLCW-1033 (Britain)

MOI Y'EN A VOULOIR DES SOUS (France, 1973) Michel Magne
Vogue 789 (France)

MOMENT BY MOMENT (Universal, 1978) Lee Holdridge
RSO SO-1-3040

MONDO CANDIDO (Italy, 1975) Riz Ortolani
CBS 80652 (Italy)

MONDO DI NOTTE, IL see WORLD BY NIGHT, THE

MONEY! MONEY! MONEY! (AVENTURE C'EST L'AVENTURE, L') (Italy, 1973) Francis Lai
United Artists 29296

MONSIEUR DE COMPAGNIE, LE (France, n. d.) Georges Delerue
Barclay 70724(45) (France)

MONTAGNA DEL DIO CANNIBALE, LA (Italy, n. d.) Guido and Maurizio de Angelis
Cometa CMT 1007-19 (Italy)

MONUGI MOUNTAIN PASS (NOMUGITOGE) (Japan, n. d.) Masaru Sato
CBS/Sony 25AH707 (Japan)

MOONRAKER (United Artists, 1979) John Barry
United Artists LA-971

MORE THAN A MIRACLE (CINDERELLA--ITALIAN STYLE/C'ERA UNA VOLTA) (Italy, 1967) Piero Piccioni
MGM SE-4514-ST
Parade JB-004(45) (Italy)

MORT D'UN POURRI see DEATH OF A CORRUPT MAN, THE

MORTE BUSSA DUE VOLTE, LA (Italy, n. d.) Piero Umiliani
Cinevox 33/25 (Italy)

MOST IMPORTANT EVENT SINCE MAN FIRST SET FOOT ON THE MOON, THE (ENVENEMENT LE PLUS IMPORTANT DEPUIS QUE L'HOMME SUR LA LUNE, L') (France, 1973) Michel Legrand
Philips 6325.403 (France)

MUORI LENTAMENTE ... TE LA GODI DI PIU (Italy, n. d.) Gianni Marchetti
CAM 10002 (Italy)

MURDER CLINIC, THE (LAMA NEL CORPO, LE) (France/Italy, 1969) Francesco de Masi
CAM CDR 33-18 (Italy)

MURDER ON THE ORIENT EXPRESS (Paramount, 1974) Richard Rodney Bennett
Capitol ST-11361

MY BROTHER ANASTASIA (ANASTASIA MIO FRATELLO) (Italy, 1973) Piero Piccioni
RCA 20 (Italy)

MY FATHER, MY MASTER see PADRE PADRONE

MY NAME IS ANDREA (LO CHIAMEREO ANDREA) (Italy, n. d.) Manuel de Sica
CAM 9045 (Italy)

MY NAME IS NOBODY (MIO NOME E NESSUNO, IL) (Italy, 1973)

Ennio Morricone
Cerberus CEM-S-0101
General Music ZSLGE-55497 (Italy)
General Music 803001 (France)

MYRA BRECKINRIDGE (Fox, 1970) John Philips
Fox S-4210

MYSTERIOUS ISLAND (Columbia, 1961) Bernard Herrmann
London SPC-21137 (Britain)

MYSTERIOUS ISLAND OF CAPTAIN NEMO, THE (ISOLA MISTERIOSA E IL CAPITANO NEMO, L') (Italy, 1974) Gianni Ferrio
Cinevox MDF 33-62 (Italy)

MYTH, THE (MITO, IL) (Italy, 1965) Armando Trovajoli
CAM 30.111 (Italy)

NAKED ANGELS (Favorite, 1969) Jeffrey Simmons, Randy Steirling
Straight 1056

NAKED APE, THE (Independent, 1974) Jimmy Webb
Playboy 125

NAPOLI SI RIBELLA (Italy, n.d.) Franco Campanino
Cinevox MDF-33-114 (Italy)

NASHVILLE COYOTE (Independent, 1974) Buddy Baker
JMI 4005

NAVAJO JOE (Italy/Spain, 1967) Ennio Morricone (Leo Nichols)
United Artists LA-292-G

NED KELLY (Britain, 1970) Shel Silverstein
United Artists 5213 and LA-300-G

NEIGHBORHOOD OF ANGELS, THE (Greece, n.d.) Mikis Theodorakis
Odeon OMCGA-38 (Greece)

NERO VENEZIANO (Italy, n.d.) Pino Donaggio
Ariston AR-LP-12338 (Italy)

NEVADA SMITH (Paramount, 1966) Alfred Newman
MCA VIM-7252 (Japan)

NEW KIND OF LOVE, A (Paramount, 1963) Errol Garner, Leith Stevens
Mercury 20859/60859

NEW YORK CHIAMA SUPERDRAGO see SECRET AGENT SUPERDRAGON

NEW YORK, NEW YORK (United Artists, 1977) Ralph Burns
United Artists UA-LA750-L2

NEXT MAN, THE (Allied Artists, 1976) Michael Kamen
Buddah BDS-5685-ST

NICHOLAS AND ALEXANDRA (Columbia, 1971) Richard Rodney Bennett
Bell 1103

NIENTE VERGINI IN COLLEGIO (Italy, n. d.) Francis Lai
Derby 20114 (Italy)

NIGHT CALLER, THE (PEUR SUR LA VILLE) (France, 1975) Ennio Morricone
Warners 56/35B (France)

NIGHT DIGGER, THE (MGM, 1971) Bernard Herrmann
Cinema LP-8016 (private)

NIGHT FLIGHT TO MOSCOW (SERPENT, THE/SERPENT, LE) Ennio Morricone
General Music ZSLGE-550497 (Italy)
RCA 440.758 (France)
RCA Victor SWK-7026 (Japan)

NIGHT OF THE GENERALS, THE (Columbia, 1967) Maurice Jarre
Colgems COMO-5002/COSO-5002

NIGHT PASSAGE (Universal, 1957) Dimitri Tiomkin
Cinema Records LO-8012 (private)

NIGHT VISITOR, THE (UMC, 1971) Henry Mancini
Citadel CT-6015

NIGHTCOMERS, THE (Britain, 1971) Jerry Fielding
Citadel CT-JF-1

9/30/55 (Universal, 1977) Leonard Rosenman
MCA 2313

1900 (NOVECENTO) (Italy, 1976) Ennio Morricone
RCA TBL1-1221 (Italy)

1941 (Universal, 1979) John Williams et al.
Arista AL-9510

NINI TIRABUSCIO, LA DONNA CHE INVENTO LA MOSSA (Italy, 1970) Carlo Rustichelli
CAM SAG-9033 (Italy)

NO WAY OUT (BIG GUNS/TONY ARZENTA) (France/Italy, 1973) Gianni Ferrio

Ariete 2013 (Italy)
Seven Seas FML-13 (Japan)

NO WAY TO TREAT A LADY (Paramount, 1968) Stanley Myers
Dot 25846

NOI DONNE SIAMO FATTE COSI (Italy, 1971) Armando Trovajoli
Beat-Music Parade 203 (Italy)

NOSFERATU (Germany, 1979) Popol Vuh
Barclay/Egg 900. 573 (France)
PUD Pld. 7005 (Italy)

NOW VOYAGER (Warners, 1942) Max Steiner
Angel S-36068

NUN AND THE DEVIL, THE (MONACHE DI SAINT ARCANGELO, LE) (Italy, 1973) Piero Piccioni
General Music 55492 (Italy)

NUN'S STORY, THE (Warners, 1959) Franz Waxman
Stanyan SRQ-4022

NUNZIO (Universal, 1978) Lalo Schifrin
MCA 2374

O LUCKY MAN (Warners, 1973) Alan Price
Warners BS-2710

OBJECTIVE BURMA (Warners, 1945) Franz Waxman
Cine Records 818 (private)

OBSESSION (Columbia, 1976) Bernard Herrmann
London SPC-21160 (Britain)

OCEANO (Italy, 1971) Ennio Morricone
RCA OLS-10 (Italy)

ODE TO BILLY JOE (Warners, 1976) Michel Legrand
Warners BS-2947

ODESSA FILE, THE (Columbia, 1974) Andrew Lloyd Webber
MCA 2084

OEDIPUS ORCA (Italy, 1977) James Dashow
Cinevox MDF 33-107 (Italy)

OF MICE AND MEN (United Artists, 1940) Aaron Copland
Mark 56 LP-606-2 (with dialog)

OH! THE NOMUGI PASS (Japan, 1979) Masaru Sato
CBS/Sony 25AH-707 (Japan)

OKLAHOMA CRUDE (Columbia, 1973) Henry Mancini
RCA APL1-0271

OLD MAN AND THE SEA, THE (Warners, 1958) Dimitri Tiomkin
Columbia 1183/8013 and ACS-8013

OLIVER'S STORY (Paramount, 1978) Lee Holdridge, Francis Lai
ABC AA-1117

OMAR KHAYYAM (Paramount, 1957) Victor Young
Filmusic SN-2823 (private)

OMEN, THE (Fox, 1976) Jerry Goldsmith
Tattoo BJL1-1888

OMICIDIO PERFETTO A TERMINE DI LEGGE, UN (Italy, n.d.) Giorgio Gaslini
Cinevox 33/51 (Italy)

ON DANGEROUS GROUND (RKO, 1951) Bernard Herrmann
RCA ARL1-0707

ON HER MAJESTY'S SECRET SERVICE (United Artists, 1969) John Barry
United Artists 5204, LA-299-G, and UXS-2-91

ON MY WAY TO THE CRUSADES, I MET A GIRL WHO ... see CHASTITY BELT, THE

ONCE UPON A TIME IN THE WEST (Italy, 1969) Ennio Morricone
RCA LSP-4736

ONE AND ONLY, THE (Paramount, 1978) Patrick Williams
ABC AA-1059

ONE BY ONE (EAST WIND) (Japan, 1975) Stomu Yamashita
Island ILS-80630 (Japan)

ONE DAY ... A TRAIN (ALLORA, IL TRENO) (Italy, n.d.) Bruno Nicolai
Edi-Pan LPX-39 (Italy)

ONE FLEW OVER THE CUCKOO'S NEST (United Artists, 1975) Jack Nitzsche
Fantasy F-9500

122 RUE DE PROVENCE (France, 1978) Ennio Morricone
General Music 803-002 (France)

ONE NIGHT AT DINNER (LOVE CIRCLE/METTI, UNA SERA A CENA) (Italy, 1969) Ennio Morricone
CBS 70067 (Britain)
Cinevox MDF 33-16 and ORL-8046 (Italy)

ONE ON ONE (Warners, 1977) Charles Fox
Warners BS-3076

ONORATA FAMIGLIA, L' (Italy, n.d.) Bruno Nicolai
Gemelli 10.017 (Italy)

OPPOSTE EXPERIENZE see ATTENTI AL BUFFONE

OPTIMISTS, THE (Britain, 1973) Lionel Bart
Paramount PAS-1015

ORA DI UCCIDERE, L' (Italy, n.d.) Carlo Savina
CAM 30.099 (Italy)

ORCA, THE KILLER WHALE (Paramount, 1977) Ennio Morricone
Tam-Cam YX-7036 (Japan)

ORCHESTRA REHEARSAL (PROVA D'ORCHESTRA) (Italy, 1979) Nino Rota
CAM SAG-9096 (Italy)

OTHER SIDE OF MIDNIGHT, THE (Fox, 1977) Michel Legrand
Fox T-542

OTHER SIDE OF THE MOUNTAIN, THE (Universal, 1975) Charles Fox
MCA 2086

OTHER SIDE OF THE MOUNTAIN II, THE (Universal, 1978) Lee Holdridge
MCA 2335

OUR MOTHER'S HOUSE (Britain, 1967) Georges Delerue
MGM SE-4495 (Canada)

OUTLAW JOSEY WALES, THE (Warners, 1976) Jerry Fielding
Warners BS-2956

OUTRAGEOUS! (Canada, 1977) Paul Hoffert
Polydor PD1-8902

OUTSIDE IN (Independent, 1972) Randy Edelman
MGM 1SE-37-ST

OVER THE EDGE (Warners, 1979) Sol Kaplan
Warners BSK-3335

OVERLANDERS, THE (Britain, 1946) John Ireland
Lyrita 45 (Britain)

PACIFIST, THE (PACIFISTA, LA) (Italy, 1972) Giorgio Gaslini
Cinevox 33/46 (Italy)

PADRE PADRONE (MY FATHER, MY MASTER/FATHER, MASTER) (Italy, 1977) Egisto Macchi
Feeling Record Italiana FR-69403 (Italy)
RCA NL-33207 (Italy)

PADRONE E L'OPERAIO, IL see BOSS AND THE WORKER, THE

PALM SPRINGS WEEKEND (Warners, 1963) Frank Perkins
Warners 1519

PAOLO AND FRANCESCA (Italy, n.d.) Bruno Nicolai
Gemelli 10.005 (Italy)

PAOLO IL CALDO (Italy, 1973) Armando Trovajoli
CAM 9052 (Italy)

PAPAVERO E ANCHE UN FIORE, IL (Italy, n.d.) Nico Fidenco
PRC 5005 (Italy)

PAPER MOON (Paramount, 1973) traditional popular music
Paramount PAS-1012

PAPER TIGER, THE (Fox, 1976) Roy Budd
Capitol SW-11475
Philips 6303-126 (Britain)

PAPILLON (Allied Artists, 1973) Jerry Goldsmith
Capitol ST-11260

PARADINE CASE, THE (Selznick, 1947) Franz Waxman
AEI-3103

PARADISE ALLEY (Universal, 1978) Bill Conti
MCA 5100

PARIGI O CARA (Italy, n.d.) Fiorenzo Carpi
CAM 30-044 (Italy)

PARIS BLUES (United Artists, 1961) Duke Ellington
United Artists 4092/5092, LA-274-G, 3158/6158, and 3197/6197

PARIS WAS MADE FOR LOVERS (France, n.d.) composer unlisted
ALA 1981

PARISIANS, LES (France, n.d.) Georges Garvarentz
Fontana 460.820 (France)

PARMIGIANA, LA (Italy, 1963) Piero Piccioni
CAM CA-2482(45) (Italy)

PARTNER (Italy, 1968) Ennio Morricone
CAM SAG-9010 (Italy)

PARTY GIRLS FOR THE CANDIDATE (CANDIDATE, THE) (Independent, 1965) Steve Karmen
Jubilee 5029

PAT GARRETT AND BILLY THE KID (MGM, 1973) Bob Dylan
Columbia S-30086

PATCH OF BLUE, A (MGM, 1965) Jerry Goldsmith
Citadel CT-6028 and CT-7008

PATRICK (Australia, 1978) Brian May
Varese Sarabande VC-81107

PATTON (Fox, 1970) Jerry Goldsmith
Fox S-4208 and T-902

PEAU D'ANE (DONKEYSKIN) (France, 1970) Michel Legrand
Paramount CO62-91975 (France)

PEBBLES OF ENTRETAT (France, 1972) Georges Garvarentz
Barclay 920. 381 (France)

PECCATO, IL (SIN, THE) Antonio Perez Olea (Italy, n. d.)
CAM CMS-30-058 (Italy)

PELE (France/Mexico, 1977) Arantes do Nascimento
Atlantic SD-18231

PEPE (Columbia, 1960) John Green; title song by Hans Wittstatt
Colpix (S)CP-507

PER AMORE (Italy, 1976) Ennio Morricone
RCA TBL1-1234 (Italy)

PER GRAZIA RICEVUTA (BETWEEN MIRACLES) (Italy, 1971) Guido and Maurizio de Angelis
It 70002 (Italy)

PERFECT MARRIAGE, THE (Germany, n. d.) Peter Thomas
Polydor 242. 217 (Germany)

PERFORMANCE (Britain, 1970) Jack Nitzsche et al.
Warners BS-2554

PERMETTE, ROCCO PAPALEO (Italy, 1971) Armando Trovajoli
CAM 9037 (Italy)

PERSECUTION AND ASSASSINATION OF JEAN-PAUL MARAT AS PERFORMED BY THE INMATES OF THE ASYLUM OF CHARENTON UNDER THE DIRECTION OF THE MARQUIS DE

SADE (Britain, 1967) Richard Peaslee
United Artists UAS 4153/5153 and LA-288-G

PERVERSION STORY, THE (Italy, n.d.) Gianni Ferrio
CAM 9021 (Italy)

PEUR SUR LA VILLE see NIGHT CALLER, THE

PHAEDRA (Greece, 1962) Mikis Theodorakis
United Artists 4102/5102, LA-280-G, 3303/6303, and 3249/6249

PHANTASM (Embassy, 1979) Fred Myrow, Malcolm Seagrave
Varese Sarabande VC-81105

PHANTOM OF THE PARADISE (Fox, 1974) Paul Williams, George Aliceson Tipton
A&M SP-3653

PICASSO SUMMER (Warners, 1969) Michel Legrand
Warners WS-1925

PIEDONE LO SBIRRO (Italy, 1973) Guido and Maurizio de Angelis
Cinevox 33/70 (Italy)

PIERROT LA TENDRESSE (France, n.d.) Guy Beart
Philips 432.511(45) (France)

PIERROT LE FOU (CRAZY PETER) (France/Italy, 1965) Antoine Duhamel
CAM SAG-9077 (Italy)

PINK PANTHER STRIKES AGAIN, THE (United Artists, 1976) Henry Mancini
United Artists UA-LA694-G

PINOCCHIO (AVVENTURA DI PINOCCHIO, LA) (France/Germany/Italy, 1972) Fiorenzo Carpi
CAM 9038 (Italy)
Pathe 2C-064-13044 (France)

PINOCCHIO'S ADVENTURE see PINOCCHIO

PIRANHA (Italy, 1979) Pino Donaggio
Varese Sarabande STV-81126

PISTOL FOR RINGO, A (Italy/Spain, 1966) Ennio Morricone
RCA INTI-1338 (Italy)

PISTOLE NON DISCUTONO, LE see BULLETS DON'T ARGUE

PIU BELLA SERATE DELLA MIA VITA, A (Italy, 1972) Armando Trovajoli
Beat LPF-035 (Italy)

... PIU FORTE RAGAZZI (Italy, 1972) Guido and Maurizio de Angelis
RCA 14 (Italy)

PIZZA TRIANGLE, THE see DRAMMA DELLA GELOSIA

PLAGIO (Italy, n.d.) Gianni Marchetti et al.
Seven Seas GXH-6032 (Japan)

PLAY IT AGAIN, SAM (Paramount, 1972) Billy Goldenberg
Paramount PAS-1004

PLAYTIME (France, 1967) Jacques Tati
United Artists UNS-15554

PLEUT SUR SANTIAGO, IL (France, n.d.) Astor Piazzola
Pathe Marconi/EMI CO66-14247 (France)

PLOT, THE see FRENCH CONSPIRACY, THE

PLOW THAT BROKE THE PLAINS, THE (Independent, 1936) (short) Virgil Thomson
Angel S-37300

PLYMOUTH ADVENTURE (MGM, 1952) Miklos Rozsa
MGM 3507 and 2353-095 (Britain)

POLICE CHIEF PEPE (COMMISSARIO PEPE, IL) (Italy, 1969) Armando Trovajoli
RCA 1008 (Italy)

POLIZIA INCRIMINA, LA LEGGE ASSOLVE, LA (HIGH CRIME) (Italy, 1973) Guido and Maurizio de Angelis
Beat LPF-020 (Italy)

POWER, THE (MGM, 1968) Miklos Rozsa
Citadel CT-MR-1 (private)

PREFETTO DI FERRO, IL see IRON PREFECT, THE

PRETTY BABY (Paramount, 1978) Scott Joplin et al.
ABC AA-1076

PRIDE AND THE PASSION, THE (United Artists, 1957) George Antheil
Capitol 873
Movie Music MM-5146 (private)

PRIMA NOTTE DI QUIETE, LA (France/Italy, 1972) Mario Nascimbene
CBS 65403 (Italy)

PRINCE AND THE PAUPER, THE (Hanna/Barbera, 1973) George

Fischoff
Pickwick SPC-3204

PRINCE AND THE PAUPER, THE see CROSSED SWORDS

PRISONER OF ZENDA, THE (United Artists, 1937) Alfred Newman
United Artists LA-374-G

PRIVATE PARTS (MGM, 1971) Hugo Friedhofer
Delos DEL/F-25420

PRIVATE VICES, PUBLIC VIRTUES (VIZI PRIVATI, PUBBLICHE VIRTU) (Italy, 1977) Francesco de Masi
Beat LPF-034 (Italy)

PRIVATE WAR OF MAJOR BENSON, THE (Universal, 1955) Henry Mancini, Herman Stein
RCA 1245

PROCESSO DI VERONA, IL (Italy, n.d.) Mario Nascimbene
CAM 2483 (Italy)

PRODUCERS, THE (Embassy, 1968) John Morris
Warners BS-2781 (Australia)

PROFESSIONAL GUN, A see MERCENARY, THE

PROFITEER, THE (SAPROFITA, IL) (Italy, 1974) Sante Maria Romitelli
Ariete 2016 (Italy)

PROMISE, THE (Universal, 1979) David Shire
MCA 3082

PROMISSI SPOSI, I (Italy, 1938) Carlo Rustichelli
CAM 30.088 (Italy)

PROPERTY IS NO LONGER A THEFT, THE (PROPRIETA NON PIU UN FURTO, LA) (Italy, 1973) Ennio Morricone
RCA OLS-19 (Italy)

PROUD REBEL, THE (Disney, 1958) Jerome Moross
C.I.F. 1001 (private)

PROVIDENCE (France, 1977) Miklos Rozsa
Pathe Marconi EMI 2CO66-14406 (France)

PSYCHO (Paramount, 1960) Bernard Herrmann
Unicorn RHS-336
UNI 75001 (Britain)

PUBLIC EYE, THE (FOLLOW ME) (Universal, 1972) John Barry
MCA 5137 (Japan)

PUFNSTUF (Universal, 1970) Charles Fox
Capitol SW-542

PURPLE TAXI, THE (TAXI MAUVE, UN) (France/Ireland/Italy, 1977) Philippe Sarde
Vogue LID. 20288 (France)

PURSUED (Warners, 1947) Max Steiner
Citadel CT-MS-5 (private)

QUANDO LE DONNE AVEVANO LA CODA see WHEN WOMEN HAD TAILS

QUANDO LE DONNE SI CHIAMAVANO MADONNE (Italy, n. d.) Giorgio Gaslini
Cinevox 33/58 (Italy)

QUANTO COSTA MORIRE (Italy, n. d.) Francesco de Masi
Beat LPF-019 (Italy)

40 GRADI ALL'OMBRA DEL LENZUOLO (Italy, n. d.) Guido and Maurizio de Angelis
Cometa CMT 1008-20 (Italy)

QUATTRO DELL'AVE MARIA, I see ACE HIGH

QUEEN, THE (REGINE, LA) (Italy, n. d.) Francesco Lavagnino, Raymond Lovelock
Seven Seas 634 and GXH-6032 (Japan)

QUEL NEGOZIO DI PIAZZA NAVONA (Italy, n. d.) Riz Ortolani
CAM 9015 (Italy)

QUELLA SPORCA STORIA NEL WEST (Italy, n. d.) Francesco de Masi
CAM MAG-10-012 (Italy)

QUELLA STRANE OCCASIONI (Italy, n. d.) Piero Piccioni
Cinevox MDF 33/106 (Italy)

QUESTA SPECIE D'AMORE (Italy, 1972) Ennio Morricone
General Music ZSLGE-55077 (Italy)

QUIET MAN, THE (Republic, 1952) Victor Young
MCA VIM-7244 (Japan)

QUO VADIS? (MGM, 1951) Miklos Rozsa
London SPC-21180
MGM 3524, 103 and (S)4112

RACE IN THE HEAD, THE (COURSE EN TETE, LA) (France, 1974) David Munrow
EMI 64. 22789 (France)

RAGA (Britain, 1971) Ravi Shankar, Colin Walcott
Apple-Capitol SWAO-3384

RAGAZZA DALLA PELLE LA LUNA, LA see SEX OF THEIR BODIES

RAGAZZO CHE SORRIDE, IL (Italy, n. d.) Carlo Rustichelli
Cinevox 33/14 (Italy)

RAGING MOON, THE see LONG AGO TOMORROW

RAILWAY CHILDREN, THE (Britain, 1970) Johnny Douglas
Capitol SW-871

RAINBOW (Italy, n. d.) Sante Maria Romitelli
CAM SAG-9005 (Italy)

RAINMAKER, THE (Paramount, 1956) Alex North
Cinevox 33/24 (private)

RAINTREE COUNTY (MGM, 1957) John Green
Entr'acte ERS-6503-ST
Sound Stage SS-2304-2 (private)

RANSOM (Britain, 1975) Jerry Goldsmith
DART ARTS-65376 (Britain)

RAPPORTO FULLER, BASE STOCCOTMA (Italy, n. d.) Armando Trovajoli
Beat 001 (Italy)

REBECCA (United Artists, 1940) Franz Waxman
Cine Records 818 (private)

REBEL WITHOUT A CAUSE (Warners, 1955) Leonard Rosenman
Columbia CL-940 and ACL-940

RED BEARD (Japan, 1966) Masaru Sato
Toho 1001 (Japan)

RED LANTERNS (Greece, 1964) Stavros Xarchakos
Odeon OMCGA-37 (Greece)

RED MANTLE, THE (Finland, 1973) Marc Fredericks
RCA LSP-5815

RED SUN (SOLE RUSSO) (France/Italy, 1971) Maurice Jarre
General Music ZSLGE-55065 (Italy)
Motors 44008

RENDENZIONE, LA (Italy, n. d.) Roman Vlad
PCC 075 (Italy)

RENE THE CANE (RENE LA CANNE) (Italy, 1977) Ennio Morricone
Polydor 2393-152 (France)

REPULSION (Britain, 1965) Chico Hamilton
CAM 1 (Italy)

REQUIEM FOR A GRINGO (Italy, n.d.) Francesco Lavagnino
Cinevox 33/6 (Italy)

RETURN OF A MAN CALLED HORSE, THE (United Artists, 1976) Laurence Rosenthal
United Artists UA-LA692-G

RETURN OF THE PINK PANTHER, THE (United Artists, 1975) Henry Mancini
RCA ABL1-0968

RETURN OF THE TALL BLOND, THE (France, 1974) Vladimir Cosma
Philips 6325-179 (France)

REVENGE OF THE PINK PANTHER (United Artists, 1978) Henry Mancini
United Artists UA-LA913-H

REVENGERS, THE (FECCIA, LA) (Italy, 1972) Pino Calvi
CBS 70120 (Italy)

REVOLVER (BLOOD IN THE STREETS) (Italy, 1973) Ennio Morricone
General Music ZSLGE-55496 (Italy)
Seven Seas CAM FML-86 (Japan)

RICHARD III (Britain, 1956) Sir William Walton
Seraphim S-60205

RIDERS OF VENGEANCE (CAVALIERI DELLA VENDETTA, I) (Italy, n.d.) Carlo Rustichelli
CAM 30.096 (Italy)

RIFIFI IN PANAMA (DU RIFIFI A PANAME) (France, n.d.) Georges Garvarentz
Barclay 70972(45) (France)

RINGARDS, LES (France, n.d.) Francis Lai
Warners 56555 (France)

RIVELAZIONE DI UN MANIACO SESSUALE (Italy, n.d.) Giorgio Gaslini
Cinevox 33/59 (Italy)

RIVER, THE (Independent, 1937) (short) Virgil Thomson
Angel S-37300

RIVER OF NO RETURN, THE (Fox, 1954) Lionel Newman
Fox T-901

ROAD TO SALINA, THE (QUANDO IL SOLE SCOTTA) (Italy, 1970) Michel Magne
Delta ZSLD-55016 (Italy)

ROBERT ET ROBERT (France, 1978) Francis Lai
Warners 56507 (France)

ROBIN AND MARIAN (Columbia, 1976) John Barry
Sherwood SH-1500 (private)

ROCKET TO THE MOON see THOSE FANTASTIC FLYING FOOLS

ROCKETSHIP X-M (Lippert, 1950) Ferde Grofe
Starlog SR-1000 (private)

ROCKY (United Artists, 1976) Bill Conti
United Artists UA-LA693-G

ROCKY II (United Artists, 1979) Bill Conti
United Artists LA-972

ROLLERBALL (United Artists, 1975) Andre Previn orchestrations of classical music
United Artists UA-EA470-H

ROLLERCOASTER (Universal, 1977) Lalo Schifrin
MCA 2284

ROMA BENE (France/Germany/Italy, 1971) Luis Enrique Bacalov
Delta 55046 (Italy)

ROMANCE OF A HORSE THIEF (Allied Artists, 1971) Mort Schuman
Allied Artists 110-100

ROMEO AND JULIET (Paramount, 1968) Nino Rota
Capitol 2993 and 400 (with dialog)

ROVER, THE (L'AVVENTURIERO) (Italy, 1967) Ennio Morricone
RCA SP-8022 (Italy)

RULING CLASS, THE (Britain, 1972) John Cameron
Avco Embassy AV-11008

RUN OF THE ARROW (RKO, 1957) Victor Young
Varese Sarabande AE1-3102

RUNAROUND (Italy, n. d.) Vasile
Cinevox MDF-132 (Italy)

SABATA (Italy, 1969) Marcello Giombini
United Artists 455

SACRED IDOL, THE (1959) Les Baxter
Capitol 1293

SAILOR WHO FELL FROM GRACE WITH THE SEA, THE (Embassy, 1976) Johnny Mandel, Kris Kristofferson
Polydor MPF-1025 (Japan)

SALLAH (Israel, 1964) Yohanan Zarai
Philips 200177/600177

SALOME (Columbia, 1953) George Duning, Daniele Amfitheatrof
MCA-15 (Japan)

SALUT D'ARTISTE (HAIL THE ARTIST/BIT PLAYER, THE) (France, 1973) Vladimir Cosma
Deesee DDLX-77 (France)

SAND CASTLE, THE (Japan, n. d.) Kanno
Polydor MR-1517 (Japan)

SANS FAMILLE (D'HECTOR MALOT) (France, 1958) Paul Misraki
Philips P-77. 506-L (France)

SAPHO see WARRIOR EMPRESS, THE

SARTANA NON PERDONA (Italy, n. d.) Francesco de Masi
Beat CR-4 (Italy)

SATYRICON (Italy, 1971) Carlo Rustichelli
Cinevox 33/17 (Italy)

SAUL AND DAVID (Italy/Spain, 1968) Teo Usuelli
CAM 30. 127 (Italy)

SAUVAGE, LE (France, 1975) Michel Legrand
Barclay FML-60 (Japan)

SAVAGE (Independent, 1974) Don Julian
Money MS-1109

SAVAGE PLANET, THE (France, 1973) Alain Goraguer
Pathe Marconi EMI 2CO66-12698 (France)

SAVAGE WILD, THE (American International, 1970) Jaime Mendoza-Nava
AIR A-1032

SAYONARA (Warners, 1957) Franz Waxman; theme by Irving Berlin
Entr'acte ERS-6513-ST

SCACCO ALLA REGINA (Italy, n. d.) Piero Piccioni
Cinevox 33/24 (Italy)

SCACCO INTERNAZIONALE (Italy, n. d.) Carlo Rustichelli
CAM 10017 (Italy)

SCANDALO, LO see SUBMISSION

SCANDALOUS JOHN (Disney, 1971) Rod McKuen
Buena Vista BV-5004

SCARLET STREET (Universal, 1945) Hans J. Salter
Medallion ML-303

SCHIAVA IO CE L'HO E TU NO, LA (Italy, 1973) Piero Umiliani
Ved. 8182 (Italy)

SCIENTIFIC CARDPLAYER, THE (SCOPONE SCIENTIFICO, LO) (Italy, 1972) Piero Piccioni
General Music 55124 (Italy)

SCORPIO (United Artists, 1973) Jerry Fielding
Film Music Collection FMC-11

SCOUMOUNE, LA (CLAN DEI MARSIGLIESI, IL) (France/Italy, 1972) Francois de Roubaix
CAM 9046 (Italy)

SCOUNDREL, THE (MARIES DE L'AN DEUX, LES) (France, 1972) Michel Legrand
Bell 92428 (France)

SEARCH FOR PARADISE (Cinerama, 1957) Dimitri Tiomkin
Film Music Collection 14 (private)

SEARCHERS, THE (Warners, 1956) Max Steiner
Citadel CT-MS-5

SEASON IN HELL, A (France, n. d.) Maurice Jarre
Eden Roc 55001
General Music 55061

SEASON OF THE SENSES (STAGIONE DEI SENSI, LA) (Italy, 1969) Ennio Morricone
Ariete ARLP-2005 (Italy)

SECRET AGENT SUPERDRAGON (NEW YORK CHIAMA SUPER-DRAGO) (Italy, 1966) Benedetto Ghiglia
CAM 33/16 (Italy)

SEDUCED AND ABANDONED (SEDOTTA E ABBANDONATA) (Italy, 1964) Carlo Rustichelli
Seven Seas/CAM GXH-6036 (Italy)

SEDUCERS, THE (TOP SENSATION) (Italy, 1968) Sante Romitelli
CAM 9013 (Italy)

SEDUCTION (SEDUZIONE, LA) (Italy, 1973) Luis E. Bacalov
Cetra 27 (Italy)

SEDUCTION OF MIMI, THE (MIMI METALLURGICO FERITO NELL'-ONORE/MIMI THE METAL-WORKER, WOUNDED IN HONOR) (Italy, 1974) Piero Piccioni
Cinevox 33/53 (Italy)

SELFISH GIANT, THE (Britain, 1972) (short) Ron Goodwin
EMI-One Up 054.95850/OU-2060 (Britain)

SENILITA (Italy, 1962) Piero Piccioni
CAM CMS-30037 and CA-2399(45) (Italy)

SENTENZA DI MORTE (Italy, n.d.) Gianni Ferrio
CAM MAG 10-009 (Italy)

SEPOLTA VIVA see WOMEN BURIED ALIVE

SERPENT, THE see NIGHT FLIGHT TO MOSCOW

SERPICO (Paramount, 1973) Mikis Theodorakis
Paramount PAS-1016

SERVIZIO DALL'ORIENTE (Italy, n.d.) Gino Marinuzzi
Gemelli 10-018 (Italy)

SETTE BASCHI ROSSI (7 RED BERETS/CONGO HELL) (Italy, 1969) Gianni Marchetti
CAM MAG 10.021 (Italy)

7 DOLLARI SUL ROSSO (7 DOLLARS ON THE RED) (Italy, n.d.) Francesco de Masi
CAM CDR-33-19 (Italy)

7 FRATELLI CERVI (Italy, n.d.) Carlo Rustichelli
CAM 10013 (Italy)

7 UOMINI E UN CERVELLO (Italy, n.d.) Carlo Rustichelli
CAM 10017 (Italy)

SETTIMO PARALLELO (Italy, 1963) native Venezuelan music
Italian RCA 10327

SEVEN ALONE (Doty/Dayton, 1975) Robert O. Ragland
Seval 101 (private)

7 DOLLARS ON THE RED see 7 DOLARI SUL ROSSO

SEVEN GOLDEN MEN STRIKE AGAIN (GRANDE COLPO PEI SETTE UOMINA D'ORO, IL) (Italy, 1966) Armando Trovajoli
CAM 4 (Italy)

7 HEROIC BASTARDS (7 EROICHE CAROGNE) (Italy, n. d.) Francesco Lavagnino
Cinevox 33/18 (Italy)

SEVEN HILLS OF ROME, THE (MGM, 1958) Victor Young, George Stoll
RCA LM-2211

SEVEN PER CENT SOLUTION, THE (Universal, 1977) John Addison
Citadel CT-JA-1

7 RED BERETS see SETTE BASCHI ROSSI

SEVEN SAMURAI (Japan, 1972) Fumio Hayasaka
Toho 1002 (Japan)

SEVEN WONDERS OF THE WORLD (Cinerama, 1956) David Raksin, Jerome Moross, and Emil Newman
Coral 57065

17 see ERIC SOYA'S 17

SEVENTH VOYAGE OF SINBAD, THE (Columbia, 1958) Bernard Herrmann
London SP-44207
Request LP-13001 (private)

SEX CRAZY (SESSO MATTO/SEXEFOU) (France/Italy, 1973) Armando Trovajoli
Duse 52 (Italy)
Vogue 863 (France)

SEX OF THEIR BODIES (RAGAZZA DALLA PELLA LA LUNA, LA) (Italy, 1972) Piero Umiliani
Beat 24 (Italy)

SHAFT IN AFRICA (MGM, 1973) Johnny Pate
ABC 793

SHANGHAI JOE (MIO NOME E SHANGHAI JOE, IL) (Italy, 1974) Bruno Nicolai
TAM YX-8018 and 8010 (Japan)

SHANGO, LA PISTOLA INFALLIBILE (Italy, n. d.) Gianfranco di Stefano
Cinevox MDF 33-39 (Italy)

SHE (RKO, 1935) Max Steiner
Cinema LP-8004 (private)

SHOCK, THE (Italy, n. d.) Libra
Seven Seas FML-118 (Japan)

SHORT EYES (Independent, 1977) Curtis Mayfield
Curtom CU-5017

SHOT FROM THE VIOLIN CASE, THE (Germany, 1966) Peter Thomas
Polydor 237. 493 (Germany)

SHOT IN THE DARK, A (United Artists, 1964) Henry Mancini
RCA 47-8381 (45)

SHOUT AT THE DEVIL (PAROLE D'HOMME) (France, 1976) Maurice Jarre
Barclay 900-534 (France)

SILENT MOVIE (Fox, 1976) John Morris
United Artists UA-LA672-G

SILENT PARTNER, THE (Canada, 1979) Oscar Peterson
Pablo 2312103

SILENT RUNNING (Universal, 1973) Peter Schickele
Decca DL-79188

SILVER CHALICE, THE (Warners, 1954) Franz Waxman
Film Music Collection FMC-3

SIMON BOLIVAR (Italy, n. d.) Carlo Savina
CAM 9022 (Italy)

SIMPATICO MA GLI ROMPEREI IL MUSO see CESAR AND ROSALIE

SIMPLE HISTOIRE, UNE (SIMPLE STORY, A) (France, 1957) Philippe Sarde
Cobra COB-37020 (France)

SINCE YOU WENT AWAY (United Artists, 1944) Max Steiner
Angel S-36068
Citadel CT-MS-3-4 (private)

SISTERS (American International, 1973) Bernard Herrmann
Entr'acte ERQ-7001

SISTERS, THE (SORELLE, LE) (Italy, n. d.) Giorgio Gaslini
Cinevox 33/22 (Italy)

633 SQUADRON (United Artists, 1964) Ron Goodwin
Sunset SLS-50203 (Britain)
United Artists LA-305-G

SLAUGHTER'S BIG RIP-OFF (American International, 1973) James Brown
Polydor PD-6015

SLEUTH (Fox, 1972) John Addison
Columbia S-32154 (with dialog)

SLIPPERY WHEN WET (Independent, 1959) Bud Shank
World Pacific 1265

SLOW DANCING IN THE BIG CITY (United Artists, 1978) Bill Conti
United Artists UA-LA939-H

SMALL CHANGE (ARGENT DE POCHE, L') (France, 1977) Maurice Jaubert
EMI-Pathe 20066-14567

SMASHING BIRD I USED TO KNOW, THE (Britain, 1969) Bobby Richards
NEMS 6-70059 (Britain)

SMOKEY AND THE BANDIT (Universal, 1977) Bill Justis, Jerry Reed, and Rich Feller
MCA 2099

SODOM AND GOMORRAH (Fox, 1963) Miklos Rozsa
Citadel CT-MR-1 (private)

SOLARIS (Russia, 1977) Eduard Artemiev
Columbia YX-7212MK (Japan)

SOLDAAT VAN ORANGE see SOLDIER OF ORANGE

SOLDIER BLUE (Embassy, 1970) Roy Budd
Pye 18389 (Britain)

SOLDIER OF ORANGE (SOLDAAT VAN ORANGE) (Holland, 1979) Rogier van Otterloo
Polydor 2925-059 (Holland)

SOLE DELL'AMORE, I (Italy, n.d.) Piero Umiliani
Cinevox 33/42 (Italy)

SOLIMANO IL CONQUISTATORE see SULEIMAN THE CONQUERER

SOLO GRANDE AMORE, UN (Italy, n.d.) Francesco de Masi
Beat LPF-011 (Italy)

SOLOMON AND SHEBA (United Artists, 1959) Mario Nascimbene
United Artists UASF-5061 (France)

SOME LIKE IT HOT (United Artists, 1959) Adolph Deutsch
United Artists 3122/6122, 4030/5030, LA-272-G, and 3158/6158

SOME PEOPLE (Britain, n. d.) Ron Grainer
Pye 24158(45) (Britain)

SOMEBODY KILLED HER HUSBAND (Columbia, 1978) Alex North
Seven Seas FML-108 (Japan)

SOMEONE IS KILLING THE GREAT CHEFS OF EUROPE see WHO IS KILLING THE GREAT CHEFS OF EUROPE?

SOMETIMES A GREAT NOTION (Universal, 1971) Henry Mancini
Decca DL-79185

SON OF DRACULA (Cinemation, 1974) Harry Nilsson, Paul Buckmaster
RCA-Rapple ABL1-0220

SONG OF BERNADETTE, THE (Fox, 1943) Alfred Newman
Cinema LP-8008 (private)
MCA VIM-7213 (Japan)

SONNY (Italy, n. d.) Ennio Morricone
Music for Pleasure 2M-026-13330 (Britain)

SORCERER (Universal/Paramount, 1977) Tangerine Dream, Charlie Parker, and Keith Jarrett
MCA 2277

SORRELLE MATERASSI, LE (Italy, n. d.) Piero Piccioni
Beat-Music Parade 051 (Italy)

SORRISO DEL GRANDE TENTATORE, IL see TEMPTER, THE

SOUL HUSTLER, THE (MGM, 1973) Harley Hatcher
MGM SE-4943

SOUL OF NIGGER CHARLEY, THE (Paramount, 1973) Don Costa
MGM 1SE-46-ST

SOUND AND THE FURY, THE (Fox, 1959) Alex North
MCA VIM-7209 (Japan)

SOUT KIESKA see DEDICATION TO TITO

SPELLBOUND (United Artists, 1946) Miklos Rozsa
AEI-3103
Stanyan SRQ-4021

SPIDER'S WEB, THE (Britain, 1965) Tony Crombie
Roulette 804

SPIRIT OF ST. LOUIS (Warners, 1957) Franz Waxman
Entr'acte ERS-6507-ST
Film Archives F-4761 (private)
RCA LSP-14721

SPOILED CHILDREN see ENFANTS GATES, DES

SPY WHO LOVED ME, THE (United Artists, 1977) Marvin Hamlisch
United Artists UA LA774-H

SPY WITH A COLD NOSE, THE (Britain, 1966) Riz Ortolani
Columbia 6670/3070

SQUADRA ANTIGANGSTER (Italy, 1978) Goblin
Cinevox MDF 33/131 (Italy)

STAGIONI DEI SENSI, LA see SEASON OF THE SENSES

STAR IS BORN, A (Selznick, 1937) Max Steiner
United Artists LA-375-G

STAR TREK--THE MOTION PICTURE (Paramount, 1979) Jerry Goldsmith
Columbia 36334

STAR WARS (Fox, 1977) John Williams
Fox 2T-541
London 2M-1001
RCA ARL1-2698

STARCRASH (New World, 1979) John Barry
Durium DAI 30. 314 (Italy)

STARDUST (POLVERE DI STELLE) (Italy, 1974) Piero Piccioni
General Music 55498 (Italy)

STATE OF SIEGE (France, 1973) Mikis Theodorakis
Columbia S-32352

STAVISKY (France/Italy, 1974) Stephen Sondheim
RCA ARL1-0952

STEELYARD BLUES (Warners, 1973) Mike Bloomfield, Paul Butterfield, Nick Gravenites, and David Shire
Warners BS-2662

STING, THE (Universal, 1973) Scott Joplin music arr. by Marvin Hamlisch
MCA 390

STONE KILLER, THE (Columbia, 1972) Roy Budd
Project 3 PR-5085-SD

STORIA DE SAN MICHELE (Italy, n. d.) Mario Nascimbene
Cinevox 33/11 (Italy)

STORY OF ADELE H., THE (France, 1975) Maurice Jaubert
Pathe 2C-066-14216 (France)

STORY OF "O," THE (France, 1975) Pierre Bachelet
CAM SAG-9065 (Italy)

STRANGER RETURNS, THE (MAN, A HORSE AND A GUN, A) (Italy, 1968) Stelvio Cipriani
CAM SAG-9004 (Italy)

STRAW DOGS (Cinerama, 1971) Jerry Fielding
Citadel CT-JF-2/3

STREETCAR NAMED DESIRE, A (Warners, 1951) Alex North
Angel S-36068

STREGHE, LE (Italy, 1966) Ennio Morricone, Piero Piccioni
United Artists 3113(45) (Italy)

STRIDULUM (Italy, n. d.) Franco Micalizzi
RCA 31433 (Italy)

STROGOFF (Italy, 1970) Teo Usuelli
Cinevox M. D. F. 33-38 (Italy)

STUDY IN TERROR, A (Columbia, 1966) Patrick John Scott
Roulette (S)R-801

STUNTMAN (Italy, n. d.) Carlo Rustichelli
CAM 10020 (Italy)

STUNTS (New Line, 1977) Michael Kamen
Amerama ST-251

SUBMISSION (SCANDAL, THE/SCANDALO, LO) (Italy, 1977) Riz Ortolani
Polydor MPF-1059 (Japan)

SUGAR, THE (SUCRE, LE) (France, 1978) Philippe Sarde, Hubert Rostaing
Pathe Marconi/EMI CO68-14705 (France)

SULEIMAN THE CONQUEROR (SOLIMANO IL CONQUISTATORE/ FORTEZZA DI SAMOGRAD, LA) (Italy, 1963) Francesco de Masi
Beat CR-6/7 (Italy)

SULL'ALTRA, UNA (Italy, n. d.) Riz Ortolani
Beat-Music Parade 202 (Italy)

SUMMER PLACE, A (Warners, 1959) Max Steiner
Film Music Collection FMC-1 (private)

SUMMERTIME KILLER (VERANO PARA MATER) (Italy, 1973) Luis E. Bacalov
Seven Seas 6 (Japan)

SUN ALSO RISES, THE (Fox, 1957) Hugo Friedhofer
MCA 7207 (Japan)

SUN ON THE SKIN (SOLE NELLA PELLE, IL) (Italy, 1972) Gianni Marchetti
RCA 5 (Italy)

SUNDOWNERS, THE (Warners, 1960) Dimitri Tiomkin
Cinema LP-8014 (private)

SUNRISE AT CAMPOBELLO (Warners, 1960) Franz Waxman
Entr'acte ERS-6506

SUNSET, SUNRISE (Italy, n. d.) Nino Rota
Cine Disc M3001 (Japan)

SUPERFLY T. N. T. (Paramount, 1973) Osibisa
Paramount BDS-5136

SUPERMAN (Warners, 1978) John Williams
Warners 2BSK-3257

SUSANNA ... E I SUOI DOLCI VIZI ALLACORTE DEL NAP (Italy, n. d.) Gianni Ferrio
CAM 10. 019 (Italy)

SUSPIRIA (Italy, 1977) Goblin, Dario Argento
Cinevox MDF 22-108 (Italy)

SVEGLIATI E UCCIDI see WAKE UP AND DIE

SWARM, THE (Warners, 1978) Jerry Goldsmith
Warners BSK-3208

SWASHBUCKLER (Universal, 1976) John Addison
MCA 2096

SWEDEN--HEAVEN AND HELL (Italy, 1969) Piero Umiliani
Ariel (AS)LP-216 and ARS-15000

SWEET BODY OF DEBORAH, THE (France/Italy, 1969) Nora Orlandi
CAM 10011 (Italy)

SWEET MOVIE (Yugoslavia, 1975) Manos Hadjidakis
Spot 69624

SWEET RIDE, THE (Fox, 1968) Pete Rugolo
Fox (S)4198

SWEET SMELL OF SUCCESS, THE (United Artists, 1957) Elmer Bernstein, Chico Hamilton, and Fred Katz
MCA 7132 (Japan)

SWEPT AWAY (Italy, 1975) Piero Piccioni
Peters International PLD-1005

SWINDLE, THE see BIDONE, IL

SYMPHONY FOR TWO SPIES (SINFONIA PER DUE SPIE) (Italy, 1966) Francesco de Masi
CAM CDR-33/5 (Italy)

T. R. BASKIN (Paramount, 1972) Jack Elliot
Paramount PAS-6018

TAKE A GIRL LIKE YOU (Britain, 1970) Stanley Myers
Pye 18353 (Britain)

TAKE CARE, FRANCE (A NOUS DEUX, FRANCE) (France, 1972) Francis Lai
WEA WB-56664 (France)

TALL BLOND MAN WITH ONE BLACK SHOE, THE (France, 1973) Vladimir Cosma
Deesse DDLX-77 (France)

TARAS BULBA (United Artists, 1963) Franz Waxman
United Artists 3249/6249, USAF-5100 (France), 3303/6303, and 4100/5100

TAROT (ANGELA) (France, n. d.) Michel Colombier
A&M FML-12 (Japan)

TARTARS OF THE DESERT (DESERTO DEI TARTARI, IL) (Italy, 1962) Ennio Morricone
General Music GML-10005 (Italy)

TASTE OF VIOLENCE, A (France, 1963) Jean-Michel Demase
Philips 200071/600071

TAXI DRIVER (Columbia, 1976) Bernard Herrmann
Arista AL-4079

TAXI MAUVE, UN see PURPLE TAXI, THE

TELL ME THAT YOU LOVE ME, JUNIE MOON (Paramount, 1970) Philip Springer
Columbia OS-3540

TEMPTATION (Italy, 1967) Piero Piccioni
CAM AMP-64(45) (Italy)

TEMPTER, THE (DEVIL IS A WOMAN, THE/SORRISO DEL GRANDE TENTATORE, IL) (Italy, 1975) Ennio Morricone
Beat LPF-026 (Italy)

TEMPTRESS, THE (MGM, 1926) Ernst Luz
Pelican LP-2011

"10" (Warners, 1979) Henry Mancini
Warners BSK-3399

TEN COMMANDMENTS, THE (Paramount, 1956) Elmer Bernstein
Paramount PAS-1006-2

TENDER COP (TENDRE POULET) (France, 1977) Georges Delerue
Deesse DDLX-159 (France)

TENDER MOMENT, THE (LECON PARTICULIERE, LE) (France, 1968) Francis Lai
Columbia AZ-2227 (France)

TENTACLES (Italy, 1977) Stelvio Cipriani
CAM SAG-9079 (Italy)

TENTATIVO SENTIMENTALE, UN (Italy, 1963) Piero Piccioni
CAM CMS-30064 and CA-2512(45) (Italy)

TEOREMA (THEOREM) (Italy, 1968) Ennio Morricone
Ariete ARLP-2002 (Italy)

TERRORIST, THE (TERRORISTA, IL) (Italy, 1963) Piero Piccioni
RCA SP-8008 (Italy)

TERRORISTS, THE see RANSOM

THAT'S THE WAY OF THE WORLD (Independent, 1975) Philip Bailey, Larry Dunn, and Maurice White
Columbia PC-33280

THEOREM see TEOREMA

THEY CALL ME TRINITY (Italy, 1971) Franco Micalizzi
Ariete 2011 (Italy)

THEY CAME TO ROB LAS VEGAS (Warners, 1969) Georges Garvarentz
Philips 7898

THIEF OF BAGDAD, THE (United Artists, 1924) James C. Bradford
Pelican LP-2011

THIEF OF BAGDAD, THE (United Artists, 1940) Miklos Rozsa
Film Music Collection FMC-8
RCA LM-2118
United Artists UAS-29725 (Britain)

THIEF WHO CAME TO DINNER, THE (Warners, 1973) Henry Mancini
Warners WS-2700

THINGS TO COME (Britain, 1935) Sir Arthur Bliss
EMI ASD-3416 (Britain)

13 DAYS IN FRANCE (France, 1968) Francis Lai
Seven Seas-Saravah GXH-6022 (Japan)
Sonet SNTF-605 (Britain)

39 STEPS, THE (Britain, 1978) Ed Welch
United Artists UAG-30208 (Britain)

THIS EARTH IS MINE (Universal, 1959) Hugo Friedhofer
Varese Sarabande VC-81076

THIS IS CINERAMA (Cinerama, 1952) Max Steiner et al.
Peter Pan 152 (private)

THOMAS CROWN AFFAIR, THE (United Artists, 1968) Michel Legrand
United Artists 5182, LA-295-G and 69

THOSE FANTASTIC FLYING FOOLS (BLAST-OFF/ROCKET TO THE MOON) (Britain, 1967) Patrick John Scott
Polydor 583.013

THREAT, THE (MENACE, LA) (Canada/France, 1977) Gerry Mulligan
CBS 70154 (France)

3 DAYS OF THE CONDOR (Paramount, 1975) Dave Grusin
Capitol SW-11469

3 IN THE CELLAR (American International, 1970) Don Randi
AIR 1036

THREE INTO A THOUSAND (TRE NEL MILLE) (Italy, 1970) Ennio Morricone
Cometa CMT-1006-16 (Italy)

THREE MUSKETEERS, THE (Fox, 1974) Michel Legrand
Bell 1310

THREE NIGHTS OF LOVE (TRE NOTTI D'AMORE) (Italy, 1964) Giovanni Fusco, Piero Piccioni, and Carlo Rustichelli
CAM CMS-30117 and MDG-2004 (Italy)

3:10 TO YUMA (Columbia, 1957) George Duning
Citadel TT-GD-2

THREE THE HARD WAY (Allied Artists, 1974) Richard Tufo
Curtom 8602

THREE TOUGH GUYS (Paramount, 1974) Isaac Hayes
Enterprise ENS-7504

3 WORLDS OF GULLIVER, THE (Columbia, 1959) Bernard Herrmann
London SPC-21137 (Britain)

THRONE OF FIRE (TRONO DI FUOCO, IL) (Italy, n. d.) Bruno Nicolai
Cinevox 33/32 (Italy)

THUNDER ALLEY (American International, 1967) Mike Curb
Sidewalk (S)T-5902

TI HO SPOSATO PER ALLEGRIA (Italy, 1967) Piero Piccioni
Cetra SP-1353(45) (Italy)

TIFFANY MEMORANDUM, THE (Italy, n. d.) Riz Ortolani
Beat 001 (Italy)

TIKO AND THE SHARK (TI-KOYO E IL SUO PESCECANE) (MGM, 1966) Francesco de Masi
CAM-Seven Seas GXH-6035 (Japan)

TI-KOYO E IL SUO PESCECANE see TIKO AND THE SHARK

TILT (Warners, 1979) Lee Holdridge, Bill Wray, and Randy Bishop
ABC AA-1114

TIME AFTER TIME (Warners, 1979) Miklos Rozsa
Entracte ERS-6517

TIME FOR LOVING, A (Britain, 1971) Michel Legrand
RCA 8253

TIME OF INDIFFERENCE (INDIFFERENTI, GLI) (France/Italy, 1965) Giovanni Fusco
Campi-Editore 100. 002 (Italy)

TIME TO LOVE AND A TIME TO DIE, A (Universal, 1958) Miklos Rozsa
MCA VIM-7204 (Japan)

TO BED ... OR NOT TO BED (DIAVOLO, IL) (Italy, 1963) Piero Piccioni
CAM 30. 061 (Italy)

TO KILL A MOCKINGBIRD (Universal, 1962) Elmer Bernstein
Film Music Collection FMC-7

TO THE LAST DROP OF BLOOD (ALL'ULTIMO SANQUE) (Italy,

n. d.) Nico Fidenco
CAM 10016 (Italy)

TOGETHER BROTHERS (Fox, 1974) Barry White
Fox S-101

TOM JONES (Britain, 1963) John Addison
United Artists 3134/5134, 4113/5113, (S)1535, and 3376/6376

TOM THUMB (PETIT POUCET, LE) (France, 1972) Francis Lai
Gama 165 (France)

TONY ARZENTA see NO WAY OUT

TOO SOON TO DIE see WAKE UP AND DIE

TOP CRACK (Italy, n. d.) Gianni Marchetti
CAM 6 (Italy)

TOP SENSATION see SEDUCERS, THE

TOPO, EL (Abkco, 1971) Alejandro Jodorowsky
Apple SWAO-3388
Douglas 6 KZ-30920

TORN CURTAIN (Universal, 1966) Bernard Herrmann (not used in the film)
Film Music Collection FMC-10

TOSCA, LA (Italy, 1973) Armando Trovajoli
RCA 18 (Italy)

TOUCH OF CLASS, A (Embassy, 1973) John Cameron
Brut 6004

TOUCH OF EVIL, A (Universal, 1958) Henry Mancini
Challenge 602 and CH-615
Citadel CT-6015

TOUR DU MONDE DES AMOUREAUX DE PEYNET, LE (France, n. d.) Alessandro Alessandrini, Ennio Morricone
Seven Seas/General Music FML-25 (Japan)

TOURIST TRAP (Independent, 1979) Pino Donaggio
Varese Sarabande VC-81102

TOUT UNE VIE see AND NOW MY LOVE

TOWERING INFERNO, THE (Fox/Warners, 1974) John Williams
Warners BS-2840

TOWN WITHOUT PITY (United Artists, 1961) Dimitri Tiomkin
Cinema LP-8012 (private)

TOYS IN THE ATTIC (United Artists, 1963) George Duning
Citadel CT-GD-1

TRAIN, LE (France, 1973) Philippe Sarde
Polydor 2393. 072 (France)

TRAITEMENT DE CHOC (France/Italy, 1972) Rene Koering, Alain Jessua
Cine Disc M-5008 (Japan)

TRASTEVERE (Italy, 1972) Guido and Maurizio de Angelis
It 90005 (Italy)

TRE NEL MILLE see THREE INTO A THOUSAND

TRE VOLTI, I (Italy, 1964) Piero Piccioni
RCA PML-10394 (Italy)

TRIAL OF BILLY JACK, THE (Independent, 1974) Elmer Bernstein
ABC ABCD-853

TRIBULATIONS OF A CHINESE MAN IN CHINA, THE see UP TO HIS EARS

TRINITY IS STILL MY NAME (THEY STILL CALL ME TRINITY/ CONTINUAVANO A CHIAMARLO TRINITA) (Italy, 1971) Guido and Maurizio de Angelis
RCA 9 (Italy)

TRIO INFERNAL, LE (INFERNAL TRIO, THE) (France/Germany/ Italy, 1974) Ennio Morricone
Yuki 873/001 (France)

TRIP, THE see VIAGGIO, IL

TRIPLE CROSS (Warners, 1967) George Garvarentz
United Artists 4162/5162

TRISTAN ET ISEULT (France, 1979) Christian Vander
Barclay 80. 528 (France)

TROCADERO LEMON BLUE (TROCADERO BLEU CITRON) (France, 1978) Alec R. Costandinos
Casablanca NBLP-7117

TRONO DI FUOCO, IL see THRONE OF FIRE

TROP C'EST TROP (France, 1975) Jean Bouchety, Christian Chevalier
Pathe 2CO64-96661 (France)

TROPPO PER VIVERE, POCO PER MORIRE (Italy, n. d.) Francesco de Masi
Beat 001 and 003 (Italy)

TROUBLE MAN (Fox, 1973) Marvin Gaye
Tamla T-322L

TROUBLE WITH ANGELS, THE (Columbia, 1966) Jerry Goldsmith
Mainstream 56073/6073

TRUCK TURNER (American International, 1974) Isaac Hayes
Enterprise ENS-7507-2

TRUE AND THE FALSE, THE (VERO E IL FALSO, IL) (Italy, n.d.) Giorgio Gaslini
Cinevox 33/54 (Italy)

TU SERAS TERRIBLEMENT GENTILLE see YOU ONLY LOVE ONCE

TUTTI A SQUOLA (Italy, 1979) Gianni Ferrio
Cinevox MDF 33.130 (Italy)

TUTTI I COLORI DEL BUIO (Italy/Spain, 1972) Bruno Nicolai
Gemelli 10.014 (Italy)

TUTTO A POSTO E NINENTE IN ORDINE see EVERYTHING'S READY, NOTHING WORKS

12 CHAIRS, THE (UMC, 1970) Mel Brooks, John Morris
Warners BS-2781 (Australia)

TWISTED NERVE (Britain, 1968) Bernard Herrmann
Cinema LP-8006 (private)

TWO ENGLISH GIRLS (DEUX ANGLAISES ET LE CONTINENT, LES) (France, 1971) Georges Delerue
AZ 117 (France)

2001: A SPACE ODYSSEY (MGM, 1968) various composers
MGM (S)13 and SE-4722

UIT ELKAAR (Holland, n.d.) Van der Wurff
Polydor Harl. 292554 (Holland)

ULTIMA NEVE DI PRIMAVERA, L' see LAST SNOWS OF SPRING, THE

UNCLE JOE SHANNON (United Artists, 1979) Bill Conti
United Artists UA-LA935-H

UNDER PARIS SKIES (France, 1930) H. Giraud
Camden 233

UNESERCITO DI 5 UOMINI see FIVE-MAN ARMY, THE

UNFORGIVEN, THE (United Artists, 1960) Dimitri Tiomkin
Sonopr. United Artists 25068-82658

UNMARRIED WOMAN, AN (Fox, 1978) Bill Conti
Fox T-557

UNO DI PIU ALL'INFERNO (Italy, n. d.) Nico Fidenco
CAM 10016 (Italy)

UOMO DA RISPETTARE, UN see HEARTS AND MINDS

UOMO LIBRO, UN (France, n. d.) Francis Lai
CAM 3001 (Italy)

UOMO, L'ORGOGLIO, LA VENDETTA, L' (Italy, n. d.) Carlo Rustichelli
CAM 9002 (Italy)

UP TO HIS EARS (TRIBULATIONS OF A CHINESE MAN IN CHINA/ CHINESE ADVENTURES IN CHINA) (France/Italy, 1965) Georges Delerue
Poo LP-108 (private)
United Artists 4136

US TWO (DEUX HEUVES DE COLLE POUR UN BAISER/LIEDENSCHAFTLICHEN BLUMCHEN) (France, 1979) Francis Lai
WEA WB-56626 (France)

UTAMARO'S WORLD (Japan, 1946) Ryohei Hirose
Victor VIP-7233 (Japan)

VACATION, THE (VACANZA, LA) (Italy, 1971) Fiorenzo Carpi
General Music 55062 (Italy)

VADO ... L'AMMAZZO E TORNO see ANY GUN CAN PLAY

VALACHI PAPERS, THE (Columbia, 1972) Riz Ortolani
English Philips 6303-075
Project 3 PR-5085-SD

VALDEZ THE HALFBREED (VALDEZ NORSES) (Italy, 1973) Guido and Maurizio de Angelis
Seven Seas 24 (Japan)

VALENTINO (United Artists, 1977) Stanley Black, Ferde Grofe
United Artists UALA-810-H

VALERIA DENTRO E FUORI (VALERIE INSIDE AND OUTSIDE) (Italy, n. d.) Franco Bixio
Cinevox 33/52 (Italy)

VALISE, LA (France, 1973) Philippe Sarde
Polydor 2393. 070 (France)

VALLEY, THE (France, 1972) Roger Waters, Pink Floyd
Harvest-Capitol ST-11078

VAN NUYS BLVD. (Crown, 1979) Ken Mansfield, Ron Wright
Mercury SRM 1-3794

VENGEANCE (JOKO, INVOCA DIO ... E MUORI) (Italy, 1968) Carlo Savina
CAM 10018 (Italy)

VERGOGNA SCHIFOSI see DIRTY ANGELS, THE

VERTIGO (Paramount, 1958) Bernard Herrmann
Mercury 20384 and SRI-75117 (Netherlands)
Sound Stage SS-2301 (private)

VERY HAPPY ALEXANDER see ALEXANDER

VIAGGIO, IL (JOURNEY, THE/VOYAGE, THE/TRIP, THE) (Italy, 1974) Manuel de Sica
CAM 9057 (Italy)

VICE SQUAD (BRIGADE MONDAINE--LA SECTE DE MARRAKECH) (France, 1978) Carrone
WEA Malligator 772-811 (France)

VICTORY MARCH (MARCIA TRIONFALE) (Italy, 1977) Nicola Piovani
Beat LPF 032 (Italy)

VIE DEVANT SOI, LA see MADAME ROSA

VIGLIACCHI NON PREGANO, I (Italy, n. d.) Gianni Marchetti
CAM MAG 10.021 (Italy)

VIKINGS, THE (United Artists, 1958) Mario Nascimbene
United Artists 4003/5003 and 3122/6122

VILLAGE OF EIGHT TOMBS (YATSU HAKAMURA) (Japan, 1977) Yasushi Akutagawa
JVC-KVX-1001 (Japan)
Varese Sarabande VC-81084

VIOLENT LIFE, A (VITA VIOLENTA, UNA) (Italy, 1962) Piero Piccioni
CAM CMS-30041 and CA-2440(45) (Italy)

VIOLETTE NOZIERE (France, n. d.) Pierre Jansen
Pema Music 900-062

VIRGIN OF NUREMBERG, THE (Italy, n. d.) Riz Ortolani
CAM 30.119 (Italy)

VISIONS OF 8 (Cinema V, 1973) Henry Mancini
RCA ABL1-0231

VITA AGRA, LA (Italy, 1964) Piero Piccioni
CAM CMS 30102, CA 2569, and MDG-2004

VITA SEGRETA DI UNA DICIOTTENNE (Italy, n. d.) Gianni Marchetti
CAM 9024 (Italy)

VITA VENDUTA, UNA (Italy, n. d.) Ennio Morricone
CAM SAG-9073 (Italy)

VITA VIOLENTA, UNA (Italy, n. d.) Piero Piccioni
CAM 30. 041 (Italy)

VIVA MARIA (United Artists, 1965) Georges Delerue
United Artists 4135/5135, 3570/6570, and 3608/6608

VIVA ZAPATA! (Fox, 1952) Alex North, Manuel M. Ponce
Dot 3107
Film Music Collection FMC-9
Hamilton 108/12108

VIVI O PREFERIBILIMENTE MORTI see ALIVE BUT PREFERABLY DEAD

VIVRE LA NUIT (France/Italy, 1967) Claude Bolling
Philips B-77. 754-L (France)

VIXEN (Independent, 1968) William Loose
Beverly Hills BHS-22

VIZIETTO, IL see CAGE AUX FOLLES, LA

VOCI BIANCHE, LE see WHITE VOICES

VOGLIO MORTO, LO (Italy, n. d.) Nico Fidenco
CAM 10016 (Italy)

VOICES (MGM, 1979) Jimmy Webb
Planet P-9002

VON RICHTOFEN AND BROWN (United Artists, 1971) Hugo Friedhofer
Delos DEL/F-25420

VOYAGE, THE see VIAGGIO, IL

VOYAGE OF THE DAMNED (Embassy, 1977) Lalo Schifrin
Entr'acte ERS-6508-ST

W. C. FIELDS AND ME (Universal, 1976) Henry Mancini
MCA 2092

W. W. AND THE DIXIE DANCEKINGS (Fox, 1975) Dave Grusin
Fox ST-103

WAIT UNTIL DARK (Warners, 1967) Henry Mancini
Decca (7) 4956
RCA 9340 (45)

WAKE UP AND DIE (LUTRING/SVEGLIATI E UCCIDI/TOO SOON TO DIE) (France/Italy, 1966) Ennio Morricone
RCA SP-8018 (Italy)

WALK IN THE SPRING RAIN, A (Columbia, 1970) Elmer Bernstein
Cinema LP-8013 (private)

WALK IN THE SUN, A (Fox, 1946) Ballad by Millard Lampell and Earl Robinson
Disc 523 (78)

WALK ON THE WILD SIDE, A (Columbia, 1962) Elmer Bernstein
Choreo A(S)-4-ST

WALK WITH LOVE AND DEATH, A (Fox, 1969) Georges Delerue
Citadel CT-6025

WALKABOUT (Britain, 1971) John Barry
Poo LP-102 (private)

WARRIOR EMPRESS, THE (SAPHO) (France/Italy, 1961) Georges Garvarentz, Francesco Lavagnino
Barclay 920. 322 (France)

WARRIORS, THE (Paramount, 1979) Barry De Vorzon
A&M SP-4761

WATERHOLE #3 (Paramount, 1967) Dave Grusin
Smash 27096/67096

WATERSHIP DOWN (Britain, 1978) Angela Morley, Mike Batt, and Malcolm Williamson
Columbia JS-35707

WAY WE WERE, THE (Columbia, 1973) Marvin Hamlisch
Columbia KS-32830

WE WILL ALL GO TO HEAVEN (NOUS IRONS TOUS AU PARADIS) (France, 1977) Vladimir Cosma
Deesse DDLX-157 (France)

WEAK SPOT, THE (FAILLE, LA) (France/Germany/Italy, 1975) Ennio Morricone
Yuki 873. 003 (France)

WELCOME TO L. A. (United Artists, 1976) Richard Baskin
United Artists UA-LA703-H

WE'LL CALL HIM ANDREA (LO CHIAMEREO ANDREA) (Italy, 1972) Manuel de Sica
CAM 9045 (Italy)

WESTWORLD (MGM, 1973) Fred Karlin
MGM 1SE-47-ST

WHAT A WAY TO GO (Fox, 1964) Nelson Riddle
Fox 3143/4143

WHAT'S NEW PUSSYCAT? (United Artists, 1965) Burt Bacharach
United Artists 4128/5128 and LA-278-G

WHAT'S THE MATTER WITH HELEN? (United Artists, 1971) David Raksin
Dynamation DY-1200 (private)

WHEN WOMEN HAD TAILS (QUANDO LE DONNE AVEVANO LA CODA) (Italy, 1970) Ennio Morricone
CAM SAG-9032 (Italy)
E. M. Records 1001 (private)

WHERE EAGLES DARE (MGM, 1969) Ron Goodwin
MGM 2315-036 (Britain)

WHERE THE LILIES BLOOM (United Artists, 1974) Earl Scruggs
Columbia KC-32806

WHISPERING CITY, THE (Canada, 1947) Andre Mathiew
English Columbia 2526 (78)

WHITE ROCK (Britain, 1976) Rick Wakeman
A&M SP-4614

WHITE ROSE OF ATHENS (Greece, n. d.) Manos Hadjidakis
Mercury 20688/60688

WHITE VOICES (VOCI BIANCHE, LE) (France/Italy, 1965) Gino Marinuzzi
CAM 30. 110 (Italy)

WHITE WITCH DOCTOR (Fox, 1953) Bernard Herrmann
RCA ARL1-0707

WHO IS KILLING THE GREAT CHEFS OF EUROPE? (Warners, 1978) Henry Mancini
Epic SE-35692

WHO SAW HER DIE? (CHI L'HA VISTA MORIRE?) (Italy, 1972) Ennio Morricone

Cometa GGST-10. 017 (Italy)
Gemelli GGST-10. 017 (Italy)

WIDOW COUDERC, THE (ESCAPE/VEUVRE COUDERC/EVASO, LE) (France/Italy, 1971) Caruso
Cinevox MDG-129 (Italy)

WILD ANGELS, THE (American International, 1966) Mike Curb
Tower (S)5043 and (S)5056

WILD FOR KICKS (BEAT GIRL) (Britain, 1959) John Barry
Columbia 1225 (Britain)

WILD GEESE, THE (Allied Artists, 1978) Roy Budd
A&M SP-4730

WILD ONE, THE (CYCLIST RAIDERS) (Columbia, 1954) Leith Stevens
MCA VIM-7208 (Japan)

WILL OUR FRIENDS SUCCEED IN FINDING THEIR FRIEND WHO MYSTERIOUSLY DISAPPEARED IN AFRICA? (RIUSCIRANNO I NOSTRI EVOI A RITROVARE L'AMICO MISTERIOSAMENTE SCOMPARSO IN AFRICA?) (Italy, 1969) Armando Trovajoli
RCA 1105 (Italy)

WILLIE DYNAMITE (Universal, 1973) J. J. Johnson
MCA 393

WIND AND THE LION, THE (MGM, 1975) Jerry Goldsmith
Arista AL-4048

WINDJAMMER (Cinerama, 1958) Morton Gould
Columbia 1158/8651

WINDS OF CHANGE (Sanrio, 1979) Alec Costandinos
Casablanca NBLT-7167

WINNETOU I (Germany, 1966) Martin Boetticher
Polydor 46838 (Germany)

WITCHCRAFT (MALEFICES, LE) (France, n. d.) Pierre Henry
Philips 432. 762(45) (France)

WOMAN IS A MARVELOUS THING, A (Italy, 1964) Piero Piccioni
RCA SP-9008 (Italy)

WOMEN BURIED ALIVE (SEPOLTA VIVA) (Italy, 1973) Ennio Morricone
Beat LPF-021 (Italy)

WONDERFUL COUNTRY (United Artists, 1959) Alex North
Ascot 13501/16501
United Artists 4050/5050 and 3122/6122

WORKING CLASS GOES TO HEAVEN, THE (CLASE OPERAIA VA IN PARADISO, LA/LULU THE TOOL) (Italy, 1971) Ennio Morricone
RCA SP-8038 (Italy)

WORLD BY NIGHT, THE (TOTO DI NOTTE N. 1) (Italy, 1961) Armando Trovajoli
CAM 30.047 (Italy)

WORLD BY NIGHT II, THE (MONDO DI NOTTE, IL) (Italy, 1962) Piero Piccioni
RCA 10078 (Italy)

WORLD'S GREATEST LOVER, THE (Fox, 1977) John Morris
RCA ABL1-2709

WRITTEN ON THE WIND (Universal, 1956) Frank Skinner
Filmmusic SN-2823 (private)
Varese Sarabande VC-81074

WUTHERING HEIGHTS (United Artists, 1939) Alfred Newman
Film Music Collection FMC-6

YANKS (Universal, 1979) Richard Rodney Bennett
MCA 3181

YATSU HAKAMURA see VILLAGE OF 8 TOMBS

YESTERDAY, TODAY AND TOMORROW (IERA, OGGA, DOMANI) (Italy, 1964) Armando Trovajoli
CAM 30.076 (Italy)

YETI, IL GIGANTE DEL 20° SECOLO (Italy, 1977) Sante Maria Romitelli
Aris LM-10 (Italy)

YOU CAN'T HAVE EVERYTHING see CACTUS IN THE SNOW

YOU LIGHT UP MY LIFE (Columbia, 1977) Joe Brooks
Arista AB-4159

YOU ONLY LIVE TWICE (United Artists, 1967) John Barry
United Artists 4155/5155, LA-289-G, UXS-2-91

YOU ONLY LOVE ONCE (TU SERAS TERRIBLEMENT GENTILLE) (France, 1969) Jacques Loussier
London GXH-6040 (Japan) and 561

YOUNG BESS (MGM, 1953) Miklos Rozsa
Film Music Collection FMC-5

YOUNG GIRLS OF ROCHEFORT, THE (France, 1967) Michel Legrand
United Artists UAS-6662

YOUNG LIONS, THE (Fox, 1958) Hugo Friedhofer
MCA 7154 (Japan)
Star ST-1001 (private)

YOUNG LOVERS, THE (MGM, 1964) Sol Kaplan
Columbia OL-7010/OS-2510

YOUNG WINSTON (Columbia, 1972) Alfred Ralston
Angel SFO-36901

ZENABEL (Italy, n. d.) Bruno Nicolai
Gemelli 10.002 (Italy)

ZITA (France, 1968) Francois de Roubaix
Philips (S)600287

ZIZANIE, LA (France, n. d.) Vladimir Cosma
Warners 56493 (France)

ZOMBI see DAWN OF THE DEAD

ZORBA THE GREEK (Fox, 1964) Mikis Theodorakis
Fox 3167/4167 and T-903

ZORRO (France/Italy, 1975) Guido and Maurizio de Angelis
EMI-Pathe 2CO66-13058 (France)

ANTHOLOGIES
(Themes)

ALFRED NEWMAN CONDUCTS HIS GREAT FILM MUSIC
Captain from Castile
David and Bathsheba
Robe, The
Anastasia
Hurricane, The (1937)
Pleasure of His Company, The
Pinky
Laura (Raksin)
Love Is a Many-Splendored Thing

Angel S-36066
Capitol ST-1652

AWARD WINNING SCORES FROM THE SILVER SCREEN (101 Strings)
Love Is a Many-Splendored Thing
Moulin Rouge
Ruby Gentry
Around the World in 80 Days

High and the Mighty, The
Spellbound
Three Coins in the Fountain
Picnic
Gone with the Wind

Somerset/Alshire P-7000

BALLET MUSIC FROM MGM MUSICALS
American in Paris, An
Words and Music
Pirate, The
Band Wagon, The
Lili
Singin' in the Rain

MGM E-3148

BELLE BARDOT, LA (Ray Ventura and His Orchestra)
And God Created Woman
Man and the Child, The
Ostrich Eggs
Sans Famille
Porte des Lilas
Mefiez-vous Fillettes
Strange Mr. Stevens, The
One Never Knows
Grand Bluff
Insensiblement
Bear's Skin
Amour Descend du Ciel, L'

Dot DLP-3120

BERNARD HERRMANN CONDUCTS GREAT BRITISH FILM SCORES (National Philharmonic Orchestra)
Anna Karenina
Oliver Twist
Ideal Husband, An
Escape Me Never
Invaders, The (49th Parallel)
Things to Come

London SPC-21149

BERNSTEIN: BACKGROUNDS FOR BRANDO (Elmer Bernstein, Conductor)
Sayonara
On the Waterfront
Viva Zapata
Men, The
Guys and Dolls
Streetcar Named Desire, A

Teahouse of the August Moon
Desiree
Julius Caesar
Wild One, The

Dot DLP-25107

BEST OF THE GREAT MOTION PICTURE THEMES, THE
Gone with the Wind
Exodus
Lili
Lawrence of Arabia
Love Is a Many-Splendored Thing
Ben-Hur
Mondo Cane
Umbrellas of Cherbourg
Black Orpheus
Robe, The
Captain from Castile
King of Kings

Capitol SL-6632

BEST OF THE NEW FILM THEMES, THE (Frank Chacksfield and His Orchestra)
Fellini's 8-1/2
Charade
VIP's, The
Cardinal, The
Tiara Tahiti
Lord of the Flies
Toys in the Attic
Mondo Cane
New Kind of Love, A
Victors, The
Divorce Italian Style
Cabinet of Caligari, The

London PS-347

BIG SCREEN, LITTLE SCREEN (Henry Mancini conducting orchestra and chorus)
Nicholas and Alexandra
Sometimes a Great Notion
Summer of '42
Kotch
Shaft
Cade's County (TV)
Tonight Show, The (TV)
All in the Family (TV)
Mystery Movie (TV)
Ironsides (TV)

RCA LSP-4630

BIG SOUNDS OF RON GOODWIN AND HIS ORCHESTRA, THE
Adventures of Black Beauty, The
Deadly Strangers
Monte Carlo or Bust
Red Cloak, The
Ben-Hur

EMI TWOX-1034 (New Zealand)

BIG SUSPENSE MOVIE THEMES (Geoff Love and His Orchestra)
2001: A Space Odyssey
Godfather, The
French Connection, The
Rififi
Z
High and the Mighty, The
Shaft
Third Man, The
In the Heat of the Night
Airport
Diamonds Are Forever
Frenzy

Music for Pleasure MFG-50035 (Britain)

BIG TERROR MOVIE THEMES (Geoff Love and His Orchestra)
Jaws
Poseidon Adventure, The
Exorcist, The
Rollerball
Psycho
Eiger Sanction, The
Earthquake
Airport '75
Towering Inferno, The
Three Days of the Condor
Executioner, The
Death Wish

Music for Pleasure MFP-50248 (Britain)

BIG WAR MOVIE THEMES (Geoff Love and His Orchestra)
633 Squadron
Battle of Britain, The
Dam Busters, The
Guns of Navarone, The
Great Escape, The
Lawrence of Arabia
Bridge on the River Kwai, The
Is Paris Burning?
Where Eagles Dare
Reach for the Sky
Longest Day, The

Green Berets, The

Music for Pleasure MFP-5171 (Britain)

BIG WESTERN MOVIE THEMES (No. 2) (Geoff Love and His Orchestra)
Butch Cassidy and the Sundance Kid
For a Few Dollars More
Hang 'Em High
Wild Bunch, The
Sabata
Rio Bravo
Cat Ballou
True Grit
Once Upon a Time in the West
Man Who Shot Liberty Valance, The
Hombre
Mackenna's Gold

Music for Pleasure MFP-5204 (Britain)

BOY NAMED CHARLIE BROWN, A (Composed and conducted by Rod McKuen)
Boy Named Charlie Brown, A
Joanna
Prime of Miss Jean Brodie, The
Me, Natalie

Stanyan SR-5010

BRIAN'S SONG THEMES AND VARIATIONS (Michel Legrand)
Brian's Song
Go-Between, The
Happy Ending, The
Picasso Summer
Summer of '42
Wuthering Heights
Pieces of Dreams
Thomas Crown Affair, The

Bell 6071

CAPTAIN BLOOD: CLASSIC FILM SCORES FOR ERROL FLYNN (Charles Gerhardt conducting the National Philharmonic Orchestra)
Adventures of Don Juan, The
Sea Hawk, The
Captain Blood
They Died with Their Boots On
Dodge City
Objective Burma
Sun Also Rises, The

Adventures of Robin Hood, The

RCA ARL1-0912

CAPTAIN FROM CASTILE: THE CLASSIC FILM SCORES OF ALFRED NEWMAN (Charles Gerhardt conducts the National Philharmonic Orchestra)
Captain from Castile
How to Marry a Millionaire
Wuthering Heights
Robe, The
Airport
Down to the Sea in Ships
Anastasia
Best of Everything, The
Bravados, The
Song of Bernadette, The

RCA ARL1-0184

CASABLANCA: CLASSIC FILM SCORES FOR HUMPHREY BOGART (Charles Gerhardt conducting the National Philharmonic Orchestra)
Casablanca
Passage to Marseille
Treasure of the Sierra Madre
Big Sleep, The
Caine Mutiny, The
To Have and Have Not
Two Mrs. Carrolls, The
Sabrina
Left Hand of God, The
Sahara
Virginia City
Key Largo

RCA ARL1-0422

CHARADE ORANGE TAMOURE (Marcello Minervi and His Orchestra)
Longest Day, The
Sundowners, The
Jessica
March or Die
Town Without Pity
Leopard, The
My Uncle

London MB-104 (France)

CINEMA LEGRAND (Michel Legrand and His Orchestra)
Vie de Chateau, La
Black Orpheus
Gone with the Wind

Umbrellas of Cherbourg, The
Young Girls of Rochefort, The
Plastic Dome of Norma Jean, The
American Dream, An
Two for the Road
Fitzwilly

MGM (S)E-4491

CINEMA RHAPSODIES (Victor Young and His Singing Strings)
Moulin Rouge
Lili
Anna
Limelight
Ruby Gentry
Forever Female
Shane
Bad and the Beautiful, The
Thunderbirds
Melba
Something to Live For
Star, The

Decca DL-8051

CINEMA SANS IMAGE
Umbrellas of Cherbourg, The
Animals, The
Sweet Skin
Do You Like Girls?
Mepris, Le
Comment Trouvez-vous ma Soeur?
To Die in Madrid
Bay of Angels
D'ou Viens-tu Johnny?
Bebert et l'Omnibus
Striptease
Aine des Ferchaux, L'

Philips Deluxe P-77.233-L

CINEMOOG (The Electronic Concept Orchestra featuring Eddie Higgins on the Moog Synthesizer)
Midnight Cowboy
Happy Ending, The
Last Summer
Young Girls of Rochefort, The
Z
Sweden, Heaven and Hell
Che!
Justine
Butch Cassidy and the Sundance Kid
John and Mary

Sterile Cuckoo, The

Mercury SR-61279

CLASSIC FILM SCORES FOR BETTE DAVIS (Charles Gerhardt conducting the National Philharmonic Orchestra)
Now Voyager
Dark Victory
Stolen Life, A
Private Lives of Elizabeth and Essex, The
Mr. Skeffington
In This Our Life
All About Eve
Jezebel
Beyond the Forest
Juarez
Letter, The
All This and Heaven Too

RCA ARL1-0183

CLASSIC FILM SCORES OF BERNARD HERRMANN, THE (Charles Gerhardt conducting the National Philharmonic Orchestra)
Citizen Kane
On Dangerous Ground
Beneath the 12-Mile Reef
Hangover Square
White Witch Doctor

RCA ARL1-0707

CLASSIC FILM THEMES FOR ORGAN (Gaylord Carter playing the Simonton Grande Wurlitzer Organ)
Kings Row
Bad and the Beautiful, The
How Green Was My Valley
High Noon
Uninvited, The
Exodus
Gone with the Wind
Best Years of Our Lives, The
Spellbound
Place in the Sun, A
Raintree County

Delos DEL-F25419

CLASSIC FILM THEMES FOR SAXOPHONE (Ralph Gari, saxophonist)
Place in the Sun, A
Conversation, The
Toys in the Attic
Invitation

Streetcar Named Desire, A
Ship of Fools
Advise and Consent
Eleanor and Franklin (TV)
Torn Curtain
Killers, The
Brute Force

Citadel CT-6021

COFFRET (Ennio Morricone)
Once Upon a Time in the West
Israel (TV)
Serpent, The
Giu la Testa
Violent City
Pistol for Ringo, A
For a Few Dollars More
Moses, the Lawgiver (TV)
Oceano
For a Fistful of Dollars
Ad Ogni Costo
Pugni in Tasca, I
Menage all'Italiana
Gott Mit Uns
Battle of Algiers, The
Sacco and Vanzetti
Svegliati e Uccidi
Maestro and Margherita, The
Metello
Giardino delle Dilizie, Il
Harem, The

RCA PL-31279 (France)

DAVID RAKSIN CONDUCTS HIS GREAT FILM SCORES (David Raksin conducting the New Philharmonia Orchestra)
Forever Amber
Laura
Bad and the Beautiful, The

RCA ARL1-1490

DAVID ROSE PLAYS THEMES FROM THE GREAT SCREEN EPICS
Bible, The
Ben-Hur
Ten Commandments, The
Sodom and Gomorrah
Robe, The
Francis of Assisi
Exodus
King of Kings
Spartacus

Song of Bernadette, The
Quo Vadis
Greatest Story Ever Told, The

Capitol ST-2627

DIGITAL SPACE (Morton Gould conducting The London Symphony Orchestra)
Windjammer
Star Wars
Airport
Red Pony, The
Things to Come
Big Country, The
That Hamilton Woman
Invaders, The (49th Parallel)
Spitfire (First of the Few, The)

Varese Sarabande VCDM 1000. 20 (Britain)

DIMITRI TIOMKIN (Dimitri Tiomkin)
Alamo, The
Fall of the Roman Empire, The
55 Days at Peking
Guns of Navarone
Old Man and the Sea, The
Wild Is the Wind

CBS 66604

DR. STRANGELOVE AND OTHER GREAT MOVIE THEMES FROM COLUMBIA PICTURES
Dr. Strangelove
Victors, The
Bridge on the River Kwai, The
Picnic
From Here to Eternity
Diamond Head
Damn the Defiant!
Lawrence of Arabia
Psyche '59
In the French Style
Barabbas
Song Without End
Interns, The

Colpix (S)CP-464

DOLCE VITA AND OTHER GREAT MOTION PICTURE THEMES, LA (Ray Ellis and His Orchestra)
Dolce Vita, La
High and the Mighty, The
Misfits, The

Spellbound
Love Is a Many-Splendored Thing
Gone with the Wind
Laura
Summer Place, A
Ruby Gentry
April Love
Exodus

RCA LSP-2410

DRACULA AND THEMES (Christopher Lee, narrator)
Dracula
Fear in the Night
She
Vampire Lovers, The
Dr. Jekyll and Sister Hyde

EMI TWOA-5001 (Britain)

ELIZABETH AND ESSEX: THE CLASSIC FILM SCORES OF ERICH WOLFGANG KORNGOLD (Charles Gerhardt conducts the National Philharmonic Orchestra)
Private Lives of Elizabeth and Essex, The
Another Dawn
Sea Wolf, The
Prince and the Pauper, The
Of Human Bondage
Anthony Adverse
Deception

RCA ARL1-0185

ELMER BERNSTEIN: A MAN AND HIS MOVIES
To Kill a Mockingbird
Walk on the Wild Side, A
Man with the Golden Arm, The
Carpetbaggers, The
Rat Race, The
Sweet Smell of Success
Anna Lucasta
Sudden Fear

Mainstream 56094/6094

ENNIO MORRICONE--UN FILM UNS MUSICA
Sicilian Clan, The
Pistol for Ringo, A
Metti, una Sera a Cena
Violent City
Incontro
Vamos a Matar Companeros
Gatto a Nove Code, Il

Indagine su un Cittadino
Al Di Sopra di Ogni Sospetto
Metello
Seven Guns for the MacGregors
Gott mit Uns
Attentato, L'
Tepepa
Once Upon a Time in the West
Sacco and Vanzetti
Battle of Algiers, The
Maestro e Margherita, Il
Fistful of Dollars, A
Working Class Goes to Heaven, The
Giu la Testa
Maddalena
Avventura, L'
Hawks and the Sparrows, The
Cosa Avete Fatto a Solange?
Veruschka
For a Few Dollars More

RCA Italiana DPSL-10599

ENOCH LIGHT AND HIS ORCHESTRA--GREAT THEMES FROM HIT FILMS
West Side Story
Never on Sunday
Cid, El
Dolce Vita, La
Exodus
King of Kings
Tender Is the Night
Four Horsemen of the Apocalypse
Hustler, The
Satan Never Sleeps

Columbia Harmony H-30549

EXCITEMENT (Ron Goodwin and His Orchestra)
2001: A Space Odyssey
Women in Love
Tender Is the Night
Doctor Zhivago
Z
Where Eagles Dare
Lawrence of Arabia
Apartment, The
Ben-Hur
Romeo and Juliet
Battle of Britain
plus popular orchestra standards

World Record International SLZ-8346 (New Zealand)

FANTASTIC FILM MUSIC OF ALBERT GLASSER, THE (VOLUME 1)
Cisco Kid, The
Big Town
Boy and the Pirates, The
Amazing Colossal Man, The
Buckskin Lady, The
Beginning of the End, The
Cyclops, The
Top of the World

Starlog SR-1001 (private)

FANTASY FILM WORLD OF BERNARD HERRMANN, THE (Bernard Herrmann conducting the National Philharmonic Orchestra)
Journey to the Center of the Earth
Seventh Voyage of Sinbad, The
Day the Earth Stood Still, The
Fahrenheit 451

London SP-44207

FERRANTE & TEICHER PLAY "TONIGHT" AND OTHER FAVORITES
Strada, La
West Side Story
King of Kings
Breakfast at Tiffany's
City Lights
and popular movie songs

United Artists UAS-6171

FESTIVAL DE PARIS DU FILM FANTASTIQUE ET DE SCIENCE-FICTION, LE
Malpertius
Horror Rhapsody

Decca/Pascal Bertrand Music 900.411 (France)

50 YEARS OF FILM
Don Juan
Captain Blood
Midsummer Night's Dream, A
Adventures of Robin Hood, The
Sea Hawk, The
Kings Row
plus dialog and songs from Warner Brothers films

Warners 3XX-2737

50 YEARS OF FILM MUSIC
Sea Hawk, The
Kings Row
Adventures of Robin Hood, The

All This and Heaven Too
Treasure of the Sierra Madre
Nun's Story, The
Sayonara
Streetcar Named Desire, A
Who's Afraid of Virginia Woolf?
Land of the Pharaohs
High and the Mighty, The
Casablanca
plus popular movie songs

Warners 3XX-2736

50 YEARS OF MOVIE MUSIC FROM FLICKERS TO WIDESCREEN
(Jack Shaindlin, conductor)
First Film Music (medley)
Chase, The
Slapstix
Newsreel in Medley
Charmaine
If I Had a Talking Picture of You
Beyond the Blue Horizon
Carioca
King Kong (Suite)
Informer, The
Spellbound
Man with the Golden Arm, The

Decca DL-79079

FILM DELLA VIOLENZA, I (Ennio Morricone)
Violent City
Sicilian Clan, The
Vorta Notte delle Bambole di Vetro, La
Uomo a Uomo, Da
Diavolo nel Cervello, Il
Escalation
Giordano Bruno
Grazie Zia
Milano Odia
Polizia Non Puo Sparare, La
Mussolini, Ultimo Atto
Proprieta non e Piu'un Furto, La
Pugni in Tasca, I
Quattro Mosche di Velluto Grigio
Queimada (Burn!)
Revolver
Sacco and Vanzetti
Zensa Movente
Spasmo
Storie di Vita e Malavita
Svegliati e Uccidi
Tarantola del Ventre Nero, La

Uccello Dalla Piume di Cristallo, L'
Ultimo Treno della Notte, L'
Uomo da Rispettare, Un

RCA TPL-2 1174 (Italy)

FILM FAME. MARVELOUS MOVIE THEMES (Enoch Light and the Light Brigade)
Camelot
To Sir with Love
Gone with the Wind
More Than a Miracle
Valley of the Dolls
Bonnie and Clyde
For a Few Dollars More
Long Duel, The
In the Heat of the Night
Wait Until Dark
Live for Life
Bobo, The

Project 3 PR-5013-SD

FILM MUSIC (Harlan Ramsey conducting the Cosmopolitan Orchestra)
Moulin Rouge
Limelight
Story of Three Loves, The
Under Paris Skies
Blithe Spirit
Lydia
Love Story
Spellbound
Laura
Flesh and Fantasy

Camden CAL-233

FILM MUSIC (Werner Janssen conducting the Janssen Symphony of Los Angeles)
Hangover Square
Laura
Flesh and Fantasy
plus themes from Showboat

Camden CAL-205

FILM MUSIC BY ALEX NORTH
Unchained
Racers, The
Viva Zapata!
Bad Seed, The
Streetcar Named Desire, A
Bachelor Party, The

13th Letter, The
Stage Struck
I'll Cry Tomorrow
Miserables, Les
Rose Tattoo, The
Desiree

Citadel CT-6023

FILM MUSIC FROM FRANCE (Original soundtracks from the 12 best French films)
Jules and Jim
Lovers of Tereul, The
Cleo from 5 to 7
Trial, The
Taste of Violence, A
Gamberge, La
Lafayette
Button War, The
Liberte 1
Girl with the Golden Eyes, The
7 Capital Sins, The
Sweet Ecstasy

Philips 600-071

FILM MUSIC OF BRONISLAU KAPER (Bronislau Kaper, piano)
Mutiny on the Bounty
Lili
Glass Slipper, The
Butterfield 8
Auntie Mame
Chocolate Soldier, The
Invitation
Brothers Karamazov, The
Green Dolphin Street
Swan, The
Lord Jim
San Francisco

Delos DEL-F25421

FILM MUSIC OF HANS J. SALTER, THE
Ghost of Frankenstein
Magnificent Doll, The
Bend of the River
Against All Flags

Citadel TT-HS-1/2

FILM MUSIC OF HERBERT STOTHART, THE
Mutiny on the Bounty (1935)
David Copperfield

Anna Karenina (1935)
Viva Villa!

Citadel TT-ST-1/2

FILM MUSIC OF MIKLOS ROZSA, THE (Miklos Rozsa) (Hamburg Concert Orchestra and Chorus, conducted by Richard Muller-Lampertz)
King of Kings
Ben-Hur
El Cid

Stereo Fidelity SF-16400
Varese Sarabande VC-81104

FILM SPECTACULAR (Stanley Black conducting the London Festival Orchestra)
Exodus
Breakfast at Tiffany's
Samson and Delilah
Around the World in 80 Days
Longest Day, The
Henry V
Big Country, The

London SP-44025

FILM SPECTACULAR (Vol. II) (Stanley Black conducting the London Festival Orchestra)
My Fair Lady
Spellbound
Cleopatra
Summer Place, A
On the Waterfront
Gone with the Wind
Lawrence of Arabia
Magnificent Seven, The

London SP-44031

FILM SPECTACULAR (Vol. III) (Stanley Black conducting the London Festival Orchestra)
Thunderball
From Russia with Love
Goldfinger
Mary Poppins
Charade
Mondo Cane
Sound of Music, The
Man with the Golden Arm, The
Black Orpheus
Zorba the Greek

London SP-44078

FILM SPECTACULAR (Vol. IV) (Stanley Black conducting the London Festival Orchestra and Chorus)
- Stagecoach
- For Whom the Bell Tolls
- Doctor Zhivago
- Ben-Hur
- 2001: A Space Odyssey
- Sea Hawk, The
- Alamo, The
- Patton

London SP 44173

FILM SPECTACULAR (Vol. V) (Stanley Black conducting the London Festival Orchestra)
- Casablanca
- Man and a Woman, A
- Intermezzo
- Blood and Sand
- Strada, La
- Love Story
- Gone with the Wind

London SP-44225

FILM THEMES (Orchestra conducted by Henry Loges)
- East of Eden
- Breakfast at Tiffany's
- Johnny Guitar
- Bebo's Girl
- Chateau en Suede
- Charade
- From Russia with Love
- Alamo, The
- How the West Was Won
- Strada, La

Polydor 184023

FILM THEMES BY ALFRED NEWMAN
- Royal Scandal, A
- Man Called Peter, A
- President's Lady, The
- Letter to Three Wives, A
- Come to the Stable
- Life Begins at 8:30
- Trade Winds
- Mark of Zorro, The
- Captain from Castile, The
- Wuthering Heights
- Razor's Edge, The
- All About Eve
- How Green Was My Valley

David and Bathsheba
Bluebird, The
12 O'Clock High

Capricorn CP-1286

FILM THEMES OF ERNEST GOLD (Ernest Gold conducting the London Symphony Orchestra)
It's a Mad, Mad, Mad, Mad World
Exodus
On the Beach
Judgment at Nuremberg
Inherit the Wind
Young Philadelphians, The
Pressure Point
Child Is Waiting, A
Last Sunset, The
Too Much, Too Soon
Saddle Pals

London PS-320

FILM UNA MUSICA, UN (Ennio Morricone)
Sicilian Clan, The
Pistol for Ringo, A
Metti, una Sera a Cena
Violent City
Incontro
Vamos a Matar Companeros
Gatto a Nove Code, Il
Indagine su un Cittadino al di Sopra di Ogni Sospetto
Metello
7 Guns for the MacGregors
Gott Mit Uns
Tepepa
Attentato, L'
Once Upon a Time in the West
Sacco and Vanzetti
Battle of Algiers, The
Maestro and Margherita, The
For a Fistful of Dollars
Working Class Goes to Heaven, The
Giu la Testa
Maddalena
Avventuriero, L'
Hawks and the Sparrows, The
Cosa Avete Fatto a Solange?
Veruschka
For a Few Dollars More

RCA DPSL 10599 (Italy)

FILMMUSIC
All the President's Men
From Noon till Three
Reincarnation of Peter Proud, The
Victory at Entebbe
Up the Sandbox
Midway
Mackintosh Man, The
Marseilles Contract, The
Pete 'n' Tillie
Long Goodbye, The
Scorpio
Rio Conchos
Harry and Walter Go to New York
Birdman of Alcatraz, The
Cheyenne Social Club, The
Man in the Grey Flannel Suit, The
Ballad of Cable Hogue, The
Class of '44, The
Mr. Sycamore
Our Time
Coogan's Bluff
Poseidon Adventure, The

Centurion CLP-1600 (private)

"FOR A FEW DOLLARS MORE" AND OTHER MOTION PICTURE THEMES (Leroy Holmes and His Orchestra)
For a Few Dollars More
Fistful of Dollars, A
Zorba the Greek
Topkapi
Viva Maria
Train, The
Tom Jones

United Artists UAL-3608

FORBIDDEN GAMES. THEMES OF LOVE AND LONGING (John Perrone, guitarist)
Forbidden Games
Romeo and Juliet
Doctor Zhivago
and popular songs

Citadel CT-6014

FOTOGRAMMA PER FOTOGRAMMA
Absolutely Natural
Forza G
Giu la Testa
Metti una Sera a Cena
Indagine Su Di un Cittadino al Disopra di Ogni Sospetto

Moglie piu Bella, La
Anche se Volessi Lavorare, Che Faccio?
Mussolini, the Last Act
Cosa Buffa, La
Giu la Testa
Uccello Dalle Piume di Cristallo, L'
4 Mosche di Velluto Grigio

Cinevox MDF-33/74-75 (Italy)

FRANCIS LAI PLAYS FRANCIS LAI
Love Story
Rider on the Rain
Dans la Poussiere du Soleil
Love Is a Funny Thing
13 Days in France
Live for Life
Man and a Woman, A
Crook, The
Madly
Du Soleil Plein les Yeux
Hello, Goodbye

United Artists UAS-5515

FRENCH THEMES--FRANCIS LAI
Odeur des Fauves, L'
Legend of Frenchie King, The
Early Morning
Man and a Woman, A
Golden Claws Cat Girls, The
Smic, Smac, Smoc
Love Story

United Artists UAS-5630

FROM RUSSIA WITH LOVE (Jimmie Haskell and His Orchestra)
From Russia with Love
Prize, The
Great Escape, The
Dime with a Halo
Ticklish Affair, The
Boys, The
Flipper
McLintock!
Gunhawk, The
Cleopatra

Capitol ST-2075

GEOFF LOVE AND HIS ORCHESTRA PLAY BIG WAR MOVIE THEMES

Bridge on the River Kwai, The
Lawrence of Arabia
Guns of Navarone, The
Battle of Britain, The
Longest Day, The
Where Eagles Dare
633 Squadron
Dam Busters, The
Great Escape, The
Green Berets, The
Is Paris Burning?
Reach for the Sky

Music for Pleasure MFP-5171 (Britain)

GOLDEN AGE OF BRITISH FILM MUSIC, THE

Vice Versa
History of Mr. Polly, The
Eureka Stockade
Floodtide
Adam and Evelyne
Christopher Columbus
Tight Little Island (Whiskey Galore)
Rocking Horse Winner, The
Bitter Springs
They Were Not Divided
So Long at the Fair
Man in the White Suit, The
Pool of London
Promoter, The (Card, The)
Titfield Thunderbolt, The
Little Kidnappers, The
Up to His Neck
Touch and Go
Tale of Two Cities (1958)
Thirty-nine Steps, The (1959)

Citadel CT-OFI-1 (private)

GRANDI TEMI DA FILM DI ENNIO MORRICONE, I (Ennio Morricone and His Orchestra)

Once Upon a Time in the West
For a Few Dollars More
Fistful of Dollars, A
Menage all'Italiana
Battle of Algiers, The
Pugni in Tasca, I
Gott Mit Uns
Metello
Svegliati e Uccidi
Giardino delle Delizie

Ad Ogni Costo
Violent City

RCA Italiana PSL-10486

GRANDI WESTERNS ITALIANI, I (Ennio Morricone)
Fistful of Dollars, A
For a Few Dollars More
Good, the Bad and the Ugly, The
Once Upon a Time in the West
Giu la Testa
My Name Is Nobody
Tepepa
Pistol for Ringo, A
Vita e Voltere'Molto Dura, La
Vera Provvidenza?
Pistole Non Discutono
Return of Ringo, The

RCA TPL2-1077 (Italy)

GRANDS THEMES DU CINEMA FANTASTIQUE ET DE SCIENCE FICTION, LES (Dick Jacobs and His Orchestra)
Son of Dracula
Incredible Shrinking Man, The
This Island Earth
Mole People, The
House of Frankenstein, The
Horror of Dracula
Creature from the Black Lagoon, The
It Came from Outer Space
Creature Walks Among Us, The
Deadly Mantis, The
Tarantula
Revenge of the Creature

Coral CRL-757240
MCA 410.064 (France)
Varese Sarabande VC-81077

GREAT CLASSIC HITS FROM THE FILMS
Clockwork Orange, A
Sunday, Bloody Sunday
Elvira Madigan
Great Waltz, The
Zardoz
Sting, The
Red Shoes, The
Brief Encounter
Dangerous Moonlight

CBS/Harmony 30052 (Britain)

GREAT FANTASY FILM MUSIC (Various composers and orchestras)
Circus of Horrors
Daughters of Darkness
Dunwich Horror, The
Dead Ringer
Convulsions
Children of the Damned
Chosen, The
Kingdom of the Spiders
Message from Space, A
Sinbad and the Eye of the Tiger
Solaris
Seven Faces of Dr. Lao, The
Snow Devils
Scars of Dracula, The
Son of Blob
Varan, the Unbelievable
Witches, The

POO LP-106 (private)

GREAT LOVE THEMES FROM MOTION PICTURES (Max Steiner and His Orchestra)
Bird of Paradise
Bill of Divorcement, A
Little Women
Star Is Born, A
Life of Emile Zola, The
Dark Victory
Saratoga Trunk
Adventures of Don Juan, The
Johnny Belinda
Helen of Troy
McConnell Story, The
Last Command, The

RCA LPM-1170

GREAT MOTION PICTURE THEMES FROM JEAN HARLOW FILMS
Saratoga
China Seas
Dinner at Eight
Girl from Missouri, The
Reckless
Personal Property
Hold Your Man
Suzy

World Artists WAS-3007

GREAT MOVIE SOUNDS OF JOHN BARRY, THE
Thunderball
From Russia with Love

Goldfinger
Dr. No
King Rat
Chase, The
Knack, The
Seance on a Wet Afternoon
Ipcress File, The
Born Free

Columbia CL-2493/CS-9293

GREAT MOVIE THEMES (The Norman Luboff Choir)
Moulin Rouge
Ruby Gentry
Affair to Remember, An
Green Dolphin Street
Days of Wine and Roses
David and Lisa
Uninvited, The
Lili
Streetcar Named Desire, A
Unchained
My Foolish Heart

RCA LSP-2895

GREAT MOVIE THEMES COMPOSED BY MIKLOS ROZSA
Sodom and Gomorrah
Spellbound
King of Kings
Lydia
Quo Vadis
Ben-Hur
Madame Bovary
Diane
Cid, El

MGM (S)E-4112

GREAT MOVIE THEMES IN HI-FI (Cyril Templeton and His Orchestra)
Love Is a Many-Splendored Thing
Limelight
Three Coins in the Fountain
Street Scene
Laura
Love in the Afternoon
High Noon
Affair to Remember, An
Lili
Around the World in 80 Days

Master (Columbia) XTV-65002

GREAT SCIENCE FICTION FILM MUSIC
Jack the Giant Killer
Kiss of the Vampire
Godzilla
Theater of Blood
Danger: Diabolik
Return of Dracula
Omega Man, The
Time Machine, The
Green Slime, The
First Men in the Moon, The
Blob, The
Damnation Alley
Mysterians, The
Dracula Has Risen from the Grave
War of the Worlds
Kronos
I Bury the Living
Mothra
Incredible Shrinking Man, The

Poo LP-104 (private)

GREAT SONGS FROM ITALIAN FILMS (Gian Stellaru and His Orchestra)
Anna
Girl from San Frediano, The
Uomini Che Mascalzoni, Gli
Nights of Cabiria
Farewell to Youth
Open City
Impossible Family, An
Strada, La
Anna of Brooklyn
Seven Hills of Rome
Souvenir of Italy

Epic LN-3593

GREAT WESTERN THEMES
Return of the Seven
Big Country, The
Scalphunters, The
One-Eyed Jacks
High Noon
Duel at Diablo
Way West, The
Wonderful Country
Hour of the Gun
Unforgiven, The
Alamo, The
McLintock!
Good, the Bad and the Ugly, The

How the West Was Won
Big Gundown, The
Hang 'Em High
Young Billy Young
Fistful of Dollars, A
For a Few Dollars More
Misfits, The
True Grit
Navajo Joe
High Chaparral (TV)

United Artists UA-LA082-F2

GREEK FILM MUSIC (Stavros Xarchakos. Music from five unlisted Greek films composed by Xarchakos)

Columbia SX-6135 (Greece)

HENRY MANCINI CONDUCTS THE LONDON SYMPHONY ORCHESTRA IN A CONCERT OF FILM MUSIC
Romeo and Juliet
Boccaccio '70
Strada, La
Amarcord
Godfather, The
White Dawn, The (TV)
Earthquake
Towering Inferno, The
Jaws
Thomas Crown Affair, The
Man and a Woman, A
Love Story
Summer of '42
Great Waldo Pepper, The

RCA APL1-1379

HI-FI MUSIC FROM HOLLYWOOD (Paul Weston)
Gone with the Wind
Love Letters
Indiscretion of an American Wife
Duel in the Sun
Song of Bernadette, The
Quo Vadis?
Since You Went Away
Ruby Gentry
Streetcar Named Desire, A
Portrait of Jennie, A
For Whom the Bell Tolls

Columbia CL-612

HISTORY OF MGM MOVIE MUSIC, THE (Vol. I)
Gone with the Wind
How the West Was Won
Ben-Hur
Mutiny on the Bounty
Raintree County
plus songs from MGM film musicals

MGM 2-SES-15-ST

HIT THEMES FROM FOREIGN FILMS
Dolce Vita, La
Strada, La
Ronde, La
Romance d'Amour
Black Orpheus
Never on Sunday
Saturday Night and Sunday Morning
Bonjour Tristesse
Anna
Rocco and His Brothers
Tunes of Glory
Rising of the Moon, The

London SP-44020

HOLLYWOOD BYRD (Charlie Byrd with Orchestra and Chorus)
American Dream, An
Georgy Girl
Alfie
Hawaii
This Property Is Condemned
Born Free
What Did You Do in the War, Daddy?
Any Wednesday
Moment to Moment
Spinout

Columbia CS-9452

HOLLYWOOD MAESTRO--ALFRED NEWMAN
Royal Scandal, A
How Green Was My Valley
Song of Bernadette, The
Razor's Edge, The
Pinky
Letter to Three Wives, A
All About Eve

Citadel CT-6003

HOLLYWOOD RHAPSODIES (Victor Young and His Singing Strings)
Robe, The

So Big
Gog
Jubilee Trail
Moonlighter, The
Glenn Miller Story, The
Belle Le Grande
Cynthia
Geraldine
Lost Moment, The
Perilous Journey

Decca DL-8060

HOLLYWOOD STRINGS DOUBLE FEATURE FILM HIT SPECTACULAR, THE
Dangerous Moonlight
Spellbound
Hawaii
Is Paris Burning?
Bible, The
Greatest Story Ever Told, The
Ten Commandments, The
King of Kings
plus Hollywood film musical themes

Galaxy 2DP723

I LOVE MOVIES (Michel Legrand and His Orchestra)
Blue Angel, The
Under the Roofs of Paris
Visiteurs du Soir, Les
Third Man, The
High Noon
Orgueilleux, Les
River of No Return
Porte des Lilas
plus popular film musical songs

Columbia CL-1178

IMMORTAL FILM MUSIC (Russ Case and His Orchestra)
Slaughter on Tenth Avenue
While I Live
Tale of Two Cities
Spellbound
and other music

Rondo-lette SA-160

INSPIRED THEMES FROM THE INSPIRED FILMS (The Fantastic Strings of Felix Slatkin)
Samson and Delilah
Cid, El

Man Called Peter, A
Francis of Assisi
Prodigal, The
King of Kings
Ten Commandments, The
Song of Bernadette
Ben-Hur
David and Bathsheba
Quo Vadis?
Robe, The

Liberty LSS-14019

INTERNATIONAL FILM FESTIVAL (Werner Mueller and His Orchestra)
Sundays and Cybele
Last Year at Marienbad
Black Orpheus
Saturday Night and Sunday Morning
Fellini's 8-1/2
Room at the Top
Shoot the Piano Player
Dolce Vita, La
Jules and Jim
Ballad of a Soldier
Strada, La
Loneliness of the Long Distance Runner

Warners W-1548

ITALIAN THEMES
Col Cuore in Gola
7 Fratelli Cervi, I
Giorno della Civetta, Il

CAM MAG 10.013 (Italy)

JAZZ FROM THE MOVIES
I Wake Up Screaming
Criminal, The
Nightmare
Captain from Castile
Wild One, The
Room 43
Big Operator, The
West Side Story

Cinema LP-8002 (private)

JAZZ GOES TO THE MOVIES (Manny Albam and His Orchestra)
Exodus
High Noon
Paris Blues

Dolce Vita, La
Majority of One, A
Alamo, The
Guns of Navarone
Cid, El
Fallen Angel

Impulse A-19

JOHN BARRY CONDUCTS HIS GREATEST MOVIE HITS
You Only Live Twice
Born Free
Goldfinger
Whisperers, The
From Russia with Love
Wednesday's Child
Thunderball
Dutchman
Wrong Box, The

Columbia CL-2708/CS-9508

JOHN BARRY REVISITED
Zulu
From Russia with Love
Four in the Morning
Elizabeth Taylor in London

Ember SE-8008 (Britain)

"KING OF KINGS" AND ELEVEN OTHER GREAT MOVIE THEMES
(Clebanoff and His Orchestra)
King of Kings
Parrish
Ben-Hur
By Love Possessed
Spartacus
Back Street
West Side Story
Tender Is the Night
Apartment, The
Alamo, The
Where the Hot Wind Blows
Unforgiven, The

Mercury MG-20640

LA DOLCE VITA AND OTHER CELEBRATED FILMS BY FELLINI
(Nino Rota, with orchestra directed by Carlo Savina)
Dolce Vita, La
Strada, La
White Sheik, The
Vitelloni, I

Bidone, Il
Nights of Cabiria
Juliet of the Spirits
Boccaccio '70

RCA NL-33204 (Italy)

LEROY HOLMES: ONCE UPON A TIME IN THE WEST
Days of Anger
Hang 'Em High
100 Rifles
Mackenna's Gold
Stranger Returns, A
Stalking Moon, The
Big Gundown, The
Man from Nowhere, The
Once Upon a Time in the West
True Grit
Bandolero
Heaven with a Gun

United Artists UAS-6710

LOST HORIZON: THE CLASSIC FILM SCORES OF DIMITRI TIOMKIN (Charles Gerhardt conducting the National Philharmonic Orchestra)
Lost Horizon
Friendly Persuasion
Big Sky, The
Fourposter, The
Search for Paradise
Guns of Navarone, The

RCA ARL1-1669

LOVE MUSIC FROM HOLLYWOOD (Paul Weston)
My Foolish Heart
Laura
Ramona (1927)
Samson and Delilah
Spellbound
Odd Man Out
King's Row
Seventh Heaven
Now Voyager
Wuthering Heights
Dark Victory
Lost Horizon

Columbia CL-794

LOVE STORY (The Philadelphia Orchestra conducted by Eugene Ormandy)

Love Story
Elvira Madigan
Thomas Crown Affair, The
Romeo and Juliet
Heart Is a Lonely Hunter, The

RCA LSC-3210

LOVE THEME FROM CLEOPATRA AND MUSIC FROM OTHER GREAT MOTION PICTURES STARRING ELIZABETH TAYLOR (David Rose and His Orchestra)
Cleopatra
VIP's, The
Cat on a Hot Tin Roof
Butterfield 8
Giant
Father of the Bride
Girl Who Had Everything, The
Raintree County
Julia Misbehaves
Little Women

MGM E-4144

LUSH THEMES FROM MOTION PICTURES (Leroy Holmes and His Orchestra)
High and the Mighty, The
Bullet Is Waiting, A
Land of the Pharaohs
Strategic Air Command
Rear Window
Tight Spot
Gone with the Wind
Bridges at Toko-Ri, The
Prodigal, The
Unchained
President's Lady, The
Spellbound

MGM E-3172

M-G-M PARADE OF HITS
Dr. Kildare
Lolita
King of Kings
Walk on the Wild Side, A
Cid, El
Four Horsemen of the Apocalypse
plus popular movie songs

MGM SE-4078

MGM YEARS, THE
Gone with the Wind
Invitation
Ben-Hur
Four Horsemen of the Apocalypse, The
Mutiny on the Bounty
Prize, The
How the West Was Won
Cincinnati Kid, The
Doctor Zhivago
plus songs from MGM film musicals

MGM P4S-5662

MAGIC OF MAX STEINER, THE
Garden of Allah, The
Tovarich
Gold Is Where You Find It
They Died with Their Boots On
Saratoga Trunk
Deep Valley
Young Man with a Horn
Rocky Mountain
Woman in White, The

Citadel CT-MS-6 (private)

MAGICAL MUSIC OF WALT DISNEY, THE. 50 YEARS OF MOTION PICTURE SOUND TRACKS
STEAMBOAT WILLIE through
PETE'S DRAGON and the
MICKEY MOUSE CLUB

Ovation 5000

MAGNIFICENT MOVIE MUSIC
Knack, The
Greatest Story Ever Told, The
Zorba the Greek
Thunderball
Hallelujah Trail
How to Murder Your Wife
Train, The
Rage to Live, A
Help!
Sound of Music, The
Marriage, French Style
What's New, Pussycat?
I'll Take Sweden
Glory Guys, The
Return from the Ashes

United Artists 3476/6476

MAIN TITLE
Man with the Golden Arm, The
Catered Affair, The
Congo Crossing
Seven Wonders of the World, The
East of Eden
Proud Ones, The
Picnic
Away All Boats
Proud and the Profane, The
20,000 Leagues Under the Sea
While the City Sleeps
Nightfall

Coral CRL-57065

MARCHES FROM THE MOVIES (Band of the Grenadier Guards)
Dr. Strangelove
Longest Day, The
Ben-Hur
Inn of the Sixth Happiness
Music Man, The
Babes in Toyland
Victors, The
Captain from Castile, The
Guns of Navarone
How the West Was Won
Bridge on the River Kwai, The
King and I, The
Guns at Batasi

London PS-434

MAX STEINER CONDUCTS HIS ACADEMY AWARD WINNING GREAT FILM MUSIC
Since You Went Away
Now Voyager
Informer, The
(plus) Streetcar Named Desire, A (Alex North)

Angel S-36068

MAX STEINER--MUSIC FOR WESTERNS
Virginia City
Lion and the Horse, The
San Antonio
Jim Thorpe, All-American
Raton Pass
Distant Trumpet, A
Charge at Feather River, The
Violent Men, The
Dallas
Oklahoma Kid, The

Silver River

Max Steiner Music Society TT-MS-9/10

MAX STEINER REVISITED
Lady Takes a Sailor, The
So Big
Ice Palace
Spencer's Mountain
City for Conquest
Operation Pacific
Life of Emile Zola, The

Citadel CT-MS-7 (private)

MAX STEINER: THE RKO YEARS (1932-1935)
Symphony for Six Million
Bird of Paradise, The
King Kong
Morning Glory
Lost Patrol, The
Of Human Bondage
Little Minister, The
Three Musketeers, The

Citadel CT-MS-1 (private)

MAX STEINER: THE WARNER YEARS
Dive Bomber
Santa Fe Trail
One Foot in Heaven
Adventures of Mark Twain, The
Glass Menagerie, The
Flame and the Arrow, The

Citadel CT-MS-2 (private)

"MEDICAL CENTER" AND OTHER GREAT THEMES (Lalo Schifrin, conductor)
Medical Center (TV)
Kelly's Heroes
Liquidator, The
Once a Thief
Haunting, The
Sol Madrid
Cincinnati Kid, The
Venetian Affair, The

MGM SE-4742

MEL BROOKS' GREATEST HITS, FEATURING THE FABULOUS FILM SCORES OF JOHN MORRIS
High Anxiety

Producers, The
12 Chairs, The
Blazing Saddles
Young Frankenstein
Silent Movie

Asylum 5E-501

MIKLOS ROZSA CONDUCTING THE ROYAL PHILHARMONIC ORCHESTRA
Knight Without Armor
Bad and the Beautiful, The (Tribute to a Bad Man)
Asphalt Jungle, The
Moonfleet
Double Indemnity
Lust for Life
Men of the Fighting Lady

Polydor 2383-384 (Britain)

MIKLOS ROZSA CONDUCTS HIS GREAT FILM MUSIC (Miklos Rozsa conducting the Royal Philharmonic Orchestra)
Thief of Bagdad, The
Double Life, A
Lost Weekend, The
Time to Love and a Time to Die, A
Naked City
Knights of the Roundtable
Diane
Story of Three Loves, The
Young Bess

Polydor 2383-327 (Britain)

MIKLOS ROZSA CONDUCTS HIS GREAT THEMES
Ben-Hur
Cid, El
Quo Vadis
King of Kings

Capitol ST-2837

MORE GREAT MOTION PICTURE THEMES
Goodbye Again
Gone with the Wind
Elmer Gantry
One-Eyed Jacks
Houseboat
Naked Maja, The
Some Like It Hot
Porgy and Bess
Paris Blues
Never on Sunday

Moulin Rouge
Misfits, The
Bonanza (TV)
God's Little Acre
Odds Against Tomorrow

United Artists UAL-3158

MORE LUSH THEMES FROM MOTION PICTURES (Leroy Holmes and His Orchestra)
War and Peace
Place in the Sun, A
Friendly Persuasion
Helen of Troy
Limelight
Lola Montes
Living Idol, The
Duel in the Sun
These Wilder Years
Last Wagon, The
Proud Ones, The
Baby Doll

MGM E-3480

MORE SOUNDS OF HOLLYWOOD (Emmanuel Vardi and His Orchestra)
Lisa
Parent Trap, The
West Side Story
Majority of One
Dolce Vita, La
King of Kings
Wonderful World of the Brothers Grimm, The
Ballad of a Soldier
Rome Adventure
Return to Peyton Place
Butterfield 8
Cid, El

Kapp KL-1289

MOTION PICTURE MUSIC (Alfred Newman and the Hollywood Symphony)
American in Paris, An
Wuthering Heights
All About Eve
Pinky
Razor's Edge, The
Song of Bernadette
Letter to Three Wives, A

Mercury MG-20037

MOVIE AND TV THEMES, COMPOSED AND CONDUCTED BY ELMER BERNSTEIN

Rat Race, The
Take Five (TV)
Sudden Fear
Anna Lucasta
Saints and Sinners (TV)
Sweet Smell of Success
Man with the Golden Arm

Choreo A(S)-11

MOVIE MOODS (George Cates, conductor)

Picnic
Friendly Persuasion
Man on Fire
This Could Be the Night
Anastasia
Man Who Knew Too Much, The
Strange One, The
Barretts of Wimpole Street, The
Boy on a Dolphin
To Catch a Thief
Giant
Rebel Without a Cause

Coral CRL-57125

MOVIE THEMES (John Carlton and the Craftsmen All-Stars)

Around the World in 80 Days
Third Man, The
Bells of St. Marys, The
Merry Widow, The
Spellbound
Man with the Golden Arm
Quiet Man, The
Young at Heart
Gigi
South Pacific

Craftsmen C-8002

MOVIE THEMES FROM HOLLYWOOD (Dimitri Tiomkin and His Orchestra)

High and the Mighty, The
Champion, The
Bullet Is Waiting, A
Strange Lady in Town
Dial "M" for Murder
Return to Paradise
High Noon
Land of the Pharaohs
Adventures of Hajii Baba

Duel in the Sun
I Confess
Lost Horizon

Coral CRL-57006

MOVIES 'N' ME (John Dankworth)
Modesty Blaise
Darling
Morgan!
Return from the Ashes
Servant, The
Look Stranger (TV)
Bird's Eye View (TV)

RCA LPL1-5092

MUSIC BY ERICH WOLFGANG KORNGOLD (Conducted by Lionel Newman)
Kings Row
Anthony Adverse
Private Lives of Elizabeth and Essex, The
Sea Hawk, The
Prince and the Pauper, The
Constant Nymph, The
Adventures of Robin Hood, The

Warners WS-1436

MUSIC FOR FILMS (Charles Williams and Sidney Torch conducting the Queen's Hall Light Orchestra)
Stairway to Heaven
Spellbound
Loves of Joanna Godden
Wanted for Murder
This Man Is Mine
Idol of Paris, The
That Dangerous Age
Nicholas Nickleby

Columbia Entre RL-3029

MUSIC FOR FRANKENSTEIN, DRACULA, THE MUMMY, THE WOLF MAN AND OTHER OLD FRIENDS (Hans J. Salter/John Cacavas)
Horror Rhapsody (Medley of themes from the album title)
Horror Express

Citadel CT-6026

MUSIC FOR SILENT FILM CLASSICS: D. W. GRIFFITH (Composed and performed by organist Lee Erwin on the Fox-Capitol Theatre Wurlitzer Pipe Organ)

America
Birth of a Nation, The
Intolerance

Angel S-36092

MUSIC FROM GREAT FILM CLASSICS (Bernard Herrmann conducting the London Philharmonic Orchestra)
Snows of Kilimanjaro
Citizen Kane
Devil and Daniel Webster, The
Jane Eyre

London SP-44144

MUSIC FROM GREAT FRENCH MOTION PICTURES (Frank Pourcel and His Orchestra)
Carnet du Bal, Un
Under the Roofs of Paris
My Uncle
Rififi
Eau Vive, L'
Stowaway in the Sky (Voyage en Ballon, Le)
Forbidden Games (Jeux Interidits)
Devil in the Flesh (Diable au Corps, Le)
And God Created Woman
7 Capital Sins, The
Black Orpheus

Capitol SP-8603

MUSIC FROM GREAT ITALIAN MOTION PICTURES (Pino Calvi and His Orchestra)
Four Days of Naples, The
Strada, La
Dolce Vita, La
Leopard, The
Basilisks, The
Street of Dreams, The
Divorce, Italian Style
Anna
8-1/2
Crimen

Capitol P-8608

MUSIC FROM GREAT SHAKESPEAREAN FILMS (Bernard Herrmann conducting the National Philharmonic Orchestra)
Hamlet (Russia)
Richard III
Julius Caesar

London SPC-21132

MUSIC FROM HOLLYWOOD. THEMES FROM GREAT MOTION PICTURES (Al Goodman and His Orchestra)
Snows of Kilimanjaro, The
High Noon
Ivanhoe
David and Bathsheba
Fourposter, The
Moulin Rouge
Happy Time, The
Place in the Sun, A
Shane
Quo Vadis?

RCA LPM-1007

MUSIC FROM MOTION PICTURES (David Rose and His Orchestra)
Love Is a Many-Splendored Thing
Giant
Summertime
Julie
Catered Affair, The
Strada, La
Glass Slipper, The
Friendly Persuasion
Swan, The
Public Pigeon No. 1
Serenade
Forbidden Planet

MGM E-3397

MUSIC FROM THE FILMS (Cleveland Pops Orchestra conducted by Louis Lane)
Fanny
Gigi
State Fair
Exodus
Bridge on the River Kwai, The
Henry V
Louisiana Story

Epic BC-1147

MUSIC FROM THE FILMS (London Variety Theatre Orchestra conducted by Gilbert Vinter)
Dangerous Moonlight (Suicide Squadron)
Tale of Two Cities
Night Has Eyes, The
While I Live (Dream of Olwyn)
Story of Three Loves, The
Love Story
Legend of the Glass Mountain, The
Spellbound

Slaughter on Tenth Avenue

Saga XID-5018 (Britain)

MUSIC FROM THE FILMS (Mantovani and His Orchestra)
Dangerous Moonlight (Suicide Squadron)
Legend of the Glass Mountain, The
Love Story
Story of Three Loves, The
While I Live (Dream of Olwyn)

London PS-112

MUSIC FROM THE FILMS (Michel Legrand and His Orchestra)
Strada, La
Lost Continent
Lovers and Lollipops
French Can-Can
Lola Montes
Gervaise
Friendly Persuasion
Empire of the Sun
Holiday for Henrietta
Touchez Pas au Grisbi
Modern Times

Columbia WL-107

MUSIC FROM THE FILMS (Vol. 1) ACADEMY AWARD WINNING SONGS (Hollywood Sound Stage Orchestra)
Love Is a Many-Splendored Thing
High and the Mighty, The
Gone with the Wind
Around the World in 80 Days
plus popular movie songs

Stardust SDS-107

MUSIC FROM THE FILMS OF JAMES DEAN (Leonard Rosenman)
Rebel Without a Cause
East of Eden
Giant

Sunset SLS-50420

MUSIC FROM "THE GOOD, THE BAD AND THE UGLY," "A FISTFUL OF DOLLARS" AND "FOR A FEW DOLLARS MORE"

RCA LSP-3927

MUSIC FROM THE GREAT MOVIE THRILLERS (Bernard Herrmann conducting the London Philharmonic Orchestra)
Psycho

Marnie
North by Northwest
Vertigo
Trouble with Harry, The

London SP-44126

MUSIC FROM THE MOTION PICTURE "THE BIBLE" (The Metropolitan Pops Orchestra conducted by Henry Rene)
Bible, The
Ten Commandments, The
Greatest Story Ever Told, The
King of Kings
Ben-Hur

MGM SE-4417

MUSIC FROM THE ORIGINAL SOUND TRACKS OF "A FISTFUL OF DOLLARS" AND "FOR A FEW DOLLARS MORE"

RCA Camden CDS-1052 (Britain)
RCA Victor SHP-5562 (Japan)

MUSIC FROM THE SOUND TRACK OF THE MOTION PICTURE "OF HUMAN BONDAGE" AND OTHER GREAT SELECTIONS
Of Human Bondage
Love Is a Many-Splendored Thing
Bad and the Beautiful, The
Cat on a Hot Tin Roof
Butterfield 8
plus popular movie songs

MGM SE-4261

MUSIC OF GREAT WOMEN OF FILM (Clebanoff Strings and Symphonic Orchestra)
Gone with the Wind
Spellbound
Indiscretion of an American Wife
Captain from Castile
Laura
Ruby Gentry
Blithe Spirit
Samson and Delilah

Mercury SRW-16399

MUTINY ON THE BOUNTY: THEMES FROM THE MGM MOVIE (Nicholas Andriano, conductor)
Mutiny on the Bounty
Cid, El
Cimarron

King of Kings

Diplomat DS-2276

MYSTERIOUS FILM WORLD OF BERNARD HERRMANN (Bernard Herrmann conducting the National Philharmonic Orchestra)
Jason and the Argonauts
Mysterious Island
Three Worlds of Gulliver, The

London SPC-21137 (Britain)

NHK (JAPAN) TELEVISION DRAMA THEME MUSIC
God of Flower, The (Hanagami)
Wind, Cloud and Rainbow
Story of Peaceful Genroku Era, The
Katsu Kaishu
Story of the Age of Wars, The
Story of Taira Family, The
Slope in Spring, The
Fir Is Left, A
Heavens and the Earth, The
Ruma Is Going
Three Sisters
Minatomo Yoshitsune
Story of Taikoh, The
First Star, The
In the Fire Land
Carpet on the Cloud, The
Good Morning
Time of Blue, The
Hatoko's Sea
Family of North Country, The
More Blue Than Blue Color
Mayuko, The Only One
Rainbow, The
Nobuko and Her Grandmother
Absolutely Tomorrow
Journey, A
Ohanahan

Crown GW-7089M (Japan)

1961 THEMES (Cambridge Strings)
Tunes of Glory
Pepe
World of Suzie Wong, The
Midnight Lace
Where the Boys Are
Murder Inc.
French Mistress, A
Singer, Not the Song, The

Key Witness

London LL-3238

NINO ROTA MUSICHE DA FILM
Neapolitan Millionaire, The
Legend of the Glass Mountain, The
Dolce Vita, La
Sunset Sunrise
White Nights
War and Peace
Romeo and Juliet
Leopard, The
Rocco and His Brothers
Taming of the Shrew, The
Purple Noon
Godfather, The

CAM SAG-9054 (Italy)

NINO ROTA PLAYS THE MUSIC OF THE FILMS OF FEDERICO FELLINI
Boccaccio 70
Dolce Vita, La
Juliet of the Spirits
Spirits of the Dead (Toby Dammit)
Clowns, The
Satyricon
Roma
Amarcord
8-1/2

Polydor 2393-084 (France)

NORTH OF HOLLYWOOD (Alex North, conductor)
Streetcar Named Desire, A
Wall Street Ballet (short)
Hot Spell
American Road (short)
Unchained
Racers, The
Rose Tattoo, The
Member of the Wedding

RCA LSP-1445

NOW VOYAGER: THE CLASSIC FILM MUSIC OF MAX STEINER (Charles Gerhardt conducts the National Philharmonic Orchestra)
Now Voyager
Big Sleep, The
Charge of the Light Brigade, The
Since You Went Away

Four Wives
Fountainhead, The
Johnny Belinda
Informer, The
Saratoga Trunk

RCA ARL1-0136

O CANGACIERO--ORIGINALMELODIE AUS DEM FILM "DIE GESETZLOSEN" UND ANDERE GROTSE FILM-THEMEN
O Cangaciero
For a Few Dollars More
Sacco and Vanzetti
Fistful of Dollars, A
Rosemary's Baby
Good, the Bad and the Ugly, The
In the Heat of the Night
Hang 'Em High
Valley of the Dolls
Delitto di Regime
Flying Through the Air

RCA PJL-8035 (Germany)

ORIGINAL MOTION PICTURE HIT THEMES
Breakfast at Tiffany's
Town Without Pity
West Side Story
Guns of Navarone
King of Kings
Fanny
Paris Blues
One, Two, Three
Happy Thieves, The
Judgement at Nuremberg
Cid, El
Pocketful of Miracles

United Artists UAL-3197/UAS-6197

ORIGINAL MOTION PICTURE SOUND TRACKS
Rain People, The
Great Bank Robbery, The
Damned, The
Learning Tree, The
Wild Bunch, The
Madwoman of Chaillot, The

Warners PRO-329

ORIGINAL MOTION PICTURE SOUND TRACKS AND OTHER GREAT THEMES (Manhattan Pops Orchestra conducted by Elias Breeskin)

Sandpiper, The
Shop on Main Street, The
Blue Max, The
Harper
Can-Can
Doctor Zhivago
Cleopatra
Chaplin's Art of Comedy
Patch of Blue, A
plus popular movie songs

Time S-316

ORIGINAL MUSIC FROM THE FILMS OF FRANCOIS TRUFFAUT
Green Room, The
Story of Adele H., The
Argent de Poche, L'
Man Who Loved Women, The

EMI/Pathe 2CO66-14567

ORIGINAL SOUND TRACKS AND HIT MUSIC FROM GREAT MOTION PICTURE THEMES
Exodus
Never on Sunday
Magnificent Seven, The
Alamo, The
City Lights
Big Country, The
I Want to Live
Unforgiven, The
Apartment, The
On the Beach
Horse Soldiers, The
Vikings, The
Wonderful Country, The
Some Like It Hot
Solomon and Sheba
God's Little Acre

United Artists UAL-3122/UAS-6122

ORIGINAL SOUND TRACKS AND RECORDINGS OF ORIGINAL MUSIC FROM GREAT MOVIES
Mutiny on the Bounty
Ben-Hur
Cleopatra
Quo Vadis
Butterfield 8
VIPs, The
Robe, The
Farewell to Arms, A
Cid, El

King of Kings
Madame Bovary
Lili
How the West Was Won
Cimarron
Love Is a Many-Splendored Thing

MGM 2E-10

ORIGINAL SOUND TRACK MUSIC FROM THE FILMS OF JACQUES TATI
Playtime
My Uncle (Mon Oncle)
Big Day (Jour de Fete/Day Off)
Night Class (Cours du Soir)
Mr. Hulot's Holiday

United Artists International UNS-1555

PEPE LE MOKO ET JEAN GABIN
Pepe le Moko (with dialog in French)
Melodie en Sous-Sol
Belle Equipe, La
French Can-Can
Touchez pas au Grisbi
Gens sans Importance, Des
Deux Hommes dans la Ville
Sicilian Clan, The

Canyon ST-2627 (Japan)

PERSUADER, THE (John Barry)
Persuader, The
Midnight Cowboy
Goldfinger
Vendetta
From Russia with Love
On Her Majesty's Secret Service
Thunderball
Chase, The
Dr. No

CBS 64816 (Britain)

PLAY IT AGAIN, JOHN BARRY
Dove, The
Walkabout
Tamarind Seed, The
Billy (TV)
Monte Walsh
Lolita, My Love (musical play)
Orson Welles' Great Mysteries (TV)
Love Among the Ruins (TV)

On Her Majesty's Secret Service
Mary, Queen of Scots
Boom!
Glass Menagerie, The (TV)

Polydor 2383-400 (Britain)

PLUS BELLES MUSIQUES DE FRANCOIS DE ROUBAÎX, LES (Vol. 3)
Death of the Guide
Charo
Nervous Breakdown
Luna Parking
and others

Barclay 900. 577 (France)

PLUS BELLES MUSIQUES DE FILMS DE GEORGES DELERUE (Vol. 1)
Police Python 357
Jamais Plus Toujours
Compte A Rebours
Insoumis, L'
Grand Escogriffe, Le
Gifle, La

Barclay 900. 507 (France)

PLUS BELLES MUSIQUES DE FILMS DE GEORGES DELERUE, LES (Vol. 2)
Important c'est d'Aimer, L'
Mona
Monsieur de Compagnie, Un
Deux Anglaises et le Continent, Les
Peau Douce, La
Quelque Part, Quelqu'un
Heureux qui Comme Ulysse
Mepris, Le

Barclay 900. 508 (France)

PLUS BELLES MUSIQUES DE FILMS DE MICHEL MAGNE, LES (Vol. 1)
Repos du Guerrier, Le
Vice and Virtue
Melodie en Sous-Sol
Gentleman of Cocody, The
OSS 117 se Dechaine
Journal d'une Femme en Blanc, Le
Furia a Bahia
Compartiments Tueurs

Barclay 900. 509 (France)

PLUS BELLES MUSIQUES DE FILMS DE MICHEL MAGNE, LES (Vol. 2)
Fantomas se Dechaine
Brigade Anti-Gangster
Tout Coeur a Tokio, A
Coeur Joie, A
Tout le Monde il est Beau, Tout le Monde il est Gentil
If Don Juan Were a Woman
Moi y'en a Vouloir des Sous
Chinois a Paris, Les

Barclay 900. 510 (France)

PREMIERE RADIO PERFORMANCES
Double Life, A
Time Out of Mind
Bandit of Sherwood Forest
Force of Evil

Premiere PR-1201 (private)

PRIZE, THE, PLUS MUSIC FROM OTHER MOTION PICTURES
Prize, The
Caretakers, The
VIP's, The
Lord of the Flies
David and Lisa
Wonderful World of the Brothers Grimm
To Kill a Mockingbird
Twilight of Honor

MGM SE-4192

READER'S DIGEST
Love Is a Many-Splendored Thing
Laura
Road House
Three Coins in the Fountain
Zorba the Greek
Mondo Cane
Third Man, The
Never on Sunday
Ronde, La
Jules and Jim
Dolce Vita, La
Now Voyager
Casablanca
To Have and Have Not
Saratoga Trunk
Kings Row
Glenn Miller Story, The
Sandpiper, The
Sayonara

Woman Commands, A
Cleopatra
Jezebel
Magnificent Seven, The
Alamo, The
Big Country, The
East of Eden
Shane
Way to the Gold, The
My Foolish Heart
Lili
Picnic
Carpetbaggers, The
Till the End of Time
Moulin Rouge
Around the World in 80 Days
Charade
Lawrence of Arabia
Exodus
Gone with the Wind
Cid, El
Lady from Shanghai, The

Reader's Digest RD4-39-1

READER'S DIGEST
Days of Wine and Roses
Casino Royale
Papa's Delicate Condition
Prime of Miss Jean Brodie, The
Sterile Cuckoo, The
Doctor Zhivago
Happy Ending, The
Pink Panther, The
How to Succeed in Business Without Really Trying
Z
Dr. Dolittle
How to Marry a Millionaire
Love Story
Butch Cassidy and the Sundance Kid
Funny Girl
Yellow Rolls Royce, The
High Society
Great Race, The
Uninvited, The
Joanna
Oliver!
Toys in the Attic
Alfie
Cactus Flower
Easy Rider
Midnight Cowboy
Bonnie and Clyde

Goodbye, Columbus
Thomas Crown Affair, The
Airport
Graduate, The
Hush ... Hush, Sweet Charlotte
Brotherhood, The
Reivers, The
Born Free
Romeo and Juliet
Valley of the Dolls
Women in Love
Madwoman of Chaillot, The
Elvira Madigan
That Lady in Ermine
Americanization of Emily, The
Bells Are Ringing
For Whom the Bell Tolls
Big Sleep, The
Breakfast at Tiffany's
Hatari
Darling Lili
True Grit
Norwood
Cat Ballou
Hombre
Once Upon a Time in the West
How the West Was Won
Adventures of Robin Hood, The
Spellbound
Jane Eyre
Private Lives of Elizabeth and Essex, The
2001: A Space Odyssey
Rashomon
Of Human Bondage
Specter of the Rose
Julie

Reader's Digest RD4-141

READY WHEN YOU ARE, J. B. (John Barry)
Midnight Cowboy
On Her Majesty's Secret Service
Deadfall
Lion in Winter, The
Appointment, The
Born Free

Columbia CS-1003

ROBIN AND MARIAN/AUDREY HEPBURN
Robin and Marian
Wait Until Dark

Two for the Road
How to Steal a Million
My Fair Lady
Charade
Breakfast at Tiffany's
Unforgiven, The
War and Peace
Roman Holiday

CBS/Sony 25AP118 (Japan)

ROZSA CONDUCTS ROZSA (Miklos Rozsa conducting the Royal Philharmonic Orchestra)
Julius Caesar
That Hamilton Woman (Lady Hamilton)
Killers, The
Lydia
Private Life of Sherlock Holmes, The
Five Graves to Cairo
Red Danube, The

Polydor 2383-440 (Britain)

SALUTE TO BOGIE, A (MGM Singing Strings)
Popular songs from Bogart movies

MGM SE-4359

SAM "THE MAN" TAYLOR PLAYS
Bad and the Beautiful, The
Anna
Ruby Gentry
World of Suzie Wong, The
Butterfield 8
Laura
Anastasia
Barefoot Contessa, The

Moodsville MV-24

SATAN SUPERSTAR (Stanley Black conducting the National Philharmonic Orchestra and Chorus)
Dr. Jekyll and Mr. Hyde
Rosemary's Baby
Seventh Victim, The
Exorcist II, The
Omen, The
and other themes

Decca PFS-4432 (Britain)

SCREEN GOLD DISK: ACTION FILM THEMES
Gitan, Le

Flic Story, The
Zorro
Thomas Crown Affair, The
Great Escape, The
From Russia with Love
Goldfinger
Diamonds Are Forever
Man with the Golden Gun
In the Heat of the Night

United Artists GXH-2 (Japan)

SCREEN GOLD DISK: IMMORTAL THEMES
Ultima Neve di Primavera, L'
Little Prince, The
Andremo in Citta
Incompreso
Marcelino Pan y Vino
Railroad Man, The
Forbidden Games (Jeux Interdits)
Melody Fair
Mary Poppins
Lollipop
Wizard of Oz, The
Friends
Cristo del'Oceano, El
Adagio Cardinal

Seven Seas GXH-4 (Japan)

SCREEN GOLD DISK: ITALIAN WESTERNS
Django
Fistful of Dollars, A
Tempo di Massacro
For a Few Dollars More
Lunghi Giorni della Vendetta, I
Bounty Killer, The
Good, the Bad and the Ugly, The
Per Pochi Dollari per Ancora
Man ... A Story, A
Uomo, l'Orgoglio, la Vendetta, L'
Per il Gusto di Uccidere
Texas Addio
Once Upon a Time in the West

Seven Seas GXH-5 (Japan)

SCREEN GOLD DISK: PANIC AND SPECTACULAR THEMES
Jaws
Towering Inferno, The
Poseidon Adventure, The
Earthquake
Airport '75

Anticristo, L'
Exorcist, The
Longest Day, The
Gone with the Wind
Lawrence of Arabia
Ben-Hur
War and Peace
Patton
Exodus

Seven Seas GXH-6 (Japan)

SCREEN GOLD DISK: SCREEN LOVE THEMES
Story of "O," The
Emmanuelle
Amour d'Aimer, L'
Wenn Ich Mir Was Wunschen Durfte
Love Story
Man and a Woman, A
Lecon Particuliere
Blue Balloon, The
Godfather, The
Umbrellas of Cherbourg, The
Bebo's Girl
Romeo and Juliet
Eddy Duchin Story, The

United Artists GXH-3 (Japan)

SCREEN GOLD DISK: WESTERN MOVIE THEMES
Magnificent Seven, The
Johnny Guitar
Alamo, The
High Noon
Duel at Diablo
Big Country, The
Shane
River of No Return
and other traditional songs

United Artists GXH-1 (Japan)

SEA HAWK: THE CLASSIC FILM SCORES OF ERICH WOLFGANG KORNGOLD, THE (Charles Gerhardt conducting the National Philharmonic Orchestra)
Sea Hawk, The
Juarez
Anthony Adverse
Adventures of Robin Hood, The
Devotion
Deception
Kings Row
Captain Blood

Constant Nymph, The
Escape Me Never
Of Human Bondage
Between Two Worlds

RCA LSC-3330

16 BOUMS DU FILM FRANCAIS, LES (Jean Claudric and His Orchestra)
Retour a l'Aube
Jules and Jim
Private Life
Carnet du Bal, Un
Chiens Perdus Sans Collier
Carthacalla
Mr. Hulot's Holiday
Verite, La
Premier Rendez-vous
Katia
Paradis Perdu, Le
Fausse Maitresse, La
Quatorze Juillet
Fievres
Touchez Pas au Grisbi

Victor 440.138 (France)

SERENADE TO A PRINCESS (Theme Songs from the Motion Pictures Made Famous by Grace Kelly. Orchestra conducted by David Carroll)
Bridges at Toko-Ri, The
Dial M for Murder
Rear Window
Green Fire
To Catch a Thief
Swan, The
Mogambo
Country Girl
High Noon
To Catch a Thief
and two non-film instrumentals

Mercury MG-20156

SOGNI DELLA MUSIA (NO. 3), I
Roma Violenta
Bacio, Il
Nel Buio del Terrore
Lupo dei Mari, Il
Giugno '44
Sbarcheremo in Normandia

Beat LPF-036

"SOMEWHERE MY LOVE" AND OTHER ROMANTIC MOVIE MELODIES (Longines Symphonette Society)

Gone with the Wind
Chitty Chitty Bang Bang
Love Is a Many-Splendored Thing
Wait Until Dark
Three Coins in the Fountain
Magnificent Seven, The
Women in Love
Breakfast at Tiffany's
Romeo and Juliet
True Grit
Born Free
Strada, La
Pal Joey
Zorba the Greek
Summer Place, A
Love Letters
High and the Mighty, The
Madwoman of Chaillot, The
Gigi
Alfie
Easy Rider
Star Is Born, A
Midnight Cowboy
Captain Nemo
Thomas Crown Affair, The
Man and a Woman, A
Looking Glass War, The
Good, the Bad and the Ugly, The
Exodus
Sandpiper, The
Umbrellas of Cherbourg
Doctor Zhivago
Mondo Cane
By Love Possessed
Airport
Laura
Thoroughly Modern Millie
Anne of the Thousand Days
Sterile Cuckoo, The
Days of Wine and Roses
Butch Cassidy and the Sundance Kid
Molly Maguires, The
Black Orpheus
April Fools, The

Longines SYS-5312-5317

SOUND OF SILENTS: MUSIC FOR SILENT FILM CLASSICS (Lee Erwin playing the Fox-Capitol Theatre Wurlitzer Pipe Organ)

Phantom of the Opera, The
Wings

Thief of Bagdad, The
General, The
What Price Glory?
Seventh Heaven
Eagle, The
My Best Girl

Angel S-36073

SOUNDS FROM THE SILENT SCREEN (Gaylor Carter, theater organist)
Thief of Bagdad, The (1924)
Ben-Hur (1925)
Temptress, The (1926)

Pelican LP-2011 (private)

SPECTACULAR MOVIE THEMES (The Mass Brass of the Royal Artillery)
Chitty Chitty Bang Bang
Devil's Brigade, The
Charge of the Light Brigade, The
For a Few Dollars More
Magnificent Seven, The
From Russia with Love
Goldfinger
You Only Live Twice
Khartoum
Russians Are Coming, the Russians Are Coming, The
Great Escape, The
Squadron 633

United Artists UNS-15553 (Britain)

SPELLBOUND: RON GOODWIN AND HIS ORCHESTRA
West Side Story
Things to Come
Invaders, The (49th Parallel)
Spellbound
Exodus
Dam Busters, The
Frenzy
American in Paris, An
Battle of Britain

EMI SLZ-8582 (New Zealand)
EMI Studio 2 TWOX-1007 (England)

SPELLBOUND: THE CLASSIC FILM SCORES OF MIKLOS ROZSA (Charles Gerhardt conducts the National Philharmonic Orchestra)
Spellbound
Lost Weekend

Double Indemnity
Red House, The
Four Feathers, The
Thief of Bagdad, The
Jungle Book, The
Ivanhoe
Knights of the Round Table

RCA ARL1-0911

SUCCES DES GRANDES FILMS DE FERNANDEL, LES
C'est dans la Mama
On m'Appelle Simplet
Ma Creole
Je Connais des Baisers
Barnabe
Dans la Flotte
Ne Me Dis Plus Tu
Ernestito
Petite Fine, Une
Ignace

Decca 164.077 (France)

SUNSET BOULEVARD: THE CLASSIC FILM SCORES OF FRANZ WAXMAN (Charles Gerhardt conducts the National Philharmonic Orchestra)
Sunset Boulevard
Bride of Frankenstein, The
Place in the Sun, A
Prince Valiant
Rebecca
Philadelphia Story, The
Old Acquaintance
Taras Bulba

RCA ARL1-0708

SUPERALBUM SELECTIONS FROM ORIGINAL SOUNDTRACKS AND FILM SCORES
Exodus
Odds Against Tomorrow
Some Like It Hot
Apartment, The

Ascot US-16500

SUPERALBUM SELECTIONS FROM ORIGINAL SOUNDTRACKS AND FILM SCORES
Vikings, The
Wonderful Country
I Want to Live

Never on Sunday

Ascot US-16501

SUPERALBUM SELECTIONS FROM ORIGINAL SOUNDTRACKS AND FILM SCORES
Horse Soldiers, The
Paris Blues
Judgement at Nuremberg
Unforgiven, The

Ascot US-16502

SWEETHEART TREE AND OTHER FILM FAVORITES, THE (Arranged and conducted by Johnny Douglas)
Great Race, The
Sandpiper, The
What's New, Pussycat?
Hush ... Hush, Sweet Charlotte
Zorba the Greek
Summer Place, A
Ship of Fools
Crack in the World
Yellow Rolls Royce, The
Harlow

Camden CAS-926

THEATRE MUSIC WITH A FRENCH TOUCH (Michel Legrand and His Orchestra)
Modern Times
Touchez Pas au Grisbi
Johnny Guitar
Rififi
Under the Roofs of Paris
Strada, La
French Can-Can
plus French popular songs

Columbia CB-15 (private)

THEME FROM "STAR TREK" (The Jeff Wayne Space Shuttle)
Star Trek (TV)
Planet of the Apes (TV)
Batman (TV)
Superman (TV)

Wonderland WLP-301

THEME FROM "THE BIBLE" AND OTHER FILM SPECTACULARS, THE (Robert Rheims Chorale and Orchestra)
Bible, The
Cardinal, The

Greatest Story Ever Told, The
Ten Commandments, The
Robe, The
Quo Vadis?
Song of Bernadette, The
David and Bathsheba
King of Kings
Ben-Hur

Liberty LP-6011

THEME FROM "THE UNFORGIVEN" (Don Costa Voices and Orchestra)

Unforgiven, The
Affair to Remember, An
Invitation
Moulin Rouge
Laura
Third Man, The
City Lights
Apartment, The
From Here to Eternity
Picnic
Uninvited, The
Return to Paradise

United Artists UAL-3119

THEME FROM "Z" (Henry Mancini and His Orchestra)

Z
Molly Maguires, The
Prime of Miss Jean Brodie, The
Airport
Butch Cassidy and the Sundance Kid
Casablanca
Stranger Returns, The
Adventurers, The
Patton

RCA LSP-4350

THEME MUSIC FROM GREAT MOTION PICTURES (Al Goodman and His Orchestra)

Gone with the Wind
Spellbound
Duel in the Sun
Undercurrent
Love Story
Lost Weekend
Fiesta

RCA LPT-1008

THEME MUSIC FROM "KING OF KINGS" AND OTHER FILM SPECTACULARS (Frank Chacksfield and His Orchestra)

King of Kings
Samson and Delilah
Robe, The
Quo Vadis?
Alamo, The
Exodus
Ben-Hur
Francis of Assisi
High and the Mighty, The
Prodigal, The
Sundowners, The

London PS-246

THEME MUSIC FROM THE GREAT BRANDO FILMS (Elmer Bernstein and His Orchestra)

On the Waterfront
Teahouse of the August Moon
Streetcar Named Desire, A
Men, The
Sayonara
Desiree
Wild Ones, The
Julius Caesar
Guys and Dolls
Viva Zapata

Contour 2870 337 (Britain)

THEMES FROM GREAT FILMS MADE IN ROME (Riz Ortolani and His Orchestra and Chorus)

Mondo Cane
Divorce, Italian Style
Strada, La
Bread, Love and Dreams
Anna
Easy Life, The
Four Days of Naples, The
Fellini's 8-1/2
Women of the World
Yesterday, Today and Tomorrow
Dolce Vita, La

United Artists UAL-3360

THEMES FROM ITALIAN FILMS (Robert Ashley and His Orchestra)

Anna
Saluti e Baci
Bread, Love and Dreams
Bitter Rice
Woman of the River

Indiscretion of an American Wife

MGM E-3485

THEMES FROM RELIGIOUS MOVIES (The Sunset Strings)
Cardinal, The
Cid, El
Ben-Hur
King of Kings
Four Horsemen of the Apocalypse

Diplomat DS-2520

THEMES FROM THE NEW PROVOCATIVE FILMS (Leroy Holmes Orchestra and Chorus)
Fanny Hill
Sweden, Heaven and Hell
Medium Cool
John and Mary
De Sade
All the Loving Couples
I, a Lover
Arrangement, The
Bob & Carol & Ted & Alice
Women in Love
Libertine, The
What Do You Say to a Naked Lady

United Artists UAS-6742

THIS IS RON GOODWIN
Magnificent Seven
633 Squadron
Hatari
Battle of Britain
Where Eagles Dare
Story of Three Loves, The
Love Story (Britain)

EMI-EMSS-2 (New Zealand)

TRIBUTE TO CHARLIE CHAPLIN, A (Stanley Black conducting the London Festival Orchestra and Chorus)
Modern Times
Chaplin Revue
City Lights
Kid, The
Great Dictator, The
Limelight
King in New York, A
Countess from Hong Kong, A

London SP-44184

TRIBUTE TO JAMES DEAN, A
Giant
East of Eden
Rebel Without a Cause

Columbia CL-940

TWILIGHT OF HONOR AND OTHER GREAT MOTION PICTURE THEMES, PLUS SONGS BY RICHARD CHAMBERLAIN
Twilight of Honor
Murder at the Gallop
55 Days at Peking
Ride the High Country
Black Orpheus
Hud

MGM SE-4185

25 ANS DE MUSIQUE DE CINEMA
Orpheus
Quatorze Juillet
Atalante
Red Balloon, The (Ballon Rouge, Le)
Univers d'Utrillo, L'
Quai des Brumes (Port of Shadows)
Portes de la Nuit, Les
Farrebique
Actualities (newsreels)

Vega C-30-A-98 (France)

WARSAW CONCERTO (Ron Goodwin and His Orchestra)
Dangerous Moonlight
Alphabet Murders, The
Romeo and Juliet
Apartment, The
Of Human Bondage
Love Story
plus popular movie themes

Music for Pleasure SPR-90027 (Britain)

WELCOME! (Music by Guido and Maurizio de Angelis)
Milano Trema: La Polizia Vuole Giustizia
Mare
Dedicato a una Coppia
Cittadino si Ribella, Il
Altrimenti si Arrabbiamo
Delitto di Regime
Quaranta Giorni di Liberta
Piu forte Ragazzi
Anche gli Angeli Mangiano Fagioli

Private Stock PS-7004 (Italy)

WESTERN, THE
Good, the Bad and the Ugly, The
Pistola non Discutono, Le
Return of Ringo, The
Once Upon a Time in the West
Pistol for Ringo, A
7 Guns for the MacGregors
For a Few Dollars More
Fistful of Dollars, A

Peters International PILPS-4050

WESTERN, THE (Vol. 2)
My Name Is Nobody
For a Few Dollars More
Man to Man
Crudeli, I
Genio, Due Compari, un Pollo, Un
Good, the Bad and the Ugly, The
Mercenary, The
J. & S.: Cronaca Criminale del Far West
Faccia a Faccia
Vita a Voltre e Molto Dura Vero
Provvidenza, La?

RCA NL-33066 (Italy)

WHITTEMORE AND LOWE PLAY FOR THE LATE LATE SHOW
Gone with the Wind
How Green Was My Valley
Lili
Bad and the Beautiful, The
Uninvited, The
Love Letters
For Whom the Bell Tolls
Intermezzo
High and the Mighty, The
Moulin Rouge
Spellbound

Capitol SP-8634

WINDMILLS OF YOUR MIND, THE. MICHEL LEGRAND
Thomas Crown Affair, The
Swimming Pool, The
Young Girls of Rochefort, The
Play Dirty

United Artists UAS-6715

Television

ADDAMS FAMILY, THE (ABC-TV, 1964) Vic Mizzy
ABC (S)513
Audio Fidelity 2146/6146
Dot 3616/25616
Epic 24125/26125
RCA LPM-3421/LSP-3421

ADVENTURES IN PARADISE (ABC-TV, 1959) unlisted
Carlton (S)126

ADVENTURES OF SIR FRANCIS DRAKE, THE see SIR FRANCIS DRAKE

ADVENTURES OF ZORRO, THE (ABC-TV, 1957)
Disneyland 3601

AFRICA (TV, 1967) Alex North
MGM E-4462/SE-4462

AIR POWER (CBS-TV, 1956) Norman dello Joio
Columbia ML-5214

ALCOA PRESENTS see ONE STEP BEYOND

ALFRED HITCHCOCK PRESENTS (CBS-TV, 1955) Charles Gounod's "Funeral March of a Marionette"
Epic 24125/26125
London 44077
Mayfair 9961
Tops 1161

ALLE ORIGINI DELLA MAFIA (ITA-TV, 1978) Nino Rota
Dischi Ricordi SMRL-6198 (Italy)

ALVIN SHOW, THE (CBS-TV, 1961) Ross Bagdasarian
Capitol (S)1771

ANDY GRIFFITH SHOW, THE (CBS-TV, 1961) Earle Hagen
Capitol T-1611/ST-1611
Epic 24224/26224
Mercury 20706/60706
Reprise (9)6018

ANNA KARENINA (ITA-TV, 1978) Piero Piccioni
Carosello CLN-25051 (Italy)

APHRODITE INHERITANCE, THE (BRI-TV, 1979) George Kotsonis
BBC REB-356 (Britain)

ARCHERS, THE (BRI-TV, n. d.) unlisted
His Master's Voice 1565

ARREST AND TRIAL (ABC-TV, 1963) unlisted
Warners (S) 1529

AVENGERS, THE (BRI-TV, 1964) John Dankworth, Laurie Johnson
Hanna-Barbera 8056/9056
Philips 200027/600027

BARBARA STANWYCK THEATER, THE (NBC-TV, 1960) unlisted
Mercury 20706/60706

BARON, THE (ABC-TV, 1965) unlisted
Metro (S)565

BAT MASTERSON (NBC-TV, 1958) unlisted
Chancellor 7002

BATMAN (ABC-TV, 1966) Nelson Riddle, Neal Hefti
Decca (7)4754
Fox 3180/4180
Metro (S)565
Reprise (S)6210
RCA (S)3573
Warners (S)1642

BATTLESTAR GALACTICA (ABC-TV, 1978) Stu Phillips
MCA 3051

BEN CASEY (ABC-TV, 1961) unlisted
Audio Fidelity 2146/6146
Capitol (S)1771
Fox (S)4109
Mercury 20706/60706

BEVERLY HILLBILLIES, THE (CBS-TV, 1962) unlisted
Capitol (S)1869
Fox (S)4109

BEWITCHED (ABC-TV, 1964) unlisted
ABC-Paramount 513
Audio Fidelity 2146/6146
Dot 3616/25616
Epic 24125/26125

BIG VALLEY, THE (ABC-TV, 1965) George Duning
ABC 527/S-527

BILL DANA SHOW, THE (NBC-TV, 1963) unlisted
Fox 4105
Warners 1529

BLACK SADDLE (NBC-TV, 1959) unlisted
Dot 3421/25421
RCA LPM-2042

BLUE LIGHT, THE (ABC-TV, 1965) unlisted
Metro 565

BONANZA (NBC-TV, 1958) David Rose et al.
Audio Fidelity 2146/6146
Capitol 1869 and STBB-626-2
Fox 4109
Liberty 13011/14011
London 44077
MGM (S)E-3960 and (S)4285
Metro 544
Mercury 20706/60706
Reprise (9)6018
RCA LPM-2180 and (S)2583
United Artists 2158/6158

BORROWERS, THE (NBC, 1973) Rod McKuen
Stanyan SRQ-4014

BOURBON STREET BEAT (ABC-TV, 1959) various composers
RCA LPM-2180
Warners W-1321/WS-1321

BOY NAMED CHARLIE BROWN, A (CBS-TV, 1965) Vince Guaraldi
Fantasy 5017

BRANDED (NBC-TV, 1964) unlisted
Audio Fidelity 2146/6146

BROKEN ARROW (ABC-TV, 1956) unlisted
Coral (7)57267

BURKE'S LAW (ABC-TV, 1963) Joseph Mullendore
Liberty 3374/7374 and 3353/7353
Warners (S)1529

CANDID CAMERA (ABC-TV, 1948) unlisted
Epic 24224/26224

CARAVANE PACOULI, LE (FRA-TV, n.d.) Armand Gomez
Philips 77.236 (France)

CASE OF THE DANGEROUS ROBIN, THE (TV, 1960) unlisted
Mercury 20706/60706

CHARLIE BROWN CHRISTMAS, A (CBS-TV, 1969) Vince Guaraldi
Fantasy 85019

CHEATERS, THE (BRI-TV, n. d.) Bill le Sage
English Ember 5030

CHECKMATE (CBS-TV, 1960) John Williams
Columbia CL-1591/CS-8391
Contemporary 7599/S-7599
RCA (S)3491

CHEYENNE (ABC-TV, 1955) unlisted
Coral (7)57267

CIMARRON CITY (NBC-TV, 1958) unlisted
Mayfair 9661
Tops 1661

COMBAT (ABC-TV, 1962) unlisted
ABC-Paramount (S)513
Audio Fidelity 2146/6146

COMING OF CHRIST, THE (TV, 1960) Robert Russell Bennett
Decca DL-9093/DL-79093

D. A.'S MAN, THE (NBC-TV, 1958) unlisted
Warners (S)1290

DAKTARI (CBS-TV, 1966) Shelly Manne
Atlantic 8157/SD-8157

DANGER (CBS-TV, 1950) Tony Mottola
MGM-111

DANGER MAN, THE (BRI-TV, 1961) unlisted
His Master's Voice 1565

DANIEL BOONE (NBC-TV, 1964) unlisted
Metro (S)544

DANNY THOMAS SHOW, THE (ABC-TV, 1953) unlisted
Reprise (9)6018

DARK SHADOWS (TV, 1966) Robert Cobert
Philips 600-314

DAVID COPPERFIELD (BRI-TV, 1972) Malcolm Arnold
GRT-10008

DEFENDERS, THE (CBS-TV, 1961) unlisted
Capitol (S)1771
Fox (S)4109

DEPUTY, THE (NBC-TV, 1959) unlisted
RCA LPM-2180

DETECTIVES, THE (ABC-TV, 1959) Herschel Burke Gilbert
Camden (S)627
Dot 3421/25421

DICK POWELL THEATER, THE (NBC-TV, 1961) Herschel Burke Gilbert, Richard Shores
Dot 3421/25421
Reprise (9)6018

DICK POWELL'S ZANE GREY THEATER see ZANE GREY THEATER

DICK VAN DYKE SHOW, THE (CBS-TV, 1961) Earle Hagen
Capitol (S)1869
Fox 4105
London 44077
Mercury 20706/60706

DIRECTIONS (BRI-TV, 1972) Philip Green
RCA LSC-3276

DOBIE GILLIS (CBS-TV, 1959) Lionel Newman
Mercury 20706/60706

DR. KILDARE (NBC-TV, 1961) Harry Sukman
Capitol (S)1771
Fox 4109
London 44077
Mercury 20706/60706

DRAGNET (NBC-TV, 1952) Walter Schumann
Liberty 3353/7353
London 44077
Mercury 20702/60702

EAST SIDE, WEST SIDE (CBS-TV, 1963) Kenyon Hopkins
Columbia CL-2123/CS-8923

ECHO FOUR-TWO (BRI-TV, n.d.) Laurie Johnson
Philips 200027/600027

EDO NO KAZE (WIND OF EDO) (JAP-TV, n.d.) Katsuhisa Hattori
Toho AX-5012 (Japan)

87TH PRECINCT (NBC-TV, 1961) unlisted
Mercury 20706/60706

ELEVEN AGAINST THE ICE (TV, 1958) Kenyon Hopkins
RCA LPM-1618

ELEVENTH HOUR, THE (NBC-TV, 1962) unlisted
Fox (S)4109
United Artists 3315/6315

ELIZABETH TAYLOR IN LONDON (TV, 1963) John Barry
Capitol (S)2527
Colpix CP-459/SCP-459

ERIC (TV, 1975) Dave Grusin
Seven Seas FML-57 (Japan)

F TROOP (ABC-TV, 1965) unlisted
Epic 24224/26224

F. B. I., THE (ABC-TV, 1965) unlisted
Camden (S)927

FLINTSTONES, THE (ABC-TV, 1960) unlisted
Reprise (9)6018

FLIPPER (NBC-TV, 1964) unlisted
Metro (S)554

FOLLYFOOT (BRI-TV, 1978) Dennis Farnon
York 715 (Britain)

FUGITIVE, THE (ABC-TV, 1963) Pete Rugolo
Audio Fidelity 2146/6146
Fox (S)4109
Liberty 3353/7353

GENERAL ELECTRIC THEATER (CBS-TV, 1953) Elmer Bernstein
Columbia CL-1395/CS-8190
Mercury 20706/60706

GENERAL HOSPITAL (ABC-TV, 1963) unlisted
ABC-Paramount (S)513

GERTRUDE BERG SHOW, THE (MRS. G GOES TO COLLEGE) (CBS-TV, 1961) Herschel Burke Gilbert
Dot 3421/26321

GET SMART (NBC-TV, 1965) unlisted
Epic 24224/26224

GHOST SQUAD (BRI-TV, 1965) Philip Green
Philips 200027/600027

GIRL FROM U. N. C. L. E., THE (NBC-TV, 1966) Dave Grusin et al.
MGM E-4410/SE-4410

GREEN HORNET, THE (ABC-TV, 1966) Billy May
Epic 24224/26224
Fox 3186/S-3186

GUNSLINGER (CBS-TV, 1961) unlisted
United Artists 3161/6161

GUNSMOKE (CBS-TV, 1961) unlisted
Fox (S)4109

HALLMARK HALL OF FAME (NBC-TV, 1951) unlisted
RCA LPM-1020

HAMLET (NBC, 1970) John Addison
RCA VDM-119-2

HAVE GUN, WILL TRAVEL (CBS-TV, 1957) unlisted
Capitol (S)1869
Coral (7)57267
Warners (S)1290

HAWAII FIVE-0 (CBS-TV, 1970) Morton Stevens
Capitol ST-410

HAWAIIAN EYE (ABC-TV, 1959) Jerry Livingston
RCA LPM-2180
Warners W-1355/WS-1355

HENNESEY (CBS-TV, 1959) Sonny Burke
Carlton (S)126
Signature 1049/S-1049

HIGH CHAPARRAL, THE (NBC-TV, 1967) David Rose, Harry Sukman
Capitol STBB-626-2

HIGHWAY PATROL (TV, 1955) Ray Llewellyn
RCA LPM-2042

HOGAN'S HEROES (CBS-TV, 1965) unlisted
Epic 24224/26224

HOLLYWOOD PALACE, THE (ABC-TV, 1977) unlisted
ABC-Paramount (S)513

HOLOCAUST (TV, 1978) Morton Gould
RCA ARL1-2785

HONEY WEST (ABC-TV, 1965) Joseph Mullendore
ABC-Paramount (S)367

HONG KONG (ABC-TV, 1960) Lionel Newman et al.
ABC 367/S-367

I SPY (NBC-TV, 1965) Earle Hagen
Camden (S)927
Capitol T-2839/ST-2839
Warners W-1637/WS-1637

ICHABOD AND ME (CBS-TV, 1961) unlisted
Mercury 20706/60706

I'M DICKENS, HE'S FENSTER (ABC-TV, 1962) unlisted
Capitol (S)1869

INDICATIF: "LES BETES CHEZ ELLES" (FRA-TV, n.d.) F. Rabbath
Philips 77.236 (France)

INDICATIF: "MIRE 2e CHAINE" (FRA-TV, n.d.) R. David
Philips 77.236 (France)

INDIENS, LES (FRA-TV, n.d.) Armand Migiani
Philips 77.236 (France)

INTERNATIONAL DETECTIVE (TV, 1959) Leroy Holmes
Ember 5030 (England)
RCA LPM-2180

ITALIA VISTA DAL CIELO, L' (ITA-TV, n.d.) Francesco de Masi
SR SP-117 (Italy)

JACKIE GLEASON SHOW, THE (CBS-TV, 1962) unlisted
London 44077
RCA LPM-1020

JANE EYRE (Britain, 1970) John Williams
Capitol SW-749

JESUS OF NAZARETH (BRI-TV, 1977) Maurice Jarre
Pye NSPH-28504 (Britain)

JOHNNY STACCATO (NBC-TV, 1959) Elmer Bernstein
Camden (S)627
Capitol T-1287/ST-1287
Philips 200027/600027
RCA LPM-2180

JUNE ALLYSON SHOW, THE (CBS-TV, 1959) Herschel Burke Gilbert
Dot 3421/25421

KRAFT TELEVISION THEATER (NBC-TV, 1947) Vladimir Selinsky
RCA LPM-1020
RKO 127

KUNG FU (ABC, 1972) Jim Helms
Warners BS-2726

LATE SHOW, THE (TV, n.d.) unlisted
London 44077

LAW AND MR. JONES, THE (ABC-TV, 1960) Hans J. Salter
Dot 3421/25421

LAW OF THE PLAINSMAN (NBC-TV, 1959) Leonard Rosenman
Dot 3421/25421

LEGACY FOR THE FUTURE (JAP-TV, 1978) Toru Takemitsu
NHK MEF-6001 (Japan)

LIARS, THE (BRI-TV, n.d.) A. Sciascia
Ember 5020 (England)

LIEUTENANT, THE (NBC-TV, 1963) unlisted
Warners (S)1529

LILLIE (BRI-TV, 1979) Joseph Horowitz et al.
Decca MOR-516 (Britain)

LINEUP, THE (CBS-TV, 1954) unlisted
RCA LPM-2180

LOOK AT MONACO, A (TV, 1963) Percy Faith
Columbia CL-2019/CS-8819 and 2209/9009

LORETTA YOUNG SHOW, THE (NBC-TV, 1953) Harry Lubin
Carlton (S)126
Decca DL-4124/DL-74124

LOVE AMERICAN STYLE (ABC-TV, 1969) Charles Fox
Capitol SM-11250

LOVE FOR LYDIA (Britain, 1977) various composers
Weekend DFJ-20514 (Britain)

M-SQUAD (NBC-TV, 1957) Benny Carter, John Williams, and Stanley Wilson
Camden (S)522
Liberty 3353/7353
Philips 200027/600027
RCA LPM-2042 and LPM/LSP-2062
Warners (S)1290

McHALE'S NAVY (ABC-TV, 1962) unlisted
Capitol (S)1869

MAIGRET (BRI-TV, 1978) Ron Grainer
English Decca 1135
German Decca 16324
His Master's Voice 1565
RCA 1020 (Britain)

MAMA (CBS-TV, 1949) unlisted
RCA LPM-1020

MAN FROM INTERPOL, THE (BRI-TV, 1960) Tony Crombie
Ember 5030 (England)
Top Rank 327/627

MAN FROM U. N. C. L. E., THE (NBC-TV, 1964) Gerald Fried, Robert Drasnin, Jerry Goldsmith, Walter Scharf, Lalo Schifrin, and Morton Stevens
Audio Fidelity 2146/6146
Camden (S)927
London 44077
Metro (S)544 and (S)565
Verve (6)8624
RCA LPM/LSP-3475 and LPM/LSP-3574

MANI SPORCHE, LE (ITA-TV, 1978) Ennio Morricone
CAM SAG-9089 (Italy)

MANNIX (CBS-TV, 1967) Lalo Schifrin
Paramount PAS-5004

MANY LOVES OF DOBIE GILLIS, THE see DOBIE GILLIS

MARKHAM (CBS-TV, 1959) Stanley Wilson
Camden (S)627
RCA LPM-2180

MARSHAL DILLON see GUNSMOKE

MAVERICK (ABC-TV, 1957) unlisted
Coral (7)57267
Warners (S)1290

MAYA (NBC-TV, 1967) Hans J. Salter
Citadel CT-6017

MEDIC (NBC-TV, 1954) Victor Young
Decca 8285
Jubilee 1034
London 3129/193

MELINA'S GREECE (TV, n. d.) Stavros Xarchakos
Greek Odeon 46

MEN INTO SPACE (CBS-TV, 1959) David Rose
RCA LPM-2180

MICHAEL SHAYNE (NBC-TV, 1960) Leith Stevens
Dot 3421/25421

MICHAEL STROGOFF (FRA-TV, n. d.) Vladimir Cosma
Blue BLRM-15002 (Italy)
CNR 660012 (Holland)

MICKEY MOUSE CLUB, THE (TV, 1955) unlisted
Warners (S)1290

MIDNIGHT MOVIE (TV, n. d.) Stan Zabka
Laurie (S)2025

MIKE HAMMER (TV, 1957) David Kahn, Melvyn Lenard
Camden (S)522
RCA LPM-2140 and 2042

MISSION IMPOSSIBLE (CBS-TV, 1966) Lalo Schifrin
Dot 3831/25831
Paramount PAS-5002

MR. BROADWAY (CBS-TV, 1964) Dave Brubeck
Columbia 2275/9075

MR. LUCKY (CBS-TV, 1959) Henry Mancini
Camden CAL-600, (S)627, and (S)736
Liberty 12011/14011 and 3353/7353
RCA LPM/LSP-2198
Reprise (9)6105

MRS. G GOES TO COLLEGE see THE GERTRUDE BERG SHOW

MOSES THE LAWGIVER (CBS-TV, 1975) Ennio Morricone
RCA TBL1-1106

MOVIE FOUR (TV, n. d.) Stan Zabka
Laurie (S)2025

MY FAVORITE MARTIAN (CBS-TV, 1963) unlisted
Warners (S)1529

MY THREE SONS (ABC-TV, 1960) unlisted
ABC-Paramount (S)513
Capitol (S)1771
Epic 24224/26224
Mercury 20706/60706

NAKED CITY (ABC-TV, 1958) Billy May
Camden (S)522
Capitol (S)1771, (S)1869, and (S)1990
Colpix 505
Liberty 7195
Mercury 20706/60706
RCA LPM-2042
Warners (S)1529

NATIONAL VELVET (NBC-TV, 1960) unlisted
Ava (S)6

NEWCOMERS, THE (BRI-TV, n. d.) John Barry
Ember 5030 (England)

NIGHT PEOPLE (TV, n. d.) unlisted
Metro (S)544

NOI LASSARONI (ITA-TV, 1978) Ennio Morricone
CAM SAG-9086 (Italy)

ONE STEP BEYOND (ALCOA PRESENTS) (ABC-TV, 1959) Harry Lubin
Decca DL (7)8970

OUTER LIMITS, THE (ABC-TV, 1963) unlisted
Epic 24125/26125

PATTY DUKE SHOW, THE (ABC-TV, 1963) unlisted
Warners (S)1529

PERRY MASON (CBS-TV, 1957) Fred Steiner
Audio Fidelity 2146/6146
Camden (S)522
Fox (S)4109
Mayfair 9661
RCA LPM-2042
Reprise (9)6018
Tops 1661
Warners (S)1290

PETE KELLY'S BLUES (NBC-TV, 1959) unlisted
Warners (S)1290 and (S)1303

PETER GUNN (NBC-TV, 1958) Henry Mancini
Camden (S)522 and (S)736
Contemporary 3560
Dot 3204/25204
Hamilton 112
London 44077
Mayfair 9661
Metro (S)520
Liberty 12011/14011
RCA LPM/LSP-1956, and LPM/LSP-2040, LPM-2042, (S)2693, and (S)2604
Tops 1661
Warners (S)1290

PETTICOAT JUNCTION (CBS-TV, 1963) unlisted
Warners (S)1529

PEYTON PLACE (ABC-TV, 1964) Franz Waxman, Randy Newman
ABC-Paramount (S)513
Audio Fidelity 2146/6146
Epic 24147/26147

London 44077
Metro (S)544

PHIL SILVERS SHOW, THE (CBS-TV, 1955) unlisted
Fox (S)4105

PHILCO TV PLAYHOUSE (NBC-TV, 1948) unlisted
Warners (S)1290

POLY (FRA-TV, n. d.) J. Hajos
Philips 77. 236 (France)

QB VII (ABC-TV, 1974) Jerry Goldsmith
ABC 822
RCA LSPX-1003

RACCONTI DI MARE (ITA-TV, 1978) Bruno Zambrini
RCA 1011 (Italy)

RACKET SQUAD (CBS-TV, 1951) Joseph Mullendore
RCA LPM-2042

RAWHIDE (CBS-TV, 1958) Dimitri Tiomkin
London 44077
RCA LPM-2042

REAL McCOYS, THE (ABC-TV, 1957) Harry Ruby
Reprise (9)6018
Warners (S)1290

REPORTER, THE (CBS-TV, 1964) Kenyon Hopkins
Columbia 2269/9069

RESTLESS GUN (NBC-TV, 1957) unlisted
Coral (7)57267

RICH MAN, POOR MAN (ABC-TV, 1976) Alex North
MCA 2095

RICHARD DIAMOND, PRIVATE DETECTIVE (CBS-TV, 1957) Pete Rugolo
Mercury 36162/80045
RCA LPM-2042
Warners (S)1290

RIFLEMAN (ABC-TV, 1958) Herschel Burke Gilbert
Dot 3421/25421

RISE AND FALL OF THE THIRD REICH, THE (MGM-TV, 1968) Lalo Schifrin
MGM 1(S)E-12

RIVERBOAT (NBC-TV, 1959) Elmer Bernstein
RCA LPM-2180

ROARING TWENTIES, THE (ABC-TV, 1960) unlisted
Philips 200027/600027

ROBERT MONTGOMERY PRESENTS (NBC-TV, 1950) unlisted
RCA LPM-1020

ROBERT TAYLOR'S DETECTIVES see DETECTIVES, THE

ROCAMBOLE (FRA-TV, n. d.) Jacques Loussier
Philips 77. 236 (France)

ROGUES, THE (NBC-TV, 1964) Nelson Riddle
ABC-Paramount (S)513
RCA LPM/LSP-2976

ROOTS (ABC-TV, 1977) Gerald Fried, Quincy Jones
A&M SP-4626

ROUTE 66 (CBS-TV, 1960) Nelson Riddle
Capitol (S)1771 and (S)1990
Fox (S)4109
Liberty 3195/7195
London 3298/298 and 4407
Mercury 20706/60706
Philips 200027/600027

SAINT, THE (NBC-TV, 1967) Edwin Astley
Metro (S)565
RCA LPM/LSP-3467

SAINTS AND SINNERS (NBC-TV, 1962) Elmer Bernstein
Ava (S)11

SAM BENEDICT (NBC-TV, 1962) unlisted
Capitol (S)1771

SANDOKAN (ITA-TV, n. d.) Guido and Maurizio de Angelis
RCA TBL1-1191 (Italy)

SCOPERTA DELL'AFRICA, LA (ITA-TV, n. d.) Francesco de Masi
Duse ELP-061 (Italy)

SEA HUNT (TV, 1957) Ray Llewellyn
RCA LPM/LSP-2042

SECRET AGENT (CBS-TV, 1965) Edwin Astley
Victor LPM/LSP-3467 and LPM/LSP-3630

77 SUNSET STRIP (ABC-TV, 1958) Jerry Livingston
Camden (S)522

Mercury 20702/60702
Philips 200027/600027
Warners (S)1289, (S)1290, and (S)1529

SHOTGUN SLADE (TV, 1959) Gerald Fried
Mercury 20575/60235

SHOW STREET (TV, n. d.) unlisted
ABC-Paramount (S)513

SING ALONG WITH MITCH (NBC-TV, 1961) Mitch Miller
Capitol (S)1771

SIR FRANCIS DRAKE (BRI-TV, 1962) unlisted
His Master's Voice 1565

SIX PROUD WALKERS (BRI-TV, n. d.) unlisted
RCA LPM-1184

SOPHIA LOREN IN ROME (TV, 1964) John Barry
Columbia OL-6310/OS-2710

SPACE: 1999 (TV, 1976) Barry Gray
RCA ABL1-1422

STACCATO see JOHNNY STACCATO

STONEY BURKE (ABC-TV, 1962) unlisted
Capitol (S)1869

STRAIGHTAWAY (ABC-TV, 1961) unlisted
Roulette Birdland (SR) 52076

STUDIO ONE (CBS-TV, 1948) Bernard Herrmann
RCA LPM/LSP-1020

SUGARFOOT (ABC-TV, 1957) unlisted
Coral (7)57267

SUNDAY SHOWCASE (TV, n. d.) Stan Zabka
Laurie (S)2025

SUPERCAR (TV, n. d.) unlisted
Capitol (S)1869

TALES OF WELLS FARGO (NBC-TV, 1957) unlisted
Coral (7)57267

TARGET: THE CORRUPTORS (ABC-TV, 1961) Rudy Schrager, Fred Steiner
Dot 3421/25421

THIERRY LA FRONDE (FRA-TV, n. d.) Jacques Loussier
Philips 77. 236 (France)

THIN MAN, THE (NBC-TV, 1957) Pete Rugolo
Camden (S)522

THRILLER! (NBC-TV, 1960) Pete Rugolo
Time (S)2034

THURSDAY NIGHT AT THE MOVIES (TV, n. d.) unlisted
Epic 24224/26224

TIGHTROPE (CBS-TV, 1959) unlisted
Camden (S)627
Philips 200027/600027

TOI LE VENT MON AMI (FRA-TV, n. d.) Armand Gomez
Philips 77. 236 (France)

TOM EWELL SHOW, THE (CBS-TV, 1960) Jerry Fielding
Dot 3421/25421

TONIGHT SHOW, THE (NBC-TV, 1954) Stan Zabka
Laurie (S)2025

TOP SECRET (TV, n. d.) Taranteno Rojas
Philips 200027/600027

TOURISME ET CULTURE (L'AGE HEUREUX) (FRA-TV, n. d.) A. Kerr, Rudy Castro
Philips 77. 236 (France)

TRAVELS OF JAMIE McPHEETERS, THE (ABC-TV, 1963) unlisted
Fox (S)4109

TRIALS OF O'BRIEN, THE (CBS-TV, 1965)
Camden (S)927

TURN THE KEY SOFTLY (TV, n. d.) Stan Zabka
Laurie (S)2025

12 O'CLOCK HIGH (ABC-TV, 1964) unlisted
Audio Fidelity 2146/6146
Metro (S)544

20 MULE TEAM (TV, n. d.) unlisted
Coral (7)57267

TWILIGHT ZONE, THE (TV, 1962) Bernard Herrmann
RCA LPM-2180

UNTOUCHABLES, THE (ABC-TV, 1959) Nelson Riddle
Camden (S)627

Capitol (S)1430, (S)1771, and (S)1990
Carlton (S)126
RCA LPM/LSC-2180

UOMO E LA MAGIA, L' (ITA-TV, 1976) Ennio Morricone
Cometa CMT-1 (Italy)

VALIANT YEARS, THE (ABC-TV, 1960) Richard Rodgers
ABC-Paramount (S)387

VICTORY AT SEA (TV, 1952) Richard Rodgers
Columbia CL-810
Quintessence PMC-7032
Somerset 10900
Stereo Fidelity 10900
RCA LM/LSC-2335, LM/LSC-2226, LM/LSC-2523, LM-1779, and VCS-2-7064

VIRGINIAN, THE (NBC-TV, 1962) Percy Faith, Bernard Herrmann
CineSound CSR-301
Columbia 2209/9009

VOICE OF FIRESTONE, THE (NBC-TV, 1949) Mrs. Harvey Firestone
RCA LPM/LSC-1020

VOYAGE TO THE BOTTOM OF THE SEA (ABC-TV, 1964) unlisted
Audio Fidelity 2146/6146

WAGON TRAIN (NBC-TV, 1957) Jerome Moross
Coral (7)57267
Mercury 20502/60179
Reprise (9)6018

WANTED: DEAD OR ALIVE (CBS-TV, 1958) Rudy Schrager
Dot 3421/25421

WASHINGTON: BEHIND CLOSED DOORS (TV, 1977) Dominic Frontiere
ABC AB-1044

WATERFRONT (TV, 1954) Alexander Laszlo
RCA LPM/LSP-2042

WICHITA TOWN (NBC-TV, 1959) Hans J. Salter
Citadel CT-6022

WIDE, WIDE WORLD (NBC-TV, c1954) David Broekman
RCA LPM-1280

WILDERNESS TRAIL (TV, 1975) Walter Scharf
National Geographic Society 07708 (private)

WORLD AT WAR, THE (BRI-TV, 1978) Carl Davis
Decca 325 (Britain)

WORLD TONIGHT (BRI-TV, n. d.) A. Sciascia
Ember 5030 (Britain)

WORLD WAR I (CBS-TV, 1964) Morton Gould
RCA LPM/LSP-2791 and ANL1-2334

WYATT EARP (ABC-TV, 1955) unlisted
Coral (7)57267

YOUNG AND THE RESTLESS, THE (CBS-TV, 1973) Don McGinnis, Jerry Winn, Bob Todd, Barry De Vorzon, and Perry Botkin Jr.
PIP 6812

YOUNG SET, THE (TV, n. d.) unlisted
Camden (S)927

ZANE GREY THEATER, THE (CBS-TV, 1956) Joseph Mullendore
Dot 3421/25421

Television Anthologies

AMAZING TV THEMES, THE
Green Hornet, The
Tarzan
King Kong
Batman
Flipper
It's About Time
Daktari
Man from U. N. C. L. E., The
Alice Through the Looking Glass

Leo CH-1023

FAVOURITE TV AND FILM WESTERN THEMES (Cinema Sound Stage Orchestra)
Bonanza
High Noon
Butch Cassidy and the Sundance Kid
Maverick
Virginian, The
Good, the Bad and the Ugly, The
Magnificent Seven, The
Shenandoah

Stereo Gold Award MER-353 (New Zealand)

FAVOURITE TV THEMES (The City Lights Orchestra and Strings)
Onedin Line, The
Bonanza
On the Buses
Doctor at Large
Big Match
This Is Your Life
Owen M. D.
Paul Temple
Please, Sir
Fenn Street Gang, The
Match of the Day
Persuaders, The

Maestro TRO-184 (Britain)

JAZZ THEMES FOR COPS AND ROBBERS (Leith Stevens and His Orchestra)
Thin Man, The
M-Squad
Private Hell 36
Perry Mason
Peter Gunn

Coral CRL-75728

ORIGINAL MUSIC FROM GREAT BBC TV SHOWS
Pallisers, The
Six Wives of Henry VIII, The
War and Peace
Lord Peter Wimsey
Likely Lads, The
Take Another Look
World Cup '74
Mighty Continent, The
Clochemerle
Elizabeth R
and other themes

BBC REB-188 (Britain)

TV THRILLER THEMES (Johnny Gregory and His Orchestra)
Route 66
Tightrope
Roaring Twenties, The
M Squad
Top Secret
Ghost Squad
Avengers
Echo 4-2
Perry Mason
77 Sunset Strip

Johnny Staccato

Philips PHS 600-027

TELE MUSIQUE (Billy Stark and His Orchestra)
Thierry la Fronde
Caravane Pacouli
Toi le Vent Mon Ami
Rocambole
Indicatif: "Mire 2e Chaine"
Indiens, Les
Poly
Indicatif: "Les Betes Chez Elles"
Tourisme et Culture

Philips DeLuxe P-77. 236-L (France)

THEMES FROM THE GENERAL ELECTRIC THEATER (Conducted by Elmer Bernstein)
Opening Theme
Man on a Bicycle
And One Was Loyal
Stone, The
At Miss Minner's
Girl with the Flaxen Hair, The
World's Greatest Quarterback, The
Robbie and His Mary
Train to Tecumseh
Shoes for a Small Sinner
Nobody's Child
Closing Theme

Columbia CS-8190

ZABKA'S THEMES FROM TELEVISION
Tonight Show, The
Movie Four
and other melodies by Stan Zabka

Laurie LLP-2025